AVID

READER

PRESS

UFO

The Inside Story of the US Government's Search for Alien Life Here — and Out There

GARRETT M. GRAFF

AVID READER PRESS

New York London Toronto Sydney New Delhi

Avid Reader Press
An Imprint of Simon & Schuster, LLC
1230 Avenue of the Americas
New York, NY 10020

First Avid Reader Press trade paperback edition November 2024

AVID READER PRESS and colophon are
trademarks of Simon & Schuster, LLC

Simon & Schuster: Celebrating 100 Years of Publishing in 2024

For information about special discounts for bulk purchases,
please contact Simon & Schuster Special Sales at
1-866-506-1949 or business@simonandschuster.com.

The Simon & Schuster Speakers Bureau can bring authors to
your live event. For more information or to book an event, contact
the Simon & Schuster Speakers Bureau at 1-866-248-3049
or visit our website at www.simonspeakers.com.

Interior design by Lewelin Polanco

Manufactured in the United States of America

1   3   5   7   9   10   8   6   4   2

Library of Congress Cataloging-in-Publication Data has been applied for.

ISBN 978-1-9821-9677-6
ISBN 978-1-9821-9678-3 (pbk)
ISBN 978-1-9821-9679-0 (ebook)

To my son Christopher—
It's a big world out there,
bigger than we can imagine,
and I hope you are always fascinated
by the wonders around you.

Contents

PART 3: THE INTERSTELLAR AGE

War of the Worlds

Just after 8 p.m. on the East Coast on Sunday, October 30, 1938, millions of American families tuned into CBS Radio had heard just seventeen seconds of Ramón Raquello's orchestra playing the tango "La Cumparsita," live from the Meridian Room of the Park Plaza Hotel in New York, when a voice interrupted:

> *Ladies and gentlemen, we interrupt our program of dance music to bring you a special bulletin from the Intercontinental Radio News. At twenty minutes before eight, central time, Professor Farrell of the Mount Jennings Observatory, Chicago, Illinois, reports observing several explosions of incandescent gas, occurring at regular intervals on the planet Mars.*

After a note about spectroscope readings and a confirmation by a Professor Pierson at the Princeton Observatory that Farrell's reports were indeed correct, Raquello's orchestra returned to the air. A few minutes later, another news bulletin. "Ladies and gentlemen, following on the news given in our bulletin a moment ago, the Government Meteorological Bureau has requested the large observatories of the country to keep an astronomical watch on any further disturbances occurring on the planet Mars," the announcer said, adding that the network was working to set up an interview with the nearby Princeton Observatory.

Again, the orchestra returned. Again, a bulletin provided an update.

And then, about eleven minutes into the broadcast, a breathless series of news reports and man-on-the-street interviews about a Martian craft landing near Princeton, New Jersey, started to play.

Sirens, crowd murmurs, and shouted orders from concerned police punctuated the audio delivered by the field correspondent and a Princeton astronomer who had rushed the eleven miles to the scene. The reporter, Carl Phillips, said breathlessly, "Well, I hardly know where to begin—to paint for you a word picture of the strange scene before my eyes, like something out of a modern *Arabian Nights*." Phillips was obviously confused and struggling to get his bearings while live on air. "I guess that's it—yes, I guess that's the thing, directly in front of me, half buried in a vast pit. Must have struck with terrific force. The ground is covered with splinters of a tree it must have struck on its way down. What I can see of the object itself doesn't look very much like a meteor, at least not the meteors I've seen. It looks more like a huge cylinder. It has a diameter of. . . . What would you say, Professor Pierson?"

The Princeton astronomer was clearly trying to wrap his head around the scene, too. "What's that?" he said, caught off guard by the question.

"What would you say—what is the diameter of this?"

"About thirty yards," the professor said.

A cylinder, that is, nearly the length of a football field. Phillips moved on as the police began to push the crowd back and he located the farm's owner, Mr. Wilmuth, who recounted the experience of the object crashing into the field. They edged closer to the object as Phillips tried to capture on his microphone a strange humming sound coming from inside. Pierson proclaimed the object, whatever it was, definitely extraterrestrial.

Then the top of the craft opened and the Martians emerged.

First came the tentacles.

"Good heavens, something's wriggling out of the shadow like a gray snake," Phillips declared from the farm in Grovers Mill, New Jersey. "Now it's another one, and another. They look like tentacles to me. There, I can see the thing's body. It's large, large as a bear and it glistens like wet leather. But that face, it . . . Ladies and gentlemen, it's indescribable. I can hardly force myself to keep looking at it."

Moments later, a police officer was reportedly approaching the craft with a white flag—"If those creatures know what that means," Phillips wondered on air—when the Martians suddenly fired a heat ray, killing everyone nearby and spreading fire across the field from the extraterrestrial craft.

The transmission cut off. The music resumed.

At around eighteen minutes into the hour—8:18 p.m.—the news returned, with reports of burned bodies, mobilized militias and troops, and emergency care rushing to the scene. Another bulletin from Trenton stated that Carl Phillips had been found dead and charred. The radio studio itself, the new announcer explained, had been turned over to the state, as the military operations commenced. Eight battalions—seven thousand soldiers—had surrounded the pit in New Jersey, attempting to surround and isolate whatever the strange creatures were that had caused such destruction.

A Captain Lansing, from the Signal Corps, said that "all cause for alarm, if such cause ever existed, is now entirely unjustified." The creatures, he promised, could hardly survive the military's heavy machine-gun fire, but even as he spoke, his voice began to fill with wonder and alarm. "It's something moving . . . solid metal . . . kind of shield-like affair rising up out of the cylinder. . . . It's going higher and higher. Why, it's standing on legs . . . actually rearing up on a sort of metal framework. Now it's reaching above the trees and the searchlights are on it. Hold on!"

The field report cut off.

No one ever heard from Captain Lansing again.

Just after 8:24 p.m., listeners were given terrifying news: "I have a grave announcement to make," the voice said over the radio. "Incredible as it may seem, both the observations of science and the evidence of our eyes lead to the inescapable assumption that those strange beings who landed in the Jersey farmlands tonight are the vanguard of an invading army from the planet Mars."

By 8:30 p.m., word came that the US Army in New Jersey had been defeated, with just 120 soldiers—of seven thousand!—having survived the heat ray attack. Communication networks were down. More Martian cylinders were reported to be hitting Earth—Buffalo, Chicago, St. Louis. People were beginning to flee cities. Martial law had been declared. They were everywhere. The nation was crumbling.

The secretary of the interior, live from Washington, addressed the unfolding national emergency: "I shall not try to conceal the gravity of the situation that confronts the country, nor the concern of your government in protecting the lives and property of its people."

And then, around 8:40 p.m., some forty minutes into the broadcast, normality returned as a station identification break made an even more stunning proclamation: "You are listening to a CBS presentation of Orson Welles and the Mercury Theatre on the Air in an original dramatization of *The War of the Worlds*, by H. G. Wells. The performance will continue after a brief intermission. This is the Columbia Broadcasting System."

There had not been, listeners soon realized, an invasion, or epic battle, or lives lost. There had not been a Ramón or even an orchestra—just a phonograph record playing in an empty CBS studio, the tango especially chosen for its tedium. The most dramatic night of radio in American history had been a scripted performance.

• •

A spectacular dramatist, twenty-three-year-old Orson Welles had thrived in the entertainment industry amid the darkest days of the Great Depression thanks to a unique artistic collaboration with a producer named John Houseman, forged through FDR's Federal Theatre Project. In 1937, the pair launched the Mercury Theatre as a place to experiment with innovative productions and adaptations—and before long, the efforts and vision had paid off. Mercury Theatre was a wild success in its first year, and CBS picked it up to air on the radio beginning on July 11, 1938. "On the broad wings of the Federal eagle, we had risen to success and fame beyond ourselves as America's youngest, cleverest, most creative and audacious producers to whom none of the ordinary rules of the theater applied," Houseman wrote later.

One of their biggest opportunities came that same year, when Houseman and Welles realized a possible use for the Sunday night literary adaptations lineup, which was still so new that it didn't even have a corporate sponsor. For the week of Halloween, Welles had wanted to do something bold and new, and "conceived the idea of doing a radio broadcast in such a manner that a crisis would actually seem to be happening," he recalled—"a dramatized form as to appear to be a real event taking place at that time, rather than a mere radio play." Adapting H. G. Wells's old and somewhat heavy-handed science fiction novel, *The War of the Worlds*, to the modern age of radio, he thought, might do the trick. Once it was decided, the Mercury Theatre team had only a week to translate the 1897 first-person novel about a Martian invasion of England into radio fodder and prepare for their roles. (To do so, some actors playing the announcers listened to archival broadcasts of the crash of the Hindenburg, attempting to mimic the growing terror of the announcer's voice, as the airship had crashed and burned in real time, killing thirty-six people.)

The hard work paid off. It sounded like a real invasion. On the evening of the broadcast, roughly a dozen actors stood behind microphones, playing a score of characters—Welles himself played Professor Pierson, among other roles—and delivering an impressively convincing performance. At the end of the hour, his show complete, Welles took a moment to make a statement. "This is Orson Welles, ladies and gentlemen, out of character to assure you that *The War of the Worlds* has no further significance than as the holiday offering it was intended to be," he said cheerfully. "The Mercury Theatre's own radio version of dressing up in a sheet and jumping out of a bush and saying *Boo!*"*

By that point, though, the damage had been done.

In those forty minutes, some chunk of the nation had apparently actually panicked, setting aside the disbelief that events could ever unfold so quickly—that in less than an hour, other beings could make it from Mars and land on Earth, that state leaders and troops could mobilize emergency efforts, identify the dead and triage the wounded, the military launch bombing raids, and ready and deploy artillery batteries in between a few bars of tango music, and issue a national address from Washington. By 8:48 p.m., the Associated Press had felt it necessary to issue a national "Note to Editors" clarifying that any "Queries to newspapers from radio listeners throughout the United States tonight, regarding a reported meteor fall which killed a number of New Jerseyites are the result of a studio dramatization." The NYPD, similarly, felt the need to release a citywide teletype with the assurance that there was "no cause for alarm," as did the New Jersey State Police, who reported, "Note to all receivers: WABC broadcast as drama re this section being attacked by Mars. Imaginary affair."† Newspaper headlines on Halloween and the days after made it sound like America had nearly succumbed to anarchy, fueled by mass hysteria. Telephone switchboards had been overwhelmed, they claimed, and

---

* The excitement certainly worked for Welles: His show finally landed a sponsor—Campbell's Soup—and he landed a role directing a new movie, called *Citizen Kane*.

† With time, more careful study led scholars to wonder how much—if any—real panic ensued. One of them, W. Joseph Campbell, wrote in 2010, "These reports were almost entirely anecdotal and largely based on sketchy wire service roundups that emphasized breadth over in-depth detail." Did a few confused people panic? Certainly. Did millions? Maybe not.

terrified families had fled into the streets—some covering their faces with wet towels to avoid the spreading poisonous gas. The *New York Times* reported that the broadcast had "disrupted households, interrupted religious services, created traffic jams, and clogged communication systems."

In the following days and months—and, really, for the remainder of his life—Welles maintained that he hadn't meant for the program to run so long before announcing that the events being described were fictional. The team had just been working so fast, and the changes and edits to the scripts had come so late and so quick, he explained, that no one had realized the standard station ID segment, a routine element of live radio, had been pushed back. Instead of hearing the disclaimer on the half hour, as was expected, listeners who had tuned in to *The War of the Worlds* late hadn't received any notice that the broadcast was a performance until the bottom of the hour, an inconsistency that only heightened the belief it could be breaking news.

As the years passed, *The War of the Worlds* became a somewhat-inflated legend of popular culture, cited as a prime example of the power of the media to spread disinformation, and our population's susceptibility to panic, especially when it came to potential invasion and the subject of aliens. Its recipe of equal parts fact, sketchy details, public confusion, media hype, and outright myth, all helped along by a showman's instincts and—looming in the background—some government money, would come to define discussion and debate about that very subject for decades to come.

After Welles had turned his microphone off, the Martians may have been done with Earth—but Earth was far from done with the Martians.

There's no doubt that UFOs exist, but that's not what most people mean when they ask if UFOs are real. As folklorist Thomas Bullard notes, UFOs are a particularly alluring sociological topic, "at once so popular and so despised," that fascinates us even as polite society continues to dismiss the true believers. The hunt and identification of "unidentified flying objects" has been confused over the years in part because the term has become popular shorthand for alien spacecraft, what so-called "ufologists" actually refer to as the interplanetary theory, or extraterrestrial hypothesis (ETH). Instead, all "UFO" technically implies is exactly what it stands for: something in the sky of unknown origin.

Even so, UFOs, ETH, aliens, and space travel have dominated our popular culture for decades, pushing boundaries of understanding and fueling our human imagination; it is not a coincidence that many of the most popular and iconic TV shows and movies—from *Star Trek* and *Star Wars* to *E.T. the Extra-Terrestrial* and *Close Encounters of the Third Kind* to *Predator* and the *Alien* franchise to *Alf* and *The X-Files*—all feature space travel, aliens, and the paranormal. The idea of other intelligent life, either visiting here or existing far away, astounds and captivates. Historian David M. Jacobs observes, "It is difficult to name another subject so quickly identifiable, so widely debated, so easily dismissed, and yet so little understood" as the one regarding intelligent, extraterrestrial life. It is a self-sustaining cycle: interest fuels attention, and attention fuels interest, and a mystery that on any given day, any of us could solve. There's not much at the bounds of human knowledge that I can participate in—and even less that I might stumble onto solving. I don't understand string theory or dark matter, my math abilities are quite limited, and I'm unlikely to invent nuclear fusion in my garage on a weekend. And yet each time any of us look out a window, glances into the night sky, or drives down an empty highway, we might spot that one glowing light that changes everything. Waves of sightings, what are known in ufology parlance as "flaps," have unfolded regularly over the last seventy-five years, defining more than one generation's understanding of its place in the world, and the universe at large, and creating memories that have lasted a lifetime.* When for research I tracked down a battered used copy of Harold Wilkins's 1955 *Flying Saucers Uncensored*, it bore a touching inscription inside that hinted at our collective great mystery: *December 19, 1955, to my dear boy, in remembrance of the Flying Saucer we saw on June 22, 1954, at 9:07 p.m.—Daddy.* Wrapped up in that simple inscription was one of the biggest and most important unanswered questions of human existence, the question that people really are asking when they ask if UFOs are real: Are we alone?

• •

"In the beginning there was an explosion. Not an explosion like those familiar on earth, starting from a definite center and spreading out to engulf more and more of the circumambient air, but an explosion that occurred simultaneously everywhere, filling all space from the beginning, with every particle of matter rushing apart from every other particle," writes Steven Weinberg, the 1979 Nobel Prize winner in physics. In short: before we were stardust, we were nothing. Space and time began about 14 billion years ago, with the big bang, and as Weinberg explains in his book *The First Three Minutes*, that explosion filled everything—everything being defined either as an infinite universe or a finite one that curves back on itself like the surface of a sphere. ("Neither possibility is easy to comprehend, but this will not get in our way; it matters hardly at all in the early universe whether space is finite or infinite," he writes.) One one-hundredth of a second later, the earliest moment in time that scientists can discuss confidently, the universe's temperature was a hundred thousand million degrees Celsius. There were no galaxies, stars, or planets in that instance, just a giant pool of what Weinberg calls an "ionized and undifferentiated soup of matter and radiation." In the first three

---

* "Ufology" today and the "ufologists" who practice and study it is a phrase that captures a field that's something more than a hobby and something less an academic field. As Thomas Bullard describes it, "Ufology is more nearly synonymous with the sum of UFO beliefs than with anything like a well-defined academic discipline."

minutes of the universe's life, temperatures cooled rapidly—it was then only one thousand million degrees, about seventy times hotter than the center of today's sun—and with time, a concept that now existed and has forever since unfurled only forward, protons and neutrons began to form together, creating nuclei that over a few hundred thousand years would become the atoms we now know as things like helium and heavy hydrogen, the building blocks of stars, dust, and, well, us.

It took some seven hundred thousand years after that for anything interesting to occur.

Over and across eons, worlds formed. Objects that we can recognize and classify—life—emerged. As astronomers view it, everything beyond our planet's atmosphere is referred to as "outer space," and the term "solar system" refers to a star and the objects that orbit around it; our solar system is about 4.6 billion years old and consists of our sun—a relatively average G-type main-sequence star, informally known as a yellow dwarf—and eight major planets (Mercury out through Neptune), as well as what astronomers generally accept are nine dwarf planets, including the once-upon-a-time-planet Pluto, some 650 "natural satellites," commonly referred to as moons, and over a million other items, from comets to asteroids.

Our solar system, in turn, is just one tiny corner of the Milky Way galaxy, that thick band of stars visible in the darkest night skies stretching far over our heads. We're about 25,000 light-years away from the center of the rotating galaxy, which astronomers estimate contains somewhere between 100 and 400 billion stars—and at least that number of planets—and stretches across some 87,400 light-years. What we see in our skies from Earth is the equivalent of staring at the side of the Milky Way stretching off before us, as if we're looking at the edge of a plate or a Frisbee. It is spiral-shaped, like an enormous spinning pinwheel, first mentioned, as far as we know, by the Persian astronomer Abd al-Rahman al-Sufi in AD 964, recorded in his *The Book of the Fixed Stars*. In 1610, Galileo was the first astronomer to piece together, using a telescope, that the Milky Way visible in our skies was a collection of faint stars; a century later, Immanuel Kant surmised that it was a rotating body of stars, and over the next two hundred years, astronomers came to begin to grasp how enormous the universe truly is.

Now we understand that our Milky Way is about 2.5 million light-years from the next closest galaxy, known as Andromeda. Together, these two massive galaxies—and all the stuff in between them, including a number of so-called dwarf galaxies and satellite galaxies, as well as a third large galaxy known as Triangulum—make up what astronomers call the "Local Group," which is one corner of a larger cosmic structure known as a "supercluster."* For most of the last fifty years, our particular galactic neighborhood was believed to be part of the "Virgo Supercluster," a gathering of about one hundred galaxies, but in 2014 a team of astronomers led by Hawaii's R. Brent Tully realized we were more connected to our neighbors than anyone had realized; they redrew the boundaries of the galactic map after realizing that our supercluster was far more vast and in fact consisted of what had been four separate superclusters that all moved in the same gravitational rhythm.

They dubbed the new supercluster "Laniakea," Hawaiian for "immense heaven," and we now believe it encompasses about one hundred thousand other galaxies that astronomers define as "nearby," despite the fact that they stretch across more than 520 million light-years of outer space. Laniakea, in turn, is now understood to be part of the Pisces-Cetus Supercluster Complex, an enormous structure of about sixty superclusters that together stretch across a billion light-years. The Pisces-Cetus Supercluster Complex is what's known as a "galaxy filament," the largest structures known to exist in our universe, in which NASA now estimates there are about 200 billion galaxies stretching across 46 billion light-years.† (Each of those galaxies is estimated to have perhaps 100 million stars—although the largest, known as supergiants, can contain 100 trillion.)

On the one hand, Earth seems unique—and yet when set against the scale of the universe, even if the odds of intelligent life are literally astronomical, the universe seems likely large enough for there to be many such possible planets. Recent estimates imagine that there are one sextillion—a

---

* In 1959, Harlow Shapley had proposed an alternate name for this structure, "metagalaxy," but science stuck with the supercluster name chosen by French American astronomer Gérard Henri de Vaucouleurs.

† Next door to us, metaphorically speaking, is the Perseus-Pegasus Filament, which was discovered in 1985 and itself stretches for another billion light-years.

billion trillion—of habitable planets in the universe. Sure, the odds of life are long, but does it really seem like humans are a one-in-a-sextillion chance? "There's good and growing reason to expect cosmic company. The past hundred years have witnessed a slow but inexorable spring tide of discoveries that encourage the idea that Earth may have many, many analogues," SETI astronomer Seth Shostak wrote.

• •

The spies and analysts who work in earthly intelligence always try to draw distinctions between secrets and mysteries; their realm and strength, they say, is primarily in uncovering secrets—knowable facts purposefully concealed from public view. (The capabilities of the latest Chinese hypersonic weapon, for example, is a secret; how the Egyptians built the pyramids is a mystery.) Much of the story and history of the popular culture, media, and governmental focus on UFOs has been trying to understand where that critical line is between knowable secrets and unknown mysteries: How much of the UFO phenomena is attributable to secret human technology or visiting extraterrestrial activity versus simple physics, meteorology, and astronomy that we just don't yet fundamentally understand?*

UFOs surely continue to confound us, in part because we know so little about the world around us. As much as we now know about meteorology, astronomy, the heavens, and physics, it's worth remembering how new (and still evolving) much of that knowledge truly is. Most of the core principles we have uncovered about physics, time, space, and astronomy have been discovered in just a human lifetime or two. In fact, before you even get to the mysteries of space, much of our understanding of our own planet is startlingly new. Western scientists have only known about the existence of gorillas, our closest living relative, for about 150 years; before 1847, reports of their sightings were dismissed as stories of a mythical

---

* This secret/mystery line was a key part of why the US government recently "rebranded" UFOs as UAPs, unidentified anomalous phenomena, understanding that while some portion of UFO sightings are surely secret advanced aerial craft from the US, China, Russia, or elsewhere, that surely much—and perhaps most or nearly all—of today's UFO sightings simply reflect basic principles and phenomena of physics, meteorology, and astronomy that today are mysteries.

creature akin to a yeti or a unicorn. The first "dinosaur" was discovered and identified in 1824, and it's effectively only been in my lifetime that we've come to recognize they were wiped out in an asteroid collision and that many dinosaurs were feathered. Giant squids existed as a myth for thousands of years, traceable to Aristotle and ancient Greece, until a French ship actually caught one in 1861, and it wasn't until 2004 that biologists actually spotted one in its natural habitat. My high school geology teacher, Mr. McGraw, would remind us that the theory of plate tectonics—now widely understood as the way the entire Earth moves—wasn't even proven when he himself was a student. We still know less about the bottom of the oceans than we do the surface of the moon. "There is a tendency in 20th-century science to forget that there will be a 21st-century science," J. Allen Hynek, one of the world's most influential astronomers and ufologists said, "and, indeed, a 30th-century science, from which vantage points our knowledge of the universe may appear quite different."

• •

This book intertwines two threads from across the last seventy-five years: the military's on-again-off-again hunt for UFOs here on Earth, and the increasingly serious work conducted by scientists, astronomers, and eventually NASA to search for extraterrestrial intelligence in the universe. These stories have been traditionally told separately, the UFO tale usually relegated to conspiratorial whodunits and self-published books by obscure small presses, while the more official "Search for Extraterrestrial Intelligence," known as SETI, is the subject of more scholarly work and memoirs by well-respected scientists—but that artificial divide fails to recognize the parallel tracks these two stories have led since World War II, as advancing technology has allowed us to understand the heavens in ways that our ancestors never could have imagined. Both threads are fundamentally stories of believing—the human desire, at a basic and almost cellular level, to hope even against the longest of odds—and they are different sides of the same coin, the line between the believability of one and the reality of the other deeply intertwined. "The common thread is a sincere desire to understand the universe, to find truth and meaning in a time when we are overwhelmed with astronomical data," journalist Joel Achenbach writes.

What follows is not an attempt to tell the full, exhaustive story of UFOs, alien contact, and the search for extraterrestrial intelligence—there are some famous "sightings" that barely merit mention, and others that don't get any mention at all, and many of the incidents, sightings, and reported encounters in this book have resulted in entire stand-alone books or even shelves of books themselves—nor does it purport to offer comprehensive solutions to every sighting. Instead, it is an effort to tell the story of how the US government, military, and leading scientists have approached these questions over our collective lifetime. I've tried to narrow my focus to those incidents, sightings, and reported encounters that changed the arc of the broader history of UFOs in America and the world beyond during the latter half of the twentieth and the first two decades of the twenty-first centuries. It is a story populated by some of the biggest figures of modern American history, from Harry Truman to Jimmy Carter, and some of most famous minds of the twentieth century, from Enrico Fermi to Carl Sagan, as well as all manner of strange and colorful characters who span the spectrum from serious scientists to outright grifters, from the nation's leading nuclear scientists to the man who inspired talk radio conspiracist Alex Jones. It is a story, as one of the field's most notorious practitioners, James Moseley, once described the field of ufology, of "genuinely mysterious events that always remain somehow just beyond solution while becoming impossibly tangled in a web of wacky human failings and yearnings."

Part of the challenge in putting it all together is that the government absolutely is covering up the full extent of its interest and investigation into UFOs. Plenty of revelations, declassified documents, and public reports prove an active, ongoing cover-up over decades, and even today, the US government is surely hiding information from us about its knowledge, beliefs, and working theories about what exists in the skies above and beyond us. I know this not because I have any special visibility into what they're hiding, but simply because the US government routinely hides information important and meaningless on all manner of subjects, regardless of whether there are legitimate national security concerns involved. Every book I've ever written has run up against classified information and decades-old secrets still locked inside archives. Today, especially, the US government remains coy about the extent to which modern-day "UAPs," an acronym that in recent years first referred to "unidentified *aerial* phenomena" and now refers to "unidentified *anomalous* phenomena," are drones or unmanned vehicles launched by adversaries like Russia and China. What is unclear is whether the government is covering up *meaningful* information about UFOs or UAPs—the verdict is much more mixed about whether the government has intelligence that would forever alter our understanding of ourselves and our universe.

At the same time, as someone who has spent two decades researching and reporting on US intelligence, national security, and the military, one of my maxims is that government conspiracy theories generally presuppose a level of competence and planning that isn't on display in the rest of the work that the US government does: sure, secrets can be held for a few years or a few decades, particularly if they're focused on a small group, but the government just isn't secretive, creative, or thoughtful enough to execute the grandest conspiracies we see lurking behind the darkest interpretation of events like Roswell, the Kennedy assassination, Watergate, or 9/11. The deeper I got into this particular subject, the more I came to realize that the government's UFO cover-up has primarily been a cover-up motivated not by knowledge but of ignorance. It's not that the government knows something it doesn't want to tell us; it's that the government is uncomfortable telling us it doesn't know anything at all. It's a bafflement that hints at a more exciting and intriguing truth: there is something out there, and none of us yet know what it is. As Philip Morrison, one of the inventors of the SETI field, said, "Either we're alone in the universe or we're not, and either possibility boggles the mind."

For now, we are left with math, physics, astronomy, and a mystery. Carl Sagan dedicated his life to his hunt, wondering whether humans were alone, a hunt that popularized him even as it caused his peers to sneer at his scientific credentials. As he saw it, "In a very real sense this search for extraterrestrial intelligence is a search for a cosmic context for mankind, a search for who we are, where we have come from, and what possibilities there are for our future—in a universe vaster both in extent and duration than our forefathers ever dreamed of."

As it turns out, in the end, the story of the hunt for "them" is mostly actually a story about us.

PART 1

The Saucer Age
(1947–1960)

1

Flying Saucers

From the moment he saw it, Colonel William Blanchard knew something was odd about the wreckage spread out before him. The jagged wooden pieces and scraps of reflective material, hastily gathered from a crash site discovered days earlier, were not from any aircraft he could identify, and the strange symbols weren't any language he recognized—they looked, if anything, like hieroglyphs.

The wreckage had been found, he had been told, by a local rancher named Mac Brazel. The sheriff, guessing it was military, had sent Brazel onward to the nearest air base to report the find, and soon after, two military intelligence officers, Major Jesse Marcel and an anonymous man who Brazel would describe as being in plainclothes, had traveled back with him to investigate, wandering around the field and gathering up the fallen "rubber strips, tinfoil, a rather tough paper, and sticks" before transferring them back to the headquarters of the 509th Bombardment Wing.

The United States military had designed and produced a wide variety of aircrafts—as one of the most respected and decorated airmen in the Army Air Forces, Blanchard knew this for sure—but this definitely wasn't one of them. It also didn't seem to resemble anything atomic weapon–related, another area with which he had deep experience.* The idea that it was an amateur inventor's design was unlikely, given that the base was in a relatively remote area of New Mexico. Maybe it was some kind of test. Maybe it was Russian.

Or, maybe, he thought, it was something else.

---

* As a graduate of West Point, Blanchard had flown the first B-29 bomber into China in 1944, part of the first US efforts to bomb the Japanese mainland, and then in 1945 he'd served as the backup pilot to Colonel Paul Tibbets on the Hiroshima bombing.

The commanding colonel, known by the nickname "Butch," had a long-standing reputation as a bold, decisive man with a knack for pushing the envelope (a fact his detractors would sum up more negatively as a "loose cannon"), and to this particular moment, he applied his trademark decisiveness. He knew exactly what he was looking at.

This wreckage, he thought to himself, was one of those things that everyone was talking about.

He ordered his public affairs officer, Lieutenant Walter Haut, to put out a press release: The US Army Air Forces at Roswell, it announced, had captured the first flying saucer.

• •

While Mac Brazel's discovery would someday be the most well-known of its time, it was far from the first or only report of strange objects flying through American skies in the years following the Second World War. Just two weeks prior, a Boise businessman named Kenneth Arnold had had a similarly odd experience in Washington State, setting off a "flap," as waves of sightings would come to be called, that would kick off the modern UFO phenomenon.

While flying on June 24, 1947, the thirty-two-year-old Arnold, an experienced rescue pilot with some four thousand hours of mountain high-altitude flight time, had decided to take a detour to search for a suspected downed military transport plane near Mount Rainier. (He had heard that there was a $5,000 reward for anyone who could locate it, and he had some time to kill on his trip between Chehalis and Yakima.) But, as he had navigated his two-seat CallAir A-2 prop plane toward the area, he later recalled, he had begun to see a bright light. At first, he assumed it was just a glare from another plane—but then he realized he was looking at as many as nine objects, seemingly in formation and moving at tremendous speed through the air, stretched out over perhaps five miles. "I could not find any tails on these things," Arnold said. "They didn't leave a jet trail behind them. I judged their size to be at least 100 feet in wingspan. I thought it was a new type of missile." As the lights continued to move together "like the tail of a Chinese kite, kind of weaving and going at a terrific speed," he used his dashboard clock to time how long it took them to fly from between Mount Rainier and Mount Adams. It was astonishing. According to the measurements, these things—whatever they were—were moving somewhere around 1,200 to 1,700 miles per hour, far faster than anything known at the time.* Altogether, Arnold watched the objects for about three minutes—during which time he even opened his airplane window to make sure he wasn't catching a reflection off his windshield.

When he landed at Yakima, he told friends at the airport about the strange sighting, and a day later, repeated the story to reporters at the *East Oregonian*. The first version of the article referred to the objects as "saucer-like aircraft," and headline writers across the country subsequently shorthanded the label to "flying saucers."†

When the two reporters returned from lunch after filing their story to the wires, they found the small newspaper office besieged by follow-up inquiries, and within hours, the story flew coast-to-coast. Eager for more information, one of the *East Oregonian* reporters hustled down the road to Arnold's hotel for a second interview. The conversation lasted two hours. Other reporters followed, and by the twenty-sixth, the pilot was telling his story on the radio.

It was a fantastical tale, one primed for debunking and disproving. But, as the details of the account were more closely studied, those who initially questioned Arnold were ultimately convinced that he was telling the truth. As part of an investigation, Frank M. Brown, an army intelligence officer assigned to evaluate the case, pulled highly detailed files that

---

* One of the major points of Arnold's report later called into question was how accurately he could have judged his distance from the objects—based on how big items have to be in order to be seen by the regular human eye, it's possible that the objects were closer than he thought. He might have seen something around fifty feet long moving at more like 400 mph, which is to say he might have seen something plane-sized, moving at a normal plane speed.

† The idea of a "flying saucer" was in and of itself a somewhat new and unexpected concept. As folklorist Thomas Bullard wrote, "The disk shape had appeared from time to time in illustrations for science fiction and on the cover of magazines like *Popular Science* to depict futuristic aviation designs, but images of round craft enjoyed no special favor in mass or popular culture."

the Army Air Forces kept of the region—maps that Arnold would have never had a chance to access—and determined, "After having checked an aeronautical map of the area over which Mr. Arnold claims that he saw the objects it was determined that all statements made by Mr. Arnold in regard to the distances involved, speed of the objects, course of the objects and size of the objects, could very possibly be facts."

"It is the personal opinion of the interviewer that Mr. Arnold actually saw what he saw," Brown continued in a then-secret report. "To go further, if Mr. Arnold can write a report of the character that he did while not having seen the objects that he claimed he saw, it is the opinion of the interviewer that Mr. Arnold is in the wrong business, that he should be writing Buck Rogers fiction."

Whatever the objects were, the news of their interaction with Arnold kicked off the biggest aerial fever the nation had ever seen. That summer, spotting flying saucers seemed to overtake baseball as the national pastime, with newspapers tracking the now daily reports from across the country of one strange sight in the sky after another. Appearances of other anomalies came from countless other pilots, both military and commercial. On June 28, an F-51 Mustang pilot near Lake Mead, Nevada, reported a half-dozen circular objects in the air around 3:15 in the afternoon; that same night, air force officers in Alabama reported a bright light passing overhead and making a sharp ninety-degree turn before heading south. At 11 a.m. on July 4, four disk-shaped objects allegedly streaked across the sky near Redmond, Washington. At 1:05 p.m. the same day, a Portland police officer said he saw five large disks over the city, a claim supported by two other officers who soon reported their own sighting, as did the harbor patrol. Citizens also called in, describing objects of "aluminum or chromium color, disc or hubcap or pie-pan or half-moon shape flashing in the sun, no vapor trail, no noise (except possible humming)." That afternoon, a Coast Guard yeoman in Seattle snapped the first-known photograph of a suspicious object in the sky overhead—a circular bright dot. (It was later deemed by investigators to be a weather balloon.)

At first, the military didn't know what to make of the deluge; the incidents seemed to be happening everywhere, but details were scarce and none seemed hostile. Were these bizarre floating entities friend or foe? And did they even exist at all?

To know one way or another, the military readied P-61 fighters to attempt to intercept the mystery disks, and began flying specially equipped "camera patrols" with telescopic lenses in the hope of encountering and photographing whatever they found. Other military bases placed fighters on ground alert; California's Muroc Army Air Field kept a P-80 jet fighter at the end of the runway, ready to chase a flying disk at a moment's notice. For days, eight P-51 fighters and three A-26 bombers patrolled over the Cascades and the Pacific Northwest, finding nothing but empty sky.

Even as the military came up empty, the sightings continued to stream in from dozens of states—at least thirty-nine reported anomalies within a matter of weeks. Some, ultimately, were easier to dismiss than others: when over four hundred callers contacted the police in Birmingham, Alabama, with reports of lighted disks, investigators quickly determined they were just decorative searchlights from a nearby circus, lighting up low-hanging clouds. Meanwhile, in Portland, Oregon, a Fourth of July flyover of B-29 bombers and P-80 fighters led to a police alert as citizens misidentified the planes overhead as suspicious flying objects. "Flying 'Whatsits' Supplant Weather as No. 1 Topic Anywhere People Meet," read a *Los Angeles Times* report. One Oregon minister preached that the mystery objects "were the advance guard of the second coming of Christ."

Eventually, the military accepted that something had to be done. That July 4, Wright Field, the headquarters of the Army Air Forces' technical intelligence and laboratory, issued a press release saying that, despite its skepticism, it would now officially be investigating the sightings, at the order of the air force chief of staff. "As things stand right now, it appears to be either a phenomenon," the statement concluded, "or the figment of somebody's imagination."[*]

The same evening, around 8 p.m., the crew of United Airlines Flight 105, flying from Boise to Oregon, reported a fast-approaching light in the sky; they had turned on their DC-3's landing lights to warn the

---

[*] Since, as the book explains, the initial years of the flying saucer reports took place amid a rapidly evolving postwar military establishment, I have in a few places standardized place or unit names to avoid confusion; Wright-Patterson, for instance, went through three name changes in 1945, 1947, and 1948 before settling on what it's known as today.

approaching craft, but then realized it wasn't any normal plane. Instead, Captain Emil Smith and copilot Ralph Stevens saw somewhere between four and nine disks—news reports varied in their summary, objects that paced them for about twelve minutes as the commercial propeller plane cruised across about forty-five miles of the Pacific Northwest. Smith described the objects as "smooth on the bottom and rough appearing on top," but in the darkness, they couldn't define whether the flying objects were "oval or saucer-like." *

And then, on July 8, came Roswell. In the wake of Blanchard's announcement that a saucer had been found and relocated to the 509th Bombardment Wing, the official announcement dominated the local paper. Under a two-level banner headline declaring "RAAF Captures Flying Saucer on Ranch in Roswell Region," the *Roswell Daily Record* noted how "the disk was recovered on a ranch in the Roswell vicinity, after an unidentified rancher had notified Sheriff Geo. Wilcox, here, that he had found the instrument on his premises." Major Jesse Marcel had then inspected the recovered craft and then it was taken onto "higher headquarters," but had thus far refused to release any details about the saucer's construction or appearance.

The article also quoted two locals, Mr. and Mrs. Dan Wilmot—the latter of whom was identified as "one of the most respected and reliable citizens in town"—who said they had been sitting on their porch the previous Wednesday, July 2, when they saw a fast-moving "large glowing object" zip overhead. "In appearance it looked oval in shape like two inverted saucers, faced mouth to mouth, or like two old type washbowls placed, together in the same fashion," the Wilmots explained. "The entire body glowed as though light were showing through from inside, though not like it would inside, though not like it would be if a light were merely underneath."

By 2:30 p.m. local time, Blanchard's statement was picked up by the Associated Press, prompting reporter visits to Roswell and a bombardment

---

* When an army counterintelligence officer interviewed the United pilot, the agent concluded that the pilot "would have to be very strongly convinced that he actually saw flying disks before he would open himself for the ridicule attached to a report of this type."

of telephone calls from across the country, and even around the world—one came, very long distance, from the London *Daily Mail*—upon Sheriff Wilcox's office.

Amid the bedlam, the *San Francisco Examiner* reached Blanchard's boss, Brigadier General Roger Ramey, the commander of the Eighth Air Force in Fort Worth, Texas, where the debris had been subsequently moved. Ramey quickly refuted the reports of unidentified material, claiming that his base experts had examined the debris sent from Roswell and easily identified it as belonging not to any foreign or unknown craft, but to a lowly weather balloon instead. At 5:30 p.m. New Mexico time, the AP put out an updated story, datelined Fort Worth: "Roswell's celebrated 'flying disk' was rudely stripped of its glamor by a Fort Worth army airfield weather officer who late today identified the object as a weather balloon." From there, the military continued to double down on the assertion that nothing had happened out of the ordinary at Roswell, culminating in an appearance by Ramey himself that night on the local NBC station in Fort Worth. Once again, the general explained that the crash debris was "a very normal gadget," one that upon examination appeared to be little more than "remnants of a tinfoil covered box kite and a rubber balloon."

The nation's interest quickly moved on—there were so many other sightings to cover and whatever had landed in Roswell clearly didn't solve the mystery. One state over, the *Arizona Republic* reported on the "dud" New Mexico disk on its front page on July 9, but gave much of its front page over to what it thought was an even bigger scoop: one of the first photos of a flying saucer—two grainy images, shot by local resident William Rhodes, that appeared to show a disk-shaped object that Rhodes said had been flying south and then banked into a series of tight turns near his house at an altitude of about one thousand feet before disappearing into the western sky at high speed.

Aviation experts agreed that Rhodes's photo didn't match anything known to be flying in the United States—the one attempt by the military to field a similar saucer-shaped plane, the Vought V-173, nicknamed the "Flying Pancake," had never been put into production and the test planes had never been known to fly outside of Connecticut, where they'd been under development during World War II. In fact, the navy had formally given up on the program in March 1947 after the planes failed to ever be able to achieve proper fighter speeds.* *So what had Rhodes photographed?* The military's inability to answer the question was becoming an embarrassment—and in the summer of '47, the last thing the US military wanted was to be embarrassed on the national stage.

• •

The national focus on flying saucers came at a critical moment in the postwar evolution of the US government, the US military, and aviation in general. In just a few short wartime years, planes and aviation had gone from a curiosity to the central vehicle of battle, and the public and government fascination with the new unexplained flying objects was all but inseparable from the larger security concerns of that moment.

In 1945, the United States had emerged from World War II more powerful and better positioned economically and militarily than any other country, adversary, or ally. With the traditional European powers devastated by war and famine, global security was, for the first time, now left to the United States to protect and defend, but the country was only now readying itself to assume that role—and it became all too clear that such supervision would be necessary when, throughout 1946 and 1947, the shadows of a new conflict had settled in across Europe.

In 1946, diplomat George Kennan started calling for a policy of "containment" of the Communist and Soviet menace, which he felt would emerge from the ashes of broken governments and war-torn nations, and in March 1947, President Harry S. Truman committed US support to Greece and Turkey, who had been experiencing Communist takeovers in the region, declaring it the policy of the United States "to support free peoples who are resisting attempted subjugation by armed minorities or by outside pressures."† In April, statesman Bernard Baruch coined the

---

* Even with the passage of far more time and far greater access to aviation records and declassified files, there's no evidence that the US had access to any aircraft in the late 1940s that would mimic the behavior, speed, or shape of the flying disks.

† The so-called Truman Doctrine would come in the 1950s to encompass the "domino theory" that would lead the US into Korea and Vietnam.

phrase "Cold War" to describe the increasingly chilly relations between the Soviet Union and the West. And in early June, just three weeks before Kenneth Arnold's fateful flight and sighting, Secretary of State George Marshall had outlined a sweeping plan to invest in rebuilding and securing Europe during his speech at Harvard University's spring commencement.

Confronting all of these issues required new thinking about the function of a peacetime military. Traditionally, the US had kept little standing military in between wars—and what army and navy did exist over most of the preceding seventy-five years had hardly been a world-class fighting force. At the start of World War I, the US had possessed the world's largest economy, but only its seventeenth largest army, a force smaller than Portugal's. (A military historian characterized that force as "old, drunk, and stagnant.") Now, after a war that had engaged nearly every corner of the globe on land, sea, and by air, such unpreparedness and underdevelopment was no longer an option.

Luckily, Truman had a unique vantage point on what his successor would call the "military-industrial complex." As a senator, he had led the congressional committee charged with auditing the vast wartime spending, rooting out fraud, and identifying waste, and seen the military—which had long consisted of entirely separate Navy and War Departments, each overseen by its own cabinet secretary—sprawl. At the start of World War II, the US military had established the Army Air Forces, a third, confusing, and semiautonomous service branch. In 1944, he had published an op-ed titled "Our Armed Forces MUST Be Unified," in *Collier's Weekly*, arguing that it was long past time to combine the theretofore separate Departments of the Army and the Navy. "Our scrambled professional military setup has been an open invitation to catastrophe," he argued. "All of our defensive and offensive strength [must be] under one tent and one authoritative, responsible command." As president, he had followed through on his proposal for a unified command—known as the War Department, Department of National Security, or the Department of National Defense—that would, among other chances, bring together the two existing military services and plan for a future of an independent air force, too.

General Dwight Eisenhower endorsed the same restructuring; World War II had demonstrated the critical importance of airpower, and the arrival of the atomic bomb had made it seem possible that wars would begin and end with airplanes. It had also created the unsettling sense that future wars might take place within a more compact time frame, meaning the country would need to keep a larger standing force and wouldn't have time to ramp up its industrial manufacturing for a year or two as it had at the start of both world wars. "The war had ushered in a new era that would be dominated by air power, both conventional and atomic," an official air force history explained. "The new peacetime military establishment must be geared to deter conflict by maintaining adequate forces in-being."

With all of this in mind, as newspapers filled with saucer sightings throughout the summer of 1947, the full US Senate in Washington, DC, debated groundbreaking legislation that would come to be known as the National Security Act of 1947, and ultimately prepare the military establishment for the impending Cold War. The legislation unified the army and navy into a single department and created new entities like the National Security Council, Joint Chiefs of Staff, and the Central Intelligence Agency—the nation's first peacetime intelligence agency. The bill also established a fully independent US Air Force and a new post that would be known as the secretary of defense to oversee the combined three-branch military. Within days that July, it sailed through the Senate, the official recognition from Congress that "peace" in the atomic age would look unlike any peace America had experienced before, and in many ways, the saucer frenzy was its first test. Harry Truman signed the legislation, a law that promised "a comprehensive program for the future security of the United States," just eighteen days after the Roswell crash.*

---

* At its start, the new entity was called the National Military Establishment, and led to an abbreviation—NME—that many pronounced like "enemy," which seemed exactly counter to the new department's goal. In 1949, it was officially renamed the Department of Defense, a two-year gap that would become, decades later, an important detail in the story of ufology.

• •

In the midst of this geopolitical uncertainty and evolving technologies, it was crucial that the department quell national anxiety. Day after day, military leaders disavowed any knowledge of the disks. Major General Curtis LeMay, the legendary World War II air leader who now headed the air force's research program, told reporters, "Whatever these people have seen it hasn't been anything resulting from experiments by the Army Air Forces. As far as I'm concerned there's nothing to it at all. The whole thing is unfortunate." Another military spokesman laughably suggested the "flying disks" were "large hailstones which might have flattened out and glided a bit." In early July, officials at the US Naval Observatory in Washington announced that the disks, as described, could not be astronomical phenomena; David Lilienthal, the head of the Atomic Energy Commission, followed up with the confirmation that the sightings were unrelated to any secret nuclear weapons project, adding a personal statement that he, too, was "anxious to know" more about them. That reassurance, though, seemed undermined when a spokesman for the Army Air Forces' Wright Field in Ohio said that if "some foreign power is sending flying discs over the United States, it is our responsibility to know about it and take the proper action."

These disconnects only fueled the fire, and now a new question—and anxiety—hung over the entire controversy: *Was the US being probed by a secret Soviet space weapon?*

While at first LeMay and others had brushed off civilian reports of these "flying saucers," a series of sightings in and around sensitive facilities in the Mojave Desert the same day as the Roswell hullabaloo had made them suddenly quite concerned.

The Muroc Army Air Field* was one of the military's most secret facilities, home to research and development operations and offering 300,000 secluded acres across which experimental plane testing and elite training schools could be conducted without notice or disruption—out in

---

* In 1950, it would be renamed Edwards Air Force Base.

the desert nearby, a full-scale replica of a Japanese heavy cruiser known as "Muroc Maru" and constructed entirely of lumber and chicken wire covered in tar paper, sat by Rogers Dry Lake, used during World War II to train pilots on attacking naval vessels.

On July 8, around 9:30 a.m., Lieutenant Joseph McHenry had just left a base exchange, where he'd been discussing with other airmen his dubiousness about the flying saucer reports pouring in around the country. "Someone will have to show me one of these discs before I will believe it," he had told his colleagues—when, upon entering his office, he had glanced skyward and saw what he later described as two "spherical or disc-like" objects, moving, by his estimate, at about three hundred miles an hour at around eight thousand feet. Three people nearby—two sergeants and a secretary—all spotted the same thing. Moments later, after the original two objects had passed from view, McHenry spotted a similar silver sphere or disk-like object circling to the north. "From my actual observance the object circled in too tight a circle and too severe a plane to be any aircraft that I know of," he later wrote in an affidavit given to counterintelligence officers.

Just thirty minutes later, around 10 a.m., a test pilot named J. C. Wise was warming up the engines of a XP-84 Thunderjet prototype when he saw what he first assumed was a weather balloon traveling west far overhead; with a start, though, he realized the object appeared to be moving against the prevailing wind. "The object was yellowish white in color and I would estimate that it was a sphere about 5 to 10 feet in diameter," Major Wise said. Other officers and airmen reported as many as three similar objects heading west.

Around noon, an observer crew out by Rogers Dry Lake stationed there for an ejection-seat experiment, noticed a round, aluminum-colored object moving through the sky, also against the prevailing wind. "As this object descended through a low enough level to permit observation of its lateral silhouette, it presented a distinct oval-shaped outline, with two projections on the upper surface which might have been thick fins or nobs," the crew's report read. "No smoke, flames, propeller arcs, engine noise, or other plausible or visible means of propulsion were noted." (One of the observers, Captain John Paul Stapp, noted defensively in his affidavit, "Seeing this was not a hallucination or other fancies of a sense.")

The day ended with yet another P-51 pilot, south of Muroc, spot-ting a "flat object of a light-reflecting nature" high above him. He tried to give chase, but his plane couldn't climb high enough to reach what-ever it was.

To the military, the idea that these disks—whatever they were, who-ever they were—seemed so intensely focused on one of the air force's most secret facilities set off alarms anew through the Pentagon ranks. One rumor circulated in the media that the "flying saucers" were a new supersonic atomic-powered Russian plane. In the media, the Soviet for-eign minister even played up his country's involvement in what the *New York Times* dubbed the summer "Dither of the Disks": he joked that maybe the objects were a "Russian discus thrower training for the Olym-pic Games who didn't realize his own strength." The military was begin-ning to think, though, the saucers weren't anything to joke about.

Again, the objects, whatever they were, appeared to have no harmful intent—nor did they seem to have any particularly friendly intent. What were these things appearing in the sky all over the country?

In the end, it didn't matter. A new national obsession—and govern-ment headache—had taken hold. The age of saucer obsession had begun.

2

The Foo Fighters

As the flying saucer frenzy dominated the summer of 1947, what was perhaps more shocking and scattered than the sightings themselves was the United States military's response to them. Individual military bases across the country made their own statements and sent out their own counterintelligence agents to investigate, but there was little national-level reaction or even apparent interest from the larger government structure. This was largely due to the fact that, at the time, there was no formalized approach to studying strange things in the sky—not because they were rare, but precisely because they *weren't*. Humans, after all, had been reporting odd sightings in the sky for millennia—there are those who believe that Ezekiel's heavenly vision in the Bible of a "wheel within a wheel" was itself a reference to a biblical-age flying saucer*—and officials had weathered a few flying object contagions over the last century.

One period in particular—about six months from November 1896 through April 1897—had created quite the stir, during which American newspapers had been filled with sightings of mysterious airships passing through the skies over California and as far east as West Virginia, at speeds that varied from a lazy five miles an hour to an astounding 150 miles per hour (the latter estimated by an Iowa railroad engineer, who reported pacing the object with his train). One Illinois report described a witness working in his field, when "an airship alighted near him and . . . six people

---

* His Old Testament vision in Ezekiel 1:1–6 references "I looked, and I saw a windstorm coming out of the north—an immense cloud with flashing lightning and surrounded by brilliant light. The center of the fire looked like glowing metal, and in the fire was what looked like four living creatures. In appearance their form was human, but each of them had four faces and four wings."

disembarked therefrom, remained a few minutes and conversed with him, and then jumped aboard, ascended and sailed away."

Simultaneous or near-simultaneous sightings in multiple locations gave rise to the perception that it might be a whole fleet of mystery aircraft overflying the continent at the same time—or maybe just one aircraft slowly crossing the country. While witness reports varied in detail and astonishment, they coalesced around a nighttime description of a bright white or red light; during the daytime, it was a flying blimp-like craft, usually with a basket or vehicle suspended below it, powered by something like a propeller, evoking something more akin to an aerial sailing yacht than an out-of-this-world spaceship. "The strange aerial craft has been seen by every operator and station agent along the line between West Liberty, Iowa, and Cedar Rapids, and they all report the same condition," the *Detroit Free Press* noted on April 10, 1897. That same day the *Chicago Tribune* reported, "Either the long-expected airship from the Pacific Coast reached Chicago at 8:30 o'clock last evening or the fixed star, Alpha Orionis, shone with unusual brilliance."

Once again, theories abounded. While some posited that perhaps a mysterious inventor—a Howard Hughes or Tony Stark of his or her time—had created a secret flying machine, others, inspired by the Jules Verne and H. G. Wells science fiction of the era, believed that the craft might be of Martian origin.* Speculation only grew when, despite widespread written and oral reports, no hard proof—no photographs, no recorded imagery, no wreckage—ever emerged of the craft or crafts, nor did any technology that could be mistaken for it. Though real-world inventors were standing at the cusp of flight in the late 1890s—European inventors were known to have been tinkering with real-life rigid dirigibles, and in May 1897, US professor Arthur Barnard took off from the Tennessee Centennial Exposition in Nashville in a bicycle-powered airship that reportedly flew twelve miles toward Memphis—the characteristics of the mystery airship or airships didn't align with any known inventions then (or now).

---

* One rumor circulated that the inventor's name was Wilson, as a series of landings and sightings around Texas from April 19 to 30, including one by the sheriff in Uvalde, involved one of the craft's passengers introducing himself as "Wilson."

By summertime, the sightings trickled off and there was no real sign of the aircraft ever again, leading newspapers to conclude that the entire thing was a hoax, perhaps a prank played by bored telegraph operators that got out of hand.

It wasn't the last time a mystery would come and go with no convincing explanation.

· ·

Over weeks and months in late 1944 and 1945, US fighters and bombers alike had faced unknown objects in the sky over Europe, generally described as balls of light that appeared off wingtips or behind aircraft, and then proceeded to follow them through seemingly impossible maneuvers. Around Christmas, a pilot and radio observer from the 415th Night Fighter Squadron were on an early-morning flight at ten thousand feet in eastern France near the German border when something approached them. "We saw two lights climbing toward us from the ground. Upon reaching our altitude, they leveled off and stayed on my tail," the baffled pilot reported. "The lights appeared to be large orange glows. After staying with the plane for two minutes, they peeled off and turned away, flying under perfect control, and then went out."

Back on the ground, some flight crews chalked the lights up to a bad meal in the chow hall, combat fatigue, or simply nerves and stress—and yet, more and more planes continued to encounter the aerial balls of light, which were eventually named "foo fighters," after a nonsense word popularized by characters in the *Smokey Stover* comic strip.

Intelligence officers and military leaders were equally stumped—were they a new kind of flare? A rocket? Some sort of magically powered enemy plane? A jet? Nothing made sense. Shooting at the objects appeared to do nothing and evasive maneuvers seemed pointless. The lights followed nearly anywhere, seeming to pose no danger to the fighters and bombers, but nevertheless still appeared ominous to the confounded flight crews. One pilot had an encounter so unsettling that even twenty-four hours later, the crew said the radio observer was still hyperventilating. Even stranger was that similar reports arrived in lesser numbers from US pilots and aircrew fighting in the Pacific theater, too.

The first news reports of the puzzling events finally made it into US newspapers on January 1, 1945, prompting a quick dismissal by scientists that the sightings were only exaggerated views of St. Elmo's Fire, the luminous plasma that sometimes appeared in stormy weather near church steeples, ships' masts, or other tall pillars. The affected pilots, in turn, angrily responded they knew all about St. Elmo's Fire—what they'd seen wasn't *that*. Curious journalists also disagreed with the explanation, noting that they had found the pilots and flight crews to be totally credible and clearly high-functioning, among the best aerial aces in the European skies.

Ultimately, reports of the foo fighters all but disappeared from Europe as the war ended. Some suspected that this meant they'd been secret German weapons all along, but as Allied scientists, engineers, and military personnel swarmed captured Nazi factories, airfields, and offices during the Liberation, they never found any trace of something that might have been responsible for the unknown aerial phenomenon. The army eventually wrote off the entire episode as a "mass hallucination," which seemed to satisfy officials until the following year, when what was described as cigar-, rocket-, or meteor-like objects started to appear over Sweden—on July 9, 1946, one large daytime meteor-like light prompted the Swedish government to convene a special committee to study the events. The US military and US intelligence panicked, too, worrying that the rockets, whose locations seemed to be bordering the Soviet Union, were secret tests of a new weapons systems, perhaps updated versions of the German V-1 and V-2 missiles that Soviet scientists were developing with the help of captured Nazi engineers. The Swedish "ghost rockets" provoked widespread fear, especially as concerns about possible atomic weapon development grew in the wake of the Manhattan Project.*

By that August, the *New York Times* wrote that the "mysterious missiles" had brought the country "almost at the boiling point" and that the

---

* A V-2 fired from the Baltic seaside proving ground at the Peenemünde Army Research Center toward the end of the war had become the first man-made object to cross into space as it passed over the Earth-space boundary known as the Kármán line, one hundred kilometers above sea level.

military was racing to install advanced radar that might be better at tracking the unknown projectiles. On August 20, the US semi-covertly dispatched two of its leading aerial warriors to Stockholm: former general James Doolittle, who had led the daring and morale-boosting carrier-based bomber raid on Tokyo early in World War II, and David Sarnoff, a former member of Eisenhower's London staff who had become the president of the Radio Corporation of America. Doolittle was touring Sweden in his new postwar role as vice president of Shell Oil, and Sarnoff was exploring the European radio market, but both men arranged to be in the capital city at the same time and meet quietly with Swedish defense officials. Doolittle would decline to comment for the rest of his life on the existence and content of the meeting, but shortly after, the head of the US military's Central Intelligence Group (CIG), Lieutenant General Hoyt S. Vandenberg, wrote President Truman that it was possible the objects were coming from a former secret seaside German rocket proving ground that had fallen to the Soviet army and now was part of East Germany. "The weight of evidence pointed to Peenemünde as origin of the missiles," he wrote. "It is the belief of CIG that scientific experimentation is the primary Soviet objective and that political considerations, although thoroughly appreciated, are secondary" —but no proof or concrete sign of whatever was flying through the skies was ever established or released.

Finally, on October 10, 1946, the Swedish Defense Staff publicly stated that it suspected that almost all the sightings were actually just normal meteors and astronomical phenomena with some errant exceptions: "Most observations are vague and must be treated very skeptically. In some cases, however, clear, unambiguous observations have been made that cannot be explained as natural phenomena, Swedish aircraft, or imagination on the part of the observer. Echo, radar, and other equipment registered readings but gave no clue as to the nature of the objects."* In

---

* In terms of numbers, about 80 percent of the sightings over Sweden quickly resolved themselves as actual meteors or other mistaken sights, but a stubborn 20 percent remained mysteries, a number that could still have been misleadingly high, since the Swedish government had begun censoring exact details of public reports, fearing that the rockets were indeed secret Soviet tests and the sightings would help the

December, the inquiry was closed. "There is no actual proof that a test of rocket projectiles has taken place," the government's official concluding report declared.

In the end, all three episodes—the 1890s airships, the foo fighters, and the ghost rockets*—had all amounted to little more than bizarre, unexplained mysteries, with neither a sign of any hostile intent nor evidence that the mysterious objects in the end represented some exquisite advanced adversarial technology. At the time, throughout the sightings of foo fighters and ghost rockets, virtually no one publicly or privately speculated that the objects were alien spaceships. Now, though, with the saucers flap of the summer of '47, the government faced a new conundrum. The idea that the Soviets might be testing new rocketry over waters neighboring the Soviet Union was one thing, but it was something else entirely to wonder if someone—or some *thing*—was flying over the continental United States itself. Were these hostile craft? Or was this another mass hysteria—perhaps even one riled up by tricky Communist provocateurs?

• •

In the summer of 1947, sightings arrived from seeming every corner of the country—Butte! Philadelphia! Birmingham! Long Beach! Vermont!—and as they piled up, the press coverage shifted. For the first few weeks, newspaper and magazine editors had eaten up the stories, running one banner headline after another and cataloging the sightings as they flowed in around the country and across the world. Altogether, more than 850 mysterious objects were reported over the course of the year. By August, Gallup reported that 90 percent of American adults had heard of the flying saucers.

As more weeks passed, the breathless reports from across the country

---

enemy military calibrate its missiles. All the while, the Soviet government denied they were responsible for the sightings.

* While the episode is usually referred to as "Swedish ghost rockets," other "ghost rocket" sightings took place in Greece, Portugal, Belgium, and other European countries during the same time period.

and around the world that had followed Arnold's initial UFO sighting gave way to a more tempered (and even mocking) coverage. No proof of a crashed disk emerged, nor did any photos materialize with any greater level of detail than Rhodes's grainy Phoenix image.* One newspaper editor even offered a $3,000 reward for proof of the saucers' existence, a large sum that accelerated a wave of hoaxes that made it increasingly difficult to differentiate between "real" sightings and fake ones. One particularly elaborate hoax, whereby two men said they'd seen a disk and recovered debris from it on Maury Island in Puget Sound, Washington, ended in tragedy when the B-25 plane dispatched to pick up the debris and take it for further analysis crashed on its return flight, killing two counterintelligence officers.† As UFO historian Jacobs summed up, "By the end of July, newspaper reporters automatically placed any witness who claimed to see something strange in the sky in the crackpot category." *Life* magazine compared the reports to sightings of the Loch Ness Monster.

Arnold, for his part, grew ever more frustrated with the government's inability to answer the mystery of what he and others were seeing in the nation's skies. "It is with considerable disappointment you cannot give the explanation of these aircraft as I felt certain they belonged to our government," he wrote the head of Wright Field in Dayton, Ohio, that summer. "They have apparently meant no harm, but used as an instrument of destruction in combination with our atomic bomb the effects could destroy life on our planet." Arnold explained that he'd compared observations directly with the two United Airlines pilots, Smith and Stevens, "and [we] agreed we had observed the same type of aircraft as to size shape and

---

* Other sightings poured in from around the world—South Africa! Iran! Australia! Mexico! England!—and the press stories mocked the now-international trend. One wire report joked, "Several homesick Americans in Nanking found a formula today for locating 'flying saucers' in Chinese skies. The formula: Shortly before dawn, you *gambei* (Chinese for 'bottoms up') eleven cups of local yellow wine immediately followed by one stiff shot of American bourbon. Then fall to your knees, bow three times towards San Francisco and out of the dawn come flying saucers, some green, some yellow, but mostly purple."

† One of the officers who died in the crash was Lieutenant Frank Brown, who had also responded to Arnold's original sighting in June. Brown's death would spark numerous conspiracy theories in the years ahead.

form. We have not taken this lightly. It is to us a very serious concern as we are as interested in the welfare of our country as you are." *

No less an authority than Orville Wright, the coinventor of the airplane and the namesake of the military airfield where many of the sightings were being collected, declared that the saucer flap was nonsense: "It is more propaganda for war to stir up the people and excite them to believe a foreign power has designs on this nation." If it was propaganda, though, that was news to the government.

With the sightings showing no sign of slowing down, the air force called in J. Edgar Hoover's FBI. Two days after the multiple saucer sightings at the Muroc airfield, a bureau executive met with Brigadier General George F. Schulgen, the head of the Army Air Corps' intelligence requirements branch, to discuss the flying disks and how they were preparing to deal with them in a new military era. "The Air Corps has taken the attitude that every effort must be undertaken in order to run down and ascertain whether or not the flying disks are a fact," the FBI representative noted in an internal memorandum, "and if so, to learn all about them." The air force also explained how military scientists were hard at work ascertaining whether "the flying objects might be a celestial phenomenon . . . [or] they might be a foreign body mechanically devised and controlled." There was also a possibility, the memo added, "that the first reported sightings might have been by individuals of Communist sympathies with the view to causing hysteria and fear of a secret Russian weapon." The military, Schulgen had explained, was running down every lead they could; he had personally interrogated one pilot who adamantly reported seeing a disk, and neither the navy nor the War Department had any research projects that could be contributing to or involved in the situation. He asked the FBI for help investigating the claims all over the country, offering all of his office's resources to help run down the source of the sightings.

---

* Becoming the face of the sighting flap took a personal toll on Arnold, disrupting his business and causing him to become an object of ridicule as week after week went by with no vindication or clarity about whether he'd seen anything real at all. As he confided, he regretted speaking up at all—and would never make the same mistake again: "If I saw a ten-story building flying through the air, I would never say a word about it."

The request for help touched off a debate inside the bureau. Airborne anomalies, some argued, was neither their focus, nor their jurisdiction, while others considered them FBI domain by definition, dealing directly with what the bureau pledged to do: protect the nation from attack. Assistant Director Daniel Milton "D. M." Ladd recommended that the issue be avoided entirely—too many of the sightings, in his opinion, had turned out to be "pranks."* Director J. Edgar Hoover's closest deputy, Clyde Tolson, thought it was important for the bureau to engage, and ultimately Hoover agreed, handwriting a note that indicated a confusing but fascinating level of interest: "I would do it, but before agreeing to it we must insist upon full access to discs recovered. For instance, in the La. case the army grabbed it and would not let us have it for cursory examination."†

As was custom, the director's word was law. The FBI sent a national bulletin to field offices across the nation, asking them to start investigating "flying disk" sightings as they came in. In response, dozens of sightings and news clippings poured in to headquarters. In mid-August 1947, the FBI and army began working together to sort through the daily piles of fresh reports—some more reliable than others—and compiling a list of the names of the individuals who had sent them, to investigate their backgrounds and confirm none were Communists, subversives, or just plain practical jokers.

Before long, a new, quiet question started to emerge between investigators: *What if their own government was responsible for the sightings?* At one point, an FBI agent subtly approached a lieutenant colonel in air

---

* One of the reports that landed on Ladd's desk that July concerned a Laurel, Maryland, "flying disc" that the police quickly determined was comprised of a Gulf Oil sign and the top of a garbage can. The paint, in fact, was still wet when investigators examined it.

† The mention of an "La. case" appears to refer to a July 7 sighting in Shreveport, Louisiana, that proved to be a hoax after the sixteen-inch aluminum "wreckage" was found to include a "Made in USA" stamp. In that incident, according to the "very urgent" teletype sent to FBI headquarters by the New Orleans field office, army intelligence from the Barksdale air base took possession of the wreckage before the FBI arrived.

force intelligence with the now-growing theory, suggesting it would be embarrassing to the country, the military, and the FBI if the saucers were later determined to be of its own making, but as the inquiry bounced up the ranks of the military, each successive rank of command promised they knew nothing that could account for the sightings.* Eventually, the head of air force intelligence agreed to draft a memo to General LeMay, asking him to attest that the sightings weren't of the US's own making.

In early September, the head of the FBI's San Francisco Field Office obtained an internal Pentagon memo dismissing the FBI's services as merely an attempt "to relieve the numbered Air Forces of the task of tracking down all the many instances which turned out to be ash can covers, toilet seats, and what not," infuriating Hoover and his leadership team. The FBI was no one's junior partner, and as Assistant Director Ladd pointed out, the bureau had participated in this endeavor as a good faith favor to the air force, despite the fact that the efforts had "failed to reveal any indication of subversive individuals being involved in any of the reported sightings." This hostility left them no choice but to "discontinue all activity in this field," and the nascent joint effort collapsed before it could really make much progress.

In late September, Hoover sent a terse letter to the air force, formally cutting off cooperation. In turn, the bureau issued its field offices a national bulletin announcing, "Effective immediately, the Bureau has discontinued its investigative activities."

The FBI was out of the flying saucer business. For the next twenty years, the problem would be the air force's alone.

---

* It was hard even for the FBI and more junior officers to know whether to trust the denials—according to the internal FBI memo, the intelligence colonel to whom the question was originally brought "not only agreed that this was a possibility, but confidentially stated it was his personal opinion that such was a probability."

The Rocket Age

As the fall unfolded, the air force struggled to find its footing in the aftermath of the FBI debacle. With the National Security Act of 1947 now law, the new branch was set to become an independent military service on September 18, an undoubtedly positive outcome, but the influx of flying saucer sightings was continuing to be a source of frustration and outright embarrassment for its leaders. Here they were, making a political case that their group deserved pride of place among the military branches—that it could serve simultaneously as both the nation's leading defender and its leading attacker—and yet they could not solve the mystery playing out every day on the front pages of the nation's newspapers. Finally, a strategy was put in place. "Air Force officials could not confirm nor deny the existence of the objects," according to historian Kate Dorsch, so "the foremost goal was to determine whether they were piloted aircraft. If foreign, they could only come from one place. Was the Soviet Union flying experimental, high-speed aircraft over the Pacific Northwest in anticipation of some larger assault? Or were they domestic, indicating some advanced aircraft the Air Force higher ups had no knowledge of?"

The fears of surprise from the sky were real and were a big driver of the reorganization of the nation's defense apparatus then underway. James Forrestal took over as the first secretary of defense on September 17, as the National Security Act took effect; the air force was created formally on the following day; and a week later, on September 26, the personnel of the Army Air Forces were officially transferred to the new department.*

---

* While the air force became its own branch, military officials griped that the new legislation really "legitimized four military air forces," since not only did both the army and navy keep some aviation capability, but so did the marines, which was part

The moves were a major part of the nation's answer to the ominous birth of the atomic age.

As victory celebrations abated following the war, a deep sense of doom had permeated the public and government consciousness, especially after the publication of a thirty-thousand-word story by journalist John Hersey in the *New Yorker* the previous summer about the personal stories of six Hiroshima survivors and the hell they'd lived. An initial US media blackout had kept Americans from learning the true horror in Hiroshima and Nagasaki, but now the dedicated issue had broadcasted the stark and horrific details across the nation and the world; it sold out nationwide almost immediately, and was read aloud on the radio. "[Hersey's story was] the first truly effective, internationally heeded warning about the existential threat that nuclear arms posed to civilization," explained his biographer Lesley Blume.

The details and implications of the article that were shocking to the public were less so to government officials and others within the military and intelligence infrastructures, who had understood the true effects of the atomic power and held private concerns about what it meant for the future. One army lieutenant who had journeyed to Hiroshima to film the damage for a classified government review walked away thinking, "This kind of weapon cannot exist on earth and people live on earth too." In 1947, the Bulletin of the Atomic Scientists, an organization founded by scientists fearful of the new nuclear power, many of whom had played a role in its invention during the Manhattan Project, created what they called the "Doomsday Clock," a striking visual tracker of how close the world seemed to Armageddon, denoted by a simple clock sketch with the minute hand approaching "midnight." The clock, at its debut, was set initially at seven minutes to midnight. Anyone who hoped to save the world would have to act fast.

• •

Lieutenant General Nathan Twining, one of the longest-serving air officers in the US military, had tried to ignore the flying saucers. After all, he

---

of the navy, leading to generations of jokes about why exactly did the navy's army require its own air force?

had other things to worry about. As head of the Air Force Materiel Command, the air force's logistics organization, he was in charge of research, development, procurement, maintenance, and supplies—a massive operation headquartered at Wright Field in Ohio. He was a traditional military man, having started his career in the Oregon National Guard, graduating from West Point in the midst of World War I, and serving in every one of the air force's predecessor iterations from the Air Service to the Army Air Corps to the Army Air Forces, rising along the way from a private to a three-star general. In World War II, as a brigadier general, he'd been rescued by the navy in the South Pacific after six days in a life raft when his transport plane had to ditch in the ocean. After the war, he'd led a flight of three B-29s on a dashing adventure, flying from Guam to Washington, DC, via India and Europe, in just under sixty hours. And he was just as baffled by the waves of saucer sightings as anyone. On September 23, he and his team sat down and wrote the head of the air force with an official opinion "concerning 'flying discs.'"

As Twining's team saw it, it was possible that what many people were experiencing or witnessing was natural phenomena, like meteors, but some could indeed have been seeing "objects probably approximating the shape of a disc, of such appreciable size as to be as large as man-made aircraft." The described capabilities of those craft, "such as extreme rates of climb, maneuverability (particularly in roll), and action which must be considered evasive when sighted or contacted by friendly air-craft and radar," the report stated, "lend belief to the possibility that some of the objects are controlled either manually, automatically, or remotely," not paranormal or extraterrestrial. To test the theory, air force scientists wanted to engineer and build an aircraft that roughly fit the profile of the flying disks, and though it would require "extensive detailed development" and the research and construction costs would be "extremely expensive [and] time consuming," Twining thought it was worth it. His official recommendation was that the air force move ahead with a more formalized approach to monitor the situation and "issue a directive assigning a priority, security classification and Code Name for a detailed study of this matter to induce the preparation of complete sets of all available and pertinent data." A preliminary report, he added, should be completed within fifteen days and more detailed reports should follow every thirty days thereafter.

Within a short period, perhaps a few months or a year, they might have the answer to the question of the disks.

What would come to be known as "the Twining letter" was classified at the time, and it serves as an important indication that the government really did not know anything beyond its official findings, or feel the need to conceal its knowledge. It would be years before freedom of information laws were enacted (or even imagined), and even amid such secrecy, one of the nation's top air force officers, writing to the service's top officer—both men presumably in a position to know just about anything and everything concerning any known aircraft in the US fleet or that of foreign militaries overseas—expressed neither a hint nor a wink that the public controversies had roots in known US programs or planes. The nation's top flying minds were just as befuddled by the situation as anyone else.

• •

The creation of the US Air Force led to changes big and small, both cultural and administrative—all the service's "pursuit" planes, for example, were renamed "fighter" planes, with P-51s becoming F-51s. Just weeks after the air force became its own stand-alone service, Captain Chuck Yeager took to the air on October 14, 1947, in a $6 million craft known as the XS-1 (X for "research," S for "supersonic") in a tiny, highly secret project to fly faster than the speed of sound.

Since August, a crew of just thirteen personnel had been running familiarization flights with the plane, named the *Glamorous Glennis* after Yeager's wife, out of Muroc Air Force Base; the flights were harrowing—the straight-winged X-1 was dropped from the bomb bay of a B-29—and the equipment a mix of cutting-edge and highly primitive. In an era before hard-shell flying helmets, Yeager fashioned his own out of an army tank helmet, and he sat on an apple box inside the belly of the B-29 as the bomber climbed to altitude. The delicate X-1 was filled with liquid oxygen fuel, stored at 296 degrees below zero Fahrenheit, making the entire plane bitingly cold, which it then devoured at a rate of a ton of fuel per minute of flight. "Anyone with brain cells would have to wonder what in hell he was doing in such a situation—strapped inside a live bomb that's about to be dropped out of a bomb bay," Yeager joked. The only acknowledgment of their work on base was that the base closed operations every time they took off, given the volatility of the X-1 load.

On Yeager's first flight, the team had expected him to fly it to just .82 Mach, but he enjoyed himself so much that he hit .85 Mach, much to the chagrin and worry of his commanders. "Do you want to jeopardize the first Air Corps research project?" Colonel Albert Boyd had chided him after one test. No wind tunnel exceeded .85 Mach, so no one knew the aerodynamics or science of what came next. Each subsequent flight pushed the X-1 faster in roughly twenty-mile-an-hour increments; the flight team learning in turn about new shock waves, air ripples, and stability issues introduced as they neared the sonic barrier.

On the fourteenth, Yeager had been in particularly rough shape—he'd broken his ribs in a horse-riding accident over the weekend, causing him pain and making it difficult for him to turn around, but had avoided confessing it to military doctors so he wasn't sidelined from the program. With a friend, he snuck into the X-1 hanger and practiced locking the cockpit door behind him using a piece of broomstick. In flight, he'd only planned to hit .97 Mach—just under seven hundred miles per hour—but now, as he neared .965 Mach, his instruments began to wobble, and his Machmeter, which only went up to 1.0, went off the scale. Down below, the tracking van heard the rumble of a sonic boom—the first one ever heard on Earth from an airplane.

In the cockpit, though, flying faster than sound, Yeager recalled, was an anticlimactic, fairly smooth ride. "There should've been a bump in the road, something to let you know that you had just punched a nice clean hole through that sonic barrier," he later said. He'd hit Mach 1.07; when he landed on the dry lake bed below minutes later, his main reaction was that his ribs ached.

Ultimately, Yeager's faster flight topped out at about Mach 1.45, roughly 945 miles per hour, more than double the top speed of the P-51 Mustangs he'd flown during World War II—and as tests continued, the challenges soon became routine and predictable. "Light buffet and instability between .88 and .91 Mach; decrease in elevator effectiveness between .94 and .97 Mach, and a single sharp bump, similar to flying through 'prop wash,' while accelerating through .98," Yeager recalled. "Decelerating from supersonic speed, I would experience all of these effects in reverse."* The monumental achievement was initially kept secret to give the air force as much of a lead in flight development over the Soviets as they could get, and so the team celebrated privately that night with a pitcher of martinis.

• •

Secret, world-changing projects like Yeager's were a big reason that the military was so concerned about the waves of flying saucer sightings around facilities like Muroc, as well as near the White Sands Proving Ground and other facilities relevant to the ongoing development of atomic weapons. The sightings, which seemed likely to be surveillance flights, prompted the somewhat-terrifying question of whether what they were seeing weren't just random orbs, but unique Soviet spy aircraft. Had the Soviet Union procured some experimental German Nazi design that the US was unaware of?† The fact that these mysterious objects—whatever they were—had appeared over the skies of the White Sands Proving Ground seemed hardly serendipitous. There, amid the brilliantly white deposits of gypsum and calcium sulfate that made up the striking, deserted New Mexico desert, America was slowly tiptoeing itself into the space age. The military base there, which would grow to 3,200 square miles, was the largest in the United States and had been the site of the

---

* Word of the achievement finally leaked to *Aviation Week* in December, but the air force didn't confirm the success until June 1948. Then Yeager was summoned to the White House, where Harry Truman presented him with the 1948 Collier Trophy, the nation's highest award for aeronautical achievement. At the reception, Yeager's father stubbornly refused to shake Truman's hand. His mother tried to cover up the awkwardness by talking corn bread recipes with the Missouri president, but air force secretary Stuart Symington noticed. "My husband is a little firm in his ways," Mom Yeager said. Symington doubled over in laughter.

† It was, in some ways, an obvious question, because the US had done the same thing. As US and Allied forces had pushed across Europe, intelligence officers had collected every document and file about the Nazi rocket program they could find and whisked every German rocket scientist they located out of the war zone and back to the United States as part of what came to be known as "Operation Paperclip," an initiative to enhance its own standing in the technology race.

world's first-ever atomic explosion, the first nuclear test, code-named Trinity, whose heat had in an instant violently melted the signature sand into a unique glass known thereafter as trinitite.

In the wake of the war that the atomic weapon had so unexpectedly cut short (scientists and military planners unaware of the Manhattan Project had been expecting World War II to continue for another year or longer), the New Mexico base had been quickly transformed to a new, equally secret and equally ambitious project. Formally known as the Upper Atmosphere Research Panel, but known to most simply as the V-2 Panel, it pulled together citizen scientists and military engineers in a major peacetime effort to study how the US could capitalize on Nazi ballistic missile design and expertise. "The V-2 Panel was born of a wartime marriage of widely differing worlds," wrote historian David DeVorkin. "Unlike nuclear physics, astronomy, and chemistry, which had established institutional bases before the war . . . space science lacked an institutional infrastructure experienced in the technology it exploited. The V-2 Panel acted as a substitute for a disciplinary infrastructure." At the time, America had no one experienced in rockets and rocket-borne experiments and was in the early stages of a contract with General Electric to build its first rockets.

The V-2 Panel, organized quickly in the beginning of 1946 by army ordnance Colonel Holger Toftoy, brought together about forty thinkers, including civilian scientists, as well as the army, navy, and their various laboratories, to plot how the military could utilize some twenty-five captured V-2 rockets it intended to test-fire over the course of the next two years.[*]

One of the first experiments grew out of the Johns Hopkins Applied Physics Laboratory, led by James Van Allen, whose lab had helped develop the proximity fuse. Now, as part of the V-2 Panel, Van Allen's team raced to use the V-2s to study the upper atmosphere and near space, developing a cosmic ray detector that rode on one of the first V-2 flights in 1946.

---

[*] Over the course of the program, which would extend from 1946 to 1952, the effort yielded a total of sixty V-2 missile launches, carrying more than twenty total tons of scientific experiments in fields from meteorology to solar physics to specialized studies of cosmic ray physics and missile control.

To help develop the new experiments, Van Allen knew he needed another member of the team that had helped with the proximity fuse during the war, an astronomer who could help the V-2 team understand what they needed to pack aboard the rockets for scientific purposes, a man who, though no one knew it yet, would go on, over the decades ahead, to be one of the most critical connections between the military and the community of what would come to be known as "ufologists."

He needed J. Allen Hynek.

• •

Josef Allen Hynek had been fascinated by outer space since he was seven. Born in 1910 to a multigeneration cigar manufacturer family, he'd contracted scarlet fever in 1917 and, during that time, his mother had spent weeks reading to him, eventually resorting to an *Elements of Astronomy* textbook when she ran out of other options. He was hooked almost instantly. "The system, the law, and order of things, grabbed me," he recalled. Three years later, his parents gifted him a Sears, Roebuck telescope, and his fate was sealed. He pursued science at the University of Chicago, graduating with a degree in astronomy in 1932, landing a graduate student slot at the university's Yerkes Observatory in Wisconsin, at the height of the Great Depression.

The observatory looked far grander than it was—the roof leaked and the heat was turned off on winter weekends, making for a cold, long forty-eight hours for the students living there—but Hynek had loved the "sort of mystical quality" it held, and he demonstrated his dedication to the cause by almost immediately overworking himself into exhaustion. "The doctor said [Hynek] was run down due to overwork & improper eating," a Yerkes staffer wrote the observatory's director, Otto Struve, a few weeks into Hynek's employment. "It seems he ate very infrequently and worked half or more of the night."

Impressed by the young man's commitment, Struve, one of the world's leading astronomers, soon became a mentor of sorts. A genius born to an aristocratic family in Ukraine in 1897, Struve had one of the most colorful and prestigious pedigrees of any astronomer in the twentieth century. His great-grandfather had been the royal astronomer to Czar Nicholas I, a pioneer who had helped prove Copernicanism, and both his father and grandfather had forged careers of distinction themselves. The fourth-generation Struve had started working with his father in the telescope tower when he was just eight, and had gone on to fight on the Turkish front of World War I and then on the side of the White Russians in the Russian Civil War, before escaping ahead of the Bolsheviks to Turkey, where he had finally immigrated to the United States. In 1944, he received the Gold Medal from the Royal Astronomical Society, the fourth in his family's history.

Now a renowned scientist at the University of Chicago, Struve specialized in studying the spectrum of stars, a field that could be traced back to the 1800s, when scientists had figured out that they could use a star's light with a spectroscope to determine the elements that it was made of as well as its age. Different elements registered light differently, so a spectroscope could break a star's light apart with a prism and convert it into what amounted to be a unique barcode made up of lines representing the elements present inside the star. Older stars were made up of almost exclusively hydrogen and helium, while younger stars—like our sun—had a much more varied composition. Further information could be gleaned from the Doppler effect, the principle of how sound and light waves moving away from you are stretched, while waves moving toward you are condensed.* By studying whether the light from a star was pushed toward the red end of the spectrum (the longer end) or the blue end (the shorter end), scientists could also tell whether an object was moving toward earth or away. Struve had taken this decades-old science to a new level, conducting research that would identify for the first time the presence of hydrogen in interstellar space, itself a landmark achievement that would prove even more important in the years ahead.

Hynek loved working alongside the inspiring—but distant—Struve, who often displayed a gruff outlook on life and philosophy (once, Hynek

---

* The Doppler effect, discovered by mathematician Christian Johann Doppler, in 1842, is easily and best understood by modern ears as why passing cars and emergency sirens change in pitch as they approach and pass a listener. It revolutionized astronomy in 1868 as astronomers began tracking Doppler shifts in the spectral lines of stars, a breakthrough that scientists were then able to use to begin to calculate the speed and direction of light sources.

had asked his mentor as they drove up to the Wisconsin observatory from the Chicago campus what things might be like if the human race had developed emotionally rather than intellectually, to which Struve had quickly snapped, "Oh, it would be much better if you didn't think of such things!"), and at the end of his term at Yerkes, he received his PhD and left for Ohio State University, where he rose through the ranks until World War II, when his work was shifted to aid the war effort. He became part of Van Allen's team at Johns Hopkins University's Applied Physics Laboratory, which developed the proximity fuse, a critical weapon aid that transformed their construction and use moving forward. Hynek had felt uncomfortable with the whole enterprise, calling his team's invention "the Devil's own business," and lamenting "how inspiring if even part of [the lab's $750,000-a-day budget] could be directed into constructive channels instead of weapons of destruction."

Now, at the White Sands Proving Ground, it seemed like he would have a chance to do just that. Van Allen had sought him out to help turn the Nazi V-2, a weapon of destruction, into a tool that would alter humanity's knowledge of the world around us, work that Hynek quickly came to love. He and his colleagues felt they were inventing an all-new field and had freedoms few other scientists did—freedom driven in part by the knowledge that most of their instruments were blown up in each launch experiment, which allowed them to iterate and experiment more widely than the culture of earthbound science usually encouraged. It was an exciting time to be a scientist, he couldn't help but think. The sound barrier had fallen—and rockets and outer space wouldn't be far behind. America was entering a new era of aviation and, ahead, loomed a race for space. Technologies that even just a decade or two earlier had seemed the realm of science fiction were now becoming realities. The country's future—humanity's very destiny!—seemed to lie for the first time in the skies above.

Project Sign

I n the final months of 1947, it seemed like the air force had finally found a possible explanation for their mysterious flying disks. During the height of World War II, two German aerospace designers known as the Horten brothers—Walter and Reimar—had been developing a long-range bomber, what the Nazis called an *Amerikabomber*, that could target the US mainland all the way from Europe. The Hortens' design, by all accounts, happened to look like a flying wing. Although the Nazi regime had been running short of turbojets at the time, they'd managed to build three prototypes that looked remarkably like the descriptions of the craft and rushed them into large-scale production in the last weeks of the conflict. The Nazi regime had hoped one of those so-called *Wunderwaffe*, or "Wonder Weapons," would turn the tide of the Allied advance, but the construction effort had come too late. The US captured one of the prototypes, what the brothers named the H.XVIII, and brought it home for study. What if, the air force now wondered, the Russians managed to do the same and were now testing their aircraft in US skies? It was an option, per a report from the military attaché in Moscow that stated roughly 1,800 Soviet bombers might be under construction based on the Horten design, but no one could find any evidence of actual Russian flight tests.

Meanwhile, others wondered if the answer was more obvious. Word had spread some time ago that the navy had been developing a plane nicknamed the Flying Flapjack, but that it had been scrapped—perhaps contrary to public reports, it was still alive? "Are you positive that the Navy junked the XF-5-U-1 project?" one analyst scrawled across a memo.

Whatever the truth was, getting closer to it remained a priority by year's end. In late December, an air force intelligence memo on the "flying disks" confirmed that "continued and recent reports from qualified observers concerning this phenomenon still makes this one of concern to

Headquarters, Air Material Command." Days later, Major General L. C. Craigie weighed in on the situation. He wrote, "It is Air Force policy not to ignore reports of sightings and phenomena in the atmosphere but to recognize that part of its mission is to collect, collate, evaluate and act on information of this nature.

"In implementing this policy, it is desired that the Air Material Command set up a project whose purpose is to collect, collate, evaluate and distribute to interested government agencies and contractors all information concerning sightings and phenomena in the atmosphere which can be construed to be of concern to the national security."

As a final signal of his intention, the major general assigned the new project "Priority 2A," the second-highest priority in the air force, and a code name: Sign.

Within two weeks, it had its first assignment.

• •

The first telephone calls had started coming into the Kentucky State Police in the early afternoon on January 7, 1948, reporting an unusual aircraft in the skies over Maysville, a small town on the Ohio River northeast of Lexington. It was something circular, locals said, perhaps as large as 250 to 300 feet in diameter. The police, in turn, called Godman Army Airfield across the state at Fort Knox, and further reports about what would come to be known in government parlance as "UFO Incident 33" began to trickle in from Irvington and Owensboro. At Godman, detachment commander Lieutenant Paul Orner was summoned to the air traffic control tower. He was able to spot "a small white object" in the southwest sky around 1:45 p.m. "It appeared partially as [a] parachute with bright sun reflecting from [the] top of the silk, however, there seemed to be some red light around the lower part of it," he related later to investigators.

The men in the control tower were reluctant to make a flying saucer report, but within a few minutes they had peered through their 6x50 binoculars long enough to be sure the object wasn't a normal aircraft. The base commander, Colonel Guy Hix, was particularly baffled. "The object observed could be plainly seen with the naked eye, and appeared to be about one-quarter the size of a full moon, white in color."

Meanwhile, four Kentucky Air National Guard P-51 fighters, en route from Marietta, Georgia, were asked by the tower's chief operator, Technical Sergeant Quinton Blackwell, to take a closer look at the strange object. One fighter was too low on fuel to pursue, but the other three took off after it. The object appeared initially to be around fifteen thousand feet, or higher, and moving at about half the speed of the P-51 fighters.

Around 2:45 p.m., the fighters headed south and began to climb to intercept the object; flight leader Captain Thomas Mantell radioed that he had it in sight "ahead and above, I'm still climbing," whatever "it" was. ("What the hell are we looking for?" the other pilot responded.) The chase continued ever higher, and Mantell pulled ahead of the other fighters, climbing into ever-thinner air even though he had no oxygen equipment in his plane for high-altitude operations. A Kentucky native, Mantell was an experienced combat pilot—earning a Distinguished Flying Cross and four Air Medals over Europe during World War II, where he'd piloted C-47 transport planes that delivered paratroopers into battles like D-Day and Operation Market Garden, the invasion of the Netherlands—but relatively new to this type of flyer, with just sixty-seven hours of logged practice time.

Around 3:15 p.m., the tower asked for a description of what Mantell was chasing. The flight leader radioed back that he was still in pursuit, approaching twenty thousand feet, but the second part of the message remains disputed by the four witnesses. While some recollections have him reporting, "It appears to be a metallic object . . . of tremendous size," others hold that his final report was a more ambiguous "It's above me and I'm gaining on it." The other fighters attempted to contact him, asking him to level off and let them catch up, but about five minutes later, unable to spot Mantell or the object, they became concerned about their own low fuel and high altitude and decided to head back to the airfield.

"I was seeing double," Lieutenant B. A. Hammond later reported. "I pulled alongside [the other pilot, Lieutenant A. W.] Clements and indicated with gestures that I didn't have an oxygen mask. In fact, I circled my finger around my head to show him I was getting woozy. He understood the situation, and we turned back." As they passed over Godman, one of the returning pilots told the tower he'd never spotted anything in the sky other than a reflection on his canopy.

Soon after, another plane—now refueled and equipped with oxygen—took off to join the hunt, eventually working its way one hundred miles south of the airfield and all the way up to thirty thousand feet without ever finding sight of anything.

Within an hour, the base received word that Mantell was dead. A state police officer had responded to a plane crash ninety miles south and found the fighter on a farm outside Franklin, Kentucky, on the Tennessee border. Investigators surmised that the pilot had lost consciousness due to a lack of oxygen as he climbed through twenty-five thousand feet; his plane had then spiraled and plummeted to the ground, the speed of the descent ripping it apart in the air. At the crash scene, firefighters noted that Mantell's wristwatch had stopped at 3:18, apparently the time of impact.

In a moment, the national perspective on flying saucers—a story that had long seemed more a curiosity than a concern—had taken on a dark and tragic tinge. "The fact that a person had dramatically died in an encounter with an alleged flying saucer dramatically increased public concern about the phenomenon," historian David Jacobs explained. "Now a dramatic new prospect entered thought about UFOs: they might be not only extraterrestrial but potentially hostile as well." Investigators immediately wrote the incident off as an overzealous pilot chasing Venus, but many dismissed the notion that an experienced flyer would lose his life by mistaking a star for something else. A Vanderbilt astronomer later came forward, claiming he had seen "a pear-shaped balloon with cables and a basket attached" through binoculars between 4:30 and 4:45 p.m., seemingly supporting the idea of a flying object.

• •

Project Sign, aka Air Force Project No. XS-304, officially began work on January 22, 1948, just weeks after the crash. Based with the Wright-Patterson intelligence unit, which had started in World War I as the Foreign Data Section of the Army Signal Corps' Airplane Engineering Department, the Project Sign staff quickly began a collection and study effort that would lay the groundwork to explain cases like Mantell's, enlisting the Weather Bureau at the Department of Commerce to understand the meteorological phenomenon of "ball lighting," which was suspected behind at least some sightings, and turning to scientists at GE and MIT to help categorize and group the types of sightings across the country. It also collected specialized design and technical reports from

Air Force Materiel Command to understand the flight characteristics of known aircraft, worked with the Air Weather Service to map and trace known weather balloon launches, and assembled lists of blimp flights and guided-missile tests. It asked the air force's Aeromedical Laboratory for a comprehensive study about the possibility of plain old human error and optical illusions—one of the project's core principles soon became that it wouldn't start an engineering analysis of a possible sighting before ruling out "psychological factors." (Interestingly, though, as historian Kate Dorsch has noted, "There were initially no social scientists or philosophers on-board at Sign, despite project personnel acknowledging mass hysteria as a possible 'source' of the sightings.") Overall, Sign's investigation procedures, David Jacobs said, "were fairly good. The main problem was that the staff was too inexperienced to discriminate between which sightings to investigate thoroughly." Plus, they worried about the reliability of witnesses—Sign repeatedly turned to the FBI for help with investigating the background of observers and double-checking whether they were otherwise known to be subversives, or else staff wasted seemingly countless hours interviewing friends, family, and coworkers.

· To better understand the design or performance characteristics of a so-called "spaceship" and the reality of whether any planets in the known universe might be in the "physical or cultural position of [its] development," Sign turned to the newly created RAND, a division of Douglas Aircraft. Originally called "Project RAND," for "Research ANd Development," the organization had started in the month after the end of World War II, when General Hap Arnold had begun to worry about how the rapid demobilization of the war's science efforts might stall the military's progress on key innovations—particularly items like missiles and rockets that had only appeared in the war's closing chapters and yet now seemed so critical to securing the peace ahead. Arnold had teamed up with former test pilot Franklin Collbohm and in just two days' time, they had outlined details of the new initiative for approval.*

In March 1946, James E. Lipp, an aeronautical engineer who had

---

* The plans had come together so rapidly that the only plane available to fly the Douglas executives to Arnold's meeting turned out to be the late president Roosevelt's personal plane, a C-54 named "Sacred Cow."

spent thirteen years at Douglas, became one of RAND's first four employees. Given the paltry size of the research center, his title as "director" of the Missiles Department seemed more aspirational than anything, but that year he helped author RAND's first paper, a landmark study with the bland title of "Preliminary Design of an Experimental World-Circling Spaceship," that laid out the first serious engineering concept for an orbital launch vehicle. The work quickly established him as one of the nation's leading thinkers on the possibility of reconnaissance satellites, pushing the country's military establishment to move into what would come to be known as the space race.

"Before long, someone will start on the construction of a satellite vehicle, whether in the United States or elsewhere," he wrote the following year in a follow-up RAND report. "History shows that the human race does not allow physical development to lag very far behind the mental realization that a step can be taken." The nation's dominance in air and naval power meant that adversaries like the USSR would focus on developing rockets as the "quickest shortcut for challenging this country's position. No promising avenues of progress in rockets can be neglected by the United States without great danger of falling behind in the world race for armaments."

Now, as RAND become a stand-alone nonprofit called the RAND Corporation, Lipp began to pour over everything he knew about rockets and propulsion systems to understand and imagine how a spaceship might fly and travel from another planet—work that "may have been the first U.S. government sponsored study of non-human life in the universe," according to aerospace historian Curtis Peebles.

At first, Lipp approached his study as a simple engineering and math problem: How likely was life on other planets and how likely was it that someone or something else had mastered technologies that humans hadn't? Back-of-the-envelope math pointed to both answers as "very likely," but the deeper he got into his work the more dubious he was that the flying objects in question were of interstellar origin.

Instead, he turned his focus to answering questions from the perspective of public speculation. The first was whether the flying objects of 1947 were directly related to the atomic bomb explosions in the years prior, and whether they could have caused some kind of interstellar alarm or reaction. By the time the first objects appeared to Kenneth Arnold, the United States had exploded five atomic weapons, and Lipp calculated that likely only two of them would have been visible from Mars. While it seemed highly possible Martians could have built such telescopes, it seemed unlikely to Lipp that they were just now checking in on Earth and reacting for the first time. Beyond Mars, the math seemed to indicate a range of possible truths. It was probable that intelligent life existed elsewhere (if it did on Earth, he figured, why not elsewhere, too?), but less so that those civilizations would be traveling vast distances to visit Earth. Lipp also assumed that "man is average as to technical advancement," meaning that half of any habitable planets would be behind Earth in development, while the other half would be more advanced. That meant that of the roughly twenty-two stars within sixteen light-years of Earth that shared the properties of our sun, there would be eleven civilizations capable of space travel.

Next, he turned to how a craft capable of reaching Earth from another solar system could be built. It was in this segment of the argument that Lipp felt the possibility of outer space visitors fall apart. The size and weight of a craft necessary to travel to Earth, using the most efficient systems imaginable to man—a nuclear, hydrogen-propelled vehicle—would still be too large, too inefficient, and too slow to be successful, according to his calculations. "A trip from another star system requires improvements of propulsion that we have not yet conceived," he wrote as he studied. "Conceivably, among the myriads of stellar systems in the Galaxy, one or more races have discovered methods of travel that would be fantastic by our standards. Yet the larger the volume of space that must be included to strengthen this possibility, the lower will be the chance that the race involved would ever find the earth." As special as Earth might feel to humans, it was a pretty undistinguished planet in the scheme of the vast galaxy. "A super-race (unless they occur frequently) would not be likely to stumble upon Planet III of Sol, a fifth-magnitude start in the rarified outskirts of the Galaxy," Lipp concluded.

Lipp's work was helpful, though it didn't answer all of the military's new questions about outer space; the air force knew that unlocking the mystery of the flying disks would come from one of two realms, science or intelligence, and while it had its own intelligence operatives, it was keen to enlist other outside science minds like Lipp's, particularly one who could help the air force analysts understand how humans viewed outer space.

For that, it enlisted J. Allen Hynek, now the director of the observatory at Ohio State University in Columbus. With a decade of astronomy study under his belt, mixed with his time helping on the wartime research and the V-2 project, the scientist had earned a reputation for diligence in what his mentor Struve called "your studies of unusual stars." As Hynek's biographer wrote, "Wherever there was a star exhibiting unexpected properties—the confounding velocities of mass escaping Beta Lyrae, the 'paradox' of Zeta Tauri's variable hydrogen curve, Phi Persei with its 'remarkable' hydrogen lines, the 'attractive astrophysical problems' of P Cygni, and the 'striking variations in the spectrum' of Gamma Cassiopeiae were especially striking and tantalizing—Hynek was either at the telescope making observations or being called in to interpret puzzling photographic plates or spectroscopic readings."

That resume made him the perfect candidate for a second set of expert eyes—one who could sort through the sighting reports and dismiss those that seemed clearly to be astronomical phenomena—but it took some convincing for Hynek to agree. In fact, the scientist actually thought quite little at first of the request to consult on the new Project Sign effort—he wasn't exactly the world's leading expert on flying saucers or a brand-name astronomer and wasn't even sure if he believed in them. "When I first heard of the UFO's, I thought they were sheer nonsense, as any scientist would have," he wrote later. "Most of the early reports were quite vague: 'I went into the bathroom for a drink of water and looked out of the window and saw a bright light in the sky. It was moving up and down and sideways. When I looked again, it was gone.'" It wasn't likely anything serious, therefore, would come from the work, but to be involved in it would be a unique opportunity. After some consideration, he agreed to help, figuring he was at least the top astronomer in central Ohio within driving distance of the Wright-Patterson Air Force Base. Plus, it could be fun. "The sky and stars have always been symbolical of that which is above human comprehension and this circumstance has led to a great deal of unscientific speculation," he had once said during a 1936 lecture. So why not get just a little closer?

• •

As it turned out, the air force's zeroing in on astronomical phenomena as a possible source of the sightings was proven correct when, that spring, British scientists offered up a breakthrough that could explain much—perhaps most or even all—of the 1947 flying saucer wave.

The new discovery came as scientists realized they could use radio echoes to identify and track meteor showers during the daytime, which until then had largely only been trackable in the night's darkness. Until then, little serious scientific work had gone into studying or cataloging meteor events and only a few regular events were tracked, like the Geminid shower in December, and the Perseid meteor stream, which unfolded in Earth's August skies, but thanks to somewhat accidental advancements made during the war, progress was now being made. The realization had come in the final months of the conflict, as British army officials had used radar to track incoming German V-2 rockets and been repeatedly puzzled at the "many occasions [radar] warnings were given in the absence of rockets." Once they were released from their wartime research endeavors, a team of British scientists turned their attention back to that mystery and launched a new observation station at Jodrell Bank, in Cheshire, relying in part on donated surplus wartime radar equipment to do their work. In May 1947, they observed a wondrous and heretofore unknown meteor shower, known as Mu-Aquarids. "A new daytime stream in itself was not unexpected but it soon became evident that this was not just one more meteor shower, but a whole new set of showers of great activity. They continued all through the summer, reaching a peak of activity in June and finally ending in early September," explained a 1948 article in *Physics Today*. In other words, British scientists had been tracking a previously unrealized and dramatic meteor shower that peaked precisely during the time window that Kenneth Arnold had spotted his bright lights over the Cascades and when the first "flying disk" flap hit the United States.

Perhaps the summer sightings in '47, including Arnold's original sighting that kicked off the whole phenomena, had been particularly bright meteors, but there was only one way to find out.

The Classics

The Mantell case became the first of three incidents in 1948 that Project Sign would eventually label "The Classics." The second came on July 24, 1948, when an Eastern Airlines DC-3, en route from Houston to Atlanta, saw a bright light closing in in the evening darkness. "Look, here comes a new Army jet job," pilot Clarence Chiles said as he noticed the disturbance—but in just a moment, he realized whatever it was was too fast to even be another jet, and put the plane into a sharp left turn as the unidentified object whizzed past about seven hundred feet away. Over his shoulder, copilot John Whitted saw the object begin to climb steeply as it passed. "As if the pilot had seen us and wanted to avoid us," Chiles recounted later, "it pulled up with a tremendous burst of flame out of its rear and zoomed up into the clouds."

Together, the men were sure of what they saw: something shaped like a wingless fuselage of a B-29, with a "deep blue glow" on the underside, and "two rows of windows from which bright lights glowed," appearing to be powered by a "50-foot trail of orange-red flame" shooting off the back end. Interestingly, "no disturbance was felt from air waves, nor was there any wash or mechanical disturbance when the object passed," which would be expected given the size, proximity, and speed of the passing object. That same evening, another pilot flying near the Virginia–North Carolina border independently reported a "bright shooting star" in the direction of Alabama; a crew chief at Robins Air Force Base near Macon, Georgia, also noted seeing a high-speed bright light passing overhead. Investigators triangulating the sightings found them all credible and consistent.

Inside Project Sign's home at Wright-Patterson's intelligence center, confusion reigned; too many sightings that weren't adding up, analysts feared, and researchers were confounded the deeper they went into the issue. Luckily, the media had largely given up on run-of-the-mill "fly-ing saucer" sightings and public ridicule of such events had increased the more time passed without real confirmation of such sightings, enabling them to work privately and without outside interference.* The contro-versy, though, remained on the mind of the nation's leaders—not even President Truman was immune from curiosity. One afternoon in 1948, he summoned his air force aide, Colonel Robert Landry, to the Oval Of-fice and "talked about UFO reports and what might be the meaning for all these rather way-out reports of sightings, and the subject in general," Landry recalled. "All manner of objects and things were being seen in the sky by people."

Truman told Landry that he hadn't given much serious thought to the reports but was worried about the possibility of new and underesti-mated threats. "If there was any evidence of a strategic threat to the na-tional security," the president said, "the collection and evaluation of UFO data by Central Intelligence warranted more intense study and attention at the highest government level." Moving forward, he wanted a quarterly oral report from Landry and the air force on whether any of the UFO sightings presented any real danger.

Over the rest of Truman's presidency, Landry regularly provided the briefings, but as he later recalled in an oral history, "Nothing of substance considered credible or threatening to the country was ever received from intelligence." Nor, it seemed, were any definitive conclusions about what

---

* During the same period, the air force was beginning its biggest test yet as an inde-pendent military branch. In June 1948, a Soviet blockade of West Berlin prompted UK and US air forces to mobilize in the greatest resupply mission ever conceived. C-47 and C-54 transport airplanes raced in and out of Germany—at the height of the effort, a supply plane was landing every thirty seconds—delivering everything from coal to candy twenty-four hours a day, each plane carefully staggered in flight and on the ground. As the summer progressed, though, and the US and its allies realized it was in for a long grind and not a short endeavor, the airlift began to falter; maintenance suffered, and crews were tiring. The air force appointed a new com-mander, only to have him forced to circle Berlin Tempelhof Airport after a series of errors amid clouds and rain led to multiple crashes ahead of his arrival; in the weeks ahead, revamping the airlift would speed the air force's maturation, but it was still a service that was a long way from becoming the global force and defender of freedom it pained to be.

exactly was happening "up there." Even if the vast majority of sightings were simple meteorological or astronomical quirks or mistaken natural phenomena, enough of the sightings came from seemingly reliable observers who provided a deep enough level of detail that the Sign team didn't think they'd simply seen a planet on the horizon, and while the researchers were relatively convinced that the "flying saucers" weren't a US government program—or, at least, not all of them—it didn't make sense that the Russians would be testing secret designs so brazenly over US airspace. There was never any indication that the objects were truly hostile, and no crash, landing, or terrestrial encounter had allowed for the recovery of any physical debris. No known propulsion system on Earth could accelerate an aircraft to the reported speeds; what scientists were beginning to learn about high-speed aircraft and the g-forces of high-speed turns made the air force's Aeromedical Laboratory dubious that any human could survive such maneuvers. In one memo, project scientists speculated that perhaps the craft were being flown by "some unknown race": "As far as the effect on the human body was concerned, why couldn't these people, whoever they might be, stand these horrible maneuver forces? Why judge them by earthly standards?"

In the face of all the questions and theories and ideas, the Sign research team—according to Edward Ruppelt, who would later head the project—authored that summer what was known as an "Estimate of the Situation," a thick, legal-sized, top secret intelligence analysis document that was sent onward to the highest levels of the Pentagon. The report pulled together the many sightings from seemingly reliable observers—scientists, pilots, military leaders themselves—that were consistent in their descriptions and clearly outside the realm of known aviation capabilities or cosmic phenomena. They had left them with only one conclusion: extraterrestrial. "The situation was the UFO's; the estimate was that they were interplanetary!" Ruppelt recorded later, exclamation point included.

The Pentagon disagreed. Officials up to chief of staff General Hoyt Vandenberg thought the Project Sign conclusion was, at best, premature and lacking in any meaningful proof. "The general wouldn't buy interplanetary vehicles," Ruppelt reported, and so Project Sign and the air force decided that the document was too explosive to exist.

Within a few months, the military apparently burned every copy in existence.[*]

• •

As the "Estimate of the Situation" ricocheted around the Pentagon, the most dramatic incident of 1948—the third in what would come to be known as "The Classics"—occurred in the skies over Fargo, North Dakota. Lieutenant George Gorman, a veteran World War II pilot and tractor salesman who had moved into service in the North Dakota Air National Guard after the war, was flying over the city in his F-51 Mustang around 9 p.m. on October 1 when he reported back to air traffic control that a bright light had whizzed past him.[†] Despite assurances by the controller that there was nothing in the area other than the Piper Cub he could see below him, Gorman decided to investigate, and for some thirty minutes, engaged in a dramatic aerial duel with the light—pushing the Mustang to its top speed and closing in fast to about one thousand yards before it zoomed away. He estimated that the ball-shaped object was less than a foot wide, and whatever it was, it seemed able to turn faster and sharper than his top-of-the-line fighter jet—at one point, Gorman said he blacked out in a turn when trying to match the sharp trajectory of the ball. Not even the best living pilots, Gorman felt, could survive

---

[*] The only proof of the report's existence comes from the personal testimony of Edward Ruppelt and J. Allen Hynek, who evidently confirmed its existence in a February 1971 interview. No sign of the document has ever surfaced and no text from it has ever been quoted directly. As historian Kate Dorsch wrote in 2019, "No other corroborating evidence suggesting even the existence of this document—let alone its contents—has ever been uncovered. No drafts, no mentions either before or immediately after from either military personnel or consulting scientists, not a single surviving copy (even though Ruppelt claims a few were saved 'as mementos of the golden days') of the many that were allegedly distributed." Dorsch concluded that she's unconvinced the document existed at all, writing, "It does, however, demonstrate how little evidence considerable parts of the UFO lore from their period is built on."

[†] Gorman is usually referred to in UFO literature as a "construction manager," but according to his interview file with counterintelligence agents, he listed his occupation as "Dairy Line Salesman, International Harvester Co."

and execute the turns being made. At one point, he closed on it head-on and only dove off when he felt they were about to collide. "I guess I got scared," he told investigators. "I went into a dive and the light passed over my canopy at about 500 feet. Then, it made a left circle about 1,000 feet above, and I gave chase again."

The aerial ballet ranged over dozens of miles at speeds up to four hundred miles per hour and altitudes from 1,500 feet up to 17,000 feet (at times, he said, he was below the light, at others he said it appeared below him). Gorman only broke off the dogfight and headed for the air-field around 9:30 p.m. after his plane stalled at fourteen thousand feet. "It is hard to believe your own eyes when something with no wings walks off and leaves you standing still," he said later.

The entire incident was observed by both the pilot and passenger aboard the Piper Cub, as well as air traffic controllers at the airfield. The Piper pilot, a local doctor, said, "The object was moving very swiftly, much faster than the 51," and the controllers, tracing the dogfight through bin-oculars, said they saw "an object or a light traveling at a high rate of speed, apparently on a southwest heading. The F-51 was some distance behind and the object was traveling fast enough to increase the spacing between itself and the fighter. The object appeared to be only a round light, per-fectly formed, with no fuzzy edges or rays leaving its body. The edges were clear cut. No other shape was observed. The main identifying char-acteristic was the high rate of speed at which it was apparently traveling."

After he was on the ground, Gorman met with commanders and in-vestigators and told them unequivocally that he'd interacted with some-thing that was driven with "thought or reason": "I am convinced that there was definite thought behind its maneuvers. I am further convinced that the object was governed by the laws of inertia because its acceleration was rapid but not immediate and although it was able to turn fairly tight at considerable speed, it still followed a natural curve."

The Gorman sighting—known to the air force as "Incident 172"—made national headlines and further stoked interest in flying saucers. Meanwhile, Project Sign investigators pieced together a theory: the weather service had released a lighted weather balloon by Fargo around 8:50 p.m. that night, which would have been visible in the area near Gor-man and the Piper Club by around 9 p.m., when the "dogfight" began.

The fast maneuvering of the balloon, investigators believed, was actually just Gorman's misperception and visual illusion as he maneuvered his plane quickly around the object at increasingly fast speeds. Later, as the balloon continued to ascend and move away from Fargo, Gorman must have confused the weather balloon's receding light with the planet Jupiter and raced south after the planet in the sky. The investigators also noted that while the other observers—the Piper Cub pilot and the air traffic controllers—had reported seeing a fast-moving light, those "other witnesses of the incident did not observe the complex tactics reported by Lieutenant Gorman." The fancy turns were, perhaps, Gorman just being confused by his own fancy turns.

The pilot remained unconvinced; that December, he wrote Kenneth Arnold—the original flying saucer spotter had written Gorman asking for more details on the dogfight—that he was prohibited from speaking about the incident because it had been classified. "I have a normal amount of curiosity and I have a lot of questions to ask. But then I had a lot of them answered that nite. The rest of that I have will have to wait until they get ready to answer them," he said.

In the weeks following Gorman's incident, news spread of other oddities, including a case involving a F-61 Black Widow pilot who had tried to chase a suspicious object that appeared on its radar over Japan. That pilot watched his radarscope as the object evaded six separate interception efforts, each time accelerating away as the fighter plane drew near, and the pilot could only vaguely make out a silhouette he described as like a "rifle bullet." Then a landmark report from Germany arrived: on November 23, two F-80 "Shooting Star" pilots had spotted something that appeared to be a "reddish star," moving south over Munich. A radar operator had reported the contact at twenty-seven thousand feet, traveling about nine hundred miles per hour, and followed up, minutes later, that, according to the radar, it had risen to fifty thousand feet. No known aircraft could perform anything like such a maneuver, let alone hit that speed, and it was the first time a suspicious flying object had been both visually identified and captured on radar.

It was an exciting development, but not one that Project Sign could make too much of—radar was not, after all, proof of a flying saucer. And they needed proof if they were to make any progress. By 1948 it had collected 167 reports deemed ultimately reliable, but the Pentagon's rejection had left the program troubled, and led, gradually, to a rebalancing of its estimates.

In February 1949, after barely a year in existence, Project Sign issued its final report on "Unidentified Aerial Objects," a forty-five-page compendium of work, process, sightings, and conclusions based on a study of a total of 243 domestic and 30 foreign incidents. To start, the report noted that sightings tended to group into four categories:

1. Flying disks, i.e., very low aspect ratio aircraft.
2. Torpedo or cigar-shaped bodies with no wings or fins visible in flight.
3. Spherical or balloon-shaped objects.
4. Balls of light.

All of the first three categories were at least "readily conceivable by aeronautical designers," even though some of the apparent control features would be more speculative. Sign's in-depth engineering studies had largely convinced its analysts that few of the flying objects made much sense aerodynamically, and that it wasn't even clear "these configurations would develop much speed and allow a sufficient duration of flight and adequate range to be of practical use as aircraft." (For instance, wind-tunnel tests had never shown "flying disk"–style aircraft to be particularly efficient at lift and the idea of using such shapes for long-range travel was all but unthinkable based on earthly propulsion systems; similarly, the fuel-hungry engines of a jet-propelled cigar-shaped aircraft, like what Whitted and Chiles said they saw, would require a "method of propulsion . . . far in advance of presently known engines.") As for the last, fourth, category, Sign had "no reasonable hypothesis of the true nature of the balls of light."

In an appendix to the main report, physicist George E. Valley, who was a founding member of the air force's science advisory board, broke down the characteristics and patterns of the most reliable sightings. The flying disks, he explained, were largely reported during the daytime, and were sometimes sighted in groups, whereas nighttime reports almost always featured single objects. He gave deep thought to the possibility of new technologies—including that the flying objects were aided by an antigravity shield proposed by writers like H. G. Wells—but in the end thought it was more likely that the witnesses were just confused about what they saw. "One would like to assume that the positions held by many of the reported observers guarantee their observations. Unfortunately, there were many reports of curious phenomena by pilots during the war—the incident of the fire-ball fighters comes to mind. Further, mariners have been reporting sea-serpents for hundreds of years yet no one has yet produced a photograph."

All told, about 20 percent of the sightings were identified as "conventional aerial objects," so far as the Sign researchers could determine, and many of the rest could be explained by sightings of "weather and other atmospheric sounding balloons" or other astronomical phenomena. Some chunk of the sightings, too, were undoubtedly the result of what the Aeromedical Laboratory called "errors of the human mind and senses," including vertigo-induced dizziness and "swimming of the head" that came with the disorientation of flying at night.

"The possibility that some of the incidents may represent technical developments far in advance of knowledge available to engineers and scientists of this country has been considered," the team asserted, but "no facts are available to personnel at this Command that will permit an objective assessment of this possibility. All information so far presented on the possible existence of space ships from another planet or of aircraft propelled by an advanced type of atomic power plant have been largely conjecture."

In the end, Project Sign was left unable to prove or disprove the sightings, or provide evidence that flying objects existed at all—even the most reliable observers fell short in offering inconvertible evidence of what they'd seen. "[The air force] just couldn't get the kind of 'hard data' the military was used to getting," Hynek recalled later. "They wanted close-up photos, pieces of hardware, detailed descriptions, and so forth. Instead, a military pilot would report that he saw a metallic-looking object, possible 'disc-shaped'; a wingless craft which 'buzzed' him and then shot away at incredible speed—and that was about all."

Still, the report made clear that it hadn't detailed enough sightings to chase down and solve every mysterious claim: "Proof of non-existence is equally impossible to obtain unless a reasonably and convincing explanation is determined for each incident." It also notably articulated that it remained unconvinced that witnesses really were reporting some new advanced technology unknown to the American military, which at the time, after all, was the most advanced industrial nation in the world. "It would be necessary for any other country to conduct research and development work in extreme secrecy for any such project to have reached such an advanced state of development without a hint of its existence becoming known here," Sign posited, saying that there was little evidence that the USSR was capable of such a cutting-edge project, given that the majority of its aeronautical "innovation" actually came from copying craft from other countries. "An objective evaluation of the ability of the Soviets to produce technical development so far in advance of the rest of the world results in the conclusion that the possibility is extremely remote," it concluded. Recommendations for further research filled barely a third of a page, a clear indication of the group's disheartenment, frustration, and general bafflement. Future investigations, they advised, "should be carried on at the minimum level necessary to record, summarize, and evaluate the data," until enough incidents were able to "indicate that these sightings do not represent a threat to the security of the nation." At that point, it suggested, the project could be stopped altogether and folded into the routine intelligence work of the air force.

The final nail in the proverbial coffin was delivered with a nine-page follow-up report, written by James Lipp and included in the portfolio as "Appendix D." In it, Lipp ran through the math of the galaxy, rocket propulsion, and more, explaining that no evidence had been found that Earth was likely under the active study of an advanced civilization—and while such visits might make sense in the abstract, given the recent arrival of the nuclear age, it just didn't seem to square that such visits were actually occurring. "Such a civilization might observe that on Earth we now have atomic bombs and are fast developing rockets. In view of the past history of mankind, they should be alarmed," Lipp explained. "We should, therefore, expect at this time above all to behold such visitations. Since the acts of mankind most easily observed from a distance are A-bomb explosions we should expect some relation to obtain between the time of A-bomb explosions, the time at which the space-ships are seen, and the time required for such ships to arrive from and return to home-base." This, he argued, was all conjecture, though. Any observed behavior of the flying saucers made little sense in reality. Based on the reports gathered by Project Sign, the flying objects also weren't acting with any apparent meaningful purpose—especially considering that sightings seemed to inexplicably come almost entirely from the United States, whereas surely any advanced civilization visiting Earth would "scatter their visits more or less uniformly over the globe." Even if the outer space visitors were probing Earth's defenses, surely the paltry pursuits of the best and most advanced aircraft of the US Air Force had shown how little they had to fear from human technology. "It is hard to believe that any technically accomplished race would come here, flaunt its ability in mysterious ways, and then simply go away," he continued. "They must have been satisfied long ago that we can't catch them. It seems fruitless for them to keep repeating the same experiment."

As a final note, Lipp stated that, "[a]lthough visits from outer space are believed to be possible, they are believed to be very improbable. In particular, the actions attributed to the 'flying objects' reported during 1947 and 1948 seem inconsistent with the requirements for space travel." The notion that the flying objects were "visitors from another planet" should only be seriously considered once "all other solutions" had been eliminated.

Lipp's final verdict—and the Project Sign report overall—marked a key shift in how the US government and scientific community had progressed in its thinking about outer space. The more astronomers and scientists learned about the sheer vastness of the universe, the more likely it seemed that life existed out there—it just didn't seem likely that those other life-forms, whoever or whatever they may be, were the cause of the weird sightings in our own skies.

As far as the military was concerned, if the "flying objects" weren't a threat, figuring out what they really were could only be left to the scientists. Project Sign was over; the military's interest would go forward in a new project, known now as Project Grudge.

Project Grudge

Though the government had tried now for a year to downplay or publicly dismiss the nation's flying saucer fascination—the final Sign report remained classified—there was a lot of evidence it was far more interested than it let on, evidence, in turn, that led to speculation among those interested that something big was being hidden. "Whenever a reporter went to interview a person who had seen a saucer, he found the Air Force had already been there," aerospace historian Curtis Peebles later explained. "It was clear that the Air Force was intensely interested in flying saucers. The implication was that behind all the questions, there was something there." Those reporters, in turn, had no issue relaying that involvement to the masses, via a new medium that would come to define the alien information age.

Even as Sign's investigators had fanned out across the country in 1948 to try to infuse some reality into the situation, pulp entertainment magazines had begun to feverishly stoke the flying saucer craze. The genre of cheaply printed monthlies, filled with stories of science, danger, love, heroes, and detectives, with names like *Thrilling Adventures*, *Astounding*, *Unknown*, and *Popular Detective*, had taken off in the 1920s, featuring brightly colored covers of scantily clad women, dashing men, and a whole lot of robots. The flying disks were like magazine editor catnip, especially for publications like *True* magazine, which combined science fiction, mystery, *and* adventure, and the newly launched *Fate*, which focused specifically on the paranormal—the first issue of the latter, in March 1948, featured a cover story on the "flying disks" and an article by Kenneth Arnold about his encounter.

The air force, uneasy from the attention, organized and executed their own media strategy, offering Sidney Shalett, a writer for the *Saturday Evening Post*, high-level access for a two-part series in the April 1949 issue that promised to tell readers "What You Can Believe About Flying Saucers." The *Post* was at its peak in popularity, reaching something like 5 million readers, the perfect vehicle for a widespread countercampaign.

Shalett's reporting was the first in-depth exploration of the so-called "Classics"—Mantell's death, the Chiles and Whitted sighting, and the Gorman dogfight—and featured the first real public confirmation and discussion of Project Sign, even the code name of which was still secret (Shalett referred to it only as "Project Saucer"). He was given access to eyewitness accounts, select details, and even air force officials, including former general Carl Spaatz, who dismissed the entire "saucer hysteria" wave on the record: "If the American people are capable of getting so excited over something which doesn't exist, God help us if anyone ever plasters us with a real atomic bomb," he told Shalett, adding, "I can tell you unequivocally that the reported sightings of so-called saucers were completely unconnected with any form of secret research that the Air Force was conducting during my term as Chief of Staff." Shalett also interviewed Dr. Irving Langmuir, a Nobel Prize–winning scientist who served on the air force's Scientific Advisory Board, and he had some friendly advice for the service's flying saucer hunt: "Forget it!"

"I have found that if there is a scrap of bona fide evidence to support the notion that our inventive geniuses or any potential enemy, on this or any other planet, is spewing saucers over America, the Air Force has been unable to locate it," Shallet said. The article finished with detailed instructions about how to report future sightings to the air force—"If you've really seen something and can prove it, you may scare the wits out of the United States Air Force, but it will be grateful to you"—but the tone implied a less than receptive attitude to further discussion.

The effort, to some extent, backfired. Public interest in and debate on the subject continued—and now they had something more concrete to dissect and react to. As the *Saturday Evening Post* article sat on newsstands, the *New York Times* picked up a story from the Dayton *Journal Herald*, the hometown paper of Wright-Patterson, where Project Sign and Grudge were based, which reported the air force had concluded that flying saucers "are not a joke." Reports of continued miscommunication and crossed signals between local military bases and the investigators actually working the cases also contributed to the confusion and suspicions, like an incident in which two strange flying devices were found in a Maryland barn. An air force officer from Bolling Air Force Base had quickly released a statement saying there was a "good chance" the devices were old prototypes of flying saucers, but less than twenty-four hours later, air force special agents dispatched to the site pieced together that the experimental craft was the work of a failed Maryland inventor, abandoned long before World War II. Was it a cover-up or incompetence? And which would be worse?

Perhaps one of the most vocal critics of the whole situation was Kenneth Purdy, the editor of *True* magazine, who didn't believe the *Saturday Evening Post* story for a second and had no problem saying so. On May 9, 1949, after two years of chasing the flying saucer story (Arnold's original sighting had kick-started his interest), he decided he needed more help and telegraphed for Donald Keyhoe, one of the top aviation writers:

HAVE BEEN INVESTIGATING FLYING SAUCER MYSTERY. FIRST TIP HINTED GIGANTIC HOAX TO COVER UP OFFICIAL SECRET. BELIEVE IT MAY HAVE BEEN PLANTED TO HIDE REAL ANSWER. LOOKS LIKE TERRIFIC STORY. CAN YOU TAKE OVER WASHINGTON END?

The next day, Keyhoe arrived in Purdy's New York office at 67 West Forty-Fourth Street. He hadn't been following the news much when Purdy's telegraph arrived, and had "half forgotten the disks," he recalled later, but he was indeed interested. Born in 1897 in Iowa, just weeks after the series of mysterious airship sightings had overtaken the state, he'd been one of the nation's earliest military pilots, graduating from the US Naval Academy in 1919 and later flying for the Marine Corps. He'd been injured in a crash in Guam in 1922, and taken up writing as he recovered, a hobby that soon grew into a thriving career as a short story writer—during the 1920s and '30s, he published fictional stories like "The Master of Doom" and "The Mystery of the Singing Mummies" in pulp publications like *Weird Tales* and *Weird Fantasy*, and helped manage a coast-to-coast publicity tour for Charles Lindbergh after the aviator's groundbreaking 1927 transatlantic flight, an experience he turned into a book, *Flying with Lindbergh*. In the 1930s, he wrote air adventure stories starring a series of superhero World War I pilots. When World War II arrived on America's doorstep, he'd returned to active duty with the marines, working in the navy's aviation training division, and rising the ranks to major before V-E Day.

Now, as he walked into the magazine editor's office, Purdy stubbed out his cigarette and shook hands. "There's something damned queer going on," he told Keyhoe. "For fifteen months, Project Saucer is buttoned up tight. Top secret. Then suddenly Forrestal gets the *Saturday Evening Post* to run two articles, brushing the whole thing off." To Purdy, it all didn't square with the air force's public statements saying that the phenomena required further study and active attention from citizens. It seemed like there was something the air force was worried about.

Sitting in the club car of the Congressional Limited train back to DC, Keyhoe began to read through the files Purdy had collected over the previous two years, including detailed accounts of sightings, military documents, and timelines. There were far more incidents, from far more places than he'd realized—Paraguay, Belgium, Turkey, Holland, Germany—and more than fifty additional cases stateside he'd never seen before. Before long, he was hooked. "The evidence was more impressive than I had suspected," he recalled thinking. "There was something ominous about it." His mind began to race. Could it all be an unknown US weapons system? Was the US capable of developing something so fantastic as a gigantic flying disk with the public completely unaware? He knew, in the end, the answer was yes: "We had produced the A-bomb in comparative secrecy, and I knew we were working on long-range guided missiles." Then he had another thought: "If it were a Soviet missile, God help us."

The next day, back at the Pentagon, he started his own investigation, talking to officials he knew there and pointing out the apparent contradiction between the public brush-off and the statements about remaining vigilant. Quickly, he realized that air force officers were genuinely more divided than the public statements had made it out to be. Some claimed to know of or suspect a cover-up ("I've been told it's all bunk," one officer told him, "but you get the feeling they're trying to convince themselves"), while others swore up and down it wasn't a US project.

Over the weeks and months ahead, Keyhoe kept researching, traveling around the country and interviewing pilots who had seen the suspicious objects in the sky, many of whom still expressed genuine confusion at what they'd seen. By the end of his fact-finding mission, he had amassed four possible hypotheses, all of which he presented to Purdy and the magazine's aviation editor, John DuBarry:

"One, the saucers don't exist. They're caused by mistakes, hysteria, and so on. Two, they're Russian guided missiles. Three, they're American guided missiles. Four, the whole thing is a hoax, a psychological-warfare trick."

"You've left out one answer," Purdy added. "Interplanetary."

Keyhoe quickly objected, but as the debate continued, his protestations wavered. It did, he had to admit, seem less and less crazy that other societies could have figured out space travel—after all, look at how far the aviation industry on Earth had advanced. Fifty years earlier, when he was born, the first dirigibles had been taking to the sky, and within fifty years in the future most people imagined that humans would be exploring outer space. "If by any chance it's true, it'll be the biggest story since the birth of Christ," Purdy told Keyhoe as they talked.

"It could set off a panic that would make that Orson Welles thing look like a picnic," Keyhoe replied.

The most convincing piece of evidence—at least to Keyhoe—emerged two months later, when the government released a report from the newly designated Project Grudge, which had continued Sign's process of collection and analysis of suspicious sightings, but with a more intellectual and systemic approach, starting with the expectation that unidentified objects in the sky had an earthly and knowable answer. The first red flag was in the report's designation: the group had only been created six months prior, and yet the four-hundred-page secret report, which included large portions simply reprinted from Sign's report earlier in the year and relied substantially on the same stable of experts, including MIT's George Valley and Ohio State's Hynek, as well as the Air Weather Service, RAND, and the air force's Aeromedical Laboratory, had been marked "final." Out of 228 cases rapidly studied and accounting for various readily identifiable answers, just thirty were officially determined "unexplained," while the Air Weather Service had tentatively identified about 14 percent of the 220-odd cases as weather balloons. Hynek estimated that at least an additional one-third of the cases appeared to have astronomical explanations—perhaps even as much as half, if normal inaccuracies of scattershot reports were allowed—but the report generally dismissed even that number as too conservative, claiming that

Hynek "cautiously accepted each case at face value, without discounting evidence that sometimes 'verged on the ludicrous.'"

"We have found nothing which would seriously controvert simple rational explanations of the various phenomena in terms of balloons, conventional aircraft, planets, meteors, bits of paper, optical illusions, practical jokers, psycho-pathological reporters, and the like," RAND added in its portion of the document.

The conclusion felt far more definitive than Sign's—but the former investigation's "position that unexplained sightings were classed as such only because of a lack of sufficient and reliable witness data and evidence was repeated throughout Grudge like a mantra," historian Kate Dorsch wrote. "Unexplained cases, the report implied, were the fault of the observer who reported the sighting, not the methods of the scientists and technicians mobilized to evaluate and analyze the case report."

Again, it was concluded that the flying objects did not constitute a direct threat to the US national security apparatus, but with a pointed addition: the most imminent threat, Grudge noted, seemed to be the "war nerves" and "mild form of mass hysteria" found in many public reports." Having apparently satisfied its own intellectual curiosity, Grudge recommended that the study of unidentified flying objects be curtailed and scaled back, and that reporting systems be developed and revised such that they focused only on collecting "those reports clearly indicating realistic technical applications." It also encouraged the declassification and public release of its major conclusions and supporting evidence, in order to temper public curiosity. In December, the Defense Department did just that, issuing a press release saying, effectively, that it was getting out of the flying disk business.

Soon after, the project went into something approaching bureaucratic hibernation. As more reports and sightings accumulated—about ten good ones a month, by one estimate—most went uninvestigated, and after cooperating with the *Saturday Evening Post*, it proceeded to turn down other magazine writers chasing the same story, referring them to the existing press releases, and refusing additional interview requests.

For Keyhoe, the apparent stonewalling confirmed he was onto something hot: since meeting with Purdy, he had been gradually coming to his own conclusion that the disks were interplanetary—the deeper he got into his research, the more compelling he found the explanation that the mystery objects in Earth's sky weren't earthly at all. If some of the modern sightings were covering up a secret government project or two, he reasoned, what about the older reports of fantastic things in the sky?

As he traveled around the country, interviewing pilots about their experiences, he became convinced that Project Sign—still only known publicly as Project Saucer—was meant to be a cover-up, a whitewash of the government's "real" theory. "More and more, I became convinced that Secretary Forrestal had persuaded some editors that it was their patriotic duty to conceal the answer, whatever it was," he later recalled, and began to study how giant flying saucers could be powered, quickly realizing it was far beyond anything humans could have created. He began to think deeply and thoughtfully about the patterns of past sightings, going back centuries, and how they mapped to the progress of human civilization, seeing a pattern that seemed to indicate that aliens, possibly from Mars, had been visiting Earth regularly—Europe, in particular, since human populations had typically been concentrated there—perhaps once a century, before expanding their visits to the US.

It made sense to Keyhoe that the saucers would be interested in military bases, and would generally stay at high altitude, and occasionally luring fighter jets into almost-playful pursuits. "The explorers would first try to get a general idea of the whole planet. Then they would attempt to examine the most densely populated areas, types of armature, any aircraft likely to attack them," he wrote.

Add it all up, Keyhoe and Purdy decided, and they had something. In January 1950, a new issue of *True* magazine announced in bold letters, "The Flying Saucers Are Real," promising a "sober, considered conviction that the conclusion arrived at in this story is a fact." In his story's opening paragraphs, Keyhoe summarized his four bombshell conclusions after eight months of research:

1. For the past 175 years, the planet Earth has been under systematic close-range examination by living, intelligent observers from another planet.
2. The intensity of this observation, and the frequency of the visits to the Earth's atmosphere by which it is being conducted, have increased markedly during the past two years.

3. The vehicles used for this observation and for interplanetary transport by the explorers have been identified and categorized as follows: Type I, a small, non-pilot-carrying disc-shaped aircraft equipped with some form of television or impulse transmitter; Type II, a very large (up to 250 feet in diameter) metallic, disc-shaped aircraft operating on the helicopter principle; Type III, a dirigible-shaped, wingless aircraft which, in the Earth's atmosphere, operates in conformance with the Prandtl theory of lift.

4. The discernible pattern of observation and exploration shown by the so-called "flying discs" varies in no important particular from well-developed American plans for the exploration of space expected to come to fruition within the next fifty years. There is reason to believe, however, that some other race of thinking beings is a matter of two and a quarter centuries ahead of us.

Over six pages of text, Keyhoe walked through the details of "The Classics"—the Mantell, Chiles-Whitted, and Gorman sightings—and said the only possible conclusion was interplanetary, though he offered no new evidence or additional information that backed up his claim. "The sudden spurt of sightings in 1947 might indicate that we have attracted attention with our V-2 rockets, A-bomb explosions, and other experiments," he explained, "and that an orbiting satellite base has been established, or re-established after an absence."

The magazine hit newsstands on December 26, 1949, and created a sensation, considered "the most widely read and discussed magazine article up to that time." Radio commentators and astronomers weighed in; mail flooded the *True* magazine offices. The response was so great that, the day after publication, the Pentagon released a statement saying that while its flying disk study had been shut down entirely, Project Grudge's final report from August would be made available in sanitized form. The subtext was clear: Keyhoe's article was wrong, and they had nothing to hide. There was nothing to worry about—that is, until two months later, *True* magazine followed up Keyhoe's sensational story with another, this one seemingly done with the full cooperation of the military.

"How Scientists Tracked a Flying Saucer" focused on the White Sands Missile Range in New Mexico and featured a navy scientist, R. B. McLaughlin, explaining how a team at the missile range had spotted a strange silver elliptical object, 105 feet in diameter, flying at an altitude of fifty-six miles that rapidly ascended some twenty-five miles in just ten seconds. "I am convinced that it was a flying saucer and, further, that these disks are space ships from another planet, operated by animate, intelligent beings," the officer told *True*. "I think it is safe to say that it wasn't any type of aircraft known on Earth today. Even if, as is likely, there are top secret models which you and I know nothing about, there is no human being in this world who could take a force of 20 G's and live to tell about it."

On the record, Commander McLaughlin proceeded to outline two other incidents where he'd seen flying saucers in his work at the White Sands range, seemingly feeding into the pervasive belief that the objects were specifically targeting locations where bomb and nuclear testing had occurred. "Where the saucers come from can only be answered by guesswork. My guess is Mars. Mars 'cooled off' and perhaps became capable of supporting some form of life millions of years before the Earth did. The Martians, if such there be, would have a big start in scientific development," he told the magazine. "So far, their behavior would indicate that they are interested only in observing us."

• •

Bolstered by the public reception to his work, Keyhoe spent the following year adapting his article into a book. *The Flying Saucers Are Real*, published in June 1950 in paperback, featured a fantastical cover illustration of three flying saucers racing over Earth, and a detailed argument that the military had purposefully, gradually let the true facts of extraterrestrial visitors leak into view to prepare the public for future revelations. The truth was too explosive to come out all at once, the author explained, and people needed to become accustomed to the incredible reality ahead. The book was an instant bestseller, an indisputable sign that the idea of extraterrestrial life had transitioned from the stuff of science fiction to accepted possible reality. After all, one of Keyhoe's sources told him, once you realize there can be life elsewhere, the other things that came with it wasn't all that shocking. "At first I had a queer feeling about it," the source said. "But once you accept it, it's like anything else. You get used to the idea."

Keyhoe's book was followed in September 1950 by another explosive book, this one by *Variety* columnist Frank Scully. The author of a series of joke books and word games known as the *Fun in Bed* series, aimed at entertaining sick people as they convalesced, Scully was an unlikely figure to participate in what he himself called one of "the greatest stories told since the creation of the world," but his argument, for the most part, seemed legitimate and rooted in evidence. From the first page, *Behind the Flying Saucers* embraced the postwar age of fear and government secrecy. The truth about the government's knowledge of flying saucers, he argued, could be traced to a lecture delivered on March 8, 1950, at the University of Denver, in which an oil magnate named Silas Newton had outlined how the government had recovered three saucers in Aztec, New Mexico, in 1948. The saucers, one of which was ninety-nine feet in diameter, had contained nearly three dozen alien bodies in total, all between thirty-six and forty-two inches tall, dressed in dark clothing. They appeared to be from Venus, according to a scientist Newton called Dr. Gee, who had been brought in by the government to study the crashed crafts and bodies.[*]

"Anything remotely scientific has become by government definition a matter of military security first," Scully wrote. The nation's very freedoms were being threatened and overrun by the loyalty test hysterias, cloaks of secrecy, and the kowtowing to official, nameless bureaucratic spokesmen. He objected to the way the government had turned the tables on its citizens, making the flying saucer witnesses prove *their* credibility instead of showcasing their own. "Every citizen who thought he saw a flying saucer had to turn in a report that left no doubt about who he was, where he was, and the alcoholic content of his blood for one week before and one week after he had observed a 'silver-like saucer whizzing through space,'" Scully wrote.

---

[*] The original 1948 "story" about the Aztec crash came from a literal parody article, published by *Aztec Independent-Review* editor George Bawra, mocking the early flying saucer reports; over time, Bawra's article morphed from satire to reality. Notably, Keyhoe had investigated the same story and decided it was a hoax.

The book sold sixty thousand copies, and received widespread coverage, though much of it was negative ("Measured for scientific credibility, Scully's science ranks below the comic books," *Time* magazine said). In the end, it took only two years for the fantastical tale to fall apart. While the University of Denver lecture had indeed taken place, Scully had been hoodwinked by the speakers; when a San Francisco reporter asked Scully's two main sources, Silas Newton and Leonard A. GeBauer (aka Dr. Gee), for a piece of the fallen craft, they delivered a piece of ordinary aluminum—Newton and GeBauer, it turned out, had a long history of running cons, and as their victims spoke publicly after the national spotlight brought by Scully's book, both men were charged with fraud, arrested by the FBI, and ultimately faced eleven other civil lawsuits. Scully, meanwhile, never admitted he'd been misled, later claiming that Dr. Gee was actually a "composite of 8 different scientists," which made the whole story even more puzzling.

As the decade came to an end, and public fascination with the saucers endured, other authors turned their attention to the extraterrestrial visitors, speculating about their origins and purpose. British humanist and theologist Gerald Heard's *Is Another World Watching?*, for example, theorized—with convincing logical constructions, syllogisms, and pseudoscience—that the alien visitors were small bees, or beelike insects, from Mars, just two to three inches in size. (Only an insect's body could survive the g-forces and aerial maneuvers that the flying saucers seemed to undertake, he asserted.) They also clearly had some degree of intelligence and awareness. "These searchers and explorers from the sky are considerate—indeed, there is every reason to suppose that they are as wise as they are clever," he wrote, and they were likely monitoring Earth's behavior out of a concern that it could be introduced on its own planet.

"When we twice struck Japan and then, not to slaughter but to astound, made the Pacific spout—when we time and again sent up great super-thunderheads of smoke, spray, and the wreckage of human industry and human bodies, right up into the stratosphere," Heard said, echoing his predecessors. "Then we put out a finger to beckon attention on any watching fellow planet that we were the little fellow out for trouble and able and itching to give it."

Captain Ruppelt Arrives

D ramatic as they were, the Keyhoe and Scully controversies of 1950 paled in comparison to the events unfolding in a world that seemed darker and more ominous than ever before, facing not just an escalating arms race but outright war. The creation of NATO in 1949 and the test of the first Soviet atomic device that following August had only drawn the global battle lines more sharply. Concerned that it needed to stay on top in the arms race, the US moved ahead in January of 1950 with developing a thermonuclear bomb that was orders of magnitude even more destructive. The crash US program to deliver the "superbomb," code-named Campbell (for the soup company), would become the largest military undertaking in history and at one point consumed 7 percent of the country's electricity. Its potential destructive capabilities injected even more anxiety into a society already filled with it. As Albert Einstein told a television interviewer: "General annihilation beckons."

Fear of war also meant fear of those who seemed to want to start it. In January 1950, as Keyhoe's *True* magazine story flew off newsstands, State Department official Alger Hiss was convicted of perjury amid a probe into his Communist sympathies and involvement in a Soviet spy ring; a month later, the UK arrested Klaus Fuchs for sneaking atomic secrets to the Soviet Union, and others would be arrested steadily as the year unfolded. A week after Fuchs's arrest, at a speech in West Virginia, Senator Joseph McCarthy ranted about a list of 207 Communists in the State Department, touching off the "Red Scare" and leading to his subsequent high-profile congressional hearings on "Un-American Activities" that would soon consume Washington's attention. Questions about who to trust, who America's true enemies were, and where the threat came from, stood front and center in political and popular consciousness.

Then, in early summer 1950, actual war began: North Korean troops poured across the 38th parallel on the Korean peninsula, following the okay of Joseph Stalin and China's Mao Zedong, and overran Seoul. Within days, the US and South Korean military positions were collapsing. Within two months, the US faced possible defeat and mobilized rapidly for large-scale combat, rushing forces not just to Korea but to the Taiwan Strait, which it feared Communist China might invade; the daring September landing at Inchon by Douglas MacArthur turned the momentum in Korea, but China responded with a counterinvasion. By the end of 1950, a quarter-million US and UN troops were locked in ferocious combat.

It was in January 1951 that a twenty-seven-year-old Iowan named Edward Ruppelt was recalled from the reserves to active duty. Ruppelt had originally been drafted into the army in 1942 and served as a bombardier, flying on submarine patrols across the Atlantic and earning a chest-full of medals across more than two thousand hours of flight time—five battle stars, two theater combat ribbons, three Air Medals, and two Distinguished Flying Crosses. After returning home, he had enrolled at the University of Iowa, part of the rush of postwar GIs in higher education, just finishing his bachelor's degree in aeronautical engineering when the air force summoned him back.

Now the newly promoted captain found himself assigned not to the front lines of the new war in Asia, but instead to the intelligence unit at Wright-Patterson airfield. On his second day on the job, he overheard a conversation about flying saucers; overnight, a lieutenant told another colleague that a DC-3 taking off from Sioux City, Iowa, had reported encountering a bright light that the pilot and copilot said looked like a wingless B-29 fuselage. The glare had also been seen by the air traffic control and a colonel in military intelligence who was a passenger on the flight. The object had briefly taken up a position flying alongside the DC-3, according to the copilot, and then disappeared, no exhaust or engines evident.

Ruppelt watched all day as the lieutenant hunted for an explanation, until eventually the whole affair was written off as a mistaken sighting (a B-36 bomber had also been in the air over Sioux City at the time, which likely accounted for the light). Ruppelt had his doubts about the conclusion—the B-36 was the largest piston-powered aircraft in the world,

with six giant engines and roughly twice the size of a B-29, but as someone who had believed the military pronouncements that it was hard at
work investigating every sighting of a flying disk, the apparent dismissal
of the sighting details was puzzling. "I'd only been at [Wright-Patterson]
two days and I certainly didn't class myself an intelligence expert," he
recalled later. "But it didn't take an expert to see that a B-36, even one
piloted by an experienced idiot, could not do what that UFO had done—
buzz a DC-3 that was in an airport traffic pattern."

He remained fascinated by the subject even as he was pulled deeper
into the center's main work on the Korean War, and found that many of
his fellow intelligence officers shared similar questions about the reality
of the flying disks, despite toeing the official line. As one colleague told
Ruppelt, "The powers-that-be are anti–flying saucer, and to stay in favor
it behooves one to follow suit."

Beyond the sleepy corner of Project Grudge, the technical intelligence division at Wright-Patterson was in the midst of a massive wartime
transition. In May 1951, it was renamed the Air Technical Intelligence
Center (ATIC), and became one of the many units that made up the
growing eight-thousand-acre Dayton, Ohio, base, which focused on research, development, and technical engineering and had ballooned from
3,700 personnel to 50,000 during World War II. (Ultimately, it would
become the largest US Air Force base in the world.)

The airfield, named in part after the local heroes and flight pioneers
Orville and Wilbur Wright, who used some of the surrounding land
for their early aeronautical experiments, was home to more than 1,500
tons of technical plans, manuals, schematics, and papers, which had been
transferred from German facilities to a five-hundred-person intelligence
team, who had then used them to jump-start America's postwar industrial
innovations. All told, an official history of the center says the base's intelligence operation was responsible for introducing "100,000 new technical
terms to the English language." Operations Paperclip and Overcast, the
government's ethically dubious efforts to recruit Nazi rocket scientists
and engineers to help America fight the Soviet threat in the Cold War,
brought German scientists to the field to help translate the captured ideas
and make them a reality.

"Besides the aviation-related advances, new designs for vacuum tubes, the development of magnetic tapes, night vision devices, improvements in liquid and solid fuels, and advances in textiles, drugs, and food preservation were made available to American manufacturers."

It also was the site of hundreds of captured enemy aircraft—special teams of Allied intelligence officers and pilots had secured Japanese and German airplanes and technology in the war, including some eighty-six German planes repatriated to the US as part of what was known as Operation Lusty (aka Luftwaffe Secret Technology).* After the war, the base often held a wildly popular open house, displaying the captured aircraft for the more than a million tourists who trooped through the airfield.

Now, amid the Korean War, a steady stream of captured and crashed Soviet MiGs passed through the center as combat unfolded on the other side of the world—the tail section of a MiG-15 arrived in May, followed the next month by a full fighter jet that had crashed—and engineers and intelligence officers like Ruppelt were tasked with carefully studying and disassembling the components, calculating speed, range, and flying characteristics, and rushing updated specs back to the battlefield.

At some point during the spring of 1951, Ruppelt got a new office mate. Lieutenant Jerry Cummings had been named head of Project Grudge and soon befriended Ruppelt. Their conversations ranged widely, and when Cummings realized that the young officer was interested in Grudge efforts, he began to share the intriguing reports that came into ATIC, including one that arrived on September 12.

From the start, the intelligence officers knew something strange had happened. The teletype filled a full thirty-six inches of text and reported that a series of radar operators around Fort Monmouth, New Jersey, had spotted fast-moving aerial anomalies on their scopes. At one point, the pilot aboard a T-33 trainer flying at twenty thousand feet had tried to chase a silver disk far below him that he'd estimated between twenty and fifty feet in diameter, but as he dived on it, the object hovered, turned, and headed out to sea.

The combination of a visual sighting with repeated radar alerts raised

---

* The "Patterson" portion of the base's name honors Lieutenant Frank Stuart Patterson, who crashed and died during an aerial experiment in 1918 at what was then Wilbur Wright Field.

alarm bells among top air force officials, and the head of air force intelligence, Major General Charles Cabell, personally ordered ATIC to
investigate the sightings; within hours, members of the team, including
Cummings, were on a plane to New Jersey, where they spent two days
interviewing witnesses and studying the events before briefing Cabell at
the Pentagon.*

When Cummings returned, he told Ruppelt that things hadn't gone
so well. The two-hour briefing in DC was apparently the first time in
months—perhaps longer—that top-level air force officers thought seriously about the flying disks and they were disturbed to realize that
Project Grudge was bureaucratically comatose. "Who in hell has been
giving me these reports that every decent flying saucer sighting is being
investigated?" one general demanded.† Tired from the seventy-two-hour
investigative marathon and early-morning trip, the lieutenant responded
more candidly than he normally would to a major general, explaining
how understaffed and ignored Project Grudge actually was and the or-
ganizational resistance he'd encountered to the subject of flying saucers.
ATIC was quickly given a new charge—take the flying disks seriously—
and a new leader. Cummings, a short-timer, had fulfilled his reserve

---

* The Monmouth sightings, further investigation quickly showed, all turned out to
  be a false alarm: the T-33 pilot had accidentally chased a weather balloon, and the
  radar reports were a strange but easily untangled combination of user error, weather
  balloons, and common meteorological interference.

† Ruppelt says in his memoir that this Pentagon briefing was recorded and that he
  listened to the meeting several times, but that "the recording was so hot that it was
  later destroyed." There's no evidence to back him up or disprove it. It's one example
  of how Ruppelt is a challenging narrator of these early days of the military's UFO
  hunt—his 1956 memoir had access to files that have been long lost to history, and
  he was undeniably an integral figure in the military's UFO program, and thus it
  remains a critical source for any history. At the same time, his memoir suffers the
  same challenges as many former government memoirs—that is, he portrays basically
  everyone who came before him as incompetent, and makes sweeping generalizations
  and statements about his predecessors' thinking and work that are not well sourced.
  At the same time, given the paucity of other records and accounts, his assertions are
  hard to disprove. Other historians who have trod this landscape, like Kate Dorsch,
  have developed doubts about some of what he asserts.

service and was leaving ATIC, and, after Cabell's frustration, the base commanders wanted someone who would take the subject seriously and invest in building a better effort. They turned to Ruppelt, and on October 27, Project Grudge was formally restarted with him in charge alongside a sole staffer, Lieutenant Henry Metscher.

With the Grudge initiative formally under Ruppelt's command, he set about streamlining its efforts, namely by restricting its technical approach and intellectual outlook. As he reread the Project Sign and Project Grudge work, he realized that the issue with the sightings largely lay in how haphazardly they arrived at ATIC's offices. The process had to be streamlined. Together, he and Metscher reread and re-sorted the piles of incidents studied by Sign and Grudge, organizing them by color, size, time of day, and so forth—by the end, the captain joked that the project had amassed so much paper that he could just pile it outside the office door as a giant aerial barrier and wait for a flying disk to crash into it. To manage it all, he built up what eventually peaked at a team of eight analysts, who were selected based on their openness to all possibilities; any analysts who either tried to jump to a conclusion prematurely or were unwilling to accept the mystery of the unknown were reassigned. "As long as I was chief of the UFO project, this was our basic rule," Ruppelt later wrote. "If anyone became anti–flying saucer and was no longer capable of making an unbiased evaluation of a report, out he went. Conversely anyone who became a believer was through. We were too busy during the initial phases of the project to speculate as to whether the unknowns were spaceships, space monsters, Soviet weapons, or ethereal visions. I had to let three people go for being too pro or too con."

From there, a clearer, new system developed. First, Ruppelt's team would sort through all existing and incoming sightings—he didn't want them wasting time trying to solve unsolvable puzzles—and place them into one of three categories: Identified ("Sufficient specific information has been accumulated and evaluated to permit a positive identification or explanation of the object"), Insufficient Data ("One or more elements of information essential for evaluation are missing"), and the mysterious Unidentified ("A report apparently contains all pertinent data necessary to suggest a valid hypothesis concerning the cause or explanation of the report but the description of the object or its motion cannot be correlated with any known object or phenomena"). Those that could be easily explained by the team of internal and external experts—balloons, stars, meteors, and the like—were marked as "Identified." Those proven not to be an ordinary mistake would be set aside into a pile marked "Unidentified," where it would largely be left alone; only when a sufficient number of "Unidentified" sightings had accumulated would the team actually begin to study them. (That's not to say that, in the interim, they were neglected. In fact, the way Ruppelt organized the process made sure those unknown cases would be revisited, with the attention they deserved.)

An area that presented a good deal of difficulty was the witnesses. Those who were considered to be "reliable" were prioritized, but the definition was very much a product of its time. "These witnesses were overwhelmingly male, familiar with (if not directly trained in) aeronautics and flight, often employed by the military in some capacity, and many had technical training or professional scientific education and degrees," historian Kate Dorsch has noted. "Their professions and training cast them as educated men of sound mind, not prone to irrational speculation or outbursts of hysteria. They had experience with aerial phenomena and could be trusted to 'know' what they were looking at and offer accurate descriptions after the fact."

All too aware of the increasingly hostile intellectual ridicule about flying saucer sightings among the larger air force and aviation community, many witnesses were disinclined to cooperate or report to investigators the suspicious things they saw in the sky—as one pilot said, "If a spaceship flew wing-tip to wing-tip formation with me, I would not report it"—and Ruppelt knew this reluctance could potentially hamper his ability to identify new threats. In order to avoid that outcome, he took one other significant step: if he was going to change how the world viewed these aerial mysteries, he'd have to change how we talked about them. "We don't like the name 'flying saucers' and only rarely use it because it seems to represent weird stories, hoaxes, etc.—sort of a joke. We don't take 'flying saucers' too seriously either, but we do take the problem of Unidentified Flying Objects seriously. The definition of an

Unidentified Flying Object is an airborne object that by performance, aerodynamic characteristics or unusual features does not conform to any presently known type of aircraft or missile, or which cannot be identified as a known object or phenomena."

The age of the UFO had begun.*

---

* Ruppelt would later claim he "coined" the term "UFO," but Grudge's 1949 report had been titled "Unidentified Flying Objects" and so the term was obviously in general use long before he arrived at ATIC. Instead, it's probably more accurate to say that Ruppelt popularized the term "UFO."

The Mysterious
Death of Captain Mantell

As part of his effort to renew and jump-start the air force's UFO effort—which in the spring of 1952 had been officially named Project Blue Book—Ruppelt sought out J. Allen Hynek, the astronomer who had worked on Project Sign, to join what he was now calling the Aerial Phenomena Group.* Though Hynek had been left out of the air force's half-hearted efforts to study UFOs since Project Sign's decline in 1948, his career had thrived at Ohio State. His astronomy class was one of the most popular on campus, driven in part by the passion and wit of the glasses-wearing professor, who would open "Astronomy 500" by announcing, "My name is Hynek, as in giraffe." Still a skeptic, he frequently told students that his goal was to teach them enough about what existed in the skies above that they would never need to report a flying saucer, and continued to focus his own research on using that information to explain and answer the questions put forth by UFO sightings. Through the McMillin Observatory, he had also worked with the air force to investigate how stars twinkled, examining the Gemini stars Castor and Pollux—the former, he was able to determine, was a binary star, meaning that it appeared on Earth as a single point of light, but was actually six stars, rotating together in three binary pairs, while the latter, a giant single star, had different scintillation patterns. (This research, in its own way, was key to future UFO identification efforts, as it recognized that not all stars look the same in Earth's night sky—and that even trained observers might misunderstand a star for a UFO in certain circumstances.)

---

* The name, Ruppelt said later, came from the blue-colored blank notebooks given to students for college exams; as Ruppelt joked, "Both the tests and the project had an abundance of equally confusing questions."

All of this work impressed and intrigued Ruppelt, but what he really was hoping for, he had admitted to Hynek, was a chance to talk about the Mantell incident, the fatal Kentucky plane crash in 1948. Ruppelt had always been unsatisfied by Project Sign's conclusion that the experienced pilot had died chasing Venus, and thought if anyone would be able to look at it, it was the famed astronomer.

Finding the air force back on his doorstep took Hynek by surprise—he had seen the original UFO flap as little more than a "fad [and] a craze" and had long assumed it would fade away like zoot suits, the mambo, and other trends of the decade. But, as he and Ruppelt began to talk about the intervening years, filled with other sightings, sustained public attention, and popular culture references, Hynek began to reconsider his dismissal. "It was the persistence of the phenomenon, not only in the United States, but over the world, that finally grabbed my attention." He retrieved and reviewed his Project Sign notes and quickly concluded that he'd been wrong: while Venus indeed had been in the direction Mantell had chased it, it almost surely hadn't been bright enough that day to attract the pilot's attention. There had to be another explanation.

Ruppelt, who had also been reexamining the case, found something else that was curious—many of the witnesses had consistently described things that sounded less to him like flying saucers and more like balloons: "The first man to sight the object called it a parachute; others said ice cream cone, round, etc.," he recalled. "Buried deep in the file were two more references to balloons that I had previously missed. Not long after the object disappeared from view at Godman AFB, a man from Madisonville, Kentucky, called Flight Service in Dayton. He had seen an object traveling southeast. He had looked at it through a telescope and it was a balloon. At 4:45 p.m., an astronomer living north of Nashville, Tennessee, called in. He had also seen a UFO, looked at it through a telescope, and it was a balloon."* A drifting balloon would also explain other

---

* The Blue Book records actually show that astronomer as even more definitive than Ruppelt's summary: "a Dr. Seyfert, an astronomer at Vanderbilt University, had spotted an object south-southeast of Nashville, Tennessee, that he identified as a pear-shaped balloon with cables and a basket attached, moving SSE at a speed of 10 MPH at 25,000 feet. This was between 1630-1645" (i.e., between 4:30–4:45 p.m. local time).

elements of the Mantell incident, like the alleged UFO's reduced speed and nearly two-hour visibility.

It was in the records of the Office of Naval Research that Ruppelt finally found a clear answer: the veteran World War II pilot had died chasing a military weather balloon launched in Ohio and run by, of all things, the cereal manufacturer General Mills. The once-secret research effort, known initially as Helios and later renamed Skyhook, grew out of the leaps and bounds made during World War II in manufacturing plastics and had started as an attempt to send manned balloons into the sky. Skyhook balloons—made of polyethylene sheets that were just 1/1,000th of an inch thick—marked a revolution over traditional rubber weather balloons. Nearly 100 feet in diameter and about 130 feet tall, they required about two dozen standard helium tanks to inflate and could soar to close to 100,000 feet, perfectly suited for high-altitude research, especially on cosmic rays. The initial goal of learning how to do so, with gondolas, quickly transitioned to unmanned flights packed with scientific instruments when it was realized that the latter approach might be more effective.

The operation and experiments had been based in Minneapolis, where General Mills technicians had worked alongside personnel from the Office of Naval Research, but as Ruppelt asked around, he was unable to find any flight records from 1948. He suspected that Mantell had crossed paths with a balloon, and understood how, to the pilot, it might have really seemed like a UFO.* Neither he nor presumably anyone at Godman air base had ever heard of the Skyhook program. A one-hundred-foot-diameter balloon looming above him would have justified

---

* Ultimately, in 1994, researchers Barry Greenwood and Robert G. Todd determined that the likely suspect was actually a Skyhook balloon launched from Camp Ripley in Minnesota around 8 a.m. on January 6, 1948. According to their investigation, which involved locating photos of the Minnesota balloon launch, plotting its southeasterly path, and speaking with Professor Charles Moore, one of the research project participants, the navy was reticent to come forward with its own Skyhook knowledge after the fatal crash because it did not want to be held responsible for Mantell's death and, subsequently, suppressed knowledge of the Camp Ripley balloon, according to Professor Moore, who was a participant in the discussion of this matter with the navy.

a radio back saying that the object "appears metallic [and] of tremendous size," as some recalled his final radio transmission to be.

Mantell hadn't died chasing a flying saucer; he'd died chasing a secret balloon run by his own military.

• •

In April 1952, the air force began to circulate word of Project Blue Book's newly organized efforts under Ruppelt, sending out a formal statement that explained how the military would be continuing its study of UFOs, and later making a public announcement with Air Force Letter 200-5, which outlined the new standardized reporting of UFO sightings across the service. Going forward, any sighting would have to be sent to the Blue Book team.*

The protocol came on the heels of the latest issue of *Life* magazine, which asked, "Have we visitors from space?," a question to which writers H. B. Darrach Jr. and Robert Ginna strongly implied that the answer might be yes. The article walked through ten major UFO incidents and outlined why it deemed existing explanations as inadequate, and featured an interview with Dr. Walther Riedel, one of the Nazi engineers brought over from Germany, who was, as *Life* said, "now engaged on secret work for the U.S.—'I am completely convinced that they have an out-of-world basis,' the scientist said."

Dr. Maurice Biot, another physicist and aeronautical engineer quoted in the article, agreed. "The least improbable explanation is that these things are artificial and controlled," he said. "My opinion for some time has been that they have an extraterrestrial origin."

Amazingly, high-level air force officers seemed to be trending in a similar direction behind closed doors; at a summer briefing in Washington, where Ruppelt outlined the latest sightings, a colonel on the intelligence staff asked a surprising question: "Isn't it true that if you make a

---

* This new standard reporting structure included a sixty-page manual for how to file suspicious sightings, which in the acronym-loving military were soon dubbed "FLY-OBRPT." To address concerns about ridicule or embarrassment for those reporting sightings, the manual emphasized that "no matter who is making the report, extreme courtesy should be shown."

few positive assumptions instead of negative you can just as easily prove that UFOs are interplanetary spaceships?" The thought was important, but the fact that it had been asked in the first place was even more so, validating the work as legitimate and of official government concern. The staff was soon doubled from two to four, and a press aide, a civilian named Al Chop, was brought on to assist. The Pentagon also assigned an official liaison for the project in DC, Major Dewey Fournet. After providing briefings around the country to research labs and science teams, an encouraged Ruppelt formulated plans to deploy technological detection tools nationwide, focusing on areas with high UFO activity—including cameras that could capture the chemical spectra of UFOs, to compare them against known stars or meteors and help eliminate astronomical confusion, as well as sound recording equipment that might capture clues about suspicious sightings.

In June, thanks in part to the new report procedures and the attention of *Life* magazine, Project Blue Book received its highest-ever number of UFO reports—149. As July began, air force chief of staff Hoyt Vanderberg told *Look* magazine that the UFO research was important for the nation's security. "With the present world unrest," he said, "we cannot afford to be complacent."

The Washington Merry-Go-Round

Saturday, July 19, 1952, was a typically blazingly hot and humid summer day for Washington, DC, the daytime high in the mid-nineties and the overnight temperatures falling only into the still-steamy mid-seventies. That morning, a smiling President Truman had posed for photographers carrying his favorite panama hat as he returned to the White House after three days in the hospital with a virus, cracking that his health was distracting the capital from the week's other big political news story, the ups and downs of the Democratic National Convention in Chicago and the political battle to see who would secure the nomination to succeed him.

Another joke landed around midnight, when air traffic controllers at National Airport, right on the Potomac, noticed multiple unidentified targets on their radars. In response, controller Ed Nugent summoned his boss, Harry Barnes, and pointed to the seven objects on the screen. "Here's a fleet of flying saucers for you."

The sightings were reported to Andrews Air Force Base, across the river in Maryland, which put aircraft departing from National on alert to the potential hazards in the sky. Not long after, the pilot of Capital Airlines Flight 807 radioed back that he'd spotted something, a half-dozen bright lights that looked, he described, "like falling stars without tails." Until about 7 a.m., the radar stations continued to pick up about a half-dozen unexplained targets, while other controllers, pilots, and airport personnel reported unusual lights in the sky—including one pilot who said a light was paralleling him as he landed. Radar tracking showed the unidentified objects passing over the city, including into the prohibited airspace over the White House and the Capitol. The aliens, it seemed, were inspecting the US capital.

While odd objects over military bases at this point had become anticipated, the appearance of one over a major city raised immediate concerns.
In the atomic age, America's physical distance from potential adversaries
no longer provided the security it had for much of the previous century,
and there was a real, legitimate fear that a single plane and a single bomb
could doom a city. "A single flight of planes no bigger than a wedge of
geese can quickly end this island fantasy," E. B. White wrote during the period. "All dwellers in cities must live with the stubborn fact of annihilation."

Army antiaircraft batteries now surrounded key targets across the country, and Truman had recently approved the creation and use of the nation's
first air raid early-warning system, which officials hoped would provide
three to six hours of warning of approaching Soviet bombers. Schoolchil-
dren would soon become familiar with the eerie optimism of the Bert the
Turtle civil defense mascot and "Duck and Cover" air-raid drills.

As much as the flying saucers proved illusory—no one had still ever
found one of these craft, as far as the public knew—the suspicion of the
sky remained a daily preoccupation. "Files filled with reports of hoaxes,
misidentified common objects, and Jupiter might make the study seem
an uninteresting waste of time and resources. But . . . Air Force officials
repeated the refrain that all that was required was one ignored report of
a legitimate aircraft to forever alter American national security, and the
nation itself," Kate Dorsch writes.

Barnes, in his report to officials, emphasized the strangeness of the
entire encounter. "It would be extremely difficult to write this so that it
is in a logical sequence due to the confusion that seems to have existed
throughout the entire affair," he wrote, before explaining that he was convinced the "pips" he'd seen on his radarscopes weren't ordinary aircraft:
"The only recognizable behavior pattern which occurred to me from
watching the pips was they acted like a bunch of small kids out playing. It
was helter-skelter, as if directed by some innate curiosity."

When Ruppelt's team began investigating the incident two days
later, on Monday, July 21, they initially deemed the sightings to be very
believable—the combination of radar returns and visual identifications
was always one of the highest levels of evidence, short of actual photographic or real-world proof of a UFO—but doubts began to creep in as
they got deeper into the research. Yes, all three radar sites in the capital

region—National Airport, Bolling Air Force Base directly across the Potomac from National, and Andrews Air Force Base, out in the suburbs—had registered suspicious objects, but only once, and for about thirty seconds, had all of them recorded and tracked the *same* suspicious object.

They were prepared to dismiss the anomaly, but then, the next weekend, it happened again. This time, more ready and more wary, the air force scrambled fighters out of Delaware to respond, and the F-94 pilots confirmed that they were seeing unidentified lights in the region. National Airport saw strange radar returns but could never get close enough to make a true determination. "I tried to make contact with the bogies below 1,000 feet," pilot William Patterson said. "I was at my maximum speed but . . . I ceased chasing them because I saw no chance of overtaking them." One object, which he estimated to be about ten miles away, was lost after a roughly two-mile chase. Members of the Blue Book team were awakened in the middle of the night, and two officers raced to Washington from Dayton, arriving in time to spot seven possible targets on the radar, but neither the original F-94 pilots nor the second set of fighters rushed to the scene when the first ran low on fuel, ever identified an object.

The string of sightings would come to be known in UFO lore as "the Washington Merry-Go-Round," after the then-popular DC-insider newsletter column of the same name by Drew Pearson and Jack Anderson, and were front-page news right across the country, right alongside reports from the Democrats' national convention, where Adlai Stevenson and John Sparkman were nominated for the presidential ticket against Dwight Eisenhower and Richard Nixon. An unnamed Pentagon spokesman (probably the UFO public affairs officer, Al Chop) tried to reassure the country: "One thing I would like to do is dispel the belief of some that we are holding something back. We are not"—but confidence was further shaken when, in a July 28 *Washington Post* article titled "'Saucer' Outran Jet, Pilot Reveals," an air force spokesman was quoted saying, "We have no evidence they are flying saucers; conversely we have no evidence they are not flying saucers. We don't know what they are."

Everyone was looking for answers, including President Truman, who had his aide, Robert Landry, call Ruppelt for updates while the president listened in. That week, the air force held a large press conference at the Pentagon to calm public nerves, "the largest and longest [it] had held since World War II," recalled Ruppelt, who spoke at the event alongside the heads of air force intelligence and air defense command, both two-star generals, as well as ATIC's chief of technical analysis.* Major General John Samford, the air force intelligence commander, actively tried to downplay any idea of a threat, explaining that "there has been no pattern that reveals anything remotely like purpose or remotely like consistency that we can in any way associate with any menace to the United States," before being forced to admit that the team did not actually have a clear answer that that was true. "There have remained a percentage of this total, about 20 percent of the reports, that have come from credible observers of relatively incredible things," he said. "We keep on being concerned about them."

The so-called Merry-Go-Round and resulting national press attention arrived at a particularly inopportune time: that summer, the air force also launched a civil defense program known as "Operation Skywatch," which sought to build a national network of 150,000 civilian volunteers who would watch for Soviet bombers at some 6,000 stations scattered across coastal and northern border states. "If an enemy should try to attack us," President Truman explained upon announcement of the new initiative, "we will need every minute and every second of warning that our skywatchers can give us."

Americans flocked to volunteer for the program, and proved eager—often too eager, it seemed—to spot suspicious objects in the sky. Within days of the first Ground Observer Corps shifts, which lasted twenty-four hours, reports of UFOs began to pour in; a Westfield, Maine, observer saw three disks, and a Coast Guard seaman in Nahant, Massachusetts, noted one circling his post. One volunteer in a remote mountain post reported an "unexpected multi-engine plane," which led to the scrambling of fighter jets before it was quickly determined that the craft was none other than President Truman's own plane, the *Independence*.

Between the Skywatch results and the public focus on the UFOs in

---

* In the back of the room, Ruppelt met for the first time the UFO-believer Donald Keyhoe, who was covering the press conference for his next book on UFOs. They shook hands, and Ruppelt explained that he'd been a fan of Keyhoe's early aviation fiction short stories as a kid in Iowa.

DC, the nation felt poised for another interest wave. Normal air force intelligence, completely overwhelmed, all but ground to a halt, the *New York Times* reported, as more than five hundred UFO reports flooded in throughout the month of July. Sixteen-hour workdays became the norm for Ruppelt's staff, who felt, given the volume of incoming information, like the country was constantly on the verge of a full-blown attack. To help alleviate the workload and pressure, the air force brought in two scientists, Richard Borden and Tirey Vickers, to map the sightings against meteorological phenomena. As they studied the weather maps and temperature records, it became clear that the visual sightings had probably been due to simple confusion, the radar sightings standard interference that typically came during humid-night temperature inversions, when warm air ends up on top of cold air—an almost nightly occurrence in DC during the summer. "The almost simultaneous appearance of the first moving targets with the [stationary] ground returns, [the latter] signifying the beginning of the temperature inversion, suggested that the target display was perhaps caused by some effects existing in or near the inversion layers," they stated in their report. Moreover, they determined that there was little correlation, overlap, or relationship between the radar targets at each of the three facilities, or the visual sightings (save that one thirty-second overlap, which Borden and Vickers chalked up to coincidence).

Their conclusion—that the entire incident was a weird mix of weather and the power of suggestion—was backed up by November tests of a new radar system in Indianapolis that "spotted" similar UFOs. "Targets were larger, stronger, and more numerous than those observed by the writers during the Washington observations," the scientists reported. "At times the clutter made it difficult to keep track of actual aircraft targets on the scope."

By the end of the fall, Ruppelt himself was doubting the reality of the DC sighting flap. And, the more he looked into it, the more he realized that DC air traffic controllers and pilots seemed to spot a lot of UFOs—weeks earlier, on a night in May, they'd seen more than fifty of them on radar over the course of a few hours. While at first glance the "visual" sightings may have seemed harder to explain away, the more the Blue Book team interviewed witnesses, the less convincing their testimony seemed. One pilot's recollection of "a falling star go[ing] from overhead to the north. A few minutes later another went in the same direction. They faded and went out within two seconds. The sky was full of stars, the Milky Way was bright, and I was surprised that we did not see more falling stars" seemed to Ruppelt to be a run-of-the-mill meteor shower. If he was going to make any progress, he was going to need more help, and a more expanded approach.

• •

As the DC sightings and Skywatch reports clogged the air force's intelligence pipeline, the Blue Book team turned to outside consultants to help make sense of the phenomena. The resulting effort, called Project Stork, was formed in early 1952 and focused on a contract with the Battelle Memorial Institute, a government research group based in Hynek's hometown of Columbus who would use Battelle's powerful and still-rare computers to sort and study UFO sightings. Battelle had had a long-standing Cold War contract with ATIC, primarily to study Soviet and Chinese military aircraft and capabilities, and Blue Book hoped their expertise could create a sophisticated statistical analysis of reported sightings, tracing the commonalities and highlighting differences across the hundreds and thousands of encounters listed in their files.

Stork, known internally as PPS-100, spent months working on their new mission, examining what Battelle called "a novel, airborne phenomenon, a manifestation that is not a part of or readily explainable by the fund of scientific knowledge known to be possessed by the Free World." Their process required four people (two from ATIC, and two from a panel of outside consultants) to review the final identification of each sighting and label each "Known" or "Unknown"; about eight hundred were ultimately rejected as either too nebulous or containing too highly conflicting witness statements. The rest were coded and fed onto punch cards, for analysis by IBM computers, resulting in hundreds of pages of charts, bar graphs, and statistical analysis—everything from the angle of the sun to the reported colors to the latitude and longitude of the sightings. Ultimately, about four thousand reports were coded and analyzed, using a complex numbering system and a translation and standardization process, the final report dryly noted, that was "extremely difficult and time-consuming," since the original sighting reports were not thorough enough for even a "quasi-scientific study."

The resulting research found, effectively, almost nothing of interest. The sightings had no apparent trends or patterns, and Battelle concluded, "on the basis of this evaluation of the information, it is considered to be highly improbable that reports of unidentified aerial objects examined in this study represent observations of technological developments outside of the range of present-day scientific knowledge."

Hynek, meanwhile, had been asked to track down what the air force might be missing. Over three weeks during the summer, he traveled throughout the US and Canada, meeting with astronomers at eight observatories, including the University of California's Lick Observatory, near San Jose, and Mount Wilson Observatory, in Los Angeles, as well as a meeting of the American Astronomical Society, in British Columbia, to ask them what they thought about UFOs. "Whenever possible, I brought up the subject in cocktail gatherings and in meetings," he later recalled, and found, perhaps not surprisingly, that among his esteemed peers "hostility was rare" to the idea of flying saucers; many astronomers privately expressed more interest and openness about UFOs than they were willing to let on publicly. With some colleagues during his national tour, he dove even deeper, explaining the details of some suspected sightings and the unanswered questions that remained—conversations, he noted, that almost always caused fellow astronomers to become quite animated and interested. "Their general lethargy," he would conclude, "is due to lack of information on the subject."

A veteran of academia himself, Hynek understood the nuances behind the seemingly hot-and-cold response: "A scientist will confess in private to interest in a subject which is controversial or not scientifically acceptable but generally will not stand up and be counted when 'in committee,'" he explained to his Blue Book colleagues upon his return. It was a fact of the environment in which they were working, and one they all had to seriously consider as their efforts continued.

There were still steps to be taken, but to Hynek, the Battelle study had been a significant milestone: UFOs were becoming the fad that never faded, proving it was a subject worthy of deeper study to be "weighed and considered, without rush, by entirely competent men," since "the number of truly puzzling incidents is now impressive." Contrary to his original expectations when he'd joined Project Sign as a consultant four years earlier, sightings had continued, and interest had sustained. "It appears, indeed," he later wrote in his Blue Book report, "that the flying saucer along with the automobile is here to stay."

The Robertson Panel

O nce the mystery of the flying saucers arrived in Washington, it seemed impossible for the confounding question to be left only to the purview of the air force. If this was a Cold War trick or some secret Soviet operation, the nation's intelligence leaders wanted to know—and the sooner, the better. The day of Ruppelt's air force press conference about the "Merry-Go-Round," the CIA's head of scientific intelligence, Ralph Clark, wrote the agency's deputy director to inform him that the CIA had decided to convene a "special study group" to review the flying saucer phenomenon. Throughout the month of August, various secret briefing papers and memos raced around the CIA offices and buildings in downtown DC. While the agency believed that the military had successfully identified the vast majority of UFO reports and sightings as explainable incidents, according to internal documents, "less than 100 reasonably credible reports remain[ed] 'unexplainable'" and "so long as a series of reports remain[ed] 'unexplainable' (interplanetary aspects and alien origin not being thoroughly excluded from consideration), caution require[d] that intelligence continue[d] coverage of the subject."

Out of the reports, CIA analysts created four major theories for UFO origin: (1) US secret weapon development; (2) Russian secret weapon development; (3) "the man from Mars—spaceships—interplanetary travelers"; and (4) user error, e.g., that all the "unexplained" sightings could be explained with better reporting and data. They then carefully began dismantling the first three categories. Via the agency's own research team, analysts confirmed that the first option was not possible—after all, why would the air force demand national reporting on something it already knew about? Plus, the CIA wrote, there was the "unbelievable risk aspect of such flights in established airlanes." It was unlikely that secret weapons would be tested where they were sure to be seen. The Soviet angle was similarly dismissed: "We have absolutely no intelligence of such a technological advance as would be indicated here in either design or energy source," it was concluded, and "there seems to be no logical reason for the security risk which would be involved and there has been no indication of a reconnaissance pattern." Geopolitics at the moment were just too fragile.

As for the theory of visitation, "Even though we might admit that intelligent life may exist elsewhere and that space travel is possible," the briefing paper read, "there is no shred of evidence to support [aliens] at present. . . . There have been no astronomical observations in confirmation—no slightest indications of orbiting which would probably be necessary—and no tracking."

In the end, the CIA agreed with the air force—UFOs were mostly the product of user error, not extraplanetary technology—but agreed that the concerns for national security and intelligence were very real, and very legitimate. At best, they caused confusion, but at worst, they could be turned into a key part of a psychological operation by the Soviet Union. Analysts and intelligence officers, in fact, had not seen a single news report about UFOs in the Soviet press, and concluded that there must have been an "official policy decision" to keep the phenomena from their public, while wreaking havoc on the United States'. Nervous that organizations on the ground could be seeking to cause exactly that kind of chaos, the air force began to closely monitor groups for UFO aficionados that had popped up around the country, including the Civilian Saucer Committee in California. "Air Force is watching this organization because of its power to touch off mass hysteria and panic," the CIA wrote in mid-August. "Perhaps we, from an intelligence point of view, should watch for any indication of Russian efforts to capitalize upon this present American credulity." It was also feared that public reports of UFOs might someday cause government officials to dismiss real sightings of incoming Soviet bombers. "We will run the increasing risk of false alerts and the even greater danger of tabbing the real as false," the CIA warned.

• •

Despite its public-facing authority, a trio of secret briefing papers and memos—documents declassified only in the 1970s—underscored that even behind closed doors, the US government remained just as puzzled about UFOs as the general population. That September, an overview of the agency's ongoing efforts presented to CIA director Walter Bedell Smith came with a suggestion from the agency's head of scientific intelligence that the CIA form a study group of its own to try to address both the scientific solutions to the "unexplainable sightings" and the real operational concerns about how the sightings, left unchecked, could disrupt or undermine US air defenses and enable a surprise attack. "I consider this problem to be of such importance," the official, H. Marshall Chadwell, wrote, "that it should be brought to the attention of the National Security Council in order that a community-wide effort toward its solution may be initiated." Smith agreed, and over the coming months, the CIA and the other US intelligence leaders, including the air force, the Atomic Energy Commission, and the FBI, moved ahead with plans for a formal study that would mitigate public concern about UFOs. To lead the new effort, the CIA recruited Caltech physicist and mathematician Howard P. Robertson.

Beloved by colleagues and one of his field's most respected pioneers, Robertson had been researching and publishing on quantum mechanics since the 1920s. In the middle of World War II, he'd been part of the National Defense Research Committee, where he'd been tasked with determining whether rumors of the V-1 were real (his work focused on what was obliquely called "enemy secret weapons"), and his involvement in the postwar interviews of Nazi engineers about the V-2 had earned him a presidential Medal for Merit in 1946. From 1950 to 1952, he had served as the head of the Pentagon's prestigious Weapons Systems Evaluation Group, which sought "to provide rigorous, unprejudiced and independent analyses and evaluations of present and future weapons systems under probable future combat conditions—prepared by the ablest professional minds, military and civilian, and the most advanced analytical methods that can be brought to bear."

The panel now under his purview consisted of a half-dozen science leaders, including physicist and radar expert Luis Alvarez (a future Nobel Prize winner), geophysicist Lloyd Berkner, nuclear expert Samuel Abraham Goudsmit, and Johns Hopkins astrophysicist Thornton Leigh Page. (Page later said he suspected he was chosen simply because he was an old friend of Robertson's and lived in the DC area.) A CIA officer and a leading expert on missiles, Frederick Durant served as the panel's secretary; J. Allen Hynek rounded out the team as an associate member.

For four days in January 1953, the panel convened at the National Academy of Sciences building near the National Mall in DC, for what was intended to be a comprehensive examination of about seventy-five cases that the air force had deemed the best and most effectively documented UFO sightings. Their collective mission was clear: debunk them and prove there was no such thing as UFOs. "H. P. Robertson told us in the first private (no outsiders) session that our job was to reduce public concern, and show that UFO reports could be explained by conventional reasoning," Page later recalled. The pile of sightings was divvied up among the members according to their expertise. Alvarez took case histories involving radar or radar and visual sightings, while Page dove into reports of green fireball phenomena and nocturnal lights.

The panel's research also consisted of watching two motion pictures—one from Tremonton, Utah, and one from Montana. The Tremonton film, taken by an experienced navy photographer, featured twelve bright objects in daytime crossing a blue sky that, after a thousand hours of frame-by-frame analysis, the men were told, the Navy Photographic Interpretation Center had determined were moving at close to the speed of sound. The Montana film, on the other hand, showed two lights moving far off, including passing at one point behind a water tower, a valuable reference point that helped show their distance and speed.

Supplementing those video sessions were briefings from Ruppelt on Project Blue Book, a report on Project Twinkle, the air force's study of the green fireball phenomenon, and a meeting with air force technical intelligence chief William Garland, who spent about forty-five minutes telling them he thought "vigorous effort should be made to declassify as many of the reports as possible"* and that air force intelligence should dedicate more resources to the cause.

It also heard from air force major Dewey J. Fournet, who had held the UFO portfolio at the Pentagon for the preceding fifteen months before he'd left the service to return to private life. Fournet had started as a skeptic, but over the course of his tenure had come to consider UFOs more worthy of serious study. "In the normal intelligence tradition, I knew I lacked some key data upon which to base an evaluation," he recalled, but it was possible, he now told the panel, that these were indeed extraterrestrials. He was far from confident, yes, but he just wasn't sure what else the objects could be. For at least a certain subset of the sightings, he and the Blue Book team had ruled out all other known explanations—the objects were either aliens or something that humans couldn't yet explain at all. To him, either answer was worthy of more intellectual study.

Through each event, film, and presentation, Hynek steamed. No aspect of the panel's approach, in his view, was taking the problem, evidence, or investigation seriously—the movies were just screened onto the wall of the conference room, hardly the high-quality projection necessary to make a serious determination about what they showed,† and the intellectual

---

* Garland had a unique background and sensitivity to the UFO issue—he'd seen one himself. As Ruppelt recalled Garland's sighting: "When he was at Mather AFB [in California] he and some other people were sitting in their yard one evening. They all saw this bright silvery, round, object. The Gen. said that it was going too fast for a balloon or an airplane. They sighted on it through some wires so they got a good idea of angular velocity. Three of the people who saw it were command pilots." Garland's wife later denied that the air force officer ever saw a UFO.

† Indeed, given the relatively primitive video technology of the time, the forty-five-second video, filmed by chief warrant officer Delbert Newhouse while he was on vacation on July 2, 1952, is incredibly hard to study, even under the best of circumstances—a jerky bright blue sky, with plenty of passing imperfections, shows the objects clearly for only a handful of seconds. Given the cloudless sky and featureless backdrop, it's impossible to judge distance or speed at all—they could be small objects relatively close by moving at ordinary speeds or giant objects far away moving at astronomical speeds. Newhouse, an experienced military observer, believed the objects were made of metal and about the size of a B-29 cruising at ten thousand feet.

environment seemed so hostile to even imagining the answer could be extraterrestrial that he didn't even bother raising evidence that contradicted the theories being developed in the room. Clearly, the panel's compressed time frame and research conditions meant that they were being asked to sit in passing judgment based on their existing scientific knowledge.

"If the whole Robertson panel was a put-up job," he later said, "then one could argue that they deliberately chose high scientific-establishment men, men who were terribly, terribly busy, could obviously not spend a lot of time examining things, and had no intention of doing their homework. . . . Their basic attitude was very clearly an attitude of 'Daddy knows best, don't come to me with these silly stories, I know what's good for you and don't argue,'" he recalled years later.

After just two days of briefings and discussion, the panel spent its final day and a half focused on coordinating its recommendations. Its members, skilled in radar and astronomy, had recognized signs that some of the sightings might have been normal tech issues or weather phenomena, and they believed that with more expertise in those areas—as well as additional, better data—probably most, if not all, of the other sightings could be similarly explained.

In some ways, Robertson argued, the longer the puzzle remained, the less surprising the final answer likely would be—the "saucer problem," for example, had displayed a lot of similarities to the V-1 and V-2 rocket waves of World War II, which had seemed mysterious until one crashed in Sweden and the use of other rockets allowed the Allies to identify and disassemble key engineering. "The absence of any 'hardware' resulting from unexplained U.F.O. sightings lends a 'will-of-the-wisp' nature to the [challenge]," Durant added. "The results of their investigation, to date, strongly indicate that no evidence of hostile act or danger exists."

In the end, the Robertson Panel concluded there was "no indication that these phenomena constitute a direct physical threat to national security," but that "the continued emphasis on the reporting of these phenomena does, in these [perilous] times, result in a threat to the orderly functioning of the protective organs of the body politic." In response, it suggested that "the national security agencies take immediate steps to strip the Unidentified Flying Objects of the special status they have been given and the aura of mystery they have unfortunately acquired."*

The panel officially determined, to Hynek's frustration, that the biggest problem and danger of UFOs was the *idea* of them and the psychological panic and pressure that placed on the American populace—and that the air force's continued efforts to solve the "puzzle" was only exacerbating the situation. To course correct, the military was advised to push a public education campaign aimed at the "debunking" and "deemphasization" of concerns over unexplained sightings, in which airline pilots, air traffic controllers, and Ground Observer Corps personnel were also encouraged to participate. More broadly, articles, television shows, motion pictures, and Disney cartoons would be used to help explain the real (and mundane) answers behind previously mysterious sightings.

The Robertson Panel's research and report would remain secret for years (its very existence wasn't made public until Ruppelt published a tell-all in 1956), but its conclusions reset the US government's posture toward UFOs for the next decade and beyond. As Fournet would later recount, "When the CIA Scientific Panel concluded in 1953 that no threat was evident the Air Force philosophy seems to have undergone drastic modifications."

While the military UFO study would continue, starting with the premise that there were no actual UFOs was enough to redirect the trajectory of Project Blue Book. In February 1953, Ruppelt left his team for another temporary assignment; when he returned, he found much of them had been reassigned. By August, he left for good. His plans for expanding scientific- and instrument-based UFO searches never got off the ground, and his replacement as head of the operation was an airman

---

* The panel argued even over whether extraterrestrial objects in general were something to be worried about. As Durant recorded, "It was noted by Dr. Goudsmit and others that extraterrestrial artifacts, if they did exist, are no cause for alarm; rather, they are in the realm of natural phenomena subject to scientific study, just as cosmic rays were at the time of their discovery 20 to 30 years ago. This was an attitude in which Dr. Robertson did not concur, as he felt that such artifacts would be of immediate and great concern not only to the U.S. but to all countries."

first class, one of the service's most junior enlisted ranks. It was hardly a vote of confidence in the importance of the work.

Hynek was left heartbroken by the panel. "They're not going to have a scientific investigation," he told his graduate student Jennie Zeidman when he returned to Ohio. "For some strange reason, they voted it down. They didn't even take a decent look at the data, and they decided to discredit them." Hynek's reaction was somewhat surprising—or at least would have surprised the vaguely disinterested rising-star astronomer who had been first approached by the US Air Force in the 1940s to contribute to its flying saucer study—and it was clear from his pained reaction to the Robertson Panel that his once-dismissive interest in the subject had shifted. It was clear now that he was invested in the answer to the underlying mystery: What were UFOs?

Saucer-Mania

If the Robertson Panel's official determination was that UFOs were unworthy of public concern, Hynek's reaction was hardly unique: the public didn't seem to reach the same conclusion, either. By the mid-1950s, aliens had firmly lodged themselves in popular culture. TV was filled with space shows, like *Captain Video and His Video Rangers* and *Tom Corbett, Space Cadet*, and toy stores were filled with ray guns and rocket ships. When Gimbels department store hosted a "Space Cadet Christmas" exhibit, with the popular Corbett's spaceship, *Polaris*, as its main attraction, six thousand kids showed up on the first day; Disney's Tomorrowland opened with the park's tallest building, the TWA Moonliner—even taller than the park's princess castle—showing a mock-up of how tourists would journey to the moon in the distant future of 1986.* As extraterrestrial-led movies, comic books, pulp novels, books, and more spread, artists, writers, and authors began to think more deeply about what an alien might look like—How tall were they? How many eyes, arms, and fingers did they have? What color was their skin? What did they eat?—but for the moment, America's most famous alien remained a tall, muscular, bespectacled man with dark, combed-back hair, and a chiseled chin.

In the fifteen years since Superman's first appearance, in June 1938's *Action Comics* #1, readers had gradually learned the origin story of the figure who would come to be the world's most famous superhero. The character's creators, Jerry Siegel and Joe Shuster, had been experimenting with the idea for years, initially imagining him in the 1930s as a superhuman time traveler from the future. Writers didn't waste much effort on continuity

---

* The attraction was designed with the help of Nazi rocket scientist Dr. Wernher von Braun, who also teamed up with Walt Disney himself to make three movies about space exploration.

in the early years of comic books, though, and backstories or side stories often contradicted themselves from issue to issue, so it was only for the character's tenth anniversary in 1948 that the superhero's backstory was told comprehensively for the first time. Superman, who went by the Earth name Clark Kent, was no longer from the future, but from another planet. "Now I understand why I'm different from earthmen!" Superman shouted in wonder in the pages of *Superman* #61. "I'm not really from Earth at all—I'm from another planet—the planet Jor-El called Krypton!!"* In the years ahead, the Krypton myth expanded—just as the Robertson Panel report reverberated through the government in the summer of 1953, Superman came to realize in *Action Comics* #182 how Krypton had given him his special powers on Earth, and as the nuclear age progressed, special note was taken of his susceptibility to kryptonite, an interesting play on the kind of radiation that many feared would result from an attack.

In 1951, the release of the hit film *The Thing from Another World,* in which an air force team finds a crashed spacecraft after a UFO report near the North Pole, further cemented the idea of alien visitation into the public consciousness. "*The Thing* was not only the first modern 'creature' film, but, more important, it was the first to link inhuman, devouring, alien beings with the Red Menace," film historian Todd McCarthy writes. "For years to come, the screen was filled with aliens and monsters that somehow carried with them the baggage of the communist, thermonuclear, antidemocratic, brainwashed, 'foreign' threat." Theater owners had been wary of the new genre—*The Thing* had no big stars in its cast—but audiences were obsessed; one woman in Pasadena fainted from either fright or excitement at the sneak preview. The movie was the nation's second-most

---

* Case Western Reserve University professor Brad Ricca, who wrote a book on the series' creation, has suggested that Siegel and Shuster might have been partly inspired by a brilliant astronomical event that roughly occurred as they were launching the idea of their superhero. On December 13, 1934, an amateur British astronomer, J. P. M. Prentice, noticed a brilliant light in the northern constellation Hercules—its brightness peaked on the twenty-second and remained visible in the night sky for months; astronomers realized with time that they were witnessing a brilliant nova, a unique kind of binary star prone to rapid changes in brightness. As Ricca says, "I think that Nova Herculis may have played a role in turning Superman from a time travel story into an astronomical one."

popular film at the box office for the entire month of May. "Not since Dr. Frankenstein wrought his mechanical monster has the screen had such a good time dabbling in scientific-fiction," film critic Bosley Crowther wrote in the *New York Times*.

Other alien disaster flicks quickly followed, including *The Day the Earth Stood Still*, where a UFO landed in Washington, DC; *Invaders from Mars*; Ray Bradbury's *It Came from Outer Space*; *Invasion of the Body Snatchers*; and *Earth vs. the Flying Saucers*, which was loosely inspired by one of Donald Keyhoe's books. All made waves in the midst of—and aligned with—a broader cultural preoccupation with possible Armageddon. As shooting started for an adaptation of H. G. Wells's *The War of the Worlds*, Truman's Federal Civil Defense Administration was at the height of its push for backyard fallout shelters and emergency preparedness; a nationwide tractor-trailer convoy called "Alert America" traveled city to city with exhibits and films encouraging citizens to stock up on canned goods, water, and supplies in the event of a Soviet attack. At all levels, the Cold War had become the central organizing event of both American politics at home and geopolitics beyond, and tensions had mounted further upon Joseph Stalin's death in March 1953, as well as the Korean War stalemate that summer, which happened to coincide with "The World's First Flying Saucer Convention" in Los Angeles, which brought thousands of people to Hollywood Boulevard. The convention, sponsored by the nonprofit Flying Saucers International, launched the organization's magazine *Saucers*, and featured letters of greeting from now vice president Nixon, the secretary of defense, and LA's mayor.

It was against this rush of popularity that the Robertson Panel's plans for a countercampaign needed to be implemented, and they started out strong with a Harvard astronomer, Donald Menzel. Menzel, who had seemingly made discrediting any public fascination with UFOs his personal mission. He had been quoted liberally in press reports about the various sightings and even faced off with Hynek at a public meeting of the Optical Society of America. He was also the author of a book, *Flying Saucers: Myth-Truth-History*, the first book published by a major scientist about the UFO question.

"Why, then, have so many civilized people chosen to adopt an uncivilized attitude toward the flying saucers?" he asked the reader. "I think there are three reasons. First, flying saucers are unusual. All of us are used to regularity. We naturally attribute mystery to the unusual. Second, we are all nervous. We live in a world that has suddenly become hostile. We have unleashed forces we cannot control; many persons fear we are heading toward a war that will destroy us. Third, people are enjoying this fright to some extent. They seem to be part of an exciting piece of science fiction."

The truth, Menzel argued, was that flying saucers could be both unexplained and also not threatening or supernatural. To support this argument, he pointed to a long history of hoaxes, like the 1897 airships and Frank Scully's visitors from Mars and strange sightings that could be attributed to natural phenomena like meteors, comets, auroras, ice crystals, and air ripples. The unknownness of certain sightings, he explained, was akin to the mysteries of thunder and lightning—phenomena that scientists still didn't quite understand. "The meteorologist cannot tell you exactly how many flashes of lightning will occur tomorrow or where they will strike," but that didn't mean we needed to "reinstate our belief in the pagan god Thor and his thunderbolts." Instead, we should trust Occam's razor—hearing hoofbeats, we should imagine horses not zebras. "This game of 'cosmic hide-and-seek' that the flying saucers appear to engage in does not carry much weight, and seems to be inane for a civilization allegedly much more advanced than ours," Menzel wrote. What superintelligent, technologically sophisticated interstellar society would bother coming to Earth and then not make their presence clear?

Hynek, however, wasn't as quick to dismiss the whole thing as public confusion. "We can define a flying saucer as any aerial phenomenon or sighting that remains unexplained to the viewer at least long enough for him to write a report about it," the astronomer rebutted. "Each flying saucer, so defined, has associated with it a probable lifetime. It wanders in the field of public inspection like an electron in a field of ions, until 'captured' by an explanation which puts an end to its existence as a flying saucer."

Sure, many—even most—sightings were ordinary phenomena, from Venus to weather balloon, and for someone like him, it was easy to sort through a pile of two hundred reports and reject those that appeared astronomical. But, even then, you would be left with some that still weren't easily explainable. "My concern is with flying saucers of long lifetime—those which have not, as yet, been 'captured' or demolished by an explanation," Hynek said. "Let us further limit them to those that have been observed by two or more people, at least one of whom is practiced in the making of observations of some kind, that is, to pilots, control tower operators, weather observers, scientific workers, etc. Also, let us limit cases to sightings lasting a minute or more, again for obvious reasons." There was something clearly afoot in such sightings—something that science didn't grasp, and reactions of uncertainty or ridicule from eminent scientists like Menzel should be condemned. There had been incidents over centuries in which scientists had dismissed meteorites, not trusting the very real testimony of untrained, ordinary citizens.

"Now, it is clear that stories of real flying saucers, visitors from space, and strange aircraft violating the laws of physics are as reprehensible to the scientist of today as stones that fell from heaven were to the scientist of yesteryear," he wrote, "but, of course, stones did not fall from heaven—that was poor reporting and a wrong slant on a perfectly natural phenomenon. And we don't have space ships that disregard physical laws. But, do we have a natural phenomenon?" As Hynek saw it, there was one pattern in "flying saucer" reports that bore no ready explanation: the reliable, multi-observer sightings of a "hovering nocturnal light" or "nocturnal meandering lights" across the country; some lasted fifteen minutes or longer, or sometimes even appeared throughout a given night. Occasionally they mixed with radar returns.

"There is no question in my mind—just to make this point exceedingly clear—that there exists a relatively simple, natural explanation for them, perhaps even ordinary aircraft under special test conditions," he concluded. "The chief point here is to suggest that nothing constructive is accomplished for the public at large—and therefore for science in the long run—by mere ridicule and the implication that sightings are the products of 'bird-brains' and 'intellectual flyweights.'"

It was, for Hynek, yet another small public step in a personal transformation from skeptic to informed sympathizer. Nature and the universe beyond, he knew, was weirder and more complex than we understood. But that shouldn't stop anyone from trying to.

• •

As Menzel's book hit the market in October 1953, Donald Keyhoe published his second. Titled only slightly differently than his debut, *Flying Saucers from Outer Space* sold nearly five hundred thousand copies, and operated around the premise that saucers were extraterrestrial in nature, and that answers could be found through details of the "baffling cases" in the Blue Book files he had been given access to by Al Chop. The book kicked off with the unsourced assertion that the May 1953 crash of BOAC Flight 783 departing Calcutta, killing all forty-three aboard, had been caused by a collision with a UFO, and continued with first-person reportage of Keyhoe's conversations with Pentagon insiders, pilots, and other witnesses to incidents, proliferating the idea of a grand conspiracy by the air force, and his belief that the government "was keeping the answer secret until the country could be prepared." Such assertions were supported by quotes from sources—"Don, I swear it's nothing the U.S. is doing. I'm in on all special weapons programs," one said, while another revealed, "We're years from anything like the saucers' performance."—and editorialized narratives (at one point, he appeared to, without evidence or sourcing, imagine the inner thoughts of General Samford as he decided ahead of the Washington, DC, press conference to knowingly cover up the truth of the origins of the Merry-Go-Round sightings.)* Keyhoe's book concluded dramatically with a reported conversation with Chop, after the public affairs officer had left the government and Project Blue Book, in which the spokesman admitted to being convinced by the interplanetary theory. "There's no other possible answer," Chop said. "One thing's absolutely certain: We're being watched by beings from outer space. You've been right from the very start." It was imperative that the government admit that the flying saucers were real and extraterrestrial—if only, in Keyhoe's mind, to deflate

---

* Keyhoe would ultimately write five flying saucer books, with others to follow in 1955, 1960, and 1973, all with the same unwavering belief that the conspiracy was clear—and enormous. As James Moseley, a fellow ufologist and Keyhoe critic described the books, "fictitious characters and fictitious 'reconstructions' of fictitious conversations dramatizing UFO cases and Keyhoe's own musings on the Significance of It All."

the possibility that sightings could be used as a psychological weapon by the Soviet Union.

It was a jaw-dropping read—so much so that Keyhoe's publisher wrote the air force for reassurance that Keyhoe wasn't crazy. "[We're] aware of Major Keyhoe's conclusion that the flying saucers are from another planet," the response from Blue Book stated, and "The Air Force has never denied that this possibility exists. Some of the personnel believe that there may be some strange natural phenomena completely unknown to us, but that if the apparently controlled maneuvers reported by many competent observers are correct, then the only remaining explanation is the interplanetary answer." (In fact, the air force's reception to Keyhoe's work was far less sanguine than its statement made it appear. When the book was excerpted in *Look* magazine, the air force insisted on placing parenthetical comments in the article text to dispute various Keyhoe conclusions.) Most readers would see the statement for what it was— carefully crafted government doublespeak, neither a denial nor a confirmation. But for Keyhoe, it was the admission he'd been waiting for: the cover-up was real, and he'd exposed the truth for all to see.

Soon thereafter, perhaps in response to this latest round of UFO hullabaloo, Air Force Regulation 200-2, yet another new directive for reporting and releasing the details of sightings, was put into effect. Going forward, the military would only provide information after establishing origin, e.g., "when the object is positively identified as a familiar object." "For those objects which are not explainable," the new protocol mandated, "only the fact that ATIC will analyze the data is worthy of release, due to many unknowns involved."

That December, the Joint Chiefs of Staff, too, further tightened up sighting procedures with a thirteen-page document. Known as Joint-Army-Navy-Air Force Publication (JANAP) 146, it outlined procedures for civilian and military pilots (mariners, too) in the US and Canada to report what it called "vital intelligence sightings"—not just unknown or enemy aircraft, but missiles, submarines, and UFOs as well. It was, at one level, a seemingly routine update of World War II operations that had enlisted civilian pilots and mariners on both sides of the border to reporting important security sightings, but to generations of ufologists that followed, the timing of the new revisions, and the provision that the public release of a designated "vital intelligence sighting" could be subject to prosecution in the US under Title 18, Chapter 37—the Espionage Act—or Canada's equivalent, the Official Secrets Act of 1939, would be seen as evidence that the government was firmly locking away UFO reports from prying eyes.

• •

Even as the government lost interest in the possibility of visitors coming to Earth, it took the first serious steps toward exploring what might lie beyond our own planet. In 1954, the air force began exploring options for a satellite reconnaissance program, and a year later the Eisenhower administration formally green-lit development of "earth-circling satellites" that would launch sometime in 1957 or 1958, during what would be known as the International Geophysical Year, a massive effort celebrating scientific cooperation. Lloyd Berkner, the force behind the so-called IGY, hailed Eisenhower's announcement as the biggest advancement in aviation since the Wright brothers' flight. "When man talks of artificial satellites and of conquering the immensity of interstellar space, he is transformed into a defiant, creative Prometheus tearing at the chain that binds him to this rock of an earth," a New York Times editorial praised.

The navy's Vanguard project, the US hoped, would also make progress in its mission to launch a satellite to orbit—but the US technological lead was already slipping and the US was farther behind than it realized. As it turned out, the nation year by year in the 1950s was squandering its postwar research lead when it came to space. "The United States did not exploit its initial postwar advantage over Soviet technology. There is significant evidence to support the conclusion that American science could have pushed the nation into the space age in advance of the Russians. The key event was the successful launch of a satellite, and here the United States clearly failed to take the initiative," the air force's own history of its space program concluded in 1961.

It was a disappointing truth, one that the US would only realize after a brutal shock in 1957. Even as its space lead dwindled, though, unbeknownst to many, another mission, closer to home, was underway: the US was, in secret, trying to build its own flying saucer.

Frost's Flying Saucer

S ince 1947, John Carver Meadows "Jack" Frost, a British aircraft designer, had been thinking about doing the seemingly impossible. He was an expert designer—during World War II, he had worked on the design teams for the Hornet fighter and the UK's first jet fighter, known as the Vampire, as well as its first swept-wing jet, the Swallow, and the gliders that had carried troops to the Normandy countryside on D-Day. After the war, he had been tasked with building a supersonic fighter called the Arrow, working with the Canadian firm Avro. There, as reports of flying saucers filled the newspapers, he'd begun to wonder what it would take to actually build such a futuristic design. At Avro, he eventually developed a team, known as the Special Projects Group, to dream big about precisely that type of question.

On the surface, building a flying saucer didn't seem as complicated as one might think. From his experience in aeronautics, Frost believed that a real flying saucer could rely on what was called the Coandă effect, the tendency of air to stick to curved surfaces (the kind of thing that keeps a ball spinning aloft with a stream of air). And he believed, too, that the US was likely already behind in the search for knowledge about the crafts, thinking "that the Germans had [already] developed some form of flying saucer–like aircraft," an aircraft that he believed the Soviets had probably stolen and locked away behind the Iron Curtain, according to aeronautics historian Palmiro Campagna. "He didn't want North Americans to lag behind."

Indeed, beyond the futuristic design challenge, a flying saucer actually seemed remarkably practical, too: the idea of craft that could hover and accelerate up and down—what would come to be known as vertical take-off and landing (VTOL)—seemed a promising solution to the question of how to build aircraft capable of fighting a nuclear war. War planners assumed that many, if not all, of the US's airfields and runways would be immediately targeted, destroying the ability to get planes aloft from normal bases; designers, therefore, were challenged to imagine options that required no runway or that could operate from more primitive facilities scattered around the country that could be utilized in a second strike.

Frost's team imagined a craft whose exhaust was channeled all around it to provide the air cushion for a vertical launch, and then transition to forward flight as the exhaust was redirected to the rear. They began development work in earnest at Avro's sprawling manufacturing facility, adjacent to today's Pearson International Airport in Toronto, in 1952. When the Canadian government abandoned the effort just two years later, deeming it too costly, Frost was undeterred. As US Air Force officials visited the plant to see Canada's new CF-100 fighter, he hijacked the tour and took them to his laboratory, showing mock-ups of what he called Project Y-2. Over the course of testing, Frost's calculations showed an astounding performance capability—a top cruising speed of between Mach 3 and Mach 4, a top altitude ceiling of 100,000 feet, and a range of about 1,000 miles. It would be one of the best-performing aircraft ever built. Intrigued, they picked up the $750,000 bill for further work, motivating Avro to keep up its support.* By 1956, $2.5 million had been committed to the building of a prototype of Frost's saucer, which could now lift about twenty feet off the ground straight-up and then transition to forward flight. The Air Force imagined the Avro to be the future of flight. Walking out of a meeting where the military was discussing the start of its new helicopter program, what would become the long-flying UH-1 "Huey," aeronautical engineer Bernard Lindenbaum later recalled overhearing a departing general declare, "The Huey was to be the last helicopter the army would buy."

The Avro flying saucer was the future.

• •

To the outside world, however, Frost's efforts had to remain top secret, and the government had to appear unmoved by the cresting wave of

---

* The Project Y-2 effort would go by a dizzying number of names over its decade-long history: The US Air Force called it, at various times, WS-606A, Project 1794, and Project Silver Bug, while the army's later involvement gave it the name VZ-9 Avrocar.

sighting reports and pop culture obsession. Following the conclusions of the Robertson Panel, agencies worked quicker than ever to shut down any remaining mystery around the subject of flying saucers. In March 1955, the air force revised its "UFOB Reporting Manual," to state that, under new policies, intelligence officers could "solve" cases using a preponderance of evidence and, notably, apply "common sense" to the process (this read to many as "rational thought," which in turn read as "dismissal"). The air force also reorganized who was in charge of investigating saucer reports, assigning the task to the 4602nd Air Intelligence Service Squadron, a Colorado-based collection of seven-man detachments spread across seventeen military bases nationwide that focused on interviewing enemy pilots and exploiting captured enemy documents and material in times of war. (Before leaving Blue Book, Ruppelt identified it as a perfect fit. It had no other distinct peacetime mission and its personnel could benefit from the interviewing experience that came from tallying saucer reports.) They would now take the lead in investigations, "solve" everything possible, and turn over the true "unknowns" to the Project Blue Book team at ATIC in Ohio, which had also reorganized itself in 1954 into a two-person staff, headed by Captain Charles Hardin.

The message was clear to everyone involved: there was no mystery to solve, just paperwork to process.

Unsurprisingly, the results that followed were what the government had hoped for. "The new methods of investigating and identifying UFO reports worked marvelously," historian David Jacobs said. "The percentage of unknowns fell from 60 percent in August 1954 to 5.9 percent in 1955 and then to 0.4 percent in 1956." Out of 335 potential sightings that air force intelligence studied in the second half of 1956, only two were forwarded to Hardin as truly "unsolved."* At a December 1954 press conference, President Eisenhower answered a question about reports of flying saucers by saying, "Nothing has come to me at all, either verbally or

---

* In the years ahead, the responsibility for UFO reports would be continually shuffled by the air force—first from the 4602nd to the 1006th Air Intelligence Service Squadron, in July 1957, and then onto the 1127th Field Activities Group, at Virginia's Fort Belvoir, in July 1959. By then, the 1127th would do almost no investigation at all and would consider the mission all but over.

in written form." The air force, he added, had reassured him that it was "completely inaccurate to believe that they came from any outside planet or otherwise." In 1955, the military also released what it called "Special Report No. 14," the results of the Battelle Institute's giant statistical study of UFO sightings, which confirmed the Battelle scientists found nothing of interest.

Many Americans, though, still remained largely unconvinced. Motivated by the apparent disinterest of official investigators, UFO enthusiasts, and self-proclaimed ufologists had begun to take the mantle and formalize their own hunts for the truth. Over the 1950s, dozens (and perhaps hundreds) of UFO clubs popped up in various states and cities, some focusing on more "technical" investigations and interest in the UFO phenomenon and attracting people interested in or working around aviation, aeronautics, and rocketry, sometimes with military backgrounds, while others veered into the more spiritual and paranormal elements of the UFO question (a Berkeley sociologist found that run-of-the-mill UFO clubs seemed more likely to attract women who had a history of interest in the occult, many of whom had previously been associated with small religious sects or cults). In 1954, a technical writer for North American Aviation, the manufacturer of the P-51 and F-86, among other planes, named Ed Sullivan* launched what he called the Civilian Saucer Intelligence (CSI) with Dr. Walther Riedel, the German rocket scientist from Peenemünde, by asking people to send in sightings to a Los Angeles PO box. They collected more than a thousand sightings (though most were quickly dismissed as either unreliable or easily identifiable confusions).

Meanwhile, in Wisconsin, Coral and Jim Lorenzen started the Aerial Phenomena Research Organization (APRO), which sought to examine sightings through a scientific lens, not just in North America, but South America as well. Coral, a Wisconsin-born technical writer and editor, had been fascinated with UFOs since childhood, after seeing one in 1934—a white disk crossing the western sky—and another just two weeks before Kenneth Arnold's famous June 1947 sighting. The Lorenzens strongly

---

* Not to be confused with the popular television personality of the same name, who at the time was hosting his own Sunday night variety show in New York City.

rejected both the idea of a government cover-up as well as the more faddish paranormal and occult theories that would come to accompany much of ufology in the years ahead, and as a result, APRO became one of the country's most respected UFO research organizations, with a well-read newsletter and a membership that peaked around three thousand. "APRO was shaped by Coral's strong personality, with the gentle-natured Jim serving as a calming influence on his wife's occasional volatility," Jerome Clark would write. "She thought ufology was better served by concentrating on investigation and documentation of cases and making the subject palatable to scientists." On many issues, APRO would stand in opposition to other big names like Donald Keyhoe, but Keyhoe wanted allies wherever he could find them. In one letter to Coral, he outlined the conspiracy and his hopes for them to team up.

"Actually the Air Force is not the only agency involved; the CIA, National Security Council, FBI, Civil Defense, all are tied in at top levels. The White House, of course, will have the final word as to what people are to be told, and when," he wrote. "If enough intelligence believers could get together and use all possible influence, through their congressmen, senators, and any other means at hand, it might force a quick policy change in Washington."

As their interest continued in parallel, Keyhoe also expressed concern that they might get too close to the truth, and the government might try to "muzzle" him by recalling him to active duty and put pressure on Coral to silence her, too. In one letter, he outlined a code for her to use in correspondence with him if she was writing under duress.

Ironically, Keyhoe's prediction was almost exactly wrong—far from any government "muzzling," the next phase of the UFO story would not be dictated by the powers that be, but instead by a new flood of media publicity from all manner of people who claimed they spoke to visiting aliens.

13

The Contactees

Just like UFO sightings themselves, reports of seeing aliens up close was not in and of itself new. For years, military efforts like Sign, Grudge, and Blue Book had fielded claims of two different types of encounters—one that produced highly unreliable and easily dismissed narratives of strange occurrences, contacts, and conversations that seemed more in line with rumors of the Loch Ness Monster than serious technological wizardry, and others that seemed more credible. These accounts would describe experiences—sometimes with corroborating witnesses or physical evidence, like scorched earth, or reported side effects, like stalled automobiles, or interactions with aliens themselves. In general, Blue Book had been quick to skip over reports of both varieties, considering them too far-fetched to believe—"We're simply not bothering with monster stories. We've got enough trouble with confirmed sightings," Al Chop said dismissively at one point—but from 1953 onward, public dissemination of contact stories began to dominate the culture and demand more focused and formal attention.

"The contactees represented an entirely different type of UFO witness," historian David Jacobs wrote, who had "no fear of ridicule and eagerly sought publicity." Indeed, these individuals generally seemed more interested in the attention (and profit) of their stories than in examining the science or wizardry behind them—none, for instance, reported their contacts first to the government or military, choosing instead to publicize them through books and speaking tours—but in time they became responsible for driving the new era of growth in the UFO conversation, keeping the issue alive as the Robertson Panel sought to suppress its influence.[*]

---

[*] Thomas Bullard, one of the leading scholars of UFO contacts, was blunter in his analysis: "The contactees acquired a cult following and an angry dismissal from serious UFO-ologists as more con artists out to make a buck."

The phenomenon began in earnest with the publication of George Adamski's *The Flying Saucers Have Landed*, a 1953 account of the author's various encounters—including one night, over the course of which he claimed to have seen 184 crafts—that culminated in a landing he witnessed in the California desert on November 20, 1952. "I fully realized I was in the presence of a man from space," he wrote in the book. "A HUMAN BEING FROM ANOTHER WORLD!" that looked like a more Nordic version of the model Fabio, with long blond hair. Through gestures and telepathic communication, Adamski said he learned that the visitors were Venusian (from the planet Venus), and was shown their "Scout Ship" before the craft simply flew off. "I felt that part of me was going with it," Adamski wrote. "The presence of this inhabitant of Venus was like the warm embrace of great love and understanding wisdom."

Following that first meeting, his contact with the Venusians—as well as a growing number of Martians and even Saturnians—deepened. He met some of them in California bars and restaurants, as they hid among ordinary humans; Orthon, a Venusian Adamski had met in November, returned to arrange a tour of the solar system, and warned against the threat of nuclear war. These extraterrestrials, as well as the clear leader of the space people, a thousand-year-old sage known as "the master," had chosen to bring a message of peace to the human race, he explained to his new human friend, because the rest of the inhabited solar system feared that conflict on Earth would not only destroy the planet but also spread dangerous radiation to other planets, putting universal balance in jeopardy. Jerome Clark, the author of the comprehensive *The UFO Encyclopedia*, summarized Adamski's book as a collection "of long, verbatim conversations with assorted benevolent space people, with an occult philosophy identical to the one with which Adamski had long associated himself, and a surprisingly tedious account of a voyage into outer space," but both the FBI and the military were forced to give it a bit more consideration.* On the one hand, Adamski's reports seemed so much more

---

* Notably, Adamski's contacts were dismissed by UFO enthusiast Donald Keyhoe, who saw Adamski as a con man. "To put it politely, Adamski had a vivid dream," Keyhoe told one person.

detailed than other flying saucer reports. But, on the other, they strained credulity at every turn.

As they dug deeper into the author's background, it became increasingly clear that he may not be the most reliable narrator. An occultist and would-be science fiction writer (a 1946 novel he wrote, featuring a trip to the Moon, Mars, and Venus, bore in some ways a striking resemblance to his later testimonies about alien contact), Adamski had worked at a four-stool café near Mount Palomar, the famous California observatory, and, in 1950, published an article in *Fate* magazine about two photographs he claimed to have taken of UFOs. He also founded the Royal Order of Tibet, a mystical cult; toyed with astronomy; and openly stated his beliefs that the government knew that "all planets are inhabited" and that Mars was crisscrossed with canals "built by an intelligence far greater than any man's on earth." A photograph he provided to government investigators was quickly identified as "a Spanish style hat (sombrero) with the sweat band pulled out"; air force intelligence also noted that the "flying saucer" was likely hat-sized based on a comparison to a fence also visible in the image. Another photograph he produced looked like the UFO had three lightbulbs or ping-pong balls as landing gear.

The FBI had met with Adamski as early as January 1953, before his first book was published, to hear his stories of Venusian contact, but after Adamski started implying in lectures that the bureau and military had given him "clearance" in those meetings to speak about alien contacts, an FBI agent and two air force investigators had him sign a statement saying, "I have not and do not intend to make statements to the effect that the US Air Force and Federal Bureau of Investigation have approved material used in my speeches." (Months later, Adamski began to represent a seemingly doctored version of the signed government statement as an endorsement of his tale. In response, an FBI agent and air force investigator sought him out again and, according to an internal FBI report, "read him the riot act.")

Before long, there was more than just Adamski to worry about. In the wake of *The Flying Saucers Have Landed* and its follow-up, *Inside the Space Ships*, other self-proclaimed contactees had started to make their own testimonials public. Truman Bethurum, a fifty-five-year-old California equipment operator who worked road construction, published *Aboard a Flying Saucer*, a work of "Non-Fiction—A True Account of Factual Experience" (as the subtitle defended) that detailed the author being awakened from a nap at work in the Nevada desert by eight men who "seemed to be of Latin extraction from their appearance," and ushered aboard a parked saucer, commanded by a hundreds-of-years-old "gorgeous" woman named Aura Rhanes. Aura explained they were from a nearby planet called Clarion, which was in our solar system, but hidden from view as it existed on the far side of the moon.* They were there, as Adamski's Venusians had been, to warn against a destructive nuclear war. Soon after, Bethurum had been encouraged by the visitors to start soliciting donations—$10 for the first year, followed by $6 annually—to fund a "Sanctuary of Thought," a commune-style property he bought and established outside Prescott, Arizona. (Bethurum's wife ultimately divorced him in 1956, naming Aura Rhanes as a corespondent and cause of the marriage's unraveling.) In 1957, he published another book, *The Voice of the Planet Clarion*, which recorded his conversations with "the lady saucer pilot"; a third book, *Facing Reality*, followed a year later.

Then there was Daniel Fry and *The White Sands Incident*, a book that grew out of his experience at the secret missile range on July 4, 1950. Fry, a hardworking engineer in his mid-forties, had largely educated himself by studying at the Pasadena Public Library during the Great Depression, and worked as an explosives expert on projects like the Salinas Dam before ending up with Aerojet at the White Sands Missile Range after World War II. On that Fourth of July weekend, he said, he'd been exploring the desert when a flying saucer appeared and a being named Alan (pronounced "A-lawn") began to speak to him. (The craft, Fry learned, was just a remote-controlled cargo carrier. Alan was in the mothership, some nine hundred miles above the Earth, piloting around as he waited to become adjusted to the atmosphere and gravity, a process that would take four more years.) Fry was offered a ride, and he took the opportunity.

---

* Needless to say, the idea of a planet existing in orbit on the other side of the moon has some astronomical difficulties to it.

In just a half hour, it whisked him from New Mexico to New York City and back.*

A fourth contactee, Orfeo Angelucci, had his first encounter in 1946, when a saucer stopped to study some balloons he'd released into the air, and another on May 24, 1952, when they returned for a more in-depth visit. At the time, Angelucci was working at a Lockheed assembly plant in Southern California, and while driving home, noticed a red glowing object in the sky. He followed it, and eventually met a large craft that ejected two objects that spoke to him: "Don't be afraid, Orfeo, we are friends," they said. When he stopped his car, the craft delivered him the "most delicious beverage I have ever tasted," a beverage that wiped away his lifetime of physical ailments, and a screen appeared, through which two beings delivered a message hoping for peace and love on Earth directly into Fry's mind. Two months later, Fry came across a luminous thirty-foot-high, igloo-shaped craft and went aboard. Lifted into the sky, he found himself gazing down at Earth. "Orfeo, you are looking upon Earth—your home!" the voice gently told him. "From here, over a thousand miles away in space, it appears as the most beautiful planet in the heavens and a haven of peace and tranquility. But you and your Earthly brothers know the true conditions there."

Tears filled Angelucci's eyes. "Weep, Orfeo. Let tears unblind your eyes," the voice continued. "For at this moment we weep with you for Earth and her Children. For all of its apparent beauty Earth is a purgatorial world among the planets evolving intelligent life. Hate, selfishness and cruelty rise from many parts of it like a dark mist."

---

* Fry would fail a polygraph in 1954, and he later said the event happened in 1949, not 1950, but by then he had gained enough of a following that it didn't matter. He had used the attention of his book to lecture widely throughout the late 1950s and '60s, and eventually created a group called Understanding, which offered a mix of occult and New Age spirituality; its monthly newsletter would publish until October 1979, and its membership would peak in the 1960s with about 1,500 dues-paying members split among sixty national chapters, known in the group as "units." According to Fry, contact with Alan continued in the years ahead—though inexplicably Fry would say that the two didn't meet in person until the early 1960s, long after the four-year acclimation period would have concluded.

The craft turned, shifting his view away from the planet, and as he recalled, "Gradually the heavens came into view—an awesome, breathtaking sight from that tiny craft. All space appeared intensely black and the stars incredibly brilliant, set like jewels against black velvet—large, small; single and clustered. I felt lost in a strangely beautiful, ethereal world of celestial wonder." As the out-of-this-world experience continued, he learned the mystery of life and "drifted in a timeless sea of bliss" before being returned to consciousness back aboard the craft on Earth. The only evidence of his trip, he claimed, was a red burn on his hand where he'd held a piece of glowing metal picked up from the floor of the spacecraft.

A few weeks later, the same Nordic-style being who had appeared on the screen in the desert—who Angelucci had begun to call Neptune—summoned him for an in-person conversation. Pulsing with energy, Neptune explained that he and others existed in dimensions unknown to Earthlings, and warned of a coming conflict: "Communism, Earth's present fundamental enemy, masks beneath its banner the spearhead of the united forces of evil," he explained.

"War will come again to your Earth. We are powerless to prevent it. Millions in your land will fight to the end for their cherished ideals and freedom of the human mind, with only a minimum on their side for victory." It would be catastrophic, and yet, Neptune promised, it would result in a "New Age of Earth," where "all will forget their bitter hurts and build constructively together upon the solid foundation of the Brotherhood of Man."*

This was perhaps the most notable—and consistent—detail in Angelucci's and others' accounts during the 1950s and '60s: mysticism and calls for love and understanding amid what was then considered the dark days of the Cold War. The contactees offered, in place of Earth's trials and

---

* New York overnight radio personality Long John Nebel, who often covered UFOs and other unexplained phenomena in the 1950s and '60s on his wildly popular show, which reached about half the US population, once said, "As far as I'm concerned, although I don't buy any of these bits, this man's was, and is, the most imaginative, the most beautiful, and the most fascinating of them all."

conflicts, a vision for utopias beyond, from seemingly advanced societies that humans could achieve if humankind set aside its differences.* Their moment of hope, though, would be short-lived. Soon, the story would take a darker turn.

---

* Beyond the most famous four contactees, there were other notable ones—like George Van Tassel, who actually worked at the same manufacturing plant as Ange-lucci, and, later, Howard Menger, whose 1959 book recounted a lifetime of contacts that included tours of the Moon, Mars, and Venus that led him to understand that he was a reincarnated Jupiterian placed on Earth to offer peace. Then there were even more minor contactee figures who abounded—including a Missouri farmer, Buck Nelson, who wrote a booklet about his journey to Venus, along with three humanlike aliens and a friendly 385-pound Saint Bernard, and offered for sale hair from the Venusian dog, whose name was Bo. Nelson found the interest in his story a small fraction of what he'd anticipated—when he announced a UFO convention at his farm, just three hundred people showed up, leaving him with nine thousand uneaten hot dogs.

Van Tassel, for his part, founded the Giant Rock Spacecraft Convention in 1954, bringing together the UFO-curious as well as hard-core believers. More than five thousand people flocked to the event its first year, held in the shadow of the epony-mous seven-story boulder in the Mojave Desert near Landers, California, purport-edly the largest freestanding boulder in the world. The annual convention's audience peaked in 1959 to around ten thousand people, though it continued until the late 1970s. The conventions became huge draws for commerce, with stalls selling all manner of books, pamphlets, and UFO souvenirs of varying degrees.

14

The Men in Black

Despite the ubiquity and excitement of widespread contact narratives in the postwar era, doubts began to creep in as it became clearer that, while those who claimed to have seen and communicated with aliens could explain their interactions, they lacked an answer to a major question: Why, if the alien beings were so powerful and so wise, had they chosen such unlikely and down-on-their-luck vessels for their messages on Earth? And why, if their own fate depended on humans heeding their warnings, had they provided so little concrete proof of their existence? Surely if their own civilizations hung in the balance, they'd have been able to come up with some meaningful, demonstrable proof of life, right?

As more seemingly far-fetched accounts spread, new lines of defense emerged to protect the integrity and legitimacy of others, further widening the gulf of belief on either side of the spectrum. Individuals like Isabel Davis, a ufologist who was part of the Civilian Saucer Intelligence club, argued that the contactee literature was all a scam— comparing their stories showed a continuous stream of contradictions in the descriptions of the extraterrestrials, their technologies, and their home planets. "Everything about these books is inconsistent with the theory they are true," she asserted, "and fatally consistent with the theory that they are inventions." Adamski, she pointed out, for instance, never saw Clarion in his tour of the solar system, nor had asked Orthon about its whereabouts, despite having met with Bethurum before his supposed galactic trip.

Swiss psychiatrist Carl Jung also found himself particularly fascinated by the phenomenon and grew to develop a nuanced view of contactee documents. As he devoured their books and personal testimonials, he recognized what most had overlooked: the birth of a new mythology. UFOs, he would explain in his own book—translated into English as

Flying Saucers: A Modern Myth of Things Seen in the Sky—were as much a social phenomenon as a physical one, a collective response to the anxiety of the Cold War, fears of war, and hopes for peace.

Ruppelt came to share a similar view. As the air force officer wrote in his memoir of running Blue Book, "Consciously or unconsciously, they want UFOs to be real and to come from outer space. These individuals, frightened perhaps by threats of atomic destruction or lesser fears—who knows what—act as if nothing that men can do can save the earth. Instead, they seek salvation from outer space, on the forlorn premise that flying saucer men, by their very existence are wise and more advanced than we are." It was an insight that would explain much of the decades of ufology to come.

It was the space between all of these perspectives that a bizarre, less regulated, and far less official area of inquiry and belief began to take hold, leaving opportunities for nefarious behavior. Contact became a for-profit industry, and as the 1950s advanced, more serious ufologists ran up against cons and stunts, most notably from two of the field's great tricksters: James Moseley and Gray Barker.

Moseley had gotten into ufology partly out of boredom; growing up in a privileged cocoon had spared him much of the pain of the Great Depression—his father was an army general and his mother the heir to a family steamship fortune—and his age had spared him from serving in World War II, so, without much motivation or purpose, he attended the tony St. Albans private school in DC before going to Princeton. Later, with his family fortune in hand, he'd begun what he'd later describe as "a rather frantic and neurotic search for something—anything—interesting to do," which brought him back to a long-held obsession. As a student at St. Albans, he'd heard the story of Captain Mantell's crash in Kentucky and immersed himself in the subsequent tidal wave of UFO books. Why, now, couldn't he write one himself?

In October 1953, he decided to collaborate on a UFO book, which would involve driving to California and back, interviewing people who had seen flying saucers along the way. ("This will solve my problem of what to do until February," he noted in his journal.) Through the experience, he became an almost full-time investigator; one of his first interviews was with the deputy commander of Keesler Air Force Base,

Brigadier General J. P. Kirkendall, who had once spotted a UFO and "believed UFOs were real, solid objects but had no idea where they were from." The interaction, for Moseley, was perspective altering: if a senior official would tell a run-of-the-mill aspiring author that UFOs might be real and were certainly a mystery, he thought, then how real of a government conspiracy could there be?

He came to subscribe to the "Earth Theory," a line of thinking that argued that many (or even most or all) saucers were not alien beings, but secret US military experiments. After he finished the short-term book project, he launched the group SAUCERS—the Saucer and Unexplained Celestial Events Research Society—a scientifically minded organization that did little, but managed to last for years. In November 1954, he was elected president of Civilian Saucer Intelligence, and in the years following, edited *Saucer News*, the field's "publication of record."* ("Nationally there was a vacuum in ufology," he would later explain in his memoir. "Saucer fans of all stripes needed a journal where they could read the latest sighting reports and insider dope, trumpet their views to their associates, and enjoy a chuckle or two.")

Gray Barker's own interest in UFOs had begun in September 1952, after some boys near his hometown of Flatwoods, West Virginia, reported seeing a falling flying saucer. Near the site of the supposed crash, curious onlookers saw what was described as a "ten-foot, red-faced monster, which sprayed a foul, sickening gas," with "claw-like hands" and a hooded head shaped like an "ace of spades"—"It looked worse than Frankenstein," one woman, Kathleen May, said later—and ran when the monster made a hissing sound and "glided" toward them.†

---

* The group's primary contribution to the field would end up being the work of member Leon Davidson, who—a time long before the internet, when government reports were hard to come by—republished Blue Book's "Special Report No. 14," the Battelle study, and other documents into ever-larger collections of key documents for ufologists. The compiled documents were offered to members at $1.50 a copy.

† Later, investigators would surmise that the boys probably saw a meteor, if it was anything at all, and that in the dark woods, the group had stumbled upon a barn owl sitting in a tree branch that swooped down on them.

Intrigued, Barker wrote up the story for *Fate* magazine. A short time later, when he saw an announcement about the creation of the International Flying Saucer Bureau, a new club for UFO enthusiasts founded by a Connecticut man named Albert Bender, he signed up and became the group's "chief investigator," working alongside a handful of other aeronautical experts and other IFSB regulars, and writing for its magazine *Space Review*, which went out to several hundred members. The work, Barker later recalled, felt engaging, and exciting: "The eye-witness accounts piled up in our files. We analyzed them and assessed them and compared them, looking for corroborative details and sometimes succeeding, looking for contradictions, looking for hoaxes, looking for a key that would unlock the mystery."

Then, in the fall of 1953, Bender abruptly disbanded the International Flying Saucer Bureau and *Space Review*. "The mystery of the flying saucers is no longer a mystery," he declared to confused members. "The source is already known, but any information about this is being withheld by orders from a higher source." But to Barker, he disclosed the real story: three dark-suited men had visited him, apparently on behalf of the US government, and told him the full truth about the saucers. They had also threatened to send him to prison if he told anyone else.

Barker became consumed by the shocking tale, and in 1956, fueled by the obsession, wrote and published an explosive book titled *They Knew Too Much About Flying Saucers*. In it, he alleged a wide-ranging cover-up by the "Silence Group," a group of government agents working in concert with alien civilizations to suppress the truth about their existence. These "Men in Black," as he dubbed them, repeatedly targeted UFO witnesses, believers, and investigators to shut down their curiosity, not just in the United States but overseas as well—even in countries like Australia, Barker argued, there were accounts of shadowy and intimidating figures appearing just as a witness or researcher was getting too close to the full truth. He also recounted his own experience being visited by an FBI agent in West Virginia in the fall of 1953 (just around the time Bender had had his meeting), which had left him wondering why the government would dispatch an even more clandestine group to silence them when they had already made their efforts so public. Perhaps the men weren't just government agents, but officials from a religious order of some kind—in fact, the men in black, Barker realized, could be representing almost any powerful entity on the planet. (That would explain the black garb, he speculated.) After all, what would change religion on Earth more than the knowledge that there were other inhabited planets and other beings?

In the years ahead, the legend of the "Men in Black" transformed into something more ominous, as it became a favored theory among UFO followers. Occult journalist John Keel, who would become famous as the author of *The Mothman Prophecies*—the story of a huge, winged creature in West Virginia that was turned into a 2002 movie with Richard Gere and Laura Linney—spread extreme interpretations of the theory, positing in the late 1960s and '70s that the "MIB" weren't merely shadowy US government agents, but actually a dark, sinister, and timeless force from the underworld, "not real people but some kind of phantasms," whose existence and presence helped explained not just UFOs, but vampire lore, ghosts, and all manner of other paranormal reports stretching throughout human history.

Barker would remain a prominent ufologist well into the 1970s, including as publisher of the *Saucerian Bulletin,* one of the nation's other most prominent UFO magazines—though how much he ever believed his own writing was an open question, particularly once he struck up a friendship with Moseley. While both were known separately for editing "serious" ufology magazines, together they were responsible for some of the field's most notorious forgeries and pranks, including a soon-to-be infamous hoax in 1957, in which they mailed letters on State Department letterhead to various targets to cause dissension and uproar in the community of enthusiasts. One such note was sent to George Adamski, assuring the contactee that the government had full knowledge of and believed the stories of his meetings with the Nordic Space Brothers.[*]

---

[*] In 1959, Barker actually published Howard Menger's contactee book, and in 1962, would publish Bender's account of his encounter with the men in black, *Flying Saucers and the Three Men,* which told an incredible tale of how Bender had actually been kidnapped by aliens and taken to the South Pole, which didn't exactly square with the story that Barker had told in his own book.

Adamski had trumpeted the letter as vindication and a sign that the government would eventually come clean before realizing it had all been part of a scheme.*

"Those drawn to saucers, believers and skeptics alike, always have been a remarkable bunch of characters. Many are highly credulous, easy targets for practical jokes and highly susceptible to kooky theories and tales of conspiracy, cover-up, and assorted weirdness. For better or worse, both Gray Barker and I quite happily took advantage of this," Moseley wrote in his memoir, *Shockingly Close to the Truth!*, which was colorfully subtitled *Confessions of a Grave-Robbing Ufologist*, an allusion to his seasonal work literally looting the graves of South American ancient civilizations and selling the antiquities on the black market.

To mitigate and combat this growing stream of hoaxes and paranoia, a number of additional groups tried to position themselves alongside APRO and CSI, in part to distinguish their "serious" approach from the grifters they saw populating lectures and conventions. The first was the National Investigations Committee on Aerial Phenomena (NICAP), which began in 1956 as a monthly DC meetup, led by a sixty-seven-year-old widow, Clara John, a friend of contactee George Adamski. The Flying Saucer Discussion Group, as it was initially called, consisted of a treasurer (a retired chiropractor), a corporate secretary (a George Washington University law professor), a PR man, and an office assistant, a fifty-four-year-old Maryland grandmother of five who edited the *Maryland Saucer Magazine*, but soon grew into a cohort of "approximately 75 scientists, educators, and church leaders," and a nine-member board of governors including multiple former military generals and admirals, as well as Keyhoe, an Indiana broadcaster named Frank Edwards, a Pittsburgh minister, an Ohio physics professor, and the wealthy Boston hotelier Abraham Sonnabend. In October 1956, the group opened an office at 1536 Connecticut Avenue NW in Washington, DC, just north of Dupont Circle—"The time

---

* APRO's Coral Lorenzen, for her part, hated Barker, telling colleagues that "he wore too much lipstick," a knowing nod to his then-scandalous homosexuality. Moseley, in turn, thought Lorenzen "opinionated, prejudiced, and just not a very nice person—but she was a hoot to drink with, and once matched me martini for martini."

has come," John noted during one meeting, "to coordinate [our] activities into a pattern that will prepare humanity for this startling new event in human existence. Where better than in Washington for this movement to take shape and direction?"—complete with a brass plaque outside, and from the start, displayed an apparent eagerness to cause confusion about whether their activities were government sanctioned: staff answered the phone, "National Investigations Committee," and its director was not an overzealous UFO believer, but a former navy researcher and inventor named Thomas Townsend Brown, who had spent much of his life trying to develop antigravity devices.* Once at the helm, Brown gave himself the exalted title of "executive vice chairman *pro tempere*," and told reporters, "I wince whenever anybody refers to 'flying saucers,' but actually that's what we're after. We want to know whether they exist. If they do, we want to know what they are. And we think it's high time." Its primary investigation, Brown announced, would be known as Project Skylight.

It would be his first and only act in the role. Brown lasted only about ninety days as NICAP's leader, before the board ousted him amid concerns of financial mismanagement and a suspicion that he was taking membership fees and channeling them into his own antigravity research. He was replaced by the board chair, retired rear admiral Delmer S. Fahrney, who had once headed the navy's guided-missile program and now began his tenure at NICAP with a high-profile news conference, during which he announced—with no new supporting evidence—that UFOs were both real and guided by "an intelligence" unknown to man. "There are objects coming into our atmosphere at very high speeds," he told a room full of reporters on January 16, 1957. "No agency in this country or Russia is able to duplicate at this time the speeds and accelerations which radars and observers indicate these flying objects are able to achieve." The objects, he continued, were "not entirely actuated by automatic equipment" and "the way they change[d] position in formations

---

* Brown's probably best remembered today as a star player in the so-called Philadelphia Experiment, the legend that in the middle of World War II the US Navy turned the destroyer USS *Eldridge* invisible and teleported it from Philadelphia to Norfolk, Virginia. The fantastical experiment has been widely seen as a hoax, and no evidence has surfaced in seventy-five years to support it.

and [overrode] each other would indicate that their motion is directed," relying on "a tremendous amount of technology of which we have no knowledge." He concluded with a call for the country to be vigilant and look out for intelligent beings piloting flying saucers, before announcing that retired general Albert Wedemeyer would serve as NICAP's "evaluations advisor."

The press conference received widespread national attention, mainly due to Fahrney's respected military career and the fact that he was the highest-ranking former government official yet to speak publicly and positively about flying saucers. Despite the lack of fresh evidence or testimony, some saw the event as a formal declaration of position within the UFO conversation, and publicized it as such. "Flying Saucers Now Respectable," exclaimed an editorial in the *Victoria* (Texas) *Advocate*. "The near future may hold the biggest story since Christ," it continued, as UFOs had been "rescued from fantasy and formally installed as possible reality after assaulting the public consciousness for a whole decade without official recognition. . . . It seems improbable that something completely fantastic, visionary, and lacking in substance could command the interest and support of men like Wedemeyer and Fahrney." An editorial in Vermont's *Bennington Banner* similarly concluded, "Don't laugh. These gentlemen aren't kidding."

The attention—and inferences—evidently surprised Fahrney. Soon after the press conference, he resigned from the organization in a slight panic, leaving other NICAP leaders and members to explain and emphasize that their former director hadn't precisely said that the UFOs were extraterrestrial in origin—just that they were under intelligent control from an unknown source.* Soon after, Donald Keyhoe stepped into the director role. Under his tenure, NICAP started welcoming new associate members with a letter asking for a $7.50 membership fee, in exchange for "a monthly newsletter containing recent UFO (or flying saucer) sightings, reports on secret developments, exciting articles by scientists, pilots,

---

* It's not clear when Fahrney's resignation, which he attributed to his wife's ill health, took place; an April announcement said that it had been effective on January 23, just days after the press conference, but in February he was still giving interviews to his local newspaper seemingly cheerfully associated with NICAP.

and UFO researchers, a new serialized history of flying saucers, and many other features."

"Most important of all," Keyhoe's welcome letter proclaimed, "you will be playing a vital role—not only in aiding to end the censorship—but in helping to find all the answers to the UFO mystery." NICAP leadership praised those efforts, but also made clear that it hoped that the organization could grow by moving even further into the mainstream—and so, Keyhoe set out on speaking engagements and a relationship-building tour, encouraging the founding of new UFO society chapters around the country that would coalesce under NICAP's umbrella. "Our UFO-reporting network grew rapidly," Keyhoe recalled. Hundreds of interested citizens—both NICAP members and not—wrote and called to offer help investigating local sightings.

To manage the new influx of information, NICAP developed a two-page questionnaire for sighting reports, comprised of both the typical questions asked by the air force and other military and intelligence agencies, and its own supplementary queries that ran through a number of details, including a sighting's position in the sky, its movement, and the witness's professional background and military or aviation training. A syndicated feature story that ran in more than sixty newspapers over the summer of 1957 said the group was offering "secret" memberships and reporting tools so people could subscribe to the magazine or report a sighting "without being tagged as the neighborhood nut."

In 1957, the first issue of the *UFO Investigator*, NICAP's new magazine newsletter, was finally released, with thirty-two black-and-white mimeographed pages assembled by Keyhoe that contained sightings, NICAP personnel announcements, reporting forms, and page after page of what Keyhoe presented as evidence that governments the world over were hiding the truth about flying saucers. The most significant portion of the booklet, though, was dedicated to the summer's biggest UFO news: Captain Edward Ruppelt had published a tell-all about his work inside Project Grudge and Blue Book. *The Report on Unidentified Flying Objects* chronicled his time navigating the air force bureaucracy and Washington corridors of power, and was the first publication on the subject from a government insider. While the narrative stopped short of endorsing the idea of flying saucers as interplanetary, Ruppelt did expose genuine secrets and presented real evidence that the air force had taken flying saucers far more seriously than it had previously let on, including General Twining's 1948 letter establishing air force saucer reporting, the supposedly squashed "Estimate of the Situation" prepared by Project Sign that held the flying saucers to be extraterrestrial in nature, and the Robertson Panel's work.

At first glance, the book was the exposé the UFO community had been waiting for, but upon closer examination, it fell far short in presenting a smoking gun that the government was covering up interplanetary visits or out-of-this-world technology. In some cases, Ruppelt even undermined his own argument, explaining in one instance that in all its "unknown" cases, Blue Book had "never found measurement of size, speed, or altitude that could be considered to be even fairly accurate," a remarkable statement that underscored the sheer uncertainty and vagueness of many of the seemingly most incredible reports.

That detail didn't stop Keyhoe and others, though, from using it in pursuit of their own goals. As part of its reviewing and reporting on Ruppelt's book, NICAP outlined an "eight-point plan of cooperation to end the controversy over flying saucers" in their newsletter, which was eventually delivered to the air force. Most of the plan consisted of NICAP reviewing the military branch's work thus far on flying saucers, including the 1948 "Estimate of the Situation" and the Robertson Panel's final report, which was still classified; in exchange, the group would "help educate and prepare the public for whatever conclusions and developments may later be officially disclosed."*

The Report on Unidentified Flying Objects would fuel conspiracies for years to come, especially once the air force vigorously denied many of

---

* To say that the air force was less than welcoming of NICAP's offers of assistance and oversight would be an understatement; as Ruppelt wrote, "This went over like a worm in a punch bowl." In fact, one of the air force spokesmen who had worked on Blue Book, Lawrence Tacker, published his own book in 1960 filled with government press releases, key documents, and official correspondence related to the flying saucer search to help debunk the sightings. "Certainly the experience gained over the past 13 years points up to the fact that flying saucers are not space craft from other worlds, but, rather, represent convention objects or aerial phenomenon seen under confusing conditions," he wrote.

Ruppelt's (truthful) revelations, deploying technicalities and carefully worded statements that went over the heads of ordinary readers and refusing to release the documents Ruppelt cited, and again in 1960, when the captain published a new version of his book with three additional chapters that more definitely downplayed the extraterrestrial possibility of UFOs, calling them a "space age myth." Keyhoe blasted him as a turncoat and a heretic and, soon after the new edition came out, Ruppelt died of a heart attack at just thirty-seven, ending his ability to defend or explain his work.

As time went on, the divide and suspicion between the government, military, and civilian researchers continued to grow. After years of confusing and perhaps under-resourced but largely good-faith efforts to determine what, if anything, the flying saucers represented, the air force and government hadn't found anything noteworthy, leading to the conclusion that they were mostly a figment of the public imagination—and that giving any energy or attention to the subject only fueled a vicious cycle that encouraged more reports and further clogged up valuable intelligence channels and resources. These shifty, hesitant statements and dismissive comments were precisely what made civilian researchers and even military insiders like Keyhoe feel that something nefarious was afoot. There were some genuine (but routine) intelligence processes and procedures hidden among the military's classified files, but largely NICAP was demanding access to an empty vault, and the chicken-and-egg debate continued.

Even so, the quest for "truth" continued, helped along by an intriguing piece of news, buried by the Ruppelt revelations in that first NICAP newsletter: Admiral Roscoe Hillenkoetter, one of Keyhoe's Naval Academy classmates, had freshly retired from the service that spring and was set to join NICAP's board of directors. It was a high-profile addition, to be sure, but Hillenkoetter's membership in the UFO truth-seeking group was notable less for his academic and military pedigree and more for his most recent job title: from 1947 to 1950, Roscoe Hillenkoetter had been the director of the CIA. Soon, a question emerged that would haunt ufology for years to come, and remains a mystery to this day: Was Hillenkoetter on the board to support a friend or because he knew the truth? What did he know about UFOs that the rest of America didn't?

15

Sputnik

A s revelations about NICAP's new leadership spread and spurred questions about UFOs throughout the fall of 1957, Americans, for perhaps the first time in a decade, found themselves preoccupied with an entirely different kind of troubling spacecraft. For about a decade, the US and the Soviet Union had been racing to build and launch a rocket capable of delivering a satellite to orbit, and after early failed starts and much push and pull, the US Navy's Vanguard rocket program could comfortably state that it was in the lead. The effort had been staffed by leading minds in the military, technology, and scientific communities, including one in particular that would have been familiar to anyone in the UFO community: J. Allen Hynek, the astronomer from Projects Sign, Grudge, and Blue Book, had been given a leave of absence from his teaching role at Ohio State to lead the segment of the project that would create the new Optical Tracking Program, a satellite tracking initiative that was part of the larger international effort known as the International Geophysical Year.* The IGY, modeled on two previous "International Polar Years" in 1882 and 1932 that had focused on Arctic and Antarctic explorations, was "perhaps the most ambitious and at the same time most successful co-operative enterprise ever undertaken by man," according to its creator, Lloyd Berkner, bringing together sixty thousand scientists and facilities in sixty-seven countries to study Earth, the atmosphere, and the sun.

The hope was that the collaboration would underscore the power of international cooperation and use the avenue of science to advance peace and geopolitical harmony. Hynek's $3.3 million slice of the effort was

---

* The project made Hynek colleagues for the first time with Donald Menzel, the UFO debunker-in-chief, who was the assistant director of the Smithsonian observatory through Harvard.

directed toward identifying tracking sites around the world, as well as fielding a truck-sized $100,000 camera capable of photographing orbiting satellites—a project made even harder when the navy announced that their Vanguard model would be only twenty inches in diameter rather than the planned thirty. ("The manufacture of the camera was one of the proudest achievements of American industry," the Smithsonian later bragged.)

Beyond establishing sites where the new high-tech cameras would be installed, Hynek needed a global network of humans who could tell the cameras where to look for them.* The resulting effort, known as Operation Moonwatch, relied on eighty thousand volunteers around the world who could use their amateur telescopes at sunset and sunrise—when satellite visibility would be best—to note and track the position of an orbiting object and then report those sightings to Hynek's team at the central clearinghouse, the Smithsonian Astrophysical Observatory in Cambridge, Massachusetts. This was hardly just casual backyard astronomy. It required large teams of observers at each location, working in coordinated, fixed viewing locations in order to build what was called a picket fence in the sky; the Moonwatch post in Terre Haute, Indiana, for instance, had a specially designed building, complete with red interior lighting to ease night vision, with sixteen observing locations.† Many Moonwatch recruits came from the Ground Observer Corps, the network of aerial watchposts established to announce incoming Soviet bombers, and it even stretched to the British research post in Antarctica and drifting ice station in the Arctic, known as Fletcher's Ice Island. In May 1957, Hynek and the Moonwatch team ran a national practice exercise, "the largest organized astronomical observation ever to be made in this country," with the air force and Civil Air Patrol, their planes flying

---

* Twelve of the so-called Baker-Nunn cameras, named after their pioneering inventors, would end up being located all around the globe, including in New Mexico, Florida, Hawaii, Spain, Japan, India, South Africa, Iran, Peru, Argentina, Australia, and in the Antilles.

† As W. Patrick McCray, who wrote the definitive book on the project, noted, there were hardly any minority volunteers in the effort: "Moonwatch in the United States primarily engaged the interest and participation of white, mostly middle-class people."

designated routes and trailing long ropes with rubber toilet plungers on the ends to mimic the size and speed of a potential satellite track.

It was perhaps the most expensive ongoing mission in recent memory—which is why it was a total shock when around 6:30 p.m. on the evening of October 4, 1957, the phone rang in Harvard's Kittredge Hall with the news that the Soviets had succeeded with launching a satellite.

Sputnik—Russian for "fellow traveler"—was in orbit.

Within hours, reporters descended on Hynek's office and the observatory, but the team had almost nothing to show, and nothing to track the new satellite with—the sole camera that existed was being overhauled in Pasadena at the manufacturer. All they could do was rush to rig up a way for reporters to hear Sputnik's beeps as it passed overhead, reducing Hynek's office to "a shambles of extension cords, cigarette butts, and used-up flashbulbs," as he later recalled. The night became more chaotic when Cambridge fire trucks roared up on scene in the narrow streets outside, responding to a neighbor's mistaken report that the building was on fire (it wasn't—the unexpected nighttime brightness of the camera flashes and movie lights had just given the impression it might be). It was a shocking moment for the nation, but one where scientists like Hynek couldn't help but to recognize also the significance it held: "I remember staying until 4 a.m. to listen in fascination to the weird chirp of the Soviet satellite as it passed overhead every 96 minutes." A member of Hynek's team remembered "the sound that captivated the world and shocked the United States into an educational and scientific revolution."

• •

Revolution, indeed. In the coming weeks and the wake of what Hynek called an "intellectual Pearl Harbor," the observatory ran twenty-four hours a day and Hynek hosted twice-daily press conferences alongside director Fred Whipple to keep the public abreast of ongoing efforts to lock a signal onto Sputnik. "We had a world-wide nerve center focused in one room on the second floor at Kittredge," Hynek recalled, and even though people could tune in to hear the beeps, it would be four days before the satellite was spotted in the sky for the first time by a Moonwatch team over Woomera and Sydney, Australia. Two days later, another group in New Haven, Connecticut, made the first North American sighting as it passed over the Atlantic coast.

Two weeks after the launch, Hynek and Whipple were on the cover of *Life* magazine, plotting Sputnik's orbit around a giant globe; beyond examining the geopolitics of the launch, the issue featured photos of the "space fashion" and "space toys" inspired by the news. Weeks after that, the Soviet Union made headlines again with the launch of a second satellite, and the sending of the first living thing in orbit, a dog named Laika. The successive achievements represented a worrisome milestone, one that called into question not just America's immediate defensive capabilities but even more so its commitment to and investment in science and technology. The nation that invented the atomic and thermonuclear bombs had suddenly, embarrassingly, and *publicly* fallen behind. The article in *Life* that featured Hynek opened its report with a definitive, disappointed statement that summed up how most Americans felt about the situation: "The U.S. should have been and could have been the first nation to launch a satellite."

"This is really and truly 'the shot heard round the world,'" rocket scientist G. Harry Stine told reporters in a separate statement. "I wonder what the dead veterans of Lexington and of Korea are thinking." (The somewhat extreme comment led to his immediate dismissal from a job designing ICBMs, but that didn't stop him from continuing to speak openly about his feelings on the subject: "We lost five years because no one would heed rocket men. We're a smug, arrogant people who just sat dumb, fat, and happy, underestimating Russia.")

Amid the public outrage, Hynek and his team retreated into their work with little time to pursue his normal UFO interest. Still, a steady stream of UFO sightings came, including one that would become one of the most significant flaps of the period. Just hours after the Soviet Union had launched Sputnik 2 and Laika, two farmworkers near the Texas prairie town of Levelland had called the local police to report that a fast-moving blue streak of light had started coming toward them from a nearby field, seemingly killing their truck's electrical system and engine as it got closer. As the light approached, one of the farmworkers dove out of the vehicle—"The thing passed directly over my truck with a great sound and rush of wind," he recalled. "It sounded like thunder and my truck rocked from the flash. I felt a lot of heat"—where he watched it disappear to the east, toward town.

Before the responding officer, A. J. Fowler, had time to fully process the story, others started pouring in from across the region. A college student reported that his car had died while he was driving, and when he got out to check the engine, he had seen a hundred-foot-long "egg-shaped object" in the road ahead; it wasn't until the UFO rose up into the sky that he was able to restart the vehicle. The local sheriff, who had gone out to investigate, had also spotted an object "like a brilliant red sunset" pass over the road ahead of him, as had the local fire marshal—the object seemed to affect his vehicle's electrical system, too. Later, a couple reported their car dying as they watched a bright streak of light across the sky during the same time frame. All told, more than a dozen local residents encountered something strange that night, and similar sightings continued over the following day farther west, near White Sands in New Mexico; one reporter dubbed the object "Whatnik."

Based on the witnesses' seemingly genuine fright, the distance involved, and apparent independent corroboration across town, it was clear that something unusual was in the area's skies for more than two hours that night. But what?

Two weeks later, the air force issued a terse sixty-word statement "solving" the sightings, attributing the Texas event to ball lightning and St. Elmo's Fire (the vehicle problems, it suggested, were perhaps overblown, some routine wet electrical circuits or flooded engines). Locals doubted the explanation, and Hynek, distracted by the Sputnik tracking, would later lament not investigating it further. The breadth of sightings and the engine interference, he said, were "out of the statistical universe."

• •

In the month after Sputnik's launch, the air force reported 361 sightings, almost equal to the 406 it had received between January and September that year, and the highest one-month total since July 1952 and the month of the "Washington Merry-Go-Round." Another kind of space race, it seemed, was coming to a head.

After a near-decade, tensions between the transparency-focused NICAP and the secrecy-focused air force threatened to bubble over when Keyhoe was scheduled to appear on *Armstrong Circle Theatre*, a long-running popular series on CBS that tackled contemporary events. The January 1958 episode, titled "UFOs: Enigma of the Skies," was set to feature a variety of guests, including Keyhoe, Ruppelt, UFO witnesses Kenneth Arnold and Captain Chiles, and debunker-in-chief, Harvard astronomer Donald Menzel, each discussing their perspective, along with representatives from the air force. Arrangements had begun calmly enough, but in the run-up to the show, things had started to unravel. First, Keyhoe started a brawl with the producers, who insisted on a scripted conversation and, in Keyhoe's view, were likely planning to edit out his documented evidence of a cover-up. (Adding insult to injury was the realization that Menzel and the air force were set to have twenty-five minutes of airtime, while Keyhoe would be relegated to just seven.) Then the air force made a statement in advance of filming that it would deny on-air the existence of the documents that Ruppelt had made public, prompting the former Blue Book head to drop out of the broadcast just before the on-air date. Chiles followed, as did Arnold, who argued that the episode was rigged in the air force's favor. Suddenly, Keyhoe was on his own against Menzel and an entire branch of the US military.

On January 22, 1958, the 10 p.m. broadcast started as planned, with Keyhoe set to follow an air force lieutenant colonel who spent his segment pooh-poohing the whole phenomenon and reassuring the American people that there was nothing to worry about. For a few minutes, the author and UFO advocate stuck with his prepared, agreed-upon statement. And then he started to ad-lib: "And now I'm going to reveal something that has never been disclosed before," he began. "For the last six months, we have been working with a congressional committee investigating official secrecy about UFOs. . . . If all the evidence we have given this committee is made public in open hearings, it would be proved—"

For the audience at home, the program went silent, though Keyhoe remained on-screen, his mouth still moving. CBS had muted him. Unaware of the technical difficulty, Keyhoe confidently finished his sentence on set: "—that it will absolutely prove that the UFOs are real machines under intelligence control."

The apparent act of public censorship sparked national headlines and a deluge of angry letters to CBS. To the conspiracy-minded, the act confirmed their worst fears. "What makes me boil is that the powers that be consider the American public too stupid and childish to take this thing in stride," one letter writer said. "Just what were your last words that we weren't allowed to hear?" In response, the network calmly admitted that it had, indeed, muted Keyhoe's reckless words, but for a legitimate and important reason. "This program had been carefully cleared for security reasons," its director of editing, Herbert Carlborg, explained to one writer. "It was the responsibility of the network to insure performance in accordance with predetermined security standards."

In the end, it didn't matter. What a later generation would call the Streisand effect had already taken hold: censoring Keyhoe spread his message far more widely than it would have happened had CBS just let him finish his sentence, and the incident hadn't initially seemed to disturb him much. In the hours after the broadcast, he had chalked up the muting to a misunderstanding, only finding his anger a few days later when he learned for the first time from a congressional source that the CIA had created and hosted the Robertson Panel years earlier. Convinced anew that the cover-up was real, he pried loose the first sanitized version of the panel's report in April 1958 and published it in the NICAP newsletter and continued to fume at the cover-up all around him for the remainder of the spring, blasting the air force whitewash, and saying he and CBS were victims of what he called "censorship by intimidation" during an interview appearance with a young, cheery, smoking Mike Wallace.*

Any headlines about the issue, however, were swiftly scrubbed from the public discourse when the US finally succeeded in launching a satellite a week after Keyhoe's TV appearance. Until that point, the US effort to follow Sputnik had been deemed a farce, and the navy program an ongoing embarrassment. A first launch attempt on December 6, 1957, of the Vanguard rocket had failed, as the craft lifted just four feet off the launchpad before sinking back and exploding live on television sets

---

* Between puffs, the host's intro line on the show was "My name is Mike Wallace and the cigarette is Parliament!"

across the country—its damaged satellite, TV-3, landed on the ground and started beeping away, its regular rhythm seeming to mock the entire US space program. The press had called the mission "Flopnik" and "Kaputnik."* Determined to change course, the program rushed a modified army Jupiter rocket into use, a decision that paid off when Explorer 1 lifted off and reached orbit on January 31, 1958. As the ship moved into space, James Van Allen, Hynek's former rocket colleague at the White Sands Proving Ground, held a triumphant press conference in Washington with a full-scale model of the craft and the father of America's rocketry program. The former Nazi scientist Wernher von Braun, who assisted in the endeavor, stood beside him.

Two days later, Hynek's Operation Moonwatch team picked up Explorer's signal over the skies of Texas and New Mexico. Cameras were now finally in operation and could track and calculate its orbit; others in South Africa, Japan, and New Mexico all successfully photographed the satellite.† The cameras they used, the so-called Baker-Nunn cameras, had been developed by Hynek for the satellite tracking project, and became the basis for a whole new field of astronomy; Hynek and Whipple had hooked one of the cameras, in Las Cruces, New Mexico, up to a television camera, founding a field called "image-orthicon astronomy," an effort that revolutionized the detection of supernovas and faint galaxies and that Hynek would later regard as perhaps his greatest contribution to the field.

It was a victorious moment for Hynek's program, but one that would, ironically, lead to its diminishment. With the creation of the National Aeronautics and Space Administration (NASA) later that spring, satellite tracking efforts at the Smithsonian observatory wound down, and Hynek felt that priorities were shifting, both for the government and

---

* The satellite, its antennas still bent, is on display today at the Smithsonian's National Air & Space Museum.

† Finding and photographing the US's much smaller satellites was no easy feat; after Explorer 1 came a successful launch of a grapefruit-sized Vanguard 1, and Explorer 2. As one Moonwatcher said, "Hells bells, why couldn't they put a larger one up there?"

for himself.* "I came here to work with you on STP on January 1, 1956, when satellites were just a gleam in the scientific eye," he wrote to observatory director Fred Whipple in his resignation letter. "Now they are commonplace and we are tracking them with success. Time clearly for me to turn to more challenging things." The astronomer, now a father of five, returned to academia, taking the chairmanship of Northwestern's astronomy department, a job that would give him more freedom to pursue his own research, including his ongoing fascination with UFOs and to advocate for what he called the "invisible college" of scientific peers who believed the phenomenon deserved more serious attention.

• •

Unlike the now-orbiting Explorer 1, the Avro flying saucer was proving to be nearly impossible to get going. In 1958, the Canadian company and designer Jack Frost had presented the latest design to the US military, and received another $2 million for development, but as the army and the air force teamed up to imagine both a fighter aircraft version and a more traditional battlefield version that could replace helicopters, the incoming resulting tests had been troubling.

Despite promising wind tunnel tests of a scale model at MIT's Naval Supersonic Laboratory,† a one-twelfth-scale model of AVRO was just barely making it off the ground. The first army version of the craft—known as the VZ-9 Avrocar—was manufactured in May 1959, but the three-wheeled, three-ton craft, which carried a crew of two and was eighteen feet in diameter, was equally unreliable. Its first tethered flight was a failure, as the craft experienced "an uncontrollable oscillation," and each of its wheels alternately bounced on the ground. Design changes appeared to improve the situation, but that November, as test pilot Wladyslaw "Spud" Potocki took it into the air for the first time untethered

---

* Moonwatch itself would continue for almost two decades, closing only in 1975, after some four hundred thousand volunteer observations of the ever-widening number of satellites.

† "The aircraft can be satisfactorily controlled and manoeuvred [sic] from engine idling to maximum thrust at supersonic speed through a satisfactory supersonic flight envelope," the 112-page development report concluded.

and snow and ice driven by the powerful engines whipped across the field, it quickly became clear that the craft still couldn't lift much more than about four feet off the ground before losing control and whipsawing up, down, and around—a dynamic engineers came to call "hubcapping," after the way car hubcaps spun on their rim when dropped.

Eventually, stability improved, making slow forward travel possible—its top speed was about thirty-five miles an hour—but the height was still an issue, and further test flights showed it wouldn't be particularly useful on the battlefield or even pleasant to fly. ("The cockpit was cramped, noisy and became excessively hot during a 15-minute flight," a program history noted.) Ultimately, the whole project was canceled in 1961 when funding ran out; the dream of a high-performance military flying saucer had never amounted to anything more than a battlefield hovercraft capable of moving at the speed of a jeep.*

If anyone could make a flying saucer fly, it probably wasn't going to be the US government. The question was, who could?

---

* While *Popular Mechanics* published a photo of the Avro craft in 1960, the full history of the program wouldn't be known to the American public until its files were declassified and released in 2012.

Briefing Capitol Hill

In the wake of the Sputnik launch and the dawn of the intense new space race, there seemed plenty of reason for morale to be high at NICAP: the country cared, deeply, about outer space all of a sudden, and newsletter headlines proclaimed that big revelations about UFOs were just around the corner; thanks to increasing pressure on the government for more investigations, UFO surveillance programs were ever-expanding; and sightings were as prevalent and routine as sunrises.

Behind the scenes, however, it was a different situation entirely. The group was surviving year to year largely due to the energy and personal financial contributions of Keyhoe himself; bills were often overdue (at one point in the early 1960s, records showed it had about 5,500 recipients of its newsletter, though nearly 2,000 of those were overdue in their membership fees), membership fees were cut to $5 to encourage more sign-ups, and its newsletter shrank to just eight pages.

Though ideological battles with the contactees continued, Keyhoe remained convinced that the truth wasn't to be found in investigating random sightings so much as it was prying loose what the government already knew. Their focus, he reminded his team, had to be on Washington and influencing the powerful to take saucers seriously. One of NICAP's long-prioritized goals had been to focus congressional attention, specifically high-profile hearings, on the air force's treatment of flying saucers, which the military branch had long resisted, understanding that a public airing and the resulting media coverage would almost certainly lead to further spikes in UFO sightings.* And in 1957, it got its wish. As part

---

* Interestingly, in an incident that wouldn't be declassified until 1985, the chair of the Senate Armed Services Committee, Georgia's Richard Russell, had reported a UFO during a tour of the Soviet Union in 1955. Arriving by train from Ukraine to Prague, he'd raced to the US embassy to meet with the air force attaché there and explain

of the national panic over space, the House of Representatives finally set up what it called the Select Committee on Astronautics and Space Exploration,* which in turn included the Subcommittee on Atmospheric Phenomena—more commonly referred to as the "UFO subcommittee, made up of Reps. William Natcher and Les Arends." In August 1958, the committee chair, Massachusetts representative John McCormack, announced that there would be a week of sessions on UFOs, calling on various air force officials, including its chief science adviser and the current head of Blue Book, to testify. There were also plans to include Menzel, Keyhoe, and Ruppelt, but as the committee convened, things again took a turn: McCormack announced that the closed-door sessions weren't formal hearings and that no stenographer would be present to record the events. As Congress's own history of the event summarized, "By the end of the [first] day Congressman McCormack announced that he was satisfied with the Air Force's handling of the subject and no formal hearings would be necessary," and it added in a comment that surely a frustrated Keyhoe agreed with, "The Air Force had once again averted publicity."

As time went on, Keyhoe found himself increasingly in opposition with the government and officials in the halls of the Capitol. While the FBI and J. Edgar Hoover had always maintained a relatively cordial—albeit unhelpful—relationship with the former military officer and NICAP, it was far from welcoming of the group, and had seemingly taken

---

that his traveling party had seen "something that you may not believe, but something that we've been told by your people [the military] doesn't exist." As the train passed through the Transcaucasia, Russell had seen a disk-shaped object appear a mile or two south of their train. "One disc ascended almost vertically, at a relatively slow speed, with its outer surface revolving slowly to the right, to an altitude of about 6,000 feet, where its speed then increased sharply as it headed north," the military's Prague report stated. "The second flying disc was seen performing the same actions about one minute later." Hurriedly, train personnel closed the curtains. The CIA and air force both took seriously the possible sighting, wondering whether Russell had glimpsed secret Soviet technology, but eventually decided that Russell and his colleague had just misidentified normal fighter jets in a steep climb.

* This committee would, in the years ahead, evolve to be the Science and Astronautics Committee and, eventually, the modern-day Science, Space, and Technology Committee.

steps to distance itself in recent months; when the head of the New Orleans Field Office wrote to Hoover about a staffer's interest in NICAP, the director wrote back tersely that Keyhoe had "openly attempted to capitalize upon [the] names and military titles" of some of its former military members, and "NICAP is not the type of organization with which the Bureau's name should become connected."*

The Pentagon was more direct with its disdain. In 1960, the secretary of the air force's office wrote Hoover, asking whether the FBI and government could prosecute NICAP using a new law that aimed to prevent private citizens and organizations from creating the "false impression" that they were aligned with the federal government. "As you well know, the National Investigation Committee on Aerial Phenomenon has done this for many years," Lieutenant Colonel Lawrence Tacker explained in the missive, "and has been a thorn in the side of many governmental agencies during this period including the FBI, the Air Force, Department of Defense, various Congressional Committees and individual Congressmen and Senators." In response, the bureau demurred, saying the law didn't apply to NICAP, but the letter succeeded in capturing the growing frustration military and service leaders felt about the UFO situation—and before long their ire turned even to the government's own sanctioned efforts to find answers.

As the 1960 presidential campaign neared and the nation debated fears of a "missile gap" with the Soviet Union, a restricted ATIC analysis of Project Blue Book deemed it "an unproductive burden upon the Air Force," one that had "resulted in unfavorable publicity." The program had sorted through 6,152 cases since its inception, critics argued, and found precisely zero credible evidence "that these objects constitute a threat to national security or are space vehicles controlled by men or alien beings

---

* In a statement of the times, a large percentage of the FBI's total files on NICAP represent letters from "concerned citizens," writing to Hoover to inquire whether NICAP was a subversive or Communist-backed organization. Hoover always demurred, saying—not entirely truthfully—that the bureau hadn't investigated it and instead pointing the writers to various anti-Communism pamphlets and to Hoover's own books on Communism, which, like all of his works, were ghostwritten by FBI agents at taxpayer expense, even as he profited from the sales personally.

from another world"—so why did it still exist? "Complete elimination is desirable," the report concluded, "but it should certainly be disassociated with the intelligence community where it is extremely dangerous to prestige." Attempts in the months ahead to transfer the program to the air force's research command or to its public information office were both rejected; no one wanted the hot potato. Blue Book stayed at ATIC.

Door after door, meanwhile, had appeared to close to Keyhoe—and limited resources meant he couldn't even lobby as effectively as he hoped. In 1960, he tried to fund sending a ten-page paper, "NICAP's Confidential Digest of Documented UFO Evidence," to every member of Congress, along with another five hundred copies to prominent media figures, reporters, and commentators, but could only raise the money to send thirty-one.

In a final attempt to keep the UFO question alive, a handful of congressional committees pushed for better official briefings in July, but were met with hesitation from McCormack, who was now the House Majority Leader. He was dubious that there was anything more to be pried from the military; even in his role overseeing the space committee, he'd felt he couldn't get adequate information on UFOs in closed, confidential sessions—how would more hearings be any different? "I feel that the [Air Force] has not given out all the information it has on Unidentified Flying Objects," he told one reporter, despite the fact that "it was pretty well established by some, in our minds, that there were some objects flying around in space that were unexplainable." Finally, the House agreed to form a new three-member UFO subcommittee, under the Science and Aeronautics Committee, headed by Representative Joseph Karth. Keyhoe was momentarily thrilled—"Majority Leader Support Indicates Early Congressional Action," NICAP's newsletter enthusiastically declared—but after an August 1961 air force briefing tour of ATIC to House committee staff, the energy for both public and closed hearings evaporated. Keyhoe responded with vocal disappointment, which Karth in turn criticized, saying the NICAP president wanted the hearings only for "grandstand[ing] acts of a rabble-rousing nature where accusations may be made THAT COULDN'T BE ANSWERED BY ANYONE— the Air Force or NICAP."

While attention on Capitol Hill would occasionally flare up and, in several instances in the early 1960s, it would push unsuccessfully the air force to take UFOs more seriously, the dream of a congressional hearing—a grand, high-profile moment that would squeeze the truth out of reluctant uniformed witnesses sitting under hot TV lights—would ultimately disappear for nearly a decade. Not long after, the long-simmering tensions between NICAP and APRO in the early 1960s followed a similar trajectory: Coral Lorenzen published an editorial dismissing NICAP as a less serious, lobbying-focused organization whose only talking point was a military cover-up; APRO, she reminded readers, was committed to research and a science-based agenda. As historian David Jacobs wrote, "The two organizations were never able to cooperate again."

Keyhoe's greatest effort had gone kaputnik once and for all.

PART 2

The Space Age
(1960–2000)

Fermi's Paradox

A s the military and intelligence communities did their best throughout the postwar era to distance themselves from the UFO conversation, another began to engage with it more directly. For centuries, scientists had sought to explain and understand various natural phenomena, but now a new generation set out for answers beyond what they could see, considering for the first time what multitudes the heavens may include. The quest existed within a rare intersection of science and spiritualism, and was inadvertently tinged with the militaristic ubiquity of the 1940s and '50s. After all, some of the most influential people and decision-makers during the period, building bombs and estimating their impact, were not generals, but physicists, engineers, and mathematicians—and, in fact, one of the most famous and consequential scientific conversations of our time had taken place at a laboratory dedicated to studying the most famous and consequential forms of weaponry of the modern age.

The discussion occurred sometime in the summer of 1950, as scientist Enrico Fermi and three other scientists, Emil Konopinski, Edward Teller, and Herbert York, were walking to lunch at the Los Alamos National Laboratory. The men were in New Mexico preparing for the latest set of the nation's nuclear tests in the South Pacific's Enewetak Atoll, a critical part of the march toward a full thermonuclear device—but that day, interest had shifted to an amusing cartoon that Konopinski had seen in a recent issue of the *New Yorker*. Referencing a spate of unexplained trash can thefts that had bedeviled New York City, the illustration by Alan Dunn showed a flying saucer landing on a faraway planet and a stream of aliens carrying off their souvenirs from Earth: wire trash cans with the New York logo on them. None of the men took seriously the idea of alien visitors—as physicists they knew the speeds necessary for interstellar travel were unachievable—but that didn't stop curious minds from playing out the puzzle before them.

Fermi turned to Teller. "Edward," he asked, "what do you think—how probable is it that within the next ten years we shall have clear evidence of a material object moving faster than light?"

Teller considered, then answered: "Ten to the sixth." *One in a million,* in scientist-speak.

"This is much too low," Fermi scoffed. "The probability is more like ten percent," odds that he usually referred to as a miracle. Neither Teller nor Konopinski could argue. The debate was settled—one in ten—and moved on.*

Later, at lunch in Fuller Lodge, the group was deep in a new conversation when, seemingly apropos of nothing, Fermi chimed in to ask: "Where is everybody?"

The group all laughed heartily. "In spite of Fermi's question coming from the clear blue, everybody around the table seemed to understand at once that he was talking about extraterrestrial life," Teller later recalled. Intrigued by the idea, the table discussed the subject for a moment or two longer, eventually agreeing that "the distances to the next location of living beings may be very great and that, indeed, as far as our galaxy is concerned, we are living somewhere in the sticks, far removed from the metropolitan area of the galactic center."

The intellectual challenge—if life was so prevalent in the universe beyond, why didn't we see more of it?—came to be known as the Fermi Paradox, and gave way to more questions that would define the new scientific era of the UFO age: Was interstellar travel too difficult, too far, or too advanced? Was visiting Earth or our solar system not worth the effort? Or, perhaps most haunting of all, was life on Earth in fact alone?

• •

While historically astronomy and naval power had long been linked, the two entities had come together during World War II as never before,

---

* Many accounts of this now-famous conversation place it as happening during the Manhattan Project in World War II, but astronomer Eric Jones firmly established it happening around 1950, when the *New Yorker* published the cartoon in question.

including through the work at Los Alamos, but few case studies were more emblematic of that cooperation than the rise of radio astronomy, a field very different than the night-oriented optical work long done by astronomers for centuries.

The discipline had only emerged in earnest in 1933, after Karl Jansky, a Bell Labs scientist, first detected radiation coming from the Milky Way. Jansky, who was twenty-five years old at the time, had been studying atmospheric interference in the signals of radio-telephone calls, rigging up a one-hundred-foot-long antenna atop a turntable made of old Ford Model-T wheels in a New Jersey potato field in order to pinpoint the static's location. After a year, he'd successfully identified static from lightning storms, but remained puzzled by another mysterious form of output that repeated every twenty-three hours and fifty-six minutes. It was weak, and difficult to trace—Jansky couldn't tell if it was coming from nearby power lines, equipment, or even the sun, until an astrophysicist friend pointed out that the time signal interval was equivalent to the length of time it took an object overhead in the heavens to rotate around to the same spot in the sky, known as "sidereal day." The breakthrough inspired Jansky to use astronomical maps for future tracing, which in turn revealed that the static was actually faint radiation emanating from near the constellation Sagittarius.

The announcement of the discovery stirred great initial attention—the *New York Times* ran a story on its front page, under the headline "New Radio Waves Traced to Centre of the Milky Way"—but a lack of science funding during the height of the Great Depression and Jansky's amateur credentials delayed further study. The field of radio astronomy remained at a standstill for much of a decade, until two key discoveries made it possible to further evolve.[*]

The first was a creation of the radio telescope, initiated by radio hobbyist Grote Reber in Wheaton, Illinois, in 1937. Using a parabolic piece of metal nine meters in diameter, shaped in what would be familiar to later generations as a TV satellite dish, Reber had been able to carefully

---

[*] According to his son, Jansky died in 1950, just forty-four, without ever hearing the phrase "radio astronomy," the field he is now credited with founding.

track his findings, and eventually submitted them to Otto Struve's *Astrophysical Journal* in 1940. Upon seeing the research, Struve was stunned. They were extraordinary, revealing something professional astronomers had never realized: outer space was loud—far louder than anyone imagined. But why? And how? ("A universe of radio sounds to which mankind had been deaf since time immemorial now suddenly burst forth in full chorus," recalled John Kraus, who started a radio astronomy observatory at Ohio State University.) For years, Reber continued to map the sounds of the sky, but "hearing" the stars was difficult—the signals were incredibly weak, requiring vast arrays of telescopes that resembled TV satellite dishes to collect them. Until more progress could be made in the tools' sensitivity and precision, many lamented, further advancement seemed impossible.

Luckily for Reber, Struve, and others who would follow them, a new discovery was waiting just around the corner.

• •

While it's easy to oversimplify and declare the atomic bomb the most important technology to emerge from World War II, the weapon that led to the defeat of Nazi Germany, perhaps more than any other, was what the Brits called RDF, for radio direction finding. The process, which relied on bouncing electromagnetic radio waves off potential targets and measuring the reflection time to calculate distance and location, had only been in practice since the 1930s, when engineers at the British Post Office working on shortwave communications had begun noticing that airplanes flying nearby disrupted their signals.

Before long, eight countries—the UK, US, Soviet Union, Germany, Japan, Netherlands, France, and Italy—were all racing, in secret, to bring the new technology into the field. By the time war began, the UK had built an elaborate series of towers, known as the Chain Home system, that allowed it to roughly locate incoming Luftwaffe bombers (a critical aid to maximizing the efforts of its dramatically undermanned Royal Air Force), but what would truly turn the tide against Nazi Germany came through an incredible UK-US partnership, a unique effort forged between Vannevar Bush—the head of the US's National Defense Research Committee—and his UK counterpart, Sir Henry Tizard, during one of the war's darkest hours. That September in 1940, a secret British delegation, including Tizard, escaped the Blitz to travel to Washington, DC, and over dinner at the Cosmos Club, a private bastion for the capital's leading thinkers, he and Bush planned a collaboration unlike any seen in world history—a joint defense effort to harness the UK's scientific wizardry with the American manufacturing that could make it a reality.

A cornerstone of the effort would be a device the British had secretly brought with them—a small disk-sized piece of hardware known as a resonant cavity magnetron, a direction-finding device a thousand times more powerful than anything the Americans possessed. Hidden inside a regular metal briefcase carried by an unassuming Welsh physicist, it had spent its first night in the American capital locked inside the UK ambassador's wine cellar before being delivered to eager NRDC scientists.

Soon, the magnetron was on its way to Tuxedo Park, the suburban New York laboratory created by the wealthy (and eccentric) philanthropist and inventor Alfred Lee Loomis. Loomis had already been working on the problem of radio detecting and ranging (or, as the Americans called it, radar), for some time—that summer, he had invented the first radar gun, to catch speeding cars on the roads around the estate. Now, in the weeks and months that followed, he helped bring together some of the nation's smartest men, ten of whom would go on to win the Nobel Prize, at the Tuxedo Park lab and a newly created facility at MIT, known as the Radiation Laboratory, to participate in a mission to place a working prototype of radar aboard a fighter plane by February 1941. By the end of the war, what had started with just twenty staff would balloon to an effort larger than the Manhattan Project.[*]

In this endeavor, radar quickly proved itself to be a multipurpose and necessary tool, usable over land and sea to detect German U-boats in the North Atlantic and defend critical convoys. A plane using the Rad Lab's breakthroughs could search three thousand square miles of ocean an hour. Coupled with the Allies' cryptological success in breaking the

---

[*] Altogether, the Rad Lab had three specific charters: an airborne radar interception capability, an antiaircraft gun sight, and a navigation system. The team's evening drinking sessions at the nearby Commander Hotel in Cambridge were known as "Project Four," radar historian Robert Buderi noted.

Nazi's Enigma code, the Allies were able to go from sinking one out of every forty submarines spotted to one out of every *four* by 1943. That fall, U-boats sank just nine ships out of 2,500 that passed through hostile waters—and lost twenty-five submarines themselves, an unsustainable ratio that all but silenced the German menace and allowed for a massive military buildup that would lead to the success of D-Day in June 1944. (By then, radar had proven so critical to air defenses as well that a massive Microwave Early Warning system was delivered to Omaha Beach just six days after the initial invasion.)

As the war ended, the transformative impact of radar continued to evolve. On January 25, 1946, the front page of the *New York Times* announced that radar had been used to successfully detect the moon, a true first small step for man that fundamentally changed the way many saw outer space. Since the first time a human looked skyward, all astronomers had been limited to the visible wavelengths of light in studying stars, planets, and the universe beyond, but as the military began to speculate about whether Earth would someday be able to detect aliens—"If intelligent human life exists beyond the earth such signals could be answered," air force Major General Harold McClelland said. "We might even find that other planets have developed techniques superior to our own."—it adopted the use of radar into its ongoing attempts to track UFOs. A small group of astronomers studying the depths of outer space for possible alien civilizations also brought it into their practice. Suddenly, the seemingly silent night sky roiled with violence and mystery. "[Radio astronomy] led to information that overturned the idea of a rationally developing universe and replaced it with a relativistic, ultra-high-energy cosmos of scary, violent, uncontrollable forces like black holes and quasars. It was a revolution," recalled Jesse Greenstein, a pioneer in the field.

Radio astronomy centers dedicated to further implementing the method and studying its results appeared quickly around the globe, helped in many cases by military surplus equipment—in the UK, physicist Bernard Lovell put together his apparatus at the University of Manchester with more than a million pounds' worth of transmitters and equipment set to be dumped after the war. The Australians relied, in part, on an old army gunlaying radar system, which ended up delivering one of the biggest surprises and astronomical breakthroughs yet: intergalactic signals.

"No one believed radio noise could be picked up from external galaxies: the sheer power implied was mind-boggling," technology historian Robert Buderi explained, but an Australian team's sky survey revealed that it was possible to be from two galaxies, NGC 5128 and M87, the latter of which was five million light-years away. The astronomers, Buderi wrote, "hedged enormously in their final paper, afraid . . . of being denied publication because it was too unbelievable."

By the mid-1950s, it was well accepted that radio astronomy was the key to the future; in 1954, the Office of Naval Research and the US Air Force began to pour money into the field and four universities opened new graduate programs to focus on the discipline; a national symposium also took place in January.* The Naval Research Laboratory constructed a fifty-foot telescope on the roof of its Washington, DC, building, creating a striking new landmark for travelers arriving across the Potomac at National Airport that, in short order, delivered major new contributions, including discovering new thermal radiation from the Orion Nebula and the planet Venus.

That surge of new investment directly benefited a rising generation of scientists, including a young man who arrived at Harvard's observatory just as that revolution began.

---

* "The number of active radio astronomers in the United States has increased in the past five years from half a dozen to twenty or more," a *Scientific American* article excitedly noted.

Project Ozma

E ven though he wouldn't hear of the Fermi Paradox until years later, its basic underlying principle had captured Frank Drake's interest from a young age. Preternaturally bright and raised Baptist in a scientific and curious Chicago family, Drake's view of the enormity of the world had always been expansive—his Sunday school teachers had been some of the world's leading Egyptologists and their lessons mixing religion and ancient history no doubt sparked in him far more intellectual rebellion than they intended.

On a trip to Adler Planetarium while in elementary school, he had glimpsed and understood for the first time that our star was one among many. ("Not only was it one of many, it was also unspectacular," he'd note in his memoir decades later), and almost instantly, he had begun contemplating the possibility that those worlds beyond likely included intelligent life. Later, as a student at Cornell University, he looked through the school's fifteen-inch telescope and saw Jupiter for the first time—colorful, surrounded by its four Galilean moons: Io, Europa, Ganymede, and Callisto. "Everything I had read or heard about astronomy suddenly became three-dimensional," he said. "I was smitten."

In December 1951, during his junior year, he sat in on a set of endowed lectures given by a particularly notable visiting astrophysicist: Otto Struve, the famous one-time head of the Yerkes Observatory who had become known for his work on spectrography. Drake marveled at the astronomer's ability to wring vast information and grand theories from the tiny amount of their light that was detectable on Earth. "He raised the practice of stellar spectroscopy to an art form," Drake remembered, as he listened and watched the astronomer lead the audience through a series of charts and calculations that used the minute changes in the light of stars to show how fast they spun in space. Large hot stars, Struve explained, spun fast, but more modest stars like our sun spun more slowly because they were being circled by objects like our planet. Stars like our sun were, in fact, numerous, so numerous stars therefore had objects in orbit around them. At this revelation, Drake felt an almost electric shock.

"In the space of a few moments in the lecture hall, Struve had raised the number of planets in the Galaxy from the nine we knew to more than ninety-nine billion," he recounted with wonder.* In that moment, he realized he wasn't alone in believing—scientifically—that there must be life beyond Earth.

After graduating from Cornell, Drake spent three years in the navy (a condition of the ROTC scholarship he'd received), before heading to Harvard for graduate school, where he took a job as a summer research assistant in radio astronomy. Studying the signals emitted from stars wasn't the kind of work he'd imagined for himself—the glory of optical telescopes seduced him with that view of Jupiter, he later said—but his background in naval electronics proved vital in keeping Harvard's radio astronomy machinery functioning, and he had a key brainstorm in his first year that further propelled the discipline. "I realized that a radio telescope was the prime instrument for detecting and even communicating with extraterrestrial beings," he wrote, meaning that it was now possible for other civilizations and beings to beam specific messages out into the galaxy.

Sitting alone at night in the Harvard observatory, listening and watching the stars, he calculated precisely what signals might arrive from outer space and from where, until one night, when he was twenty-six, he heard it: a sound seemingly sent from another planet.

It was regular and new, something he'd never seen in his previous studies of Pleiades, the constellation known as the Seven Sisters, part of Taurus, a rare constellation visible all over Earth. The signal was also in the region of what was known as the "21 cm hydrogen line"—a band of the radio spectrum linked to the radiation of hydrogen that astronomers had surmised would be the most logical choice for broadcasting by aliens attempting to attract attention. The frequency was particularly attractive,

---

* The significance of Struve's talk flew right over the heads of most audience members; the *Cornell Daily Sun*'s write-up of the lecture didn't even mention Struve's stunning conclusion.

astronomers believed, because such radio waves existed in a quiet corner of outer space, appearing above the low-frequency background radiation of interstellar space, but below the high-frequency noise from Earth's atmosphere (and, presumably, the atmosphere of other similarly situated planets). It was an enormously valuable signal, one useful for mapping the structure of the universe, peering deep back into the universe's history—even detecting dark matter—and, possibly, just possibly, communicating with other advanced civilizations. As Drake recalled, "Any scientifically savvy civilization would know that, and would expect others to know it, too, so they might choose the hydrogen channel as an interplanetary common ground." Because of its importance to astronomy, terrestrial radio signals in that band were generally prohibited, so a signal as regular and strong on the hydrogen line, he thought, almost surely had to be extraterrestrial—and, he noted with excitement, it seemed to be clearly coming from Pleiades because the signal demonstrated the same high-velocity Doppler shift as the stars.

For the rest of his life, Drake struggled to recapture the feeling he experienced in that instant. "What I felt was not a normal emotion. It was probably the sensation people have when they see what to them is a miracle: You know that the world is going to be quite a different place—and you are the only one who knows," he said.

The feeling, unfortunately, would be short-lived—as Drake conducted his first quality integrity test, he realized that the signal remained even as he turned the telescope away from Pleiades, meaning that contact was probably routine military interference, high off in the sky somewhere. "I sat down, sweating and shaking from the heady moments spent almost believing I'd been in touch with a distant and alien mind," he recounted in his memoir. The energy and inspiration of the moment never left him. "From then on, whenever I looked at a radio telescope, I would ask myself as an aside, 'Could this one be used to search for life?'"

• •

In April 1958, Drake arrived in Green Bank, West Virginia, to start his new job at what would soon be the National Radio Astronomy Observatory. As he pulled into the valley in a '53 white Ford loaded with all of his life's possessions, the young scientist was immediately struck by the beauty of the isolated Allegheny Mountain hillsides. The facility, still under construction, was a physical reminder of how his entire scientific field was changing. Astronomy had long been a uniquely lonely form of science—primarily conducted at night, usually solo, and often as far from urban centers as was possible. For centuries, visual astronomers had sought out darkness, and as radio astronomy advanced, its pioneers had realized that listening to the universe required more atmospheric silence than any corner of the country could provide as it became crowded with radio, television, and electronic signals. The size and scale of radio astronomy now required more money and investment than any single institution or university could support. "Radio telescopes needed big collecting dishes because cosmic radio sources shed so little power on Earth—even the strongest radio sources in the sky shed only a few watts," Drake wrote decades later. "In fact, all the energy collected in the history of radio astronomy barely equals the energy released when a few snowflakes fall on the ground."

It was out of these conditions that the idea for a national radio observatory, governed by a consortium of colleges and universities and funded by the US government, had been born. After a nationwide survey of thirty suitable locations, the National Science Foundation had moved forward in the summer of 1956 with the $3.5 million purchase of five thousand acres surrounding Pocahontas County, a flat, shallow valley that would experience less than one-tenth of 1 percent of the radio interference that the Naval Research Laboratory faced in DC. Construction for the remote site would run about $9 million, and engineering plans were put in place for a telescope, larger than anyone in the US had yet seen. The town of Green Bank, population twenty-one, some four hours' drive from DC, would be transformed into radio astronomy's "Shangri-La," one report declared, and scientists began to line up what experiments and investigations they wanted to pursue, from studying the sun to understanding the hydrogen line. The groundbreaking took place in the local high school gym at the height of the space race, just thirteen days after the Soviet launch of Sputnik.

To preserve the radio silence around the facility, the Federal Communications Commission designated the "National Radio Quiet Zone," a giant rectangle that would eventually encompass roughly 108 miles north and south and 120 miles east and west, stretching across 8.3 million acres of West Virginia, Virginia, and a sliver of Maryland, within which electronics and broadcast transmitters were severely restricted. The US Navy also began secret construction of its own giant $79 million antenna inside the quiet zone, a few valleys over near the village of Sugar Grove. Ultimately, though, the scale of the six-hundred-foot antenna—so wide that the Washington Monument could be laid sideways inside with room left over, and an engineering feat compared to the construction of the Brooklyn Bridge—was too massive to be kept secret, and news reports revealed it as part of the effort to explore outer space and the origins of the universe. *Popular Mechanics* called the antenna "the biggest machine that men have ever built," but construction was abandoned in the 1960s after the military had spent $63 million alone on it, with no tangible results.*

• •

Drake was one of Green Bank's first three staff members, and upon his arrival the site's grand title was more aspirational than reality—construction hadn't even started on the site's two main telescopes, and so Drake and his colleagues quickly started building a much more modest model, effectively copying an eighty-five-foot instrument from other existing designs in order to get the observatory up and running.

As he watched the new tool rise from the hillside out his window, Drake marveled at the advancement he had seen in just a few short years. The two telescopes he'd used at Harvard would likely have not been able to detect signals from other civilizations more than just a few light-years away, but between the larger sizes at Green Bank and new advances in radio technology—like the invention of a solid-state maser, which improved sensitivity a thousandfold and would lead to the 1964 Nobel Prize

---

* With time, the secret life of Sugar Grove would become one of the military's most important eavesdropping sites, as it became a central part of the global listening network by US intelligence and the National Security Agency, established by Harry Truman in 1952 but not publicly acknowledged by the US government until 1975. In reports by the *New York Times* published after the terrorist attacks of September 11, 2001, James Bamford called Sugar Grove Station the nation's "largest eavesdropping bug" and later revelations from Edward Snowden would show that the facility intercepted millions of calls, emails, and text messages per day for the NSA.

in Physics for its inventing trio, and a parametric amplifier, which increased Green Bank's sensitivity a hundredfold—the theoretical detection scale had been pushed out as far as twelve light-years, an amount of space that included multiple sun-like stars. Earth could now realistically detect signals from other civilizations.

"It was a remarkable idea whose brilliance has been dulled by long familiarity," wrote astronomer Seth Shostak decades later. "Hardware that we've already built for other purposes, accessible right here on the ground, could discover sentient beings living on unseen worlds. We could find cosmic company with no more effort than turning a dial."

Over burgers and fries at a nearby diner, Drake pitched his colleagues on using the new technologies to look for life beyond Earth. After an awkward silence, the observatory's director, Lloyd Berkner, responded enthusiastically. "He had a reputation in science for being an optimistic gambler, and he loved the idea," Drake recalled. "In fact, before the waitress brought our check, he gave me authorization to proceed."

Drake named the effort Project Ozma, after Princess Ozma, the ruler of Oz ("I, too, was dreaming of a land far away, peopled by strange and exotic beings," Drake wrote later), stepping fully into one of the oldest intellectual quests of humanity, the chance to figure out whether we are alone in the universe, what science fiction writer Arthur C. Clarke has called "one of the supreme questions of philosophy."

• •

The idea that we're alone in the universe as humans is largely a Western one—and the debate that we're not is a mostly recent one. From almost the dawn of human time, early scholars and scientists had considered the origin of the universe, including Lucretius, who early in the first century BC had imagined the existence of atoms and speculated, "We must realize that there are other worlds in other parts of the universe, with races of different men and different animals." Indeed, the seemingly controversial idea that would consume Drake and the modern scientific community is a debate largely unique to Western, Judeo-Christian traditions. Many Eastern and Indigenous traditions, like Buddhism, have long recognized and embraced what's formally known as the "plurality of worlds" or "cosmic pluralism," the idea that there are many inhabited worlds, perhaps even many of them "human," spread about the universe. Pythagoreans even believed that the moon and stars were peopled by other humanlike beings.

In the Western tradition, though, the school of thought known as Ptolemaic-Aristotelian dominated for centuries, a belief that the heavens revolved around Earth (not the sun) and that humanity was special, unique, and—as Christianity advanced—a gift from God. "For centuries Platonists, Aristolians, and Christians in their metaphysical speculation refused to accept that there were other 'Earths' analogous to our own," Karl Guthke wrote in his defining intellectual history of humanity's embrace of other worlds.

This worldview was challenged—and ultimately upended by Copernicus, who in the sixteenth century first posited that the Earth revolved around the sun and that, perhaps, some of the bright lights in the night sky were other neighboring planets and not just stars. It was a theory with dramatic implications for science, theology, philosophy, and even literature. Goethe wrote, "Of all discoveries and convictions none could have had a more powerful effect on the human mind than the teaching of Copernicus." As Guthke traces, it took nearly a half millennium for Copernicus's new science to evolve, as "the dangerous heresy ha[d] become a new gospel." Only with the observation of Galileo in the early 1600s that the moon was similar to Earth and that Jupiter had moons of its own did Copernicus's idea begin to gain more widespread acceptance, even as he sidestepped the implications of his observations. As Guthke notes, "Galileo himself, soon widely hailed as the 'new Columbus,' was sufficiently worldly wise to make a point of evading the delicate question of whether the planets were inhabited."

For hundreds of years, as astronomy advanced and writers and thinkers began to play around with imagining worlds beyond, Christian scholars—whose entire faith tradition would be upended by the idea of other beings and planets—were primarily concerned with how such a discovery would be treated doctrinally: How does one square other worlds and other beings with the Christian teachings that God sent his own son to redeem us, sacrificing him for our sins, and that God created everything for the benefit of humans? What if the other inhabitants of other worlds somehow were better than humans, more advanced, happier, more blessed? In many ways, the debate for centuries paralleled the challenge the Catholic

Church faced as European explorers discovered the Americas teeming with indigenous life. Would alien beings be animals, "humans" (that is, descendants of Adam and Eve), or something else—perhaps humans of a different lineage, not descendants of Adam, and thus untouched by original sin, thus beings who did not need to be redeemed?[*]

By the 1700s and 1800s, amid the Enlightenment, the debate began to progress on more scientific lines; Edmund Halley, as an aside in one of his works, declared "it is not taken for granted that the Earth is one of the Planets, and they are all with reason suppos'd Habitable." Discoveries around 1860 by Gustav Kirchhoff and Robert Bunsen about spectrum analysis—that is, the science of breaking apart light to determine what elements are present in the light's source in far-off celestial bodies—established for the first time that not only were there other planets and stars, but that they were made of the same elements as our solar system, planet, and sun, proof of a literal universality that the chemicals that make up us and our world also make up all the rest as well. It was becoming hard not to imagine that there might be other worlds out there.

Now, as Drake saw it, the group's efforts inaugurated a third era of what he called the Search for Extraterrestrial Intelligence (SETI). "For the first time, SETI embodied philosophical, qualitative, and quantitative elements," he wrote. Project Ozma had the potential to be its defining effort.

Fate aligned again just as Drake began Project Ozma: Otto Struve, the man whose lecture long ago had inspired Drake to realize he wasn't alone in imagining other life in the universe, stepped in as director of the observatory in July 1959. The new director's outlook and support was all Drake could hope to have as he started his observations, building a receiver that studied that 21 cm hydrogen line where astronomers most imagined other civilizations would share signals—the interstellar water hole.[†]

---

[*] The Bishop of Chester, John Wilkins, wrote in the 1630s a treatise, *The Discovery of a World in the Moone, or, A Discourse Tending to Prove That 'tis Probable There May Be Another Habitable World in That Planet*, about whether the residents of the moon were likely to live in a state of blessedness and how best to bring them to salvation.

[†] As Drake recalled, "There's something aesthetically appealing about the idea of communicating with aliens at an interstellar waterhole, just the way so many species

Drake had intended to keep his research secret until completion—the idea of using government resources to search for extraterrestrial life still seemed too controversial to him—but in September 1959, the Green Bank team was startled to read a *Nature* paper, written by two Cornell physicists, proposing just the type of study Drake was already leading. Radio telescopes, the Cornell team suggested, were now advanced enough to be capable of detecting interstellar signals, and "the probability of success is difficult to estimate, but if we never search, the chance of success is zero," Giuseppe Cocconi and Philip Morrison wrote.

Their hypothesis had grown out of their own work in gamma rays, which crossed the galaxy before arriving at Earth, and Cocconi had first started to wonder if that was how other civilizations might communicate—but as they learned more, they concluded that radio waves made more sense.* Cocconi and Morrison even surmised in their piece that aliens would use the same frequency Drake had zeroed in on: the 21 cm hydrogen line.

Suddenly, Drake and Struve realized, their crazy idea might not be quite so crazy.

---

of animals have traditionally gathered at the waterholes of Earth, to share another vital resource. We suspect that water is very important to life elsewhere in the universe as well. What's more, the electromagnetic waterhole occupies a very quiet region, containing the least possible extraneous noise from the Galaxy (and the Earth's atmosphere). This fact makes it a logical choice as a frequency for transmitting signals over great distances. That is, it appears logical to us. Time will tell if the logic has truly universal appeal."

* Their paper in *Nature* was titled "Searching for Interstellar Communications," and Morrison for decades would maintain it was a better—and more accurate—name than SETI. "SETI has always made me unhappy because it somehow denigrates the situation," he told an interviewer in 2003. "It wasn't the intelligence we could detect; it was the communications we could detect. Yes, they imply intelligence, but that's so evident that it's better to talk about getting signals from them."

Phantom Signal

While Frank Drake was elated at the press attention that the *Nature* paper received, Otto Struve fumed. Others were about to claim the credit and notoriety that should belong to the Green Bank observatory, and to preserve that authority, he seized upon a lecture opportunity at MIT to preempt the announcement of Project Ozma, rewriting one lecture to focus on the new search for extraterrestrial intelligence. In November 1959, he laid out a grand vision to a rapt audience in MIT's Kresge Auditorium as part of its Compton Lecture Series. "It is probable that a good many of the billions of planets in the Milky Way support intelligent forms of life," the astronomer said. "To me this conclusion is of great philosophical interest. I believe that science has reached the point where it is necessary to take into account the action of intelligent beings, in addition to the classical laws of physics."

The announcement made headlines in the science community, and colleagues came out of the woodwork to support Drake's flight of fancy. One day, an English electrical engineer came by the observatory; Drake set him to work on the receiver he planned to use for Ozma, calibrating it to make sure it could differentiate between real interstellar signals and random electrical fluctuations. The head of a Boston firm, meanwhile, offered Drake a prototype parametric amplifier that would significantly boost the receiver's sensitivity—the equipment was so delicate that one of the firm's engineers drove it to Green Bank, nestled in the passenger seat of a Morgan sports car.

Early on the morning of April 8, 1960, the first formal observations began. Assisted by his two female student assistants—Ellen Gundermann and Margaret Hurley,* Drake spent about forty-five minutes crouched

---

* The presence of the two women on the team was hardly a coincidence; Drake's thesis adviser at Harvard, Cecilia Payne-Gaposchkin, was the first female astronomy PhD at Harvard, the first promoted to tenured professor, and, later, the first

five stories off the ground inside a garbage can–sized device installed inside the eighty-five-foot telescope dish, turning the amplifier. "It had the
simplest possible output device: a chart recorder, consisting of a pen that
wiggled with each sound received from space, leaving squiggles describing
sounds on a moving strip of paper," Drake later recalled in his memoir.

By 5 a.m., all there was to do was sip coffee, and wait. The room was
filled with tension and excitement. "What we were doing was unprecedented, of course, and no one knew what to expect," he remembered. "It
was as though we expected the aliens to speak to us at any moment." Just
in case, he had a loudspeaker and audiotape recorder at the ready.

They began with Tau Ceti, a star in the Cetus the Whale constellation, that was roughly similar to the sun and about twelve light-years
away. Hours passed with nothing and finally Tau Ceti set over the horizon around noon. Then the team moved to Epsilon Eridani, a young star
in the southern constellation of Eridanus that is just ten light-years away
and the third-closest star visible to the naked eye.

Within just five minutes, the room erupted into chaos. "A burst of
noise shot out of the loudspeaker, the chart recorder started banging off
the scale, and we were all jumping at once, wild with excitement," Drake
said. "I felt I was reliving my encounter with the Pleiades all over again,
only this time I wasn't alone, and I was actively searching. Could discovery really be this easy?"

After the moment of collective elation, the team got to work to verify the possible signal, testing their equipment and moving the telescope
away from the star to test its direction. Immediately, they saw the noise
disappear, and for a moment, hope rose even higher—that seemed to
indicate the signal indeed had come from Epsilon Eridani. But when
they moved the telescope back, the room fell silent, and stayed that way.
"We couldn't tell if it had come from the star, or if it was some kind of

---

woman to head a department at Harvard. He, in turn, had similarly championed
some young female PhD students, choosing two women—out of twelve slots—to
participate in the observatory's summer program and earning the opprobrium of a
colleague, who chastised him, "This is a total waste of resources and contrary to all
tradition!"

terrestrial interference that just happened to quit the moment we moved the telescope," Drake recalled.

Though the team still had questions, word spread that Ozma had heard a signal. Press calls poured in, hoping for more information, but Drake waved them away, solely focused on the work in front of him. Each day, the telescope was tuned on Epsilon Eridani as soon as the start broke the horizon, and before long, a new tool was added—an ordinary antenna that would pick up normal terrestrial interference was set out the window and tied to its own recorder to double-check any other incoming signals. The days settled into a quiet routine; it became, Drake later said, almost boring, until, on the fifth day, the signal returned, same as before, pulsing eight times a second—this time, though, the ordinary antenna picked it up, too, meaning that the source was on Earth. The team was crestfallen. They'd stumbled upon nothing more significant than a plane passing overhead, though as they calculated the height and speed of the detected plane, they realized the aircraft must be flying at a stratospheric altitude literally unheard of at the time.

"The rate at which the phantom signal traversed the sky suggested that it was emanating from an aircraft cruising at unprecedented altitude— perhaps 80,000 feet," recalled H. Paul Shuch, who would later be the executive director of the SETI League. It was, to them, a literal unidentified flying object, just not one from an alien civilization like they'd hoped.

Over the next two months, with pauses for other experiments and observations, Project Ozma searched the skies for more than two hundred hours, frequently visited by a steady stream of scientists and luminaries. One day, the president of Notre Dame, Theodore Hesburgh, "came to ponder the religious significance" of discovering life beyond Earth; and on another, Barney Oliver, the head of research at Hewlett-Packard, phoned to tell Drake that he'd read about the project in *Time* magazine and wanted to come by when he was in the area on a trip to the capital. Drake pooh-poohed the idea, saying there was no way to do a day trip from Washington, DC, to Green Bank, to which Oliver only laughed: "You underestimate me." A longtime fan of science fiction and a successful inventor, Oliver saw Ozma as a dream come to life and arranged for a private plane to bring him to the facility.

Despite the attention, though, Ozma's recorders remained silent—the celestial silence uneventfully unfurled across thousands of yards of paper. Drake was disappointed but knew the realities of the work he and his team were doing. He often compared their efforts to the apocryphal story of a drunk searching for his lost keys under the streetlight: they'd looked only where it was easy. "We had failed to detect a genuine alien signal, it was true, but we had succeeded in demonstrating that searching was a feasible and even reasonable thing to do," he recalled.

Overall, Project Ozma could—and would—still be considered a success, having established numerous lessons for the nascent field, including, Drake noted, how quickly boredom could set in, and how future efforts should be mixed and balanced with other observations and experiments. After all, work so far had only been conducted over just two months—a blip in the grander scheme of space and time. What if the period when his team had been looking coincided with when those civilization's messages had been down for maintenance or pointed at planets on the other side of the galaxy? This was reason enough, he argued, to continue.

• •

What Drake didn't quite realize at the time was that Ozma had inadvertently uncovered a giant secret: that mystery plane detected in the opening hours had likely been one of the government's best-kept secrets. As the Cold War intensified, the US had desperately needed to see behind the Iron Curtain to understand the Soviet military's buildup, and military and intelligence leaders proposed to Dwight Eisenhower that a long-range plane, equipped with cameras, be developed to fly above the limits of the Soviet air defenses; Ike refused to allow the effort to be flown by actual air force personnel, fearful of the escalation of such incursions by uniformed military, but allowed the project to proceed under the cloak of the nation's intelligence agency. Thus, since 1955, on the other side of the country in the Nevada desert, the CIA had been developing a secret reconnaissance plane to penetrate the deepest regions of the Soviet Union, what historian Annie Jacobsen called "the country's first peacetime aerial espionage program."

The effort, code-named Project Aquatone, was overseen by the CIA's benign-sounding Development Projects Staff, and started after two CIA officials, Richard Bissell and Herbert Miller, took an administrative lead, flying across the deserted corners of the West to identify a new test facility. Existing air force test sites, like Edwards Air Force Base, where Chuck Yeager had broken the sound barrier, had been deemed too populated for such a secret effort, so they surveyed California and across north and east, up through Nevada and past Las Vegas, toward the remote desert known as the Nevada Test Site, where the Atomic Energy Commission and the military were conducting aboveground tests of the country's nuclear weapons. Finally they found Groom Lake, a salt flat that had once been used as an emergency landing strip for World War II pilots. It was perfect for the new secret project—isolated and already adjacent to one of the most secure corners of the entire US. The new secret base would eventually be known as Area 51.

The task of building the plane itself was delegated to the Lockheed Corporation, an American aerospace manufacturer, and the parts and money required for the effort were stolen and hidden across the entire military's budget; to kick things off, Bissell personally wrote a $1,250,000 check from one of the agency's accounts and mailed it to the home of Lockheed's chief engineer. Development work began in 1943 in Burbank, California, at the company's so-called Skunk Works, a vast series of hangars, warehouses, and offices set amid the rising postwar prosperity and suburban sprawl of Los Angeles.* Through World War II and the Cold War, the Skunk Works was where many of the country's best planes were born, including America's first jet fighter, the F-80, and its fastest, the F-104 Starfighter, which in 1958 would break the world speed, topping 1,404 miles per hour.

"The entire project became the most compartmented and self-contained activity within the agency," Bissell reflected in his memoirs decades later, cloaked in secrecy and achieved by any means necessary. Information was so sensitive that the Lockheed janitors weren't allowed into offices, leaving engineers to police their own trash; when Lockheed needed altimeters that went up to eighty thousand feet from a company

---

* Project staff could dine at the nation's first McDonald's restaurant, which opened nearby just as the Aquatone work began.

whose equipment normally only went as high as forty-five thousand, the CIA secured them with a story about experimental rocket craft. In order to produce twenty planes, each costing around $1 million, pieces were separately shipped to Area 51 at Groom Lake, where a newly paved runway awaited.

The craft, officially dubbed the U-2 (with the *U* for "utility label" purposefully chosen to be as bland as possible) resembled an ungainly albatross, with incredibly long, drooping fuel-filled wings that required extra wheels during takeoff. It could stay in the air for ten hours at a time, gliding along through the stratosphere for long portions of the flight with its engines off, consuming just a thousand gallons of specially designed fuel, known as JP-7.* The planes were remarkable feats of engineering, equipped with the most advanced and powerful cameras ever built in the United States; to demonstrate their readiness, Bissell sent one over Eisenhower's farm outside Gettysburg and displayed to the president images of his cows drinking, taken from seventy thousand feet above the ground. "With 12,000 feet of film, the cameras were considered able to photograph a path from Washington to Phoenix in one flight," historian Michael Beschloss noted.

Pilots for the program were plucked from the Strategic Air Command, who in a flurry of paperwork were then removed from the rolls of the air force and reemployed by the CIA for eighteen months, at a salary of $1,500 a month ($2,500 while deployed overseas). After their service, they were promised a return to the air force, with no time lost promotionwise.† That did not mean, however, that the job was all perks. The pilots had to wear special pressure suits, since their blood would likely vaporize

---

* "Manufacturing this special fuel required petroleum byproducts that Shell normally used to make its 'Flit' fly and bug spray. In order to produce several hundred thousand gallons of LF-1 for the U-2 project in the spring and summer of 1955, Shell had to limit the production of Flit, causing a nationwide shortage," a once-secret CIA history noted.

† To preserve secrecy, CIA cable traffic referred to the pilots only as "drivers," using the code name KWGLITTER-00, where the two-digits identified the specific pilot, and ensured that, if the cable codes were broken, the Soviet Union would be unable to understand who or what was involved.

above sixty-five thousand feet under normal conditions. The long missions, during which food and drink were limited, were grueling—pilots usually lost between three and six pounds of weight during a flight.

As the planes took to the sky, there was also the issue of visibility. "Once U-2s started flying at altitudes above 60,000 feet, air-traffic controllers began receiving increasing numbers of UFO reports," a secret 1992 CIA history, which was only declassified in 2013, revealed. "Such reports were most prevalent in the early evening hours from pilots of airliners flying from east to west . . . and appear to the airliner pilot, 40,000 feet below, to be fiery objects.

"Even during daylight hours," the report continued, "the silver bodies of the high-flying U-2s could catch the sun and cause reflections or glints that could be seen at lower altitudes and even on the ground." (Later, the planes were painted black.)

The air force, of course, knew about the secret missions and Project Blue Book staff regularly cross-checked their incoming reports of UFOs with U-2 flight logs. By the CIA's secret estimate, U-2 flights "accounted for more than one-half of all UFO reports during the late 1950s." In July 1956, "Angel" and its fellow crafts began flying over the Soviet Union, providing invaluable intelligence about its military readiness—as it turned out, the Soviet air force lacked any meaningful bomber capacity at all, despite public political debates and warnings of a "bomber gap." As one CIA memo noted after the first blockbuster flight, "For the first time we are really able to say that we have an understanding of what was going on in the Soviet Union." The flights rightly irked the Soviet Union—more than twenty MiG fighters tried unsuccessfully to intercept the high-flying American craft on its first mission, but each plane fell away after their engines flamed out in the climbing altitude—but Nikita Khrushchev and the military kept silent about the incursions, not wanting to demonstrate their own impotence at being unable to defend their own airspace.

Unable to hide the existence of the planes for much longer, the US eventually announced in 1956 that the National Advisory Committee for Aeronautics (NACA)—the forerunner to NASA—had developed a new high-altitude weather research plane, although they vastly underplayed its performance capabilities, saying the plane could only reach fifty-five thousand feet. The cover story held until just a month after Frank Drake and Project Ozma had seemingly picked up one of its overflights; in early May 1960, President Eisenhower and US officials gambled on another U-2 reconnaissance mission, set to be the twenty-fourth over the Soviet Union, taking off from Pakistan and aiming to photograph two space sites, including the cosmodrome where Sputnik itself had been launched.

All seemed well, until, midway through the mission, pilot Francis Gary Powers, a veteran of twenty-seven U-2 flights, was hit by a Soviet SA-2 missile. The plane crashed, but Powers survived and was captured quickly. The incident and resulting public exposure of the crashed plane caused immense embarrassment to the US government and caused the collapse of a scheduled Khrushchev-Eisenhower summit in Paris weeks later. The U-2 overflight program, as a result, was abandoned.[*]

---

[*] U-2s, of course, would continue to be a vital US surveillance tool and another would be shot down over Cuba in one of the tensest moments of the Cuban Missile Crisis in October 1962. The planes continue to fly today, and one was used to surveil the Chinese spy balloon in the winter of 2023.

The Drake Equation

I n the aftermath of Project Ozma, Frank Drake's profile in astronomy circles had been sharply elevated, and he felt that he'd earned some space to have some fun. He hung a sign on his office door at Green Bank: "Is there intelligent life on Earth?" It made people chuckle, but the truth was his new status meant he was now regularly hearing from some of the sharpest and most interesting minds in science. One of the many new pen pals he had was a budding young planetary scientist named Carl Sagan.

Born in the working-class Italian and Jewish neighborhood of Bensonhurst, Brooklyn, in 1934, Sagan had become fascinated by astronomy and science fiction through the novels of writers like Edgar Rice Burroughs, featuring his Mars explorer John Carter, and comic books that imagined worlds beyond. By age ten, he later recalled, he was confident that life existed elsewhere: "I had decided—in almost total ignorance of the difficulty of the problem—that the universe was full up. There were too many places for this to be the only inhabited planet."

He sent away for a mail-order book called *Interplanetary Flight* and marveled at its contents. The final two sentences, in particular, struck a chord: "The challenge of the great spaces between the worlds is a stupendous one; but if we fail to meet it, the story of our race will be drawing to its close. Humanity will have turned its back upon the still-untrodden heights and will be descending again along the long slopes that stretches, across a thousand million years of time, down to the shores of the primeval sea." As a high school student, he took great interest in Kenneth Arnold's flying saucer tales, and desperately watched the skies himself in the evenings, hoping to spot one—he raced through school, graduating two years early, and during his senior year in 1952, he won first place in a Knights of Columbus essay contest, choosing as his subject "the question of whether human contact with technologically advanced extraterrestrials would be as disastrous as contact with Europeans had been for Native Americans." To him, an obsession with the possibility of life beyond was not unusual—it was the lack of interest by so many others that felt odd. "Not a single adult I knew was preoccupied with UFOs," he wrote later. "I couldn't figure out why not."

At just sixteen years old, Sagan entered the University of Chicago, where he managed to attach himself to three of the leading thinkers about life on Earth: geneticist Hermann Muller, best known for his work on fruit fly evolution; molecular biologist Joshua Lederberg, known for his work on microbial genetics; and physicist Harold C. Urey. Urey, the recipient of the 1934 Nobel Prize for his work discovering deuterium, had been a key figure in the Manhattan Project, helping to create the process that yielded enriched uranium for use in the first bombs, but postwar, he'd become a fierce critic of atomic weapons, refocusing his work on biology with a grad student named Stanley Miller to further understand how life began on earth—"I don't like rocks, I like life," he later quipped.

The resulting Urey-Miller experiment built upon relatively new advances and interest in the field of paleobiology, and sought to address and answer questions that several scientists around the country had begun to ask: How did life emerge from the stew of chemicals present in Earth's early atmosphere, and what combination of processes had led to the organic compounds that would over eons become the building blocks of carbon-based life? They wanted to build on work by UC Berkeley professor Melvin Calvin, who had spent much of his career focused on plants and photosynthesis, but had become particularly intrigued by the question of how life started on Earth after reading a 1949 book on evolution by George Gaylord Simpson, the century's most influential paleontologist. Inspired by some of Simpson's theories and approaches, Calvin's team devised an experiment to zap a mixture of carbon dioxide and water with radiation, in an attempt to re-create what they imagined the atmosphere had looked like on Earth as life began; the findings were somewhat inconclusive, although tiny traces of formaldehyde and formic acid were found, leading Calvin to believe that their experiment had failed.

Miller and Urey thought that Calvin had the right idea, but the wrong chemical mixture—they believed early Earth was composed of more methane, ammonia, water, and hydrogen—and in August 1952, they tried to replicate the experiment with that combination instead. Almost instantly, it was clear that something amazing happened. When they hit the chemical-filled tubes with an electrical spark, the tubes clouded, meaning they were filled with amino acids, the basic components of DNA.* It would become one of the most famous experiments of all time, establishing in the public consciousness the idea that the building blocks of life could have emerged almost spontaneously from the "prebiotic soup" that existed on early Earth.

It was around this time that Sagan had arrived on the University of Chicago's campus, and he was immediately captivated by the work of his soon-to-be mentor.† As his studies advanced, he dove ever deeper into physics and astronomy, working at one point at the University of Texas's McDonald Observatory under Gerard Kuiper, the only full-time planetary scientist in the country at the time. Then, in the wake of Sputnik's launch, a moment when astronomy and space was where the money, energy, enthusiasm, and ambition all came together in science, Sagan seized a moment of opportunity. "The scientists who designed NASA experiments tended to be young, and in a single mission they could eclipse the patient work of elders who headed observatories or academic departments," Sagan's biographer wrote; and Sagan was perfect for a role in the organization. With a vote of confidence from Lederberg, he "sort of glided effortlessly between some kind of bull sessions late at night to advising the government," and by 1960, Sagan was contributing to the experiments around the Mariner missions to Venus, what would be the first US probe sent to another planet as part of a new initiative introduced by John F. Kennedy. "I believe that this nation should commit itself to achieving the goal, before this decade is out, of landing a man on the moon and returning him safely to the earth," the newly elected president

---

* In fact, later analysis after Miller's death in 2007 found that his experiments actually created more than twenty amino acids.

† By 1958, Calvin viewed the results of this experiment as conclusively pointing to the possibility of life—or at least its building blocks—all over the galaxy and the universe beyond: "We can assert with some degree of scientific confidence that cellular life as we know it on the surface of the Earth does exist in some millions of other sites in the universe."

had told Congress in May of 1961. "No single space project in this period will be more impressive to mankind, or more important for the long-range exploration of space; and none will be so difficult or expensive to accomplish.

"I believe we should go to the moon. But I think every citizen of this country as well as the Members of the Congress should consider the matter carefully in making their judgment, to which we have given attention over many weeks and months, because it is a heavy burden, and there is no sense in agreeing or desiring that the United States take an affirmative position in outer space, unless we are prepared to do the work and bear the burdens to make it successful."

Sagan was rapt, feeling the course of human history changing before his eyes. This, he thought, was how we would find the answers to all of our questions.

• •

That same summer, Frank Drake got a telephone call from a staffer on the National Academy of Sciences' Space Science Board. In a strong Oxford accent, J. Peter Pearman explained to the astronomer that he had been quietly testing support within government and science circles for a more focused quest to identify intelligent life, and that he believed it was "crucial that a meeting be organized as soon as possible to investigate the research potential." Pearman asked Drake to host the meeting at Green Bank—symbolic, given Ozma's roots—and within moments, they were enthusiastically talking dates and invitees.

The three-day conference came together quickly, with only one notable twist: mid-planning, Pearman informed Drake that one of its attendees, Melvin Calvin, was likely set to receive the Nobel Prize for Chemistry for his work describing photosynthesis. This news was exciting, but presented a logistical challenge: How do you celebrate a Nobel Prize in the middle of nowhere?

Drake knew that procuring spirits would be difficult in the mostly dry state of West Virginia—there was only one state liquor store in each county, and ahead of the conference, he couldn't find it even in the small town. Confused, he asked the only person in sight if he knew the location of the liquor store. "Yup," the man replied, "but I ain't gonna tell you." (Looking up, Drake realized the man was sitting outside the local Baptist church.) After more wandering, he finally found the store and purchased a case of champagne.

The conference began on Halloween 1961. Scientific luminaries descended on Green Bank, filling every available room at the observatory. Many had kept word of the gathering—and their participation in it—private, in part to avoid ridicule and unwanted attention, but now, meeting their intellectual colleagues for the first time, they marveled at the opportunity they'd been given and the company they found themselves in; several of them noted how striking a figure Drake cut. He had gone prematurely gray by thirty, and with swept-back hair, bold glasses, bushy eyebrows, and his navy pedigree, he seemed a natural leader for the group, despite being the second-youngest attendee.

Altogether, there were ten of them: Drake, J. Peter Pearman, Otto Struve, Carl Sagan, Melvin Calvin, and Cornell's Philip Morrison, as well as Boston radio expert Dana Atchley, who had helped donate his firm's parametric amplifier to Ozma, Hewlett-Packard executive Barney Oliver, and neuroscientist John C. Lilly, who was experimenting with consciousness and communication by attempting—semi-successfully—to communicate with dolphins.* Rounding out the group was one of Struve's former students, a Chinese optical astronomer named Su-Shu Huang, who had joined NASA and conceived of the idea that stars had "habitable zones" that could support life within specific bands of planetary orbits. At the time, the group constituted the totality of the scientists known to be interested in the field.

As everyone settled in, attention turned to the centerpiece of the conference's discussion: a rough equation that Drake had scribbled down in advance:

$$N = R_* \cdot f_p \cdot n_e \cdot f_l \cdot f_i \cdot f_c \cdot L$$

---

* Lilly's book *Man and Dolphin* had caused a national sensation upon publication earlier that year, and Pearman considered him as the closest scientist they could find who had, in effect, communicated with an alien species.

This, he now explained, could break down the likelihood of life else-where by calculating that the number of detectable civilizations in space (N), equaled "the rate (R) of star formation, times the fraction (f_p) of stars that form planets, times the number (n_e) of planets hospitable to life, times the fraction (f_l) of those planets where life actually emerges, times the fraction (f_i) of planets where life evolves into intelligent beings, times the fraction (f_c) of planets with intelligent creatures capable of interstellar communication, times the length of time (L) that such a civilization re-mains detectable." It was a remarkable leap of deduction and imagination, one clearly born of its time, as the existential risk of the Cold War and the nuclear arms race forced the realization that humanity might be capable of its own utter destruction.[*]

As the scientists at Green Bank eagerly debated the various factors of the calculation over the next three days, they realized that small changes in the numbers could lead to vastly different estimates of the universe's hab-itability. Just considering the possibilities of our own solar system—where in theory three of nine planets, Venus, Mars, and Earth, all existed in that habitable zone—and where thousands of years ago advanced civiliza-tions had arisen separately in China, the Middle East, and the Americas, the math seemed encouraging. Closer examination, though, raised more questions. The Incas and Aztecs, some argued, lagged hundreds or thou-sands of years behind European civilization in scientific development; Philip Morrison also pointed out that the Renaissance, which had kicked off the modern technological and scientific revolution, had occurred in only one of those three independent centers of civilization. Would China or the Americas have ever had their own Renaissances someday in the future, if they had continued to develop in isolation? Perhaps, but perhaps not, or perhaps it would have taken many more millennia.

Together, John Lilly and Morrison were particularly focused on the trickiness of (f_c). Lilly used the sophistication of dolphins, whose

---

[*] The concern was hardly abstract for the group: Morrison had worked on the Man-hattan Project, driven the core of the world's first nuclear bomb to its test site in New Mexico, and helped arm the Nagasaki bomb. He'd walked, too, through the ruins of Hiroshima as part of the US government's damage-assessment team and become an outspoken critic of nuclear weapons afterward.

enormous brains seemed perhaps even more complex than humans, who had a communication system all their own, and who clearly demonstrated concern and care for each other (and even, in some cases, for humans), as evidence that they would meet the standards of "intelligent life." Morrison agreed that the cetaceans did meet all the traditional markers of "intelligent life," but pointed out that they were still a long way from contacting alien civilizations—no dolphin had ever glimpsed a star and thus pondered what life might look like beyond our solar system. The universe might have all manner of dolphin-equivalent species, incredibly smart animals that would never communicate beyond their own planet. At one point, Su-Shu Huang joined in the debate, adding that dry land and the ability to make fire seemed almost prerequisites for interstellar communication—the idea of a purely aquatic world communicating beyond itself seemed far-fetched, almost no matter how intelligent the life within those oceans could be.

At 4 a.m. West Virginia time, on November 2, the night watchman at the observatory received a call from Stockholm: Melvin Calvin had indeed been awarded the Nobel Prize in Chemistry. Drake retrieved his champagne and the men celebrated together.[*]

Over the next two days, conversations continued about the Drake equation, and other topics, like what life might be like among intelligent extraterrestrial beings. "Let's imagine what these creatures are," Calvin said during one session. "We have no idea what they look like, of course, but I think we can safely assume that they'll have organs for sight and sound, because the universe in which they live is a universe of light and sound. Maybe they don't see what we call visible light. Maybe they see in the ultraviolet or the infrared, but they must see and hear something. They probably have sensing organs for touch, so they don't bump into each other, and they must have some way to process the information from their sensors—something like a brain, though what shape it might take, I can't tell."

Morrison argued that considering human evolution itself was another piece of the puzzle—man had eliminated all close competitors and

---

[*] Calvin's own recollection of the events are slightly different and involve a phone call from his wife notifying him of the prize, but I've used Drake's story here.

humanlike species so long ago that we don't even understand why: Was it done with violence or simple out-competition? If intelligent life on a planet only ended up with one or two truly advanced species, that math would fundamentally alter the equation. Life might take many forms and thrive almost anywhere—from frozen arctic peaks to deep in the ocean—but advanced intelligent life was another matter. And would the nature of further civilizational and technological advancement lead to ever-greater curiosity—or to slothfulness and laziness? Lilly, for his part, raised a final challenge from his work with dolphins: he had only come to understand how dolphins communicated by observing the effects of dolphin sounds on other dolphins. Perhaps mankind would need to find two alien civilizations in conversation with one another to understand either—seemingly a vanishingly and impossibly rare proposition.

As they talked, they came to understand that basically the entire discussion hinged on the L in Drake's equation, the length of time an advanced civilization capable of interstellar communication could sustain itself. Civilizations that imploded quickly, even on the scale of thousands or tens of thousands of years, would effectively be forever unknown across the universe, while intelligent beings who managed to sustain their civilization for millions, tens of millions, or even hundreds of millions of years, might have the time and inclination to search beyond their own solar systems, sending or receiving messages or even exploring in interstellar crafts.

By the conference's end, Drake saw things generally as $N = L$. The group concurred, estimating that across the Milky Way there were probably "somewhere between one thousand and one hundred million advanced extraterrestrial civilizations." In any case, it was clear that they'd together arrived at a massive project, one that surely would consume not just their professional lives but generations yet unborn. "This is work for society, not for individuals," Barney Oliver concluded. "The distances we're talking about mean that communication will proceed over decades, maybe even centuries. It isn't going to be one human talking to one alien. The search itself must be a group effort." And they, the ten of them, would be the first to take on the effort. Just before they went their separate ways, they cheerfully dubbed themselves the Order of the Dolphin, splitting the final bottle of champagne to make it official.

(Sagan also offered a name for the larger effort: CETI, Communication with Extraterrestrial Intelligence.*)

"To the value of L," Struve toasted. "May it prove to be a very large number."

A few weeks later, Calvin mailed each of the participants a little memento: a lapel button made from an ancient Greek coin, depicting a dolphin.

---

* CETI would be used in the field for a decade, then replaced with the term SETI, the Search for Extraterrestrial Intelligence, of which CETI was reconceived as a single branch of SETI. For ease of reading, I primarily use SETI in the book.

21

The Search Expands

As isolated as members of the Order of the Dolphin may have felt, they were hardly alone in considering life beyond planet Earth. In fact, among others, scientists in Europe and behind the Iron Curtain were hard at work solving the very same puzzle in what a later generation of scientists would define as the "adjacent possible," the idea derived from biological evolution that human knowledge and curiosity similarly can only evolve a bit at a time, building on the shared knowledge of humanity at any given moment.*

Luckily, it didn't take too long before some of them found one another. Drake, for one, found a thrilling new colleague at Green Bank in 1962, the German radio astronomer Sebastian von Hoerner; the two men shared a passion for exploring caves and as they explored the dark reaches on Earth, they discussed the darkness beyond. Drake shared his equation with von Hoerner, who began to eagerly unpack the qualities of L, for the longevity of detectable civilizations. Before long, von Hoerner came to the conclusion that while many—or even most—civilizations might fail in relatively short order, even a few small outliers could dramatically change Drake's calculations. At some point in their evolution, he argued, civilizations might very well establish a healthy stasis that would allow them to survive for eons. The hiccup for most civilizations was probably

---

* The concept helps explain why breakthrough innovations often are invented independently by multiple people around the same time—the knowledge and imagination to make the necessary leaps of creation come into view at similar times as other creations open up new avenues of knowledge. "The adjacent possible is a kind of shadow future, hovering on the edges of the present state of things, a map of all the ways in which the present can reinvent itself," science author Steven Johnson wrote. "[It] captures both the limits and the creative potential of change and innovation."

getting to that stasis in the first place, but once achieved there'd be nothing to stop it from surviving not just tens of millions of years, but hundreds of millions or even a billion years.

He showed Drake that if just 1 percent of alien civilizations made it to a billion years, the value of L would leap by orders of magnitude, soaring from ten thousand to ten million. "It makes a compelling argument to continue the search," the German asserted.

Others far from Green Bank agreed. In fact, as the 1960s unfolded, the search for extraterrestrial life was proceeding in the Soviet Union much faster than it was in the United States, seen by Soviet astronomers as another area of Cold War and space race competition in which the Soviets could potentially best the US. Astronomers and scientists had read Cocconi and Morrison's 1959 paper in *Nature*, and in 1962, as part of the celebrations marking the fifth anniversary of Sputnik, Soviet astronomer Iosif S. Shklovsky had published a book, *Universe, Life, Intelligence*, based on an article he had published in the Soviet journal *Nature* in 1960 about communicating with extraterrestrial civilizations.* The book was a huge success, selling out its entire initial fifty-thousand-copy print run in the Soviet Union, and was rushed into translation by NASA and delivered to curious US government agencies, including the CIA. "The early world-leading space exploration program was the most remarkable positive achievement of the USSR in the post–World War II period," noted one history of Russia's SETI efforts. "Not surprisingly, in those years, anything related to space used to attract a lot of attention in the USSR among scientists and general public alike."

Among the key differences between the US's and USSR's approaches to the UFO question was how the involvement of the scientist in the

---

* Shklovsky, one of the great characters of Soviet science, would later declare that he'd offered up the monograph in part because he assumed—rightly—that his colleagues were too busy and lazy and would never complete their own projects on time, thus limiting the ability of the editor and the space program's dedicated censor, a bureaucrat named Kroshkin—both facing an otherwise embarrassingly empty inbox in the run-up to an important milestone—to bury his provocative work. "Under normal circumstances . . . the book would run considerable risk of suppression," he wrote in his posthumous memoir.

quest was viewed. While Sagan, Drake, and others had to meet in near-secret to avoid ridicule, the fact that an astronomy luminary like Shklovsky would be curious about extraterrestrial intelligence largely legitimized focus on the field in the Soviet Union. Born in Ukraine to a rabbi, he hadn't finished middle school, and spent his teen years building railroads in Siberia. A talented artist—lacking paper or pencils, he'd started drawing on his family home's walls with coal—he'd never given much thought to science until the age of sixteen, when he read an article in a magazine on the discovery of the neutron. He was instantly fascinated, and found his way to the university in far-flung Vladivostok, where it was mandated that the twenty-five boys in his class study astronomy instead of physics. Later, married, poor, and desperate for a job, he pursued graduate work in astronomy that took him to Moscow; when World War II began, his poor eyesight saved him from conscription into the military and he ended up at the Sternberg Astronomical Institute rather than on the brutal front lines of the Nazi invasion.

By the mid-1940s, Shklovsky established a name for himself in the discipline when he predicted the existence of the hydrogen line, the twenty-one-centimeter part of the radio spectrum, a central discovery that would ultimately help astronomers map and understand the spiral shape of the Milky Way itself.* After reading the Cocconi and Morrison paper in 1959, he immediately understood that the hydrogen line might be a communication corridor for other civilizations, too.†

The following year, in 1960, Shklovsky and Sagan met for the first time at a gathering of the International Astronomical Union in Moscow. ("It was impossible not to like him—impossible not to be won over by

---

* As technology improved, Harvard astronomer Harold "Doc" Ewen would go on to make the first observations of the hydrogen line in 1952, an accomplishment that helped earn him his PhD with the shortest thesis ever from the Harvard physics department, just twelve pages.

† According to Sagan's biographer, the US scientist always suspected that Shklovsky's accomplishments went far deeper than the West realized, and that he had "invented a technique or device of military significance," perhaps a special radar system, that gave him unique contacts inside the defense establishment and protected him from political repercussions of his criticisms of the Soviet Union on human rights.

his warmth and optimism," Sagan recalled. "I thought he'd make a great maitre d'.") At first, neither of them realized the other was interested in extraterrestrial intelligence, but when Sagan learned of Shklovsky's forthcoming book, he made clear his desire to translate it into English for a general audience, beginning a yearslong collaboration. When *Universe, Life, Intelligence* was published stateside in 1966 as *Intelligent Life in the Universe*, it was a landmark achievement—Sagan made contributions that doubled the book's size, each addition with his name printed alongside to shield Shklovsky from Soviet censors. The book went through fourteen printings over the next decade, and many still consider it to be Sagan's best book, "a chance to write at length on his personal and passionate subject," his biographer noted.

In May 1964, the next major milestone in the US-USSR quest for intelligent life was reached when the Soviet Union hosted its own scientific gathering, known as the First All-Union Conference on Extraterrestrial Civilizations, at Armenia's Byurakan Astrophysical Observatory. There, over three days, perched on the southern side of the thirteen-thousand-foot Mount Aragats—and looking out at the distant Mount Ararat, the rumored resting place of Noah's ark—"Such a rare conference had to take place against the background of the ancient stones of Armenia, witness to bygone civilizations," Shklovsky wrote later—astronomers, physicists, and mathematicians debated the details of communicating with interstellar civilizations, from the likelihood of such civilizations existing to the question of what language might be shared, and adopted a resolution together "emphasiz[ing] that the problem of establishing contact with extraterrestrial civilizations is a perfectly mature and timely scientific problem." Together, they called for a systematic, experimental, and theoretical SETI study, and, in doing so, embraced the Cold War ethic underlying their work: Soviet philosophy, as they saw it, all but guaranteed the existence of other civilizations, as their Marxist "materialistic philosophy has firmly rejected the concept of anthropocentrism."

One of the conference's most notable presentations, many recalled, featured a star Shklovsky student named Nikolai Semyonovich Kardashev. Known as "Kolya" to his friends, the young astronomer was an unlikely success in the Soviet science system—his parents had been Bolshevik revolutionaries, arrested in Stalin's purge when Kardashev was five years old in the late 1930s. His father was executed and his mother spent nearly two decades in a forced labor camp; the aunt who eventually took him in died during World War II, forcing him to live on his own as a teen. By then, though, he'd fallen in love with astronomy, attending meetings at the Moscow Planetarium at as young as twelve, and his mind and hard work had delivered him to Moscow State University. By 1964 he possessed a PhD from the Sternberg Astronomical Institute.

Now, at the conference in Armenia, Kardashev proposed a three-tier scale to measure the relative sophistication and evolution of advanced civilizations. Later published that fall in a five-page article in the Soviet Union's main astronomical journal, it would come to be known globally as the Kardashev scale, one of the seminal brainstorms of its time.

Type I civilizations, Kardashev now explained, had harnessed all of the energy that reached the home planet—this was, in his mind, roughly where Earth was, though later scientists have refined and downgraded the scale to place Earth at about a .7 of a Type I civilization. Type II, meanwhile, had succeeded in harnessing the full energy of their local star. And Type III civilizations had harnessed all the power in their galaxy. Thinking in those rough orders of magnitude—mastery of a planet, a star, and a galaxy—helped explain the complexities of locating other civilizations and communicating with them.

It would be near impossible, Kardashev thought, for Earth to detect and communicate with another Type I civilization—like two fireflies blinking in the night hundreds or thousands of miles from one another—but signals from a Type II or Type III would be more visible, easily detectable, and potentially a huge boon to Earth's own development. More advanced civilizations' huge reserves of energy would presumably allow them to broadcast much stronger and much more consistent signals much more widely than Earth could imagine. In fact, it was entirely possible that Earth could hear from such a civilization without having the capability to send a response, he posited. It was of the "utmost importance," therefore, to expand Earth's listening program.

"Should there even exist one Type II civilization within the local system of galaxies, there will be a realistic possibility of securing an enormous quantity of information," Kardashev wrote. "It is entirely reasonable to assume that Type II and Type III civilizations would be in possession of information many orders of magnitude in excess of what we have available at the present time."*

In response to the conference in Armenia, the Soviet Academy of Sciences formally created a project called the Search for Extraterrestrial Civilizations, and named Kardashev vice-chair of the effort. In the new role, he was able to piece together a national network of Soviet antennas, stretching across 3,700 miles of the country from Vladivostok, near Japan, to Murmansk, near Finland, that filtered out earthly interference. He heard nothing that seemed alien, at first, but one signal consistently held his interest.

Kardashev had long been intrigued by the outputs from two star formations, known as CTA-21 and CTA-102, stars that he'd even singled out for further study in his paper outlining concepts for measuring advanced civilizations.† "It is speculated that even some sources known to us today (notably CTA-21 and CTA-102) may be artificial radio sources," he'd written in the Soviet astronomical journal in the wake of the Armenian conference. Perhaps, he wondered, were the powerful radio signals emanating from the stars actually signs of a Type II or Type III civilization that Earth hadn't recognized yet?

Now, with the broader resources available post-conference, Kardashev

---

* In the years ahead, other scientists—including Sagan—would add to and amend Kardashev's scale, suggesting the addition of other metrics and measurements. Sagan, for one, suggested adding a Type 0 classification, which would account for Earth and other less-developed worlds that hadn't even fully mastered their own energy sources. Physicist Michio Kaku later estimated that Earth might achieve full Type I status in the next century or two. "Growing at the average rate of about 3 percent per year, however, one may calculate that our own civilization may attain Type I status in about 100–200 years, Type II status in a few thousand years, and Type III status in about 100,000 to a million years." As Kaku wrote, "These time scales are insignificant when compared with the universe itself."

† The names of many celestial objects refer to official catalogs—in these cases, objects that had been recorded by a radio survey of the skies by Caltech, 21 and 102 representing the order in which the objects had been observed and recorded.

and other Soviet scientists, including another Shklovsky student, Gennady Sholomitsky, continued to study the puzzling stars, namely CTA-102. Using a secret Crimean military radar site, a deep-space telescope cobbled together with pieces of a Soviet battleship, a bridge, and the hull of an Italian submarine, Sholomitsky found remarkable results—the strength of the signal varied by nearly a third over just one hundred days, a then-unheard-of variance—and excitedly published them in an international astronomical telegram in February 1965, the then-standard tool for sharing observations and discoveries internationally.*

Though Sholomitsky's observations were accurate, the announcement of the findings quickly spiraled into chaos and confusion. At an April 1965 colloquium, a reporter for TASS—the Soviet state-run newswire service—heard Sholomitsky say that the signals from CTA-102, located in the Pegasus constellation, could be an advanced extraterrestrial civilization, effectively the same statement that Kardashev had printed in his original 1965 article, and on April 12, 1965, published a story titled "We Are Signalled by a Friendly Civilization." "Radio signals, detected from an object in space, might belong to the technology of a highly developed extraterrestrial civilization, declare Moscow astronomers," the report said, quoting Kardashev without nuance when it stated that "a supercivilization is discovered." Astronomers celebrated, believing they had made "one of the most outstanding discoveries in the history of radio astronomy," but none of the Soviet scientists had meant their comments to be as definitive as the selected quotes made it seem.

The breathless (and overhyped) news bulletin set off precisely the furor one might imagine, and at a hasty press conference the next day in Moscow, more than 150 foreign journalists pressed Shklovsky, Sholomitsky, and Kardashev for details. The trio did their best to downplay the

---

* Sholomitsky was limited, to some extent, by the military about what he could say about precisely what and how he'd made his observations. "Many of the details of Sholomitsky's observation were left out of the publication for security reasons, making it difficult for scientists in the West to verify his claimed results," astronomy historian Rebecca A. Charbonneau wrote, "and was upheld as an example of why Soviet science was untrustworthy, further cementing a culture of distrust between scientists on either side of the Iron Curtain."

conclusiveness of the research thus far, but it was too late.* For a few brief days, CTA-102 became the most famous astronomical phenomena in the world. On April 13, 1965, the potential contact ran on the front page of the *New York Times*, with a companion news analysis by the paper's leading science writer declaring that, if true, the discovery "could prove to be the most revolutionary event in human history."†

It was an embarrassing experience for all involved, and became even more so when Western scientists publicly doubted the TASS announcement—unbeknownst to the Soviet scientists, researchers at Caltech had discovered that CTA-102 was not a supercivilization, but instead a new kind of phenomena, known as a quasar, an extremely massive and extremely bright stellar object that emitted radio signals from the center of a far-off galaxy. "It is rather sad," the British astronomer Sir Bernard Lovell told reporters. "Russians are in some ways given to extravagant interpretations of their results."

---

* The elder Shklovsky even said his student Kardashev was filled with "adolescent optimism."

† The brief false alarm would go on to be immortalized in the rock band the Byrds' 1967 album, *Younger Than Yesterday*, in "C.T.A.-102," a song inspired by the band's lead guitarist Roger McGuinn, who was so fascinated by astronomy that soon after the incident, he attended one of Drake's lectures in California and invited Drake to join him that night at a star-studded Hollywood party. "I saw Jane Fonda wearing a fishnet non dress, and so many other movie stars in wild garb that my business suit and tie looked nothing short of weird," Drake recalled. "It was the first and only time in my life that I felt like an extraterrestrial."

The Socorro Incident

D espite the widening circles of global interest and the increasingly illustrious scientific names associated with the search for extraterrestrial intelligence, J. Allen Hynek still found the hunt for UFOs here on Earth an isolating experience—the subject still raised more eyebrows and snickers from "serious" scientists than Hynek felt he deserved, and, too often, he wasn't even sure how he felt about the entire phenomena himself. Whatever brusque dismissals he'd once been inclined to make at the start of his work with the air force had faded into more uncertainty as the years passed. It really seemed to him that there was something out there, mysteries he couldn't explain—"UFOs had been reported in more than 140 countries," his biographer later noted, "and there was confoundingly little variety in the types of objects reported: what witnesses described seeing in the skies above Rio were essentially identical to what was being reported by witnesses in Turkey, Canada, France, and Japan, as though they were all manufactured on the same UFO assembly line."

For Hynek, it often seemed like his book-lined home near the Northwestern campus in Evanston—the rooms piled high with classical records and old copies of the *New Yorker*—was the inner clubhouse of ufology, the one place where fresh sightings could be chewed over and discussed with full openness, and in the fall of 1963, he welcomed a new convert into the haven, a leading French astronomer named Jacques Vallée, who had long been fascinated by UFOs.

Vallée had once dabbled in science fiction—his first novel, *Le Sub-Espace*, published under a pseudonym in 1961, had even won the Jules Verne Award—but found the astronomy field in France too stifling. A move from Paris to Austin, Texas, in 1962 had offered an environmental paradise with huge butterflies and lots of woods, but still failed to deliver the intellectual jolt he wanted. "Professional astronomy is a field with only a small number of scientists who dislike each other and fight over tiny budgets, ignoring the big questions that are reshaping the world around them," he wrote in his journal that summer of '63. "They underestimate the potential of computers, a fast-changing technology to which I am increasingly attracted."

All around him, he could sense that the end of an era was coming in astronomy and planetary studies; in Austin, as he was working on a Mars mapping project, one that would be ten times more accurate than any map before it, he came to understand that, from this point forward, traveling space probes, orbiting satellites, and space-based telescopes would surely outclass in detail any work that could be done from inside the atmosphere. "The great tradition," he wrote, "which comes to us from Galileo and Kepler . . . ends in our machine." Moreover, he knew that he could never fully pursue his interest in UFOs in Austin—the observatory worked too closely with Harvard and "arch-skeptic" Menzel, and it would be too awkward for his colleagues. He had been fascinated with them since a major wave of sightings in France in 1954 that prompted hundreds of reports of a *cigare volant*, a "flying cigar," often with occupants inside. A Grenoble farmer spotted a glowing lighted engine moving quickly across the sky; beachgoers at Carry-le-Rouet saw a "half-cigar in the sky," belching smoke; a seaman in the Bay of Biscay saw a moving disk giving off a green glow; actress Michèle Morgan reported a glowing disk over the Paris airport.[*] French mathematician Aimé Michel had compiled the sightings as part of a hit book in France, *Flying Saucers and the Straight-Line Mystery*, but Vallée knew that even in the more comparatively intellectually open country, Michel had felt peer pressure to downplay the occupant sightings lest his reports be dismissed by scientists.

Vallée shared Hynek's wonderment at how uniform the sightings were. So many people in so many places reporting the same or highly

---

[*] Worried about the sightings and the potential for damaging the wine-making region's famous grape vines—or merely hungry for publicity—the mayor and village council in Châteauneuf-du-Pape had passed an ordinance amid the sighting wave prohibiting "the overflight, the landing and the takeoff of aircraft known as flying saucers or flying cigars, whatever their nationality is."

similar encounters couldn't all be making up the same thing, could they? Restless, Vallée had contacted the astronomer at Northwestern and flew out with his pregnant wife to Evanston to meet him. "[Our first meeting] lasted all day and into the whole of Sunday," Vallée recalled. "Above all I want to work closely with Hynek."*

Hynek felt the same way, and quickly secured an opportunity at Northwestern for the French scientist as a systems programmer, working with the new computers that so intrigued him. Less than a week after their first visit to Chicago, the Vallées were packing for Northwestern, and a month later settled into a three-bedroom apartment. Finally, Vallée thought, he'd found a place where he could be himself. In less than a month, Hynek enlisted him to start helping with Blue Book reports, and within their first month working together, they hosted the first meeting of what they called their UFO Committee, at Hynek's home, bringing together the small team of researchers who would push forward the study of what Vallée still wanted to brand "The Arnold Phenomenon."† As time went on, Vallée and Hynek became a dynamic team, the only scientists with direct access to the air force's official UFO records.

Hynek, meanwhile, found himself drawn even deeper into the intellectual aspect of the work—the puzzle at the heart of the sightings seemed just as challenging as ever. In January, he and Vallée met with Blue Book's Captain Hector Quintanilla, who had taken over the program that year and summed up his mission narrowly: "What are we looking for? Enemy prototypes, spy craft, anything unusual that we can understand in terms of technology." (Vallée was entirely unsure what the saucers were, just

---

* "He is a warm and yet a deeply scholarly man, with much energy and a great sense of humor, an open mind, and a deep sense of culture," Vallée wrote. "We are impressed by his sharp ideas and his eagerness for action. He has a lively face where piercing ideas are softened by a little goatee that makes it hard to take him completely seriously."

† Hynek's wife, Mimi, argued vociferously against Vallée that UFOs could or would ever be able to be studied seriously at a major university—the ridicule factor was just too high. Vallée remembered, "Hynek watched us fight, cleaned his pipe, and refilled it in silence. Wisely, he avoided getting into the dispute."

that they seemed worthy of scientific study that the air force wasn't interested in doing. "We only have vague theories about the nature and origin
of the saucers. . . . We could speculate that they may be coming from a
temporal rather than a spatial source," he mused. "The saucers observed
on the ground do not seem adapted to long-term interstellar flight as we
understand it.")

Even as the conversations evolved that winter, Hynek remained unsure, too, telling Vallée repeatedly, "All this is very interesting, but there
isn't any evidence here that I could take before the National Academy of
Sciences."

Then came the Socorro incident.

• •

On the afternoon of April 24, 1964, in Socorro, New Mexico, police officer Lonnie Zamora was in Cruiser 2, a white 1964 Pontiac, pursuing a
speeding Chevrolet—as a good local cop, he thought he recognized the
habitual seventeen-year-old speeder—when he "heard a roar and saw a
flame in the sky to the southwest some distance away—possibly a 1/2
mile or a mile." He immediately drove toward the sound of the explosion,
thinking it might have been a local dynamite shed, and as he arrived in
the desert he could see a flame.

When his cruiser was about 150 yards away, he spotted a metallic
object that he first judged to be a car on its side. Then, he saw "two figures in what resembled white coveralls, pretty close to the object on its
northwest side, as if inspecting it." The figures—he'd thought upon approach that they were young boys, given their size—turned at the sound
of his police car, and one "must have seen me, 'cause when I turned and
it looked straight at my car, it seemed startled—almost seemed to jump
somewhat." The terrain was uneven, and the object kept coming in and
out of view as he drove through dips, depressions, and rises. "10-44 [acci-
dent]," he radioed to his dispatcher. "I'll be 10-6 [occupied out of the car]
checking the car down in the arroyo."

As he got closer, though, the object looked more football-shaped and
aluminum-colored, rather than a car's standard chrome. It had red letter-
ing or an insignia of some kind, about two feet high on the side, but had

no visible doors or windows. He heard a couple quick loud thumps—
"like someone possibly hammering or shutting a door"—and then a load,
growing roar. "Flame was under the object. Object was starting to go
straight up—slowly up," he explained later. He turned and ran, unsure
what he was seeing or what was happening, and ended up colliding with
his own car, losing his glasses in the commotion. After running about
seventy-five feet and jumping over a hill, he heard the roar stop. "I lifted
up my head," he said, "and saw the object going away from me.

"It appeared to go in straight line and at same height—possibly 10
to 15 feet from ground," he recounted. "Object was traveling very fast. It
seemed to rise up, and take off immediately across country."

Zamora raced back to his cruiser and radioed a local amateur radio
operator, unsuccessfully asking him to look out his window and verify the
object, as it disappeared over the mountains. A New Mexico state police
sergeant, M. S. Chavez, arrived moments later and commented, "You look
like you've seen the devil."

"Maybe I have," Zamora said.

Socorro was near the northwest corner of the White Sands Missile
Range, and the sighting gained widespread attention—especially after
Chavez, Zamora, and other responding officers said they found seared
bushes and impressions in the desert where Zamora had seen the legs of
the object. The FBI began looking into the incident that night, and it was
reported to the local army commander. Neither White Sands nor nearby
Holloman Air Force Base had any operations that seemed to square with
what the officer had reported, but everyone involved had reason to trust
the account. The local FBI agent, who happened to be at the local office
of the New Mexico State Police when the sightings were called in, had
known Zamora for five years and reported to the bureau's headquarters
that he was "well regarded as a sober, industrious, and conscientious officer and not given to fantasy."

The local FBI agent responded to the scene that evening, as did
Captain Richard Holder with the army's military police, to search the
sighting's location by flashlight, and found disturbances in the dirt and
burned bushes. The FBI report described the four indentations as "sixteen by six inches rectangular," all "going into the earth at an angle from

a center line." The next morning, a colonel in the Pentagon's command center called unexpectedly and demanded Holder read his report out loud on the phone. (As he told an interviewer later, he always wondered, "Why in the world were they so interested?") The UFO community responded quickly: the day after the news broke, Coral and Jim Lorenzen—the APRO founders—were also in town, as was an investigator for Blue Book.

As word spread farther about the happenings in the New Mexico desert, Hynek, by chance, was with Vallée at Wright-Patterson wrapping up a two-day meeting with Blue Book's commander, Hector Quintanilla. (At the meeting, Vallée had been little impressed with the air force officer; the two couldn't even agree on music and spent the first evening of the visit arguing about the Beatles, which Quintanilla saw as too violent and encouraging the "wrong kind of behavior" in youth. "The attitude of the Air Force in the face of the phenomenon remains consistent: open and motionless, like a lazy schoolboy yawning in the back of the class," Vallée noted.) When the meeting was over, Quintanilla promptly dispatched Hynek to Socorro.

A local air force officer met Hynek in Albuquerque on the twenty-eighth to drive to Socorro, but their vehicle got a flat tire en route and Hynek hitchhiked the rest of the way by himself.* He thought that arriving alone would benefit him in the long run—Zamora and Chavez seemed wary of the military, and might be more likely to speak with him if he didn't arrive with an entourage. He was right. The next morning, they took him to the site of the "landing" (where they ran into a NICAP investigator doing his own report) to examine the gouges in the ground.

In a confidential memo afterward, Hynek observed, "Z. is an unimaginative cop of an old Socorro family, incapable of hoax, and pretty sore at being regarded as a romancer." He added, "There's never been a strong case with so unimpeachable a witness."

---

* As historian Jerome Clark notes, the "symbolism" of the flat tire and Hynek thumbing his way into a UFO sighting amid how underresourced Blue Book was by the 1960s amid the giant defense bureaucracy "seems a little too perfect."

The air force never figured out what was seen that day.* Writing in the CIA's own internal journal, *Studies in Intelligence*, Quintanilla would later conclude, "There is no doubt that Lonnie Zamora saw an object which left quite an impression on him. There is also no question about Zamora's reliability. He is a serious police officer, a pillar of his church, and a man well versed in recognizing airborne vehicles in his area. He is puzzled by what he saw, and frankly, so are we."

Despite the remarkable and widespread cooperation of government and private-sector industries in his probe, Quintanilla remained committed to the theory that Zamora had stumbled upon a secret experimental lunar lander being tested by the space program, though searches for more information and proof came up empty after contacting NASA and more than fifteen private-sector contractors. "During the course of the investigation and immediately thereafter, everything that was humanly possible to verify was checked," he wrote, explaining that they checked the scene with Geiger counters; analyzed soil; checked on possible launches with the Holloman Air Force Base's Balloon Control Center, as well as with local authorities; cross-checked helicopter and plane flights across New Mexico; interviewed personnel at the Pentagon and range controllers at White Sands, as well as "industrial companies engaged in lunar vehicle research activity." All to no avail. As Quintanilla wrote, "The findings were altogether negative."

Local legend eventually settled on an experimental aircraft from one of the nearby military bases as an explanation, but as Blue Books's leader then told the CIA, "This is the best-documented case on record, and still we have been unable, in spite of thorough investigation, to find the vehicle or other stimulus that scared Zamora to the point of panic."

The "unusual case," as historian David Jacobs wrote, "had important ramifications," including widespread public press attention and ongoing government puzzlement, but even as "by the end of 1964 the UFO

---

* Interestingly, one of the FBI reports on the incident, released only decades later, cites specifically that the sighting was not connected to Operation Cloud Gap, a then-classified military research project to determine the feasibility of dismantling nuclear weapons as part of a hypothetical arms control agreement. It's not clear why that specific military project, among all possible ones, was specifically ruled out.

controversy had reached a type of stalemate," with the unmoving tension between NICAP and Keyhoe on one side and government and the military on the other, Hynek "now came to virtually the opposite position to that which he had held when he started as an Air Force consultant in 1948." He was ready privately to accept some sensational cases as being legitimate mysteries—he couldn't get past why people like Officer Zamora, people with nothing to gain and much to lose from reporting an encounter, continued to come forward. What exactly they were seeing, well, he still didn't know. But he was more and more convinced they saw *something*.

Exploring Mars

As the 1960s began, it was time for mankind to finally explore Mars—and, again, the Cold War race was on for who would do so first. Mars, as our closest neighbor, has always held a specific fascination for earthlings. Records of observing the red planet go back some four thousand years, to both the early Egyptian astronomers on one side of the planet and Chinese astronomers on the other. Even then they understood Mars was somehow different—it and seven other celestial bodies moved against the backdrop of the rest of the stars—and its red light led the Chinese to call it the "fire star." The Greeks called the celestial object Ares, the name for their god of war, but later it was the Roman version of the name that stuck.

Throughout the 1500s and 1600s, scientists and astronomers Nicolaus Copernicus, Johannes Kepler, and Tycho Brahe all studied the planet; their observations reoriented how we understood the solar system and our own place in the heavens, namely that the sun did not revolve around us, we revolved around it. In 1610, Galileo Galilei looked at the red planet for the first time through a telescope, seeing in more detail than anyone ever before him. He had no idea what might lurk on it—or any other heavenly body. "If we could believe with any probability that there were living beings and vegetables on the moon or any planet, different not only from terrestrial ones but remote from our wildest imaginations," he wrote in 1612, "I should for my part neither affirm it nor deny it, but should leave the decision to wiser men than I." (It would be another almost half century before a Dutch astronomer, working with a more powerful convex telescope, was able to map the first surface feature on Mars, and another half century after that, a British Astronomer Royal, William Herschel, was finally able to identify its polar ice caps and apparent clouds.)

The planet fully came into mainstream public imagination when it reached its closest position to Earth, about 56 million kilometers, in the summer of 1877. Discoveries during that time abounded; the US Naval Observatory used its sixty-six-centimeter telescope to uncover two new Martian moons, and Italian astronomer Giovanni Schiaparelli went to the rooftop of the Brera Palace in Milan to sketch the planet through his own telescope, drawing the most detailed map to date. "During those nights up on the rooftop observing Mars, Schiaparelli noticed curious features crisscrossing dark patches—lines that would entrance and bedevil scientists for decades," planetary science professor Sarah Stewart Johnson later wrote. "He interpreted each dark patch to be a sea, 'the saltier the water, the darker it appears.' He conjectured that the lines linking them were waterways." He named the lines *canali*, an Italian word for "channels," but French astronomer Camille Flammarion began to popularize the notion that the lines were in fact canals—infrastructure like the Erie, Suez, and Panama projects, Earth's greatest engineering feats in the 1800s.

Across the Atlantic, American astronomer Percival Lowell had also spent some time considering the Mars question, imagining the lush vegetation that surely spread out from the irrigation and navigation canals. To learn more, he funded an elaborate new observatory in Arizona in May 1894 and set out on an effort to better map the pathways—and the more he studied them, the more convinced he became that the planet represented a unique, more advanced civilization. The canals went everywhere, apparently without borders, indicating a peaceful society that had solved Earth's geopolitical and warring rivalries. "The evidence of handicraft, if such it be, points to a highly intelligent mind behind it," Lowell wrote. "Party politics, at all events, have had no part in them for the system is planet wide. Quite possibly, such Martian folk are possessed of inventions of which we have not dreamed. . . . Certainly what we see hints at the existence of beings who are in advance of not behind us in the journey of life."

In 1895, Lowell outlined his thesis of an advanced civilization on our closest planetary neighbor in *Mars*, a book that experienced its own mini-phenomenon. As one of Lowell's reviewers wrote soon after the book came out, "The world at large is anxious for the discovery of intelligent life on Mars and every advocate gets an instant and large audience." His sheer confidence and exuberance in some ways was the greatest selling point for his theory—especially as his Martian maps proliferated. How could he be wrong if there were such detailed maps of the red planet's surface? Even as pieces of evidence from other astronomers accumulated that questioned whether Mars really was packed with advanced Martians, it was "Lowell's tour de force of popular science [that] would hold sway over the public for years," as Sarah Stewart Johnson wrote.

A few years later, one of the world's leading scientists took the discourse even further, revealing that he'd potentially received a message from Martians. Inventor Nikola Tesla, in 1899, had built a giant experimental laboratory in Colorado Springs, funded by J. Pierpont Morgan, to advance his new work in high-voltage electricity, and that December, as he was studying the wireless transmission of electricity, he was surprised to actually *receive* a signal on his transformer—a noise that was described as either a chirping or three distinct dots. "My first observations positively terrified me, as there was present in them something mysterious, not to say supernatural, and I was alone in my laboratory at night," Tesla recalled. "It was some time afterward when the thought flashed upon my mind that the disturbances I had observed might be due to an intelligent control." He said that he'd been later able to rule out that the signals were of earthly origin, leaving him even more sure that he'd made contact with a civilization beyond—especially since, as he saw it, there was no particular reason to imagine it would be technologically complicated to send a message from Mars or vice versa. As he wrote in 1901 in *Collier's Weekly*, "The feeling is constantly growing on me that I had been the first to hear the greeting of one planet to another."*

Tesla's suggestion that he'd heard from Mars did not seem like an "out of this world" proposition to many people at the time. Science fiction was a popular part of culture, and at the end of the nineteenth century "it was a popularly held belief among sane, educated, sensible people of Earth that

---

* There's good evidence that Tesla heard for the first time what later scientists now understand are "whistlers," basically faint electromagnetic echoes of far-off lightning flashes that spread through the Earth's magnetic field. One of Tesla's biographers has also posited that he heard something much more mundane: the three-dot Morse code *S* that his electricity and radio competitor Guglielmo Marconi was transmitting in Europe as part of his own experiments during the same period.

intelligent beings existed on the planet Mars." The more scientists—and the public—learned, Sarah Stewart Johnson wrote, the observations "all fit with the idea of Mars as another Earth, a planet with its own oceans to sail and lands to walk, a place we could recognize, relate, to, and imagine."

While subsequent astronomical observations in the twentieth century had increasingly cast doubt on the possibility of thriving Martian civilizations, more than a few scientists and astronomers held out hope that the space race of the 1960s might finally discover that vegetation or other more simple life-forms existed on our closest neighbor.

• •

As had been the case with the satellite contest, the Soviet Union was determined to make history first—and in 1960, as Premier Nikita Khrushchev was set to be appearing before the United Nations General Assembly, scientists readied two probes for launch, a dual display of the triumph for Soviet science; to hammer the point of victory home, the leader had had models created and sent for display in New York. As they saw it, they had always been one step ahead in the continuing march of space exploration dominance: Sputnik; the first space animal, the dog Laika; the first human, cosmonaut Yuri Gagarin; and the first woman, cosmonaut Valentina Tereshkova. Mars, naturally, would be next.

And then, the mission failed. Spectacularly. The first craft was destroyed in launch; the second made it 120 kilometers up before it, too, stopped working. The New York–bound models never saw the light of day, and Soviet scientists tried to cover up the evidence that they had not succeeded in their quest.* Two years later, three more flybys of the red planet were attempted. The first, known to the US as Sputnik 22, launched on October 24 amid global tensions over the Soviet missiles in Cuba, but exploded (causing quite the scare, as a US early-warning radar in Alaska picked up the falling debris and alerted incoming nuclear missiles), while the second, launched a week later, made it five months into

---

* This trip by Khrushchev is remembered for the "shoe-banging" incident, although it's not actually clear that Khrushchev ever actually banged his shoe in frustration, but the failure of the Soviet Mars mission was certainly part of his anger and frustration during the New York visit.

space and 100 million kilometers from Earth before the communications systems went silent, ninety days before it was supposed to reach Mars. The third exploded prematurely.

In 1964, it was the US's turn to make a move, and although its attempts at interplanetary study were barely more successful, it did by the narrowest of miracles manage to send a probe by Venus, known as Mariner 2. (Mariner 1, aiming for Venus, and Mariner 3, aiming for Mars, had failed.) On November 28, 1964—after hurried repairs to remedy the problems that doomed Mariner 3—Mariner 4, a 575-pound probe, filled with 168,000 parts, was at once cutting-edge and unbelievably primitive, with vacuum tubes, magnetic tape, and 28,224 solar cells that collectively provided just 310 watts of power—e.g., the equivalent of three 100-watt lightbulbs—lifted off successfully. It was a major scientific leap, using the star Canopus—the second-brightest star in the night sky—as a reference point for navigation, instead of locking onto Venus or Earth. Two days later, the Soviet Union launched the Zond-2 probe, which lost communication with Earth.

President Johnson touted the $83 million mission in his inaugural address: "Think of our world as it looks from that rocket that is heading toward Mars. It is like a child's globe, hanging in space, the continent stuck to its side like colored maps." As he saw it, the view from space should motivate a recommitment to the peace process on Earth: "We are all fellow passengers on a dot of earth," he said. "How incredible it is that in this fragile existence we should hate and destroy one another. There are possibilities enough for all who will abandon mastery over others to pursue mastery over nature. There is world enough for all to seek their happiness in their own way."

On July 14 and 15, Mariner 4 became the first spacecraft to photograph the red planet, skimming by at just six thousand miles above the surface and transmitting data back to Earth at just eight and a half bits per second, so slow that as the first images came in at NASA, scientists actually hand-colored the image themselves rather than wait for the official digital image to render—the first images came to life pixel by pixel on the wall with colored Rembrandt pastels purchased from a Pasadena art store. "Looking at a planet for the first time . . . that's not an experience people are likely to have very often in the history of the human race," one of the scientists, Bruce Murray, recalled. As staff waited and watched, a second image followed, then a third. Altogether twenty-one new low-resolution photos of the planet streamed slowly back to Earth—a total of just 634 kilobytes of data, about one-sixth the size of a single modern iPhone picture.

Once scientists had the chance to more closely examine the photos supplied of Mars, it didn't take long to see that earthlings had no neighbors. Mars's crust was barren—there was no sign of advanced life, no sign of the "canals," no evidence, in fact, of water of any kind. ("My God, it's the moon," one system engineer thought.) The meteorological sensors on Mariner 4 found only the scantiest atmosphere and bone-crushingly cold surface temperatures.

Standing in the East Room of the White House at a press conference with NASA scientists seven months after the optimism of his inaugural, LBJ started the briefing about the mission with some humor at his own expense. "As a member of the generation that Orson Welles scared out of its wits, I must confess that I am a little bit relieved that your photographs didn't show more signs of life out there," he began, before shifting courses: "It may just be that life as we know it, with its humanity, is more unique than many have thought." The next day's *New York Times* filled nearly a quarter of its front page with a photo of the red planet's craters, declaring them "a heavy, perhaps fatal, blow . . . to the possibility that there is or once was life on Mars."

• •

Though the Mars missions had largely been a disappointment, there was a silver lining to renewed attention on the space program—after a decade of relative stasis in the government's hunt for UFOs and study of flying saucers, the period from 1964 to 1967 saw a wave of fresh, high-profile sightings and growing outside pressure for a reinvigorated study of the unexplained phenomena in our skies. "Those who had been on the periphery of the controversy became actively engaged in it," historian David Jacobs writes. "The press, public, Congress, and the scientific community all entered the debate over UFOs."

A year after the Socorro incident, ATIC, operating Blue Book in a highly diminished capacity (at that point, almost everything was investigated over the phone), was steadily receiving about thirty to fifty sightings a month, about a sighting or two a day. The summer of 1965, in particular, saw a flurry of nearly four hundred cases in July and August. One night, multiple people in Sherman, Texas, reported a large glowing object hanging in the sky, and a news photographer, who had been listening to the police radio dispatches, rendezvoused with the local police chief and photographed the object in the skies north of Dallas. "The picture was overexposed, possibly due to the brilliance of the UFO," a report read, but witnesses later described the object as "a cylinder with 'Mercury capsule' shape at one end, possibly rounded at other end. Several distinct bands around the diameter of cylinder, with disc shaped 'bosses' on surface. Bands of luminosity."

That sighting and others that summer attracted press attention, and as reports mounted, the public's patience with the air force's usual talking points seemed to run thin. "Something is going on 'up there' and we rather suspect the Air Force knows it," the *Charleston Evening Post* wrote in an editorial. "Maybe it's time for more people to get serious about the UFO question," the *Denver Post* agreed in the days after the Sherman sighting. "If we still choose to be skeptical, we nevertheless are not nearly so ready as we once were to dismiss all reports of variously shaped but elusive flying objects as products of midsummer night dreams"; "They can stop kidding us now about there being no such thing as 'flying saucers.' . . . Too many people of obviously sound mind saw and reported them independently. . . . Their descriptions of what they saw were too similar to one another, and too unlike any familiar object," concluded the *Fort Worth Star-Telegram*.

Even some who had dismissed earlier sightings remarked that their continued presence had made them reconsider their earlier positions on the issue: I. M. Levitt, the director of the Fels Planetarium, who had been part of the community in 1952 that dismissed the "Washington Merry-Go-Round" sightings as just normal radar interference amid summer temperature inversions, now publicly stated his belief that "there are natural phenomena taking place under our noses of which we know nothing. . . . The Air Force is trying to explain something that isn't susceptible to explanation."

That fall, another high-profile incident in Exeter, New Hampshire, raised further questions about the US government's commitment to serious UFO investigation. On September 3, two civilians reported spotting a large hovering object with blinking lights, a claim supported by the two investigating patrolmen who were dispatched to the scene, and encountered "this huge, dark object as big as a barn over there, with red flashing lights on it." One officer drew his revolver, but decided against attempting to shoot it, and retreated. Eventually, it flew away. The Exeter police reported the sighting to the nearby Pease Air Force Base, who sent officers to interview the witnesses, but ultimately came up short of a rational explanation. "At this time I have been unable to arrive at a probable cause of this sighting," an officer reported back to the Pentagon. "The observers seem to be stable, reliable persons, especially the two patrolmen. I viewed the area of the sighting and found nothing in the area that could be the probable cause. Pease AFB had five B-47 aircraft flying in the area but I do not believe that they had any connection with this sighting."

Quickly—too quickly, some would argue—both the air force and Project Blue Book came out with separate and conflicting reasons for the incident. The air force blamed a temperature inversion, while Blue Book's Hector Quintanilla (now newly promoted to a major) suggested that the confusion had been caused by a nighttime aerial refueling operation conducted by Strategic Air Command bombers in the night sky. The responding officers took umbrage at the approach, writing repeated (and unanswered) letters articulating the "considerable trouble" they went to on their own that night to confirm that their sighting wasn't mistaken. The so-called Incident at Exeter was closed, but unlikely, many realized, to be forgotten—as researchers and advocates of the UFO persuasion emerged, ready to reengage.

··

J. Allen Hynek, for his part, was ready to push the air force for more thoughtful engagement and resources, suggesting the military convene a team of outside scientists "to see whether a major problem really exists."

The idea ultimately helped nudge the service's head of information, General E. B. LeBailly to recommend the creation of what would be known as the Ad Hoc Committee to Review Project Blue Book, and a one-day panel was set for February 3, 1966, chaired by the founder of the Air Force Studies Board, Brian O'Brien, and featuring a coterie of esteemed experts, including astronomer Carl Sagan, former air force chief scientist Launor F. Carter, military psychologist Jesse Orlansky, rocket scientist Richard Porter, and computing pioneer Willis H. Ware. The group convened at 8 a.m. and spent the morning with two briefings on the air force's UFO study and Blue Book, as well as a ninety-minute review of selected case histories. They broke for lunch at 11:45 a.m., and were expected to write their conclusions by 1:15 p.m.

Given the tight time frame and the truncated briefings, it's perhaps no surprise that the findings mirrored those of the Robertson Panel a dozen years before. "In 19 years and more than 10,000 sightings recorded and classified, there appears to be no verified and fully satisfactory evidence of any case that is clearly outside the framework of presently known science and technology," the ad hoc committee concluded. "Nevertheless, there is always the possibility that analysis of new sightings may provide some additions to scientific knowledge of value to the Air Force"—to that end, they suggested that focus on the UFO question be moved out of the realm of national security and "strengthened to provide opportunity for scientific investigation of selected sightings in more detail and depth than has been possible to date." They also suggested that perhaps one hundred sightings a year, the strangest and most unknown, might be subjected to a close study by air force intelligence and a university-led team made up of multidisciplinary experts from around the country, including clinical psychologists, physical scientists, and astronomers seeking to "bring to light new facts of scientific value." Reports, they also suggested, should be made publicly available and "given wide unsolicited circulation" among members of Congress and other opinion leaders,* which would

---

* UFO researchers have obtained over the years three slightly different copies of the O'Brien committee's final report, the major difference being that a master copy had an "Appendix I," not released to the public, that included three additional recommendations: a study of false radar sightings by NORAD, the air force's North

ensure deeper study of the more valuable and scientifically interesting cases, while removing the work from the uncomfortable—and seemingly counterproductive—veil of military secrecy.*

While the committee's report was general and brief, it's hard not to see Sagan's fingerprints all over it. As the youngest member and the only one who wasn't part of the air force's scientific advisory board, his ability to direct the trajectory of the discussion signaled an important shift in the collective outlook on the issue, and a personal investment in the cause. Indeed, Sagan's views of UFOs and their place in the current political landscape had been deeply informed by his own encounter with one. One night after giving one of his popular lectures at Harvard and fielding audience questions about UFOs, he'd hurried outside to dinner, only to run into two policemen on the street pointing at the sky, where "a strange brilliant light mov[ed] slowly overhead." He'd kept walking—in part to escape the audience trickling out after him, who would surely ask him more questions—but when he got to the restaurant, the light was still there. "There's something terrific outside," he told his friends, and the group quickly piled out to the sidewalk and watched the object, "slowly moving, fading and brightening, no sound attached to it." When someone produced binoculars, though, it was determined that the seemingly celestial event was nothing more than a high-flying NASA weather plane.

"The uniform response was disappointment," Sagan recalled, but the experience itself, the possibility it held, had been perspective-shifting. "That's not a memorable story. But suppose no one had a pair of binoculars. Then the story goes, 'There was this great light out there and it was circling the city and we don't know anything about it. Maybe it's visitors from somewhere else.' That's a story worth talking about. Despite the

---

American air defense system; a few experiments involving unannounced balloon launches or air force refueling exercises and then tracking the subsequent associated "UFO" reports; and finally, more involvement with local police and participation by the FBI in UFO investigations, although the committee noted, "This might involve problems or difficulties not within the knowledge of the Committee."

* Jacques Vallée was less sanguine about the O'Brien committee: "In spite of our progress with the day-to-day research I have reached a pessimistic conclusion: Nothing significant is going to happen here. The Air Force has other fish to fry."

novelties of our times, there is a kind of drudgery to everyday life that cries out for profound novelties; and the idea of extraterrestrial visitation is a culturally acceptable novelty." More and more, he had come to realize that his scientific work didn't exist in a vacuum—there were tinges and threads of human psychology and geopolitics that influenced almost everything he and his colleagues did. That belief was only strengthened by an experience when he was invited by the air force to meet a visiting Soviet science delegation that included Alexander Imshenetsky, one of its leading voices on extraterrestrial life. After a day of conversations about the process for detecting life and how best to sterilize the growing number of earthly probes headed into outer space, Sagan learned the secret of the Soviet program: they'd sterilized their Lunik 2 probe with a mix of formaldehyde and superheated steam. Later, while bidding goodbye to the delegation, an American translator—purportedly a staffer from the Library of Congress—complimented Sagan on his good intelligence gathering and asked who Sagan worked for. With a start, the astronomer realized that the person who had been shadowing him all day was likely a US intelligence officer.

The next day, Sagan called the San Francisco office of the CIA to complain about the spy's intrusion on a peaceful science delegation, but the CIA disavowed any knowledge of an interloper. Over several days and with a rising degree of alarm, agency officers repeatedly returned to speak with Sagan, trying to discern if there had been an impostor, a double agent, or anyone interfering with intelligence gathering. Finally, after two weeks of research, an answer emerged: the translator had been an undisclosed, undercover intelligence officer in the air force.[*] The two institutions had not communicated with one another. For Sagan, the episode was quite a jolting reminder that his happy-go-lucky life of astronomical inquiry held very real implications down on Earth.

---

[*] Two years later, at another international space conference in Florence, Imshenetsky and Sagan stumbled upon a familiar face, now sporting a beard, during a tour of the Uffizi for the conference-goers. Standing in a gallery of Botticellis, Imshenetsky said, "Isn't that the fellow who was with us in Los Angeles?" Sagan nodded. "Very stupid fellow," the Soviet scientist opined.

1

Air Force intelligence officer Jesse Marcel poses with debris from the "flying disc" in Roswell.

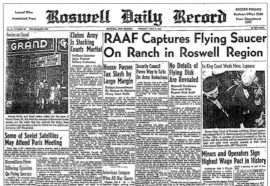

2

3

It was Kenneth Arnold's June 1947 sighting that kicked off the national craze—a story he'd famously retell in *Fate* magazine.

4

5

Major Donald Keyhoe would become convinced the government was hiding the truth about flying saucers.

6

7

Capt. Edward Ruppelt (*standing, center*) would become the face of Project Blue Book.

8

For decades, Wright-Patterson Air Force Base in Ohio was the center of the government's UFO tracking.

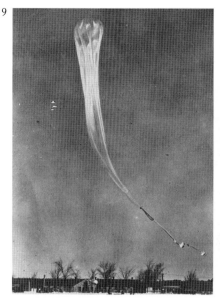 

Many UFO sightings in the late 1940s and 1950s later turned out to be Skyhook balloon launches, including, left, a balloon launched from Minnesota's Camp Ripley that Capt. Thomas Mantell died chasing.

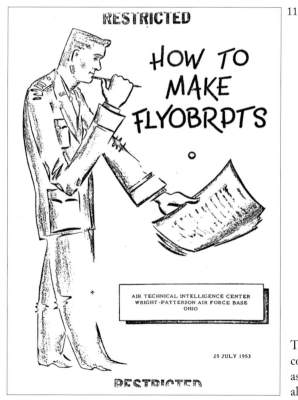

The Air Force tried to collect as many sightings as it could in the 1950s—although most it dismissed.

12

"Contactee" George Adamski poses with a painting of the alien woman he said visited him.

13

Police officer Lonnie Zamora's sighting in Socorro, New Mexico, baffled Blue Book investigators.

The US military briefly tried to build its own flying saucer, codenamed Project 1794, but it barely ever got off the ground—literally.

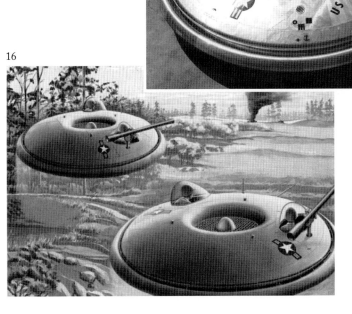

J. Allen Hynek considered his "swamp gas" press conference in Michigan his lowest professional moment; there, the Dexter, Michigan, sheriff shared his sighting.

17

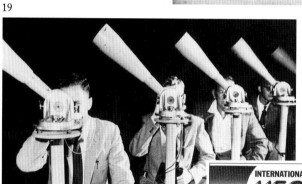

19

18

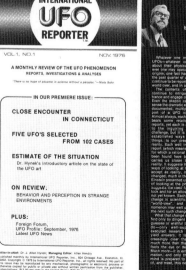

20

Hynek's "Operation Moonwatch" relied on civilian volunteers all over the world to track the early satellites, like Sputnik.

Hynek's *International UFO Reporter* would become one of the field's bibles.

Frank Drake's Project Ozma efforts at the Green Bank observatory led the way for SETI.

22

21

The equipment used for Ozma hardly looked exotic.

23

24

Otto Struve, mentor to both Hynek and Drake.

Edward Condon

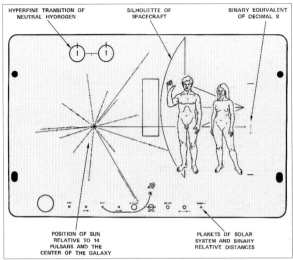

Frank Drake and Carl Sagan helped place a primitive drawing aboard the Pioneer spacecraft they hoped would communicate about Earth if any alien found it.

The Arecibo message consisted of 1,679 binary digits that could be translated into information about Earth.

26

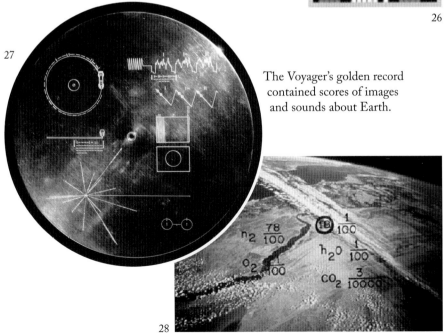

The Voyager's golden record contained scores of images and sounds about Earth.

27

28

Swamp Gas

Aside from perhaps rock and roll, no industry was more pervasive or impactful throughout the early years of the 1960s than aliens-as-entertainment. TV shows like *The Twilight Zone*, which ran for five seasons on CBS from 1959 to 1964, and *The Outer Limits*, a similar series that ran for forty-nine episodes from 1963 to 1965, kept the strange and paranormal front and center in popular culture, as did new literature by emerging figures in the discussion. One, writer and TV producer John Fuller, would become particularly notable, as he spent the month following the Exeter incident embedded in the New Hampshire community, interviewing witnesses and reviewing NICAP's investigation, piecing together the puzzle of what had happened in the skies over several nights. To him, it didn't seem likely that just air force tankers and refueling operations from the nearby Pease Air Force Base had been the source of disruption. He wrote an article for the *Saturday Review*, and expanded it into *Incident at Exeter*, which would become a standard text in the UFO canon, in part because after years of battling books seemingly of all the same voices—Keyhoe and the contactees on one side and "serious" scientists like Menzel on the other—Fuller's work appeared "sober, well written, well researched, and nonsensational."

He also helped capture and shape an evolving public curiosity, and concern about the lack of solid investigation and answers. "The unwillingness of government and of organized science to concede that anything is unknown has heightened popular anxiety," Harvard historian Oscar Handlin noted in his review of Fuller's book in the *Atlantic Monthly*. "To dismiss out of hand the evidence for the UFOs will not quiet the fears that we may be living through the first stages of exploration from elsewhere."

Handlin was right. With the idea of alien interaction—or, at worst, invasion—more solidly rooted in cultural consciousness, more and more scientists were taking the question of extraterrestrial intelligence and un-known natural phenomena seriously, with public debates at conferences—even the prestigious journal *Science* changed its publication policy in 1966 to allow debate about UFOs in its pages—and more newspapers beginning to openly question the reasons for all the mystery.* In a six-part series about Blue Book and the nationwide rise in sightings, the *Portland Evening Express* declared that the air force's "persistent endeav-ors to explain all the UFO sightings as misidentifications of ordinary objects, such as stars and balloons, has become so conspicuous as to raise questions in the minds of a growing number of citizens. Some of these explanations seem to run counter to both logic and common sense. Running along with these explainings-away is an apparent Air Force lack of enthusiasm—especially at high levels—to do a thorough job of investigating sightings."

James Moseley, the editor of *Saucer News*, also had felt the ground shift: since the Zamora sighting, interest in his work had steadily grown, and by 1966 his list of paying subscribers contained nearly eight thou-sand names. Regular radio attention on shows like New York host Long John Nebel's nightly talk-a-thon also kept up public interest. "For anyone who didn't live through it, it is hard to imagine just how widespread and intense saucer excitement was during the mid- and late 1960s," Moseley remembered. "For the first time since 1953, saucering was profitable."

Amid this shift in opinion the nation experienced one of the high-est-profile—and consequential—sightings of the decade, as nearly one hundred students at the Hillsdale College in Michigan watched a glow-ing object hover over a swampy area outside McIntyre Hall, its women's dormitory. Over the course of some four hours, the local civil defense

---

* These changes happened in part because the UFO debate was seemingly increas-ingly inescapable; the editors of *Science* and newspaper reviewers saw the sustained sales and multiple printings of a score of new UFO books that poured into the marketplace in the late 1960s, including new offerings from Keyhoe, Frank Scully (he of the previous *Behind the Flying Saucers* hoax), and Jim and Coral Lorenzen, as well as Hynek's rising-star student Jacques Vallée, whose works *Anatomy of a Phe-nomenon* and *Challenge to Science* would also prove to be thoughtful, lasting classics in the field.

director and local police also saw the object, which seemed to dim and brighten as automobiles approached and left.

"We saw a real brilliant light in the sky at a low altitude," Officer Harold Hess recounted years later. "You couldn't look at it, it was so bright. It wasn't a chopper. There was no humming." Nervous, Hess took his weapon out of its holster, but his partner chided him that surely a mere pistol was going to be ineffective at whatever they encountered: "Whatever it is, I don't think it'll bother it one bit what you've got at your side."

The next night, just about sixty miles away, in Dexter, Michigan, five other people, including two police officers, reported seeing a similar glowing object over a farmer's field. The back-to-back sightings, so geographically close and seen by so many people, quickly attracted national attention, and forced Blue Book to get involved. "All three networks are talking nothing else" one air force officer explained. "The brass is having a fit."*

In response, J. Allen Hynek was dispatched to handle the case. Lately, Hynek had seen his public profile and day-to-day work become increasingly dominated by UFOs—his family Christmas tree was decorated with lights in the shape of flying saucers—but the environment into which he arrived in Michigan was unlike anything he'd experienced before. Crisscrossing the area in a government jeep with a military escort, he found himself often competing with journalists to interview witnesses. Recollections weren't particularly consistent and he soon realized that aside from the sheer number of witnesses involved, there was nothing any more compelling and intriguing than what he already had in his files in Michigan. When he was given a photograph of the glowing light, he could immediately tell that it was simply the moon and Venus rising together in the sky. There was also a clear and genuine fear permeating the region, which made it "impossible for me to do any really serious investigation," he later explained. On one of his first nights, he found himself in a local police car in a high-speed pursuit of another reported sighting; multiple squad cars chased the supposedly moving object until they all convened at a single intersection. "Men spilled out and pointed excitedly at the sky,

---

* The *Washington Post* headline said, "First UFOs of the Season Are Sighted," and began, "Spring's first flying saucers have sprouted right alongside the forsythia."

'See—there it is! It's moving,'" Hynek recalled. "But it wasn't moving. 'It' was the star Arcturus, undeniably identified by its position in relation to the handle of the Big Dipper." He noted, "A sobering demonstration for me." "So far," he said at the time, "all I've been able to come up with is reports of a variety of lights."

Matters were only made worse when, over the course of his visit, Hynek was pressured into holding a press conference to share his impressions; standing at a bank of microphones in the Detroit Press Club, he faced a "circus," the largest gathering of journalists the venue had ever seen. He knew in his heart that he hadn't had time to investigate thoroughly but was equally aware that people wanted answers. Half-heartedly, he settled on a theory that had been shared with him by a University of Michigan botanist: burning "swamp gas," a mixture of methane, carbon dioxide, and phosphine, among other elements, that emerged from the rotting vegetation that covered wet, swampy lands, was known to spontaneously ignite, casting an eerie flickering light in the dark marsh night. Hynek had followed up with a few other Michigan scientists, who confirmed that swamp gas was a possibility, especially given that the sightings had occurred during the spring thaw, as rotting and decomposing vegetation emerged from the ice.

"Swamp gas" it was. "It would seem to me that the association of the sightings with swamps, in these particular cases, is more than coincidence," he told the reporters.

While the media ran with the explanation nationally—newspapers and magazines would run mocking cartoons and editorials about it for decades—no one in Michigan believed it for a second. "I'm just a simple fellow, but I seen what I seen and nobody's going to tell me different," said a Dexter witness named Frank Mannor. "That wasn't no old foxfire or hullabillusion. It was an object"; the *Ann Arbor News*'s story the next day reported that Hynek's reaction "sent tempers flaring and triggered angry reactions" from people questioning his findings, including the local sheriff. Hynek fled as quickly as he could.

It was perhaps the astronomer's lowest moment in the entirety of his UFO experience, but the situation resulted, inadvertently, in a small bit of progress on Capitol Hill: intrigued by what was happening in his home state, House Republican leader Gerald Ford, along with another

Michigan congressman, Weston Vivian, called on the Armed Services Committee to open the first-ever hearings on UFOs.* Ford acknowledged his "special interest" in the subject, and the possible controversy it would create—"I am most serious about this; but, of course, this is the kind of subject that lends itself to some flak," he admitted in a weekly radio address to his district—but, as he told reporters, he had not been satisfied with Hynek's explanation, particularly after receiving a wave of telegrams from UFO believers and sightings, and reading press columns that called for a more objective analysis of the air force's work behind closed doors. "We owe it to the people to establish credibility regarding UFOs and to produce the greatest possible enlightenment on this subject," he wrote in a statement for hometown media. "Are we to assume that everyone who says he has seen UFOs is an unreliable witness?"†

• •

Ford's intention was noble, but after so many years of waiting, Hynek, Keyhoe, and the others who had pressed the government forward found the resulting hearing on April 5, 1966, to be nothing more than deeply frustrating. The briefings primarily consisted of Hynek's report on the Michigan swamp gas sightings and the O'Brien committee's finished report suggesting a new phase of university-focused research, a small fraction of the existing body of research and reports,‡ and the structure seemed tailor-made to avoid the possibility that the inquiry would pry

---

* UFOs became something of a running theme in Ford's press comments at the time. When the White House's latest inflation numbers came out, Ford cracked, "Acting like the Air Force with flying saucer reports, Johnson administration economists are trying to explain about the 0.5 of one per cent increase in the consumer price index for February."

† The quick, dismissive, and seemingly ridiculous verdict led the community to turn on their witness: Vallée recorded that the main witness faced "ridicul[e] and harass[-ment] in his own community. Overnight his neighbors vandalized his house, broke his windows, threw stones on his car, and phoned at all hours to call him 'Head Martian!'"

‡ NICAP submitted voluminous materials and sighting reports to the committee, which ended up comprising the majority of the hearing's eighty-seven-page transcript, but there was no actual testimony from pro–saucer believers.

loose new facts. Adding insult to injury, only three witnesses—three!—were called to answer questions and provide insight: air force secretary Harold Brown, Blue Book head Major Quintanilla, and Hynek himself.

"Let me assure you that the Air Force is both objective and thorough in its treatment of all reports of unusual aerial objects over the United States," Brown said. "Although the past 18 years of investigating unidentified flying objects have not identified any threat to our national security, or evidence that the unidentified objects represent developments or principles beyond present-day scientific knowledge, or any evidence of extraterrestrial vehicles, the Air Force will," he promised, "continue to investigate such phenomena with an open mind and with the finest technical equipment available." It was a powerful declaration, but any hope Hynek, Keyhoe, or others held of a formal military or scientific inquiry was dashed when the chairman, Representative L. Mendel Rivers, asked whether "anybody, in authority or of stature, allege that these things, whatever they may be, have come from other planets or from somewhere outside of this universe?"

"I know of no one of scientific standing or executive standing, or with a detailed knowledge of this, in our organization who believes that they come from extraterrestrial sources," Brown replied. Denial and dismissal once again.

Hynek tried to salvage things, taking time in his statement to emphasize twenty "well-reported UFO cases" that he hadn't been able to explain yet—not because he didn't have any ideas, but because the reason for the oddities may simply lie beyond the boundaries of science. "In dealing with the truly puzzling cases, we have tended either to say that, if an investigation had been pursued long enough, the misidentified object would have been recognized, or that the sighting had no validity to begin with," Hynek said. "The UFO public, on the other hand, is equally prone to poverty of hypotheses: Either UFOs mean utter bilge and nonsense, or they jump to the far-out conclusion that the earth is host to space visitors. Surely, in scientific fairness, we must examine other hypotheses."

Later, he added, "Puzzling cases exist, but I know of no competent scientist who would say that [these] objects come from outer space."

"Then what you are looking for is an explanation in natural phenomena, [but] thus far you have not determined the factors involved in it?" Congressman Bates queried.

"Yes," Hynek answered simply.

One by one, over the hour-long hearing, the congressmen called for more serious attention to the UFO situation. "In seriousness, the people in Vermont are very much concerned over the sightings that have occurred in our State," Representative Robert Stafford said, "and reputable people have seen phenomenon which they cannot understand," a sentiment that was roughly echoed in testimony and statements by representatives from a half-dozen other states. At the end of the hearing, Brown adjourned the gathering with a statement that he planned to move forward with the O'Brien committee's recommendation to embrace a deeper university-led study.

A few weeks later, in May 1966, national attention still high, Walter Cronkite hosted a special documentary titled *UFOs: Friend, Foe, or Fantasy*. Featuring many of the topic's well-known names, including Menzel and Keyhoe, the show was mainly comprised of interviews with attendees at the contactees' Giant Rock convention, various radar operators, astronomers, and government officials. "The theme of the show came across clearly: UFOs were misidentifications, delusions, hoaxes, and products of the will to believe and of societal stress," historian David Jacobs observed. Cronkite, though, seemed to offer a more hopeful note at the end of the broadcast, reminding viewers that "Yesterday's fantasy is tomorrow's reality."

That summer a Gallup poll found that nearly half of Americans—46 percent—felt flying saucers were real. A new era of the UFO had begun.

The UFO Gap

Heightened visibility and support of UFO research in the wake of the Michigan hearings helped the cause in some ways, but were ultimately detrimental in others—including the constant scrutiny faced by scientists and researchers who were often left alone to defend themselves. Hynek, particularly in the aftermath of the Michigan incident, was starting to find the UFO hunt both mentally and emotionally exhausting and isolating. "There were times when I would get a simply marvelous and tremendous case and then a whole run of terribly bad cases, like a gambler who suddenly has a run of bad cards, case after case of nothing, and I said, 'Well, it looks like it is full of nonsense after all,' and I would go down into a UFO depression phase, and a few weeks later a hot case would come in and the barometer would go zooming up again," he recalled years later. Even teamed up with Vallée, he often felt that he was a lone traveler, constantly mitigating his personal interests and professional trajectory— with his own career still on the rise, he knew he could never be quite as honest as he wanted about what he believed if he wanted to maintain his position in projects like the Smithsonian satellite tracking project, which had been brought to him because he was a "serious" scientist. He was also conscious of the fact that he was already on the outside of astronomy's inner circle—"Ohio State is not Harvard," he noted, bluntly—and didn't want to further push his luck. He'd seen much more powerful men falter when it came to this issue: NICAP's board member, Admiral Roscoe Hillenkoetter, had been just as unsuccessful at pushing for in-depth congressional hearings—and if a former CIA director couldn't move the levers of power in Washington, how could anyone expect him to?

After his latest appearance in Michigan, Hynek had become the target of public ire, and individuals seeking answers about UFOs and lack of government action thought nothing of confronting him. In June of 1966, an atmospheric physics professor from the University of Arizona showed up in his Evanston office unannounced, full of anger that Hynek wasn't doing more to force science and the military to deal more directly with the mysteries of UFOs.

The unexpected visitor, forty-five-year-old James McDonald, had spotted a UFO in 1954 while driving with four other meteorologists in the desert outside Tucson. No one in the car could identify it—a bright object in the skies over the Santa Rita Mountains to the south—and later, the university's astronomy department would assure him that, direction-ally, it was impossible that it was a star or planet. When McDonald re-ported the incident to the air force, he received only a note thanking him for "such a thorough account from an expert observer."

The polite rejections had little impact. That spring, in the wake of the O'Brien committee meeting, McDonald contacted Brian O'Brien to sug-gest an academic, summerlong study of the military's old UFO reports; with O'Brien's encouragement and endorsement, he was able to finagle his way into the Blue Book files at Wright-Patterson and got a $1,300 grant from NASA to dive in. Sorting through the files, sightings, witness accounts, and the government reports, he became convinced there was more to the subject than he'd ever understood—and more than the public had been told. "You've been involved in a foul-up," he told the Blue Book team after reading the full, unredacted version of the Robertson Panel report (the first nongovernment individual to do so). Using his high-level contacts he arranged a meeting directly with the base's commanding gen-eral during which he lit into the official, telling him repeatedly during a forty-five-minute meeting that the air force's efforts were a joke at best.

Now, as he walked along the lake edge outside the Lindheimer Ob-servatory with Hynek and met up with Vallée and a grad student, he continued to expel his frustrations, accusing the men of being at least partially responsible for a nearly two-decade-long cover-up. "The expla-nations [are] pure bullshit," McDonald said. "How could you remain si-lent so long?"*

---

* "This man has many contacts, many ideas, and is afraid of nothing," Vallée noted in his journal.

For Hynek, the verbal assault was something of a relief, and an opportunity. Instead of turning McDonald away, he spent hours in his office and over lunch with him, articulating his own issues with the process and offering opinions on the air force's string of unserious and disinterested Blue Book leaders—namely Ruppelt's replacement, who Hynek thought had coasted to retirement in the role, while only caring about monitoring the stock market (after leaving the military, he'd quickly opened a brokerage office). The conversation, Hynek recalled, was "like taking off a pair of very tight shoes." Even if McDonald thought he hadn't done everything quite right, just the experience of having a sympathetic ear had been invigorating.

In the days after the visit, Hynek traveled to New York and met with John Fuller, the author of the book on the Exeter incident, and UN Secretary-General U Thant, who was curious about the government's approach to UFOs, in large part due to his faith.

"I am a Buddhist," he told Hynek during their chat. "We believe there is life throughout the universe."

"Most astronomers would agree with you," Hynek said. "The question is to know how 'they' would ever come here, given the enormous distances involved."

"Perhaps their lifespan is measured in centuries rather than years," the diplomat replied. "Coming here could be as simple for them as going around the block is simple for us."

• •

Though McDonald was convinced that the military had largely decided to willingly disengage from the UFO discussion, the air force and government had, in fact, been working for months to find a university interested in partnering on the more in-depth study called for by the O'Brien committee. After Harvard, MIT, and the Universities of California and North Carolina all declined,* officials finally found the initiative a home

---

* Northwestern University had actually been interested in hosting and Hynek had enlisted Lyle Boyd, Menzel's regular skeptic coauthor to lead the project with him, but to Hynek's frustration, the military rejected the Northwestern bid. The Pentagon decreed that it wanted a school that had no previous record on the issue, a view

at the University of Colorado, and—with some cajoling—a leader in Edward Condon, a renowned nuclear physicist and former head of the National Bureau of Standards. The creation of what would soon come to be known as the Condon Committee in October 1966 marked the third time in two decades that the government had assembled a team of scientists to evaluate the UFO question, and would prove to be a critical and fateful turning point in the Cold War chapter of flying saucers.

Condon, a former president of the national physics association, appeared to have both the scientific and political credentials for the controversial job. In 1929, he'd cowritten the first US textbook on quantum mechanics, been a veteran of World War II's atomic race (where he'd helped isolate the uranium needed for bombs), and became a key figure in the public postwar debate over nuclear weapons, pushing for civilian control and international cooperation. His international ties had also brought him under suspicion with FBI director J. Edgar Hoover, a young and ambitious anti-Communist congressman named Richard Nixon, and the House Un-American Activities Committee, prompting multiple investigations into his security clearances—a 1948 HUAC report deemed him "one of the weakest links in our atomic security,"* but every inquiry cleared him, and in the midst of the controversy he was elected president of the American Association for the Advancement of Science, the nonprofit that publishes the journal *Science*, a remarkable testament to his colleagues' belief in him. A few years before he assumed the role of the new UFO committee chair, a *Saturday Review* profile described him as "a moral, impassioned man, with a depth of concern for mankind not common in scientists; a man fiercely principled and anti-diplomatic; a

---

Hynek saw as "like opening a restaurant and looking for a chef who has not had any previous involvement with cooking." In a meeting at the Pentagon that June, a frustrated Hynek told the air force that he felt like Moses—he'd achieved the promised land of the scientific study he'd spent years pushing for, but would not be allowed to enter it.

* Condon responded, brusquely, "If it is true that I am one of the weakest links in atomic security that is very gratifying and the country can feel absolutely safe for I am completely reliable, loyal, conscientious and devoted to the interests of my country, as my whole life and career clearly reveal."

man who believes and feels in sharp contrasts, and who will let the world know his position without ambiguity. Fuzzimindedness is an anathema to him and he insists on saying so at every opportunity."

Even though he wouldn't participate in the project himself, Hynek celebrated the formation of the committee as a "personal triumph and vindication," a sign that his personal fascination was truly worthy of serious scientific study. After decades, the questions of the saucer phenomenon would finally be put to real scientists, open to possibility, and with the time and staff needed to properly study the problem. The night of the committee's announcement, he and his wife went out for drinks, and weeks later, as he had dinner with some of the newly chosen committee, he felt, almost for the first time, like he was among peers—people, he recalled, who didn't look at him like he was a Martian himself.

As the committee started its work, Hynek laid out what he saw as the four possible explanations for UFOs in an independent, unsanctioned article for the *Saturday Evening Post*: First was the theory that the saucer reports were "utter nonsense, the result of hoaxes or hallucinations," one he dismissed by saying that "enough evidence has piled up to shift the burden of proof to the critics who cry fraud." Second was the possibility of "some kind of military weapon being tested in secret," which he said was unlikely due to the sheer geographic reach and breadth of sightings. Third was the option that the UFOs really were from outer space, though he "agree[d] with the Air Force. There is no incontrovertible evidence, as far as I can see, to say that we have strange visitors," until he noted, "it would be foolish to rule out the possibility absolutely.

"We all suffer from cosmic provincialism—the notion that we on this earth are somehow unique," he continued. "Why should our sun be the only star in the universe to support intelligent life, when the number of stars is a 1 followed by twenty zeros? . . . Some skeptics who scoff at reported UFO sightings often ask why the 'flying saucers' don't try to communicate with us. One answer might be, Why should they? We wouldn't try to communicate with a new species of kangaroo we might find in Australia; we would just observe the animals."

Finally, Hynek said, there was the possibility that "we are dealing with some kind of natural phenomenon that we as yet cannot explain or even conceive of." In some ways, he explained, this seemed the most likely, especially given the revolutions of science that his generation had lived through already. "Think how our knowledge of the universe has changed in 100 years," he said. "In 1866 we not only knew nothing about nuclear energy, we didn't even know that the atom had a nucleus. Who would have dreamed 100 years ago that television would be invented? Who can say what startling facts we will learn about our world in the next 100 years?" As far as Hynek had come to believe, and as he now reiterated to *Saturday Evening Post* readers, the air force had continued to hide behind the fact that "most" UFO sightings turned out to have reasonable explanations—weather balloons, stars, or, as in Sagan's case, ordinary high-flying airplanes—and just because it could explain "most" sightings, it didn't equal the logical leap that the military or scientists could explain "all" of them. Sure, there was no "proof" of advanced, out-of-this-world technologies or extraterrestrial visitors, but there also remained some highly detailed and seemingly reliable sightings that were unsolved, the true unidentified flying objects.

Now Edward Condon had about $500,000 to determine which of the four made sense—money that would go not just to field interviews, research, and case file reviews, but to actual experiments, including the use of social psychology experiments on "rumor phenomena" (like the H. G. Wells *War of the Worlds* panic), and a test of Hynek's own personal bête noire: swamp gas.

In mid-November 1966, Hynek and Vallée made their way to Boulder, renting a white sports car for the hour drive to the university from the Denver airport. Upon arrival, they spent nearly an entire day briefing the fifteen members of the committee—Hynek insisted on stopping the running tape recorder at various times to give a candid, off-the-record appraisal of the sorry lot of Blue Book officers—and as they did, Vallée was dismayed to note Condon nodding off to sleep after lunch.* The next day, in a more informal session, the committee talked through its agenda and its goals, which soon turned into a lively and unproductive debate. (As they left, Hynek said to Vallée, "I think we've done all we could.")

That fall, buoyed by some of the interest and attention shown during

* Project coordinator Robert Low later explained this was a common occurrence.

the committee sessions, as well as encouragement from Vallée and McDonald, Hynek decided to revisit some of his older cases with fresh eyes, "no longer assuming that the chances are strong that it's all a lot of junk. I must take the viewpoint that after all these years," he explained, "the data may be genuine, as poor as it is."* Such work, he felt, was crucial to the survival of the discipline at large.

In an article in *Playboy* about his new outlook, Hynek admitted his worst fear—after a bomber gap, a missile gap, and even Dr. Strangelove's 1964 "mineshaft gap," what if the US was about to experience "a UFO gap"? Although the global community had accumulated UFO reports and sightings from more than seventy countries, precisely zero came from behind the Iron Curtain, a fact that seemed logically inconceivable. So what was the Soviet Union doing with the UFO sightings that were surely occurring, but not making their way to the Western scientific community? What if the Soviets solved the UFO question first? "What little 'hard' information I have—and my intuition—tells me that the U.S.S.R. may have been studying UFOs with dispassionate thoroughness for years," he wrote, whereas, he knew from personal experience, the US "is only now beginning to *consider* treating the problem seriously." For all anyone knew, the West's disinterest meant it was spiraling toward another Sputnik-like surprise. At best, Hynek warned, the Soviets could find "some previously unthought-of, unstartling explanation for unidentified flying objects; at worst, they could make first contact with an alien civilization conducting reconnaissance to our planet."

To keep the United States in the race, Hynek encouraged the creation of a yearlong national study and a manned twenty-four-hour hotline, where people could dial UFO-1000 (this, of course, was in the era before the creation of area codes) that could immediately dispatch authorities, including local police pre-equipped with suitable cameras, to the scene of any sighting. He also advocated for the use of special UFO-tracking planes and helicopters, with trained technicians and scientists, on standby around

---

* That December, a sympathetic profile in the *Chicago Sun-Times* of Hynek, titled "The Flying Saucer Man," gave him credit for "challeng[ing] the vitality and flexibility of the American scientific establishment," and credited him as the driving force behind the creation of the Condon Committee.

the country—because events seemed to occur over days and weeks, they could be dispatched to "hot spots" at a moment's notice and stay as long as necessary, capturing even more physical evidence, from videos to casts of indentations. "The expense is trivial if study of the best reports indicates that there is, indeed, valuable scientific pay dirt hidden in the UFO phenomenon," he confidently argued. The results of such an effort in either direction would be meaningful. Either it would collect nothing of interest, thus allowing the country to more confidently "shru[g] it all off" as mass hysteria—or, he said, "mankind may be in for the greatest adventure since dawning human intelligence turned outward to contemplate the universe."

• •

If Edward Condon thought that battling J. Edgar Hoover and the House Un-American Activities Committee was inconvenient, he soon realized it was a walk in the park compared to adjudicating the UFO phenomenon and satisfying figures of all sides of the debate. Unlike the Robertson Panel or O'Brien Committee before it, the Condon members had little interest in going back over the "classic" cases of years past, figuring at this point that the witness reliability was questionable at best and recognizing that in almost all historical "unidentified" cases that the data would be insufficient for new determinations.

Instead, they focused on building their own investigative capability—identifying a network of civilian observers across the country, with help from NICAP and APRO, who could collect information, details, and statements about new sightings, using field kits that included cameras and tools to take "35mm photographs and 8mm motion pictures, check the spectrum of a light source, measure radioactivity, check magnetic characteristics, collect samples, measure distances and angles, and to tape-record interviews and sounds." (By May 1967, such investigators would be capable of reaching any event in the country within twenty-four hours.) To help with the photographic data, the committee enlisted the CIA's Photographic Interpretation Center to help with the photographic data—a fact it intended to leave out of its final report.

Controversy erupted almost immediately—first, over the proposed design of a standard questionnaire to collect sighting and witness data, a project started by the team's psychologist, William Scott, that stretched to twenty-one pages, only one of which asked for information (the rest dealt with forensic examinations of the witness). Staff rebelled, deeming Scott more interested in disproving accounts than trying to find answers about the sightings. Shortly after, "he picked up his questionnaire and went home," recalled committee staffer David Saunders.

It was a sign of the squabbles, big and small, still to come. Before long, the twelve-member staff had broken down into familiar factions—those open to the extraterrestrial hypothesis and those convinced the UFO question was primarily mundane misidentifications. Project coordinator Robert Low, who outside of the committee was an assistant dean in the UC grad school with a background in electrical engineering, was firmly in the latter camp—during a research trip to Europe to attend the 1967 International Astronomical Union meeting in Prague, he had passed up meeting with European UFO researchers and instead journeyed to Loch Ness, later explaining to his colleagues, in Saunders's words, that the detour "was relevant to UFOs because neither one exists and it was important to see how they were studying something that does not exist." Perhaps even more troubling than the apparent conflation of intelligent space life with a mythical swamp monster was the fact that Condon himself was regularly quoted in the press downplaying the endeavor; the day after his appointment as committee chair, he told reporters that there was "no evidence that there is advanced life on other planets" and that he would "need a lot of convincing" that saucers existed. In January 1967, he told another professional association, "It is my inclination right now to recommend that the government get out of this business."

As the committee's research expanded—researchers traveled to the NORAD bunker in Cheyenne Mountain for a classified briefing on the nation's air defenses, and to Ohio to visit Wright-Patterson Air Force Base. Many committee staff began to understand just how little the air force would cooperate in the project; as he monitored sightings and reports, Saunders realized that Keyhoe's civilian organization was compiling more detailed, more thorough materials, and doing it faster and more comprehensively across the country than the military branch had ever even attempted.

As the weeks went by, more trouble and tension began to permeate Hynek's conversations and follow-up meetings with the Condon team, especially after he learned that Keyhoe and NICAP had apparently bad-mouthed rival APRO's "eccentric" Coral and Jim Lorenzen so intensely to the committee that Condon was now refusing to have anything to do with the New Mexico ufologists, closing the committee off from APRO's best-in-the-field records of witnesses and sightings. In July, unmitigated chaos erupted when an explosive memo penned by Robert Low came to light. The confidential internal document, which had been drafted before the University of Colorado and Condon had agreed to the UFO project, weighed the pros and cons of UFO investigation, as was standard, but also included a fateful sentence that infuriated some committee members: "The trick would be, I think, to describe the project so that, to the public, it would appear a totally objective study but, to the scientific community, would present the image of a group of nonbelievers trying their best to be objective but have an almost zero expectation of finding a saucer."

Saunders, floored by the comment, shared the memo with Keyhoe, who in turn told fellow UFO researcher James McDonald. McDonald confronted Low about his bias—leading Condon, furious about what he saw as an internal betrayal, to fire Saunders and the original staffer who had leaked the memo. In protest, other staff members quit.[*] And, to make matters worse, the dysfunction was made public almost immediately in a *Look* magazine article authored by John Fuller. "Flying Saucer Fiasco" included a statement from Keyhoe that NICAP had withdrawn its co-operation with Condon's committee. Soon Saunders, the original staffer Norman Levine, and Condon were trading accusations and threats of libel lawsuits in the press. The controversy eventually became so apparent that the journal *Science,* which had long eschewed the subject, began re-porting its own article; Condon, the past president of the nonprofit that published the journal, resigned in protest over its publication. To Hynek's dismay, the UFO effort was once again at a standstill.

---

[*] Just three of the original twelve-member committee staff, including Low, ended up staying on for the entire two-year project.

The Condon Report

As the dysfunction of the Condon Committee spilled over into mainstream consciousness, members of Congress did something entirely unexpected—they intervened. On Monday, July 29, 1968, the House Committee on Science and Astronautics, led by Representative J. Edward Roush, convened what was meant to be a wide-ranging "symposium" on UFOs, bringing together a half-dozen serious in-person voices—including experts like Hynek, James McDonald, and Carl Sagan, as well as a social psychologist and a civil engineer—and prepared papers by a half dozen more, including Harvard's skeptic-in-chief, Donald Menzel.*

The goal, Roush said, was a scientific discussion—criticism of the air force or the Condon Committee was out of bounds, as that was the purview of the Armed Services Committee. With more humility than normally appeared in such conversations, he added that the very subject of the hearing on unidentified flying objects was intended to be "a reminder to us of our ignorance on this subject and a challenge to acquire more knowledge thereof," before quoting John Dewey's maxim that "every great advance in science has issued from a new audacity of imagination."

To start, Hynek—introduced as a witness by his local Illinois congressman who served on the science committee, a young Republican named Donald Rumsfeld—told those assembled in the hearing room in the Rayburn House Office Building that "it would be difficult to find another subject which has claimed as much attention in the world press, in the conversation of people of all walks of life, and which has captured the imagination of so many over so long a period of time. The word UFO

* Perhaps not surprisingly, Menzel complained about "so unbalanced a symposium, weighted by persons known to favor government support of a continuing expensive and pointless investigation of UFOs."

or flying saucer can be found in the languages and dictionaries of all civilized peoples."

Then, taking a more scientific approach, he tried to draw the distinction between cases with easy explanations ("These have little scientific
value. . . . It matters not whether 100 or 100,000 people fail to identify an
artificial satellite or a high-altitude balloon") and "those reports of aerial
phenomena which continue to defy explanation in conventional scientific
terms." In his view, the government and scientists needed to spend a lot
more time focused on the latter, the truly unexplainable cases, and stop
paying as much attention to the cases that were clearly just misidentifications.

"When one or more obviously reliable persons reports—as has happened many times—that a brightly illuminated object hovered a few
hundred feet above their automobile and that during the incident their
car motor stopped, the headlights dimmed or went out, and the radio
stopped playing, only to have these functions return to normal after the
disappearance of the UFO, it is clearly another matter," he told the committee. "By what right can we summarily ignore their testimony and
imply that they are deluded or just plain liars? . . . There appears to be a
scientific taboo on even the passive tabulation of UFO reports. Clearly no
serious work can be undertaken until such taboos are removed."

The next witness, McDonald, echoed the same themes from Hynek's
testimony, emphasizing that, contrary to the public perception, most
people who reported UFOs didn't appear to have anything to gain from
doing so. "We are not dealing with publicity seekers," he said confidently.
"We are not—and I here concur with Dr. Hynek's remarks—we are not
dealing with religiosity and cultism." Then he evoked the words of a key
member of the institution seemingly seeking to discredit those witnesses:
"[Air Force] General Samford, then Director of Intelligence, said, and
I would concur 100 percent, 'Credible observers are observing relatively
incredible objects.' That was said 16 years ago, and it is still occurring."

The testimonies and witnesses continued, covering a wide range of
topics within the UFO space, from technology—"The possibility that
these are extraterrestrial devices, that we are dealing with surveillance
from some advanced technology is a possibility I take very seriously," Mc-
Donald noted—to time travel, which Sagan took his time to explain the

limits of, and whether UFOs inherently had to be of alien creation. "I do not think the evidence is at all persuasive that UFOs are of intelligent extraterrestrial origin," the astronomer testified, "nor do I think the evidence is convincing that no UFOs are of intelligent extraterrestrial origin," he said.

Put simply, it was all too soon to tell.

• •

The congressional hearing in July 1968 was notable for its existence alone, but it also marked a particular moment in Sagan's life. His in-person testimony had been one of his first public outings since being denied tenure at Harvard—an upsetting development that would ultimately take the popular and rising-star academic years to navigate professionally and personally. As it turned out, Harold Urey, the former Nobel laureate who had seemed an "enthusiastic booster" of Sagan in public, had intervened behind the scenes to scorch the young scientist's trajectory, issuing a blistering two-paragraph negative review to the university that called Sagan, still in his early thirties and seemingly on the fast track to academic significance and success, unserious and trivial as a scholar. As if that weren't enough, he intervened again when Sagan approached MIT about a position: "[He] has dashed all over the field of the planets—life, origin of life, atmospheres, all sorts of things," his one-time mentor told administrators in a shocking letter. "Personally I mistrust[ed] his work right from the beginning."

Unable to find work in Cambridge, Sagan eventually relocated to Ithaca, New York, where he was welcomed into the Cornell University astronomy department by Thomas Gold. Gold loved boldness and saw Sagan's focus on big questions and prominent media appearances as a benefit, not a hindrance, to his team's research efforts. One of Gold's maxims was "In choosing a hypothesis, there isn't any virtue in being timid." The opportunity and vote of confidence was transformative.*

---

* Urey would come to regret his criticism, writing Sagan in 1973, "As a matter of fact, I have not always been nice to you, and I have tried my best to catch you alone and tell you so, and in addition tell you that I have been completely wrong. I admire the things you do and the viguor [sic] with which you attack them." Harvard, though,

Now, with support and an explicit guarantee of future tenure, Sagan concentrated his work—and congressional testimony—on the vastness of the universe and the relative insignificance of Earth. One of the strongest arguments against Earth being visited by UFOs, he explained, was the simple truth that it was unlikely that any alien civilization even knew we existed. To demonstrate how hard it would be for us to locate life elsewhere, he walked lawmakers through the growing body of photos of Earth from space. Weather satellites, like the new TIROS-1 and Nimbus satellites, had a one-mile resolution (meaning anything less than a mile wide wouldn't be visible to the cameras), and from that resolution there was zero sign of life across the US's entire Eastern Seaboard. "We have looked at several thousand photographs of the earth, and you may be interested to see that there is no sign of life, not only in New York or Washington, but also in Peking, Moscow, London, Paris, and so on," Sagan pointed out. "The reason is that human beings have transformed the earth at this kind of scale very little, and therefore the artifacts of human intelligence are just not detectable photographically in the daytime with this sort of resolution."

But it didn't stop there. Even at ten times better resolution (like in the photos, for instance, taken by Apollo and Gemini astronauts), one of the only signs of human existence could be found in the tic-tac-toe logging roads visible in the forests of remote Ontario—hardly what someone might be looking for as a sign of civilization. Sagan noted that such an advanced camera resolution, where each pixel represented about a hundred meters, was still better than any photo yet taken of Mars, and yet "there are only about one in a thousand photographs where this resolution of the earth gives any sign of life." And that was only true even with all the population and construction and technology of modern times—go back even a few centuries or even a few millennia and human life, even as intellectually and spiritually rich as it might have been, would have been even harder to spot. Go back one hundred thousand years, and there were

had missed its chance for good. Sagan never looked back from Ithaca; Cornell, as promised, gave him tenure in 1970, and he spent the most famous years of his career as its David Duncan Professor of Astronomy and Space Sciences.

hundreds of thousands of *Homo sapiens* already building the first build-ings. None of this, he made clear, "would be detectable by photography."

It was a deeply profound argument and one with as many implica-tions for life beyond as it had for us at home—we shouldn't write off life on Mars (or anywhere else) too quickly, Sagan said, because as advanced as life on Earth felt like it was, we, too, would be all but invisible to even Mars, our closest and best hope for interstellar life. An alien race could have looked at Earth not that long ago and even with relatively advanced technology missed that we existed at all.

• •

The Condon Committee's final report came out in late fall of 1968, fol-lowing a review from the National Academy of Sciences. At about 1,490 pages, including six main sections and nearly two hundred pages of ap-pendices, A through X, it included chapters by thirty-six contributors, the bulk of which examined ninety-one UFO cases. Sixty-one had been identified by the expert panel as misidentifications or hoaxes.[*]

In his portion of the document, Condon was blunt: "Our general con-clusion is that nothing has come from the study of UFOs in the past 21 years that has added to scientific knowledge," he wrote on the opening page. "Careful consideration of the record as it is available to us leads us to conclude that further extensive study of UFOs probably cannot be justi-fied in the expectation that science will be advanced thereby." The remarks continued, seemingly ignoring both the professional pressures that had faced early pioneers in the field like Hynek, and the dawning of serious searches for extraterrestrial intelligence in the stars beyond. He even went on to argue that UFOs weren't that scientifically interesting to begin with, saying that "the reason that there has been very little scientific study of the subject is that those scientists who are most directly concerned, astron-omers, atmospheric physicists, chemists, and psychologists, having had ample opportunity to look into the matter, have individually decided the UFO phenomenon does not offer a fruitful field in which to look for major

---

[*] "For varying reasons, UFO-related pranks are commonly perpetrated by the young, the young at heart, and the lonely and bored," the committee concluded.

scientific discoveries." A few pages later, he issued a final, definitive blow: "We know of no reason to question the finding of the Air Force that the whole class of reports so far considered does not pose a defense problem."

The controversy that followed was swift and predictable, with the usual suspects lining up on both sides. Keyhoe, McDonald, and Saunders held a press conference blasting Condon's report, while Hynek and McDonald both publicly and privately lamented what felt like another wasted opportunity—why had the committee spent time and effort studying cases that were easily determined to be wrong? Why not dedicate more of its resources and investigation instead to the ones that remained the hardest to solve? The lack of urgency, open-mindedness, and creativity in the Condon Committee report was beneath such an esteemed scientist: "Mozart producing an uninspired potboiler, unworthy of his talents," Hynek later wrote.*

There was, however, one very concrete outcome. In March 1969, military officials convened in DC for a status review of Project Blue Book, and "from the moment the meeting opened," spokesman Captain David Shea recalled, "there was no doubt that Project BLUE BOOK was finished."

Indeed, it was. Later that year, air force secretary Robert Seaman announced that twenty-two years after the launch of the original Project Sign, the air force was taking itself out of the UFO business, due to the fact that the effort "cannot be justified either on the ground of national security or in the interest of science," as an explanation.

The US Air Force was done, permanently, with UFOs.

Or so it said.

• •

In a twist of timing and irony, the Condon Committee's final report and Project Blue Book's disbanding came just as the nation found itself completely riveted by outer space. Throughout the summer of 1969, Mariners

---

* Condon took the criticism in stride, even giving a lecture the following year titled, tongue-in-cheek, "UFOS I Have Loved and Lost," in which he derided the phenomenon as powered by "flying saucer buffs who have been making money from sensational writing and lecturing to gullible audiences, and collecting dues from the membership of their pseudo-science organizations."

6 and 7 flew by Mars, delivering some two hundred more detailed pictures than we'd ever seen, and confirming, once and for all, that there was actually no truth to the linear "canals" that had been identified on its surface seventy years earlier. "There was no geometric pattern on the surface," Sarah Stewart Johnson explained. "For all that time, the lines we'd seen simply weren't there." There was also no vegetation, as indicated by two Mariner photo missions, along with another flyby by Mariner 9 later in 1971 revealing that the seasonal dark splotches were simply shifting dust clouds. "Just like that, the concept of a vegetated Mars fell away, just as the idea of a civilized Mars had slipped through our fingers," Johnson wrote, but any disappointment about Mars was overshadowed by July 20, 1969, when Apollo 11 landed on the moon's Sea of Tranquility. It was a massive victory for the United States, and effectively the final cannon shot in the race for technological supremacy.

What many may not have realized, however, watching Neil Armstrong descend the ladder onto the lunar surface, was how much NASA had been worried right up until the end about the possibility of life on the moon, and how intertwined the government's incredibly official moon mission had been with its black sheep initiatives to study UFOs. Carl Sagan was one of many who had been working hard on the problem of what NASA called "back contamination," the fear that the astronauts might inadvertently return to Earth with moon microbes and introduce novel devastating germs or bacteria to Earth. It was a long-shot risk, but as was the case with so much of space exploration, the government preferred to err on the side of caution. NASA had wrestled with the challenge throughout the 1960s, with one committee concluding, "Negative data will not prove that extraterrestrial life does not exist; they will merely mean that it has not been found," to which another NASA reviewer penciled in editorially, "Like witches."

As part of their research and recommendations, Sagan and colleagues had pressed for an extensive quarantine and sterilization program—the Apollo capsule, they suggested, should be picked up intact from the ocean by helicopter, shipped to Houston with the astronauts still inside, and opened only inside a sealed, secure lab. The plan was ultimately rejected after the astronauts themselves protested the extreme danger of such a lengthy, multistage journey trapped inside the sealed capsule, and NASA realized from a public-relations perspective that they couldn't exactly treat the returning astronauts—set to be vaunted as national heroes—as a bio-hazard. In the end, NASA decided that navy frogmen would open the capsule in the ocean, then toss inside to the astronauts "biological isolation garments," into which the astronauts would change before stepping out. To Sagan, the plan wasn't sufficient, especially in the wake of a cultural fervor caused by a new novel called *The Andromeda Strain*, about a deadly organism arriving from space. Michael Crichton readers had flooded NASA with worried letters. "Maybe it's sure to 99 percent that Apollo 11 will not bring back lunar organisms," Sagan told *Time* magazine, "but even that one-percent uncertainty is too large to be complacent about."

In the end, none of the contingencies were needed. Apollo 11 returned safely to Earth; Armstrong, Buzz Aldrin, and their command module colleague, Michael Collins, emerged unscathed from quarantine; and NASA's tests on potted plants, brown shrimp, mice, and quails found no harmful effects or mysterious pathogens. Barely two decades into the rocket age, humans had successfully visited their first celestial body and confirmed, apparently, there was no life nearby.

The Byurakan Conference

In September 1971, a decade after the original meeting of the Order of the Dolphin in Green Bank, Soviet astronomers convened the first forum regarding communication with extraterrestrial intelligence, known as CETI. In a remarkable display of cross-border collegiality and collaboration, Sagan, Philip Morrison, Barney Oliver, Frank Drake, and select international scientists from other countries, like György Marx (Hungary), astronomer Rudolph Pesek (Czech Republic), and anthropologist Richard Lee (Canada)—traveled to the Byurakan Observatory in Armenia, where Shklovsky and Kardashev had hosted their first conference in 1964. "Never, before or afterward, have I taken part in a more imposing scientific gathering," Shklovsky recalled.[*]

There, for a full week, the roughly thirty scientists, including two Nobel Prize winners, were led by Sagan and Viktor Ambartsumian, the head of the observatory and president of the Armenian Academy of Sciences, in various discussions about their progress and new thinking about the best way to find and detect alien civilizations (albeit under heavy KGB surveillance).[†] Such an occasion was unprecedented, and, as Ambartsumian pointed out, had the potential to change more than just outlooks on alien life: "Professor Shklovsky was right when he said to me that before we are able to solve the problem of communicating with extraterrestrial civilizations," he said in his opening remarks, "it might

---

[*] The proceedings were almost derailed before they started by the stenotype machine the Americans brought to record the conference discussions, which waylaid them at Soviet customs as authorities worried it could be used as a photocopying machine.

[†] As Drake recalled, "Our American contingent immediately dubbed Ambartsumian 'Smokey the Bear' because of his uncanny resemblance to that character, although, naturally, we didn't say so out loud in his presence."

be a good thing for there to be communication on the subject among nations." He also noted how challenging the subject would be from a simple practical perspective—pointing out that the conference's acronym, CETI, was the Latin genitive for "whale," and given that humans couldn't even communicate with cetaceans, undoubtedly another intelligent species inhabiting our own planet, what hope did we have to think we'd be able to communicate with extraterrestrial civilizations?

Over the days that followed, the scientists debated topics arranged around each of the variables in the famous Drake equation, from the planetary systems beyond our own solar system and the possible biologies of non-carbon-based life-forms to the evolution of technically advanced civilizations and techniques for possible contact.* All of it was presented in rapid synchronous translation by Boris "Bob" Belitsky, a science editor for English-language programming on Radio Moscow who was widely considered to be the country's best scientific translator and who—incredibly—had been in the same freight car as Shklovsky and other science students during the 1941 evacuation from Moscow ahead of the Nazi advance. (Almost exactly thirty years later, the conference was the first time the two men had crossed paths since.)

As the conversations unfolded, the American contingent found themselves wildly jealous of the progress made by their Soviet counterparts—there were almost no active SETI projects in the United States at the time, but here there were multiple efforts underway. Ironically, under the Soviet system, where there was no real "peer review" structure and little incentive to criticize others' pursuits, senior scientists faced less social pressure in their work, and funding came mostly by fiat, so one institution's project wasn't necessarily being weighed against another's. It also meant that information could be somewhat more freely shared, and now, for the first time, the scientific Iron Curtain parted, allowing different groups to see how others had been inspired by, or built upon, their work—the American

---

* The conference-goers agreed that the wisest response to the question of the effect of alien contact on earthlings actually came from someone who wasn't even present. The dissident Soviet nuclear physicist Andrei Sakharov had written the group with a simple response: "To an intelligent and good person contact will be useful; to a stupid and bad one, harmful."

and Europeans, for example, learned that in 1968, Vsevolod Troitsky had used the forty-five-foot telescope at the Radiophysical Research Institute in the closed-city of Gorky (now Nizhny Novgorod) in 1968 to conduct a multiple-night search for signals among the twelve nearest stars. The results crossed twenty-five different channels, far more than the one that Ozma had been able to examine. He'd then assembled, through great scientific and collegial effort, a larger network of other Russian sites that allowed him to examine huge swaths of the sky.

Sagan, Drake, and other members of the delegations were shocked. Using broad-band receivers was effectively the opposite of their narrow-band listening strategy. "They did not make any educated guesses about which frequencies might make the most sense as alien broadcast bands," Drake recalled. "Instead, they concluded that the extraterrestrials would realize the inherent difficulty in selecting a particular frequency, and transmit a signal that could be picked up on *any* frequency."

One of the conference's most intriguing new ideas came out of a lunch conversation between Sagan and fellow attendees, Francis Crick— the legendary codiscoverer of the double-helix structure of DNA—and British chemist Leslie Orgel, one of the leading thinkers on the origins of life, about "directed panspermia," that life in our galaxy had been seeded by visiting ancient alien civilizations. Crick and Orgel's argument, which they now positioned to Sagan more as a credible alternative rather than a theory they personally believed in, was that the building blocks of life on Earth didn't look like what one might expect.

At that point, the theory of "panspermia," the idea that life on Earth actually had extraterrestrial origins, had been kicked around scientific circles for more than a century—several early astronomers and scientists, including Lord Kelvin, had long suggested that the first microbes had arrived on Earth from space, effectively "infecting" Earth with life, perhaps from Mars or by tagging along on a meteorite (later Sagan and Shklovsky's research would disprove this, showing instead that the radiation of outer space would have likely killed any spore traveling through its vacuum), until Thomas Gold, the astronomer who had so enthusiastically recruited Sagan to Cornell, proposed in 1960 that life on Earth was effectively "cosmic garbage," biological material left behind billions of years ago by another exploring civilization.* After all, he pointed out, "the universe was old enough that several cycles of billion-year civilizations could have risen and fallen, able to explore whole solar systems and galaxies and leave behind hardy microbes on previously lifeless planets." Now, in Armenia, Crick and Orgel took the idea one step further: Gold's hypothesis had held that "the time available makes it possible, therefore, that technological societies existed elsewhere in the galaxy even before the formation of the Earth." What if one of those societies had launched a special unmanned craft toward us? What if past civilizations had *meant* to seed life on Earth?

The two men even had an idea for what such a spacecraft might be like. An unmanned craft, packed with say one thousand kilograms of blue-green algae that could grow on CO_2 and water, wouldn't need to travel all that fast—a trip of "just" a million years, at "only" sixty thousand miles per hour, could encompass several thousand stars within a hundred light-years of Earth. Such a spacecraft would have to be relatively sophisticated and able, for instance, to home in on a star and then a specific planet—otherwise the odds were literally astronomical that in the vastness of space it would just travel forever without ever intersecting a new potential home. It also would have to be designed simultaneously to withstand the fiery entry into Earth's atmosphere, while also dissolving in the oceans sufficiently to allow the blue-green algae to spring to life and spread. According to a 1973 article that further detailed their theory, Crick and Orgel believed "that within the foreseeable future we could, if we wished, infect another planet, and hence it is not out of the question that our planet was infected," and that "We might well be tempted to infect other planets if we become convinced that we were alone in the galaxy."

There were, the scientist suggested, two things that didn't quite line up with the established understanding of early microbes' evolution on Earth. First, why was there only one genetic code? Normal science held that life should evolve in such a way that there were many versions—much like

---

* In colorful conversations, Gold was known to lightheartedly imagine aliens eating a picnic on a lifeless, rocky Earth, dropping microbe-packed cookie crumbs around them before blasting off for further adventures.

human language evolved using similar patterns and symbols, but endless variations of spellings and words—but in this case there was only one pattern of DNA, "The universality of [which] follows naturally from an 'infective' theory of the origins of life," as Crick and Orgel later argued. By that measure, "life on Earth would represent a clone derived from a single extraterrestrial organism."

The scientists were also puzzled by the "anomalous abundance" of the trace element molybdenum in organic life—despite being relatively rare on Earth, it was critical to numerous enzyme reactions. If one presupposed that the hallmarks of life would look similar to the environment into which life evolved, why did life on Earth rely so heavily on such a comparatively rare element? Maybe our version of life had begun in an environment where molybdenum was much more common?

From there, more questions emerged—were the descendants of life's senders still alive somewhere out there, or had the intervening 4 billion or so years been too much for their civilization? And did we have "sister" planets, civilizations that had grown out of the same seeds from the same extraterrestrial effort? It was the same question that had captivated the Order of the Dolphin in Green Bank: How big was L in the Drake equation, and what was the length of time that an advanced civilization survived? "Perhaps the galaxy is lifeless except for a local village, of which we are one member," the two scientists wondered, knowing that the answer would likely not be found before the Soviet conference adjourned—but that an environment in which they could ask them in the first place had been created was a victory in itself.*

---

* For much of the rest of their careers, Crick and Orgel would dance around just how seriously they'd ever intended for the suggestion of "distributed panspermia" to be taken—was it a serious scientific hypothesis or just a fantastical astronomical joke? (Even Crick's wife told him, "It is not a real theory, but merely science fiction.") They readily admitted that their arguments in favor of such a theory were "somewhat sketchy," but that available evidence also didn't allow for the theory to be "rejected by any simple argument." Later, Crick published a book on the origins of life in the early 1980s, and in Crick's 2004 obituary in the *New York Times*, his suggestion warranted two paragraphs, and the *Times* wrote, "Only the most eminent and secure of scientists would dare flirt with the idea that earth may have been seeded with life by a rocket ship from another planet."

All in all, the conference was a perspective-shifting experience, generating new crucial friendships and useful scientific breakthroughs, including a collective outline for a "master plan" of future Soviet searches for extraterrestrial intelligence that included a global network of antennas to contribute to future searches. Every night, the foreign visitors were bused back to the InTourist Hotel in Yerevan, while the Soviet delegation spent the night at the observatory.

At the final dinner on September 11, Shklovsky rose to give a toast, looking out at the group settled at large banquet tables. Behind them was a glorious panoramic view of the banks of Lake Sevan, upon which an eighth-century monastery was perched. "This joyful event serves to convince us that somewhere, far beyond the limits of the constellation Tau Ceti, so expressively sung by the Russian poet Vysotsky, a banquet like ours is taking place," he said. "Let's drink to that."

The Arecibo Message

B ack in the United States, news of the Armenia conference marked a particularly exciting moment in extraterrestrial science. A decade after Drake's first tentative steps with Project Ozma, the field seemed to be maturing in multiple ways and imaginations were stretching to answer some of its most pressing questions. One, in particular, seemed to be front of mind—part of the challenge had always been that no one really knew what to look for (as Sagan had demonstrated to the congressional committee, even relatively detailed satellite photos could gloss over fairly advanced civilizations), so how did one go about looking for the signs of a civilization many light-years away?

Freeman Dyson, an extravagantly imaginative British American theoretical physicist, provocatively responded to the paradox by suggesting that our conceptions were inherently too small to fully grasp the potential for civilizational growth—we were still a tiny unambitious undeveloped immature dot in the vastness of space, a people hundreds of thousands of years old in a universe that measured itself by the billions. A true advanced civilization, he argued, would never content itself by just harnessing the energy that reached it from its closest star or sun—nor would such a small energy source allow a civilization to achieve its own interstellar ambitions. Instead, it would build a giant solar-panel orb to encapsulate its entire local star and fulfill its energy needs. "It is . . . overwhelmingly probable that any such beings observed by us will have been in existence for millions of years, and will have already reached a technological level surpassing ours by many orders of magnitude," Dyson wrote in his research. "One should expect that, within a few thousand years of its entering the stage of industrial development, any intelligent species should be found occupying an artificial biosphere which completely surrounds its parent star."

These Dyson spheres, as they came to be known, would dwarf any earthly engineering capabilities (imagine surrounding our sun with a sphere of solar panels and habitats constructed in between it and Mercury, a sphere that might stretch across ten, twenty, or even thirty million miles of outer space), and the energy captured by such an endeavor would be equally enormous, Dyson estimated, giving off specific, unique infrared heat signatures in space that astronomers could seek out, and separate from "normal" stars. Perhaps we should be looking for them, he said, if we wanted to find the universe's most advanced civilizations.

In that heady time of the early 1970s, Barney Oliver—the Hewlett-Packard executive and Order of the Dolphin member whose plane had dropped out of the sky to surprise Drake in the midst of Project Ozma—was asked to co-lead a study with NASA's head of biotechnology, John Billingham, on how to conduct a "realistic effort" to detect extraterrestrial civilizations and intelligent life beyond, and determine the hallmarks, signs, and clues that might signal to other planets teeming with life and intelligence. Billingham had become particularly fascinated with the work of the exobiologists at the Ames Research Center, but realized in the course of his study of their approach that they might be asking the wrong questions. "The Exobiology Division was worrying about the chemistry of life, and even looking for life within our solar system," he recalled, "but what about intelligent life around other stars?"

Over ten weeks during the summer of 1971, he and Oliver, plus nearly two dozen additional researchers and scientists, piled into temporary offices on a spare floor at Ames and calculated the hardware, manpower, time, and funding necessary to create an experiment that might reasonably locate signals from the depths of space. Oliver, who had long been fascinated by radio and had worked on developing radar during World War II, became the driving force behind the study's audacious vision—a series of one thousand interconnected smaller antennas stretched over one hundred square kilometers, working together as one to vacuum up the sounds of space across hundreds of light-years. To him, NASA's building interest in the initiative was coming at the perfect time. In the decade since Drake had tiptoed into the search for extraterrestrial intelligence with Project Ozma, science had seemed to grow ever-more confident that life might exist far away. The understanding of "cosmic evolution" was also pointing more toward the likelihood that our solar system was not especially unique—that planets existed elsewhere and that life on our own had begun and evolved through understandable laws of physics and chemistry that would apply throughout the galaxy and universe beyond.

To advance understanding, the scientists zeroed in on the twenty-one-centimeter, so-called hydrogen line, and the eighteen-centimer line for OH, hydrogen and oxygen—the same frequency that had intrigued Drake, Shklovsky, and many other scientists who had examined the problem—for further study. This band, Oliver wrote, would be known and significant to any advanced civilization and provide an "uncannily poetic place for water-based life to seek its kind." Surely, the NASA team agreed, it would be where any intelligent life-form would consider communicating with others beyond; so many human settlements and animal species congregated around water sources on Earth.

The effort was dubbed Project Cyclops, and its resulting 250-page report, published on January 1, 1972, would become a classic in the field.[*] "The search for extraterrestrial intelligent life is a legitimate scientific undertaking," it concluded, "and should be included as part of a comprehensive and balanced space program." And to that end, the US should "establish the search for extraterrestrial intelligent life as an ongoing part of the total NASA space program, with its own budget and funding," a recommendation seconded by the National Academy of Sciences' prestigious Astronomy Survey Committee, which met every decade to study and outline what it considered to be the field's most important and pressing priorities.

"Each passing year has seen our estimate of the probability of life in space increase along with our capabilities of detecting it," the group justified. "More and more scientists feel that contact with other civilizations is no longer something beyond our dreams but is a natural event in the history of mankind that will perhaps occur within the lifetime of many of us. The promise is now too great either to turn away from it or to wait much longer before devoting major resources to a search for other intelligent

---

[*] In announcing a reprint in 1992 marking the long out-of-print report's twenty-fifth anniversary, the SETI League wrote, "It is probably safe to say that every major player in SETI today cut his or her teeth on this document."

beings. In the long run, this may be one of science's most important and most profound contributions to mankind and to our civilization."

It was a clear and passionate statement, but it unfortunately came down too late. With the race to the moon won and the conflict in Vietnam devouring the nation's political appetite (and the government's treasury), NASA's budget had been falling steadily. Once the last two Apollo missions, 16 and 17, were complete, America no longer had the vision to dream big in space. The quote-unquote reasonable budget of $6 billion to $10 billion that Oliver and Billingham suggested to fund their post-Cyclops work was a nonstarter. There would be no well-funded celestial search; the SETI effort would have to continue as it had started—as a jury-rigged pursuit by curious minds.

The next step would instead come, again, from Frank Drake, whose day-to-day work had continued to mix "serious" astronomy with his interest in extraterrestrial intelligence. As the field of radio astronomy advanced, he had sought to better understand Earth's closest neighbors, helping at one point to calculate a new surface temperature of Venus (about 890 degrees Fahrenheit, which was about 400 degrees warmer than scientists had previously believed), but he had never lost interest in the information that telescopes could capture. Determined to reengage with his passion, he left the Jet Propulsion Laboratory in Pasadena for an opportunity at Cornell's new Center for Radiophysics and Space Research, which was beginning to operate an enormous radio telescope in Puerto Rico. "You have to see it to believe it," Thomas Gold had told him, and when Drake finally did, he knew there was something amazing in store.

The so-called Arecibo telescope was a long way from the technology he had seen at Green Bank—stretched across a full thousand feet, the half sphere was built into an isolated sinkhole to protect it from passing hurricanes and featured the three towers, each about three hundred feet high, with eighteen wire cables stretched between them to support the main collection platform, reflectors, and antennas over the center of the dish. Scientists had poured over aerial photographs and topographical maps of US territory along the equator to find the best location, and settled on one about a full day's drive from San Juan (quite a feat for an island that was only 110 miles by 40 miles wide).

Development had begun in 1963 as part of a Cold War–era Pentagon effort known as Project Defender, which was intended to study how to detect incoming Soviet missiles as they passed through the ionosphere, the layer of electrically charged molecules and atoms that surrounds the Earth about thirty miles above the surface.* Through intensive lobbying, Gold had succeeded in securing both institutional and financial support to allow for the expansion of the telescope's capabilities beyond looking just at Earth's upper atmosphere. Eventually, the whole contraption—all 625 tons of it—could be steered toward deep space to listen and study far away radio waves.

In 1966, Drake had been named the director of the observatory—an opportunity that required some familial sacrifices, but was ultimately too scientifically exciting for the academic to pass up—and under his watch the telescope gave way to a number of discoveries, including the first accurate tracking of Mercury's full rotation, early radar maps of the surface of Venus, and the existence of "pulsars," superdense neutron stars. He'd even weathered Hurricane Inez at the observatory, using the high winds as a chance to test his hypothesis that a reflector was actually much more structurally sound than imagined, and could therefore observe much shorter wavelengths than previously realized—indeed, instead of moving a few inches in routine high winds, as its engineers originally believed, the telescope actually moved only a few millimeters, opening up all new avenues for cutting-edge research. In 1971, the observatory became part of the National Science Foundation, and Drake quickly secured the new role as director of the newly named National Astronomy and Ionosphere Center. Now he was able to more freely explore questions he and others had struggled with at the original meeting of the Order of the Dolphin, including perhaps the most basic of all: Could one communicate across vast distances with a civilization that surely spoke a different language?

---

* The telescope, Drake learned, existed because of an incredible engineering mistake: its designers, focused on the ionosphere, had screwed up their math and build a one-thousand-foot dish when all they needed was a one-hundred-foot dish, but didn't discover the error until construction was already underway—and that error then paved the way for radio astronomers to use its incredible scope for their purposes.

• •

By that time, scientists had been struggling with the challenge of how to communicate with extraterrestrials for more than a century. In 1820, German mathematician Carl Friedrich Gauss proposed the creation of a symbol, something akin to a right triangle, built large enough that it could be seen by civilizations on the moon or Mars and planted in a wheat field in Serbia, surrounded by three square-shaped stands that would prove the Pythagorean theorem—the square of the triangle's hypotenuse equaled the sum of the squares of the other two sides*—while, around the same time, a Viennese astronomer suggested digging giant circles and triangles in the Sahara, before filling them with kerosene and lighting them on fire. In France, a scientist thought arraying giant mirrors across Europe to reflect sunlight at Mars—he suggested perhaps arranging them in the shape of the Big Dipper—and in 1875, a Finnish Russian mathematician named E. E. Neovius published a booklet titled *The Greatest Mission of Our Time*, proposing contact via beaming symbols of mathematics or physics by large, lit beacons that would likely be universally understood.

Interesting as those projects might have been, no one ever received money or made it anywhere off the drawing board of their imaginations. It was only around the turn of the century, as radio was discovered, that the possibility of speaking directly to alien civilizations became more concrete. Drake compared the conundrum to trying to write "a love letter to a woman I'd never met, who not only spoke a foreign language but lived at an unknown address. She might not be able to read, or even to see. She might turn out to be not a woman at all—but a whale perhaps, or a flower, or maybe a spider, or a virus, or something I simply could not imagine," and the only answer that seemed to make sense: math. Language meant

---

* Whether Gauss himself actually suggested this has been open to some recent debate—sourcing is thin and generally attributed just to a "German astronomer," and Michael J. Crowe's 1986 book, *The Extraterrestrial Life Debate, 1750–1900*, argues that "The history of this proposal . . . can be traced through two dozen or more pluralist writings reaching back to the first half of the nineteenth century. When this is done, however, it turns out that the story exists in almost as many forms as its retellings."

something different to every civilization on Earth, but everyone had, with time, come to understand and share calculations—maybe that would be true of aliens as well.

The best approach he could imagine was creating a photograph—a black-and-white image for other civilizations using the same style of simple binary code that television used to draw moving images. He sketched, for hours, on a piece of graph paper, coloring in some boxes and leaving others blank, gradually learning how to draw without curves in the tight, regimented boxes. With time, he settled on a series of 551 ones and zeros that, in binary, indicated whether the pixel was filled in or not. He hoped that another civilization would recognize that 551 was divisible only by 29 and 19, two prime numbers, cluing them in to the idea that the message translated into a drawing 29 pixels high and 19 across. Buried inside the message, Drake encoded all manner of details, from a schematic of the solar system to a crude drawing of a human and a list of the numbers 1 through 5. To test its efficacy, he mailed copies to his fellow members of the Order of the Dolphin with a challenge: "Here is a hypothetical message received from outer space. It contains 551 zeroes and ones. What does it mean?"

None of his colleagues could decipher it. Only Barney Oliver even seemed to understand the concept, sending Drake back a new series of 1's and 0's, which Drake managed to decode as an image of a martini glass and olive.

Unwilling to give up hope, Drake sent his original message out again, this time to a wider circle of scientists. All of them failed to decipher it. Finally, he published the puzzle in a magazine for amateur codebreakers. Shortly after, he received a single correct response from an electrical engineer in Brooklyn—"the only person who ever interpreted it correctly," Drake recalled.* It was a disappointing start, but not quite the end of the road. Three years later, in 1969, Drake was attending a conference

---

* One of Drake's conclusions from the project was that if Earth ever did receive a coded message from beyond, the receiving government and scientists should publish it widely in the interest of involving as many amateur codebreakers as possible. "Their minds are uncommonly well prepared for seeing patterns, symbols, and abstractions," he concluded.

held by the American Astronomical Society in Puerto Rico, when he ran into Carl Sagan in the lobby of their hotel. The two began talking, and Sagan was soon relaying the details of a conversation he'd had about the upcoming Pioneer 10 mission, which aimed to travel to Jupiter, skim along its surface, and take thousands of photographs as it gained enough velocity to launch itself out of our solar system; the first human object to travel potentially forever across the universe. Maybe someday a far-off civilization would detect it, intercept it, or find it crashed somewhere, Sagan excitedly told Drake. What if they could make it mankind's first interstellar message in a bottle?

As conference-goers moved around them, the two men immediately began discussing ideas; Sagan had already settled on engraving a picture message onto a metal plate, which Drake noted would "probably remain readable for a few billion years," adding it would change the weight and balance of the probe and force NASA to reconfigure its thrusters, but the agency had already made clear that it was happy to do so, given the idea's importance. The only catch was that it had to be done quickly.

Drake and Sagan agreed that they should somehow include drawings of humans and other messages in the vessel, but got stuck debating how to identify Earth's place in the galaxy—mapping our planet to the Big Dipper, Drake estimated, would pin down the launch date for other civilizations to within about ten thousand years, plus or minus, and narrow down our position in the sky to within twenty or thirty light-years, which in the grand scheme of space and time seemed relatively precise, but he soon had a better idea: they could map the Milky Way using the pulsars, the rare and distinct stars that formed the core of much of his research.

After many refinements, a four-ounce gold-anodized aluminum plaque was drawn by Sagan's wife, Linda, consisting of anatomically detailed drawings of a male and female body, silhouetted against the outline and scale of the Pioneer spacecraft so future discoverers could understand how tall humans were. The male waved, to show how limbs moved, and also to display a greeting and sign of goodwill (if any alien could grasp that).* A series

---

* In the years since, the plaque has come in for some criticism about the human drawings appearing too Anglo-Saxon and not panracial enough, and while the male's genitalia is included in the drawing, there's a long-standing debate about whether

of sophisticated astronomical maps were also featured, depicting Earth as the launching point for Pioneer, and our solar system's position in the fourteen-legged, spiderlike map of pulsars that Drake had created. Each leg was mapped with binary numbers showing the pulsars' bursts. Depending on where and when the plaque was ever found, Drake hoped that by including fourteen different notable stars, he would be offering an advanced civilization enough options to triangulate our solar system. As a key, the scientists included a drawing of hydrogen, outlining how its characteristics could be used to divine the distances and numbers on their maps.

When Pioneer 10 launched in March 1972, NASA made Sagan and Drake's message public, proud of the work they had done for all mankind. But instead of praise and admiration, the efforts were met with controversy—letters to the editor lambasted NASA for spreading pornography, and in Canada, the message could barely be broadcasted, since naked humans had never been shown on their networks. In the end, though, the attention gave Drake and Sagan what they ultimately wanted: "We had already started to think of it more as a message *to* Earth than as a message *from* Earth," Drake recalled. "We had hoped it would hammer home the idea that we are not alone in the universe, that others will learn of our existence someday, and that some forms of contact and communication are possible."

The following year, when Pioneer 11 launched in April, the same plaque went with it.

• •

In 1974, Drake was presented with another exciting opportunity: as director of the National Astronomy and Ionosphere Center, he'd been overseeing a three-year renovation and rebuilding of the Arecibo telescope, and as the rededication approached, his assistant, Jane Allen, suggested they use the newly improved machine not just to listen to outer space but to broadcast a message into it. The telescope's concentrated broadcast power equaled about 20 trillion watts, meaning that against the backdrop

---

NASA itself nixed a detailed drawing of the female genitalia as too controversial to be included in the more prurient political environment of the Nixon administration. Sagan maintained that the less-detailed female body was in keeping with Greek statutory traditions.

of outer space, a receiving civilization far-off would be able to see Earth's message more brightly than the sun itself.[*]

Drake was ecstatic at the idea, and began to draw and redraw what ultimately turned out to be a 1,679-bit message, rendered into a seventy-three-by-twenty-three pixel image by relying again upon prime numbers. Successfully decoded, it contained seven parts, starting with the numbers one through ten, and the atomic numbers of the five elements critical to human life and DNA—hydrogen, carbon, nitrogen, oxygen, and phosphorus—as well as a graphic representing DNA's double helix, and the chemical formula for DNA. He also included a stick-figure drawing of a very generic human, which he struggled to keep from looking too gorilla-like.[†] Finally, he rendered the rough population of Earth (4 billion people), the rough estimated number of genes in the human genome (3 billion), a rough map of the solar system, with Earth's position highlighted, and a crude sketch of the Arecibo telescope itself. When he shared the draft with Sagan, Drake was thrilled to see that his colleague was able to understand it, giving some hope that aliens might be able to someday as well.

At the telescope dedication ceremony on November 16, 1974, the chair of the House science subcommittee, Georgia's John Davis, delivered the keynote address to 250 guests. Davis, who had been a junior congressman on the House science committee in 1968 during the UFO hearing with Sagan, Hynek, and others, now confidently proclaimed that Earth would probably receive a response in fifty thousand years—"Back where I come from," he said with a smile, "a man doesn't plant an acre of millet seed and expect to get only one sprout."

Then a loud siren signaled the antenna's movement into position, followed by beeps of the three-minute message being broadcast toward

---

[*] How far out Arecibo could detect a message has long remained an open debate. Drake believed that it could detect a signal from another Arecibo-type transmitter as far as 25,000 light-years away, although calculations by other SETI scientists estimated it effective only at smaller distances, perhaps 10,500 down to as little 400 light-years.

[†] The height of the figure, he later admitted, happened to coincide with his own: five feet, nine inches tall.

its intended target, a cluster of stars known as M13, within the constellation Hercules, that was roughly twenty-four thousand light-years away. "The sound of the message—which was transposed into eerie alternating tones for those present at its transmission—filled up the air over the site," recalled Dava Sobel, who covered the event for the *Cornell Chronicle*. "I remember seeing women in sleeveless dresses rub chills from their arms as we all looked at the telescope and thought about the conversation it might be initiating at that moment."

By the time the ceremony participants had eaten lunch and returned to their buses, the greeting from Earth was already passing Pluto's orbit, only twenty-four thousand or so more light-years to go.*

---

* Far beyond the island, the Arecibo message touched off a heated debate. Sir Martin Ryle, the UK's astronomer royal, blasted Drake's seemingly presumptuous message—saying it was "very hazardous to reveal our existence and location to the Galaxy," and that, "For all we know, any creatures out there might be malevolent—or hungry." Drake immediately hit back, pointing out that it was already too late—earthlings had been broadcasting their whereabouts by that point for decades through radio and television transmissions, and that aliens who might detect the Arecibo message would likely be too far away to do anything about it. The debate about the ethical considerations of what would come to be known as METI—messaging extraterrestrial intelligence—would rage for decades to come in a number of forms.

Close Encounters
of the Third Kind

The 1970s were an unprecedented decade in American history, an unexpected onslaught of controversies and chaos as headlines about Vietnam, the Pentagon Papers, and Watergate eroded trust in government and led to institutional collapse; new details about past events like the Kennedy assassination were relitigated through the Warren Commission, giving rise to ever more fantastical theories of cover-ups and shadowy behavior; and social unrest and anti-government protests, from the draft, civil rights, and the environment to women's rights and gay rights, from Kent State to Wounded Knee, forced a feeling of uncertainty upon the entire population.

During this period, conspiracy theories, especially regarding intelligence and military behavior, were at their peak. It became easier for many to imagine organizations like the CIA and the FBI were hiding dark truths because congressional hearings and investigative journalists had shown that they had done it before. The bombing of Cambodia had been built on lies and disingenuous intel—even the airmen who had carried out the raids had not known the true details of the mission—and the CIA had sponsored coups, organized assassinations, and spread disinformation around the world; the FBI (sometimes at the behest of the Oval Office, as was soon learned) was regularly spying on ordinary Americans and illegally targeted dissidents, antiwar activists, and political opponents. Even the president and his staff had found themselves caught up in all manner of illegal conspiracies, from dark-of-night burglaries to campaign dirty tricks to money laundering, largely with the attitude that their positions made them immune to consequences. Maybe the government really was hiding the truth. Maybe there were real "men in black." Maybe there were hidden aliens. "If that kind of thing was going on, why not a saucer cover-up?" James Moseley recalled.[*]

From this mindset, a more sinister and conspiratorial edge of the UFO phenomenon emerged from another strain of ufologists, a darker trend that began most notably with the publication of Leonard Stringfield's *Situation Red: The UFO Siege!*, a book that alleged that the country was in the midst of a wave of increasingly violent UFO encounters, incidents that had led to physical injuries and abductions—and that a US government cover-up was not only alive and well but far bigger, deeper, and more nefarious than anything the enthusiasts of the 1950s and '60s had ever imagined. "For too long, the general public has been misled by official denials claiming that a real UFO—a 'nut and bolt' alien craft—does not exist," Stringfield wrote. Not only, he claimed, did such crafts exist but the US government possessed some of them.

To a general reader or observer, Stringfield seemingly had the credentials to back up such assertions. He was a longtime ufologist who had worked with Keyhoe at NICAP in the 1950s, and in the 1960s had actually been part of the early-warning network set up by the Condon Committee to gather UFO sightings. He possessed rare insight into the phenomenon, and contacts that others lacked, as well as actual ties to some official efforts. Nevertheless, it was an explosive allegation—one that was taken even further at a 1978 ufology conference in Dayton, Ohio, just across town from Wright-Patterson. There, Stringfield presented a paper called "Retrievals of the Third Kind," alleging that the military had aliens and alien craft in their custody. Altogether, by his count, there had been

---

[*] That thought process was certainly reflected in the public response to UFOs and aliens at the time. In 1973, a German named Erich von Däniken published *Chariots of the Gods?*, a book that suggested alien civilizations had been visiting Earth for millennia, profoundly shaping human history and even serving as the inspiration for early deities. Von Däniken's book, which would sell more than 7 million copies in the years ahead, joined other chart-topping books that sought to explain strange phenomena, like Charles Berlitz's *The Bermuda Triangle* and John Wallace Spencer's *Limbo of the Lost*, two 1974 titles that popularized the mystery around an area of the Atlantic and Caribbean Oceans where ships and airplanes disappeared. Berlitz's book would go on to sell more than 20 million copies around the world, in some thirty languages.

nineteen such cases, and nearly two dozen witnesses had already filled him in on the government's darkest secret. In a stunning twist, he also alleged that there was a special air force unit, known as the "Blue Berets," solely dedicated to UFO retrieval and security duty.*

In the years ahead, Stringfield became infamous for his too-good-to-verify stories, which always seemed to emerge from anonymous sources through a game of telephone, like, as the newly formed Midwest UFO Network (MUFON) noted, one account of a UFO crash sourced to a reliable person in a technical position at a large General Electric plant who had heard the story from his brother in the air force. The tales were often long on detail, short on evidence, but created a new narrative. "More than any other single ufologist, Stringfield was responsible for restoring credibility to the notion that saucers from space had crashed and, along with the bodies of their crews—and maybe even a survivor or two—had been scooped up and secreted away by the U.S. Government," James Moseley wrote in his memoir.

The theory laid the groundwork. In many ways for seemingly blockbuster reporting in 1980 by Stanton Friedman and William Moore that the US government had long covered up the truth about that 1947 crash in Roswell. That incident in New Mexico just weeks after Kenneth Arnold's first sighting had been almost entirely forgotten when *The Roswell Incident* was published, mentioned only twice in all of the UFO books released in the intervening decades (one of which was an explicit mention in a 1967 book of the crash as a hoax and myth).

The Roswell Incident, authored by Moore and Charles Berlitz, with Friedman as a main source, was largely built around testimony Friedman had obtained from Jesse Marcel, the long-retired air force intelligence

---

* Later, he alleged that plainclothes policemen unexpectedly met him as he left the Dayton stage and told him his life was in danger. After he attended a planned press conference, they whisked him back under guard to a new hotel room. Stringfield would also purport to have collected testimonies from numerous vaguely placed insiders who had knowledge of the military's stable of aliens. "Time, with its influx of new data and new and old reliable sources, now affirms my belief that beyond my fingertips and perhaps forever unreachable, is the evidence extraordinaire—the alien cadavers and craft," he wrote in 1980.

official who had retrieved the crash wreckage from the New Mexico ranch. Now, though, Marcel had a very different story to tell: what he'd taken from the ranch three decades before was no ordinary weather balloon, but exotic materials from outer space, dotted with hieroglyphs and possessing properties unlike anything known on Earth. The debris he'd posed with for news photographers back then had been a ruse.[*]

To bolster their argument, Friedman and Moore cited witness testimony from a long-dead civil engineer named Grady "Barney" Barnett, who had recounted stumbling upon the crashed disk in the desert, surrounded by archaeology students from an unnamed eastern university who had chanced upon the wreckage. Together, they had examined the alien bodies—hairless, with round heads and small, oddly spaced eyes.[†]

The book sold widely, but the initial evidence Berlitz and Moore offered was thin (Jerome Clark called the book "premature and sketchy"), and the rise of Roswell as the ultimate deep-state conspiracy would continue in the years ahead.[‡] Friedman, though, believed he was onto the biggest story in human history. He called it "Cosmic Watergate." As he said, "The UFO Story is the most important story of the past millennium."

• •

When Richard Nixon finally resigned the presidency in August 1974, after months of controversy, a feeling of relief swept the nation, and a feeling of hope galvanized the UFO community, in particular—perhaps, some thought, this was the beginning of a new age, in which truth and transparency could take hold. The same month, APRO's Jim Lorenzen

---

[*] This claim, alone, was easy enough to disprove: there were seven photos taken in 1947 at the air base, two with Marcel, and the wreckage is the same in all images.

[†] Barnett's testimony was questionable from the start; although *The Roswell Incident* quoted him in the first person, he'd died a decade earlier and his story was related secondhand to the authors by a couple who said he'd told them about it in the 1950s.

[‡] "If one accepted these tales, then in the late 1940s and early 1950s saucers were dropping out of the air like flies," James Moseley wrote. "If the saucer beings were smart enough to travel safely through space over distances of billions and billions of miles, how likely was it that they'd be dumb enough to crash by the dozens once they got here?"

announced in an interview in *National Tattler* that "a program has been undertaken that will over the next few months make it obvious that the government has reversed its position ... [and] will release all its information [on UFOs] within the next three years."

The shift came as the UFO movement—almost exactly a quarter-century old by the time the burglars entered the Watergate building in 1972—faced its own generational transition as two of its loudest and most influential voices fell silent. After more than a decade leading NICAP, Donald Keyhoe was ousted by its board in 1969; two years later, James McDonald died by suicide. With Blue Book and the air force officially out of the conversation, organizations like APRO and MUFON stepped in and took the lead—sightings were now filtered through them and the media, with little involvement from the government. MUFON had been founded in 1969 and managed to amass several hundred new members in the early years of the 1970s, thanks in large part to its magazine, *Skylook*, which had quickly become one of the most important reads for the country's remaining ufologists, including Hynek, who felt an intellectual kinship among MUFON's members in a way that he hadn't been able to with NICAP or APRO.

At the time, the renowned astronomer was becoming something of a star in the community. The closure of Blue Book had been his final dance with the military on UFOs, and the Hynek now unleashed on the world was a far different man, thinker, and scientist than the one the air force had first approached in the 1940s.* "He's gone from initial hostility toward the subject to skepticism and misgivings, to cautious calls for more study, to muted criticism of the Air Force, and eventually to open hostility toward the Air Force and complete acceptance of the idea that UFOs represented potentially one of the most serious problems he had confronted," historian David Jacobs related.

In 1972, he had published a groundbreaking book called *The UFO*

---

* Though he may have been done with official projects, Hynek did end up staying close to the air force as a secret consultant; the branch felt his satellite-tracking knowledge amid the growth of Soviet spy satellites would be valuable, and the astronomer was willing to help, given that the nature of the relationship would allow him to speak freely in public about his thoughts on UFO investigation efforts.

Experience: A Scientific Inquiry, which was unlike anything the field had yet seen—three hundred pages outlining the intellectual and scientifically rigorous approach to the phenomenon that the author had long wished others would follow. Hynek's open and questioning nature led him down paths that other scientists didn't dare, even if they had felt odd to him—like the abductions and so-called "occupant" cases, a particularly vexing and long-standing logical challenge for the scientists in the ufology community. Written for a popular audience, and with an accessible and approachable tone, it solidified Hynek's role as the nation's unparalleled authority* on the subject in all its facets, the one consistent public and official presence across a quarter century of sightings, government efforts, and public controversies, despite his concession that "after more than twenty years' association with the problem, I still have few answers and no viable hypothesis."†

Comprehensive and rooted in deep, authoritative research, *The UFO Experience* stood in stark contrast to other books in the category authored by skeptics or conspiracy theorists and had a massive practical impact—fundamentally changing the classification framework for UFO sightings by organizing their commonalities into six levels of rising seriousness and witness proximity.

The three lowest categories dealt with most common and least reliable distant sightings: nocturnal lights (odd lights, moving or stationary, spotted in the night sky); daylight disks (oval- and saucer-shaped objects

---

* With his book and soon-to-be-famous categories of sightings, Hynek was firmly established as a star, perhaps *the* star, of the ufology world—besieged by fans, the curious, and the kooky whenever he spoke, including Gray Barker and Jim Moseley, who he met at a convention in the early 1970s. To avoid being interrupted by Hynek's many fans, the trio retreated to the closest bar they could find, only to end up at a strip club. They huddled into a corner table, hoping to escape notice, but as Hynek talked and smoked his pipe, one of the strippers came over and sat down in his lap. As Moseley recalled, "Hynek just kept puffing his pipe and talking quietly, as if nothing unusual was happening. The woman finally shot him a puzzled and shocked look—as if to say, 'My God! Are you dead?'—and flounced away in a huff."

† The positive review of Hynek's book in *Science* surely proved a major victory to him, after years of the prestigious journal rejecting articles and studies about UFOs.

spotted during daytime hours); and radar-visual (UFO sightings that are confirmed both visually and by radar; seemingly more trustworthy sightings that indicated a solid object). The second grouping gathered the so-called "close encounters," in which a UFO or flying saucer was spotted less than five hundred feet away and the witness was able to provide considerable detail, and could be further sorted into three sublevels: "Close Encounters of the First Kind" were up close but noninteractive visual sightings where witnesses could perceive shape and describe movement, and other various details; "Close Encounters of the Second Kind" were sightings that also came with physical effects—changing environments, agitated livestock or animals, electrical interference with nearby vehicles, or trace impressions on the ground, like burn marks, indentations, or scorched vegetation; and "Close Encounters of the Third Kind" were "the most bizarre and seemingly incredible aspect of the entire UFO phenomenon," the cases where the witness actually reported seeing "the presence of animated creatures," e.g., occupants, humanoids, alien beings, "UFOnauts," or "UFOsapiens."* It was a category that Hynek admitted to struggling with—as a scientist, he explained, he would gladly have omitted it entirely from his research were it not for the "offense to scientific integrity" it would create. Even in the face of doubt or dismissal, he wrote, "we must study the entire phenomenon or none of it."

"It is in Close Encounter cases that we come to grips with the 'misperception' hypothesis of UFO reports," he further explained, adding that while all of the first three categories could often be attributed to planes, balloons, astronomical, atmospheric, or meteorological phenomena, simply writing off more detailed "close encounters" was "virtually untenable"—"My own

---

* Later in the 1970s, UFO researcher Ted Bloecher proposed a further refinement of six subcategories of the third-kind close encounters that captured a more precise and wider range of associated paranormal activity: A—Aboard (where an entity was observed inside a UFO); B—Both (where an entity was observed inside and outside a UFO); C—Close (where an entity was observed only near a UFO, but not actually going in or out of it); D—Direct (where a strange entity was seen in an area of reported UFO activity); E—Excluded (where a strange entity was observed in an area with no reported UFO activity); and F—Frequence (where a witness reported experiencing an "intelligent communication" with no associated UFO activity).

opinion, and I believe the reader will agree is that accepted logical limits of misperception are in these cases exceeded by so great a margin that one must assume that the observers either truly had the experience as reported or were bereft of their reason and senses," he said.

Acknowledging these cases was also important, it was noted, because a surprisingly high number of sightings were of the "third kind," including those at military bases and many that Project Blue Book had either failed to ever hear or catalog—"clearly it is not only kooks who report humanoids." In fact, drawing on a semi-comprehensive catalog that Jacques Vallée kept of "close encounter" cases, Hynek estimated that about 300 of 1,247 tracked cases involved a report of a humanoid-type creature, and about a third of those were multiple-witness sightings. These were, he emphasized, the cases that most confounded investigators and that the government preferred to pretend didn't happen at all,* but "when the long-awaited solution to the UFO problem comes, I believe that it will prove to be not merely the next small step in the march of science but a mighty and totally unexpected quantum jump."

To keep pushing for that jump, Hynek founded the Center for UFO Studies in Illinois in 1973, an almost entirely volunteer-run effort comprised of engineers and scientists who simply wanted to see the kind of in-depth study Hynek had long advocated for. Its five major areas of research were, according to its founder, (1) analyzing soil and plants disturbed by UFOs (so-called "trace cases"); (2) physical examinations of animals and people who had contact with UFOs, as well as (3) witness credibility studies; (4) photographic and spectrographic analysis of UFO sightings; and (5) theoretical physics research about reported movement and luminescent properties of UFOs.

"The interdisciplinary nature of the UFO problem is clearly apparent," the MUFON newsletter explained in an article about the new organization. "There are aspects of the problem which are of interest to psychologists, sociologists, medical practitioners and others." The center

---

* In the years ahead, Vallée would also propose a "Fourth Kind," to capture reported alien abductions, and others would propose a "Fifth Kind," a sighting where there was direct communication between aliens and humans.

launched with a toll-free number for "UFO Central" that Hynek distributed to local police nationwide, promising "a ridicule-free avenue for the
natural desire on the part of the witnesses to communicate their experience to someone in authority."

The incredible admission, reading between the lines of his book and
his new center, was that, a quarter century into his work on the subject,
not only did Hynek still have unanswered questions about the entire UFO
phenomenon but that his questions were bigger and more fundamental
than when he'd started the work in the 1940s. In fact, given the rise of
abduction stories, the UFO phenomenon was actually even weirder than
when he'd started.

• •

Though sightings, encounters, and even telekinetic conversations had
become a widely accepted and expected part of UFO lore, the question
of alien abductions had remained largely underexamined. The first real
significant spotlight was cast on the rare occurrence in 1967, when a
new book by John Fuller, called *The Interrupted Journey*, publicized the
story of Barney and Betty Hill, an interracial couple who claimed they'd
been taken by aliens during a drive home through the New Hampshire
mountains on September 19, 1961. A bright light following them for
miles, seeming to grow larger, until Betty—a social worker for the state—
could see double rows of windows through her binoculars. The couple
stopped the car abruptly and Barney, a postal worker, got out and walked
toward the saucer-shaped craft. When he saw humanoids inside, he ran
back to the car, screaming, and tried to drive away, but suddenly, neither
of them could see the stars above them. A strange beeping filled the car.

The next thing they knew, they were home, in Portsmouth, about two
hours later than they had anticipated.

The experience left them feeling strange, but confident they had seen
a UFO. To better understand what may have occurred, Betty sought out
one of Keyhoe's books at the local library, and began to try to reconstruct
the evening's events. She and Barney spoke publicly about their terrifying journey in some groups during the spring of 1963, but as the couple's anxiety worsened, they sought treatment with Dr. Benjamin Simon,

a Boston-based psychiatrist who used hypnosis on his patients. During a session, Barney—weeping and writhing—described a memory of a strange humanoid with wraparound eyes appearing in the road and pulling him from the car. In the minutes—perhaps hours—that followed, the beings, who spoke English, had poked and prodded the Hills aboard their craft; he and Betty were attached to examining machines, one of which inserted a long needle into Betty for what she was told was a pregnancy test. Betty was also able to converse telepathically with one of the beings, who seemed to be the leader. At one point, she asked them for proof of their existence, saying no one would believe their story without it. She was shown a star chart that the beings had evidently used to navigate themselves from their home to Earth.

The tale astounded Simon. As far as he could tell, it was unlike any other ever documented by another human, and far outside the realm of what other "contactees" had described during the 1950s. The Hills were not willing participants, had received no message for mankind, and seemed traumatized by their encounter—desperate, even, to avoid the memory of it. There were some apparent physical traces of an interaction, including scuff marks on Barney's shoes and a tear and pink substance on Betty's dress, but none of it was conclusive or even seemingly out of the ordinary. Simon put great stock in his patients' perspectives and feelings, and after evaluating the situation, saw four possible explanations before him: "Betty and Barney were lying (unlikely); it was a dual hallucination (improbable); it was a dream or illusion, some kind of experience enhanced by fantasy (conceivable); or it actually happened (unthinkable)." While the case, Simon decided, "could not be settled in an absolute sense," he did come to the conclusion that Betty and Barney's experience, "was a dream. . . . The abduction did not happen."

The couple, the world's first and, to this day, most famous abductees, sat uncomfortably with their fame as the years passed by.* Barney died in 1969, and Betty later reported that, beginning in the early 1970s,

---

* In 1975, the abduction of the Hills became the basis for a movie, *The UFO Incident*, starring James Earl Jones and Estelle Parsons, prompting a tidal wave of Hollywood attention that brought the question of alien abductions to a national audience for the first time.

she'd frequently journeyed to a spot about twenty miles from their home in Portsmouth, where she could see UFOs almost any night she visited. (When a UFO investigator from Hynek's Center for UFO Studies joined her, he gently informed her that she was simply looking at planes.)

Over the years, believers like Keyhoe tried to keep the couple at arm's length, dubious about the plausibility of Close Encounters of the Third Kind, while others, like the NICAP team, offered a bit more flexibility, suggesting that the couple may have suffered a true UFO sighting that then triggered "subconscious fears of what might have happened," which then worked their way into subsequent nightmares and hypnosis sessions—but on a larger scale, many came to believe that the Hills were telling the truth. In the mid-1970s, *Astronomy* magazine reported that an Ohio schoolteacher named Marjorie Fish identified a sketch Betty had drawn from memory of the star map shown to her by the aliens as Zeta Reticuli, a southern constellation about forty light-years from Earth,[*] implying that the aliens had come from the double-star system. The article nearly demolished the credibility of the then-year-and-a-half-old magazine when Carl Sagan, among others, blasted the conclusion, saying that the Hills' star map was little more than randomly placed dots on a piece of paper, and that its alignment with Zeta Reticuli was random chance—the sky, after all, was so full of stars that if you randomly drew dots on a piece of paper you could probably line it up with some constellation somewhere, he argued. Fish, presented with later evidence, eventually recanted her own hypothesis.

Whatever the truth was, it would likely be a while before it was found. As UFO expert Jerome Clark concluded in his own study of the case, "The resolution of the Hill case awaits the resolution of the UFO question itself. If UFOs do not exist, then Barney and Betty did not meet with aliens. If UFOs do exist, they probably did. The evidence available to us from this incident alone provides no answers surer than these."

---

[*] Betty Hill had actually "recovered" the memory of the star map after seeing a similar star map featured in the coverage of the infamous 1966 press conference by Shklovsky and other Soviet scientists about spotting a possible extraterrestrial signal from CTA-102.

• •

Cases like the Hills were rare, but they occurred all over the world. For Hynek, getting to the truth of such abduction narratives seemed likely to yield larger insights about the whole world of ufology, and intrigued to learn more, he journeyed to Papua New Guinea in 1973 to study one of the oddest foreign cases ever recorded, involving an Anglican minister, Father William Gill, and dozens of parishioners in a remote town called Boianai.* The lengthy saucer sighting had unfolded over the course of two nights, and featured both smaller crafts and a larger "mother ship," all seemingly populated by humanoid figures; at one point, Gill recounted that when he had waved, a figure had waved back. The sighting lasted so long that Gill at one point went inside for dinner even as the craft stayed in the sky. Over the years, no convincing explanation had ever emerged for the reports ("Efforts to explain Gill's experience convention-ally have not been notably successful," Jerome Clark wrote dryly), and so they fell into what Hynek had come to call "the Festival of Absurdities," a term first coined by French UFO researcher Aimé Michel to describe all the strange effects reported amid UFO sightings—electronic interfer-ence with car engines, panicked livestock, and other bizarre occurrences that didn't make any logical sense. The Gill case intrigued him, in part because, over a long correspondence with Menzel, the Harvard profes-sor had remained convinced that the case could be explained by normal causes. Perhaps even that the entire sighting was a mystical invention on the part of the minister to influence the native islanders, he suggested. But Hynek was dubious the case was really that simple, and "wanted to check his theories."

Landing on the beach in a small boat—there was no port in Boianai—Hynek interviewed a half-dozen witnesses on the remote island through a translator, struggling to get as clear answers as possible through a

---

* Hynek had first learned of the incident during his Blue Book work in 1960, while visiting the British Air Ministry. At the time, the British military had all but closed its own UFO investigations arm, figuring that the American effort would deliver a result one way or another, and had been happy to give their materials on the Gill case to Hynek to examine.

language and cultural barrier—one witness, for example, caused a good deal of confusion by not distinguishing between evening and night in their testimony. Not long into the trip, the Northwestern professor found himself generally convinced that something had indeed happened back in 1959. "From the facial expressions and gestures of the natives, I sensed that the event had been real as far as they were concerned," he wrote. When his time in Boianai came to an end, he traveled to Australia to meet with Father Gill, who Hynek found "a painstaking, methodical, un-excitable person—just the sort to stand calmly by and take notes at the height of the exciting action." When Hynek asked Gill how he had been able to just go ahead with dinner while the object loomed outside, the minister explained that he didn't initially process the sighting as a UFO. New technology was being tested all the time—"I thought it was some new device of the Americans," Gill said.

All in all, Hynek came away equal parts impressed and puzzled by what he'd learned. Gill had made a strong case for what he'd seen, and it was fairly clear that what he and others had seen had not been any kind of astronomical phenomena. By all accounts, it had been a casual alien drive-by—but then why had there been such chaos? "Why would they frighten animals, stop cars, douse headlights, unless it is a purely second-ary effect and it wasn't intentional? Why did they just wave casually to Father Gill?" Hynek wondered. "Perhaps they are trying to tell us some-thing symbolically; on the other hand, if they are so smart, why don't they tell it to us directly? Why didn't they land in Boianai?"

Upon his return to the US, Hynek found himself immediately im-mersed in another strange case, this time involving two fishermen in Mississippi who had reported that they'd been kidnapped and probed by claw-handed humanoids who approached them while fishing. There were already some holes to consider—the sight of the alleged abduction was in full view of nearby twenty-four-hour tollbooths and none of the staff there reported anything unusual in the sky—but one piece of evi-dence had swung the pendulum of belief in the two men's favor.

Unbeknownst to them, the sheriff had left a tape recorder running in the interrogation room when he stepped out after their initial interview, expecting that the so-called abductees would change their tune when they thought they were alone. But to his great surprise, Charles Hickson and Calvin Parker continued talking with seemingly real fear, discussing their experience, most notably the wonder they had felt watching the craft's door opening up before them. "It just laid up and just like that those son' bitches—just like that they come out," Parker said, his voice still tinged with disbelief.

"They won't believe it," Hickson agreed. "They gonna believe it one of these days—might be too late. I knew all along they was people from other worlds up there. I knew all along. I never thought it would happen to me."

Over the course of six interrogations—including by local authorities, their employer, a local UFO researcher, and at the local air force base—the story had never seemed to budge, and after Hynek listened to the recording and taking his recent experience in the southern hemisphere into account, "My thinking was altered completely," he recalled. "The tales told by these rugged shipyard workers held up under grueling cross-examination."

As he told the press, "There's simply no question in my mind that these men have had a very real, frightening experience, the physical nature of which I'm not sure about." But now, unlike when he stood before the media in Michigan during the "swamp gas" debacle, Hynek's role with the government was over, and he spoke only as a private citizen. His conclusion carried no official weight, other than to the Pascagoula men, who felt their story had been vindicated.

For Hynek, the Pascagoula episode—and the Gill episode and a whole host of other such encounters in the 1970s—was particularly frustrating. More of the same, with more of the same frustration. Sightings came and went and nothing seemed to change, the story never moved forward. As he wrote late in the decade, "Unless we develop drastically new ideas and methodologies for the study of the baffling UFO cases and the human context in which they occur, we will watch the next thirty years of UFO report gathering simply mirror the futility and frustration of the last thirty years."

30

The Dick Cavett Duel

On October 18, 1973, John Chancellor declared on his nightly NBC newscast that "many people would like the UFOs to go away, but the UFOs won't go away and many scientists are taking them very seriously. It's likely that we will hear more and more." It was one of the first large-scale acknowledgments that the extraterrestrial conversation was a popular and legitimate one, and a slew of documentaries and interviews on the subject swiftly followed on mainstream media programs, including a ninety-minute episode of *The Dick Cavett Show* in November 1973 that featured Hynek, Sagan, astronaut James McDivitt, and witnesses to two separate sightings—including the forty-two-year-old Mississippi man who claimed he'd been taken aboard a craft during a fishing trip in Pascagoula, and an army helicopter pilot, Captain Larry Coyne, who had been part of a four-person close-up encounter with an otherworldly craft that had attempted to take control of their army Huey helicopter in the dark night sky over Ohio that October 1973.*

Sagan, who was becoming an outspoken skeptic on UFO visits to Earth even as he championed the scientific search for life beyond, ridiculed the guests and witnesses without hesitation; "one by one, Sagan disposed

---

* The military never seemed as interested in the Huey incident as would seem typical for a report of an unknown craft seizing control of a military aircraft over US soil, yet UFO researcher Jerome Clark would later describe it as "one of the most important UFO events ever recorded," given that it was "never satisfactorily explained [and] extraordinary in its implications." Similarly, the Pascagoula abduction never attracted the attention that the witnesses/abductees hoped; APRO investigators poked a couple meaningful holes in the story, and the two abductees, Charles Hickson and Calvin Parker, were never able to sell their stories for the payday they felt they deserved. "I don't understand it—their exclusive story is bigger than Watergate and nobody wants to buy it," their representative complained.

of the other guests by mocking their testimony," Vallée later recalled, "and he did it with real flair." Hynek, meanwhile, often seemed to stay quiet, looking, as Vallée said, "indecisive, timid, and tired." (At one point, arguing over the Huey's episode, Hynek said, "Altimeters don't hallucinate," and Sagan shot back, "I don't mean to attack Captain Coyne, but people who read altimeters hallucinate.")

The showdown on *The Dick Cavett Show* between Sagan and Hynek was the first public battle in what would come to more closely resemble open scientific warfare between the two as the 1970s progressed, as the men increasingly found themselves on opposing ends of the debate.

Newspapers began to explore (and exaggerate and exploit) the intellectual tensions between the two esteemed scientists—one the nation's leading expert on UFOs, the other its leading expert on extraterrestrial civilizations, both seemingly open, if not enthusiastic, boosters of the idea of existence of other life in the universe, yet deeply and fundamentally disconnected regarding the possibility that Earth would ever receive visitors. In 1975, the two men formally faced off again at a futurism conference at the Chicago Hilton. Ahead of the event, Hynek had written Sagan to propose "a sort of mutual nonaggression pact," in what he saw as an "unfortunate misunderstanding" involving a comment he had made about believing UFOs were hardware from other planets—when in fact, in Hynek's view, all he publicly argued was that the UFO phenomenon was real and deserved study. "If this is clear between us," Hynek offered, "then we can have some fun discussing the subject."

Sagan, however, had little interest in onstage peace. He began the conference with a dismissal of the entire ufology field as pseudoscience, seizing on outlandish and atypical theories, like the disappearances around the Bermuda Triangle and the ancient aliens hypothesis, which posited that aliens had been standing in the shadows of human history, guiding progress. To mitigate further damage, Hynek took a moment in his opening presentation to express his evolving position—"I think we have to be open to the possibility that we cannot fashion a hypothesis yet. There may be things that we just don't know about"—but once the two men were onstage together, the tension was palpable. A reporter noted, "They sat with arms folded, at opposite ends of the forum like negative and positive poles," animating only when defending their own point of view. Sagan, in particular, was on fire, telling the audience, "The fact that people talk about it doesn't mean that it really happened," and snidely asking at one point, "Where have all the angels gone?" Finally, he broadly dismissed the idea of funding any research into UFOs, saying that it only made sense if there was hard evidence,* a semi-astounding statement from a scientist who had spent so much time on SETI projects that had borne precisely as much "hard evidence" as Hynek's work had so far. The comments were an early sign of a fissure that would follow the field for years to come—the "serious" scientists, who struggled enough with the giggle factor of their quest for far-off extraterrestrial civilizations, trying to set themselves above and beyond the ufologists. To them, one was academic, the other fantasy.

---

* "A standard," Hynek's biographer notes, "that surely would come as a surprise to the sounds of grant-funded scientists whose important, valuable, worthy research is, was, and will always remain inconclusive."

The Tehran Incident

Though it may at times seem otherwise, UFOs are hardly a US-only phenomenon—in fact, they are and have always been regularly seen around the world. A perfectly circular gray-colored craft moving at 4,800 kilometers an hour in the sky over Woomera, Australia; a crashed saucer in Afghanistan, reported to the US air force attaché, with no mention ever of what happened to it after the fact; an August 1956 sighting in the UK, at the NATO base RAF Bentwaters, where radar operators tracked a cluster of returns that slowly converged into a single stationary object, moving at nine thousand miles an hour, prompting fighters to scramble and investigate.

News of these odd incidents, however, had not motivated other governments around the world to dig into the subject the way that the United States had with Blue Book, Grudge, and others. Over the years, various efforts in Canada had unfolded under the auspices of the national defense and transport departments, the National Research Council, and even the Royal Canadian Mounted Police, amassing thousands of pages of inconclusive files covering more than four thousand individual sightings, a "low-level hum" as Canadian UFO scholar Matthew Hayes called it, amid the nation's security services. In the 1950s, the country established Project Magnet and Project Second Storey to further investigate the UFO question. The former was supervised by a radio engineer named Wilbert Brockhouse Smith, who so deeply believed that the UFOs were extraterrestrial craft powered in some way by the Earth's magnetic field that he tried to trace UFOs through physical tracking (he came up empty). After deciding that there was no present security threat and that the puzzle did not "lend itself to a scientific method of investigation," the government largely lost interest in the process—especially as Smith strayed ever further into his embrace of the so-called "extraterrestrial hypothesis." That did not mean, however, that the sightings stopped happening.

One day, in the spring of 1967, as Canada celebrated its centennial* a mining prospector at Falcon Lake in Manitoba spotted two cigar-shaped objects in the afternoon sky. One descended near him, emitting a purple light, and he sketched it before cautiously approaching. Inside, he recalled, he could hear humanlike voices. He touched the vessel and stuck his head inside, earning him grate-like burns as the craft hurriedly blasted away. Officials were never quite able to make sense of the case; a passing RCMP constable thought the woozy prospector was merely drunk, but in the days ahead he suffered from maladies consistent with radiation poisoning.

A few months later, in October, Nova Scotia became the center of speculation when a fleet of callers began reporting to Shag Harbour authorities that a plane appeared to have crashed around midnight. Responding officers arrived in time to see a light floating on the water, but as a boat rushed out, the light went out and appeared to sink. There were no reports of any missing military or civilian craft, and a government dive team began a search. Nothing was ever found, and both incidents remained effectively unsolved. "It was impossible to do much more with it. The investigations simply hit a wall that they could not overcome," Hayes wrote. "As a result, the Canadian government would take steps to remove itself from the UFO phenomenon altogether."

Efforts to spark official interest elsewhere also fell short in the 1970s. In 1971, an Australian military scientist, Harry Turner, wrote a classified paper titled "Scientific and Intelligence Aspects of the UFO Problem," based in part on Australian sightings, that argued UFOs both were real and that US efforts, like the Condon Committee, were specifically meant to ridicule reports of flying saucers and downplay their significance. "By erecting a façade of ridicule, the US hoped to allay public alarm, reduce the possibility of the Soviets taking advantage of UFO mass sightings for either psychological or actual warfare purposes, and act as a cover for the real US programme of developing vehicles that emulate UFO performance," he told Australian decision-makers. Turner's proposal for a national Australian UFO rapid-response team, one that could hunt down

---

* One of the ceremonies set to mark the occasion included the installation of a UFO landing pad in the small city of St. Paul, Alberta.

the truth and tear down the façade of ridicule around the subject, was met with complete disinterest.

That same year in Central America, a study team from the Costa Rican National Geographic Institute was flying on a mapmaking mission over Lake Cote in September 1971 when they happened to snap what many considered the best photograph ever taken of a UFO—while none of the crew were aware of the encounter at the time, when they developed the film, they found a photo that appeared to capture a relatively crystal clear image of a metallic disk about 160 feet in diameter over the lake, but could garner no further interest in any official investigation of what the camera appeared to capture. The image would stay buried in the Costa Rican government archives for years.

Then, early on the morning of September 19, 1976, the UFOs appeared to come for Iran. Two Imperial Iranian Air Force fighters were scrambled to intercept a mysterious light in the sky. According to a report filed by the US Air Force's Iran liaison back to the Pentagon, multiple civilians—and even an Iranian brigadier general—had seen something strange, "similar to a star bigger and brighter," prompting a military air response. As they flew toward Tehran, the F-4 Phantom jets noticed the object while still seventy miles from the capital; as the first closed in on the target (about twenty-five nautical miles away), its instrumentation and communication systems failed, forcing it to abandon the pursuit. As soon as the plane turned away from the object, the pilot later reported, the systems reengaged.

As the second fighter came within twenty-five nautical miles, the object's movement became trackable on radar, the size of the output "comparable to that of a 707 tanker," the embassy report stated. Size was hard to establish, but "the light that it gave off flashed like a strobe, arranged in a rectangular pattern and alternating blue, green, red, and orange in color, so fast that all the colors could be seen at once." As the pursuit continued across the night sky, "another brightly lighted object, estimated to be one-half to one-third the apparent size of the moon, came out of the original object" and headed rapidly toward the F-4. The pilot attempted to fire an AIM-9 air-to-air missile, but he, too, lost instrumentation and executed a high-speed turn to get away; the object trailed him for a few miles before rejoining the main light and, eventually, landing. Radio and navigation interference continued for the pilots until they touched down.* The next day, the military visited a house near an apparent landing site—and although there was no sign on the ground of anything touching down, residents did report hearing a loud noise and seeing bright light outside the night before.

When word of the encounter arrived at the Pentagon's Defense Intelligence Agency, there was a rush of interest. This was, analysts could tell, "a classic which meets all the criteria necessary for a valid study of the UFO phenomenon," an object with "an inordinate amount of maneuverability" apparently seen by multiple credible witnesses from different locations, one where radar sightings received visual confirmation, and where "similar electromagnetic effects [were] reported by three separate aircraft." As the DIA saw it, the Tehran incident was "an outstanding report."

Enthusiasm about the incident in ufology circles dwindled, however, as more time was spent evaluating it. Some noticed that the cable from Tehran wasn't even classified—a serious error if Iranian fighters were truly tangling with exotic out-of-this-world technologies—and the copy of the report circulating through Washington was classified at the lowest level, "confidential." A tape recording of the radio calls of the first F-4 fighter confirmed that it chased some bright light, but made no mention of the instrument failures listed in the written report. Follow-up newspaper and on the ground investigating in Tehran only muddled the picture further—one article featured a statement from an official source that the alternating flashing lights were an exaggeration, while members of the Westinghouse maintenance crews at the Iranian air base revealed to investigators that the second F-4 had a long-running history of experiencing serious electrical problems. Numerous airliners across the Middle East and North Africa had reported that meteors had been crossing the skies that night, likely elements of not one but two annual meteorite showers, Gamma Piscids and the Southern Piscid.

Suddenly, a picture emerged less of advanced fighter jets tussling with an aggressive UFO and more of under-trained pilots flying less-than-reliably maintained F-4s, sent off to chase Jupiter or some other natural

---

* The interference also appeared to affect a civilian commercial plane passing through the area at the time, too.

phenomenon. It was a scenario that Hynek had described in 1967, tell-ing *Playboy* that "pilots have been known to swerve their planes violently when they suddenly encounter a very bright meteor they think is on a collision course, but which later proves to have been 50 to 100 miles away." The Tehran Incident, it seemed, was bunk.

• •

One country that did continue, consistently, to take UFOs seriously was France. The French government had long maintained an unacknowledged official interest in the subject since its own sighting wave in 1954 (a period that had captured the interest of a young Jacques Vallée). A secret committee authorized by President Charles de Gaulle had coincided with the Condon Committee in the late 1960s, but the study had been derailed by political turmoil in the latter years of the decade. After the French translation of Hynek's book *The UFO Experience*, the French gendarmerie began in ear-nest to gather national records of UFO sightings, and in December 1977, the country officially launched the Groupe d'Études et d'Informations sur les Phénomènes Aérospatiaux Non-identifiés (GEPAN)—the Unidentified Aerospace Phenomena Study Group—as part of its national space agency.

The creation of GEPAN was meant to bring more rigor and orga-nization to reports of flying objects, under the direction of government engineer Claude Poher, who had read the Condon Committee report and been struck by how, beneath the seemingly staid official summaries, so many of the most curious sightings had remained unexplained.* After conducting his own unofficial research, he had presented at one of the conferences hosted by J. Allen Hynek's Center for UFO Studies, and established himself as an authority in the field. Now, as the leader of GEPAN, he and six staffers would be able to draw on hundreds of gen-darmerie records to study the country's sightings.

---

* GEPAN was later renamed in 1988 SEPRA, an acronym for Atmospheric Re-entry Phenomena Expertise Department, later changed in 2000 to the Rare Aerospace Phenomena Expertise Department, and finally in 2004 renamed a fourth time to GEIPAN, for the Unidentified Aerospace Phenomenon Research and Information Group. For simplicity and lack of confusion, I refer to the group's work throughout as GEPAN.

Unlike the Condon Committee, which had devoted so much effort to studying easily debunked sightings, GEPAN took its time going deep on more complicated reports. At the first meeting of the organization's Scientific Council in December 1977, the team studied a two-volume, 290-page report, and held long follow-up meetings that allowed for more detailed interrogation and analysis. Much of its first year was spent creating four-person teams that would study eleven cases of "high credibility and high strangeness," which ultimately would find that in ten of the eleven cases, "the witnesses had witnessed a material phenomenon that could not be explained as a natural phenomenon or a human device." The committee's final report, completed in June 1978, moved that determination one step further, stating, "Taking into account the facts that we have gathered from the observers and from the location of their observations, we concluded that there generally can be said to be a material phenomenon behind the observations. In 60% of the cases reported here, the description of this phenomenon is apparently one of a flying machine whose origin, modes of lifting and/or propulsion are totally outside our knowledge." In other words, extraterrestrial.*

Hynek had carefully tracked the French project with enthusiasm, going so far as to contact Poher and arrange for GEPAN to have access to his files at the Center for UFO Studies. To him, the French effort was closest to the kind of academic study he'd long desired, staffed with scientists who had open and eager minds, willing to entertain the possibility that the UFO phenomenon was real and truly unexplainable with existing knowledge. The two groups would remain close, even after 1979, when Poher stepped down as director.

Two years later, his successor, Alain Esterle, found himself in charge of investigating a so-called "trace case," a Close Encounter of the Second Kind, that would become France's most famous sighting yet—and "perhaps the most completely and carefully documented sighting of all time," according to *Popular Mechanics*. On January 8, 1981, Renato Nicolaï, a farmer in Trans-en-Provence, was working outside on his property when

---

* The original report was limited to around 140 copies and kept secret inside the French government.

he heard a whistling sound and then noticed an object in "the shape of two saucers, one inverted on top of the other," about ten feet wide landing about fifty yards away on a nearby road. "It must have measured about 1.5 m in height. It was the color of lead," Nicolaï recalled, with "a ridge all the way around its circumference." Nicolaï, who had lived at the property for almost fifteen years, immediately assumed the odd sighting was an experimental military craft, but was convinced by his neighbors to still report it to the gendarmerie; in short step, the police interviewed him and took photos and soil samples from the scene.

"I clearly saw the device resting on the ground," he later told police, and "right away it lifted off, still emitting a slight whistling sound. Reaching a point above the trees, it left at high speed toward the forest of Trans, that is, towards the northeast. When the device lifted off, I saw four openings below, through which neither flame nor smoke were escaping. The device kicked off a little dust when it left the ground."

GEPAN quickly followed up, and after studying the reports and the roadway, determined that the ground had been compressed by some multi-ton weight, and scorched by something approaching 500 to 1,000 degrees Fahrenheit. GEPAN's resulting sixty-six-page report, known as "Technical Note 16," concluded there was evidence of an "occurrence of an important event which brought with it deformations of the terrain caused by mass, mechanics, a heating effect, and perhaps transformations and deposits of trace minerals." While they couldn't find a plausible explanation, "We can state there is, nonetheless, confirmation of a very significant event which happened on this spot."*

What exactly, though, no one could say. French authorities were left, in the end, with the same frustrating mystery left behind after so many other previous sightings all over the globe.

---

* Skeptics would claim the roadway marks were normal tire marks, and other botanists said the GEPAN botanist was a "true believer" who made critical errors in his analysis of the effect on the nearby plants.

The Wow Signal

By the mid-1970s, Carl Sagan had managed to become the most famous astronomer in the country and its leading voice on the search for extraterrestrial intelligence without ever actually conducting his own search study. For all the meetings, conferences, and speeches over the years, he'd never sat down and listened, patiently, full of eager anticipation and wonder, to outer space himself, and then experienced the great dulling sensation familiar to Frank Drake and other SETI astronomers as that anticipation and wonder drained away amid the monotony of nothingness. "He was like the movie star cowboy who can't ride a horse," Sagan's biographer observed, and in 1975 he finally decided he needed some riding lessons.

Sagan and Frank Drake teamed up for one of the largest extraterrestrial signal searches yet, using the Arecibo telescope's giant dish to sample 1,008 channels at once. (Green Bank and Project Ozma had only been able to access one frequency.)* Each morning, the two men woke at 4 a.m. for the drive to the observatory, Drake driving while Sagan ate breakfast—often leftover garlic bread from the previous night's dinner.

For nearly one hundred hours, they listened, hopeful, to M31, the Great Nebula in Andromeda, as well as other galaxies like M32, M33, and NGC205, but their studies revealed only level, flat output—silence. As the time passed, Sagan became visibly deflated. "It was an actual feeling of depression," he remembered. "There was no one on any of those stars trying to reach us in the most obvious way."

"It was a big trip, here was the world's largest telescope, and we had

---

* In 1973, since the facility lacked a television set, Cornell's James Cordes rigged up an antenna to the observatory's video screen in order to watch the evening reruns of that summer's Watergate hearings.

the finest computers in the world," Drake later told Sagan's biographer. "I think Carl really thought we were, within one day or so, going to detect radio signals."

It took much longer than a day or two. But then, seemingly against all the odds, a message did appear from outer space. On August 18, 1977, an astronomer at Ohio State's Big Ear telescope was working at his kitchen table, reviewing the recent days' activity, when a series of letters and numbers on the printouts from August 15 stopped him in his tracks. Right in the middle of the page of data, full of *1*'s and *2*'s that denoted the normal background noise of space, there was a seventy-two-second transmission that was about thirty times louder. The scientist, Jerry Ehman, immediately circled the sequence and wrote in red in the margin, "Wow!"

On the system's normal scale, Ehman knew, signal strengths of 1 through 9 were recorded numerically, and then the letters of the alphabet were used for double digits: A stood for 10, B equaled 11, and so on. This signal read out 6EQUJ5—seeing a Q and a U, letters far down the alphabet, he knew, was literally unprecedented. "I had never seen any signal that strong before," Ehman explained.

The so-called "Wow Signal" reflected what to this day might be the clearest extraterrestrial message yet—one all the more fascinating and intriguing because it came almost exactly where Philip Morrison, Giuseppe Cocconi, and Drake had first imagined such a signal would appear nearly eighteen years earlier at the dawn of SETI efforts: The signal was right near the 21 cm hydrogen line—the so-called "water hole."* After tracing back the direction of the signal, the mystery only deepened. It appeared to have come from somewhere in the constellation Sagittarius, northwest of the globular cluster M55; while that region contained something like one hundred thousand stars, astronomers were unable to find a star or planet that precisely lined up with the site of the signal. They were also unable to locate the signal again at all.

Over the next six weeks the Ohio observatory tried more than thirty

---

* The signal was slightly higher than the hydrogen line itself, perhaps reflecting the Doppler effect—the so-called blue shift that would indicate it came from something actually moving toward Earth in the vastness of space.

times to reestablish contact, and even more detailed restudies were carried out in subsequent decades. Despite the lack of definitive evidence to explain the Wow Signal, it remains perhaps the most intriguing and mysterious message in the history of astronomy. The sheer strength, unusual pattern, and precise frequency made it difficult to explain away as a natural phenomena—Ehman eventually conceded that it was perhaps a human broadcast from Earth that had been coincidentally reflected back by some piece of space debris—but it was a much-needed jolt of excitement and hope that something could indeed come from beyond.

That same year, Drake and Sagan seized another opportunity to send a message out from Earth, placing a time capsule of sorts inside the two Voyager spacecrafts, which were set to pass neighboring planets on their route out beyond the solar system. This time, though, instead of pictures, Sagan wanted to send music.

In a shared cottage at the Kahala Hilton, the two men quickly embarked upon designing a metal phonography record that could be used to store both music and photographs, drawing on brand-new technology from a Colorado video company that could convert television signals to low frequencies. The only time they broke from their work was to attend certain sessions of the annual American Astronomical Society meeting they were in Hawaii for in the first place. When the design phase was completed, "We had room for more than one hundred photos, plus an hour and a half of music, spoken greetings, and other sounds of Earth," Drake explained.

To start, they contacted artists, musicians, and other experts to assemble as comprehensive and broad a spectrum of pictures, music, and languages as they could. ("Now, let's see if I got this straight," said an astonished Smithsonian jazz curator when he answered their call. "You're calling me up at home at eleven o'clock on a Sunday night to ask which jazz to send to the stars?") Their friend and colleague, Ann Druyan, served as the project's creative director, and was tasked with identifying and locating the best material to include: What one song would represent China? What could represent Italy? For weeks, she scouted, gathering together an eclectic selection of songs—when a Berkeley musicologist told them he thought the most important piece to feature was a recording of an Indian raga, "Jaat Kahan Ho," by Surashri Kesarbai Kerkar, Druyan found a copy in a New York hardware store.*

When the record was complete, Drake, Sagan, and Druyan couldn't help but marvel at what they had done. If they could decode the 10 million characters on the gold-plated copper record, curious aliens would hear the song of a humpback whale, the sound of a kiss, the boom of a thunderstorm, the croak of a frog, the beat of a heart, and the roar of a Saturn V rocket's lifting-off, plus snippets of Bach's Brandenburg Concerto No. 2 in F, Chuck Berry's "Johnny B. Goode," some Senegalese drumming, Navajo chants, a Peruvian wedding song, and panpipes from the Solomon Islands. There were also greetings in fifty-five earthly languages, most of which were sourced from the Cornell community, in Arabic ("Greetings to our friends in the stars. We wish that we will meet you someday"), English ("Hello from the children of planet Earth"), Thai ("We in this world send you our good will"), and Zulu ("We greet you, great ones. We wish you longevity"), among others.

Instead of a photo of a nude man and woman holding hands (everyone now knew that that wasn't an option, thanks to the Pioneer plaque fiasco), the scientists depicted humans in black-and-white silhouette. On the aluminum cover of the record was a rough diagram of how to convert the record into images and sounds.

On September 5, 1977, as the record shot off aboard Voyager 1 into space, Drake was left with one lingering concern: the experiment had rested on the giant assumption that aliens possessed the concept of music. But what if they didn't? It would take a little bit of technical guesswork to distinguish the digital encoding of the sounds and music from the encoding of the pictures. What if they did not realize the sound of the *actual* sounds was different than the visuals? After thinking it over, he settled on the belief—hope, really—that the encodings on the record would sound "so different from the music, voices, and other recorded sounds that the aliens will realize they have to interpret the *click-BUZZ* sequences [of the

---

* The engaged Druyan and married Sagan, longtime friends, fell in love during the Voyager project and, despite never even having kissed, decided in the course of a telephone call to get married; they broke the news to their respective significant others at 1 p.m. two days after the Voyager launch.

pictures] in another way," Drake said. "If they have no experience whatsoever with music, then the real music and the pictures will not seem that
different from each other."

Then he had another thought: maybe our music would sound terrible
to them. It was also possible that their musical listening preferences or
their physical capabilities were so different in tonality that they would
actually *prefer* listening to the click-buzz of the encoded pictures. He
imagined another planet, filled with Walkman-wearing extraterrestrials,
snapping their tentacles to the beat of photos of planes taking off, doctors
at work, and lines of cars in traffic.

It was probably one of the most normal things the astrophysicist had
imagined in years.

••

Aside from music sounds and other sonic elements, the Voyager golden
record contained an additional special feature: a 192-word message from
the newly elected president of the United States, Jimmy Carter, the longest on the track: "This Voyager spacecraft was constructed by the United
States of America. We are a community of 240 million human beings
among the more than 4 billion who inhabit the planet Earth. We human
beings are still divided into nation states, but these states are rapidly becoming a single global civilization," Carter explained. "We are attempting
to survive our time so we may live into yours. We hope someday, having
solved the problems we face, to join a community of galactic civilizations.
This record represents our hope and our determination, and our good will
in a vast and awesome universe."

Carter's presence in the White House in 1977 was an exciting and
welcome development for ufologists, who saw his campaign trail promise
to restore public trust and dignity in government as directly beneficial
to their cause.* Plus, Carter himself was a UFO believer—he'd seen one

---

* Carter's opponent in 1976, the incumbent Gerald Ford had, of course, encouraged
  the congressional investigation after the strange Hillsdale College sightings in his
  home state of Michigan in the 1960s, but as president had engaged minimally
  with the UFO issue. His primary contribution to the world of ufology was over-
  ruling NASA to rename America's first reusable space shuttle, set to be named the

himself. The sighting had occurred just a few years prior, on January 6, 1969. At about 7:15 p.m., Carter was waiting for an event to start at the Lions Club* with a group of about a dozen other men, when one of his club colleagues pointed to the horizon and yelled, "Look, over in the west!"

There, a bright light appeared to come toward them, before rapidly moving away—"It was about 30 degrees above the horizon and looked about as large as the moon. It got smaller and changed to a reddish color and then got larger again," Carter later recalled. He estimated the object was perhaps three hundred to a thousand yards away, set against the clear star-filled night sky, and after about ten to twelve minutes, it seemed to move away and disappear for good. Carter, who had a tape recorder on hand, captured some of his colleagues' memories of the incident immediately.

The incident stayed somewhat private until 1973, when Carter, the then Georgia governor and set to run for the presidency, was contacted by Hayden Hewes, the director of the ambitiously named International UFO Bureau. Hewes had heard that Carter had seen something suspicious, and with permission, sent him the group's standard questionnaire at the state capitol in Atlanta. Carter dutifully filled out the details, noting his previous military service in the US Navy and his training in nuclear physics—he was no crackpot. He also noted that while what he'd seen was technically a UFO, he did not believe it to be an alien spacecraft. Instead, the governor speculated that what he had seen "was probably an electronic occurrence of some sort."

As the details became more public, many wrote off Carter's sighting as confusion over the appearance of the particularly bright Venus in the night sky—but to more trained observers, it seemed unlikely that the

---

Constitution—in honor of the national bicentennial in 1976—instead to *Enterprise*, after the popular television show *Star Trek*.

* The Lions Club was one of the most important networks of Carter's life—he'd followed his father into the service group and risen in its ranks by 1969 to be a district governor, in charge of about fifty-six clubs in southwestern Georgia, a network that provided him important visibility as a rising politician and one that he'd credit later for stoking his ambition to run for governor in the first place.

Naval Academy–trained Carter, who would have known celestial navigation through and through, would be confused by a planet. The mystery
persisted: What had he seen?*

As Carter campaigned, he promised he would open up the proverbial
vault of the nation's UFO secrets. "One thing's for sure, I'll never make fun
of people who say they've seen unidentified objects in the sky," he pledged.
"If I become President, I'll make every piece of information this country
has about UFO sightings available to the public and the scientists."

Surely, ufologists believed, he would tell the nation what was really
happening. In April 1977, *U.S. News & World Report* wrote that indeed
the truth was coming: "Before the year is out, the Government—perhaps
the President—is expected to make what are described as 'unsettling disclosures' about UFOs." Once in the Oval Office, though, Carter never
followed up on his pledge—and as a result, it was up to the world of
popular culture to imagine the worlds beyond.

• •

---

* It wasn't until 2016 that Jere Justus, a researcher and former air force scientist, finally
solved the puzzle: Carter had seen a high-altitude rocket-released barium cloud.
Justus knew this because, in the 1960s, he had worked on air force and NASA atmospheric studies on winds in the upper atmosphere—and at twilight and just after
dark, particle clouds could give off a green or blue glow as the barium became electrically charged in the atmosphere. As Justus dug into the records, he found that on
the night of Carter's sighting, a similar experiment had been launched from Eglin
Air Force Base in western Florida at 6:41 p.m.; a rocket had risen into the sky and
released three different clouds of barium at various heights, through about 7:09 p.m.
The clouds—rising and growing rapidly in brightness—would have been visible
from Leary, which was about 150 miles away. "The rapid growth in apparent cloud
size and brightness, followed by the subsequent diminishment in both size and
brightness, could easily be interpreted by an observer as an 'object' first approaching
and then receding," Justus explained in a subsequent report. It could also appear to
be in close proximity, despite being a hundred kilometers up in the sky. This wasn't
entirely rare—in fact, Justus had experience with this kind of observer confusion.
During an experiment in the early 1960s, he later recalled, "An Atlanta woman saw
a sodium vapor trail, launched one evening from Eglin AFB, about 600 km distant.
She viewed the cloud through the bare branches of a deciduous tree, then called a
local Atlanta TV station to report that a 'UFO had landed in a tree at the end of her
street'!"

That same year, Hynek's own life of work crossed into pop culture for the first time. Although aliens had been a staple of entertainment for decades, the late 1970s media machine was almost single-handedly driven by stories from space, most notably through the immense popularity of the TV show *Star Trek*, George Lucas's groundbreaking *Star Wars*, and Steven Spielberg's *Close Encounters of the Third Kind*. Hynek had written the young director in January 1976 after realizing that the title of his upcoming film had the same title as one of the tiers of his classification system in *The UFO Experience*. Spielberg apologized, and eventually his production company, Amblin, optioned Hynek's book and the right to use the term for $2,000; he also hired Hynek as a technical consultant for three days at $500 each.

The movie, only Spielberg's fourth ever as director and the follow-up to his massive 1975 summer hit, *Jaws*, reunited him with Richard Dreyfuss, who played a blue-collar Indiana man whose life was changed by a series of UFO encounters.* It was a huge sensation, grossing nearly $300 million at the box office, and winning two Oscars. It also further popularized Hynek's UFO classification system, as well as the work of Project Blue Book; some of the movie's most famous scenes were inspired by real sightings, including the 1957 encounter in Levelland, Texas, and 1966 sightings in Ohio. A French character in the movie, Claude Lacombe, was modeled on Jacques Vallée, and Hynek was given a six-second cameo, during which he could be seen stroking his ever-present goatee. Contact information for the Center for UFO Studies appeared on the movie posters, and resulted in hundreds of new members, sightings, and inquiries. For the first time, Hynek's grandly named center moved out of his house and into its own office space, with enough new reports to keep its corps of two part-time and 150 volunteer investigators busy.

The movie's most profound legacy, however, would be the way it changed Americans' idea of what an alien was, or could be. Gone were

---

* It was hard not to see the entire movie as an allegory of Hynek's own personal evolution on the question of extraterrestrials, "reinforc[ing] a narrative that had been taking shape for decades," historian Kate Dorsch pointed out, that "Witnesses were rational, the government couldn't be trusted, scientific interest was legitimate, and UFOs were real."

the little green men and the tentacled body snatcher. The extraterrestrials in Spielberg's world were gray, child-sized humanoids with small noses, hairless smooth bodies, black eyes, and thin arms (setting a new visual for years to come), who offered a benevolent, consciousness-raising contact experience—not a threatening, existential encounter with nuclear-age overtones—and the citizens of Earth were maturing into their roles with a larger galaxy, a concept that, intentional or not on Spielberg's part, served as a moving tribute to the work that Sagan, Drake, Hynek, and others had been doing for decades. The movie, film critic Charlene Engel wrote, "suggests that humankind has reached the point where it is ready to enter the community of the cosmos."

When Spielberg was asked a few years later to select his favorite image from his career, he chose the moment when the young wonder-filled boy of *Close Encounters* opened his living room door to the blazing orange light from the UFO, inadvertently creating the perfect metaphor for our thoughts about what lay beyond our universe—certain and uncertain, but more convinced than ever that something was out there: "That beautiful but awful light, just like fire coming through the doorway. He's very small, and it's a very large door, and there's a lot of promise or danger outside that door."

That question of "promise or danger" was what had consumed Hynek's intellectual energies for decades—and it was one he never fully resolved for himself. He retired from teaching at the end of the 1970s, moving west to Arizona, but remained active in the international UFO community. The boy whose parents took him out to see Halley's Comet pass overhead when he was just five days old in 1910 died just as the comet passed through Earth's skies once again, never knowing the truth about the quest that had animated so much of his life—but with ever more passing time, he'd come to doubt the idea of any grand conspiracy. "There are two kinds of cover-ups," Hynek explained late in life. "You can cover up knowledge and you can cover up ignorance. I think there was much more of the latter than of the former."

Situation Red

O ne of the puzzles that had long dogged the tales of UFO crash retrievals was why, if the US government had indeed secretly captured
astounding, galaxy-traveling equipment, the military was still flying
around in gas-fueled jet planes. Thus far, attempts to transform flying
craft—like Avro's Project 1794—had delivered little more than a battlefield hovercraft, failing so significantly that they'd never even been deployed in combat. If the government had succeeded in locating crashed
alien ships, it certainly hadn't figured out how to use them.

Then, in the final months of Carter's presidency, the Pentagon announced a stunning new innovation. As it turned out, the government
had been at work for years on some of the most secret and futuristic
planes ever developed—developed not with the help of captured alien
technology as it turned out, but computers and modeling clay. The process had begun with a competition by the Defense Advanced Research
Projects Agency, the Pentagon's own big-thinking skunk works, known as
Project Harvey (after the 1950 Jimmy Stewart film featuring an invisible
bunny), which had the goal of radically reducing the ability of air defense
radar to identify attack planes. Two defense contractors, Northrop and
Lockheed, had squared off over competing designs. Lockheed, which
had built the original record-breaking U-2 spy plane in the 1950s, submitted the plans for an even more advanced, high-flying, record-setting
plane that it was already developing—the A-12 Oxcart designed for
the CIA, and its more public but nearly identical cousin known as the
SR-71, designed for the air force, had capabilities that were so secret,
DARPA had originally excluded Lockheed from the stealth competition,
not realizing how much work it had already done in the field. (The A-12
had a radar cross-section just one-twentieth that of the similarly sized
B-47 bomber.)

Northrop, meanwhile, had seized upon an observation featured in an underacknowledged 1960s technical paper from the Soviet Union, "Method of Edge Waves in the Physical Theory of Diffraction," by Russian physicist Pyotr Ufimtsev: the size of a radar return, Ufimtsev had noted, was determined not by the size of the overall object but by how the radar waves reflected off of it—meaning that, if you could design a plane to break up the radar return, you could design a plane that was effectively invisible. The realization had gone completely ignored by the Soviet military, seen as so obscure and unuseful that it hadn't even been classified, but at Wright-Patterson Air Force Base, where the Foreign Technology Division translated Soviet science publications wholesale, it attracted a good deal of attention. Once it passed into Northrop's hands, "The whole world changed," an engineer recalled. "My eyes opened, 'Oh, this is what we need.'"

In the years ahead, Lockheed and Northrop continued to face off in secret competitions, driven by computer models and engineer intuition, until the first mounted prototype radar tests at White Sands Missile Range in 1976. Flight tests, code-named Have Blue, followed at Area 51, with planes that looked like nothing aviation had ever seen before—angular, black, and futuristic.

Even following the Pentagon announcement of their creation in 1980, the first two stealth planes would remain secret for years—the B-2 bomber was unveiled to the public in 1988 and the F-117 Nighthawk only in 1990—but their presence at the remote Area 51 site in the Nevada desert, a test range that the government still refused to even publicly confirm the existence of, would add to the range's mystique, inspiring rumors that even more exotic technologies were hidden away inside the closed facility. In 1978, as the first stealth tests began, the government began actively discouraging—and sometimes even preventing—public access to the Groom mountain range near Area 51, and in the years ahead, it would swallow up more of the adjacent land, throwing a larger cloak around whatever was happening at what insiders called "the Ranch." If the government was hiding stealth planes inside Area 51, many wondered, what *else* might it be hiding there?

• •

These fears of strange technologies, secretive government tests, and extra-terrestrials gave rise to one of the more bizarre categories of paranormal phenomena: the "mutes." Starting in the late 1970s, varying degrees of belief in conspiracies and secrets had begun to divide the ufology world, and one of the defining fracture points was the question of cattle muti-lations.

Though decidedly less mysterious and exciting than abductions, en-counters, and strange signals, mutilations had always played a role in UFO lore—isolated reports of them in areas where UFOs had been spotted had circulated for more than a decade, and generally involved ranchers and farmers discovering dead cattle or horses with odd seemingly surgical in-juries, or bloodless wounds that suggested something more than normal predation—and no one, not even the ufologists, had ever really known what to make of them. In 1967, after investigating an incident in south-ern Colorado, the Condon Committee and NICAP had emerged more baffled than they had ever been. The victim was Lady, a three-year-old Appaloosa saddle horse from the King family ranch that had been found skinned and butchered around the neck, but with no traces of spilled blood (other odd details included a green substance that burned the hands of the ranch owner's sister, and ranchers reporting "exhaust marks" in the surrounding desert). Ongoing local fascination had eventually led to a *Denver Post* article, which in turn had caught the attention of official investigators, including the Colorado State University chief of veterinary surgery and a Blue Book investigator. While they found little interesting about the case—the horse, they determined, died of natural causes and the wounds all appeared to be resulting from normal predation—APRO's local leader declared that "the whole episode smacks of the strange, the bizarre, the unknown." (Its subsequent report on the matter, however, un-dermined the strength of the argument with numerous errors, including both the horse's name and gender.)

Over the next decade, the odd stories continued, many of them helped along by John Keel—the *Mothman Prophecies* writer saw them as more indications of the occult-like nature of UFOs and extraterrestrials, and called for more intense examination. In Kansas, a 1973 wave of sus-picious cattle deaths, mostly Black Angus cows within a few miles of US

81, prompted a conference of a dozen local sheriffs and state investigators; the veterinarian lab at Kansas State University again concluded that the deaths looked natural, but Ottawa County Deputy Sheriff Gary Dir rejected the idea, saying, "I've spent 25 years of my life on a farm around cattle. These cases don't match up with what coyotes do." The following year, *Newsweek* took the story national, explaining that "more than 100 cattle have been dead and gruesomely mutilated in Nebraska, Kansas, and Iowa," with the note that the animals often seemed like their eyes and genitals had been uniquely targeted and carefully excised—although for what purpose no one could ever determine.

As reports piled up, conspiracies deepened. Frustrated and fearful, ranchers began to notice unmarked black helicopters circling at night, which led to speculation that the mutilations were stemming from some mysterious, military-approved training program. ("Mutilated Livestock, Helicopters, and UFOs Source of Wonder, Worry," read a headline in the Hastings, Nebraska, *Daily Tribune*.) Armed vigilante ranchers began to stop out-of-state vehicles passing through nearby roads to check for traces of cattle blood; some began to shoot at passing helicopters. "The problem became so widespread that the Nebraska National Guard ordered all helicopters to fly at two thousand feet rather than the standard one thousand when they performed routine exercises," one historian of the phenomenon noted. Cattleman associations offered reward money for answers.

On some level, ranchers and cattlemen had the right to be suspicious: in 1968, some six thousand sheep had died in a place called Skull Valley, Utah, near a secret military facility known as the Dugway Proving Ground, and for years the army had tried to deny culpability, until the investigative efforts of a Utah senator revealed that a plane had accidentally sprayed VX nerve gas at high altitude as part of an army test, which had then drifted into the valley and destroyed the sheep flock. Perhaps the targeted cattle deaths were due to another case of the government's reckless disregard for the freedoms of the wide-open range.

As the post–Watergate Church and Pike Committees turned over the dirtiest rocks of the intelligence community's decades of abuses and scandals, it seemed easier to believe that something was amiss. After all, the cattle industry was facing one of its worst years in recent memory, with little to no support. "The federal government betrayed, targeted, and abandoned small-scale ranchers, leaving them to deal with economic uncertainty," historian Michael J. Goleman explained. "When the cattle mutilations did occur, small-scale ranchers fought back, blaming the federal government and secret agencies, while also projecting their fear, insecurities, and distrust of the government into the bizarre phenomenon." Before long, concerned state legislators and members of Congress were pestering the FBI to get involved, but despite the number of reported nationwide incidents climbing into the thousands, the bureau demurred. It was unclear if a crime had been committed, and you couldn't exactly cross-examine a cow for information.

In 1975, after much lobbying and agitating, official federal and state investigations finally began, including one conducted by ATF agents in Minnesota and another by the Colorado Bureau of Investigation. In 1979, a retired FBI agent named Kenneth Rommel received a grant from the Santa Fe district attorney and other entities to continue hunting for answers, and in Arkansas, the Washington County Sheriff's Office conducted a controlled experiment in which a dying cow was administered a lethal dose of tranquilizers and then placed in a rural ravine under constant human and camera surveillance; after twenty-four hours, the corpse had been subjected to many of the same wounds seen in "typical" mutilation incidents, and now the deputies had photographic evidence that determined normal scavenger predators had been responsible. "It is a rule rather than the exception for these animals to do a neat job and not leave either blood or mess at the site of a carcass," a Missouri University vet explained. A South Dakota social behavior professor concluded the whole phenomenon was "a classic case of mild mass hysteria," stemming from the era's "partial breakdown of normal social-control forces." Ultimately, the investigations found nothing particularly sinister—no UFOs, no government plot, no mass devil-worshipping cult,* just what folklorists called "foaftales," according to UFO historian Jerome Clark,

---

* Carl Whiteside, the CBI agent who headed the bureau's investigation, said, "I'm not ready for the U.F.O. theory. Maybe I'm narrow-minded."

stories that were passed along from a "friend of a friend" in a game of telephone that ultimately unraveled when actually investigated—but resistance to that conclusion persisted.

Unsatisfied by the first round of findings, Senator Harrison Schmitt included language in the 1979 annual Justice Department appropriations bill mandating that the FBI investigate the cattle mutilations, saying he hoped the directive would mean "that the answer to this bizarre and grisly mystery will be found." As the FBI worked, filmmaker Linda Howe collected firsthand stories into a documentary called *A Strange Harvest*, which would help transform the mystery from terrestrial conspiracy to extraterrestrial event. "We didn't know what could have happened unless it was a flying saucer or something," one rancher told Howe. A local DA investigator responded to the theory of alien participation with interest: "I'm inclined to agree . . . that who is doing this now is very possibly creatures not of this planet."

By that point, the cases had caused a real schism in the ufology community. APRO's Coral Lorenzen had decided there was indeed a UFO linkage and MUFON widely circulated "mute" stories as part of its newsletter, but the Center for UFO Studies continued to have its doubts. Unlike the broader UFO phenomenon, cattle mutilation seemed almost uniquely American, making them less like extraterrestrial sightings, which happened around the globe, and defied even basic UFO conventions and understanding. Logically, it made little sense that the government would need to rely on mutilating random far-flung private ranch cattle here and there all over a dozen western states when, presumably, it could experiment on any number of cattle it purchased on its own. In the end, the Center for UFO Studies doubted the idea that the "mutes" were an anomalous phenomenon at all—just weird folktales of random natural occurrences.

That December, the conversation was revived again when science fiction editor Ian Summers—touring to promote his latest extraterrestrial project—joined forces with writer Daniel Kagan in an exhaustive search for answers about the mutes. Over the course of four years, the pair visited the site of seemingly every major case across the nation, interviewing witnesses and investigating incidents. What they found was less a national scourge of deaths-from-the-sky and more a colorful fringe populated by self-interested ufologists, angry rural residents, and overly enthusiastic small-town journalists who had pieced together a sensational puzzle.*

In their resulting book, *Mute Evidence*, Kagan and Summers explained these realities, and connected the dots between the mutilations and larger cultural and political outlooks. "Mutilation phenomenon can tell you a lot about Americans' loss of faith in institutions that have turned out to be inept, hollow, harmful, and bureaucratically crippled in thought," they concluded. "The whole point was the believers . . . *needed* the cattle mutilations to be bizarre, they needed them to remain a mystery." As long as the cattle deaths remained a mystery, the ranchers could imagine that far away in Washington, military leaders and bureaucrats were targeting them and undermining their way of life. It wasn't the larger economic shifts that had their ranches under peril, it was personal.†

• •

For all the belief through the 1970s that the government was in on the truth, though, there was plenty of evidence that the military itself remained disconcerted and dumbfounded by sightings, too. In fact, the most famous sighting to occur in the UK happened in 1980 focused on a US military base. Early on the morning of Boxing Day 1980—the traditional UK holiday the day after Christmas—a security patrol near the rear east gate of the RAF Woodbridge military base on the UK's coast spotted a bright light crossing the sky at around 3 a.m. The base, an old World War

---

* They also determined that the media's oft-repeated estimate of ten thousand mutilation incidents was just bad, back-of-the-envelope math conducted by two "mutologists" who had added up one Colorado county's total of incidents and then multiplied it by four because they believed that only one in four incidents was likely to be reported to authorities. Then they had extrapolated data from other states to create a mumbo jumbo that declared ten thousand a reasonable number.

† The anger, though, of the western ranchers against the federal government and what they saw as its attempts to undermine their lifestyle and economic well-being would not lessen—and would over the 1980s help spark the Sagebrush Rebellion, a low-level and ultimately decades-long protest and quasi-armed insurgency that would bring them into repeated conflict with federal agents, including laying the groundwork for the infamous Bundy standoffs in Nevada in 2014 and Oregon's Malheur National Wildlife Refuge in 2016.

II airfield near the east coast of Suffolk, England, had been used by the US
Air Force through the Cold War. The two US Air Force security police
on patrol, an airman first class and a staff sergeant, reported that the light
had come down into the adjacent Rendlesham Forest, a giant, 3,700-acre
woodland that backed up against the military facility. Thinking it might
be a crashed civilian aircraft, they called for help and, when additional
personnel arrived, ventured into the forest on foot to investigate.

According to a memo written two weeks later by the deputy base
commander, the then-trio of officers quickly encountered a glowing object, "metallic in appearance and triangular in shape, approximately two to
three meters across the base and approximately two meters high.

"It illuminated the entire forest with a white light," the account continued, and "the object itself had a pulsing red light on top and a bank(s)
of blue lights underneath. The object was hovering or on legs." As the security patrol approached, the apparatus maneuvered away ahead of them
and disappeared—off in the distance, the patrol could hear animals on
the nearby farm go "into a frenzy." When local police arrived shortly after
4 a.m., they reported that the only glow they could see were from the
revolving lights at the nearby Orfordness Lighthouse, some miles down
the coast. Later, investigators wondered if the security patrol had actually
conflated a series of unrelated explainable lights—including a fiery meteor that was reported to be passing through the southern English skies
around that time that night and a glimpse of the lighthouse's beacon
passing through the forest's glades. The next day, further investigation
uncovered what the air force team believed were three depressions in the
ground near where the object had been, but the local officers were un-
impressed—they thought the depressions looked more like those made
by animals than alien craft. Locals who ventured into the forest in subsequent days found nothing particularly interesting about the glade either,
chalking the whole incident up to young American airmen, posted to a
foreign land and unfamiliar with the normal marks, broken branches, and
holes that populate a forest. Later, another red "sun-like" pulsing light
was reported in the same woods, and air force personnel reported "three
star-like" objects moving rapidly through the sky.

Decades later, the two lead air force security officers, John Burroughs
and Jim Penniston, would collaborate with an author on a book about

what was now being called "Britain's Roswell," the "best documented and most compelling UFO incident ever to have taken place." In *Encounter in Rendlesham Forest*, they added voluminous details beyond what was captured in the official contemporaneous memo—including, for instance, a claim that Penniston had actually touched the object, finding it smooth, "almost like running your hand over glass," and seen a series of hieroglyphic-like symbols along its side that were "rough," like "sandpaper."

In the years ahead, multiple additional theories about the Rendlesham Forest incident were circulated and debunked, including one that held the UFO sighting was an unfriendly prank played by British special forces on the US Air Force personnel—but like many such sightings the truth of what anyone saw in the forest that night is probably lost to history.* To the believers, though, the Rendlesham Forest incident was more proof that the aliens were visiting, and that they had technologies beyond our comprehension—craft that baffled even the military.

---

* The Rendlesham encounter today is so well known, from various documentaries and books, that the local forestry division even constructed a marked "UFO Trail" through the forest for visitors to explore, complete with a model of the object the air force purportedly saw.

34

Exploring the Cosmos

Though he had been a moderate science celebrity for some time already, Carl Sagan became a true household name in 1980 with the airing of *Cosmos: A Personal Voyage*, a thirteen-part television series on PBS cowritten by Sagan and his new love, Ann Druyan. Modeled on other popular narrator-led documentaries like David Attenborough's *Life on Earth*, *Cosmos* took viewers on a wild and imaginative journey of discovery through the worlds of space and showcased Sagan's remarkable gift for communication—his neighborly, awestruck on-screen presence quickly made him a living room sensation. The series became a landmark moment in science television, reaching hundreds of millions of viewers in ultimately sixty countries worldwide, heavy with then-novel special effects, and covered topics ranging from ancient astronomy to cutting-edge physics, mixing science, religion, philosophy, and lots of music.

Aboard Sagan's *Ship of the Imagination*, viewers journeyed through the universe, starting with the Big Bang and exploring the origins of life on Earth, the evolution of species, and the future of humanity. An accompanying oversized book—filled with images and featuring a full-page back cover photo of Sagan in all his youthful rakish glory, with a full head of hair and brown corduroy jacket, more J.Crew model than bookish PhD—became the bestselling science book of all time, spending seventy weeks on the *New York Times* bestseller list and selling nearly a million hardcover copies.* Sagan was now the most well-known scientist

---

* The show would remain the most-watched PBS series until the debut of Ken Burns's *The Civil War*, and for years to come, the series and the book would be cited by future scientists as inspiring passions and career paths. Sarah Stewart Johnson, who would go on to be one of the world's leading experts on Mars, remembered watching the show as a young child with her parents on the family's gold couch,

in the world and the closest thing the field had to a rock star, appearing on Johnny Carson's show, featured on the cover of *Time* magazine, recognized in airports and restaurants, and deluged by fan mail—including many letters carefully filed in what his office called "Fissured Ceramics," i.e., crackpots.* The newfound status helped him launch the Planetary Society, a nonprofit to champion public support for space exploration. Along with his cofounders, Bruce Murray and Louis Friedman, Sagan spoke widely about his hope that the group would fill some of the gaps in funding research, eventually catching the attention of Steven Spielberg, the *Close Encounters of the Third Kind* director, whose newest movie, *E.T.*, had become the highest-grossing film of all time. Spielberg pledged a $100,000 grant to help fund Project Sentinel—an effort that was using SETI's META, the Megachannel ExtraTerrestrial Assay, to search and listen to more than eight million channels, far more than the previous maximum of 128,000.† ("How fitting," Frank Drake later noted, "that some of the box office receipts generated by *E.T.*, whose character used radio to 'phone home,' would go to fund the radio search for the real ET.")

---

rapt as, "With the help of wild special effects, Sagan spun among the stars, cruised through the 'snowballs of Saturn,' and turned his body into a silhouette of pink lasers. He jumped forward and back through time, crawled inside a giant human brain, and floated across treetops, often to a melody of trippy music."

* His iconic catchphrase from the series, "billions and billions," was even satirized by an actual rock star, in Frank Zappa's "Be in My Video." Sagan's fame left some colleagues embittered: in 1984, he came up for membership in the National Academy of Sciences and was rejected—just as his Soviet colleague Shklovsky had been turned aside by the Russian academy. Eight years later, he was rejected a second time, even as the other fifty-nine people on that ballot sailed through. Sagan brushed the affront aside: "A scientists who devotes his life to studying something arcane like the hyperfine structure of the molybdenum atom, and whose work is ignored by everyone except the world's three other experts on molybdenum, naturally is jealous and outraged to see reporters hanging on me for my latest pronouncement about the possibility of extraterrestrial life."

† META would find a powerful burst in the favored 1420 MHz band, a signal that appeared to emanate from the center of the galaxy, precisely the direction where most of the galaxy's stars would be. The intriguing signal was never seen again. Sagan and META's Paul Horowitz would call such events "things that go bump in the night."

Sagan also leveraged his public profile for one very important mission: securing an audience with Senator William Proxmire, who had managed to bar government funds from being used for SETI. A fiscal hawk, Proxmire had started issuing monthly "Golden Fleece Awards" in 1975, highlighting what he saw as wasteful spending. More often than not, he targeted research projects that he felt were unworthy of serious study, like an $84,000 National Science Foundation study on love, and an Agriculture Department's $46,000 quest to understand how long it took to cook breakfast.* In February 1978, he'd turned his sights on SETI, announcing in a press conference that he thought NASA was capitalizing on public fascination with *Star Wars* and *Close Encounters of the Third Kind* to sucker taxpayers into funding their quixotic search for other civilizations. "The overwhelming odds are that such civilizations, even if they once existed, are now dead and gone," the senator had argued. "In my view, this project ought to be postponed for a few million light-years."

The rant might not have mattered much if he didn't chair the Senate Appropriations subcommittee that oversaw NASA's budget; his objection was all but enough to kill SETI's hope for a multimillion-dollar line item that would fund a new "all-sky, all-frequency" radio search. Furious at the dismissal of the legitimate scientific inquiry, Drake had blasted Proxmire publicly at the time, declaring, among other things, that he would be signing up the Wisconsin Democrat for a membership in the Flat Earth Society,† while more than one astronomer pointed out ruefully that the light-years the senator had joked about were actually a measure of distance, not time. Unfazed by the reaction, Proxmire pushed through an amendment banning funding for developing or analyzing techniques for extraterrestrial radio signals, further squashing any hope that NASA or other groups might squeak through research funding for receivers and computer programs through the Ames Research Center and Jet

---

* It's a bit of an irony that Proxmire made such a career of criticizing seemingly narrow research projects, since he was the first US senator to receive hair transplants for his hair loss, a $2,758 expense he claimed on his taxes as a medical procedure.

† Drake was later surprised to receive a call from the senator's staff wondering if he could actually get a membership plaque from the society for their office wall.

Propulsion Laboratory, a trivial $2 million a year for seven years that had the potential to be transformative. In Congress at the time, it seemed an easy vote—there were few willing to speak up for SETI and so, without much fanfare, government spending had been cut off, and a new existential peril spread: even if a civilization was advanced enough and lived long enough to search for life beyond, if there were enough Senator Proxmires out there across the galaxy, no one might ever find each other.

Now, though, Sagan saw the attention from *Cosmos* and the public aura of enthusiasm as a chance to right Proxmire's wrong. The two men met and spent more than an hour talking, during which Sagan educated the senator on SETI's outsized potential against its minimal cost. To Sagan, the search for other worlds might help humans understand how to navigate our own, to survive peacefully as a people, and avoid the nuclear catastrophes that still loomed large over the world—particularly so in the early 1980s, when military exercises and defense hawks in both the Soviet Union and US had brought the two superpowers seemingly closer than ever to conflict. Ultimately, Proxmire was won over and agreed to walk back his objections to SETI.* Soon after, a new National Academy of Sciences report designed to help advise Congress on research agendas endorsed spending $20 million on the group's projects.

"It is hard to imagine a more exciting astronomical discovery or one that would have greater impact on human perceptions than the detection of extraterrestrial intelligence," the committee stated. That same year, the International Astronomical Union similarly moved to support SETI as a worthy endeavor, creating a 51st subject committee, titled "Bioastronomy: Search for Extraterrestrial Life," which elevated SETI's mission to the same plane in the field as the study of the sun, meteors, planets, and galaxies. Its founding members, who gathered that summer in a sweltering air-conditioning-less schoolroom to hash out their purview, would include many of the field's biggest names: Nikolai Kardashev, Frank

---

* Convinced in private, Proxmire never quite became a public fan. As Drake ruefully noted, "He did what a good politician does in such circumstances: Instead of reversing his position and speaking in support of what he had once denounced, he just shut up."

Drake, and more. "There could no longer be any question that our pursuit was legitimate astronomical science," Drake recalled.

SETI returned to the federal budget in 1983.

• •

After his hit with *Cosmos*, Sagan's next project was a novel. *Contact* was sold to Simon & Schuster for $2 million, the highest amount ever paid for an unwritten book, and became one of the biggest commercial hits of its publication year. A four-hundred-page meditation on how humans might actually react to an extraterrestrial message and how it would transform life on earth, the story mixed science, religion, and philosophy with a host of slightly fictionalized anecdotes, experiences, and personalities from across Sagan's career, including a main Russian character who resembled Shklovsky, and a female protagonist more-than-loosely based on Jill Tarter, an up-and-coming SETI scientist.

Born in 1944, Jill Tarter—née Cornell—had grown up in a family that encouraged her to learn how to do things herself. When she expressed an interest in being an engineer, her father handed her a plastic transistor radio and told her to take it apart and then reassemble it; when she was ten, he'd taught her the constellations as they walked on the beach at night while on vacation in Florida visiting relatives. In high school, she'd applied to the Ithaca college that shared her last name, and traced her lineage to discover that the founder was a multi-great-half-uncle, only to be told by the school that she was ineligible for the family-bloodline scholarship because it was only open to male descendants. Instead, she managed to attend college on a scholarship from Procter & Gamble, but even that seemed unsteady—a corporate executive told her, bluntly, that he hoped she wouldn't expect a job from the company upon graduation and it tried to rescind the scholarship entirely when she married after her junior year, an early—albeit particularly galling—example of the steady sexism she'd experience in an age when few women were engineers or scientists. (Procter & Gamble assumed if she was getting married, she wasn't serious about a career.) Luckily, her dean—Dale Corson, a future Cornell president—went to bat for her and she kept the scholarship, graduating with a GPA high enough that she qualified for the engineering society,

Tau Beta Pi, only to be told, again, that her gender made her ineligible. In a three-hundred-student engineering class in 1965, she was the only woman.

After graduation, Tarter moved to the Bay Area with her husband and started at UC Berkeley's graduate astronomy program ("You three ladies are so lucky that all the smart men got drafted for Vietnam," the astronomy chair told her and the two other female students), where she quickly established herself as a rising star in the field. Drawn to radio astronomy, her dissertation focused on what she named "brown dwarfs," failed stars that despite their massive size were too small to sustain nuclear fusion—but when one of her professors gave her the 1972 "Project Cyclops" report, she experienced a revelation. "I just knew I'd found the right place," she recalled.

"This is the first time in history when we don't just have to believe or not believe," she remembered thinking. "Instead of just asking the priests and philosophers, we can try to find an answer. This is an old and important question, and I have the opportunity to change how we try to answer it." This, she knew, was how she wanted to spend her career.

With a professor, she began a project called SERENDIP—the Search for Extraterrestrial Radio Emissions from Nearby Developed Intelligent Populations, which planned to "piggyback" on a telescope experiment at the Hat Creek Radio Observatory in Northern California.* She also put herself on NASA's radar, introducing herself to John Billingham, who invited her to a series of small-group discussions about the challenges of interstellar communications.

In the late 1970s, SERENDIP bore the brunt of Proxmire's Golden Fleece cuts, but a few careful accounting reshuffles allowed enough funding for it to skate through and survive. NASA formally embraced the project, offering a plan to prioritize Tarter's work, which included

---

* Hat Creek was so remote, Tarter's biographer Sarah Scoles noted, that Jack Welch— then the head of Berkeley's radio astronomy lab and Tarter's future second husband—learned to fly a plane simply to avoid the hours of narrow, winding roads required to get there. Her marriage to Welch, he of the grape juice family, would lead to a sizable family inheritance when his mother died in 1988, and later allow them to donate upward of $300,000 to future SETI projects themselves.

prototyping a spectrometer machine that could analyze radio signals from space, breaking them apart and then using software to study each frequency for any unusual noise. Much of the first phase involved studying nature's normal radio backdrop, since you couldn't really identify anomalous radio signals if you didn't understand the galactic backdrop of what "normal" space sounded like as well as ordinary human-caused interference. The team called it "defining the SETI sandbox."

NASA also provided Tarter and her colleagues with a van specially equipped to identify and isolate radio frequency interference; it was enormously complex, with the ability to create 65,536 radio channels, such a desired piece of technology that, not long into the project, they got a call that England's Jodrell Bank Observatory wanted to host them. Tarter's team would be granted use of its powerful 250-foot telescope. NASA squeezed the van tightly into a US Air Force C-5 Galaxy cargo plane for the flight from California, and once in England, had it towed to the observatory in Cheshire.

In October and November 1983, as the SETI team began work in England, everything at first seemed to be going smoothly—the project was sailing along, successfully determining that the experiment's planned range was sufficient to detect anomalous signals. Tarter was thrilled, but she remained puzzled by the on-site engineers' constant tinkering with the frequencies and equipment, even when it seemed to be working fine for SETI's efforts.

"Then," she recalled years later to her biographer, "I found out it was all a sham." The observatory's legendary and longtime director, Sir Bernard Lovell—who had helped pioneer radio astronomy after World War II and assembled his first observatory at Jodrell Bank using wartime military surplus equipment—had pulled a fast one on Tarter. The observatory had long served as a key part of the United Kingdom's nuclear early-warning system, working with Western intelligence agencies to spy on Soviet spacecraft, and Lovell's interest in Tarter's work had been less about collaboration and scientific possibility, and more about the equipment she possessed—SETI's van, as it turned out, was just what US and UK intelligence needed to solve one of its most frustrating searches.

• •

Over the course of twenty years in the mid- to late twentieth century, neither the US nor the UK had ever been able to crack the broadcasts of Soviet spacecraft. Classified histories of the effort, released only in 2011 and 2014, described the Western hunt for the Soviet telemetry hookup as an almost "Moby Dick–like obsession" for analysts at the NSA, US military, and Western intelligence, starting with the first Soviet probe to Mars in 1962. In subsequent years, special NSA intercept facilities in Ethiopia, Turkey, and elsewhere had successfully found three of what was believed to be four communication channels the Soviet spacecraft used, but never located that mysterious fourth, which evidently was what the spacecraft used to send back its measurements, data, and photographs. They knew the channel existed because the Soviets consistently released photographs that US intelligence listeners had never seen come back. During the 1970s, the US lost both its Ethiopian and Turkish listening posts, the only two facilities it had that could catch a signal from outer space headed back to Soviet mission control in Crimea,* but thanks to intelligence officers' gradual snooping on Soviet satellite displays at international space expositions and some discreet inquiries from Western astronomers to their Soviet counterparts, the NSA and its UK sister agency, Government Communications Headquarters (GCHQ), was able to narrow the Soviet data link to 5.9 gigahertz.

Then, in the summer of 1983, the Soviet Union launched Venera 15 and 16, two probes set to radar-map Venus. NASA and the NSA were in a hurry to intercept their signals—the US was planning its own Venus-mapping mission for 1988 and intercepting the Soviet data might give it a leg up in their own planning. The best chance was the SETI van, and so an invitation to Tarter was issued. It had been a promising solution, but

---

* The Ethiopian signals intercept base, code-named Stonehouse, operated from 1965 to 1975 and at its peak was home to about six thousand US personnel. "Before its successful career was ended by political unrest and terrorism in Ethiopia, Stonehouse—with the aid of several collaborating sites—gave us a fairly full understanding of the Soviet lunar and planetary program," the once-classified history reads. In fact, through the intercepts, the US "even obtained some scientific data superior to any released by the Soviets."

as the Venusian probes took up their orbits of the planet throughout the fall, Jodrell Bank staff aware of the true mission had grown frustrated. On October 19, the Soviet Union released the first pictures from the mission, photos the NSA still hadn't even found.[*]

On November 8, the SETI van was fired up for another try. Remarkably, shortly after midnight on the ninth, they found the mystery channel. In a rush of excitement and relief, the NSA engineers on-site dashed off a teletype to the NSA's special unit at Fort Meade, Maryland, known as the Defense Special Missile and Astronautics Center (DEFSMAC): "We have it."

When Tarter discovered the full extent of Lovell's deception, she was less than enthusiastic. The situation had led to a beneficial discovery, she knew, but for whom? And why at the expense of her own work? "I thought we were doing SETI here, guys!" she lamented to the team, but her perspective opened up a bit when, during a final meeting with Lovell, she found him in his office, crying, looking at a book filled with photos of Dresden, bombed to ruins in World War II. Tarter had been born six months before Allied troops had stormed ashore in Normandy and only ever learned about the war in history books, but for Lovell, it had very much been a lived experience—long before setting up Jodrell Bank with surplus military equipment, he'd helped in the UK-US effort to perfect radar, an experience and the stakes of which he felt viscerally when he helped retrieve one of the Allies' secret cavity magnetrons from the wreckage of a test flight that killed a number of his scientific colleagues in 1942. Like many of the Manhattan Project personnel, he lived with constant questions about the work he'd done, but also understood what it took to defend freedom.

In his office that day, the photos of Allied destruction before him, he told Tarter, "My sister tells me I should be ashamed." The radar technology he'd helped invent during the war, after all, had been used to deliver such devastating effects on German cities.

---

[*] "The SETI specialists were given sanitized search parameters and limited feedback on results," the NSA history explained.

"I think that's the way London would have looked if not for you," Tarter replied.*

• •

Amid the instability of congressional appropriations and the paucity of overall funding, Billingham, Oliver, Tarter, and the other NASA SETI scientists began to consider other structures and funding sources outside of government loopholes and celebrity gifts. The answer, as it turned out, was both simple and incredibly daunting: leaving NASA and creating a stand-alone institute would allow them to seek private philanthropic support, apply for government funding, and save the massive overhead expenses charged by universities like UC Berkeley, Tarter's technical employer. In 1984, Billingham asked her to try her hand at writing the new group's charter.

Tarter, at first, had little to no idea about where to start, but decided quickly to make the scope of the document as broad as possible, calling for "a research support home for scientists who wanted to tackle research having anything to do with any factors of the Drake Equation."

The SETI Institute officially launched on February 1, 1985, with just two employees: Tarter and Tom Pierson, a former university grants administrator who would serve as CEO.† Its mission, built out from Tarter's original notes, was "to explore, understand, and explain the origin and nature of life in the universe, and to apply the knowledge gained to inspire and guide present and future generations." For its first project, it would embark upon building a multichannel spectrum analyzer that would aid the hunt for anomalous signals in space. To Tarter, the work was as much philosophical as it was scientific; even if SETI never found intelligent

---

* Lovell might have been intended to be a casualty of the Cold War himself, as it would turn out. When Lovell died in August 2012, the University of Manchester released long-sealed diary pages in which Lovell alleged that Soviet intelligence had tried to poison him with radiation during a trip to the Soviet astronomy center in Yevpatoria, Crimea, in 1963. Why exactly he was targeted—or if he actually was—was never clear.

† Pierson, who would serve as CEO until 2013, had gotten involved originally, in part, because he was dating—and later married—Barney Oliver's administrative assistant.

life, the mere existence of the field had the potential to help humanity think differently about itself. "In that mirror," she thought, "we are all the same. It has the effect of trivializing the differences among Earthlings, differences that we're willing to spill blood over. We have to get over that. I think SETI is a great way to do it."

The Alone Theory

After living through the arc of Earth's space race and the decades of inconclusive UFO reports, many of the early SETI pioneers had spent much of the 1980s beginning to reconsider their foundational beliefs and purpose. The giddiness of the Sputnik race, Apollo years, and glories of the space age had passed, and even as *Star Trek*, *Star Wars*, and *E.T.* dominated America's screens, geopolitical and budgetary realities no longer made colonizing the moon, Mars, and beyond mankind's inevitable destiny, causing a real existential crisis among some of the movement's leading figures.

Iosif Shklovsky, in particular, had begun to question many things, including if the Fermi Paradox was actually true. "If intelligent life was abundant in our galaxy, he reasoned that statistically that many civilizations would have advanced far beyond our space travel capabilities millions of years ago," his colleague Herbert Friedman recalled, "and would have sent robot messengers to roam the galaxy far and wide, including our solar neighborhood." As the Russian now saw it, life beyond our galaxy might be all but irrelevant to us—the yawning distances of space condemning us to never truly knowing our neighbors. "He felt that the possibility that we were the only intelligent life, at least in the local system of galaxies, was a much richer concept philosophically, ethically, and morally than the presumption of a universe teeming with life," Friedman said, leaving him somewhat unmoored against the years he had spent working to prove the contrary.

In 1984, Shklovsky and Sagan met for the last time in Graz, Austria, at a Soviet-US space collaboration session, during which Shklovsky's pessimism finally boiled over. Humans, he told his longtime collaborator, were like saber-toothed tigers, a species whose teeth had famously evolved until they were too long to effectively catch prey, leading to the animal's extinction. "Shklovsky's point was that intelligence is a freak of evolution that quickly burns itself out," explained Sagan's biographer. "We will burn ourselves out with hydrogen bombs or the weapons we devise after that. And that is why there was no one signaling in Andromeda, why the universe is empty, or will be after our spark grows cold." Sagan, ever the optimist, was stunned and saddened by the sudden reversal.

Indeed, after three decades of steadily growing enthusiasm for space exploration, there seemed a growing suspicion among some that Earth was, indeed, alone. Astrophysicist Michael H. Hart began to popularize the "alone" theory, building off the famous "Where are they?" question by arguing a concept that he called "Fact A": there are no aliens on Earth now. From that, he extrapolated that there were no other technologically advanced civilizations, at least in our own galaxy, because for any long-lasting, advanced civilization, the one-hundred-thousand-light-year-wide Milky Way would be easily explored and colonized over even a few million years. Soon after, the theory was expanded upon by physicist Frank Tipler, who added the thought that, even if a sophisticated society didn't last long enough to explore on its own, surely it could expand through space using ever larger swarms of self-replicating robots. It wasn't just that there weren't aliens on Earth that showed us to be alone, Hart said: it was that there were no swarms of obvious spacecrafts flying through our solar system.

The discussion continued and became a key part of the UFO debate among experts and newcomers alike. One of Frank Drake's students, a young astronomer named Nathan "Chip" Cohen, took on Tipler with his own logic, "proving" sarcastically that Tipler himself didn't exist, either: "Have you ever seen Frank Tipler?" he boldly wrote in a letter to the physicist. "There are only 4×10^9 people on the planet; surely an intelligent creature would find some direct way of making his presence known to at least a sizable fraction of the population. Perhaps we haven't seen Frank Tipler because we haven't looked hard enough. If we undertook a comprehensive and methodical search for him (in New Orleans?) then we may be able to make a definitive decision on his existence."

Sagan and others, though, never lost their faith. "I feel it in my bones," Sagan replied when asked for a reason for his belief in intelligent worlds, and that outlook continued to frame his approach. His counter-argument to the "alone" theory was among the most controversial—but philosophical—beliefs he held, a new take on an idea first articulated by German radio astronomer Sebastian von Hoerner in the early 1960s that "because we have no knowledge whatsoever about other civilizations, we have to rely completely on assumptions.

"The one basic assumption we want to make can be formulated in a general way: Anything seemingly unique and peculiar to us is actually one out of many and is probably average."

In other words: humans should not imagine themselves special, and if we existed, it stood to reason that others did as well. The strangest thing, statistically, would be that we were the most advanced beings to have ever emerged among the billions of planets across billions of years—in fact, by the very nature of our SETI hunt, it was almost certain that any civilization we heard from would be more advanced than ours. As Sagan argued to a conference in the 1970s, "There is almost certainly no civilization in the galaxy dumber than us that we can talk to. We are the dumbest communicative civilization in the galaxy."

Stephen Hawking later echoed the concept, albeit a bit more bluntly: "The human race is just a chemical scum on a moderate-sized planet, orbiting around a very average star in the outer suburb of one among a hundred billion galaxies. We are so insignificant that I can't believe the whole universe exists for our benefit. That would be like saying that you would disappear if I closed my eyes."

In 1981, *Good Morning America* brought Frank Drake to its studios for a segment debating the "alone" theory, giving the country its first televised discussion of the Drake Equation. Ultimately, though, the debate turned academic and did little to sway a public more fascinated with the simplified concept of aliens as they had been depicted in pop culture. Later, when the new all-news cable channel CNN aired a segment on SETI, almost nine out of ten callers still answered affirmatively to the question "Do you think there is intelligent life in space?"

That public interest, but lack of closer understanding, was one of the great frustrations of scientists who saw their field as broadly supported, but ultimately diminished, to appeal to the lowest common level of comprehension—or worse, a political talking point. The problem wasn't so much that Earth was probably alone out there, they thought, but that more than two decades after Project Ozma, the world had still only barely started looking at all. "I must confess I'm weary. I'm weary of nothing happening in SETI," said Barney Oliver in the 1980s. "It's been twenty years since Morrison and Cocconi and I frankly would've expected more to have happened."

This lack of progress and answers was in no small part, Oliver knew, due to the paucity of resources that the federal government had allocated to the biggest question in the universe. Despite widespread coverage, Congress, NASA, and the White House still underestimated just how much the quest was resonating with the public, and their budget reflected that uncertainty. "The whole NASA budget is five percent of the federal budget, and the planetary exploration is about a tenth of that, and SETI is about a hundredth of that—about one cent per year for the average taxpayer," Oliver raged. "It's so minuscule that nobody would even feel it if it were augmented by a factor of 10. I could contact extraterrestrial civilizations on what we're wasting on food stamps." Congress, he continued, was just as bad, made up of "lawyers who never looked at the stars." Until the government itself felt the enthusiasm and urgency of the UFO mission, it would be doomed—but thanks to fate, luck, and the American electorate, the tide began to turn. In 1981, a new commander in chief arrived, a man uniquely philosophically inspired by UFOs.

Voodoo Warrior

While nearly every presidency in the Cold War had interacted with the UFO story in some manner—from Harry Truman's "Washington-Merry-Go-Round" flap and Gerald Ford's Michigan hearings to Jimmy Carter's own experience outside that Georgia Lions Club—Ronald Reagan was the only president whose time in office was fundamentally shaped by the intersection of UFOs and American culture.

For much of his life, Reagan had been fascinated by science fiction and dramas of the skies, seeing the stories not so much as fiction but as a roadmap to the outer bounds of human imagination and future utopias. He loved the drama and mystery of the Kennedy-era space race, and the novels of Edgar Rice Burroughs about a Martian warlord named John Carter. His service in World War II had brought him into the motion picture unit of the Army Air Forces, and later as an actor, he'd starred in countless films focused on military operations, as well as a couple of science fiction–oriented productions, including *Murder in the Air*, in which he played a government agent who is asked to impersonate a dead spy in order to destroy a US Navy dirigible and stop a death ray.

Like his predecessor, Reagan, too, had seen a UFO personally, while flying in a private Cessna Citation near Bakersfield, California, in 1974. Reagan's pilot that night, Bill Paynter, later recounted noticing a strange object several hundred yards behind their plane, "a fairly steady light until it began to accelerate. Then it appeared to elongate. Then the light took off. It went up at a 45-degree angle at a high rate of speed. Everyone on the plane was surprised," he said. "The UFO went from a normal cruise speed to a fantastic speed instantly. If you give an airplane power, it will accelerate—but not like a hot rod, and that's what this was like." Reagan himself was in awe: "It went straight up into the heavens," he recalled.

Now, upon his election to the presidency in 1981, he had pulled to-gether a space advisory council that included leading sci-fi writers, a team he'd kept in place even after the presidential transition was complete, and governed through anecdotes and experiences from movies.[*] He had long loved the message of the 1951 invasion movie *The Day the Earth Stood Still*, that the nations of the world could set aside their differences and unite against a common foe. In the heady postwar era, he'd even joined the United World Federalists, a North Carolina–based utopian group that advocated for a single peaceful global government.

Such feelings of hope and optimism were sorely needed, as the So-viet Union appeared to be on the downslide, and fears of a nuclear war caused out of desperation persisted. Despite a hawkish first year in office, Reagan had quickly intuited that in the nuclear age, when Armaged-don beckoned, the heroes were no longer the warriors—the heroes were the peacemakers. The Cold War, he realized, was like a Western—two quick-draw gunslingers facing off at high noon, but he knew that both would fall in any shoot-out. There would be no hero left standing once the ICBMs launched. Peace, instead, was the heroic option. And he, very much, very very much, wanted to be the hero on the global stage, just as he'd long been on-screen. In 1983, influenced in part by his emotional reaction to a TV movie called *The Day After* that depicted the fallout of a nuclear Armageddon in graphic visuals, the president began a campaign for a new missile defense system called the Strategic Defense Initiative that was quickly nicknamed, pejoratively, "Star Wars," and as his second term began, met with Soviet leader Mikhail Gorbachev on the banks of Lake Geneva for a summit. Midway through, they took a private stroll outside, accompanied only by their interpreters.

As Gorbachev later recounted about their walk, "President Rea-gan suddenly said to me, 'What would you do if the United States were

---

[*] "Patti Davis describes her father as fascinated with stories about unidentified flying objects and the possibility of life on other worlds," Reagan's biographer, Lou Can-non, later wrote of the president's daughter—and clearly, the whole family loved the analogies. In her own book, Davis described the madness of a presidential in-auguration being akin to "a fifties movie in which flying saucers descend on the metropolis."

suddenly attacked by someone from outer space? Would you help us?' I said, 'No doubt about it.' He said, 'We too.' So that's interesting." To the US president, the question was an opportunity to recognize a shared desire to protect humanity on Earth, a species that might very well succumb to the horrors of nuclear war. If they'd act to protect Earth from aliens, maybe they should act now to protect the planet from similar destruction at home.

Later, Reagan would use the same analogy in a speech to the United Nations, saying, "Perhaps we need some outside, universal threat to make us recognize this common bond. I occasionally think how quickly our differences worldwide would vanish if we were facing an alien threat from outside this world. And yet, I ask you, is not an alien force already among us? What could be more alien to the universal aspirations of our peoples than war and the threat of war?"*

• •

While to some, the American leader's focus on the extraterrestrial beyond might have seemed juvenile or unnecessary, it turned out to be more relevant than ever. As the Cold War entered its final chapter, both the US and Soviet governments were once again hard at work, trying to pin down whether any such invasion might be coming—and, specifically, what the other's government knew about the reality of the UFOs.

As the president pursued his own line of alien-inspired policy, a Pentagon official named Colonel John Alexander† did the same, launching a personal and largely unsanctioned inquiry into the government's knowledge of unidentified flying objects. A former Green Beret who had served in Vietnam, Alexander had spent his postwar years at the edge of research in army intelligence, working specifically on New Age mysticism, physic

---

* Reagan's frequent references to the alien invasions did not sit well with all his staff. According to Reagan biographer Lou Cannon, National Security Advisor Colin Powell "would roll his eyes and say to his staff, 'Here come the little green men again.'"

† Alexander's work was traced, in part, in Howard Blum's book *Out There*, where he was given the pseudonym Colonel Harold Phillips.

abilities, and paranormal activities.* In 1980, after spending time on a team seeking to develop next-generation weapons systems, he'd written a boundary-pushing article for the journal of the army's Command and General Staff College titled "The New Mental Battlefield," which considered how psychic abilities might be applied to military operations. (It's "out there" ideas attracted the attention of some media, including Washington investigative columnist Jack Anderson, who sarcastically referred to the "Voodoo Warriors of the Pentagon," in an article about the potential practice.)

He also met with a Lockheed executive at Skunk Works to discuss Area 51 and its then cutting-edge work on stealth technology and the F-117—a conversation that eventually shifted to the men's shared interest in UFOs. Both, as it turned out, assumed that someone somewhere in the government was hard at work on the subject, especially when it came to the Roswell case. Knowing the ins and outs of how government operated, Alexander theorized that a crack team of government scientists had examined the downed crash, but lacked the sophisticated understanding of physics and engineering behind it, and then set it aside in a "*Raiders of the Lost Ark* scenario," a reference to the final scene of the Indiana Jones movie when the Ark of the Covenant is crated up and wheeled into a giant anonymous government warehouse to be hidden (and forgotten) amid all manner of other uncertain lost treasures. Presumably, the government reconvened a team every decade or so, with updated science, to see what it could glean from the alien craft. The executive and the official also figured that the US probably had at least two UFO efforts currently in operation—one run by the air force, and another by a group of agencies that brought in the relevant scientific and intelligence components. Since they wouldn't bust the case wide open, maybe Alexander and his new ally should be the ones to try.

Together, they began assembling a cross-agency team Alexander called the Advanced Theoretical Physics Project, a name purposely obtuse and uninteresting so as to evade any scrutiny or interest. To ensure

---

* The team's findings and experiences would later be the subject of Jon Ronson's book *The Men Who Stare at Goats*.

they remained off any bureaucratic radar and avoided leaks, Alexander demanded that no written records be kept, and that the group assembled to do the work be, in his words, "literally an old boy network" of established and trusted contacts. Everyone involved would have to at least have a minimum security clearance of "TS-SCI at SI-TK," the government notation for people cleared for top secret information and the even more restrictive "sensitive compartmented information," including so-called communication intelligence, known as "special intelligence," or SI, and Talent Keyhole intelligence, the designation for imagery from the nation's spy satellites.

The first meeting, held at the offices of the defense contractor BDM in Tysons Corner, Virginia, consisted of more than a dozen officials from the army, air force, DIA, NSA, and CIA, as well as several major aerospace manufacturers like Lockheed and McDonnell Douglas. Together they discussed the knowns and unknowns of the UFO phenomena and the extent of the government's involvement—but as their day progressed, it became clear everyone had only the same second- or thirdhand knowledge. "Everyone from an organization that seemed a likely candidate—either from the US government or aerospace industry—thought it was some other agency or group that was conducting the research," Alexander explained in his memoir.

Over the next two years, from 1985 to 1987, the group met at least four times, according to a schedule later obtained by ufologist Richard Dolan. In one meeting, they examined old classified government reports about UFOs, including original sightings reports, stunned by how little meaning the classified material contained. "What civilian UFO researchers did not know was that 99 percent of the material was actually in the public domain," Alexander recalled, and therefore either sanitized or inconsequential. When they got into the Tehran incident, for instance, they found that the only reason the government's records were classified was to protect the fact that US intelligence personnel had spoken directly to the Iranian pilots—the US didn't want it to leak back to the Shah that it had sources directly inside his military. They were also surprised at how shoddy and intellectually incurious previous efforts like the Condon Committee had been; contrary to public signs that the government had been running a highly classified UFO cover-up, the Advanced Theoretical

Physics Project found mounting evidence that the government had never cared that much about UFOs in the first place.

For the next two years, Alexander and his colleagues kept searching for more answers, approaching engineers, officials, and agencies that would typically be kept in the loop about a secret UFO effort for information—at one point, Alexander even met with Ben Rich, the president of Lockheed's Skunk Works, arguably the most prestigious position in American aviation engineering. Rich had been intimately involved in the SR-71 and F-117 stealth fighters and helped invent the very idea of stealth technology, but now he professed ignorance about UFOs, and showed Alexander his own wish list for cutting-edge technologies that Lockheed wanted to crack. Rich confessed that he'd had the same suspicions that Alexander did—surely someone *else* was working on UFOs—and had assigned one of his own Skunk Works to conduct a hunt for rival UFO projects at other defense contractors. The project hadn't secured any evidence. As a courtesy, he introduced Alexander to the former deputy director of the Pentagon's research and engineering effort, who also seemed to be clueless about any black projects. One by one, quiet, trusted, high-level inquiries at other likely government UFO homes struck out—not NORAD, not the DIA, not the CIA, not the NSA had any information or answers. NORAD personnel walked Alexander through their once- or twice-monthly encounters with "uncorrelated objects," e.g., UFOs, on their continental early-warning radars, but explained that such things weren't usually reported up the chain of command. "The emphasis of the computer codes was to distinguish *threat* from *no threat*," Alexander said. "Extraneous data were generally rejected, meaning that if the incoming objects were not following a predicated path that indicated a threat, it was rejected."

One of the key participants at ATP was a longtime NSA employee named Howell McConnell, who had come over the years to be the signals intelligence agency's unofficial in-house UFO expert. If anyone was in a position in the US government to have detected signs of a real covert UFO intelligence program—in the US or the Soviet Union for that matter—it was McConnell. In 1968, he'd authored a position paper for NSA leaders about the UFO phenomenon, and in the years since, colleagues had regularly sent relevant intelligence caught in its global information dragnet his way. McConnell had become something of a figure in UFO circles and had even befriended Jacques Vallée over the years, the two men bonding over long philosophical conversations about UFOs and religion. (In one conversation recounted in Vallée's diaries, McConnell had tried to reassure him that the intelligence community was, perhaps counterintuitively, too risk-averse to hide the truth about UFOs. "Bureaucrats are just like your scientists," McConnell told the astronomer. "I work for a bunch of bureaucrats whose tendency, too, is to deny. But an agency like ours can take no risks. So we keep an eye on things. If something does happen, they'll be able to say they were aware of the situation, that one of their analysts was informed, his documentation up to date.") Nothing McConnell had ever found, heard, or read shook him from that belief or led him to suspect there was a secret US government project.

By late in Reagan's presidency, Alexander's work had finally reached a point where real funding was needed, and so he approached the Pentagon's Star Wars effort, which seemed well-suited to house a nascent UFO study program—as Alexander saw it, SDI (the Strategic Defense Initiative) was about reducing the chances of nuclear war, and a mistaken UFO sighting or fleet of UFOs could very well trigger that kind of event. Though SDI was interested in Alexander's work, it made clear there was no budgetary room for it. He tried again, this time with the Army Science Board, which was more receptive, but at a cost: Alexander's efforts, apparently, had ruffled the wrong feathers high in the Pentagon, and so while the ASB was inclined to back his work, Alexander was informed he was being transferred out.

Instead of accepting a new dead-end role, Alexander retired, settling at the Los Alamos National Laboratory to continue his quest for the project-that-never-was. The location was no coincidence: if, Alexander thought, the Roswell crash had been real, it made more sense that the downed craft would be taken to the home of the Manhattan Project, rather than the Wright-Patterson Air Force Base, which may have been an important bureaucratic hub, but was hardly a fount of innovation. "The scientific capability at LANL would have exceeded that of the US Air Force," Alexander surmised. "My guess was that if the Roswell crash was real and only a very few people had been in the loop, Dr. Teller, the father of the atomic bomb, would have been one of them"*—yet, when Alexander finally met with the aging Teller, he did not appear to be familiar with the Roswell incident at all. After Alexander filled him in, Teller agreed that, had any craft been recovered, the likeliest home for the follow-up research at the time would have been Los Alamos.

In the end, Alexander and his team came to accept that there were no caves of hidden flying saucers or facilities filled with preserved alien bodies. They had given the government too much credit—it could barely even manage to collect existing UFO sightings and data in an organized way, much less possess the capability to be secretly holding alien crafts. "The key assumption across all agencies was that somebody else was charged with responsibility for UFOs," Alexander recalled later in his memoir. "The ultimate answer appears to be that nobody does have that responsibility."

• •

Despite having trouble answering its primary question, Alexander's team did find success in understanding how the Soviets felt about UFOs. While the NSA had precious few answers to give Alexander's team about any true origins, it was able to offer information and conclusions gathered from various conversations—namely, that the Soviets were just as baffled as US officials were when it came to extraterrestrials. In one briefing, Alexander learned that Felix Yurievich Ziegel, the so-called "Father of UFO Studies" in the Soviet Union, had felt that, in many cases, "the sightings demonstrated indisputably artificiality, strangeness, and intelligence," and that "to explain these events by natural causes is senseless." Another NSA report cited Ziegel's mention of "unusual speed and kinematic movements, luminescence, invulnerability, and paralysis of aggressive intentions," comments that seemed to US ears to indicate that the Soviet military had attempted to intercept or even attack at least one UFO unsuccessfully.

---

* In fact, following Alexander's supposition, the very existence of the Fermi Paradox, stemming from a documented conversation at Los Alamos in 1950 among three of the nation's greatest thinkers at the time, including Teller and Enrico Fermi, undermines the idea that the US had captured or spotted any truly alien craft by then.

Whatever the truth, it was clear that both amateur and official ufology was alive and well behind the Iron Curtain, perhaps as much as it was in the West. Strange sightings had steadily accumulated over decades, beginning not long after Arnold's first sighting in the US, and the Soviet government had studied the topic in fits and starts while the mythology had spread nationwide, thanks in part to public science-education lectures. The government-sponsored events had originally intended to debunk and educate audiences about the facts of science and dispel conspiracies, but it was the engaging stories and colorful, mysterious anecdotes that had attracted lasting interest. ("Ufology penetrated the Iron Curtain as if it didn't exist at all," Russian scholar Alexey Golubev said. "The audience got introduced to not just facts but also storylines from the popularizers.") Ziegel, a noted astronomer and groundbreaking textbook author, had gotten hooked on the subject after reading the Russian translation of Donald Menzel's *Flying Saucers*, and back in 1967, just as the US had been convening the Condon Committee, he had led one of the first official "Soviet UFO Study Groups" with Major General Pyotr A. Stolyarov under the cosmonautics committee of the defense ministry.

Speaking on Soviet Central Television about his new effort, Ziegel had proclaimed, "Unidentified flying objects are a very serious subject which we must study fully. We appeal to all viewers to send us details of any observations of strange flying craft seen over the territories of the Soviet Union." The statement and subsequent investigations turned up hundreds of sightings and provoked a stronger response from the public than officials were comfortable with at the time; in response, they shut it down. Efforts made by the Condon Committee and other UFO groups to interface with the Soviet study group were met with silence. Ziegel, however, never lost interest and continued to collect every sighting he could, ultimately amassing more than three thousand.* To his core, he was

---

* Ziegel, an ethnic German with a Jewish name, had, like many Soviet scientists, struggled against the racism, anti-Semitism, and general brutality of the Communist regime. He was originally expelled from university when his father was arrested based on an anonymous tip from a neighbor who coveted their apartment; his dad spent two years in prison and lost his leg to torture. The family was then deported to Kazakhstan when World War II started.

convinced the phenomena was real. In 1981, he told an Italian publication, "We have seen these UFOs over the USSR; craft of every possible shape: small, big, flattened, spherical. They are able to remain stationary in the atmosphere or shoot along at 100,000 kilometers per hour. They move without producing the slightest sound, by creating around themselves a pneumatic vacuum that protects them from the hazard of burning up in our stratosphere. Their craft also have the mysterious capacity to vanish and reappear at will. They are also able to affect our power resources, halting our electricity-generating plants, our radio stations, and our engines, without, however, leaving any permanent damage. So refined a technology can only be the fruit of an intelligence that is indeed far superior to man['s]."

Then, in 1977, a bright light that witnesses described as "jellyfish"-shaped appeared in the skies over Petrozavodsk. The incident made national headlines and prompted the Soviet Academy of Sciences to assemble a team that would study "anomalous atmospheric phenomena," a framing that sounded more scientific than "UFOs" (and would parallel the later Western phrase "unidentified aerial phenomena"). Astrophysicist Yuly Platov led the effort. It was the second time in its history that the Soviet Union had assembled such a group.

Platov's team—which came to be known as the "The Network"—brought together a number of institutions and scientific experts. But, as they dug deeper into sightings and Ziegel's files, the investigation became as circular—and ultimately as fruitless—as others before it. A national mythology around UFOs slowly began to build, but inside the Soviet Union hard evidence was just as hard to come by as it was in the US.* "If a scientist is faced with something he doesn't understand," Platov later explained, "he tries to explore and study the phenomenon, but if something isn't clear for the military, then it is a possible target, or a potential enemy."

By the time his work came to an end (perhaps it's no coincidence that the downside paralleled with the fall of the Soviet Union in the early 1990s), he had come across some wild sightings—including an Aeroflot

---

* As it was, the Soviet Union even had its own Area 51, a mysterious region known as the "Perm Triangle" in the Urals that was reported to be overrun by UFOs that was often featured in Soviet UFO-themed newspapers and a destination for ufologists.

flight in the mid-1980s that reported a UFO dancing around it—but found no credible evidence of alien visitations. Even the Petrozavodsk sighting was solved when the Iron Curtain fell: the light had been the launch of a rocket from the Soviet facility in nearby Plesetsk. As the *Moscow Times* wrote later, "It appears that the rigid compartmentalization of information in the Soviet Union prevented anyone in Russia from connecting the dots sooner."

MJ-12

On December 11, 1984, a mysterious envelope was delivered to TV producer Jaime Shandera, a colleague of ufologists Stanton Friedman and Bill Moore. When Shandera opened the thick package, closed with brown tape and no return address, he found another envelope, inside of which was a third envelope containing a canister of Kodak Tri-X black-and-white 35 mm film. Shandera raced to find Moore, and the two men quickly developed the film in Moore's bathroom sink, using a magnifying glass to study the resulting images as they hung drying on a living room curtain rod.

The first thing that caught Moore's eye was that every picture was of a different piece of paper with "Top Secret/Eyes Only" typed across the bottom. Upon closer examination, they determined that the images were of a briefing prepared for president-elect Dwight Eisenhower. Dated "18 November, 1952" it was a seemingly routine discussion of a decidedly nonroutine situation: "ONE OF ONE," outlined how the Roswell crash—and others—were real; a "covert analytical effort" had determined the crashed saucer was a "short range reconnaissance craft" and that the four dead occupants inside, while "human-like" had "biological and evolutionary processes . . . quite different from those observed or postulated in homo-sapiens," likely what the team called "Extraterrestrial Biological Entities." Similar discoveries, the briefing explained, had been made near a crash site on the Texas-Mexico border in December 1950. The briefing also contained a page referencing a total of eight attachments, A through H, but only the first of them appeared to have been leaked by the internal source: a one-page, two-paragraph letter from Harry Truman to Secretary of Defense James Forrestal on September 24, 1947, authorizing him to "proceed with all due speed and caution . . . [on] this matter [which] shall be referred to only as Operation Majestic Twelve."

The twelve purported members of what the document labeled the Majestic Group—all now dead, Moore and Shandera noticed—were a who's who of the postwar defense establishment. There was the inaugural Secretary of Defense James Forrestal, CIA director (and future NICAP board member) Roscoe Hillenkoetter, Admiral Sidney Souers, presidential science advisor Vannevar Bush, air force generals Nathan Twining and Hoyt Vandenberg, among others, plus one very notable addition: UFO debunker Donald Menzel. Had the nation's leading UFO skeptic been one of the few people to know the mystery was real all along?

As Moore and Shandera finished scanning the documents, Moore couldn't help but wonder aloud whether the package could be trusted. The optimistic view was that some government insider had trusted them to do the right thing with the most significant cover-up scoop in journalism's history, but the idea that Moore and Friedman, after years of positing that the government was hiding crashed saucers, would suddenly possess official documents proclaiming exactly the information they wanted and needed seemed a little too good to be true.

One thing leaning them toward trust was the fact that the contents of the briefing weren't exactly new: a former air force intelligence officer named Richard Doty had given Moore another supposedly leaked document that had contained a teletype between the Air Force Office of Special Investigations in Washington and a local field office at the Kirtland Air Force Base in New Mexico, discussing an analysis of photos of UFOs and a lengthy explanation of the government's then-current UFO work—including that NASA had continued to study the issue "through covert cover" and that there was a UFO Reporting Center hidden inside the US Coast and Geodetic Survey. "NASA filters results of sightings to appropriate military departments with interest in that particular sighting," the paperwork explained. "The official US Government Policy and results of Project Aquarius is still classified Top Secret with no dissemination outside official intelligence channels and with restricted access to 'MJ Twelve.'" In the wake of receiving that teletype, Moore had teamed up with Friedman and Shandera to research both a fictional novel about Project Aquarius and a TV special, but now they had a second document also appearing to outline Majestic 12. This was big.

For the next two years Friedman, Shandera, and Moore worked to-gether to confirm the documents' authenticity, eventually making their efforts public in a high-profile media rollout in May 1987. Among the evidence they presented to validate the claim was a memo they had found in 1985 in the National Archives, buried in Record Group 341, entry 267, folder T4-1846. Dated July 14, 1954, the document was addressed from National Security Advisor Robert Cutler to General Twining, and re-vealed that "the President has decided that the MJ-12 SSP briefing should take place during the already scheduled White House meeting of July 16, rather than following it as previously intended." Here was a routine scheduling memo, Moore now argued—exactly what you'd expect to find among bureaucrats who ran a supersecret team. If it was real, then MJ-12 was real, and if MJ-12 was real, then so were UFOs.

The public release of the documents caused a public sensation, cov-ered in the *New York Times* and on ABC's *Nightline*, and fueled an up-roar inside the government itself, partly because no one could quite tell if the decades-old documents were genuine. Right from the start, experts began to question their authenticity and details of the origin story and investigation process, starting with why Shandera had seen fit to enlist Moore's help in developing an unlabeled canister of film himself. They spent countless hours trying to determine the documents' validity, while FBI counterintelligence agents were dispatched to the Pentagon and the Defense Intelligence Agency to compare the MJ-12 documents to other paperwork on record and investigate whether a theft had taken place.

One by one, official investigators in both New York and Los An-geles struck out. No evidence that a crime had been committed could be found. The National Archives could find no such document in its top secret register, nor did it find any of the other documents in the file folder that purportedly held the MJ-12 memo. The Eisenhower pres-idential archive reported that there was no trace of the stated meeting on his calendar from July 1954—even on the one that would have noted secret or clandestine conversations. "After more than a year of inquiries, after months of showing the papers to officials representing each of the nation's intelligence organizations, the FBI could not find an agency or an individual willing to swear out a complaint asserting that the MJ-12 document had been stolen from their classified files," journalist Howard Blum reported in 1990.

"We've gone knocking on every door in Washington with those MJ-12 papers," one agent said. "All we're finding out is that the government doesn't know what it knows. There are too many secret levels. You can't get a straight story. It wouldn't surprise me if we never know if the papers are genuine or not."

And yet, as the months and years passed, more and more evidence accumulated that they weren't. Experts pointed to the "Top Secret Restricted Information" moniker on the memo as compelling proof that some doctoring had taken place, since the notation didn't come into existence until the Nixon administration. Then, archivists examined Robert Cutler's schedule, and found that he'd been overseas for the first half of that month, touring US installations in Europe and North Africa, which meant he wouldn't have been in a position to write a routine scheduling memo on July 14.* And, there was, of course, the question of the president. The briefing memo had been written as if the existence of aliens and UFOs would all have been news to Dwight Eisenhower. If there was indeed a cover-up of aliens and UFOs during the summer of the Arnold sighting and Roswell crash, surely it would have involved telling the man who was the commander of both the US Army and Army Air Forces.†

In the end, the most damning piece of evidence came from a UFO debunker named Phil Klass, who spotted a telling extra comma in the briefing paper's date: "18 November, 1952." No established contemporaneous government documents featured a comma after the month, but Klass could find one specific person who did routinely use such a comma in his writings: Moore himself.

---

* The briefing paper displayed similar strange errors of labeling, syntax, and wording, including a lack of standard page numbers and a garbled reference to misnamed "Roswell Army Air Base (now Walker Field)." Today, the National Archives even has a special web page FAQ dedicated to the ten specific problems it's had verifying the existence of the memo.

† The air force, of course, was not an independent service until September 1947.

At best, the images were a prank played on Friedman, Moore, and Shandera—at worse, they were an intentional outright forgery by at least one of them.

Cosmic Watergate this was not.*

---

* In 1989, at a MUFON conference in Las Vegas, Moore gave a strange and rambling speech in which he professed he'd been a government-paid double agent for much of the decades—hoping that by aligning with the government, he could get the inside scoop on the real truth. How much of that speech was true remains an open question, too.

Crop Circles

With the matter of the Moore memo largely resolved, attention shifted within the UFO community to another unique ufological mystery unfolding in the United Kingdom. Strange patterns had started to mysteriously appear in farmers' fields, where, typically, grains like barley, wheat, and canola had been flattened or bent into geometric shapes. The so-called crop circles often stretched several hundred feet in diameter and sometimes came in wildly complex shapes and symbols. Some were simple, seemingly perfect circles. Others were more like concentric rings, elaborate stars, or swooping lines or Celtic-style runes.

While there had been scattered reports of such phenomena dating back to the 1600s, more had emerged throughout the 1970s and '80s, becoming more publicly linked to UFO sightings as time went on. The area of the UK around Wiltshire, the home of Stonehenge, seemed particularly prone to the seemingly mystical anomalies—farmers would wake in the morning to find their fields transformed into intricate and inexplicable patterns.* Tourists and enthusiasts, called "croppies" or "cerealogists," would flock to the scene to walk inside the circles—effectively a paranormal corn maze—and found the experience to be transformative. "I could feel the energy from within the circle itself," a Canadian filmmaker said after journeying to his first circle. "I felt a kind of altered state." The mystery became the subject of numerous books and magazine articles, as well as enthusiast study groups—including one known as CERES (Circles Effect Research), named for the goddess of

---

* In 1990, England awoke to what was called the Eastfield Pictogram, a giant dramatic, multipart crop circle that looked like a piece of out-of-this-world space technology. The pictogram became an almost instant pop culture icon and made it that year onto the cover of Led Zeppelin's album *Remasters*.

agriculture—and even a regular quasi-scientific journal, the *Cereologist*. All of them posed similar questions: Were they coded messages from far-off civilizations? Pretty designs carved by saucers for fun or to harness some unknown spiritual energy? Some started to believe the flattened patches were actually a by-product of saucer landings and began to refer to them as "saucer nests."

The mystery was seemingly solved in September 1991, when two British artists—Dave Chorley and Doug Bower—confessed to using existing tractor rows and creating circles using boards and rope in British fields to trick farmers. Imitators soon followed, which explained the large volume of incidents. All told, they estimated they'd made two thousand crop circles across more than thirteen years.

To see if such a claim was possible, Britain's Channel 4 filmed the landscape gonzo artists making a crop circle, carefully but quickly using boards, rope, and a hat fixed with a long piece of wire to shape the field. When it was done, a self-proclaimed crop-circle expert was called in and asked to authenticate. He proclaimed the circle "genuine," a phrase they used to declare something the work of a paranormal phenomenon or UFO: "No human being could have done this. These crops are laid down in these sensational patterns by an energy that remains unexplained and is of a high level of intelligence," he confidently asserted. When the reporters informed him that it had indeed been made, his distress was evident. "We have been conned," he exclaimed. "This is a dirty trick. Thousands of lives are going to be wrecked over this."*

• •

Amid this mild crop chaos, the next evolution in the darker side of the UFO debate arrived in the form of the "whistleblowers," a new constellation of odd and mysterious characters proliferating the idea of an expansive government cover-up larger than any had previously thought or

---

* Still, though, the decidedly terrestrial phenomenon unfolds seemingly annually during "crop circle season" in southern England—and some, even the affected farmers, are convinced the circles aren't just a human hoax. As one Wiltshire farmer told the BBC in 2021, "Some of the formations are so intricate and so big that I can't see two people doing them."

imagined. The movement was strengthened thanks to a then-emerging medium: online message boards.

The FidoNet bulletin board ParaNet had been founded in 1986, and while its threads contained all manner of paranormal discussion, its most active and heated conversations all focused on UFOs. The site advertised itself as "the world's first international news organization to provide information about the mysterious UFO phenomenon" and was explicitly designed to "link the layman with the 'movers and shakers' in the UFO community," containing both active discussion threads as well as a file repository of texts contributed by researchers.

On December 29, 1987, John Lear—son of the founder of the aviation manufacturer Learjet, and himself a renowned flyer and one-time cargo pilot for the CIA—posted a startling three-thousand-word message to the site. "The United States government has been in business with little gray extraterrestrials for about 20 years," the statement began, and had "gotten far more people killed trying to state it publicly than will ever be known."

Lear had become interested in UFOs the year before, he explained, after air force personnel had told him about a secret UFO landing at Bentwaters air force base near London, England. There, the officials relayed, three small aliens had met with the base's wing commander, General Gordon Williams, and established a relationship. The first official communication between the aliens—who Lear called EBEs, extraterrestrial biological entities, an acronym pronounced *ee-buhs*—and the US government had taken place in the mid-1960s, at Hollomon Air Force Base in New Mexico, where three saucers landed at a prearranged spot, starting a conversation that opened up an eventual deal between the visitors and MJ-12 that allowed human abductions to continue in exchange for advanced alien technology; a list of intended abduction targets was even provided to the government.

For a whole half century, he told ParaNet readers, a conspiracy between the aliens and the US government had been in place under the guise of a secretive MJ-12 cabal, and they kept a shocking number of secrets. The aliens had a genetic disorder, perhaps from some home-planet nuclear war or accident, and needed to extract enzymes from humans and cattle to survive—hence the abductions and cattle mutilations. The Swedish ghost rockets, he asserted, had been actual alien craft, crewed by ugly praying mantis–like creatures a billion years more advanced than earthlings; numerous US government officials had committed suicide as they learned the "horrible truth," including Defense Secretary James Forrestal, who had leapt from a window at Bethesda Naval Hospital in 1949. Even President Truman had been complicit, keeping up the charade even as craft continued to crash in Roswell, Aztec, and near Laredo, and gaslighting the American people—and UFO believers—into believing that all was well. The US government had worked with the aliens to construct a giant underground complex at Nevada's Groom Lake, in Area 51, and another secret facility, buried under a New Mexico mesa near the town of Dulce, was run jointly by the aliens and CIA together to hold some of the humans sacrificed to alien experiments.

The deal and comity, however, had begun to unravel in the late 1970s, as the government realized the promised technology wasn't living up to expectations and that the aliens were abducting thousands more humans than agreed upon. In 1979, US special forces had tried to raid the Dulce facility and free US scientists trapped there—the vicious battle left sixty-six US troops dead.

"By 1983, MJ-12 must have been in stark terror at the mistake they had made in dealing with the EBEs," Lear wrote, explaining that MJ-12 had "subtly influenced" popular culture, through *Close Encounters of the Third Kind* and *E.T.*, movies that were actually efforts by the conspirators to ready the country and the world for the mind-blowing revelation that "'odd-looking' aliens … were compassionate, benevolent and very much our 'space brothers.'" Instead, though, the MJ-12 leadership came to realize too late that the technological superior aliens they were dealing with were anything but friendly. President Reagan's Star Wars Strategic Defense Initiative had been a corrective measure aimed at aliens, not ICBMs.

In the small-but-passionate corners of ufology, Lear's allegations hit like a thunderclap, prompting Las Vegas news reporter George Knapp to pick up the story. As part of that process, he began interviewing another "whistleblower," who made an incredible claim about captured spacecraft powered by antimatter. Knapp kept listening, and his new source, Bill Cooper, kept talking.

• •

To hear Milton William Cooper tell the story of his life, he was a seer. He'd grown up fascinated by UFOs, reading Raymond Palmer's *Fate* magazine, and returned from the navy to an America that was unraveling in the 1970s—a country beset by race wars, a failing economy, despair, and poverty. He'd been privy to some of the country's darkest secrets as a naval intelligence officer during Vietnam—not just military things and the lies from the Nixon administration about the war in Vietnam, but the *real* juicy, *real* covert stuff. Things, he said, like the US government's role in the JFK assassination. Possessing such knowledge, he felt, made him look at the world differently, and allowed him to more easily identify truth and fiction—and that had made things dangerous for him. He had tried to leak the truth about the government's duplicity to a reporter, he later revealed in a memoir, but was stymied. Soon after, while riding his motorcycle, a black Cadillac forced him off the road and nearly killed him. A month later, the same black Cadillac forced him off the road again, and he lost half a leg. When he woke up in the hospital, two men were there and asked him if he was finally going to shut up—otherwise they'd kill him next time. He knew then that the government was really after him. Maybe it was the FBI, maybe the CIA, maybe someone even more secretive, maybe even the feared MIB. Either way, he was being watched.

After a short pause Cooper began posting to ParaNet in 1988, bolstered by wider public attention to UFOs; in one entry, he recounted a sighting he'd had while aboard the submarine USS *Tiru* in 1966. "There was no doubt as to what we had seen," he wrote. "It was a metal craft, with machinery on and around the outside of it." When a commander asked what had happened, Cooper recalled that the tone of the question was odd. After several moments, he caught on. "Nothing, sir," he finally replied. "I didn't see a damn thing." The commander complimented him and sent him on his way. Later, he was privy to more government secrets.[*] According to him, aliens had actually crashed in Roswell after World War II, and Americans' freedoms had been traded for alien technology.

---

[*] His "knowledge" of many of the secrets stemmed, he said, from being part of the 1970s team that briefed Admiral Bernard A. Clarey, the then-commander of the Pacific Fleet, and a unique opportunity he had to peruse Clarey's special classified safe, a seeming Pandora's box of dark secrets.

("Without the aliens, you can't make sense of anything that has happened in this country for the past 45 years," he told the audience of the nation's main UFO convention in 1989.)

Cooper's stories began to spread and attracted the attention of other top posters on the platform, including Lear. The fact that Cooper had naval intelligence experience and was offering details that aligned with the ones in Lear's wild tales had now given the former pilot seemingly instant and independent credibility—together, they declared themselves whistleblowers, issuing a citizens' "indictment" of the US government on charges of "murder and treason against the people and Constitution of the United States" and "aiding and abetting and concealing this Alien Nation which exists in our borders."

The US government, they now warned the masses, was led by a secret cabal that needed to be stopped; in fact, basically everything since World War II had been part of an ever-spiraling plot by elites to suppress, control, and steal American freedoms. There had been some sixteen UFO crashes between 1947 and 1952 (as laid out in Cooper's 1989 document, "The Secret Government: The Origin, Identity, and Purpose of MJ-12"), in which the US government had seized at least one alien alive, and, as Cooper explained, there were in fact nine distinct species of aliens in and around Earth, including a friendly, benevolent species known as the Nordics, the blond humanlike aliens sometimes referenced in sightings, and the Grays, the ominous and malicious creatures who like to prey on humans. Eisenhower had personally signed a treaty with the aliens, who wore the triangular patch of the Trilateral Commission on their space-suits. Cooper seconded Lear's theory that the world was careening toward a confrontation with the Grays, and built on his already wild-seeming stories, alleging there was vegetation growing on the moon and that the US, Soviet Union, and aliens all ran a moon base together—extravagant programs financed by MJ-12, in part, through the CIA's control of the drug trade. JFK had tried to blow the whistle, and—as Cooper insisted—a Secret Service agent had shot him in the head in Dallas, Texas.

Even though corners of the UFO community embraced Lear and Cooper—they were, like many of the field's characters before them, briefly superstars on the speaking circuits—their collected tales quickly became too crazy even for the most ardent believers; Jacques Vallée called them "some of the best horror stories I had heard since my childhood days when my mother read me Grimm's Fairy-Tales," and raised a number of simple, logical, and direct follow-up questions, like why a technologically advanced civilization, theoretically billions of years ahead of us, had to journey to Earth and harvest humans and cattle just to collect a seemingly straightforward enzyme. Enough resistance built up that, by 1989, Cooper could not make a speech without being heckled or questioned. "Oh stop it, just stop it already. This is outrageous," he shot back at a woman who interrupted him during an appearance at the MUFON conference, "I don't care what you think of me. I don't care what you call me. I do care what you do with this information because it is important to our survival as a species." That speech, Cooper described later, was "a moment of relief and redemption," a chance to unburden his soul from the secrets he'd been forced by the government to bear for nearly two decades.

It all became so intense that, by the early 1990s, Lear himself came to believe Cooper had "UFO Disease." His whistleblowing partner was, in Lear's words, "continuing to talk long after you have passed the point of what you know," and their partnership came to an end.*

Cooper, though, was just getting started. His stories became more intricately laced with other conspiracies, including the existence of a global cabal led by the Council on Foreign Relations and the Trilateral Commission. As the 1990s began, he morphed from a focus on UFOs to the broader influence of the so-called New World Order, which would come to influence the broader rise of paranoid thinking and conspiracy in right-wing American politics. As paranormal historian Colin Dickey later observed, the Cooper-Lear partnership transformed not just the UFO field but also helped to reshape the broader American society. "[Cooper and Lear] were the tip of a spear asserting that the number one thing we had to fear was not little green men, but the government that colluded with them, appropriating their technology against us," Dickey wrote.

Although Cooper seemed a passing shooting star in the UFO community—burning brightly and then disappearing—his influence would far outlast his own story. He became a fixture on conservative talk

---

* Cooper eventually accused Lear of being a CIA plant.

radio, and his bestselling book, *Behold a Pale Horse*, helped inspire the writers of the television show *The X-Files*, which did more than almost anything in the 1990s to popularize the idea of a government conspiracy around UFOs.* The show's tagline, "The Truth Is Out There," embodied the thin line of logic that Cooper, Lear, and others had begun to straddle. Truth, after all, was a finicky thing. It would only be a matter of time before it was stretched even further.

---

* In the years ahead, Cooper continued ranting on his radio show about the New World Order and the fear of the global elites would earn him a number of fans, including a young man named Timothy McVeigh—who loved Cooper's show, *The Hour of the Time*, and reportedly visited Cooper's Arizona compound with his future bombing accomplice Terry Nichols to tell Cooper to "watch Oklahoma"—and a young Austin public access talk show host named Alex Jones. The two men became fierce enemies by the end of the decade, and Cooper grew more extreme, ceasing to pay his taxes, which inevitably sparked a feud with a rising Arizona prosecutor named Janet Napolitano. In late 2001, he was killed in a shoot-out with local police after he opened fire on deputies who came to arrest him.

The Belgian Wave

On November 29, 1989, it was Belgium's turn to step into the UFO spotlight when police and civilians reported a bright light and apparently hovering craft over Eupen, a town of about twenty thousand near the eastern German border. "Suddenly, they told me they were seeing a strange object in the sky," the dispatcher, Albert Creutz, recalled in a 1992 *Unsolved Mysteries* episode about the incidents. "It made no noise. We joked about it and said it might be Santa Claus trying to land." Local police followed the soundless craft—which witnesses described as a black triangle with orangish lights at each corner—as it passed over the town, and in the days and weeks that followed, other Belgians and communities reported sighting a similar craft.

The Belgian Society for the Study of Space Phenomena—known by its French acronym SOBEPS—began an investigation. The first question was whether the US military could be secretly testing an experimental craft overhead, and an answer came swiftly. "I forwarded the question to the U.S. Embassy," Major General Wilfried De Brouwer, the country's head of air force operations, recalled, "which quickly confirmed that no stealth flights or any other experimental flights had taken place over Belgium."

As the sightings persisted over months, the air force readied a Quick Reaction Alert team of F-16 fighters, which would scramble into the air if local police and radar technicians reported a new appearance. It took weeks for authorities to initiate a response; in a time before mobile phones, few people reported sightings in real time, so immediate police dispatch was nearly impossible.

It wasn't until March 30 that another real chance at answers was secured. That night, dispatchers received reports of the suspicious lights and were able to call for assistance. For more than an hour and over nine separate attempts, the fighters "tried to intercept the alleged crafts, and at one point recorded targets on their radar with unusual behavior, such as jumping huge distances in seconds and accelerating beyond human capacity." It was impressive work, but, "Unfortunately, they could not establish visual contact," De Brouwer wrote. Later analysis showed that "the evidence was insufficient to prove that there were real crafts in the air on that occasion."

Despite that conclusion, reports continued, all with the same strange set of characteristics: a generally triangular-shaped craft, either solo or appearing to operate as a pair, usually with a large spotlight, sometimes performing flights seemingly beyond the scope of known aviation. The craft was never hostile, made no apparent effort to hide from witnesses, and there was no reported accompanying electrical interference. Altogether, Belgium amassed around 2,000 such cases over a two-year time span, of which it investigated about 650, but the inconclusive nature of the air force's interceptions and the overall lack of hostile intent meant that the government quickly lost interest. "No priority was given to this by the Belgian government," De Brouwer explained. "No formal inquiries were conducted by any governmental bodies."

Subsequent investigations largely settled on the idea of a national mass hysteria as a cause—reported sightings generated media interest, which generated more sightings, a lengthy and self-fulfilling feedback loop. Researchers later suggested that many, if not most or all, of the objects might have been simply night-flying helicopters, but De Brouwer, writing in 2010, said he's convinced there was something more real than a national delusion. "There must have been air activities or unknown origin in the airspace of Belgium," he wrote. "The number of cases and the credibility of the vast number of witnesses leave us with an intriguing mystery."

A year after De Brouwer's account was published, the sole—and long questioned—photo of the triangular craft, a black shadow with three lights at its corners, was exposed as a workplace hoax by a Belgian TV station. "The UFO of Petit-Rechain," it was determined, was "not a spaceship from a distant galaxy but a panel of painted Styrofoam with three spots affixed." It would be nearly a decade before the "black triangle UFO" made famous in Belgium was spotted again—and that next time, it would be over the skies of the United States.

If, that is, it existed at all.

Interrupted Journey

After spending years kicking around the fringes of ufology, the question—and veracity—of alien abductions moved to center stage in the 1990s. Abduction narratives had been present in UFO circles since the 1950s, but they'd always been the most controversial of the "Close Encounters of the Third Kind" episodes and reports that made even veterans like Hynek squeamish, as he'd admitted. But they'd also never gone away.

In the years since John Fuller's book on Barney and Betty Hill, others had come forward with their own stories of otherworldly abductions—almost all of them as logically confounding as the original.* Just two weeks after *The UFO Incident*, the ninety-eight-minute movie adaptation of the Hill story had appeared on NBC in October of 1975, an Arizona Forest Service crew leader named Michael Rogers reported that one of his workers, Travis Walton, had been abducted. As he told the story, the crew had wrapped up a day of brush clearing in the Sitgreaves National

---

* As best as anyone could determine, while there were plenty of abduction stories, only one seemed to predate the Hills: In October 1957, Antonio Villas-Boas, the son of a rancher, claimed to have seen a bright light over the family corral, moving toward his window at night. A week later, as they were plowing in the evening, it returned. The following night, when the egg-shaped object returned again, it finally landed, and Villas-Boas was grabbed by four small beings with large heads. Struggling, he was brought aboard and undressed. They spread some sort of liquid all over him, and then a beautiful, naked, and not-of-this-world woman—about four feet tall, with blond hair, high cheekbones, and large slanted eyes—appeared and engaged with him in intercourse. Afterward, Villas-Boas's clothes were returned, he was given a tour of the craft, and then left outside. Nearly twenty years went by before he spoke publicly about the incident—although it had circulated in UFO circles since February 1958, when he related it to a Brazilian ufologist—and he went on to have a seemingly ordinary life, becoming a lawyer and father of four.

Forest on the evening of November 5 and were driving home when they came upon a UFO hovering in the woods. Walton jumped out of the truck and ran toward it; as he approached, a beam of light flashed—like lightning—and Rogers panicked, speeding away. Eventually, they stopped and regrouped, and after seeing another flash of light (perhaps the UFO departing?), they returned to the scene to find Walton gone. Police began an intensive search that continued for days, until finally, on November 11, Walton called his family from a gas station telephone booth in a nearby town. Reporters and investigators, including APRO's Jim Lorenzen, flocked to meet him, eventually noting numerous inconsistencies in his and his crew's stories (he also failed an initial polygraph). Many came to believe the incident had simply been invented, in the hopes of a big financial payday, but regardless of whether it was true, the story quickly entered the canon of UFO lore, where it attracted the attention of Budd Hopkins,* a painter by training and vocation who had been friends in New York with Mark Rothko and Jackson Pollock. (The *New York Times* had once labeled his art "taut and decisive.")

Hopkins had been drawn to studying UFOs in the 1960s, and soon became fascinated by the abductees.† In 1981, he published a book called *Missing Time*, its title a reference to the shared experience among many abductees, that drew on nineteen different abduction cases that he'd studied carefully, involving a total of thirty-seven people, and argued that the incidents indicated that "a very long-term, in-depth study is being made of a relatively large sample of humans" by some manner of alien beings.

"All of our thinking, all of our boundaries are anthropomorphically determined," he wrote. "The nature of other possibly 'superior' but surely different intelligences studying us is literally ungraspable. The whole business, potentially, is nothing less than a second more devastating Copernican revolution, and none of us, scientist or not, can ever truly be prepared for that."

---

* The episode would become the basis for the 1993 movie *Fire in the Sky*.

† In fact, his life had been marked with an interest in UFOs and aliens from an early age: he remembered how his parents had panicked and packed to flee their home in Wheeling, West Virginia, in 1938 as Orson Welles's *The War of the Worlds* played on the radio.

It wasn't at all clear to Hopkins what the aliens were trying to accomplish with their study—nor did he believe, really, that it was even that nefarious—but something was afoot, and he wanted to know what. Hopkins's book had kicked off further serious study of the abductee phenomenon, including work supported by the Center for UFO Studies, and what was found had been, on its surface, surprising: abductees, researchers realized, seemed to lack any shared psychological order and presented the trauma hallmarks most associated with rape victims.

That research helped inspire another more traditional academic to dive into the subject: Temple University history professor David Jacobs, who had written a definitive account of the nation's UFO controversy for his PhD dissertation in the 1970s, had come to notice that many people were reporting such similar stories, seemingly with nothing to gain and no reason to lie, and wanted to know why. He'd found Fuller's book "fascinating but highly improbable," likely the result of some strange shared dream sequence, but as his own academic research into UFO sightings continued, he felt there was a hole in the center of the field: everyone was focused on the *what* of the sightings instead of the *why*. "Why, if they were extraterrestrial, did they prefer to fly about and not make contact with humans?" he wondered. Upon meeting Hopkins in 1982, the year after *Missing Time* was published, he began to wonder whether the abduction stories held the answer. The stories were often complex and confusing, but they also evolved a customary narrative, moving the UFO story *inside* the crafts, and, in doing so, potentially providing an explanation as to why aliens or other beings were circling Earth in the first place.

Researchers writ large were still wary of the abductees—the memory of the often laughable "contactee" accounts was still relatively fresh—and many of the new stories seemed somewhat lurid, "exotic and bewildering anomalies," that could just be chalked up to a bizarre brain glitch. "After all, people have always claimed that many sorts of strange events have happened to them," Jacobs reflected. "Perhaps these paranormal phenomena arose from the human tendency to create folklore. Or they might emanate from a collective unconscious. In any case, psychology rather than objective reality would explain these stories."

And yet, as he looked into the stories and began sitting in on Hopkins's hypnosis sessions with abductees, he began to doubt whether psychology was the simple answer. There had to be something more at play. He taught himself hypnosis and by 1986 was interviewing his own subjects. "They all told the same stories," he recalled. "They were abducted by strange-looking Beings, subjected to a variety of physical and mental 'procedures,' and then put back where they had been taken. They were powerless to control the event, and when it was over, they promptly forgot nearly all of it. Most were left with the feeling that something had happened to them, but were not sure exactly what it was," expressing fear and sadness in their sessions, appearing to have suffered real psychological and emotional trauma.

Moreover, unlike the contactees, who so proudly trumpeted their encounters, the abductees mostly craved anonymity—appearing in research using pseudonyms, wary of telling even friends or family lest they be subject to ridicule. As he waded deeper into their world, Jacobs found himself overwhelmed. The stories were just so strange. "From the first few seconds of an abduction, nothing is within the realm of normal human experience," Jacobs wrote. "It is an instant descent into the fantastic and bizarre."

• •

In 1987, Hopkins released a follow-up book, *Intruders*, which dove into the even stranger aspects of the stories Jacobs had now immersed himself in—particularly those involving sexual intrusions and reports of sperm and egg harvesting, which seemed to hint that reproduction or breeding could have been a motivation in at least some of the abductions. The same year, a blockbuster memoir from one of the abductees Hopkins treated, a sixty-year-old novelist named Whitley Strieber, was also released. *Communion: A True Story* featured a particularly striking cover—a bug-eyed, hairless, androgynous gray alien being, which would become one of the most iconic depictions of extraterrestrials. ("At one point, he said the image corresponded exactly to what he had seen," the artist, who had rendered it, police sketch–style, recalled.) The book recounted a six-hour abduction that had unfolded the night after Christmas in 1985, when Strieber had been with his family at their cabin in the Catskills. He'd heard a noise in the house, and then been rushed in bed by a small figure; moments later, he was naked in a small enclosure, being poked and prodded by more strange beings. They smelled, he reported, like cardboard.

The book, which the author described as "one man's attempt to deal with a shattering assault from the unknown," received a million-dollar advance from the publisher—a point skeptics would later use to question the integrity of the story—and spent six months on bestseller lists. Strieber's subsequent books turned him into the country's new poster boy for abductions—though not everyone treated him seriously: The *Los Angeles Times* refused to list the sequel to *Communion* as "nonfiction."

It also attracted the attention of John Mack, the next of the more traditional UFO scholars to get involved in the subject. On the surface, there was little reason for Mack, a distinguished Harvard psychiatrist, Pulitzer-winning biographer of Lawrence of Arabia, and vocal anti-nuclear advocate, to venture deeper into the strangest and darkest corners of the extraterrestrial debate than any other leading academic—that he had come from the institution best associated with UFOs and their longtime skeptic, Donald Menzel, made the fact even more surprising.

A closer look of his oeuvre, though, intimated how alien abductions found their place in his work: Mack's first book had centered on children and their nightmares, delving into the ethereal borderlines of sleep and fantasy, and his other written work had focused on the role of myth and imagination in memory. He was known to be remarkably compassionate and understanding with patients, and possessed a unique combination of intense intellectual exploration growing out of seemingly impulsive fascinations—his biography of Lawrence of Arabia, which broke new ground with its detailed exploration of how a sexual trauma had rewired the legendary British warrior, had grown out of a chance viewing of the 1962 film on a night out with his wife.* "Evident in Mack's prodigious research," his biographer noted, "was his interest in occult practices of ancient cultures, altered states of consciousness, spiritual breakthroughs, and mind-body connections that he would later lament had been previously devalued in an age of scientific materialism."

---

* Interestingly, Mack won the Pulitzer in 1977, a year before Carl Sagan won the award with his *The Dragons of Eden: Speculation on the Evolution of Human Intelligence*.

As his longtime friend, Bernard Lown—the Harvard cardiologist who invented the defibrillator and went on to help found the International Physicians for the Prevention of Nuclear War—said, "John's spirit roamed so wide, it was not totally surprising."

John Edward Mack had suffered his own share of childhood trauma—born in 1929 just weeks before the stock market crashed, his mother died of mistreated appendicitis when he was less than a year old, and growing up, his new stepmother—herself widowed when her husband, the scion of the Gimbels department store family, threw himself out the sixteenth floor of the Yale Club amid the early days of the Great Depression—refused to allow him to even have a photograph of his mother.

Despite those hardships, he'd managed to find success, and friends noted that he somewhat skated through adult life—dashingly handsome with a magnetic personality ("A human black hole impossible to resist," his biographer described him), preternaturally smart, and financially cocooned in New York even amid a time of great national turmoil. In 1951, he graduated from Oberlin and went on to Harvard Medical School. From there, he'd gone on to a seemingly dazzling career as a children's psychiatrist, Harvard professor, and author. As the 1980s progressed, Mack had become more actively involved in the antinuclear movement—helping to elevate the International Physicians for the Prevention of Nuclear War from merely a research organization to a full-throated advocacy program, an effort that ultimately helped it receive the 1985 Nobel Peace Prize.

He and his wife had three sons in four years, and ultimately it was the spiritual quest of his son Danny that ended up redirecting Mack's own intellectual life.* Danny had become fascinated with Dr. Benjamin Simon, the psychiatrist who treated Betty and Barney Hill and had dabbled in the 1970s and '80s with the movement known as EST, the cult-like Erhard Seminars Training, and Silva Mind Control, a meditation technique that supposedly offered heightened awareness. (After Danny and his father had the chance to meet EST founder Werner Erhard, Mack proclaimed

---

* Mack was a somewhat distant father and seemed to approach child-rearing almost clinically: at one point, he did an in-depth three-day study of his children's sibling rivalry and filled twenty-one pages with typewritten notes.

him "the most extraordinary person I've ever met.") Mack, now opened up to more transformative spiritual and mental experiences, soon found himself entranced by the breathing techniques and psychoanalysis of Czech psychiatrist Stanislav Grof, and set out on a twelve-day training in British Columbia, pronouncing the trances that took him back to his birth "wonderful, just wonderful." He also began to experiment, rapturously, with LSD—the drug, he said, provided him an "ecstatic surrender [that] seems divine, beyond sex. All creation is there"—and other psychoactive experiments like the South American tea ayahuasca, all part of his involvement in the growing manhood movement and his participation in an increasing number of spiritual retreats aimed at stretching his own consciousness.

As their collegial relationship deepened, Grof asked Mack to take a look at a forthcoming anthology about UFO encounters. Mack initially approached the offbeat subject with great skepticism, but once it lodged in his intellectually promiscuous brain, he couldn't let it go.

On January 10, 1990, Mack met up with Budd Hopkins for the first time; as the Harvard psychiatrist would later recall, it was "one of those dates you remember that mark a time when everything in your life changes." The meeting, Mack reflected in his journal, had made him consider "UFO— what if the horror/sci Fi fantasy stuff is not Freud projection but the effort to come to terms with the nightmare trauma of our visitations from the 'other universe,' which, because we cannot accept its reality, must come to us as buried horrors do—& this we displace in horror stories, twilight zones etc." In February, he returned to New York to meet with Hopkins and four abductees, an encounter he ultimately found unsettling. "I like to be able to explain things and I couldn't," he later said. "I was troubled for the people that were going through this, and I was troubled for my profession in a sense because we haven't been available to people and I wanted to know more about it."

That winter, one of Mack's closest colleagues, Lester Grinspoon, another Harvard psychiatrist, tried to wave Mack off the subject, enlisting Sagan to his cause since Sagan knew well the delicate high-wire act of extraterrestrial life and academia. During a two-hour conversation, the academics tried to talk him into dialing things down. It was one thing to have questions and encourage inquiry, they told their colleague, but this was another matter entirely. Mack waved away their concerns. "Lester," he told Grinspoon, "the problem with you and Carl is, you're too Cartesian." His meaning was clear: *You're too linear and boring.*

In the months ahead, Mack privately began interviewing abductees on his own, convinced at every step that he was dealing with something new and unique—people who truly believed they'd had out-of-the-world experiences, people with little reason to lie, and people, like the Hills, who were living with real trauma. One could believe that someone *believed* that something happened to them, he also argued, without necessarily agreeing or believing that the thing happened at all. As he saw it, their psychological struggles emerged from their abductions, not vice versa. "In no case so far have I found a way of tying the troubling events of my clients' histories to their abduction stories," Mack concluded, deciding to call the individuals "experiencers," a term that sounded less judgmental and more neutral than "abductees."

By the fall of 1991, he had written a one-hundred-page draft of a paper, or mini-book, he called *The Abduction Syndrome*, based on his experiences and findings within the monthly support group for abductees that he'd begun hosting—altogether he'd treated and studied thirty-four patients, including one family where four children reported abductions beginning as early as age two, but for the paper he zeroed in on sixteen of his cases, supplemented by details of a 1987 study called "UFO Abductions: The Measure of a Mystery," conducted by folklorist Thomas Bullard that had pulled together nearly three hundred abductees' stories. Collectively, Mack argued, the testimonies of these "experiencers" rewrote our very picture of ourselves, our consciousness, and the centrality of humans in the universe.

The article recounted the bizarre range of experiences people reported, from being taken from beds at night to being taken from vehicles on the road. There were many common elements; bright lights, humanoid figures, a sense of paralysis or numbness, and an inability to escape their fates, wake, or alter what was happening to them. Many reported missing periods of time, and some had "returned" to find themselves displaced, either in a physically different location or with their clothing rearranged, on backward, or missing entirely. Few seemed to have contact with other abductees or any preexisting interest in UFOs, making the similarities of their stories all the more striking and puzzling.

Being an abductee was hard and it wasn't clear why anyone would wish it upon themselves. As Mack's biographer summarized, "Abductees suffered a fourfold trauma, Mack said: (1) the experience itself, (2) the isolation of knowing no one believed them, (3) the shattered sense of reality, and (4) the terror of knowing it could happen again anytime." Many, he noted, tried to bury the experience as deeply as they could. At best, it seemed some inexplicable, mass, shared psychosis—but even that leap of diagnosis seemed unsatisfying.* He'd hoped to present his paper to the *American Journal of Psychiatry*, but it was rejected due to its length.

By 1991, the psychiatrist's new passion had grown to a level that confounded his Harvard colleagues and threatened his professional identity and affiliations. In February, he presented his new theories to about forty members of the Harvard Faculty Club during a casual "Shop Club," perhaps taking the monthly session's goal of sharing "incompletely digested" research projects too literally. On another occasion, he appeared with Hopkins at the Medical School, explaining to the audience that he felt his research represented the cutting-edge of science—work that pushed beyond known boundaries and felt to modern ears just as inconceivable as the theory that rocks could fall from the sky had seemed before the existence of meteorites was explained in 1794. "I want to go forward with what I believe is the edge of this extraordinary phenomenon," he told the room of befuddled students and staff. "Personally, it is difficult to find anything these people have in common, except they've been through something traumatic."

The work continued, and his profile continued to rise. Suddenly, Mack was deluged with abductees who hoped he could make sense of their experiences. ("Clearly an abduction!" he told a friend after meeting one potential client. "I mean, no questions! Ironclad!") In April 1992, he

---

* Parts of the article strained credulity; Mack noted that estimates of the prevalence of abduction ranged from several hundred thousand Americans to 4 million, a number so mind-boggling that critics would later use it to dismiss his seriousness and scholarship entirely.

was invited by none other than the Dalai Lama to the Namgyal Monastery in India, to talk UFOs and alien abductions. Mack and other academics and experts spent three days in Himachal Pradesh talking about the oddest and most mystical corners of the phenomenon, from abductions to the terrifying reports of the other-worldly "men in black." When, toward the end, the Dalai Lama asked simply, "What you think?" Mack replied, "I think we have a lot to learn from each other [aliens and humans].... I think they connect with us to get knowledge of the heart and the spirit and of us, but we learn from them that there is a spirit world, there is a universe beyond this narrow one."

Sex with Aliens

That June, MIT hosted perhaps the oddest scientific conference in the storied university's history, a five-day gathering on alien abductions that brought together some fifty experts—scientists, academics, UFO researchers, and ten specially chosen journalists, as well as roughly a dozen experiencers themselves—including Philip Morrison, who so many decades ago had authored the original *Nature* article that helped jump-start the discussions of the Order of the Dolphin—to talk through every aspect of abductions. All told, some 150 different presentations were delivered, including one by a California physician, John G. Miller, who walked through the reports of various medical tests and probes that experiencers encountered—so many of the exams seemed distinct from any earthly procedure, which was evidence, perhaps, that the "experience" wasn't just twisted memories of real-life medical practices. Other sessions examined subjects like the key similarities and differences in abduction stories or how scientists could work to prove the veracity of the incidents.

David Jacobs was one of the conference's big names; he'd been compiling a new book, *Secret Life*, that featured the details of three hundred abductions, reported by about sixty individuals, and in which he had organized their reports into three categories: primary experiences (the most common procedures performed on the greatest number of abductees); secondary experiences (less common procedures); and ancillary experiences (seemingly irregular and specialized procedures, particularly sexual ones, that were rare among the population as a whole, but often seemed to happen repeatedly to individual abductees). Over dozens of pages of verbatim interview transcripts, covering every aspect of the strange, the lurid, and the unfathomable, Jacob made one point extremely clear: "No matter how they handle the experience, all abductees have one thing in common: They are victims. Just as surely as women who are raped are victims of sexual abuse or soldiers can be victims of Post-Traumatic Stress Disorder, abductees are victims who require sensitivity, and, if needed, help in understanding what has happened to them."

Jacobs understood that some in the field imagined the abductees were simply covering up even darker memories—many psychiatrists seemed to believe that perhaps the abductions were ways to deal with repressed memories of sexual or physical abuse—but he'd never seen a case where an abduction victim turned out to have misappropriated an experience of sexual or physical abuse as an alien abduction. Nor did it seem to be a case of so-called "hysterical contagion," since the victims mostly didn't know each other and their stories were all over the map in terms of geography and timing; many had surfaced before there was the widespread media coverage or public interest that might have spurred copycats or mass hysteria. "The more I learned about the abduction phenomenon, the more frightening it became, both personally and in the larger context of its potential effects on society," Jacobs wrote. "We must realize that the abduction phenomenon is too important to dismiss as the ravings of prevaricators or psychologically disturbed people."

In another presentation, Robert Sheaffer, from the Committee for the Scientific Investigation of Claims of the Paranormal, offered the conference-goers a far more skeptical voice. He seized on how abduction narratives differed around the world—often reports from North Americans featured victims being taken by small gray humanoids, while Europeans usually reported being abducted by tall Nordic-like creatures. Were there really different alien species responsible for the abductions depending on which continent you were from? Or what about how different hypnotists often reported their clients and patients experienced similar abductions—narratives distinct from those reported by other hypnotists seeing other clients? (As Mack's biographer summarized, "Seeking a gentle, uplifting alien experience? Consult Dr. Leo Sprinkle. Aliens that stole sperm, eggs, and fetuses; deposited implants; and left scars sent you running to Budd Hopkins.") How, Sheaffer asked, had so many cases unfolded with no more solid evidence than existed of the Loch Ness Monster, Bigfoot, or the Abominable Snowman? Wouldn't you expect at least one of the aliens to have dropped the equivalent of an intergalactic coffee cup at the scene of one abduction or another?

The days of discussions were particularly sobering for David Pritchard, the conference's cohost. The longer he listened, the less convinced he was that the answer would ever be known. "I'll never do anything like that again," he lamented. "How was I ever suckered in by the thought I had any chance of making this discovery?"

For many others, however, the conversation was invigorating—science was openly wrestling with one of the most difficult and genuinely puzzling questions humans had ever encountered. There was so much more to learn. As the conference ended, the scientific director for the Center for UFO Studies, physicist Mark Rodeghier, summed up his final impressions: "I think I know exactly where we should go from here: We should follow John Mack!"

• •

By early 1993, Mack's work had begun to cause more serious problems at Harvard—particularly as popular culture began to embrace the UFO controversy. (That September when Fox launched what would be one of the decade's biggest TV shows, *The X-Files*, some of it drew directly from the stories that inhabited Mack's world.) The next spring, his expanded book, *Abduction: Human Encounters with Aliens*, arrived in stores, and he appeared on *The Oprah Winfrey Show*. By then, his theories were stretching even the already-implausible world of abductions, and his delivery of them did not lend itself to the image of a subtle, steady academic. In 1994, a profile of Mack that ran in the Sunday *New York Times Magazine* opened with the shocking lede, "'I didn't realize that I was having sex with aliens until just a few months ago,' Peter Faust is saying over coffee in the living room of his Watertown, Mass., home. 'Things unfold: it went from sperm samples to knowing that it had something to do with hybrid children, to knowing that my sperm was somehow being used with extraterrestrials, to seeing myself with an extraterrestrial female,'" aligning the professor with those who claimed to have extraterrestrial intercourse.

An article in *Psychological Inquiry* inspired by the controversy around Mack, Hopkins, and Jacobs arrived at a similarly inconclusive conclusion—if one took the abduction narratives "seriously but not literally," than perhaps the best explanation was the stories were basically "extraterrestrial sadomasochism," a fantasy world where victims could escape the day-to-day pressure of modern life and give over their self-control to imagined beings—beings, the authors noted, that appeared regularly to offer bondage, sexual gratification, or humiliation experiences.

"The majority of accounts cannot be written off as lies, attention-getting ploys, or symptoms of mental illness," the authors, University of Illinois' Leonard Newman and Case Western Reserves' Roy Baumeister, wrote. Yet at the same time, it seemed impossible that alien abductions existed anywhere near the level that people like Mack, Hopkins, and Jacobs seemed to believe. How could it be that hundreds—even thousands—of people were being taken on a regular, ongoing basis, over decades, with zero physical proof?

They saw a possible conclusion in one of Jacobs's findings: many of the people he'd spoken with had "confessed to 'fantasies involving masochism and bondage.'" As the authors explained, "We believe that both spring from a common source—the need to escape the self. Both masochistic and UFO abduction fantasies might derive from the excessive demands and stresses associated with the modern construction of selfhood . . . [and] the desire to escape from ordinary self-awareness."

• •

A big part of Mack's arguments, in public and in writing, was that the abductions and apparent alien-human encounters were only strange in the Western canon. As he said on Winfrey's show, "Why is it that every other culture in the history of the human race has believed that there were other entities, other intelligences in the universe? Why are we so goofy about this? Why do we treat people like they're crazy and humiliate them if they're experiencing some other entities, some other intelligence that's coming across?"

As Mack told the host, "This phenomenon stands a chance to break us out of that box that Carl Sagan would keep us in." When another reporter later interviewed him in his tiny office, decorated with just a desk and chair, a couch, and a Tibetan thangka painting, and asked why he'd focused on this subject, the response was equally blunt: "Why would it not capture anybody as the most interesting story going on the planet right now?"

His confidence in the validity of abduction studies, though, did not mean he thought he knew everything. He remained confused by the way accounts seemed to exist on a continuum, perhaps as much mental as physical. Whereas Hopkins and Jacobs seemed to understand abductions as an actual event—a person's body being taken aboard a craft or vessel for study—Mack had heard of examples that seemed more ambiguous, where a person's body appeared to have stayed behind as their consciousness or mind journeyed through the abduction.

Mack was hardly alone in wondering if there was a deeper, more spiritual history afoot with the aliens. In his work and his book, *The Invisible College*, Jacques Vallée had begun to posit that perhaps abductions weren't so much interstellar visits as they were inter-dimensional or even time travels. How did one account for the ability of some flying saucers to "dematerialize," disappearing from view in an instant, and their physics-bending motions of high-speed turns, acceleration, and deceleration? And how did one account for the "psychic effects," not just the physical sightings, but the life-altering experiences visited on those who saw them or interacted with them?

In fact, Vallée argued, the more one dug into history the more it seemed that UFOs had been a constant presence in human existence—generations had interpreted oddities and unexplained sightings, just written in their own cultural frameworks. "In antiquity their occupants were regarded as gods; in medieval times, as magicians; in the nineteenth century, as scientific geniuses. And finally, in our own time, as interplanetary travelers," he wrote.

"The concept current among most flying saucer enthusiasts that the unidentified flying objects are simply craft used by visitors from another planet is naive," he concluded. "The phenomenon could be a manifestation of a much more complex technology. If time and space are not as simple in structure as physicists have assumed until now, then the question 'where do they come from?' may be meaningless: They could come from a place in *time*."

Mack's book and publicity tour jolted the scientific community and his peers, exposing him to widespread criticism. James Gleick, an accomplished science historian—himself a two-time Pulitzer finalist—went after Mack in the *New Republic*, calling the Harvard psychiatrist effectively both a charlatan, for trying to sell the public on such stories, and a misguided fool, for believing them himself. Alien abductions, Gleick said, were one of the most "tawdry belief manias," an "anti-rational, anti-science cult . . . flourishing with dismaying vigor." He laughed even at the idea that psychiatrists were anywhere close to the right people to deal with the wave of abductions—let's assume for a minute that Mack was right, Gleick said, and that the United States or Earth writ large was under "a large-scale invasion by gangs of alien sex-abusers." Wasn't that a matter for astronomers, physicists, law enforcement, the military, and even world leaders personally? How was it that presumably one of the most consequential events in all of human history was under the sole purview of one man? Everyone knew the stories couldn't possibly be true—except, perhaps, for Mack himself. "The core of Mack's belief is the following cocktail party syllogism: People think they were abducted. / They don't seem crazy. / We're experts on mental illness. / Therefore people were abducted," he wrote.

Meanwhile, warning signs mounted that Mack had pushed too far. The *New York Times Magazine* profile had featured a scathing and shockingly candid quote from his boss at Harvard—"Nobody believes it," the acting chair of the psychiatry department said. "I wish he were doing something else. This is so off-base"—and soon after the book's publication in the spring of 1994, the university informed him that they were convening a panel of outside experts to review his "work on alien abduction that relates to protocol formulation, informed consent and patient billing." The concern—officially—was only procedural, but it was not hard to read between the lines.

For the next year, Harvard conducted more than two dozen hearings that called the psychiatrist and thirteen other witnesses to justify his methods; they interrogated Mack's beliefs and practices, battling with a legal team that the professor had assembled on his own behalf. The conflict spilled out over time in the campus newspaper, the *Crimson*, as well as in the *New York Times*, which touched off a torrent of criticism of the university from MUFON and other UFO believers.

Ultimately, in a forty-one-page report, Harvard decided there was no need for any disciplinary action, though it chided Mack for overstepping in his enthusiasm. It cautioned him, too, that his work "deviates significantly from that of a clinician seeking to understand his patients' experiences and their implications," and he should be wary of crossing that line again. Mack was clearly chastened by the experience. In the paperback of *Abduction*, published as the Harvard review concluded, he wrote, "My growing conviction about the authenticity of these reports, together with a sense of their great potential significance, resulted in a tendency to write as if the fact or reality of the experiences was established before the case had been made. In so doing, I may have denied some readers, especially those who would be naturally skeptical, to make up their own minds."

Asked whether Harvard was embarrassed by Mack, a spokesman demurred, saying all of its faculty had strange interests: "They're all weird and embarrassing one way or another."

• •

Despite the turmoil, Mack's interest in the abductions continued, if not in a more measured way. He wrote a follow-up book, *Passport to the Cosmos: Human Transformation and Alien Encounters*, which reflected both his evolution of thinking and the parameters around which he clearly felt he had to operate. He also continued to work with "experiencers," but in this new phase remained just as puzzled as ever by how he viewed them. He wrote about how he'd gone from first seeing the "experiences" as a "strange, unpleasant intrusion by an unknown force," to seeing something much deeper and more profound—experiences, he said, that raised ancient and existential questions about humanity: Who are we? How did we get here? Where are we going? "I do not consider that abduction reports necessarily reflect a literal, physical taking of the human body," he wrote. "Rather, I am more concerned with the meaning of these experiences for the so-called abductees and for humankind more generally."

Any attempt to understand alien abductions with the known laws of nature and physics, the five senses, and rational analysis fell short, Mack now realized. Despite hundreds of examples, no consistent psychopathology had ever emerged; if they were dreams, fantasies, or delusions there was no shared background or consistency. He was left to think that science—and perhaps Western culture in general—fundamentally had misunderstood the world around us. "One cannot begin to consider seriously something so preposterous without at least a minimal willingness," he said, "to look at the possibility that our view of the universe and ways of knowing about it have indeed been incomplete and perhaps flawed."

Perhaps other civilizations—particularly indigenous or ancient cultures that had a more fluid understanding of the difference between physical and spiritual—had been right. Perhaps the line between here and elsewhere, wherever or whatever elsewhere might be, was not as fixed as Western science or consciousness understood. He'd seen signs and had conversations with the Ipixuna tribe in Brazil, the Dagara people of Burkina Faso, and Lakota elders in the United States that pointed to more complex understandings than "scientifically raised mind[s]" could imagine, communications with worlds and spirits beyond that might offer answers about the alien abduction experience in modern life. "What I have been finding has been, according to my own background, not possible. Yet from the standpoint of my clinical experience and judgment, it does appear in some way to be true," he wrote. In the pages of *Passport to the Cosmos*, he speculated that perhaps light bridged the physical, dimensional, and spiritual in ways thus far mysterious to science. He had come to see the phenomenon as a call to action, urging people to take a more holistic view of the world and to recognize the interconnectedness of all things.

It was a mystery that Mack himself would never solve. In London for a lecture, he was struck and killed by a drunk driver. At his memorial service in Harvard's stately Memorial Church, the university's minister, Peter J. Gomes, explained, "The transition from this life to the next is a great mystery of which we know nothing of which John Mack now knows everything."

Roswell Revisited

As the perceived possibilities of UFO and alien visitation came up once again for debate, narratives around one of the founding incidents of the phenomenon—Roswell—began to reshape and reemerge in the popular consciousness. After years of evolving low-level conspiracism among UFO conventions, tales of MJ-12, and testimony by wreckage-discoverer Jesse Marcel, the story hit its apex in 1989, when the TV show *Unsolved Mysteries* centered an episode around the crash, with interviews with Stanton Friedman and Kevin Randle. By the following year, that show, and a book by Randle and Donald Schmitt, two investigators from the Center for UFO Studies, *UFO Crash at Roswell*, had made the small New Mexico town a household name.

As what you might call the "Roswell Alien Industrial Complex" grew, it became easy to see why the incident, which had been largely forgotten by the general public for thirty years, had been resurrected: despite the decades of UFO sightings, contactees, abductions, crop circles, and cattle mutilations, despite all of the weirdness and the strangeness, Roswell alone still offered the best chance at the two kinds of inconvertible proof that could—and would—forever change our understanding of our place in the universe: "Wreckage and bodies." As "pro-UFO" ufologist Karl Pflock, who would spend much of the decade chasing the truth about what happened in the New Mexico desert, wrote, "It may be no exaggeration to say, as Roswell goes, so goes ufology."

How much (and what parts) of the story one imagined to be true varied from person to person, but national polls consistently started to show that upward of a third of Americans believed the US government was hiding the truth about Roswell. "Like all good stories, Roswell expands to accommodate whatever you bring to it. That's the nature of myths and legends—they're detailed enough to seem real, yet fuzzy enough to stay always just beyond the reach of objective proof," one author wrote. "Roswell grows a little with each retelling." Acknowledging that new truth, the town embraced its rising fame, renovating an old movie theater and opening the International UFO Museum and Research Center, which became the centerpiece of a town-wide tourism blitz that grew to include a silver saucer–shaped McDonald's, with neon lighting, UFO-themed gift shops, and more.

The change and attention was so distinct that New Mexico congressman Steven Schiff, himself an air force reserve officer, was forced to get involved; constituents kept asking him about the event, pushing him to investigate and find the "real" truth. After an unsuccessful attempt at convincing the Defense Department to look into the matter, he asked Congress's investigative arm, the General Accounting Office, to dig in instead. As he referred the case for study in January 1994, he cast doubt that it would turn up any aliens—"If I had to guess, I would say some kind of military experiment," he told his local *Albuquerque Journal.* Instead, it opened a can of worms.

His petition and the pending GAO audit, unexpectedly, prompted the Pentagon and the secretary of the air force to commission its own voluminous report—the high-level effort, tasked directly by the secretary's office, resulted in a thousand-page doorstop, *The Roswell Report: Fact vs. Fiction in the New Mexico Desert,* published in just over five months, all but oozing with bureaucratic frustration over the conspiracy-that-wouldn't-die.* (A multipage summary of the evolution of the Roswell myth took specific aim at the scope of experts' various claims, citing their sheer volume as evidence as to why there was no clear answer, and noting that it couldn't even really attempt a point-by-point refutation of all theories because "many of the above authors are not even in agreement

---

* As one example of the report's frustrated tone—it dripped with unusual umbrage—the writers noted, "The 'death threats,' oaths, and other forms of coercion alleged to have been meted out by the AAF personnel to keep people from talking have apparently not been very effective, as several hundred people are claimed to have come forward (without harm) with some knowledge of the 'Roswell Incident' during interviews with nongovernment researchers and the media."

over [them].")* Instead, the air force swiftly buried the conspiracy with mind-numbing thoroughness, including extensive record searches of "current offices where special or unusual projects might be carried out, as well as historical organizations, archives, and records centers" and "obtain[ing] an official signed, sworn statement from . . . Sheridan Cavitt, Lt Col, USAF (Retired), who is the last living member of the three persons universally acknowledged to have recovered material from the Foster Ranch."

It also produced a report demonstrating that, while the "flying saucer" rumor had ricocheted around the military that fateful day in July, there had been "no indications and warnings, notice of alerts, or a higher tempo of operational activity reported that would be logically generated if an alien craft, whose intentions were unknown, entered US territory."

Amid the government's mammoth investigation and tsunami of details, however, there was one surprising admission: there had been a cover-up at Roswell, just not the one that the UFO conspiracists wanted to believe.

• •

Just as Captain Mantell's fatal Kentucky crash in 1948 had been precipitated, it seemed, by the navy's top secret Skyhook balloon project, the Roswell crash mythology could be traced back to an air force balloon effort called Mogul, a special secret operation launched in 1947 that aimed to identify and track possible Soviet atomic tests. "Determining whether the Soviets were testing nuclear devices was of the highest national priority; it demanded the utmost secrecy if the information gained was to be useful," the air force later explained. "Mogul's objective was to develop a long-range system capable of detecting Soviet nuclear detonations and

---

* Close students of ufology came to understand that over the 1970s and '80s, the new "revised" Roswell story appeared to conflate and confuse two distinct instants from that time period—one the "actual" Roswell crash, involving Marcel, and the other a long-debunked story of a UFO crash and alien fatalities in Aztec, New Mexico, that had started as a literal parody by a local newspaper and then been picked up, credulously, by Frank Scully in his early books.

ballistic missile launches."A joint effort by the military, New York University, Woods Hole Oceanographic Institution, Columbia University, and the University of California at Los Angeles, the initiative sought mainly to develop sensors—including microphones—that could be used to detect signs of a Soviet atomic test over long distances. It was considered such a critical program that it shared the nation's highest priority designation, 1A, with the Manhattan Project.*

The project had been the brainchild of geophysicist Dr. Maurice Ewing, who had spent the war doing naval research at Woods Hole on underwater sound transmission—how the ocean's different temperature and salinity layers conducted sound differently—and as the world moved into the jet age, wondered if the atmosphere possessed similar sound-conducting layers. When he presented the idea to the Army Air Force, the military immediately recognized the potential for long-range atomic eavesdropping, and approved the project, which grew into and led to cutting-edge work, including the first uses of polyethylene balloons, which would become the standard for high-altitude research in the years ahead.

New Mexico had been the central location of the Mogul test flights. There, researchers launched the giant balloons and then technicians at the White Sands Proving Ground detonated bombs to test their detection capabilities. While it was hard to exactly keep a six-hundred-foot-tall train of thirty balloons secret, the military did what it could to keep civilians away; when one prototype crashed, the B-17 bomber acting as a chase plane buzzed nearby oil workers who had seen the landing and started to move toward it, driving the curious away and circling at a low altitude until military personnel arrived on the grounds. While two other Mogul flights in early June had unfolded normally—the balloons ascending to high altitudes and then crashing between three and six hours later, after which the military recovered the devices—a third had gone missing: NYU Flight #4 had been launched on June 4, 1947, from Alamogordo Army Air Field

---

* In fact, the possible tie of Mogul to Roswell and UFOs was already an active area of investigation by ufologist Robert G. Todd, who deserves historical pride of place for sleuthing out the balloon project as early as 1990.

and teams had tracked it as it flew north-northeast to within about fifteen miles of the Foster Ranch, when they finally lost contact with it.[*]

It was probably that balloon's wreckage that Mac Brazel had found, and it was unsurprising that neither he, nor intelligence officer Jesse Marcel, nor the officials at the Roswell air base did not immediately recognize it as such—the Mogul balloons, after all, were enormous, "giant trains of balloons—over thirty of them, plus experimental sensors, strung together and stretching more than 600 feet." A setup, in other words, that very well might have created a larger-than-normal wreckage field filled with all sorts of gadgets, gizmos, metal, and debris.

While Mogul had been declassified decades later, the program had remained obscure in part because it never went anywhere: the balloon rigs were too large and conspicuous and there turned out to be simpler ways to monitor far-off atomic explosions, including both through downwind airborne testing and through ground tremor monitoring systems. In 1949, when the first Soviet atomic test happened, it was ultimately detected by air force weather reconnaissance planes outfitted with special radioactive sensors and announced by Harry Truman to the world. The odd behavior and security that accompanied the wreckage discovery stemmed from the program's underlying secrecy requirements—secrecy so strict that it meant no one at the Roswell air base would have been able to identify the mix-up.

The air force report even had an answer for one of the strangest reports to trickle down through the history and mythology of Roswell: the "hieroglyphic-like" characters and small pink or purple flowers that had appeared on some of the wreckage were not an alien language, but a random side effect of limited engineering materials. Amid the postwar shortages, the New York contractor who made the targets also made toys and had used plastic tape with pink and purple flowers, as well as geometric designs from the latter line, to seal the target seams. The absurdity of the tape on such a sensitive military project had stood out to project veterans, which is why they could clearly remember it decades later. "It was kind of a standing joke," one project worker recalled.

---

[*] When it took off, the balloon array was 102 feet taller than the Washington Monument—plenty of material to form quite a large wreckage scene.

As one of its final points, the air force report gave a most subtle but convincing argument that ufologists had long overlooked: the entire idea of "flying saucers" had only been a couple of weeks old in July 1947, meaning that there was hardly a settled definition at that point of what even a "flying saucer" was or looked like. "It seems that there was overreaction by Colonel Blanchard and Major Marcel in originally reporting that a 'flying disc' had been recovered when, at that time, nobody knew for sure what that term even meant, since it had only been in use for a couple of weeks," the report explained. "The postwar US military (or today's, for that matter) did not have the capability to rapidly identify, recover, coordinate, cover up, and quickly minimize public scrutiny of such an event. The claim that they did so without leaving even a little bit of a suspicious paper trail for 47 years is incredible."

Colonel Richard Weaver, the director of the air force's Security and Special Program Oversight, knew that even the findings circulated in September 1994 would do little to quiet the conspiracists. "Pro-UFO groups will strongly object to the attached report and denounce it as either shortsighted or a continuation of the cover-up conspiracy," he wrote in a cover note to the report addressed to the air force secretary. "Nevertheless, the attached report is a good faith effort and the first time any agency of the government has positively responded officially to the ever-dating claims surrounding the Roswell matter."

The counterarguments, indeed, swiftly followed. Walter Haut, the army public affairs officer who had put out the infamous 1947 press release about recovering the flying saucer and was now the president of the Roswell International UFO Museum and Research Center, openly scoffed at the air force report. "It's a bunch of pap," he told the *New York Times*. "All they've done is given us a different kind of balloon. Then it was weather, and now it's MOGUL. Basically, I don't think anything has changed. Excuse my cynicism, but let's quit playing games."

Almost exactly a year later, the GAO followed up with its own report, revealing three notable pieces of documentation that ultimately backed up the Pentagon's conclusion: an FBI teletype, sent from the Dallas Field Office at 6:17 p.m. on the evening of July 8 to J. Edgar Hoover and the head of the FBI Field Office in Cincinnati, which had jurisdiction over Wright-Patterson, reported that "an object purporting to be a flying disc was recovered near Roswell" and that "the disc is hexagonal in shape and was suspended from a balloon by a cable"; a formerly classified history of the Roswell air base for the relevant time period and listing the base's major activities, called "Combined History, 509th Bomb Group and Roswell Army Air Field. 1 July 1947 to 31 July 1947," contained the brief entry: "The Office of Public Information was kept quite busy during the month answering inquiries on the 'flying disc' which was reported to be in the possession of the 509th Bomb Group. The object turned out to be a radar tracking balloon"; and, lastly, but perhaps most interestingly, the GAO reviewed the minutes of the National Security Council in 1947 and 1948, previously classified documents that were written decades before the Freedom of Information Act and presumably never intended to be viewed by the public, none of which contained reference to Roswell at all. (As the GAO noted, it seemed hard to believe that an alien spacecraft could have crashed in the US and never end up in a conversation at the National Security Council.*) To drive the point home, the CIA went on the record for the first time publicly, to state that it had no records pertinent to Roswell.†

Schiff served as the face of the GAO report release on July 28, 1995, an attempt, it seemed, to both delicately highlight its conclusions and, like a good congressman, appear sensitive to the believers and the conspiracy tourism growing in his home state. In any case, the outgoing messages from the Roswell air base, he took care to point out, were missing entirely from 1946 to 1949, messages that presumably would have shed light on how the base officials described what they'd found, and so a definitive answer may not be possible—and since what one might call the "Roswell

---

* Schiff, for his part, didn't necessarily see the lack of a Roswell mention in the NSC minutes as definitive proof of anything. As he told one interviewer, "It would be such an unusual event . . . that I'm not sure how it would be handled and even if it were presented to the national leaders and National Security Council, I'm not sure I would necessarily say that you could say how they would handle the minutes of such a meeting."

† These facts, though seemingly important, were perhaps less than meets the eye: the CIA and the National Security Council weren't created until September 1947, two months after the Roswell crash. However, again, it would seem that had aliens crash-landed in New Mexico in the summer of '47 the fallout of that event would still be in discussion among government officials later in that fall.

Industrial Complex" was a fixture of the American landscape, the GAO report nor any other would likely change the minds of the true believers. In the end, as Schiff said, "People can make their own conclusions and that was my goal all along and I have accomplished that goal."

• •

Just as the Pentagon hoped that the Roswell story was done and buried, one of its aliens surfaced on television. On August 28, 1995, Fox aired a special report about a seventeen-minute black-and-white video that purported to show the autopsy of one of the alien bodies recovered from the crash. British music producer Ray Santilli said he'd acquired the video from a secret military source, and Fox, the home of the then-popular alien-loving *X-Files*, turned it into a prime-time event hosted by *Star Trek* actor Jonathan Frakes; the show was such a hit that it was rebroadcast a second time—viewed by more than 10 million people on that second airing alone. It was a clip, *Time* magazine wrote, that had fascinated America "with an intensity not lavished on any home movie since the Zapruder film."

The film, which admittedly was a bit grainy, appeared to show a grayish-colored humanoid with a small, hairless head, large black eyes, a small, slender body, and hands with three long, thin fingers, laying on a metal table. Around it, gown-wearing doctors removed and studied its organs. The hour-long Fox special, titled *Alien Autopsy (Fact or Fiction?)*, also included interviews with experts dissecting the dissection—including Hollywood special effects masters discussing whether the whole thing might be staged. All told, only about four minutes of the actual alleged film were featured, "chopped up into MTV-sized snippets that were repeated throughout the hour," wrote *Skeptical Inquirer*, a journal aimed at debunking "nonsense" that dubbed itself "The Magazine for Science and Reason."*

---

* The magazine theorized that at some level the resurgence of interest of Roswell in the 1980s and '90s stemmed from just how outlandish so many other aspects of ufology seemed by that era. Roswell, by comparison, seemed almost a simple, straightforward conspiracy. "The details are still intriguing enough to fire the imagination, and the facts and recollections have been polished bright by the passage of time. With its simple tale of a crashed saucer, a few space aliens, and a government

As more people scrutinized the film, more and more details didn't seem to add up. The autopsy procedure shown didn't seem to be a real medical exam; the doctors were working with inappropriate equipment, and the whole thing seemed to proceed on-screen more casually than you would have imagined if scientists were seeing a being from another planet for the first time. "The fact is, an autopsy on a creature this extraordinary wouldn't be done the way this one was," the *Inquirer* writer, science journalist Gene Emery, concluded. It also seemed to speak volumes that Fox made no clear attempt to authenticate the video with government sources or do anything like the frame-by-frame analysis you would imagine would go into an actual video of an alien autopsy.

Just two years later, in an attempt to double down on their veracity, Ray Santilli publicized photos of the original film canisters, but in doing so all but exposed his own hoax: the canisters were clearly labeled "Department of Defense," a name and entity that hadn't existed at the time of the Roswell crash, when the newly unified military was called instead the National Military Establishment. By the following year, Fox was featuring its own special in a program called *World's Greatest Hoaxes: Secrets Finally Revealed*. It took nearly a decade for Santilli to fully come clean, although he maintained it wasn't a full hoax, just a re-creation—the real video, he said, had degraded too much by the time he'd raised the money to purchase it, and so he had decided to re-create the footage in order to preserve the memory of what he had seen.

One person who wasn't fooled by the video was Dana Scully, the fictional FBI agent and star of Fox's own *The X-Files*. In an episode that aired late in 1995 that featured its own dubious alien autopsy video, Scully declared that the film was "even hokier than the one they aired on the Fox network."*

---

cover-up, the Roswell story seems far more plausible (relatively speaking) than today's tales of aliens passing through walls, millions of Americans being abducted by sex-obsessed space creatures, and extraterrestrials who create alien-human babies," the *Skeptical Inquirer* article read.

* The mid-1990s were, like the 1950s, another heyday of aliens in popular culture. Among other notable films, 1993 saw the movie *Fire in the Sky*, about the Travis Walton abduction, and 1996 saw both the Tim Burton parody *Mars Attacks!* and

• •

As July 1997 and the fiftieth anniversary of the supposed crash approached, the city of Roswell fully embraced its infamy by hosting a giant party (though not quite as large as the one hundred thousand visitors it had hoped to attract). Roswell, like many smaller western communities, had suffered a hard half century. The closure of the local air base in 1965 had emptied about five thousand people from the town; it had taken nearly twenty years to rebuild the population to its postwar peak. But now the town bustled and pulsed with forty-five thousand alien enthusiasts, the curious, and the strange, and saw numerous visitors at the crash site throughout the rest of the year.

Businesses competed in an alien-themed window-decorating contest, there was a Crash-and-Burn race (e.g., a soapbox derby), a flying-saucer-eating contest (e.g., a pancake-eating competition), and an Alien Chase (e.g., an ET-themed road race, complete with costumes). As the *Tucson Weekly* recounted, "The local art museum presented a UFO quilt exhibit, and a local theatrical troupe performed *Ezekiel's Wheels*, an original stagework exploring the possibility that Ezekiel's Biblical encounter with a 'flaming wheel' may have been an early close encounter."

By now, of course, the legend had sprawled to include three different possible crash sites, not just the Brazel ranch, but also where the alleged bodies and crashed spacecraft had been found. Parking cost $15 at the Corn Ranch crash site, where Jesse Marcel Jr., the son of the one-time intelligence officer who had gathered the debris, regaled visitors with his tales of actually seeing the wreckage. "I know we're no longer the only ones," he told the *Washington Post*'s Joel Achenbach.

---

the summer blockbuster *Independence Day*, which raked in more than $800 million at the box office as audiences cheered Will Smith and Bill Pullman as they battled invading alien craft. The movie had a little bit of everything for enthusiasts and believers: Roswell truthers felt vindicated by the major plot twist, which focused on the US president learning that Area 51 was real and that the US military had recovered alien bodies and flying saucers in Roswell in 1947. James Rebhorn played the deceitful defense secretary who had been in on the cover-up over the years and only revealed it to the president when the nation was threatened. The film also featured a star character who saw the alien invasion as validation of his long-claimed abduction by aliens and a chance to get revenge on the aliens who traumatized him.

What one might call the "abduction elite" also descended on the festivities: Whitley Strieber, Budd Hopkins, and Stanton Friedman made their presences known, as did Erich von Däniken, of ancient aliens fame, who held forth for ninety minutes at the New Mexico Military Institute, hinting that the Great Pyramid of Cheops held inside it secret information about extraterrestrial visitors. Our ancient forebears, he explained, were not "so stupid and so primitive to construct temples for their entire lifetimes for nonexisting gods"—the temples were meant to honor their outer space visitors, but they didn't understand the technology of their spacecraft enough to delineate real from divine.

This ongoing fascination continued to frustrate the air force, which that same year put out a *second* giant report in an attempt to tackle the remaining conspiracies around the 1947 crash, once and for all. This time, the Pentagon actively sought to dispel the notion that any alien bodies had been recovered in Roswell: "Although MOGUL components clearly accounted for the claims of 'flying saucer' debris recovered in 1947, lingering questions remained concerning anecdotal accounts that included descriptions of 'alien' bodies," stated the new 230-page report, titled, optimistically, *The Roswell Report: Case Closed.* "The issue of 'bodies' was not discussed extensively in the 1994 report because there were not any bodies connected with events that occurred in 1947."

The air force also addressed the rumors of "bodies": the long-lost memories of locals and base personnel, of bodies turning up at the base hospital, and odd anthropomorphic remains discovered in the desert, it explained, had been a falsely connected series of unrelated events, including two human accidents in the 1950s, a KC-97 accident that had killed eleven air force personnel and a manned balloon mishap that injured two pilots. There had also been a series of ejection-seat and high-altitude parachute tests conducted in the New Mexico desert around the White Sands Proving Ground, euphemistically called "high altitude aircraft escape projects." In order to design safety systems for high-flying pilots or returning astronauts, the military had dropped hundreds of humanlike dummies over the country in the late 1940s and '50s; the two operations, known as High Dive and Excelsior, had featured one figure nicknamed "Sierra Sam," who was about six feet tall and weighed some two hundred pounds. In 1953, the military had released thirty into the desert around the east side of the military range near Roswell alone, from high-altitude balloons up to as much as ninety-eight thousand feet; they would free-fall for several minutes before a parachute deployed and, theoretically, ease them down to the ground. The air force, it now revealed, could trace at least seven of those landing sites to the area around Roswell and the other supposed "crash sites" in eastern New Mexico.

At the time, dummy-recovery operations would have looked highly suspicious to anyone who chanced upon them: "Typically, eight to twelve civilian and military recovery personnel arrived at the site of an anthropomorphic dummy landing as soon as possible following impact. The recovery crews operated a variety of aircraft and vehicles. These included a wrecker, a six-by-six, a weapons carrier, and L-20 observation and C-47 transport aircraft—the exact vehicles and aircraft described by witnesses as having been present at the crashed saucer locations." Amid the flat desert of New Mexico, such a large military presence—and the colorful parachutes on their way down—would no doubt attract locals. The dummies had to be transported in wooden shipping containers or black or silver insulation bags, precisely like the "caskets" or "body bags" that witnesses reported. Plus, often enough, the dummies weren't found immediately, were found damaged, or never found at all—one languished in the desert for three years before being located. It was entirely possible, the military said, that a witness could have stumbled upon a damaged test dummy and truthfully reported it to be an odd-looking humanlike body in the desert: "Dummies with missing fingers, appears to satisfy another element of the research profile—aliens with only four fingers."

Dozens of pages of the air force report were also given over to dissecting the witness accounts that permeated the Roswell mythology—pointing out the similarities between words and descriptions and the facts of the dummy recovery operations, with the final argument that the people who said that they'd seen something odd in the New Mexico desert were entirely correct—they had seen something extremely unusual, but it had nothing to do with aliens. Add that to the passage of decades and they'd likely forgotten when precisely they saw what. Was it really crazy to think someone might imagine, upon being asked in the 1980s or '90s, that something they'd seen in 1949 or 1953 was actually seen in 1947?

Altogether, the historical record of the Roswell-related files amounted to about forty-one documents that had been declassified across decades—seven Top Secret, thirty-one Secret, and three that were either Confidential or Restricted. The documents had been authored by officials long before the Freedom of Information Act, with little indication that any ordinary citizen would ever read them, and spanned the government security apparatus, from the military to the FBI to the CIA. As Karl Pflock, the "pro-UFOlogist" but "anti-Roswellian" skeptic wrote in his definitive book on the incident, "[The documents] were created by those whose job it was to crack the flying saucer mystery, who wrote and spoke with the certainty that no unauthorized person would ever be privy to their words . . . top-notch professionals who sat in the highest ranks of American intelligence and official science." Not a single such document lends credence to the idea that a UFO or alien bodies were recovered in the New Mexico desert.*

All of that, however, didn't matter. By then, the world believed. Roswell was now internationally synonymous with aliens and government cover-ups, whether or not anything had ever actually happened there. As the UFO prankster James Moseley gleefully said at the fiftieth anniversary party, "It's the greatest celebration of a non-event I've ever experienced."

---

* They include such testimonies as a March 1948 briefing by Colonel Howard McCoy, the head of the Air Material Command intelligence office, talking about Project Sign and saying, "We are running down every report. I can't even tell you how much we would give to have one of those crash in an area so that we could recover whatever they are." Six months later, McCoy asked the CIA for help, saying, "To date, no concrete evidence as to the exact identity of any of the reported documents has been received. Similarly, the origin of the so-called 'flying discs' remains obscure." Later, secret CIA briefings in August 1952 stated, simply, "No debris or material evidence has ever been recovered following an unexplained sighting."

"Who Killed JFK?"

As the forty-second president of the United States, Bill Clinton's framed portrait hung in nearly every government office across the country—and at least one imaginary one in Hollywood: the office of FBI Assistant Director Walter Skinner, the fictional boss of special agents Fox Mulder and Dana Scully, the protagonists of *The X-Files*. As millions tuned in every Friday night on Fox to watch the criminal profiler Mulder and medical doctor Scully work to uncover the truth about extraterrestrials, circling ever closer to an alien invasion, Clinton's very-real administration also found itself repeatedly considering the possibility of life "out there."

Like his Oval Office predecessors, the former Arkansas governor had expressed interest in aliens as soon as he had taken the oath of office. When Webb Hubbell, Clinton's longtime friend, started as the associate attorney general, Clinton gave him specific marching orders: "Webb, if I put you over at Justice, I want you to find the answers to two questions for me. One, who killed JFK? And two, are there UFOs?"

"He was dead serious," Hubbell later wrote in his memoir. "I had looked into both, but wasn't satisfied with the answers I was getting."

As the years passed, Clinton's interest in UFOs—and, specifically, the idea that the government wasn't leveling with the American people about what it knew—never seemed far from his mind. Responding to a question from a child named Ryan during a 1995 trip to Ireland, he said, "No, as far as I know, an alien spacecraft did not crash in Roswell, New Mexico, in 1947," and then quipped, "And Ryan, if the United States Air Force did recover alien bodies, they didn't tell me about it, either, and I want to know."

Behind the scenes, the interest led to more serious conversations. During a vacation in Jackson Hole, the wealthy philanthropist Laurance

Rockefeller had lobbied both Bill and Hillary Clinton to take extrater-restrials seriously.* Rockefeller had been funding some efforts to syn-thesize the existing knowledge about UFOs and life elsewhere—one of which resulted in a report called "The Best Available Evidence," which pulled together evidence from the Hynek Center for UFO Studies, MUFON, and the Fund for UFO Research, a rare collaboration by the three groups—and he pressed the White House to declassify more in-telligence around "the existence or non-existence of UFOs," a question he saw of "paramount importance." In 1995, Hillary was photographed walking with Rockefeller, carrying a recent book titled *Are We Alone?: Philosophical Implications of the Discovery of Extraterrestrial Life*, written by astrobiologist Paul Davies.†

In small ways, the administration would offer a new level of trans-parency on past UFO sightings—including the dual reports on Roswell, seemingly inspired in part by Rockefeller's lobbying, and an extensive push by the CIA to publicize its historic interest in the phenomena. But it would be best known for two extraterrestrial-focused media circuses, one focused around a dramatic announcement about life on Mars and the other a series of high-profile sightings out west that would mark the heaviest news coverage of UFOs since the 1950s.

• •

For much of the previous decade, Jill Tarter had spent so much of her time focused on raising money and negotiating and pleading with Con-gress to keep up its funding for SETI that her chosen hotel chain for

---

* A briefing memo from Jack Gibbons, Clinton's science adviser in the Office of Science and Technology Policy, ahead of the vacation warned, "[Rockefeller] will want to talk with you about his interest in extrasensory perception, paranormal phe-nomena, and UFO's." Gibbons added, "He knows that we are trying to be helpful in responding to his concerns about UFO's and human potential—and that we're keeping an open mind about such matters—but I've made no secret about my con-viction that we must not be too diverted from more earthly imperatives."

† Despite Hillary Clinton's apparent reading interest, it's worth noting there is no proof of the *Weekly World News* report, in its cover story on June 15, 1993, that she adopted an alien baby while in the White House nor evidence the Secret Service constructed a special alien nursery in the White House.

visits to the capital, a Holiday Inn in DC, began sending her Christmas presents. Her efforts had helped launch two SETI projects—one, which she led, was a vast-but-targeted search to scan stars within one hundred light-years of Earth for weaker possible signals, while the other, led by NASA's Jet Propulsion Laboratory, meant to scan the whole sky for overwhelmingly strong signals—but the situation was still dire. A decade of bruising congressional battles and attention had matured and chastened their approaches to their work. "It's hard to elevate the consciousness of Congressmen from mundane to heavenly matters," Barney Oliver said, while Drake cautioned, "SETI is always burdened with the threat of being declared flaky, or fringe, or pseudo science, so you have to be very careful that very qualified, right-thinking people are involved."

In the end, the institute had been saved by Utah senator Jake Garn, who NASA had taken into orbit aboard the space shuttle in 1985 and won over to the quest for extraterrestrial life.* While the shuttle trip had been an ordeal—he had been subjected to special tests to evaluate space motion sickness and became so sick on the mission itself that future astronauts would measure their own space sickness on the "Garn scale"—the experience of orbit transformed his own vision of the world and heavens. Soon, his colleagues began to call him "E.T. Garn," as he advocated on SETI's behalf.

"The law of large numbers ought to indicate even to an atheist mathematician that someplace out there, there just happens to be an earth the right distance from its sun for temperature, atmosphere and all that to produce human life out of the sea," Garn told a reporter for his hometown paper, the *Deseret News*. "If you believe in God as I do, would it be logical if He looks at this whole universe that he's created, and [says], 'Well I think this little speck of dust—Earth—is the only place I'll put my children'? Talk about overkill!"

Garn's patronage helped inaugurate a new era for SETI, securing more than $4 million in funding, enough to move forward with the construction of a system that could scan 14 million channels; as one of Tarter's

---

* Garn, a fifty-five-year-old former Vietnam naval aviator at the time of his shuttle trip, had probably been the best candidate for conversion: a Mormon, he had been raised in a faith that believed in celestial kingdoms.

colleagues told the *New York Times*, "In the first minute, we'll accomplish more than all the other projects combined."

"This is the big step," Drake later added. "You can theorize forever, but intelligent life is so complicated in its activities and philosophies, as we know from ourselves, that it's quite impossible to psych out the extra-terrestrials and deduce by logic how they might behave. The only way we can really learn the truth is to search."

On Columbus Day, 1992—the symbolic five hundredth anniversary of the European explorer arriving in "the New World"—SETI's biggest program yet began at the Arecibo radio telescope. The telescope pointed its massive dish at star GL615.1A, some sixty-three light-years away in the constellation Hercules and listened.

"We sail into the future, just as Columbus did on this day 500 years ago. We accept the challenge of searching for a new world," NASA's John Billingham proclaimed at the launch ceremony. In the Mojave Desert, the 112-foot Goldstone telescope also began its own work scanning the sky. The SETI program, renamed at congressional insistence as the more-respectable and obscure-sounding High Resolution Microwave Survey—although Tarter's colleagues joked the acronym HRMS meant "He Really Means SETI"—had quickly found a few intriguing signals, sending a burst of excitement through the room in Puerto Rico (though, as time passed, none panned out).

The initial ebullience, unfortunately, was short-lived, and soon over-taken by outright despair. Once again, Congress stepped in—this time in the form of Nevada senator Richard Bryan—and zeroed out SETI's re-named efforts. Their $12 million in annual funding had few other champions in the corridors of Capitol Hill—no major aerospace contractors or engineering firms with stables of lobbyists at the ready had contracts tied to the efforts, there were no major facilities with good-paying jobs located in key congressional districts. The whole effort was just a few dozen engineers, none of whom were Bryan's own constituents. (More-over, as one NASA historian ruefully noted, while the SETI program's appropriation accounted for less than one-tenth of 1 percent of NASA's funding, the total ten-year price of $100 million sounded like big money to constituents concerned about ballooning federal spending.) There was also what NASA called "the giggle factor"—"Millions have been spent and we have yet to bag a single little green fellow," Bryan crowed. "Not a single Martian has said 'take me to your leader,' and not a single flying saucer has applied for FAA approval."* The team, including CEO Tom Pierson, watched C-SPAN with dread from a conference room in California as the Senate voted on Bryan's amendment. Cosmic research lost by 77 to 23. "This number has been disconnected," the *New York Times* wrote, referencing E.T. phoning home.

Once again, SETI appeared dead; as a small gift, the federal government declared the expensive sky-hunting equipment "surplus" and donated it to the SETI Institute so at least they wouldn't have to lose what they'd already built. Barney Oliver was livid: "To save the American taxpayer about eight cents per year, we are to be denied the chance to explore the universe and the sentient life forms that fill it."

• •

Funding wasn't the only problem facing NASA and the space exploration community. In 1986, the *Challenger* explosion had dealt a crippling blow to the organization and given the world a very public view of both the dangers of space travel and the cultural flaws that had metastasized inside NASA in the decades since the glory days of the Apollo program. The incident had been so disastrous that numerous investigations and panels were convened to better understand what went wrong and hold negligible parties responsible; in the meantime, the shuttle program was put on a two-year pause. Four years later, the space shuttle *Discovery* carried aloft the Hubble Space Telescope, years behind and over budget, only to have distraught scientists realize upon its deployment that the billion-dollar telescope's main mirror was off by 2 microns, just 0.00007874 inches. Instead of unprecedented clarity of distant galaxies, the telescope provided cloudy and all but unusable images. The public mistake turned the telescope (and NASA) into a national punch line.

---

* Bryan spent two terms, twelve years, in the Senate, and at least according to his Wikipedia biography, his cancellation of SETI was his one memorable—and dubious—contribution to US politics.

It was at this critical juncture that the banner of space exploration was picked up by a new face at NASA, someone interested in reviving the agency's early joie de vivre and restarting the search for life on Mars.

Dan Goldin had spent five years at NASA, starting in 1962 at the Glenn Research Center—and then a quarter century for an aerospace company, until April 1992, when President George H. W. Bush appointed him the space agency's administrator. He had arrived back at NASA just as work was underway to launch an audacious outer space repair mission for Hubble. In December 1993, astronauts aboard the space shuttle *Endeavour* pulled alongside the telescope, latched onto it, and installed a new corrective mirror. Within days, Hubble's new images wowed astronomers and helped rewrite the age of the universe. It was able to photograph the impact of the comet Shoemaker-Levy 9 into Jupiter, confirmed the existence of supermassive black holes, and—intriguingly for the search for life—found oxygen on Jupiter's moon Europa, only the third time that Earth's life-giving element had been found somewhere other than our home planet. Sitting atop NASA was, once again, one of the most exciting places in science to be, and Goldin was grateful for the opportunity. "The human life is more than survival. You need food, you need shelter, but you also need intellectual nourishment," he said. "We ought to be humble. I mean, as I grow older, and as I learn more, I become more overwhelmed by what we don't know."

With some big successes and goodwill now under his belt, Goldin set his sights on Mars, hoping that renewed study could uncover signs of life. Though as other probes had visited the red planet—most notable the Viking 1 and Viking 2 missions in the mid-1970s—the perception that Mars was a dead planet remained unchanged. Those first color images had famously established for humans the dark red of the planet's surface and its pink hazy sky, but Viking's biology experiments had struck out—despite initial excitement that they might have found biological elements in the soil, nothing had panned out. "There was not a hint of life—no bushes, no trees, no cactus, no giraffes, antelopes or rabbits," Sagan had lamented when the first photos from Viking had transited the eighteen and a half minutes back to Earth in 1976. What had once been hailed as "the greatest experiment in the history of science," an unbelievably complex series of automated tools working millions of miles from Earth made up of forty thousand individual parts, had failed to discover anything of consequence. "That's the ball game," one of the scientists said. "No organics on Mars, no life on Mars."*

But Goldin's hopes relied on Mars' past, more than its current life. The planet, he understood, was distinct from Earth; Earth's landmasses turned over with a great deal of frequency, and many scientists doubted that we would even be able to detect if highly advanced civilizations had once populated it hundreds of millions of years ago, but Mars was effectively static, almost unchanged geologically for three billion years. Perhaps if scientists looked, Goldin told a team of scientists, "Maybe we will learn that the same building blocks of life washed over both planets simultaneously. We could find fossils of cells with elements of proteins similar to those here on Earth. We might find the one fossilized cell that is the missing link between the planets. We might find actual life—imagine that!"

It wasn't long after that Goldin became one of a tiny handful of people on Earth to know perhaps the most exciting scientific discovery of all time.

---

* The longer-term answer has proven more ambiguous. Some scientists now wonder whether those early biology experiments would have correctly identified life in a radically different form. As SETI scientist Seth Shostak wrote, "A new analysis of the Viking mass spectrometer suggests it might easily have missed the Martians' molecular building blocks. It would have been unable to find the organic material in, for instance, the salt-laced soil of Chile's Atacama desert, which is chockablock with microbes. This new work—while not proving life was missed—at least reopens the door to that possibility." Resilient Martian life, for instance, may thrive underground, in the planet's underground aquifers, but few scientists believe that life there may ever amount to much more than, in Shostak's words, "single-celled pond scum."

44

The Mars Rock

Steadily through the 1970s and '80s, research on Earth had found life in the most inhospitable places, from salty brine pools to sulfur-fueled lifeforms at hydrothermal vents deep underwater to microbes in the hot springs of Yellowstone to the irradiated pools of nuclear water around Three Mile Island.* Even in places far more hostile to existence than anyone imagined, life willed out—which meant perhaps far more of the universe was capable of sustaining it than previously imagined. Scientists were finding life almost anywhere within two kilometers of the surface and at temperatures from zero degrees Fahrenheit in the Himalayans, all the way to microbes that lived and reproduced at temperatures around 250 to 260 degrees Fahrenheit on the seafloor. Maybe not even the ingredients we considered necessary for life—water and oxygen—mattered to creatures that were anaerobic or methane-based. Aliens might be quite alien to us indeed.

In the 1990s, the field originally known as "exobiology," before being rebranded as "bioastronomy," underwent a final transformation when it was reconfigured into "astrobiology." There was another development in the fall of 1995, when Swiss and US scientists announced the discovery of seven planets outside our solar system—the first ever so-called "exoplanets" were a confirmation that our celestial arrangement may not be all that unique across the cosmos.† For three decades, SETI efforts had con-

---

* The bacteria of Yellowstone, thriving at temperatures of 160 degrees Fahrenheit and up, were named *Thermus aquaticus*, i.e., "Warm bath water dweller."

† The discovery actually confirmed a paper written by astronomer and SETI pioneer Otto Struve in 1952—a paper subsequently ignored for four decades by unconvinced astronomers who didn't want to waste their precious telescope time—that it should be relatively easy to detect giant planets orbiting their stars closely, whipping around and tugging gravitationally on the star itself.

tinued without anyone actually being sure there were any other planets out there at all, let alone inhabitable ones. Now they knew, for sure, that beyond our solar system there were perhaps other Earth-like bodies—a fact that could dramatically alter the variables of the Drake equation, and our understanding of how the universe functioned.[*]

Just as the Swiss-US team was working through its new planets, a team at the Johnson Space Center in Houston had begun working with a new electron microscope designed to inspect the tiles of future space shuttle flights, to protect against the disaster that felled the *Challenger*. It was a brilliant invention for its intended purpose, and would prove helpful in other areas as well.

Applying the new tool to biology, geochemists David McKay and Everett Gibson turned to a meteorite discovered in 1984 in Antarctica on an annual government collection mission. ALH84001 was one of the oldest Martian meteorites, somewhere around 4 billion years old, when liquid water had been on the red planet's surface. The four-pound piece of planetary refuse had been blasted off Mars's surface after a larger meteor collided with the planet somewhere around 17 million years ago, as the first apes emerged on Earth and the Arabian Peninsula slammed into Eurasia. It had landed as early humans first domesticated sheep in Mesopotamia in 13,000 BC.

Now, studying tiny flakes of the meteorite under the powerful microscope, McKay and Gibson saw something that looked, inexplicably, unexpectedly, and surprisingly like life itself. Was that a . . . worm? Or at least a tiny wormlike piece of bacteria? The duo kept the potential discovery secret as they continued to probe, not even telling their office neighbors in the Johnson Space Center's Building 31. Before long, they'd found further evidence of chemicals and elements—what Gibson called a "blanket of biology" that indicated that they were looking at something at least approaching billions-of-years-old life.

---

[*] As Tufts University professor Eric Chaisson argued, there are seven stages of "cosmic evolution": particulate, galactic, stellar, planetary, chemical, biological, and cultural. As far as we knew, we were still the only ones to make it through all seven stages, but even the simple discovery of other planets far out there leapt all the way to the fourth stage.

McKay, at first, was skeptical. A career in space study had taught him not to get his hopes up too quickly. He'd been in the stadium at Rice University as a student in 1962 when John F. Kennedy had challenged the nation to reach the moon, an experience that had inspired him to join NASA during its most exciting chapter, but working in the Johnson Space Center had shown him the realities of that journey. He'd written hundreds of papers and estimated he'd examined fifty thousand rocks. As he neared the end of a distinguished career, "caution and conservatism had allowed him to develop an admirable if not spectacular reputation in the field of planetary science."

This rock, however, was unlike any he'd seen before.

Gradually, he and Gibson brought in more experts. "We do not want you to tell anybody what you're doing," they cautioned colleague Kathie Thomas-Keprta, one of the world's leading experts on cosmic dust, "one thing we think may be in this sample is evidence of biogenic processes." Thomas-Keprta went home that evening and told her husband her colleagues were nuts, but gradually she was convinced herself. She joined the study, and for nearly two years, the team continued to test, examining and reexamining the flakes of the potato-sized ALH84001. In early 1996, Thomas-Keprta spotted tiny mineral grains known as gregite, which she knew were almost always a by-product of bacteria. "This could be the coolest day of my life," she thought.

Satisfied that their hypothesis and evidence were solid, the team began to write up their findings for the journal *Science*. Their final sentence, each word chosen precisely, was ultimately left unchanged by journal editors and nine peer reviewers: "Although there are alternative explanations for each of these phenomena when taken individually, when they are considered collectively, particularly in view of their spatial association, we conclude that they are evidence of primitive life on Mars."

"There were an infinite number of ways of saying maybe—strong maybes and weak maybes, maybes that sounded definitive and maybes that had gaping escape hatches," wrote journalist Joel Achenbach, who covered the event later. "This was a strong, firm, chest-thumping maybe."

On July 31, 1996, McKay, Gibson, and Thomas-Keprta traveled to Washington to present their findings to Goldin. The thirty-minute meeting ended up stretching to three hours as the NASA administrator listened, questioned, and contemplated the information before him, compiling twenty-seven pages of notes as he did so. At the end of the presentation, he asked one important question: Were they sure they were right? If they were, this would be perhaps the most significant discovery in the history of science.

"We have it nailed. We have it four different ways," Gibson said.

Goldin paused to take that in, before issuing a second request to McKay: "Can I give you a hug?"

NASA called the White House, and Goldin and his deputy rushed into a meeting with White House chief of staff Leon Panetta, handing him a blown-up photo of the wormlike creature. Panetta was as startled by the news as anyone, and went down to the Oval Office. A few minutes later, the NASA administrator and deputy were asked to join him. President Clinton grilled the team from his desk, and when the briefing concluded, his reaction was simple: *This is a day that we'll remember.*

Vice President Al Gore, a bit of a science geek in his own right, was incredulous: "Wait a minute—our guys, government scientists, did this?"

Slowly but steadily, the news began to trickle out. On August 7, the discovery was officially announced to the world in the pages of *Science*, in an article dryly titled "Search for Past Life on Mars: Possible Relic of Biogenic Activity in Martian Meteorite ALH84001"—over a million people tried to access the paper online, a startling number on the still-nascent World Wide Web. That same day, President Clinton stood on the South Lawn of the White House and discussed the discovery. McKay, who had been off on a prescheduled family vacation, was rushed back to Washington to stand beside him.

"Today, rock 84001 speaks to us across all those billions of years and millions of miles. It speaks of the possibility of life. If this discovery is confirmed, it will surely be one of the most stunning insights into our universe that science has ever uncovered," he said. "Its implications are as far-reaching and awe-inspiring as can be imagined. Even as it promises answers to some of our oldest questions, it poses still others even more fundamental. We will continue to listen closely to what it has to say as we continue the search for answers and for knowledge that is as old as humanity itself but essential to our people's future."

Once those remarks were complete, a NASA press conference began across town. It was the happiest moment that NASA had experienced in years. Goldin proclaimed it "a day that will go down in history for the American people, and indeed for all of humanity." The excitement of the usually unexcitable scientists was palpable as they looked out onto a phalanx of nearly three dozen camera crews. "This was undoubtedly the most exciting thing I've done in my 27 years in science," Gibson said. "It does beat Apollo, and that's pretty tough to do."

The one sour note—if one can call it that—was served by UCLA paleobiologist J. William Schopf, the staff's chief skeptic. Schopf, like Sagan, believed that life was abundant in the universe, but that we hadn't found it yet ("I'm certain we will find life elsewhere, probably within our solar system, if you give me 250 years," he would say), and had been unconvinced from the moment he'd been brought in on NASA's secret. For one thing, he thought the "worm," which looked so definitive and real on the press conference photos, so surely like a worm, was simply too small—at 360 nanometers, it would have taken 150 of such worms to equal even the width of a human hair. Life just couldn't be that small. At the press conference, he explained that on a plausibility scale of one to ten, the AHL84001 claim, in his view, was just a measly two.

The public didn't care. The rock—and the NASA scientists who found it—inspired national awe, and breathed entirely new life into the space program.* Clinton called for an all-out search for life on Mars. Earth's primary life-beyond enthusiast, Carl Sagan, declared the discovery "the most provocative and evocative piece of evidence for life beyond Earth," adding that, "If the results are verified, it is a turning point in human history, suggesting that life exists not just on two planets in our paltry solar system, but throughout our magnificent universe."†

---

* One science peer proposed to Goldin renaming it "the Sagan rock," since surely something as historic as this deserved a less cumbersome name than an abbreviation for Allan Hills 1984, Rock 1.

† McKay would come to store the flake of ALH84001 in a small Tupperware-like box on top of a filing cabinet in his office—a somewhat ignominious storage location for perhaps the first sign ever of life beyond. Ultimately, as the years passed, hope

As it turned out, Sagan's statement about the Mars rock episode in the summer of '96 would be one of his final ones. A years-long battle with cancer had weakened him so significantly that when Drake met up with Sagan for lunch in San Francisco, he was startled by the stooped, elderly man who shuffled slowly into the agreed-upon restaurant. By the time Clinton's summit on space exploration unfolded, Sagan could no longer stand.

On December 20, 1996, the most famous scientist the world had seen since Albert Einstein died at the age of sixty-two. In his final days, he admitted the great mystery of his life was still unsolved, referencing a previous famous statement of his that "extraordinary claims require extraordinary evidence," and admitting, "The evidence for life on Mars is not yet extraordinary enough."

Sagan was memorialized all over—three memorial services were held, but the one at New York City's Cathedral of St. John the Divine in Morningside Heights was perhaps the most moving and demonstrative of his impact. As part of the service, a recording of Sagan reading from his book *Pale Blue Dot* (a reference to the photo he'd persuaded NASA to have Voyager 1 take of Earth as it sailed out of our solar system in 1990 some 3.7 billion miles from the sun) played out into the packed cathedral:

> That's here. That's home. That's us. On it, everyone you love, everyone you know, everyone you ever heard of, every human being who ever was, lived out their lives. The aggregate of our joy and suffering, thousands of confident religions, ideologies, and economic doctrines, every hunter and forager, every hero and coward, every creator and destroyer of civilization, every king and peasant,

---

dimmed that the grand pronouncement of life on Mars had been correct, but it was hard to think of the whole operation as a failure; it had reawakened the nation's imagination and inspired a new generation of scientists for whom projects like Mariner and Voyager were ancient history. As planetary scientist Sarah Stewart Johnson wrote, "ALH84001 was a glimpse into a future brimming with possibility." Perhaps life beyond was even weirder than we could imagine, built on biochemistry unlike anything we've discovered.

every young couple in love, every mother and father, hopeful child, inventor and explorer, every teacher of morals, every corrupt politician, every "superstar," every "supreme leader," every saint and sinner in the history of our species lived there—on a mote of dust suspended in a sunbeam.

45

The Phoenix Lights

In the wake of Sagan's death and other news headlines that lessened the impact and urgency of ALH84001, enthusiasm waned, nationally and politically, for further exploration of Mars. NASA, adventurers, and space enthusiasts had talked of an Apollo-style mission that would reach the red planet perhaps in the 2010s, but by the mid-1990s, even in a moment when the economy was going well and government budgets climbing, it was clear the country had little appetite for such a giant undertaking, and as a result, space initiatives felt the pressure to perform.

At SETI, Jill Tarter, Tom Pierson, Barney Oliver, and their colleagues had spent months, and then years, cobbling together the funding to keep their work going from companies and individual donations. Hewlett-Packard founders David Packard and William Hewlett both put in a million dollars to support the effort, as did Intel's Gordon Moore and Microsoft cofounder Paul Allen—largesse that then encouraged Packard and Hewlett to double their original gifts. ("Damn politicians," Packard, himself a former deputy secretary of defense, lamented in one funding meeting.)

To their relief, other gifts and grants also trickled in; Lotus creator Mitch Kapor handed Tarter $10,000, and Oliver kicked in $100,000 of his own money. Soon, they'd pieced together about $7.5 million,* and found an opportunity to put their mobile radio-frequency van to work in Australia. In November 1995, the team collected their vehicle from a facility in Sydney Harbor, and set up shop at the Parkes Observatory in

---

* "In retrospect, this early, easy success at garnering monies for SETI was misleading," Shostak reflected. "If Oliver could raise $20 million in an afternoon, we foresaw little danger that SETI would ever be threatened by lack of funds. Time and experience would show how naive this assumption was."

New South Wales on the country's western coast—a storied facility that had once been a receiving station for the live images from the Apollo 11 moon landing. To outfit their quarters, they shopped at what Tarter called "this thing called Ikea" and quickly lined up another telescope 144 miles away as a so-called "follow-up detection device," giving themselves a way to double-check any interesting-looking signals and help eliminate earthly interference.* It took much of the Australian summer to line up and troubleshoot all the pieces—and then on February 1, Project Phoenix finally rose.

For the next six months, Tarter monitored the skies, often taking the night shifts and walking the mile from their lodging to the telescope under the intensely dark southern sky. Ultimately, the search turned up nothing interesting, but it served as a proof-of-technological-concept, and that success encouraged Packard, Hewlett, and Moore to all renew their support—pledging a million a year each for five years, enough to keep SETI alive until the millennium. Disappointed but hopeful, the team headed back to Green Bank and its 140-foot telescope.

It was there, on June 24, 1997, that a signal appeared while Tarter and the team were studying YZ Ceti, a red dwarf in the constellation Cetus that's just twelve light-years away—practically down the block in galactic terms. The truth was that on the monitoring equipment any signal looked initially anticlimactic—it wasn't like there were flashing red lights and alarms that sounded, nor could the scientists decipher the sounds or hear Morse code coming through space—and this one followed that trend, starting out just as a dash of white dots, a line across a fuzzy black-and-white screen. Even in such a mundane form, though, it stood out to the SETI team. "We could pick from only two plausible choices," recalled Seth Shostak, who was monitoring the search from the SETI Institute in California in a room of increasingly anxious and excited scientists. "It was either a false alarm—static from a man-made transmitter causing a useless adrenaline rush—or it was the real deal."

---

* To Tarter's annoyance, the male Australian team members seemed prone to inappropriate innuendos and "dumb blonde" jokes, which she stopped finally by leveling her gaze at one joke-maker and saying, "I don't get that one—please explain it to me?"

Unfortunately, SETI's intended backup telescope, located in Georgia, was broken and not able to cross-check the signal, so the Green Bank team had to do their best on-site: they swung the giant telescope back and forth, and each time they moved away from the signal, it vanished—the desired outcome if you wanted confirmation that it was coming from far-off space rather than an earthly signal like an airplane or orbiting satellite. Finally, the team tried moving the telescope just a tiny bit. Even moving it a tenth of a degree—as Shostak described it, "the width of a knitting needle held at arm's length"—should have caused the signal's strength to drop by half if it was a true outer space signal. At 6 a.m. California time, they woke up a software engineer on the West Coast named Jane Jordan to update the telescope software from home. When Jordan ran the test, the signal stayed just as strong. To her, that was a bad sign—they had probably found something, but not a far-off planet, but in any case, the team would have to wait until nightfall to study it again. Tarter, who had intended to fly home that morning, called her assistant to rebook the return flight.

Meanwhile, in SETI's California offices, Shostak was facing another time-sensitive question: At what point did the team have to inform others about the potential discovery in progress? The issue resolved itself, unfortunately, when William Broad, a science writer for the *New York Times*, gave him a midday call: "Seth, what about that signal you're following?"*

"We're continuing to track the star," Shostak said. "We're checking out a lead right now." He asked for three hours to get more information and promised the *Times* reporter more when he got back.

In the end, it took only two. When the team got its new round of results, it was clear they hadn't found life orbiting YZ Ceti; the telescope had, instead, happened across the Solar and Heliospheric Observatory, a

---

* As it turned out, Broad had been working that morning on an article about the legacy of Carl Sagan—who had died six months earlier—and called Sagan's widow, Ann Druyan, only to reach Druyan's secretary. She had mentioned in conversation that she'd talked that morning to Tarter's secretary and that the astronomer was in the midst of investigating a curious signal. That nugget was enough for Broad to dig deeper and call the SETI Institute.

joint European-American solar research satellite several hundred thousand miles away in space. As Shostak recounted, "This was not ET."

The whole affair made him think back to a recent public debate he'd had on TV with the editor of *UFO Magazine*, discussing what would happen if SETI ever found an unambiguous signal from space. The ufologist had insisted to him that the military would immediately show up and shut down the research effort, blanketing it all with secrecy, but Shostak had publicly doubted anything would or could stay secret for very long. He also doubted that any government would care enough to mobilize before the news broke, before pointing out that a SETI discovery was fundamentally different than an alien spacecraft appearing and hovering over, say, the White House. Any discovery of a SETI signal would be both passive—there would be no way for the alien civilization to know the message had been heard on Earth—and would almost by definition be coming from so far away that there would be no need to rush; even the "close" stars in SETI's studies were often hundreds of light-years away, meaning their civilizations, if any, probably wouldn't be racing to Earth in the next few days.

What happened in Green Bank, to him, was further confirmation of both his doubts: a false alarm that hadn't even managed to stay secret for twenty-four hours, during which time none of the SETI researchers had heard a peep of interest from any government official, let alone received a visit from the men in black. *Heck*, Shostak thought, *the mayor of Mountain View, the Silicon Valley city that's home to the SETI Institute, didn't call, and I know him personally.* *

---

* Just weeks after the false alarm at Green Bank, Tarter's public profile was transformed by the release of Robert Zemeckis's adaptation of Sagan's novel, *Contact*, starring Jodie Foster, dedicated on-screen simply, "For Carl." The director controversially used footage from Clinton's Mars news conference, verbatim, as the "president" discussed the arrival of signals from space. (As Zemeckis said later, "I swear to God it was like [Clinton's news conference] was scripted for this movie. When he said the line 'We will continue to listen closely to what it has to say,' I almost died. I stood there with my mouth hanging open.") The movie came out on July 11, 1997, just a week after another alien-themed film set to become an instant classic: *Men in Black*, the uproarious Tommy Lee Jones and Will Smith story based on one of the darkest myths of ufology, and while *MIB* would have more of a lasting cultural

• •

Even as SETI's Project Phoenix searched the skies far above, the most famous UFO sighting of the 1990s unfolded, coincidentally, in the skies over the city of Phoenix itself. Over roughly three hours on March 13, 1997, thousands of Arizona residents in and around the city reported seeing a series of what appeared to be massive crafts moving across the night sky. From 7:30 to 10:30 p.m., callers swamped phone lines at news stations, police stations, and the local military base, first reporting a giant V-shaped or triangle-shaped craft crossing overhead, then later, a series of bright stationary lights hovering over the city outskirts. (While concentrated in Phoenix, callers ranged as far afield as Nevada, too.) Witness reports varied in the color, style, and arrangement of the lights, as well as the speed of the mystery craft, but the collective outpouring of concern spurred local city officials to call for an investigation. For ufologists, the giant black, V-shaped craft in the Phoenix sky seemed like a return of the ominous object that had haunted the skies of Belgium nearly a decade earlier. Perhaps the alien visitors from that 1989 flap in Europe had returned to the skies over North America?

In the still mostly pre-internet age, it took months for the Phoenix Lights story to crack the national media—it wasn't until June that *USA Today* ran a front-page story about the strange event, prompting the Republican governor Fife Symington III to announce that he was ordering an investigation. "We're going to get to the bottom of this," he said in a morning TV news interview. "We're going to find out if it was a UFO."

That same afternoon, the governor's office came back to the public with surprising speed, declaring that it had found who was responsible for the incident. At a press conference, breathlessly covered live by an eager media, Symington revealed his six-foot-four chief of staff, led into the room by police officers, handcuffed and dressed in an alien costume. "This just goes to show that you guys are entirely too serious," Symington

---

impact, Foster's portrayal of the Tarter-esque character, Dr. Ellie Arroway, turned Tarter into something of a star herself. As Joel Achenbach wrote, "Sagan dabbled in SETI, Drake made it a serious line of study, but Tarter gave herself to it completely."

chided. The crowd laughed and groaned. The stunt quickly deflated the seriousness of the story, transforming it into a literal laughing matter as the governor intended, and the national media moved on, even as residents continued to swear that something unusual had indeed transpired.

It wouldn't be until the tenth anniversary of the sightings that Symington would make a remarkable confession: while being interviewed for a documentary about that bizarre March night, he admitted, out of the blue, "I saw it too."

As he would explain, on that night in 1997 he'd raced alone to a nearby mountain as the sightings had poured in. His security detail had gone home already for the night, so when he saw the UFO atop the mountain, he had been completely alone. "I witnessed something that defied logic and challenged my reality: a massive delta-shaped craft silently navigating over the Squaw Peak in the Phoenix Mountain preserve," he recounted. "A solid structure rather than an apparition, it was dramatically large, with a distinctive leading edge embedded with lights as it traveled the Arizona skies. I still don't know what it was. As a pilot and a former Air Force officer, I can say with certainty that this craft did not resemble any man-made object I had ever seen."

The air force, exasperated by yet another UFO obsession coming out of the woodwork just as it was trying to shut down the Roswell story once and for all, argued otherwise—neither set of "crafts" spotted by the Phoenix residents existed. According to the military, the wave of sightings was attributed to two unrelated and entirely normal incidents, both tied to a training exercise known as Operation Snowbird, underway at the time at Tucson's Davis-Monthan Air Force Base. By the air force's account, five A-10 Thunderbolt attack planes had traversed the sky that evening in a V-shaped formation, their steady white lights perfectly mirroring the reports of a giant craft. Later on, other A-10 aircraft from the Maryland Air National Guard had dropped a series of long-burning flares as part of their training exercise, the bright, slow-falling points of light that likely caused the second wave of UFO reports.

Many people, including Symington, found the explanations lacking— and the governor later stated his regrets about not coming forward sooner and missing the chance to press the military for a more thorough investigation. The incident, he reiterated, just hadn't appeared threatening; the

UFO (or UFOs) had sailed across the sky silently, so it seemed easier to brush it off as a strange experience. Plus, there were political implications to worry about—admitting that he'd seen a UFO, albeit one reported by thousands of his constituents, would have been too much of a political risk. "If I had to do it all over again," he said, "I probably would have handled it differently."*

---

* Two weeks after the Phoenix Lights, America's winter astronomical obsession and the cult of UFO conspiracies came together in a tragic way. As the comet Hale-Bopp had traversed the sky, an amateur Texas astronomer announced that he'd discovered a "Saturn-like" object trailing it. While other astronomers argued he'd just misidentified a known, far-off star, ufologists declared his discovery to be a giant world-sized alien spacecraft hiding in the comet's wake; that rumor ultimately inspired a mass suicide weeks later of a New Age cult called Heaven's Gate, who believed that in doing so, they would become immortal extraterrestrials. "Hale–Bopp brings closure to Heaven's Gate . . . our 22 years of classroom here on planet Earth is finally coming to conclusion—'graduation' from the Human Evolutionary Level," the group said in a prepared statement. "We are happily prepared to leave 'this world' and go with Ti's crew" (referencing their earthly leader). It was a headline-grabbing event—the cult members infamously all wore Nike sneakers as they killed themselves in successive waves, with surviving cultists neatly shrouding bodies with purple cloth, and each cult member had in their pockets a five-dollar bill and three quarters, an apparent reference to an apocryphal Mark Twain quote that said $5.75 was "the cost to ride the tail of a comet to heaven"—but one that broadly captured the increasingly intertwined threads of paranoia and conspiracism that had pervaded American culture.

PART 3

The Interstellar Age

(2000–2023)

46

Cometa

I n 1999, the modern UFO age began in earnest when, two years after the Phoenix Lights incident, journalist Leslie Kean was leaked a ninety-page report about a three-year French study of UFO encounters that had been conducted by thirteen former generals, admirals, scientists, and space experts.

The review, code-named Cometa, had started as a general assessment of GEPAN's progress over the prior two decades, and while technically it was an unofficial project, the caliber of the former officials involved and their ties to the French defense establishment meant that, for all intents and purposes, it was receiving the highest level of attention since the Condon Committee in the 1960s. The core findings—not only that UFOs were worthy of further study but also that there were real reasons to consider the so-called extraterrestrial hypothesis—made it nothing short of a landmark event.* "Without a doubt, the phenomenon remains and the number of sightings, which are completely unexplained despite the abundance and quality of data from them, is growing throughout the world," its introduction read.

Over the course of its research, Cometa had found that even after dismissing all the mistaken celestial objects, misidentified aircraft, misjudged astronomical events, and erroneous atmospheric phenomenon, about 5 percent of UFO sightings remained genuine puzzles, "completely unknown flying machines with exceptional performances that are guided by a natural or artificial intelligence." In fact, as the panel wrote, "A relative consistency emerges from the numerous descriptions of the

---

* In French, UFO is translated as OVNI, *objet volant non identifié*, so the French title for the study was "Les OVNI et la Défense: À Quoi Doit-On Se Préparer?" It translated as "UFOs and Defense: What Should We Prepare For?"

phenomena: saucer, luminous sphere or cylinder, hovering followed by accelerations at lightning speed, the absence of noise, easily supersonic speed with no sonic boom, associated electromagnetic effects that interfere with the operation of nearby radio or electrical apparatus. Obviously, these extraterrestrials are highly endowed intellectually and are technologically advanced over us to have been able to achieve what we do not yet know how to do. But the rest remains a mystery!"

It also further theorized that perhaps alien visits were tied to concerns about Earth's nuclear technology and its expanding explorations of space. "For the moment, they do not appear to be meddling in our affairs, but it is advisable to ask ourselves what they are actually seeking," the panel wrote, echoing the thoughts of ufologists from the decades of the early Cold War. "Do they want to invade earth? To preserve it from nuclear self-destruction? To learn about and preserve the patrimony that our civilizations have created over the span of centuries? In view of these uncertainties concerning their intentions, we can't tell what the future holds and, in particular, we cannot consider that they will continue not to intervene."

In its concluding pages, the report called for a de-stigmatization of UFO reporting, with widespread, better training among civilians and military pilots alike. Similarly, they added, information gathered by the government had to improve, as did scientific monitoring of reports, and the organization of a larger effort to consider "the strategic, political, and religious consequences of a possible confirmation of the extraterrestrial hypothesis, the bizarre connotation of which it is advisable to eliminate here and now."

Ultimately, Cometa would have a lasting impact on the world of ufology, kick-starting a two-decade revolution among policymakers across multiple continents that encouragd them to consider the possibility that there was still something worth studying.

• •

The document inspired Kean—then a reporter for a Berkeley radio station—to begin to dive deeper. A native of New York and offspring of a political dynasty dating back to abolitionist William Lloyd Garrison and Puritan Massachusetts colony founder John Winthrop, Kean had grown up in privileged circles, attending the Spence School and later

Bard. She had stumbled into journalism in the 1990s during a trip to Burma to interview political prisoners, an experience that had profoundly impacted her and inspired her to write a book.* She had been as far removed from the national security and astronomy debates about extraterrestrial life as one could be—but when her French source had slipped her the English-language copy of the Cometa report, making her the only journalist in the country to possess it, she became completely captivated. Here was an opportunity to bridge a divide, a chance to bring a rigorous and objective journalist's eye to a difficult and much-giggled-about subject by focusing tightly on what was known and what wasn't, a hole in the field that had been left largely vacant ever since Hynek's death. "The UFO story was journalistically elusive, contaminated by conspiracy theories, disinformation, and just plain sloppiness, all of which had to be carefully separated from the legitimate material," she reflected later. "It also pointed to something possibly revolutionary, something that could challenge our entire worldview."

In May 2000, she published her scoop in the *Boston Globe*, just as the newly emerging internet began to turbocharge UFO conspiracy theories. The wide-ranging freedoms of the new online universe had allowed far-flung believers and researchers to share resources, compile historical documents, and study the world in ways never before accessible—and in fact, just the month before Kean's article, a North Carolina company working with Microsoft, Kodak, and a Russian satellite company had published the first-ever public images of the mysterious Area 51, high-resolution aerial images of the secret Nevada military base near Groom Lake that the US government had only officially acknowledged in the 1990s and which had long been the subject of conspiracy theories about exotic (perhaps even out-of-this-world) technologies tested far from prying eyes.†

---

* Among the more recent branches of the family tree, her grandfather served ten terms in Congress and her uncle Tom Kean, a two-term New Jersey governor, is best known for chairing the 9/11 Commission.

† That the outer boundaries of Area 51 had been pushed back and back again since the 1980s via the government seizure and annexing of hundreds or thousands of acres at a time in an effort to make it harder for anyone to see what was happening on the desert lake bed didn't help dispel conspiracy theories about what was

Though the new images themselves didn't reveal much—just runways and buildings set amid the empty desert—the glimpse inspired only more wonder and suspicion. "There's stuff out there that is strange," the head of the imaging company, Aerial Images Inc., told reporters. "There is an aircraft on one of the airfields—not Groom Lake—covered in some kind of fabric. . . . There will be those who will look at the images and be more convinced than ever of UFOs."

What most Americans still didn't realize, however, was that decades after the government had disavowed any ongoing interest in UFOs there were murmurings of projects and studies engaging with the subject. Beginning in the mid-1990s, a daring and wealthy Nevada businessman had been working behind the scenes to renew the government's interest in UFOs and paranormal phenomena.

Robert Bigelow had spent nearly his entire life in and around Las Vegas; growing up there at the height of the Cold War, he experienced his first atomic bomb explosion at age nine, when the military tested its new weapons at the Nevada Test Site north of the city. By age twelve, he'd become fascinated with space and, knowing that his own math skills were poor, resolved to become wealthy enough to buy his way there. He followed his late father into real estate, becoming a large no-frills developer over time and eventually the force behind Budget Suites of America, a chain of extended-stay motels ("It's as suite as it gets!") that appealed to temporary workers across the Southwest. As his wealth accumulated, he indulged his interest in UFOs, attending the seminal MIT conference on alien abductions in 1992, and founding the National Institute for Discovery Science (NIDS) in 1995, an initiative focused exclusively on paranormal events from cattle mutilations to UFOs, led by a team of scientists and former law enforcement investigators. Some of the field's most notable names were on its advisory board, including Hynek protégé Jacques Vallée and Harvard abduction expert John Mack; among notable staffers

---

happening there. In the 1990s, the government further secured what was known as Freedom Ridge, the last mountainside overlooking Area 51's runways, where the hardiest of aviation buffs and conspiracists had gathered in hope of glimpsing the Pentagon's blackest projects.

was retired army colonel John Alexander, the Reagan era UFO hunter who had researched psychic abilities and other paranormal activities.[*]

Headquartered in a two-story building off the Las Vegas Strip, NIDS prided itself on its speedy response to field investigations—it had a twenty-four-hour UFO hotline, (702) 798-1700, and staff was often dispatched on Bigelow's own jet to UFO hot spots and sites of sightings and cattle mutilations. Time, they understood, was of the essence, particularly when it came to responding to animal incidents, where fresh tissue samples and necropsies were critical. UFO-wise, they tried to focus on what they saw as the highest-value sightings: multiple witnesses, more than one minute's duration, clear weather. The teams carried extensive (and expensive) instrumentation to detect magnetic, electrical, and radiation residue, as well as infrared and spectrometry equipment, believing they might finally unlock the mysteries of the phenomena. "The Holy Grail in the UFO field is to get a good light spectrum from a UFO, and that has not been possible in the last 50 years," NIDS deputy administrator Colm Kelleher told reporters.

Another of Bigelow's early contributions to the cause was the $200,000 purchase of the five-hundred-acre Utah ranch where the Mormon family of Terry Sherman once said they'd been terrorized by shadowy ghosts, giant wolves, and other mysterious figures—the family lasted just twenty months before being driven from the property by what they said was a reign of paranormal terror. Now Bigelow's team flooded the site with NIDS scientists and surveillance equipment. Initially they tried to keep the ranch's secrets secret, but word began to leak that the new inhabitants had more specific plans. ("We wouldn't be there just for the weather," Bigelow finally admitted to a local reporter.)

The property, which came to be known as Skinwalker Ranch—a reference to a Navajo legend about a witch known as a skin-walker—would

---

[*] A 2000 PowerPoint outlining NIDS's work described its dozen-member science advisory board as including an "Astronaut, Theoretical and Experimental Physicists, Statistical Scientist, Developmental Biologist, Psychologist, Computer Scientist, Physician, Engineer/Radiation Specialist, Futurist, University Administrator, Aerospace Consultant, Pediatrician, Astrophysicist, Phenomenologists."

ultimately become more like local legend, whispered about by NIDS scientists and paranormal explorers for what they said was a tidal wave of strange happenings that included "metallic UAPs, flying orbs of varying colors, otherworldly creatures, discarnate voices, poltergeist, electromagnetic anomalies, and orange 'portals.'" (Among the evidence for the strange doings, as Bigelow would later show *Bloomberg Businessweek*'s Adam Higginbotham was two 8x10 color photographs of a child's ball and jacks sitting on the ranch's kitchen table at the ranch; as he told the story, the two photos—taken minutes apart in an empty room—show that something moved the objects. "We call this the jacks experiment," Bigelow said. "Really amazing.")

Outside of Utah, Bigelow continued to invest millions more in various NIDS endeavors, even personally participating in hundreds of witness interviews. One of the phenomena that particularly interested the group was what the research center called "black triangles," large, silent craft, often with blinking lights, like those that had been reported over Belgium around 1990.* The sightings came from major roadways, near cities, and low altitudes, which made it seem impossible that the US government was trying to hide something. In 2004, NIDS released a major study on the craft, based on more than four hundred sightings, that assessed that the mystery vehicle "does not appear consistent with the covert deployment of an advanced DoD aircraft," and had to therefore be either unacknowledged Pentagon craft or operated by someone—or something—beyond the military. As Kelleher told one reporter, "I cannot say whether these are U.S. Air Force aircraft. We simply don't know. But it does not appear to be consistent with the covert patterns of deployment we saw with the F-117 and B-2 prior to their acknowledgement. This is open, even brazen."

The report would be one of NIDS's final projects. In 2004, Bigelow folded his extracurricular research activities into another of his passion projects: Bigelow Aerospace, which he had created in 1999 after becoming disillusioned with other commercial space companies. (As he said later, "They may have known rocket science, but they had no understanding of

---

* He also gave the University of Nevada–Las Vegas nearly $4 million to study whether there's consciousness after death.

the science of business.") He decided he could do better on his own, and set out with his new firm to build the space hotels he'd imagined ever since his childhood—large inflatable space station modules he hoped would be the first privately owned destinations in outer space, temporary homes available for NASA, miners, and tourists alike, a sort of Budget Suites of America in the sky. The company's brochure at one point said the habitats would be available at about $840,000 a night in low-earth orbit, which would translate into a sixty-day stay for just over $51 million.

Beyond the space station aspirations, Bigelow Aerospace was his own Skunkworks for ufology and paranormal research. (Later, a subsidiary, Bigelow Aerospace Advanced Space Studies, became the new cornerstone of the nation's unofficial-official UFO and paranormal research.)

Gradually, Bigelow's team also took steps to raise the profile of their work in media and culture. The tale of the strange happenings at Bigelow's Utah ranch laboratory was compiled into a 2005 book, *Hunt for the Skinwalker*, by NIDS's Colm Kelleher and Las Vegas investigative reporter George Knapp, who had done groundbreaking reporting on UFOs, particularly around the shadowy activities of Nevada's own Area 51. The book, as it turned out, would jump-start one of the unlikeliest collaborations in the annals of the nation's UFO history, as a wealthy Nevada mogul, a DIA rocket scientist, a senior US senator, a TV reporter, and—most confoundingly of all—a rock star frontman would come together to transform forever how the nation saw UFOs.

Skinwalker Ranch

In June 2007, Robert Bigelow received a letter from a physicist named James Lacatski, a rocket scientist who had worked in DIA's Defense Warning Office, and after reading the *Skinwalker* book, had grown concerned by the apparent existence of major, unexplained phenomenon—perhaps even craft operating in the skies of the United States itself—that didn't appear to be on the policy radar of the US government and military at all. He was hoping that Bigelow might be willing to meet, to discuss the findings and "assist me in developing a strategy on how my office can characterize the potential threat aspects of the phenomena encountered in your research efforts." Intrigued, Bigelow flew with Lacatski to Utah in July to visit the ranch. The DIA scientist would later remember the property in full summer bloom, with plentiful Russian olive trees and cedars, and lush pastures stretching away from the main homestead, but the most memorable element of the trip by far, he would later say, took place when he and Bigelow were talking with the ranch caretakers in the main building. According to him, an "unearthly technological device" suddenly appeared and hovered momentarily in the neighboring room before swiftly vanishing. The whole thing had only lasted about thirty seconds, but he was transfixed.

In Lacatski, Bigelow sensed an opportunity, and after the trip was completed, he turned to one of his state's biggest power brokers to join the conversation.

A former boxer and lawyer, rising Democratic star in the US Senate, and closet ufologist, Harry Reid had been intrigued by Bigelow's work for years, and since the late 1980s, had kept in relatively close contact with a number of figures in and around the UFO debate, including George Knapp. The US senator and the reporter made an odd pair, but Reid's religious faith, as had been the case with Senator Jake Garn, had made him more sympathetic to the concept of UFOs than many realized—"Anyone who's looked at Mormonism at all understands we believe there are other worlds," he told Knapp at one point. "It's one reason people looked askew at Mormonism for a long time. They'd ask, 'Are these people crazy, talking about other worlds?' . . . I think there is no question there are other worlds." In an age before easily available internet archives, Reid had helped Knapp track down out-of-print government resources on the subject, like the transcripts of the congressional UFO hearings in the 1960s, and Knapp, in turn, had gotten Reid involved with NIDS in the 1990s, after the reporter had presented his work and research to the organization's board.

In August 1996, Reid began a rapport with Bigelow and attended a NIDS board meeting, during which he carefully listened to deputy administrator Colm Kelleher explain how "we don't study aliens. We study anomalies. They're the same thing in a lot of people's minds, but not in our minds."

"I'm terribly interested in this," Reid told Knapp later.

He also chewed over the subject privately with his senate colleague, the astronaut and national hero John Glenn, who in casual conversations had said he, too, believed that the country needed more serious study of UFOs. As much as his staff tried to wave him off, warning him to "stay the hell away from this," Reid decided he wanted to know more.

Which is why, when Bigelow called in 2007, Reid—by then the Senate majority leader—agreed to meet with Lacatski at his home. As they sat down for their conversation, the Defense Intelligence Agency staffer explained that he was an expert in rockets and wanted to dive into what the science and military community was beginning to call not UFOs, but UAPs, unidentified aerial phenomena, a term meant both to deflate the giggle factor but also capture the possibility (or even likelihood) that some sightings were atmospheric or meteorological oddities, not just flying craft. Reid found himself agreeing—"I believed the time to focus on UAPs and related phenomena in the context of science was now," he recalled later—and committed to helping however he could.

Back at the US Capitol, Reid called for a closed-door meeting with Republican senator Ted Stevens and Democratic senator Dan Inouye, the two Appropriations Committee leaders who oversaw the nation's black budget, the pot of secret money that funded classified intelligence and military operations, from spy tech and satellites to covert surveillance programs. After deep discussion, the three men agreed to allocate $22 million for what they'd obtusely call the Advanced Aerospace Weapon System Applications Program (AAWSAP), a two-year endeavor that would mark the first official UFO study effort since Project Blue Book. As they talked, Stevens shared a story he'd kept buried for decades: as a transport pilot in World War II, he'd seen something trailing him off his wing that moved in ways he didn't think possible—perhaps one of the unexplained "foo fighters" that dogged US pilots in Europe and Asia.

"I've been waiting to do this since I was in the Air Force," he excitedly told his colleagues.

• •

While Bigelow and Reid's work proceeded largely behind closed doors, Leslie Kean had spent much of her time since the *Globe* article fighting a years-long battle in federal court to pry loose government files using the Freedom of Information Act, hoping to uncover more details about a strange incident in Kecksburg, Pennsylvania, where something—*something!*—had crashed into the woods of the small town outside Pittsburgh in December of 1965 before being squirreled out by armed military guards and large army trucks. (As the object fell, apparently, a giant fireball had been visible. The incident was reported across multiple states and even up into Canada.) The object, according to witnesses at the time, had been acorn-shaped, and rumors quickly circulated about military personnel in containment suits with Geiger counters wandering the forest. In the years since, locals and ufologists had wondered whether the case was terrestrial—perhaps a Soviet satellite crashing to Earth—or extraterrestrial. A mock-up of the supposed car-sized acorn UFO sat in the town center, created at one point for an *Unsolved Mysteries* episode.

To assist in her efforts, Kean had enlisted the help of former Clinton White House Chief of Staff John Podesta. Podesta had joined the administration in the second term (the press quickly dubbed him "Clinton's Mr. Fix-It"), and his passion topics, particularly UFOs and *The X-Files*, were an open secret in DC—he most identified with the paranoid Fox Mulder, and had decorated a table in his office with trinkets and mementos of the show. When he was promoted, Doris Matsui, one of his White House colleagues, wrote a congratulatory note that said, "You will be absolutely terrific! I knew that you were the person for the job when I found out that you were an *X-Files* fan.... [A] belief in extraterrestrials prepares us for believing that anything is possible ... and that there is always another way," and another, White House press secretary Mike McCurry, once joked on the record to the *Washington Post*, "He's been known to pick up the phone to call the Air Force and ask them what's going on in Area 51."

Now, out of the White House and able to pursue those interests more openly, he was happy to help.

"I think it's time to open the books on questions that have remained in the dark on the question of government investigations of UFOs," he explained during a press conference held to share Kean's struggle in obtaining the records. "It's time to find out what the truth really is that's out there. We ought to do it because it's right. We ought to do it because the American people, quite frankly, can handle the truth."

The support was meaningful and helpful, but as it turned out, there was little truth to find. NASA claimed that it lost some key boxes, and in the end, Kean got hundreds of pages of almost entirely useless documents that did little to shed light on the crash. "There was nothing that provided any clarity," a frustrated Podesta said later, "and after forty years there was no plausible reason for them not to come clean and just say what they thought it was."*

Kean, however, was undeterred, and as her research advanced, and more credible and puzzling UFO sightings amassed, she continued to study them. On the overcast and busy afternoon of November 7, 2006, around 4:30, ground personnel at Chicago O'Hare International Airport radioed in that there appeared to be a metallic disk hovering in the sky

---

* It wasn't until 2015, when even more military files were declassified and examined, that a semi-accepted theory of the Kecksburg crash emerged: After years of study, MUFON investigator John Ventre declared that he believed that the object was part of an early American ICBM, made by General Electric, known as the Mark 2 reentry vehicle. Two days earlier, on December 7, 1965, a Thor missile launch from Vandenberg Air Force Base in California had gone awry, leading—according to Ventre—the acorn-shaped reentry vehicle to circle the Earth for two days before crashing into the Pennsylvania forest.

low over the concourse, near Gate C17. The sighting leaked to the *Chicago Tribune* seven weeks later, and a columnist wrote a mostly joking piece about it, quoting United Airlines employees who said the object hovered for "several minutes before bolting through thick clouds with such intense energy that it left an eerie hole in overcast skies." The airline and FAA both initially denied any knowledge of the event, and a union leader used the chance to make fun of the airport's notorious delays—"To fly 7 million light years to O'Hare and then have to turn around and go home because your gate was occupied is simply unacceptable"—but when the *Tribune* filed a Freedom of Information Act request, the FAA uncovered radio transmissions showing discussion at the airport among ground personnel, pilots, and air traffic controllers about something mysterious indeed being in the sky.

"Do you see anything above United concourse?" a ground controller had radioed around at one point. "They actually, believe it or not, they called us and said somebody observed a flying disc about a thousand feet above gate Charley 17." ("I haven't seen anything," one FAA supervisor told another air traffic controller on the phone, "and if I did I wouldn't admit to it.")

The incident was ultimately written off as a strange weather phenomena—meteorologists have wondered since whether it was a rare event known as a "hole-punch cloud"—but many ufologists, including Kean, remained baffled by how just five years after 9/11, the government could be so nonchalant about a widely reported suspicious object hovering over a major airport. ("The FAA treats the smallest safety issue as very important," as the *Tribune* aviation columnist who originally broke the story told Kean. "It will investigate a coffeepot getting loose in the galley and falling while a plane is landing.") To Kean, the incident and the resulting silence was just another sign that the government wasn't taking these sightings seriously. As she'd later write, "Official distaste for dealing with the UFO phenomenon is entrenched to the point of being not only counterproductive, but possibly dangerous." But that didn't mean it was the end of the road—somewhat fatefully, her efforts to spur further interest in the issue had coincided with a general thawing of UFO-related secrecy around the world.

In March 2007, France opened up decades of GEPAN files, revealing

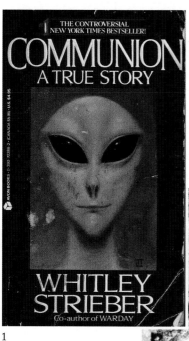

The alien being captured on the cover of *Communion* became iconic.

1

A Costa Rican survey plane captured a puzzling image of a UFO.

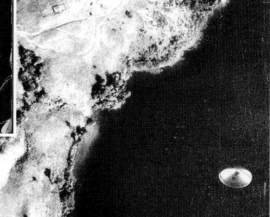

2

3

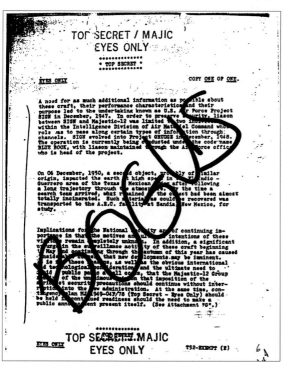

It took a Herculean effort to determine the Majestic 12 documents were fakes.

4

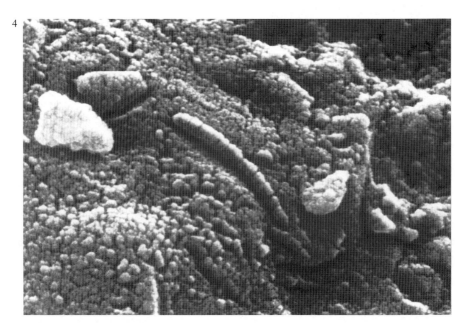

NASA scientists briefly hoped that this image captured primitive life on Mars.

5

Fig. 2. Digital printout with "Wow!" signal in channel 2.

The "Wow Signal," in 1977, was never heard again.

6

Barney and Betty Hill became the first famous "abductees."

7

Walter Haut, the military PR man from Roswell in '47, became convinced he was part of a cover-up.

8

Harvard psychiatrist John Mack upended his career to study what he called "experiencers."

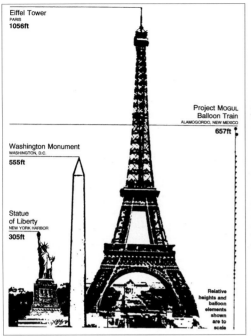

Eiffel Tower
PARIS
1056ft

Washington Monument
WASHINGTON, D.C.
555ft

Statue
of Liberty
NEW YORK HARBOR
305ft

Project MOGUL
Balloon Train
ALAMOGORDO, NEW MEXICO
657ft

Relative
heights and
balloon
elements
shown
are to
scale

9

The Roswell Report

Case Closed

Headquarters
United States Air Force

10

11

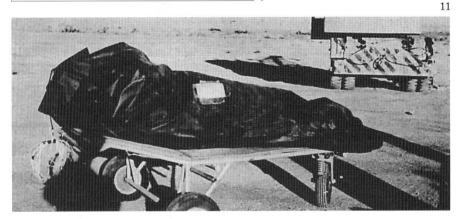

The Air Force tried in two reports
in the '90s to bury the conspiracies
around Roswell, including
explaining that the "body bags"
supposedly spotted were likely
just temperature-control bags for
transporting dummies.

SETI pioneers Jill Tarter and Frank Drake were in Arecibo in 1992 for the start of the latest listening effort.

14

13

Carl Sagan's curiosity and enthusiasm helped make him famous.

15

SETI's Allen Telescope Array.

16

Jill Tarter was the first astronomer to make SETI a full-time pursuit.

Robert Bigelow was the force behind much of the government's UFO research in the 2000s.

18

17

Blink-182 frontman Tom DeLonge helped fund UFO research.

19

Tourists now visit the Bigelow Aerospace facility outside Las Vegas to imagine its UFO secrets inside.

Yuri Milner's Breakthrough Listen
project inaugurated a new era of SETI,
with Stephen Hawking, as Sagan's
widow and producer Ann Druyan,
Freeman Dyson, and Avi Loeb look on.

THIS IS A SPACECRAFT

RADIO
GYROSCOPE
MAGNETOMETER
SOLAR CELLS
MICROCONTROLLER
ANTENNAS

Milner and Loeb hope that
the tiny "Starchips" could
help explore distant galaxies.

No one knows what
'Oumuamua actually
looks like—whether
it's shaped like a cigar,
a pancake, a rock,
iceberg, or intelligently
designed.

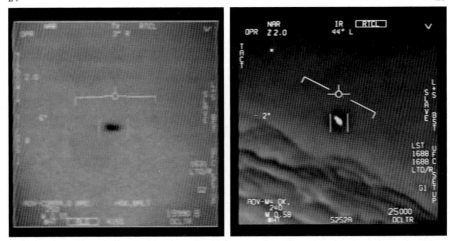

The Navy's release of new UAP images, from US aviators, including the so-called FLIR and Gimbal videos, helped touch off much more widespread interest.

The nation's fascination with UFOs is as strong as ever—as the episode with the Chinese spy balloon in 2023 showed. Here, a U-2 pilot snapped a selfie with the balloon, in some ways bringing the UFO craze full-circle, as the U-2 was responsible for many "UFO" sightings in the 1950s.

that while the vast majority of cases were explainable, about 1,600 still remained a mystery. Later that year, around the one-year anniversary of the O'Hare sighting, Kean and a documentary movie director, James Fox, assembled a symposium on sightings that would bring together credible eyewitnesses to tell their stories at the National Press Club. Amid camera flashbulbs, one speaker after another rose to give five-minute first-person testimonials about a variety of strange incidents in almost every corner of the globe; the speaker accents ranged from American to British to Belgian to Peruvian as each approached the microphone, looked up at the crowd and cameras, and noted their own sterling professional credentials.

"I believe that our government should take an active role in investigating this very real phenomenon," Fife Symington, the former Arizona governor and now-admitted Phoenix Lights witness, said as part of the event. "This panel consists of some of the most qualified people in the world with direct experience in dealing with this issue, and they will bring incredible, irrefutable evidence, some never presented before, that we simply cannot dismiss or ignore." Together, they called for the US to reopen its UFO investigation work, citing the new post-9/11 landscape as one where it was no longer acceptable to ignore or look past a possible threat to the homeland.

Later, Kean expanded those National Press Club testimonials into a book of essays—*UFOs: Generals, Pilots, and Government Officials Go on the Record*—that compiled nearly thirty years of sightings by roughly a dozen officials, mostly former military. The experiences, which ranged from the pilot of one of the F-4s in the 1976 Tehran UFO sighting to one of the security officers involved in the Rendlesham Forest incident to Symington's view of the Phoenix Lights, was, in many ways, the intellectual sequel to J. Allen Hynek's work *The UFO Experience*, effectively tracing what Kean now called the "really good cases" that had unfolded since the 1970s, and confounded even scientific investigators.[*]

---

[*] Some of Kean's arguments have not stood up to time: in a chapter focused on the Belgian wave, she spent a page extolling the blurry photograph of the triangular craft, calling it "one of the most revealing UFO images of all time," and included three separate versions of the image, only to have it exposed as a hoax in 2011 the year after her book came out.

In the main text, Kean laid out what she felt were the major premises that the collected essays proved, including the idea that "there exists in our skies, worldwide, a solid, physical phenomenon that appears to be under intelligent control and is capable of speeds, maneuverability, and luminosity beyond current known technology"; that the government's routine indifference and dismissal of sightings was "irresponsible, disrespectful to credible, often expert witnesses, and potentially dangerous"; and that "the hypothesis that UFOs are of extraterrestrial or interdimensional origin is a rational one and must be taken into account, given the data that we have." In the book's foreword, John Podesta declared, "It is definitely time for government, scientists, and aviation experts to work together in unraveling the questions about UFOs that have so far remained in the dark."*

---

* As a *New Yorker* profile of Kean summarized, "Kean is certain that U.F.O.s are real. Everything else—what they are, why they're here, why they never alight on the White House lawn—is speculation."

StarChips

In the final years of the twentieth century, SETI had mapped its future for the twenty-first. In the late 1990s, the institute had invited about fifty leading SETI thinkers and a host of Silicon Valley outsiders from places like Microsoft, Sun Microsystems, and even Walt Disney Imagineering to the luxurious Spanish mission–style Hayes Mansion in San Jose with one request: to think as big as they could. Over four three-day workshops, the group outlined "SETI 2020," a strategy for extraterrestrial science over the next two decades that was eventually published as a six-hundred-page book. The sessions, which ranged in topics from telescope design to the possibility of optical SETI—hunting for alien lasers and light signals—marked yet another unofficial handoff of the UFO question from one scientific generation to another. Philip Morrison, whose paper with Giuseppe Cocconi had helped kick off the entire field of astronomy, reminisced about how far radio had come in his lifetime—he remembered listening to the results of the 1920 election as a five-year-old, on an Aeriola Jr. radio, gifted a few days earlier from his father. Now telescopes like Arecibo listened to messages sent from the distant past.

Jill Tarter, too, marveled at how far the SETI Institute had come. What had started with just her and Tim Pierson now helped lead thirty different peer-reviewed projects examining different aspects of the Drake equation. In 1980, it had required about a million dollars and specially built computers to divide one megahertz of radio spectrum into a million narrow channels to listen for anomalous signals; by 2000, SETI had been able to accomplish the same task with off-the-shelf computers and about $1,000.

That cost and complexity, the experts knew, would continue to drop as computers improved—their report even made repeated reference to

Moore's law, the idea that computer chips doubled in power and halved in price every eighteen months. "At the conference, the attendees' main conclusion was 'SETI needs its own telescope,' closely followed by 'and perhaps we should figure out how to build it,'" wrote Tarter's biographer, Sarah Scoles. The plans, though, weren't just for any old telescope—they called for an audacious $25 million phased-array "One Hectare Telescope," one hundred meters square, that would search the skies in the 1 to 10 GHz spectrum, with 350 fully steerable identical telescopes.

It was the first time that scientists had tried to link together a whole array like that, driven by the understanding that building a field of linked telescopes that stretched across three thousand feet was just as useful as building one three-thousand-foot dish—the difference was in the computing power and the modern chips that made such linkages possible. It was, as Tarter would say, "making silicon as important as aluminum." They proposed building a test array of ten antennas and then expanding from there as budgets and resources allowed.

Altogether, the plan would need $169 million over the next two decades, an almost unthinkably large budget for a program that had effectively existed on a shoestring, but the committee was firm in its belief it would be worth it. "A concerted attempt should be made to encourage the US Congress to support the visionary nature of the SETI endeavor, which is of such profound importance to science and indeed to people from all walks of life everywhere on Earth," the report determined. "A few million dollars a year is a small price to pay for the chance to find another civilization among the stars."

SETI also embraced the era of the personal computer and the growing excitement over the rise of the internet. In May 1999, it launched a program called SETI@home, which allowed users to download software that served as a screensaver and used the idle time of a home computer to churn through small data packets looking for odd signals, power bursts, and pulses that might signal interesting corners of the sky for follow-up. The project marked only the third time anyone had tried such a crowdsourced computer-processing project, and the idea of participating in the hunt for extraterrestrial intelligence from home fascinated people. Tens of thousands committed part of their computing power to the project. In its first two years, SETI@home resulted in one sextillion calculations—that's 10^{21}, or a thousand trillion.[*]

For its new telescope, the SETI Institute settled on an old site—UC Berkeley's Hat Creek Radio Observatory, in far northern California, on the old lava fields of Mount Lassen, where Tarter and her now-husband, Jack Welch, had started working in the 1970s. Eventually, they convinced Microsoft cofounder Paul Allen, who had helped keep SETI alive in the 1990s after the congressional appropriations cutoff, to partially fund the new project; he agreed to contribute in installments as they hit certain milestones in build-out and technology development. As a first step, SETI began test construction in a horse paddock outside Berkeley, with the control center in a nearby empty barn. (Once, when Allen visited to check on the progress, he stumbled upon a pile of horse manure in the field. "At least we're not wasting your money on infrastructure," Tarter quipped.)

Things started off well enough, but as the early 2000s dot-com bubble burst, Allen's purse strings tightened; in the face of a shifting economic situation, he committed to fund an initial thirty-two telescopes, to help demonstrate the effectiveness of the phased array. He could, too, help fund the rest of the build-out to two hundred total telescopes—but only if SETI raised $13 million of outside money. SETI agreed, but struggled to raise the rest and, according to Tarter, Allen wouldn't fund the outstanding amount. Aware of their limitations, Tarter and the SETI team proceeded just with the thirty-two telescopes, as well as an additional ten that they had convinced the US Navy to fund as part of an initiative to track orbiting satellites. Construction began in 2004, and observations began in 2007, with SETI and Berkeley splitting the observation time

---

[*] This computer program was my own introduction to SETI: When I arrived at college that fall, with my first ubiquitous internet connection, several dorm mates and I downloaded the program and I competed against them with my candy-blue iMac to see who could process the most packets. SETI@home eventually became the largest computation in history, according to the *Guinness Book of World Records*, relying on a peak of about 140,000 distributed computers, and by the time it was shut down in 2020, it logged the equivalent of 2 million years of computing time.

fifty-fifty—but amid the Great Recession, the University of California shuttered its sixty-year-old observatory, deciding the wonder of astronomy wasn't wonderful enough. The closure idled the field of telescope study; an article in *Time* magazine rehashed an old joke with the headline "ET, Call Us—Just Not Collect," and quoted Seth Shostak explaining that the funding crunch was "like sending Captain Cook to the South Pacific but not giving him any food or supplies."

Eventually, the SETI Institute managed to strike a new partnership with SRI International, a nonprofit science institute that worked at the murky intersection of the government, military, and private-sector research, and saw the telescopes' potential for "space situational awareness." SRI purchased the site from Berkeley for $1, and a crowdfunding campaign raised $250,000, enough to weed and reopen the overgrown facility.

Across the same time, Tarter nominally retired from SETI, and as she did so, her career and work—ever persistent and ever optimistic, against seemingly the longest of odds both on Earth and in space—became something of a public inspiration. As the 2000s began, the pioneering female astronomer accumulated accolades and awards that marked a scientific life well-lived, including being named one of *Time*'s one hundred most influential people in 2004, and receiving public service medals from NASA. In 2009, the four hundredth anniversary of the first time Galileo used a telescope, she won the TED Prize and delivered a speech, asking, "Are we alone?" that was viewed more than a million times online, and outlined just how much more work remained. "All of the concerted SETI efforts, over the last 40-some years, are equivalent to scooping a single glass of water from the oceans. And no one would decide that the ocean was without fish on the basis of one glass of water," she said. "We need bigger glasses and more hands in the water, and then working together, maybe we can all live to see the detection of the first extraterrestrial signal." In 2005, she received one of the field's most distinct honors when an asteroid was named after her: Asteroid 74824 Tarter.

• •

Today, the Allen Telescope Array listens for just ninety seconds as it passes targets in the sky, chugging quickly through 56 million channels. "Each of these short observations was the statistical equivalent of pulling the handle on a Las Vegas slot machine day and night for 30 years," SETI astronomer Seth Shostak has calculated. If the telescope's computer detects anything anomalous, it has five autonomous checks and double checks that it runs before alerting the SETI hierarchy. As Tarter's biographer noted in 2017, "They have gotten that text message exactly once. And the signal, as usual, turned out to be just evidence of us."

But what happens if that text message arrives—and the signal keeps passing the required checks and double checks? Then the SETI Institute scientists—or, in theory, whatever astronomy team discovers such a signal anywhere else in the world—turns to the Rio scale, which, like the Richter scale for earthquakes, numerically quantifies the seriousness of a potential extraterrestrial contact. The scale grew out of a similar astronomy effort in the late 1990s, known as the Torino scale, a numerical representation of the impact threat of objects, like asteroids and comets, passing by Earth.* The original concept was developed by Tarter and Hungarian astronomer Iván Almár in 2000 and presented at the 51st International Astronautical Congress held in Rio de Janeiro, and then refined as online media and advancing science shifted the pace and understanding of a future signal. The Rio scale runs from 0 to 10—or, as the scale says, nil, insignificant, low, minor, moderate, intermediate, noteworthy, high, far-reaching, outstanding, and, at its highest, extraordinary—and is supposed to reflect a mathematical calculation between the significance of the event's consequences and the probability the event actually occurred. Judging the significance, a factor known as Q, involves three factors: the estimated distance to the signal source, the discovery type (historical, transient, or a steady communication), and the chance that the source is aware of Earth and humanity's existence (for instance, does the signal or message appear to be targeted at Earth or is it a blast message to the universe). The likelihood of the event, meanwhile, is a bit more subjective and is meant to judge the probability the signal is real, whether it's

---

* The Torino scale runs from zero, "no hazard," up through increasing levels of certainty and danger to ten, which represents certain collision of an object large enough to cause a global climatic catastrophe and threaten the future of life and civilization.

an instrument or an actual civilization, and whether it seems likely to be either human or natural.

"In many ways, a public announcement of a discovery of extraterrestrial intelligence would have societal consequences similar to the announcement of the impending impact of a large asteroid," they explained. It was critical, therefore, to create an easily understood number for the public and government policymakers that conveyed the possible significance of hearing a signal.

"It's absolutely crucial that when we talk about something so hugely significant as the discovery of intelligent life beyond the Earth, we do it clearly and carefully," echoed Duncan Forgan, a SETI scientist at the University of St. Andrews who led the subsequent revision efforts. "Having Rio 2.0 allows us to rank a signal quickly in a way that the general public can easily understand, and helps us keep their trust in a world filled with fake news."

Unlike, say, the Richter scale, which is supposed to provide fixed strengths, a Rio scale rating is intended to evolve and change as more data becomes available—downgrading or upgrading a signal as more verification and tests are run. "Throughout the life of any unfolding SETI event, as research is conducted and verification measures pursued, new information is constantly being made available which will impact our perceptions as to the significance and credibility of the claimed detection," its methodology explains. It is also meant to work with another set of principles developed by astronomers in the 1980s that outlined how an announcement should be made and what should be announced.

Following what is known as the bureaucratic "Declaration of Principles Concerning Activities Following the Detection of Extraterrestrial Intelligence," anyone discovering a newly received signal or evidence of extraterrestrial intelligence—once verified as best as possible to be valid—should share that data with other institutions, for further verification, as well as inform the secretary general of the United Nations and a host of other international institutions. "A confirmed detection of extraterrestrial intelligence should be disseminated promptly, openly, and widely through scientific channels and public media, observing the procedures in this declaration. The discoverer should have the privilege of

making the first public announcement," the principles explain.* If necessary, the Geneva-based International Telecommunication Union should
then move to protect and isolate from interference whatever frequencies
the signals are using to reach Earth. Additionally—and notably—one
of the principles also holds that no response to a signal should be issued
until after appropriate international consultations.†

---

* For fun and science, Almár and SETI Institute astronomer Seth Shostak actually
  authored a paper applying the Rio scale to popular culture, judging where different
  alien movies and books would fall on the rating system. In *Contact*, the Rio scale
  would begin at a 4 and end at a 9, whereas *2001: A Space Odyssey* would rank a 6.

† There's a similar set of standards, also developed by Iván Almár and known as the
  San Marino scale, meant to calculate the relative danger to Earth with deliberate
  transmissions from Earth aimed at communicating with or exposing us to extraterrestrial intelligence. One Russian effort to send a targeted message into space
  was initially rejected by the Arecibo Observatory in 2000, which feared the risk
  of advertising human presence to unknown civilizations beyond, only to have the
  message—a theremin concert developed by Russian teens—eventually be sent into
  the galaxy by the Yevpatoria planetary radar in Crimea. That incident helped spark
  a much larger debate about the practice of so-called "Active SETI." As critic John
  Billingham warned, "We're talking about initiating communication with other civilizations, but we know nothing of their goals, capabilities, or intent."

49

The Tic Tac Incident

Pentagon contracting is always a Byzantine process; while the Defense Department officially openly solicits bids, many are written so obtusely or narrowly scoped that only the author even understands what the document and project is. Such was the case with the Defense Intelligence Agency's Solicitation HHM402-08-R-0211 on August 18, 2008, which invited bids for an Advanced Aerospace Weapon System Applications Program that would be overseen by the Defense Warning Office. "One aspect of the future threat environment involves advanced aerospace weapon system applications," read the objective, and "this program is to understand the physics and engineering of these applications as they apply to the foreign threat out to the far term, i.e., from now through the year 2050. Primary focus is on breakthrough technologies and applications that create discontinuities in currently evolving technology trends. The focus is not on extrapolations of current aerospace technology." To this open call, only one company applied, Bigelow Aerospace Advanced Space Studies, and by the end of September, a $10 million contract for the first year of the program had been officially awarded. The manager would be James Lacatski, the same DIA official who had first contacted Bigelow and Reid about his interest in unexplained phenomena.

"This was a UFO program[,] period. That was its perfect purpose from the start," Lacatski said later. "And furthermore, this was about how UFOs might fit into the realm of what we might consider the paranormal." As the physicist saw it, hunting for UFOs was only part of the problem—the real question was how whatever those UFOs were would fit into larger questions about interstellar or interdimensional travel, unknown horizons of science and physics, and the borderlands between this world and others. "You're going to be hunting for aliens cruising by from now until doomsday and you are never going to solve anything," he said.

In its contract, the Bigelow subsidiary outlined a nine-part approach to the project, including a global survey of existing advanced aerospace characteristics, a laboratory study component, the collecting of oral histories, the study of DIA's existing data, a survey of field experts, and the installation and monitoring of remote sensors, as well as potential applications of some of the space technologies of its parent company. To begin, though, it needed to build out a facility and a staff. In 2008, Bigelow purchased a partially completed building outside Las Vegas and outfitted it with what's known as a SCIF, a sensitive compartmented information facility, to allow for the discussion and storage of top secret information, and brought on about seventy-five contract personnel.

The government money arrived soon after, and—apparently following his original NIDS philosophy on speedy investigations—Bigelow approached MUFON and offered funding to help improve their response time to sightings.* The new Star Team Impact Project would keep paid investigators ready on a moment's notice, and the FAA's formal suggestion to aviators who saw something strange was to call them: "Persons wanting to report UFO/unexplained phenomena activity should contact a UFO/unexplained phenomena reporting data collection center, such as Bigelow Aerospace Advanced Space Studies (BAASS) (voice: 1-877-979-7444 or e-mail: Reporting@baass.org)," their manual instructed.

One of the first hires onto the project was marine lieutenant colonel Douglas "Cheeks" Kurth, a key witness to perhaps the most intriguing and best-documented UFO sighting of the twenty-first century. In 2004, he had been one of a number of F/A-18 pilots aboard the USS *Nimitz* who had encountered what came to be known as the "Tic Tac" UFO.

---

* It's long been rumored that it was government money used to fund MUFON's rapid-deployment teams via Bigelow, since the timing overlapped with the award of the AAWSAP funding, but the collaboration lasted less than a year, in part because Bigelow grew frustrated at the paucity of good cases worth investigating.

The incident had occurred while the USS *Princeton*, a guided-missile cruiser, was on a routine training mission as it and a larger aircraft carrier strike force, including the *Nimitz*, prepared for deployment to the Middle East. The *Princeton* was one of the most advanced warships in the US fleet, and that day its Aegis radar system—arguably the most advanced and complex radar system in the world—had started to detect strange contacts. Worried about a malfunction, the on-board system technician shut down the radar system and recalibrated it, and "once we finished all the recalibration and brought it back up, the tracks were actually sharper and clearer," the technician said later. "Sometimes they'd be at an altitude of 80,000 or 60,000 feet. Other times they'd be around 30,000 feet, going like 100 knots. Their radar cross sections didn't match any known aircraft; they were 100 percent red. No squawk, no IFF," he added, referring to the military's "Identification Friend or Foe" system. The new tracks were so out of the realm of known flight capabilities that the naval personnel imagined them as more of a computer gremlin than a likely threat, but in the days ahead, they continued to show up. As aerial exercises began on November 14, the *Princeton* requested that the *Nimitz*'s aviators check out the radar puzzle.

It was a bright, clear, blue-sky day, and two F/A-18 fighters were vectored toward the target, about thirty miles off the coast of Baja, Mexico. When the *Princeton* announced over the radio that they'd reached "merge point," the moment where they were close enough to the target that the far-off radar operators could no longer determine who was who, they finally spotted what appeared to be frothy waves and foams far below them—and an egg-shaped object that appeared to be hovering at ocean height. As they neared, the object quickly ascended, appearing to hit supersonic speeds, and then disappeared from view. Subsequent searches of the area came up empty. "We describe [it] as a 'tic-tac' because that's what it looks like—this white oblong-shaped object that was moving very fast," recalled Lieutenant Commander Alex "Kone" Dietrich. "It appeared to respond in a way that we didn't recognize, and it surprised us because it didn't appear to have any visible flight control surfaces or means of propulsion."

"We don't know what it was, but it could have been a natural phenomenon," she added. "The point was that it was weird, and we couldn't recognize it."

Kurth, then the commanding officer of Marine Hornet Squadron VMFA-232, had also been directed to the site. Right away, he spotted the churning water, a disturbance he later estimated at perhaps the size of a football field on an otherwise calm ocean, but never saw the object itself. (A submarine nearby, the USS *Louisville*, part of the carrier strike force, reported later that it had never noticed any underwater anomalies, apparently confirming that despite the churning water, whatever the object was never submerged.) Later in the day, after a second set of fighters was dispatched, pilot Chad Underwood spotted something on his fighter's infrared radar, something stationary, hovering again with no visible means of propulsion. A recorded video, just over a minute long, showed an apparently solid object as it appeared again to accelerate out of the frame. It was never found again.

When the first set of F/A-18 aviators returned to the ship, sailors in the carrier command post had, jokingly, donned tinfoil caps and asked them about their "UFO," but the witnesses couldn't quite find the humor. That night, one of the pilots, Commander David "Sex" Fravor, told another aviator, "I have no idea what I saw. It had no plumes, wings or rotors and outran our F-18s." Whatever it was, he said, "I want to fly one." The mood definitively changed when, aboard both the ships, crew began to whisper that two unidentified personnel had arrived on board and whisked away the video and radar evidence of the encounter on hard drives. "These two guys show up on a helicopter, which wasn't uncommon, but shortly after they arrived, maybe 20 minutes, I was told by my chain of command to turn over all the data recordings for the AEGIS system," the Princeton radar tech recalled years later.*

In the moment, the encounter provoked surprisingly little attention or concern; the carrier force moved on with its training and senior officials appeared uninterested in any further investigation, and none of the

---

* The USS *Nimitz* incident would remain fully under wraps until 2015, when a lengthy account was published in *Fighter Sweep* magazine by one of Fravor's former squadron mates.

aviators were asked to sign nondisclosure agreements. "It was completely ignored," Bigelow recalled. But now, years later, with Kurth's hiring and the start of the Bigelow team's research, the *Nimitz* incident was a focus. One of its investigators interviewed the pilots, the radar operators, and other personnel, and, in the end, it would remain one of the most important—and puzzling—encounters in US history. As the Bigelow team's final report would read, "The Anomalous Aerial Vehicle (AAV) was no known aircraft or air vehicle currently in the inventory of the United States or any foreign nation."

• •

In 2009, Bigelow's DIA study was renewed for a second year, fulfilling its $22 million in funding. In response, Harry Reid wrote to the Pentagon to ask it to upgrade Bigelow's work to a so-called Special Access Program, allowing it to engage in even more classified research and development, effectively turning it into a black project. This was necessary, the majority leader explained in his letter, because of a concern that Russia and China might be advancing faster than the US on research into UAPs. "In order to support this national effort, a small but highly specialized cadre of Department of Defense (DoD) and private sector personnel are necessary," he wrote. "The technological insight and capability gained will provide the US with a distinct advantage over any foreign threats and will allow the US to maintain its preeminence as a world leader."

It was a valiant effort, but unfortunately it backfired. Rather than allowing Bigelow's purview to expand into classified areas, Reid's missive put high-level attention inside the Pentagon on Lacatski and Bigelow's project for the first time, and in the face of greater attention and resistance, he found himself unable to work his appropriations magic. While a contract offered options for annual renewals, funding was revoked. Lacatski tried unsuccessfully at one point to shift the program to DHS, thinking it might find more secure funding and support there, but soon it was clear the project was done for. Final reports trickled in through 2011, and although the AAWSAP had generated more than one hundred reports and eleven databases for the DIA, it found itself short of the meaty revelations that might have saved it at the eleventh hour. "After a while the consensus was we really couldn't find anything of substance," a Reid staffer recalled later. "There was really nothing there that we could justify using taxpayer money."

As a final goodbye and act of service to the cause, the organization wrote and compiled dozens of research papers focused on the most advanced known aerospace capabilities—what they hoped would help inform the baseline knowledge of future UFO performance. In an effort known as Project Physics, analysts and investigators poured over sighting files, creating databases of tens of thousands of cases pulled from Blue Book, Canada, the UK, and elsewhere, carefully evaluated by the standards and protocols invented by Jacques Vallée, and crisscrossed the nation as field investigators, responding to odd encounters in places like California, Oregon, Georgia, and Maryland. They wrote up detailed reports on a Soviet program known as Thread III, the Soviet Union's own UFO sighting project, which George Knapp had helped expose in the 1990s.* Meanwhile, a special team had been dispatched to Brazil to study UFO sightings there, and, according to the history of the program written by Lacatski, Kelleher, and Knapp, multiple teams of intelligence professionals rotated through the Skinwalker Ranch as part of the DIA project, all of them apparently experiencing paranormal encounters. By the time the initiative was fully shuttered, all that could be done had been done to ensure that future ufologists would have the resources they needed to continue the quest.

In May 2016, his career complete, Lacatski retired from the DIA.

• •

In the fall of 2017, mere months after the fall of AAWSAP, journalist Leslie Kean got a strange invitation: Christopher Mellon, a former deputy assistant secretary of defense for intelligence, wanted to meet at a

---

* Knapp's Soviet-era exposé stems from two research trips there in the 1990s, where he conducted interviews and said he gained access to hundreds of pages of once-secret UFO-related files. There have been doubts raised about the authenticity of some of those Soviet-era documents by Knapp, who has refused to release the archive to other researchers.

hotel bar near the Pentagon. There, on October 4, she was introduced to a man named Luis Elizondo, who explained that until weeks earlier he'd headed up another Pentagon effort to study UFOs. Kean was shocked: for years, the Pentagon had been doing the very work she had been lobbying policymakers to support.

Over a three-hour conversation, Elizondo outlined his work. His program, known as the Advanced Aerospace Threat Identification Program (AATIP), had been separate from Bigelow's research project, though he'd overlapped in meetings with the Bigelow team and had some contact with them.

After leaving the government sector, Elizondo explained he, along with Mellon, had joined up with To the Stars Academy of Arts & Sciences, an organization created by Tom DeLonge, frontman of the popular band Blink-182. DeLonge had long been a vocal UFO fanatic; one of Blink's best-known albums, *Enema of the State*, featured a song titled "Aliens Exist." (In a showing of just how knowledgeable he was about ufology, one of DeLonge's song lyrics referenced "twelve majestic lies," a reference to the MJ-12 documents of 1980s infamy.) Over the years, he'd taken his Airstream trailer to places like Area 51, using night vision goggles in an attempt to spot recovered flying saucers, and had bragged about high-level access he had to the nation's UFO secrets. After the band fell apart in 2015, he'd turned almost full-time to his UFO obsession, an eccentric mix of commercial novels and films and secret ops. "I have 10 people that I'm working with that are at the highest levels of the Department of Defense and NASA and the military," he told *Rolling Stone* in 2016. "Big shit, and no one knows this. I'm doing all this stuff already."

It seemed like an unlikely claim, or at least an exaggeration, but when Russian military intelligence hackers accessed the Gmail account of John Podesta, who was serving in 2016 as Democratic presidential candidate Hillary Clinton's campaign chair, and dumped thousands of his emails online via WikiLeaks, multiple emails between Podesta and DeLonge were right there, including one where DeLonge hinted, "I would like to bring two very 'important' people out to meet you in DC. I think you will find them very interesting, as they were principal leadership relating to our sensitive topic."* As it turned out, many of DeLonge's closest allies and partners were veterans of Bigelow's work in years prior, including Jacques Vallée.

To the Stars Academy had become a centralized hub for DeLonge's work, and a space for others to bring and conduct further research. "There is sufficient credible evidence of UAP [unidentified aerial phenomenon] that proves exotic technologies exist that could revolutionize the human experience," its website read—and DeLonge wanted to be the one to show the world the truth. In a splashy October 2017 launch event in Seattle, he had unveiled some of the brainpower and brass behind his group, Elizondo and Mellon, and they spoke about how that fall marked the sixtieth anniversary of Sputnik and how the nation once again was finding itself in a technological race with an adversary—although, this time, the who or the what of the adversary was unknown.

They also started to take more materials public to rally support and make their work more visible. Inside the military, Elizondo had collected three videos of UAP encounters, including one depicting the *Nimitz* Tic Tac incident, and gotten them declassified for release, and as the fall unfolded, he, DeLonge, and Mellon decided to share it, most notably at a Las Vegas press conference, but soon came to realize that they would need a bigger platform if they were really going to change the national conversation.

Now at the bar, Mellon and Elizondo told Kean they'd pass her the videos if she could get a piece published in the *New York Times*. She jumped at the opportunity, and even enlisted a friend and former *Times* staffer, Ralph Blumenthal, to help. (Blumenthal, she knew, had a deep interest in the subject—at the time, he was at work on the first-ever biography of John Mack.) Right away, Blumenthal emailed the paper's top editor and explained they had "a sensational and highly confidential time-sensitive story," one that would expose "a deeply secret program,

---

* Podesta, for his part, had always stayed interested in UFOs. After working in the Obama White House, he tweeted on his last day in February 2015, "Finally, my biggest failure of 2014: Once again not securing the #disclosure of the UFO files. #thetruthisstilloutthere."

long mythologized but now confirmed." On November 7, Kean and her partner met with the *Times*'s investigative editor in Washington, DC, who was impressed that they had all on-the-record sources, and teamed them up with one of the paper's own Pentagon correspondents, Helene Cooper. The story now assigned and underway, the reporters met with Elizondo again at a local hotel for a longer conversation; as they talked, the reporters noticed that the burly, tattooed former Pentagon employee kept his back to the wall, watching the hotel door intently.

On December 16, 2017, the *New York Times* ran a story on the lower front page titled "Glowing Auras and 'Black Money': The Pentagon's Mysterious U.F.O. Program." It was a blockbuster report and together with a similar in-depth story by *Politico*'s Bryan Bender, who had also been meeting with Mellon, which published the same day, the headlines seemed, in a single day, to change the national conversation and remove the decades-long national stigma around what was now generally referred to as UAPs. "Internationally, we are the most backward country in the world on this issue," Bigelow told the *Times*. "Our scientists are scared of being ostracized, and our media is scared of the stigma. China and Russia are much more open and work on this with huge organizations within their countries. Smaller countries like Belgium, France, England and South American countries like Chile are more open, too. They are proactive and willing to discuss this topic, rather than being held back by a juvenile taboo."

Midway through the article, which broke the news that the Pentagon had secretly been studying UFOs for years, was a quote from a recently retired US senator from Nevada that hinted at a much more interesting backstory than anyone had ever imagined: "I'm not embarrassed or ashamed or sorry I got this going," Harry Reid told the paper.

The *Times* article also contained, in particular, a line that left many scratching their heads: "Under Mr. Bigelow's direction, the company modified buildings in Las Vegas for the storage of metal alloys and other materials that Mr. Elizondo and program contractors said had been recovered from unidentified aerial phenomena." Had the US really retrieved out-of-this-world metals, perhaps from a real crashed saucer?

Almost just as intriguing was the video the *Times* published online of the USS *Nimitz*'s Tic Tac encounter, as well as another never-before-seen clip known as the "Gimbal" video that depicted a similarly puzzling 2015 encounter between an F/A-18 fighter off the East Coast from the USS *Theodore Roosevelt* and a fast-moving UAP. Mellon himself later also published in a *Washington Post* op-ed a third fighter-camera video, titled "GOFAST," that also appeared to show an object moving rapidly by the waves.* On the video, the flight crews can be heard talking to one another, asking: "What . . . is that thing?"

Before another exclaimed, "Oh my gosh, dude! Look at that flying!"

In the text of the piece, Mellon pushed hard for a new level of engagement, mixing history and the distant future. "As with Sputnik, the national security implications of these incidents are concerning—but the scientific opportunities are thrilling," he wrote. "The future belongs to not only the physically brave but also the intellectually agile."

---

* Years of follow-up investigation have left investigators wondering whether the infrared fighter videos are actually much more mundane—strange artifacts of camera lens distortions and misperceived distances. Mick West, a UFO skeptic, has argued that the strange radar sightings appearing both for the USS *Princeton* and the USS *Theodore Roosevelt*, of all the ships in the US Navy, is hardly a coincidence: both ships had recently undergone tech and radar upgrades prior to their supposed sightings and he suspects miscalibrated machines as part of the reason behind the radar contacts.

Life Science

Just how rare life—let alone intelligent life—is across the universe remains a mystery, but as the 2000s unfolded, science came closer to understanding at least how life began here on Earth—questions that offered tantalizing clues about how and where and why it might arise elsewhere.

In 2010, MIT geologist Linda Elkins-Tanton offered a possible solution to a long-standing debate about the most basic building blocks of life as we know it: water. Water, it turns out, is quite rare, and the type of water on Earth is even more rare. Over time, scientists had generally settled on a theory about how water came to dominate Earth known as Late Heavy Bombardment, which holds that icy comets and asteroids impacting Earth about 3.9 billion years ago, over eons, deposited millions, billions, and ultimately trillions of gallons of water. But as science writer Daniel Stone explains, "There are big holes in this theory, namely that, contrary to everything taught in high school chemistry, not all H_2O is the same. Some water contains hydrogen atoms with one proton, and hydrogen in other water molecules contains one proton and one neutron, a minuscule discrepancy that adds up to what scientists called a different 'isotopic signature.'" And, as it turns out, the "isotopic signature" of Earth's water is different from the icy water found on comets—which means that at least some of our water came from elsewhere. Plus, there's evidence that water was present on Earth much earlier than scientists originally thought; new research hinted that water's presence on Earth began as long as 4.4 billion years ago, just 164 million years after the first solid matter emerged on our early bubbling stew of planetary goo.

Elkins-Tanton, who now helps lead the interplanetary initiative at Arizona State University, had spent her career studying how planets formed in the first 100 million years of the solar system, and in 2010 she came up with an answer to where our life-giving water could have come from if not from comets: rocks. She proposed that the tiny amount of water that resided within rocks could, together, ooze off enough water to deliver us the oceans, lakes, rivers, and rain of modern Earth. Even the most solid-looking rock actually contains a fair bit of moisture and, as Elkins-Tanton calculated, planets up to five times the size of Earth could accumulate oceans as they cooled, if even just 1 to 3 percent of the rock that makes up the planetary mantle is water. That turns out to actually be a pretty low threshold: granite is 2 percent water; clay can be closer to 20 or even 30 percent water. Common minerals like chlorite, a key building block of all kinds of rocks, is between 10 and 13 percent water, Elkins-Tanton noted, and less common minerals like borax can be as much as 50 percent water. Over time, those rocks and minerals cooled and the water seeped out, rose to the surface, turned into steam, rained back to Earth from clouds, and filled in our planet's low-lying valleys.

It wouldn't even take all that much secretion to fill the Earth's oceans. Even as abundant as water may seem on Earth—70 percent of the planet, after all, is covered by water—there's still not all that much of it. The planet's oceans are geologically quite shallow, mostly just about two miles deep. "All of our planetary water is not as much water as you'd think," Daniel Stone writes. "If you picture the earth as the size of a basketball, all of the water on earth—in oceans, rivers, lakes, and ice carts—would barely fill up a marble. Freshwater alone would be even smaller, not much more than a grain of rice." According to Stone, if Earth is shrunk to the size of a basketball, its two-mile-deep oceans end up roughly the depth of a layer of dust.

The idea that water, rain, and oceans began to accumulate a half-billion years earlier than previously thought makes sense in the context of life's arrival on Earth, too. "If water oceans were present shortly after the impact that formed the moon [some 4.45 billion years ago] much more time would be available for the evolution of life, and it would explain why life was already relatively complex when we find the first traces of it in the rock record," says Washington State University astrobiologist Dirk Schulze-Makuch.

The new (and now widely accepted theory) from Elkins-Tanton transformed what scientists thought about the possibility of water elsewhere in the universe. "It is very possible that many planets are born with liquid water oceans," Elkins-Tanton says. "The evidence that we have from our solar system indicates that the chances that planets everywhere in the universe are habitable through liquid water obtained by natural accretion . . . are very high." Water may not even be as rare as we thought. Recent experiments conducted on rocks collected by the Apollo mission demonstrated that moon rocks have "as much as several thousand parts per million of water," a hundred times more than previously imagined and, as scientific methods advanced, the isotopic signature of that moon water shows it to be likely both indigenous and delivered from icy comets. Elkins-Tanton called the revelations "revolutionary," saying, "They are finding a lot more water in these minerals than would have been predicted. This now shows that primordial water was present when the moon itself formed."

The revelation that many planets may have accumulated water in their formation actually helps explain one of the other extraordinary mysteries that contributed to the development of intelligent life on Earth: we don't have more water than we do. "That shallowness, though, is the final stroke of luck for life on earth," Stone writes. Earth's size and its rock means that there might be as many as ten more oceans' worth of water still locked inside our crust—and had even twice as much water accumulated out of the Earth's crust before the planet settled into its current equilibrium, there'd be almost no land left above sea level, just a few scattered islands made up of the Earth's tallest mountain ranges.* But Earth reached a hydrological balance eons ago that left us, the dinosaurs, and all other land-dwelling creatures, figuratively and literally with our heads above water.

• •

In recent years, scientists have also come to better understand the timeline of how and when life evolved on Earth. Life got here long before

---

* This appears to be, for instance, what happened to Europa, the Jupiter moon that contains the only other known frozen sea in our solar system, where the ocean stretches perhaps a hundred miles deep and there's no land of any sort.

intelligent life—and it's not clear that life evolving into intelligent life is preordained. Life emerged here in the most primitive form, as microbes, somewhere around 4 billion and 3.7 billion years ago—an astoundingly short, only half-billion, years after the Earth formed. That timing alone makes it seem likely that life, at least at basic levels, exists elsewhere—and perhaps at least has existed elsewhere in many places. "If life arose so shortly after our world was born, a period of time that's no more than a sigh in a planet's history, then it could scarcely be a wildly improbable event," Seth Shostak observed.

It took roughly 2 billion more years before those microbes evolved into multicelled organisms. Along the way, cyanobacteria began to transform the planet, creating oxygen and collectively transforming the planet's atmosphere into the breathable, livable territory it now is. This transformation was not without its own cost—it decimated the population of anaerobic species—but worked out well for the first things we would recognize as "animals," which emerged only about 600 million years ago.

Mega volcanoes and meteors came close to extinguishing life altogether multiple times—around 250 million years ago, during the transition from the Permian to the Triassic period, something like 90 percent of all life went extinct. For several hundred thousand years, volcanoes of what paleontologist Steve Brusatte calls "preposterous" size and scale poisoned the planet, acidified the oceans, and cooked the forests. "This caused the entire ecosystem to fall like a house of cards," he writes.

That extinction gave space to the first Triassic mammals to thrive, giving them time to evolve and develop jaws that move in multiple directions, an advance that allowed them the breakthrough ability to chew—which Brusatte points out is incredibly rare and transformed mammals into "food-processing machines." That ability to consume food efficiently and begin digesting food before it reached the stomach gave mammals an important evolutionary advantage.

Along the way, dinosaurs thrived—but never appeared to evolve toward what we would call intelligent life, and had that asteroid missed Earth, coming just twenty minutes earlier or later, and sailing right by, the brontosauruses none the wiser, it doesn't seem likely that modern-day dinosaurs would be gazing at the stars through telescopes or riding oversized pickup trucks through the forest.* "The dinosaurs had 150 million years to get smart and didn't," paleontologist Niles Eldredge quipped. "So what would another 65 million years have done for them?"

So fast-forward instead through the entire history of dinosaurs and a few more mass extinctions—including, particularly, that six-mile-wide asteroid that hit near the Yucatán Peninsula with the force of a billion nuclear bombs about 66 million years ago—and mammals amazingly survived. But it was close. "Mammals almost died out," Brusatte explains in his species history, *The Rise and Reign of the Mammals.* "All they had accomplished—their entire evolutionary legacy, of hair and milk, jaw bones turned to ear bones, and all those varieties of teeth—was almost lost forever. All they would accomplish—woolly mammoths, whales the size of submarines, the Renaissance, you reading this page—was almost rendered a nonstarter. It was a close call." Just 7 percent of mammals survived.

We are all their descendants today, a class of about six thousand mammals that DNA studies show split off from reptiles about 325 million years ago, when two landmasses dominated Earth, Gondwana, by the South Pole, and Laurasia, around the equator. "All modern-day mammals belong to one of three groups: the egg-laying monotremes like the platypus, marsupials like kangaroos and koalas that raise their tiny babies in pouches, and placentals like us, which give birth to well-developed young," Brusatte writes.

For most of the history of mammals, they (and we) were hardly dominant—for almost all of mammals' history, we were more mouse-size and -scale than elephantine—and while we shape the world in profound ways, mammals remain a comparatively tiny evolutionary corner on Earth. There are twice as many bird species—themselves the descendants of dinosaurs—and nearly a million species of insects. Humans, in turn, are an even tinier corner of our own mammal class, closely related to monkeys and rabbits; nearly one in five mammal species, about 1,400 overall, are

---

* It is worth noting, though, that today's birds *are* dinosaurs and that many birds are remarkably smart: ravens can outperform chimps in many tasks and birds have large brains that feature even more neurons than mammals. That said, birds remain a long way from inventing the Cronut.

bats. And while many mammals appear to be smart—some like elephants even appearing to express feelings and complex social behaviors—and whales can communicate sophisticatedly with other whales over thousands of miles, and some, like primates, work with tools and do other humanlike things, the gulf between us and the next most-intelligent life on Earth is vast.

The split between apes and hominins happened only 5 to 7 million years ago, and we commingled genes until only about 4 million years ago. "Initially humans were an endemic group, restricted to Africa, where all our great inventions of bipedalism, braininess, and tool use took place," Brusatte writes. At first, there were *many* hominin species, only one of which evolved into us. As Brusatte says, "Our single modern human species, *Homo Sapiens*, is the lowest ebb of our diversity, and very much an exception to the historical norm."

We survived and thrived because we learned how to eat calorie-rich meat, gorging on protein that allowed our brains to grow and ensuring we had time and energy for more advanced pursuits, like socializing. Some of our close cousins—a dwarflike, vegetable-chomping *Homo luzonensis* that thrived in the Philippine islands, and *Homo floresiensis*, in Indonesia—lived until as recently as fifty thousand years ago.*

The ice ages delivered one final mass extinction of megafauna somewhere around fifty thousand years ago—which we survived, of course—and about twenty thousand years ago, we began to domesticate animals for the first time. From there, something we'd recognize as "modern life" emerged—families, settlements, agriculture. It is easy to imagine how a few incredibly minor evolutionary twists and turns would mean we never evolve at all. Life has existed on Earth for 3.7 billion years, and for only about 1/925,000th of that time have we been able to look to the stars and recognize a world beyond.

But maybe, just maybe, this is all less of a leap than we think—and that our evolution was more preordained and automatic than we currently

* Even this history is being rewritten regularly by new discoveries; about twelve years ago an entirely new branch of our family tree, the Asian-based Denisovans, who lived at the same time as the Neanderthals in Europe, about forty thousand years ago, was uncovered in a Siberian cave.

believe. To neuroscientist Lori Marino, an expert on animal intelligence, the step and fork of life we should pay attention to is as simple as the leap from single-celled organisms to multicelled. "In my view, once you have multi-cellular life, you have everything," she explained. "It may sound funny, but the difference between an annelid worm and the human brain is just variations on a theme. All multi-cellular animals have much the same brain."

The quarter century of science since ALH84001 had only underscored the prevalence of life in all of the corners of our planet, from the hottest regions to the coldest to the deepest, and as astronomy and astrobiology advanced, it seemed ever more plausible to more and more people that life might have even arrived on Earth from somewhere else. ALH84001 was hardly anomalous; scientists found that more than a hundred similar Martian fragments had made it to Earth, and as more was learned about bacteria, some species demonstrated such a high tolerance for ultraviolet light that, in the words of Harvard's astronomy chair, it seemed "likely they originated on Mars." (Calculations showed that billions of pieces of Mars had probably been broken off from the planet by cosmic collisions, perhaps carrying early bacteria and transplanting it upon extraplanetary impact.) Research showed that the reverse was true, too: meteors skimming through Earth's atmosphere even fifty kilometers above the surface could have picked up traces of floating terrestrial bacteria and carried them off into deeper space. As one astronomer would write, "Billions of such 'spoons' have stirred the Earth's atmosphere over the planet's lifetime." Scientists reported, too, that they had "defrosted" two roundworms found in the Siberian permafrost, reviving the nematodes after they had spent perhaps forty thousand years in a cryptobiotic state where all their measurable metabolic processes had stopped. In 2007, scientists even found that tardigrades, tiny half-millimeter-long creatures nicknamed "water bears" for their ursa-like appearance under a microscope, can survive the vacuum of outer space—lending possibility to the idea that life could travel planet to planet.

The deeper scientists have been able to explore it, the more amazingly resilient life turned out to be.

Breakthrough Listen

While government was becoming more amenable to the question of extraterrestrial existence, and scientists came closer to understanding life's own origins, the science around SETI became increasingly promising, too. By the 2010s, sightings and discoveries of exoplanets—a concept that had been theoretical just two decades earlier—became so commonplace that they stopped attracting headlines. In one fell swoop, the team behind the Kepler space telescope announced 306 in 2010, the first tranche of ultimately thousands discovered since, and "without a doubt, one of the most dramatic astronomical discoveries of the past two years," as Seth Shostak put it. Astronomers now were able to estimate that perhaps a third of all stars had planets similar to Earth or "super-Earths," larger versions of our planet that were not so massive, like Jupiter, that their atmosphere would be suffocating. "Today we may be on the verge of showing that our world, at least geologically, is about as prosaic as pigeons," Shostak wrote.

In 2015, a giant gift of $100 million from Russian tech billionaire Yuri Milner turbocharged SETI, funding a new project called Breakthrough Listen that would shore up the field's funding for a decade and perhaps even beyond. Milner, born in November 1961, had been named for that year's Soviet hero, cosmonaut Yuri Gagarin, and made a fortune as an early tech investor, at one point buying a 2 percent stake in Facebook for $200 million three years before it went public with a market cap of $100 billion. He'd been fascinated by extraterrestrial possibilities ever since reading Shklovsky's original *Intelligent Life in the Universe* book as a child.

Announcing the gift in London, Milner appeared with the field's pioneer, Frank Drake, as well as Sagan's widow, Ann Druyan, and Stephen Hawking. "I am fully committed to this project," he said. "If we don't find anything in 10 years, then we'll just have to extend it for another 10 years—and then for another 20, if necessary. We will just keep going until we know the answer."

"We are the beginners, the inexperienced ones," Drake added in his own statement. "We have to explore in the dark and hope there are people like Yuri Milner to keep us going for however long it takes to succeed."

Exactly how and where to look and listen, big questions about style and approach remained key puzzles for SETI. What if the aliens were trying to communicate with lasers, not radio waves?

After decades of focus on radio astronomy, the field responded to this possibility by beginning to explore what it called Optical SETI, looking for and studying lasers and bursts of concentrated light. Among these developments, an awareness that the next great discovery might take time was deeply felt. There was always the possibility that time and science and even fate had not yet aligned in a way that would allow us the capability of communicating with a potentially advanced civilization. There was always the question, Shostak explained, of "Am I too early? Is today's SETI destined to fail and be regarded—a century hence—as a quaint and novel idea that fell victim to an unknown, dead-obvious fact of the universe?" Or, as physicist Paul Davies wonders, maybe there were other less evolved civilizations out there—but they were waiting for us to con-tact *them* instead of finding ways to decode messages that had never been really sent.

Beyond simply listening, SETI started to move toward searching for what Jill Tarter first coined "techno-signatures," or hints that a gal-axy may host intelligent and ambitious civilizations. In the mid-2010s, astronomers at Penn State conducted a study they dubbed G-HAT (Glimpsing Heat from Alien Technologies), which attempted to use in-frared to search some one hundred thousand galaxies for signs of so-called Type III Kardashev civilizations—that is, civilizations so wildly advanced that they had colonized all of the galaxy's stars with enormous energy-harnessing Dyson spheres.

The researchers found precisely zero such theoretical galactic success stories—"None of them is widely populated by an alien civilization using most of the starlight in its galaxy for its own purposes. That's interesting because these galaxies are billions of years old, which should have been plenty of time for them to have been filled with alien civilizations, if they exist. Either they don't exist, or they don't yet use enough energy for us to recognize them," G-HAT founder Jason Wright explained—yet, fifty of the galaxies did show higher levels of infrared than expected. Follow-up studies, it was determined, might indicate far-off civilizations or some other much more mundane oddity. The truth, Wright pointed out, is that by searching only for the most extreme and advanced civilizations we could currently imagine, we wouldn't even have detected civilizations so vast and sophisticated that they would stagger our intelligence. There's the possibility that there are huge civilizations, larger than we can fathom, and yet still too small for us to detect.

One of the Breakthrough projects, Starshot, hoped to invent and build an interstellar craft that could travel to Alpha Centauri, reaching neighboring stars in just a generation. To lead the project, Milner recruited Avi Loeb, the chair of the Harvard astronomy department, which had once employed UFO skeptic-in-chief Donald Menzel. Loeb had been part of the growing cadre of scientists willing to question what we thought we knew about worlds beyond, namely through the push to examine techno-signatures, as a way to detect signs of far-off civilizations; the Hubble space telescope, properly focused, for example, could have detected a Tokyo-sized city on Pluto. "Looking for alien cities would be a long shot, but wouldn't require extra resources," Loeb had said in 2011, in announcing his work with Princeton's Ed Turner. "And if we succeed, it would change our perception of our place in the universe."

The Starshot Initiative's ambitious goal of reaching Alpha Centauri, the closest star, in Milner's lifetime was a fascinating and extremely challenging engineering problem; covering that distance in just a few decades required designing a craft that could travel at least a fifth the speed of light and carry no more than a few grams of a payload, yet be able to transmit photos back to Earth. (As Starshot unfolded, scientists discovered, to Loeb's extreme happiness, that Alpha Centauri featured a potentially rocky planet, eventually named Proxima Centauri, within its so-called habitable zone.)

Loeb and others came up with what would basically be an interstellar sailboat, powered not by wind but by a one-hundred-gigawatt laser that would catch a thirteen-foot-square sail on the spacecraft. Their idea was to launch about one thousand of the lightweight, relatively cheap craft, known as Starchips, toward Alpha Centauri—enough to ensure that, however many failed or were damaged by cosmic dust and collisions en route, at least some would survive to broadcast pictures back to Earth. Milner calculated it would take about $5 billion to $10 billion to launch Starshot, and that the craft could take to the heavens as early as 2036— returning photos to Earth of our closest neighbor in just about a quarter century thereafter. They'd gotten far enough along on the project by 2016 that Milner had announced it in another showy press conference atop One World Trade Center.

• •

Two years after Yuri Milner's Breakthrough Listen began, something from another galaxy came to us.

On October 19, 2017, the Pan-STARRS telescope at Hawaii's Haleakalā Observatory spotted the first-ever apparent visitor from outside our galaxy, but by the time astronomer Robert Weryk noticed, the tiny dot of light was moving too fast to be from within our solar system, it was already about 21 million miles from Earth, heading away from us and the sun. The sighting kicked off an intense eleven days as astronomers and scientists around the world raced to record and observe everything they could about the mysterious object, which was eventually named 'Oumuamua, Hawaiian for "scout."

All of the data collected about it only left the scientific community more puzzled. Telescopes got a close-up look at it, but the data showed it was either incredibly oblong—an artist's rendition of 'Oumuamua as a giant rocky cigar quickly became popular—or closer to a very thin pancake, perhaps even just a few millimeters thick. It was also highly luminous, reflecting about ten times the amount of light that a typical asteroid or comet would reflect, almost as if it were a shiny metal, and appeared to accelerate slightly, faster than what would be expected as it moved away from our sun—a common enough occurrence with icy comets that experienced so-called outgassing, as the evaporation of frozen water boosts it along, but 'Oumuamua had no apparent comet-like tail, no apparent outgassing of carbon dioxide, and scientists didn't see the expected loss of mass or slowing of its rate of spin that would be expected with a evaporating comet-like object. As Loeb wrote, "This scout was weird and mysterious and strange when compared to all other comets and asteroids previously discovered, ever. In fact, scientists could not state with certainty whether scout even was a comet or an asteroid."

At first, the International Astronomical Union officially designated the object C/2017 U1—*C* for "comet"—before amending it to A/2017 U1—*A* for "asteroid." But soon it became clear that the collected data didn't actually support either a comet or an asteroid. Finally, on November 14, the IAU designated it 1I/2017, the *I* implying it was the first observed interstellar object ever.

As Loeb kept looking at the data, he thought he recognized the object: it looked to him like precisely the type of light sail he'd been prototyping with Yuri Milner's project. Perhaps the reason that 'Oumuamua didn't match up data-wise with known natural objects was because it wasn't natural at all. Perhaps the first interstellar visitor was a piece of alien space junk. What if 'Oumuamua wasn't cigar-shaped, but a giant, superthin pancake, almost exactly like the attributes of the Starchip project? Perhaps the reason it had accelerated slightly as it moved away from the sun was because, just as a Starchip would have, it had gotten a tiny speed boost from the light of the sun.

"We determined that 'Oumuamua needed to be less than a millimeter thick for the force of the sunlight to be effective," Loeb wrote. "The implication of this was obvious: Nature had shown no ability to produce anything like the size and composition of what our assumptions suggested, so something or someone must have built such a light sail. 'Oumuamua must have been designed, built, and launched by an extraterrestrial intelligence."

In 2018, Loeb and his postdoc fellows published their findings in a paper in the *Astrophysical Journal Letters*. "Could Solar Radiation Pressure Explain 'Oumuamua's Peculiar Acceleration?" touched off a media storm not seen in the Harvard astronomy department since J. Allen Hynek's wild firetruck-laden night in Cambridge following the launch of Sputnik. "Do you believe there are alien civilizations out there?" one reporter queried Loeb.

"A quarter of all stars host a planet the size and surface temperature of the Earth," the scientist replied. "It would be arrogant to think we are alone."

In the years that followed, other incidents further complicated the 'Oumuamua narrative; a Russian astronomer spotted another interstellar object in 2019 (named 2I/Borisov, after its discoverer), a very ordinary visiting comet that behaved precisely like a comet would be expected to behave, which made 'Oumuamua stand out all the more. Without similar events, explanations couldn't quite be provided, but that didn't deter Loeb, who expanded his thesis in a bestselling book, *Extraterrestrial*, in 2021. "It's possible that the civilization is not alive anymore, but it did send out a spacecraft. We ourselves sent out Voyager I and Voyager II. There could be a lot of equipment out there," Loeb told one interviewer upon its publication. "This could be a message in a bottle, and we should be open-minded."

The object, he suspected, would look to us like a revelation, a clue from both the future and perhaps the distant past: "Humanity could build within a mere few years a spacecraft that would demonstrate every single one of 'Oumuamua's features. In other words, the simplest, more direct line from an object with all of 'Oumuamua's observed qualities to an explanation for them is that it was manufactured." Other scientists were so resistant to the hypothesis, he argued, because it was too paradigm-breaking to admit that one of the most profound discoveries in human history, one that could answer the most profound philosophical question of humanity, had literally just sailed past Earth.

That same year, two Arizona State astronomers, Alan Jackson and Steven Desch, offered a competing and far less exotic explanation: 'Oumuamua was basically an interstellar iceberg made of nitrogen, something never before seen, that was, in Desch's words, "a chunk of an 'exo-Pluto,'" a Pluto-like planet in another solar system," the *New York Times* reported. Its shininess, they argued, was consistent with Pluto and Neptune's moon Triton, both of which were covered in glaciers of nitrogen, and its acceleration might have come from the outgassing of nitrogen, which would not have been detected in the study for an ordinary comet plume of water vapor and carbon dioxide.

Yes, 'Oumuamua might have been unlike anything we'd ever seen, the scientists argued, but perhaps it was less spacecraft and more exotic iceberg.[*]

Loeb, though, has already moved on to what he hopes is his next blockbuster discovery: Working with a new effort he founded at Harvard, the Galileo Project for the Systematic Scientific Search for Evidence of Extraterrestrial Technological Artifacts, he and colleagues identified a suspicious 2014 meteor that hit off Papua New Guinea. The object, whatever it was, was moving faster than a normal meteor would—perhaps, to Loeb, an indication that it was a distant space probe. (In fact, the parameters of the 2014 meteor looked similar to how our Voyager or Mariner probes would look if they end up hitting a distant planet eons from now.) The Galileo Project combed the Pacific ocean floor for the meteor's wreckage, and in the summer of 2023, Loeb's team announced that, using a magnet, they'd retrieved dozens of spherules unlike anything they'd seen before. "It has material strength that is tougher than all space rock that were seen before, and catalogued by NASA," Loeb told the media. "The fact that it was made of materials tougher than even iron meteorites and moving faster than 95 percent of all stars in the vicinity of the sun, suggested potentially it could be a spacecraft from another civilization or some technological gadget." There was much more research to be done before Loeb's team could say whether the material was natural or artificial, but it was hard not to catch the enthusiasm of his announcement.

Perhaps, thousands or even millions of years ago, the extraterrestrial peers of Frank Drake and Carl Sagan had launched their own Golden Record off into space, only to have it find our little blue marble amid the vast blackness of the universe.

Perhaps Loeb's team had found the first piece of interstellar mail.

---

[*] Whether those two astronomers were right remains a matter of debate: other scientists, including Loeb, believe they didn't accurately account for certain variables that make the nitrogen iceberg unlikely.

The Truth Is Out There

We began in darkness and, now we are all made of stars. In the summer of 2022, new, arresting images from the James Webb Space Telescope captivated the country, as the space-based $10 billion telescope reached back through space and time to show us light and pictures of the galaxy from billions of years ago—colorful, unimaginably vast nebula, simultaneously invisible to the naked eye and yet light-years tall, unspooling through outer space and birthing stars larger than our sun. In an instant, our understanding of the worlds beyond expanded. "That was always out there," NASA astrophysicist Jane Rigby, the telescope's operations scientist, told reporters. "We just had to build a telescope to go see what was there."

It is impossible to view those images of galaxies and stars so numerous and far away that we cannot even fathom their existence without feeling incredibly small, like our tiny blue dot in the solar system, the center of so much emotion and such flurry of daily drama and activity, is an equally insignificant and unimaginable speck in the galaxy. But in fact, we are among the first generations of humans to do so.

Just five hundred years ago, most people still believed that the sun, stars, and planets revolved around the Earth. Centuries later, in the nineteenth century, another generation of astronomers began to understand that our sun was not the center of the universe—that we were but one galaxy among many, not even a galaxy that was particularly notable. And only in the last decade have we begun to peer, through technologies like the James Webb telescope, into the true depths of the universe beyond, looking backward in time across space. All of human existence, every thought, emotion, word, book, and creation of every human there ever has been is not even a microscopic dot in a microscopic blink of the eye of a universe that's 13.7 billion years old, 46 billion light-years wide, and filled with hundreds of billions of galaxies. In fact, we're coming to understand that the universe is so vast that we will never see, with the greatest of technologies, about 90 percent of the galaxy. It's too big. And we're too small.

When it comes to the likelihood of extraterrestrial life, the math certainly seems on the side of the aliens. On the clearest, darkest night, the human eye can see only somewhere around two thousand to three thousand stars, but there are actually more stars in the sky than there are all of the grains of sand on Earth. Look out at any beach in the world, visualize all the grains of sand before your eyes, and know that percentage-wise you're still seeing less of Earth's sand grains than that tiny slice of stars we see when we gaze skyward.

It's taken some 2,500 years to piece together where we stand in the universe's geography. Early astronomers have commented upon and studied the odd hazy strip of white light through the night sky ever since ancient civilizations; the Cherokee called the band "where the dog ran," imagining a dog who had stolen cornmeal, run north, and spilled it across the sky; the Chinese called it the "Silvery River" or the "River of Heaven." Egyptians, Romans, and Greeks all settled on the band's resemblance to milk and the very word "galaxy" derives from the Greek *gala*, for milk. Today, of course, astronomers understand that the Milky Way is not "the" galaxy, but in fact just one of many—many many!—galaxies. Our understanding of the universe leads to one of the oddest calculations, one argued over the years by science icons no less than Carl Sagan: It's possible, even likely, that aliens have popped by Earth—just not right now.

• •

Sagan estimated that, statistically, Earth might be visited every few hundred thousand years by passing aliens. The idea that anyone happens to be stopping by now—right now—to check on humans is all but impossible to imagine. As Seth Shostak, one of the leading scientists specializing in the Search for Extraterrestrial Intelligence (SETI), says, "If aliens have come here, it's not because they know we're here. They don't." Earth in general and humans in particular are simply too insignificant to notice. In fact, the chances that anyone has ever noticed Earth at all seem vanishingly slim. As Shostak calculated, "From Alpha Centauri, our nearest stellar neighbor, the task of spying Earth would be equivalent to noticing a mosquito circling a lightbulb 25 feet away, as seen from 10,000 miles off."

But maybe even that theory is wrong: perhaps even if there is intelligent life elsewhere, it's possible—even highly likely—that it is too far away for us to ever notice, or even exists in forms that would never think to explore beyond its own home. As biologists and astronomers frequently debate and discuss, it's hard to know what life would look like elsewhere, and our own human longing to reach for the stars may not exist elsewhere—or even occur—to other species. There could be all manner of life-supporting marine planets, filled with highly intelligent whales and dolphins, who have never glimpsed the Milky Way and wondered about journeying to the stars.

The mysteries of 'Oumuamua may well remain a permanent puzzle, but to Loeb, not treating seriously the possibility that we were visited by extraterrestrial technology is a major missed opportunity. "Humans are woefully ill prepared for an encounter with an extraterrestrial counterpart," Loeb writes. "Human science still needs to mature—in regard to SETI as well as other frontiers of our limited imagination." What, after all, is the harm in resolving at least to be better prepared for the next interstellar object? "Bet that 'Oumuamua was an exotic rock and nothing more, and on the day that more such evidence presents itself clearly, we will scramble to construct the necessary tools," he writes. "Bet that 'Oumuamua was of alien technology origin, however, and we could start tomorrow to establish such fields." Someday, Loeb posits, we may very well need academic fields like astro-linguistics, astro-politics, astro-economics, astro-sociology, astro-psychology, and more.

"Mainstream theoretical physicists now widely accept the study of extra-spatial dimensions beyond the three we are all familiar with—plainly put, height, width, and depth—and the fourth dimension, time."*

---

* It's worth noting that among the work that Bigelow's NIDS team delivered to the US government under its AAWSAP program was a thirty-four-page report titled "Warp Drive, Dark Energy, and the Manipulation of Extra Dimensions," a paper that looked at how breakthroughs in physics might one day lead to wormholes or extra-fast warp drives that could reduce travel to the Orion Nebula, some 1,600 light-years away, to just sixteen months. While theoretical physicists say such projects

Or maybe we're living in just one of many realities. "A hypothetical multiverse—an infinite number of universes all existing simultaneously in which everything that could conceivably happen is happening—occupies many of our planet's most admired minds." To Loeb, science needs to rebalance and stretch itself. The science world spent $5 billion to build the Large Hadron Collider in Switzerland, and another billion a year to operate it, a project involving ten thousand scientists in hundreds of universities and laboratories around the world that aims to study the most advanced questions of particle physics. What, Loeb wonders, would a similar investment in SETI science uncover?

"Today, a young theoretical astrophysicist is more likely to get a tenure-track job by pondering multiverses than by seeking extraterrestrial intelligence," he writes. "This is a shame, especially because budding scientists are often at their most imaginative during the early phases of their career. During this fertile period, they encounter a profession that implicitly and explicitly reins in their interests by stoking their fear of standing outside the mainstream of science." The general state of support for SETI was unfortunately encapsulated in December 2020, when, after years of budget cuts by the National Science Foundation and deepening disrepair, the once-vaunted Arecibo telescope collapsed; Arecibo was still producing groundbreaking work, just not anything the government was willing to pay for any longer.

That scientific taboo remains even as so many discoveries of science in the last two decades—everything from advancements in our understanding of physics to the confirmation of exoplanets to the passage of 'Oumuamua—seem to come together to radically reshape our place in the universe. As the *New Yorker* wrote in a 2021 article titled "How the Pentagon Started Taking U.F.O.s Seriously," "These advances—along with the further inference that ours is a mediocre or even inferior civilization, one that could well be millions or billions of years behind our distant neighbors—have lent a bare-bones plausibility to the idea that U.F.O.s have extraterrestrial origins."

---

remain distant, if ever, pipe dreams, Hynek often reflected in his speeches that there will—with some luck—someday be a "30th-century" knowledge of physics that will make our "21st-century" physics look like the Stone Age.

Even if professional science remains resistant to the serious study of extraterrestrial life, after decades of start-and-stop, often lackluster efforts, the government itself is seeming to embrace the study of UAPs here on Earth with serious resolve. In some ways, the 2017 revelations are familiar—the latest of ever-just-around-the-corner hopes of ufology that "the Disclosure" is imminent, that the government is finally about to tell all. And yet, they actually did lead to something new: a genuine—and, apparently so far, lasting—change in the public perception around UFOs. All of a sudden people stopped giggling when Kean told them at dinner parties what she did. She continued to write UFO stories and participated in suddenly high-profile prestige documentaries about them. Over the months and years that followed, Elizondo and the others involved in the program became well-known television and talk show guests and Congress began serious discussions around UAPs for the first time in a half century.

The Pentagon developed and distributed new guidelines to pilots on reporting UAPs, hoping to further break the stigma and gather better data, and announced in 2021 that it was creating a new Unidentified Aerial Phenomena Task Force, and that year's defense budget included language making the office permanent—a huge sea change in public respectability. The Senate Intelligence Committee, meanwhile, found (rare) bipartisan support for further study, as both its chair, Virginia Democrat Mark Warner, and its vice-chair, Florida Republican Marco Rubio, spoke out repeatedly on the issue. Rubio even inserted language into legislation encouraging more UAP analysis by the intelligence community, arguing that "we have things flying over our military bases and places where we are conducting military exercises, and we don't know what it is and it isn't ours, so that's a legitimate question to ask." Almost every year thereafter saw new legislative UAP provisions—including protections and encouragement for whistleblowers—and the oblique language slipped into bills sometimes created intriguing new questions. In 2022, a House Intelligence Committee authorization act included a direction that the GAO conduct a historical study of UAP activity involving US intelligence agencies, including the eye-raising clause that the study include "efforts to recover or transfer related technologies to United States–based industry or National Laboratories." Observers were left wondering: *Was this a hint the US had actually found suspicious foreign technology?*

The reporting also reshaped how senior government officials talked about UAPs, speaking openly for the first time about their professional interactions with the issue. In December 2020, US intelligence veteran John Brennan—a career CIA official who headed the agency and also served as the White House homeland security advisor under President Obama—told an interviewer, Tyler Cowen, that he was just as befuddled by the recent UFO reports as anyone. "I've seen some of those videos from Navy pilots, and I must tell you that they are quite eyebrow-raising when you look at them," he said, notably tiptoeing a step or two beyond a simple denial, saying in a roundabout way that he thought the full truth might still be elusive. "Some of the phenomena we're going to be seeing continues to be unexplained and might, in fact, be some type of phenomenon that is the result of something that we don't yet understand and that could involve some type of activity that some might say constitutes a different form of life."

The next year, former president Obama also spoke about the phenomena, telling late-night host James Corden, "When I came into office, I was like 'Alright, is there the lab somewhere where we're keeping the alien specimens and spaceship?' And you know, they did a little bit of research and the answer was no. But what is true—and I'm actually being serious here—is that there's footage and records of objects in the skies that we don't know exactly what they are. We can't explain how they moved—their trajectory. They did not have an easily explainable pattern."

Some of the *Nimitz* fighter pilots, meanwhile, appeared in a *60 Minutes* segment, talking about their encounter and bringing the story—and the permission to wonder—to millions of new viewers.

• •

The new openness to the subject has made a difference, too, creating the space for other pilots and observers who have begun to feel comfortable speaking about strange things they've seen. Many have admitted suspecting that at least some portion of UAPs have been unmanned drones built by foreign adversaries, like Russia and China, being tested near US military bases or fleets—and indeed, in one report, the intelligence community admitted that it discovered a heretofore unknown underwater Chinese drone, a so-called USO—an unidentified swimming object—as part of its newly launched UAP study, perhaps even a so-called transmedium drone that could operate in the water and air. (Indeed it's likely that a sizable percentage of modern UAPs are actually these new cutting-edge adversary technologies; as one former senior intelligence official told me, "There was always a concern out there to the extent that we were developing weird things, so were they.") Before he died in 2021, Harry Reid hinted at more and bigger secrets to come, telling the *New Yorker* that he'd heard rumors that Lockheed Martin had long studied recovered remnants of flying saucers. "I was told for decades that Lockheed had some of these retrieved materials," he said. "And I tried to get, as I recall, a classified approval by the Pentagon to have me go look at the stuff. They would not approve that."

After prodding by Congress, the US military finally released a terse nine-page report in 2021 on UAPs through the Office of the Director of National Intelligence, revealing that it had received at least 144 reports of UAPs since 2004, eighty of which had been confirmed on multiple sensors, and eighteen of which appeared to "demonstrate advanced technology." Subsequent reports now issued annually by the intelligence community have pulled back the curtain a bit more, but it still seems clear that the government is struggling to wrap its own arms around the issue*—a problem in need of a solution, since the 2022 report cited a drastically higher total of UAP reports: 510, including 247 new ones since the previous year's edition and 119 older ones that had reemerged as officials dug deeper into older time periods.

That same year, the House Intelligence Committee convened a public discussion on UFOs, the first since Gerald Ford's in the wake of the "swamp gas" controversy, followed by a closed, classified gathering to

---

* As Christopher Mellon wrote in reaction to the 2023 UAP report, "The government again demonstrated its unique and uncanny ability to transform an inherently fascinating topic into vexing bureaucratic jargon. If the intent was to make the report as anodyne, unremarkable, and boring as possible, the authors did exceptionally well."

discuss what was now euphemistically called the Pentagon's Airborne Object Identification and Management Synchronization Group. In the public hearing, two Pentagon officials tried to address one of the most notorious UFO conspiracies and testified under oath that the US had not recovered material from alien landings—nor did it have any evidence of any alien visits. "When it comes to material that we have, we have no material," one official said. "We have detected no emanations within the UAP Task Force that would suggest it is anything nonterrestrial in origin."

Beyond some broad statements, though, and some fresh and highly inconclusive videos that again appeared to show some unexplained and mysterious objects in the air, the officials stressed there was a limit to how transparent they could be—in part because it seemed likely that more of the UAPs were actually Chinese or Russian in origin, drones sent to surveil military targets and sensitive sites like nuclear bases. As it was, swarms of mysterious drones swarmed over navy destroyers over multiple nights off the California coast—unidentified flying objects that were, by all accounts, highly terrestrial and likely adversarial.

"We do not want potential adversaries to know exactly what we're able to see or understand, or how we come to the conclusion," the deputy director of naval intelligence said. "Therefore, disclosures must be carefully considered on a case-by-case basis."

In the winter of 2023, UFO fever gripped the United States yet again—showing that, as much as technology, science, aviation, and society has advanced since 1947, there's still almost nothing as collectively exciting to popular culture as a good ol' fashion UFO flap. This time, it was kicked off by an item of a known-but-still-suspicious origin: for a week, cable news channels carried live reports as a giant white bus-sized Chinese spy balloon lazily worked its way across the country. Eventually, it was shot down over South Carolina.

The balloon—an until-then-unknown adversary from that second category—made us look anew at the sky itself, discovering just how many items from the third category were floating around. The incident clearly forced the military to change its radar protocols, and in the days that followed, one UFO after another was shot down over North America. Newspapers and news shows filled with headlines about the shootdowns, with F-22 fighters and quarter-million-dollar missiles loosed on unexplained car-sized craft without visible means of propulsion, and secret military recovery missions. Days of strange official silence finally ended with a pronouncement from White House press secretary Karine Jean-Pierre: "There is no—again, no—indication of aliens or extra-terrestrial activity with these recent takedowns. Again, there is no indication of aliens or extra-terrestrial activity with these recent takedowns."

In a few days, the US military appeared to learn the lesson the hard way that Hynek, Ruppelt, and the denizens of previous UFO hunts had long known: there's a lot of weird stuff up in the sky once you start looking, most of it very terrestrial and very harmless. At least one of the US shootdowns appeared, with further research, to have been a balloon sent aloft by an Illinois hobbyist club.

The military's new engagement with UAPs encouraged NASA to launch a new project, a sixteen-person Unidentified Anomalous Phenomena Study Team, chaired by MacArthur "genius" grant recipient and astrophysicist David Spergel, along with other computer scientists, oceanographers, space experts, military and aviation experts, tech thinkers, and even former astronaut Scott Kelly. (As NASA administrator Bill Nelson said, "I've talked to those [military] pilots and they know they saw something, and their radars locked on to it. And they don't know what it is. And we don't know what it is.") In the first public hearing in May 2023, the team announced, "To date in the referred scientific literature, there is no conclusive evidence suggesting an extraterrestrial origin for UAP," and called for more, better data to be collected that could shed light on origins of UAPs and the mysteries they cloak. The push for better data and better collection seems almost certainly the key to unlocking this part of the mystery—at least, that is, short of the proverbial flying saucer landing on the White House lawn. As Kean told an interviewer from the *Guardian*, "We're [not] saying they're aliens here from other planets. But we're saying there is a phenomenon that cannot be explained. And there is plenty of data to show that. Finally, we've got our own government saying that now. So this is really an unprecedented time and there's no turning back."

• •

So, after all this, what is the truth? In 2022, Jacques Vallée—now eighty-two, the author of a dozen books on "the phenomenon," and after investigating some five hundred cases personally—told *Wired* he still wonders about the truth. He's now convinced more than ever that the prophecy he wrote in his diary as a teen will likely come true: "I will probably die without seeing any solution to this immense problem."

The truth is that there is almost certainly not one single answer to the mystery of UFOs or UAPs. The truly "unexplained" cases—that is, not counting all that are easily dismissed as mistaken planes, Venus, or the like—is almost surely a pie chart, made up of varying slices of four (or more!) answers: (1) As-yet-unknown or little-understood meteorological and atmospheric phenomena, like ball lightning or plasma*; (2) as-yet-unidentified military technologies, primarily for US purposes, and drones from adversaries like Russia and China; (3) weird terrestrial stuff floating around in the sky that we don't generally bother monitoring; and a fourth category that contains the true mystery, a secret that will only emerge as our knowledge of astronomy and physics itself evolves and lets us look anew and understand what's happening in our world that we don't understand—inter-dimensional or time-traveling visitors, extra-terrestrials, or something even weirder, what one official once called the astronomical truths that are "stranger than the strangest fiction."

We have so much left to learn, if we have the chance and can manage our way through the next fraught period of human existence. The life span of the average species on Earth is about 5 million years, meaning that if we take care of ourselves and our planet (big "ifs," to be sure), we may have not just hundreds or thousands of years of advancing knowledge ahead of us, but millions. Perhaps, somewhere along that way, there will be a fundamental principle or discovery yet to solve that will render most UAPs banal—or, conversely and perhaps even more likely, there's a fundamental principle or discovery yet to be made that will render UAPs truly extraordinary, visitors from the future, past, faraway, or even other dimensions, science that we can't even contemplate today. As British

---

* A 2019 paper in the journal *Optik* by Russian scientist Vladimir Torchigin theorized that ball lightning, a mystery since the time of the Greeks, might be light photons trapped in spheres of air, akin to a very weird soap bubble.

biologist J. B. S. Haldane wrote nearly a century ago, "My own suspicion is that the universe is not only queerer than we suppose, but queerer than we can suppose."

Determining the line between science fiction and science fact has always been the core of the UFO story, a key part of what's attracted generations of both amateur and serious ufologists to study the sky. Along the way, many of them have found a passion and meaning they never imagined, pondering what it meant if we were alone—or we weren't. After numerous conversations with Pentagon officials, Washington policymakers, journalists, and after seeing their stories told and retold by countless ufologists, former lieutenant commander Alex Dietrich—one of the *Nimitz* fighter pilots from that 2004 incident—felt she'd learned something important and fundamental about those who hunt for UFOs, summing up, perhaps, the whole journey in only a few words:

"I think they enjoy the anticipation more than actually finding answers."

Acknowledgments

I dedicated this book to my son, who I hope grows up to be as fascinated and interested in the world as the main figures of this book, but it's worth starting my acknowledgements noting that I never could have written this book except for the time *apart* from my children. The theme of acknowledgements sections is usually about how writing books is far from a solitary endeavor—and it does take a village!—but the reality is that the core craft of writing is all about solitude. Writing this book about space, time, and the mind-bending realities of space-time would have been impossible without both space *and* time.

This is the third book I've written since having kids and in each of them, I've thanked our family's nanny. During this project, Renèe Hallowell continued her exceptionally caring work doting on our kids, and we received extra help from Katey McMaster and Lexie George, but it doesn't feel enough to simply say thanks, because without the three of them—and a lot of understanding help from my in-laws, my parents, and my wife—not a single word of this would exist. Writing is an incredibly strange life, and it's one that requires a certain amount of mental clarity and space to research, read, and turn ideas into words on the page. Parenting makes those moments of clarity and acuity seemingly ever harder to fit into the week; one of the most surprising and shocking aspects of becoming a parent has been realizing how many days just never get started at all. I'm amazed as a parent how many days just end up being too narrow to squeeze into, between the mind fog of sleepless nights, the interruptions of preschool pickups, doctor appointments, unexpected colds and sniffles, snow delays, or—on the positive side—the simple joy on a nice day of saying, "Let's skip this afternoon and go do something fun." Without the peace and security that comes from having stable child care—from the actual, hard, real, caring work of Renèe, Katey, and Lexie—I know there would have been even *fewer* such days, and I'm very beyond grateful.

Many parents—too many parents—are not as lucky as I am; stable childcare is an incredible and rare gift. I wrote much of this book while my home state of Vermont debated a massive overhaul to childcare in the state and while my wife stepped in, unexpectedly, to help run our daughter's preschool—giving us an even more personal look at the broken system America relies upon to help working families raise kids in an economy and culture that doesn't make it as straightforward, easy, or affordable as it was a generation or two ago. We should do more as a country and society to support working parents and take better care of our next generation.

* * *

This book began, although I didn't know it at the time, when John Brennan spoke to Tyler Cowen in 2020. That December, in a video interview with the economist Tyler Cowen, the former C.I.A. director John Brennan admitted, somewhat tortuously, that he didn't quite know what to think: "Some of the phenomena we're going to be seeing continues to be unexplained and might, in fact, be some type of phenomenon that is the result of something that we don't yet understand and that could involve some type of activity that some might say constitutes a different form of life."

That comment, by someone I'd covered and respected, someone I knew to be a sober and thoughtful person and who had presumably been cleared into some of the deepest secrets of the US governments over a lifetime career in intelligence, made me pay more attention to the rising tide of UFO and UAP fascination in recent years—a tide that has continued right through me finishing this project in the summer of 2023, as the media heralds the arrival of new UFO "whistleblowers" and debates whether the US government actually has possession of a crashed craft. As I finished the copyedits of this book, Congress held its second hearing on the UAP mystery.

Every book I've written has been harder than I thought it would be—usually in confoundingly obvious-in-retrospect ways, and this one's surprise was just obvious, in retrospect: It's very hard to write about a subject when you don't know whether at the core of the topic is something, or nothing. Plus, it's incredibly hard to judge the veracity of many of the witnesses here. The human memory is incredibly faulty, a topic I've wrestled with in previous books facing the trauma surrounding 9/11 and the self-serving-ness of Watergate. UFOs, it turns out, mix elements of both—trauma and ego. Much of the UFO story is about the military, investigators, and scientists trying to make sense of (or debunk) witness statements that are hardly as detailed as we'd want them to be, and then journalists and historians trying to parse those scientists second- or third-hand. It's hardly the rigor one would want diving into a question as profound and important as this one is. I've tried my best to parse those parsing those witnesses, understanding that most of these sightings today will never be solved. There's just not enough evidence left to sift through.

This subject, for all these obvious reasons, is one where it's uniquely challenging to find trustworthy narrators, and so I'm incredibly grateful to the handful of respected and thoughtful historians who have tackled this subject.

The value of "real" serious study of ufology history can be found in the work of science historians like Dr. Kate Dorsch, now at the University of Pennsylvania whose dissertation "Reliable Witnesses, Crackpot Science: The UFO and American Cold War Science" was tremendously helpful in mentally organizing the early years of this story and an invaluable guide to pushing deeper into some of the serious groundbreaking work that astronomers and meteorologists were doing in the years after World War II that transformed UFO research. Similarly, Dr. Rebecca Charbonneau, currently a Jansky Fellow at the National Radio Astronomy Observatory, authored a dissertation, "Mixed Signals: Communication with the Alien in Cold War Radio Astronomy," that was so well-written I sent her a random out-of-the-blue email saying what a joy it was to read. As someone who often relies on dissertations in research, I can say that their writing rarely sparks joy.

A handful of other books and work in this space were also influential above and beyond the technical source notes and quotations throughout in the book: David Mark O'Connell's biography of J. Allen Hynek, *The Close Encounters Man*, Ralph Blumenthal's biography of John Mack, *The Believer*, Sarah Scoles's biography of Jill Tarter, *Making Contact*, and then a trio of key books about ufology—Joel Achenbach's *Captured by Aliens*, Curtis Peebles's *Watch the Skies!*, and David Michael Jacobs's *The UFO Controversy in America*, which remains the gold standard on ufology's first quarter-century. Beyond their works, I relied on Jerome Clark's exhaustive two-volume *The UFO Encyclopedia* almost every day of this project, as well as the incredible trove of documents collected over the years at the Black Vault by John Greenewald, Jr., who remains a thoughtful commentator on all the latest ufology revelations and has done so much to drive transparency and light into the most confounding of all topics. All of these works and writers helped me understand the subject and structure my own book more than the formal source notes make clear. And I'd remiss not to mention that this conversation would have never bubbled up to the point where I got interested had Leslie Kean not been pushing on it for nearly a quarter-century.

Researching this book, I found myself wowed by the everlasting hope and optimism at the core of the great books and memoirs on astronomy, from Frank Drake's *Is Anyone Out There?* to Sarah Stewart Johnson's *The Sirens of Mars.* They too deserve extra thanks for both their first-hand work in the field and then for writing memoirs that will inspire others to follow.

Tyler Rogoway's longtime leadership and writing at the website *The Drive* has provided invaluable coverage of these subjects—and so much about military minutiae and aviation over the years—that I found myself regularly ending up with his work to understand this, that, or the other strange thing.

I relied on a number of great archives across this project, from the always-incredible National Archives and multiple presidential libraries to J. Allen Hynek's still-operating Center for UFO Studies, and a lot in between, and I'm grateful to all those archivists for the hard, time-consuming work of preserving history. I'm particularly grateful to Stacy Davis and Joel Westphal at the Gerald R. Ford Presidential Library for their help digging up records on Ford's role in the "swamp gas" sightings of the 1960s. (I'm even grateful to the archivist who shall remain nameless and accidentally cc'ed me on his response to his boss about my records request on one of the early engineers studying UFOs, in which he wrote, "Did you want me to do any more work on this one? I'm thinking not because he seems pretty weird?") Yes, it's a weird subject, to be sure.

As part of my research, I spoke with a variety of senior and not so-senior government officials who provided invaluable directional help, most of whom go unmentioned in the book itself, and I'm particularly grateful to Herb Lin, who studied with Philip Morrison himself, and the other participants in a summer 2022 dinner at the annual summer meeting of the Aspen Cyber Group for helping develop some of the core themes of this book with me.

Paleontologist Stephen Brusatte warmly responded to a cold email and agreed to read portions of the book and provided helpful and thoughtful comments—demonstrating that he is just as wonderful and generous a person as he comes across in his two fabulous books, *The Rise and Fall of the Dinosaurs* and *The Rise and Reign of the Mammals.* My friends and former colleagues Bryan Bender and Shane Harris, both of whom have covered some of this material themselves, also helped with reading parts of early drafts, which I'm very grateful for.

Will DiGravio served as my day-in, day-out research assistant for this book over the last two years and became a one-man ufology expert, writing extensive research memos and tracking down ever-more-obscure sources and publications in response to my "hey, can you find this?" emails. I never ceased being amazed that he virtually always *did* find whatever it was, leaving me convinced he has access to some "Super Google" that the rest of us don't know about. He read multiple manuscript drafts and fact-checked the final draft, catching a few bone-headed misspellings and embarrassing mistakes that would have resulted in my ever-lasting shame. (I'm sure some mistakes remain—and, of course, those are my responsibility alone!)

This was the second book project where I've worked with Gillian Brassil, who both helped set up some of the initial research and then painstakingly checked quotes and endnotes at the end of the process, and she is an incredibly careful and diligent eye. I'd normally say something extra glowing about her and encourage other historians to hire her, but that would make her less available to me, so please under no circumstances try to recruit Gillian to work on your own projects.

This is the fourth book I've written with the incredible duo of Jofie Ferrari-Adler and Julianna Haubner, and the third with them at Avid Reader Press. Jofie is an unsurpassed publishing mind—I've come to understand that his greatest skill as an editor is talking me *out* of writing many of the books I'm tempted to try—and Julianna, *geez.* This book brings us to nearly 700,000 published words together, and the comfort that comes from knowing that she'll touch my words before anyone ever sees them means everything to me as a writer. There is hardly a sentence in this book—or any of my books with her—that she has not shaped or crafted in some way, and I mean that literally: In a final Herculean editing sprint, on the *third* draft of the manuscript, she still made what Microsoft Office calculated was a total of 9,000 edits. But, really, what more could I expect from an editor who sends holiday cards saying, "Looking forward to more killed darlings in the new year"?

Behind and beyond Jofie and Julianna is a veritable legion of expert publishers at Avid Reader and Simon & Schuster, including Associate Director of Copyediting Jonathan Evans and copyeditor Rob Sternitzky—who amassed a twenty-page style sheet with more than 1,500 nouns and names used throughout this book—as well as publicists David Kass and Katherine Hernandez, marketing leader Meredith Vilarello, design gurus Alison Forner and Lewelin Polanco, Caroline McGregor, Carolyn Kelly, and many more. (For the full list, see the box at the back of this book, which underscores how many people touch a project like this and how many different "publishing" careers there can be!) Jon Karp remains a great champion for my work, and I'm proud to be in his S&S stable. My now long-suffering literary agent Howard Yoon, of the incomparable Ross Yoon, was responsible for plucking this book out of the ether as we all batted around possible topics, and has been a fantastic sounding board for me for nearly a decade now, backed by Gail Ross, Dara Kaye, Jennifer Manguera, and the rest of the Ross Yoon team, now all part of the WME universe.

At The Aspen Institute, I'd also like to thank Vivian Schiller, the world's greatest boss™, for giving me the freedom to tackle "hobbies" like books, and my colleagues at Aspen Digital, especially Beth Semel, Jeff Green, and Chris Krebs. I have missed our colleague Savilla Pitt every day since January 16, 2021. More broadly, I'd like to thank my friends who have feigned interest in hearing this book develop and kept me grounded amid so much life and world turmoil, including Mary Sprayregan, Dave Schilling, Katie and Rich Van Haste, Dan Reilly, Tam Veith, Jon Murad, Meg Little Reilly, Libby Franklin, and Elizabeth Ralph.

Part of the wonder of this book was realizing how much of the story I had missed over the years despite living through many of the events described here. I was deep into my research and, specifically, deep into Ralph Blumenthal's fascinating Mack biography when I got a jolt: Mack's own literary agent was my original (and now late) literary agent, Tim Seldes. A few pages later, I found that my college minister, Peter J. Gomes, had presided over Mack's funeral. Both men have always been in the list of people who have touched my life and been critical to me being who and where I am today. Among the others: Charlotte Stocek, Mary Creeden, Mike Baginski, Rome Aja, Kerrin McCadden, and Charlie Phillips; John Rosenberg, Richard Mederos, Brian Delay, Stephen Shoemaker, and Jennifer Axsom; Kit Seeyle, Pat Leahy, Rusty Greiff, Jesseca Salky, Paul Elie, Tom Friedman, Jack Limpert, Geoff Shandler, Susan Glasser, and, not least of all, Cousin Connie, to whom I owe a debt that I strive to repay each day. My parents, Chris and Nancy Price Graff, have encouraged me to write since an early age, instilling in me a love of history and research and an intellectual curiosity that benefits me daily, and my sister Lindsay has always been my biggest fan—and I hers—although she now takes her "aunt" duties most seriously of all.

I am enormously grateful to my wonderful in-laws Donna and Paul Birrow, who help keep our family moving forward on a daily basis, and my wife, Katherine, is wonderfully indulgent and supportive of my writing, never-ending research, and the unyielding stream of increasingly odd, obscure, and sketchy research books delivered by Peter and Joel, our friendly neighborhood postmen ("What do you do with all these books?" Joel asked me in wonder not long ago in passing, handing me another stack of thick padded manila envelopes.). Her patience has never been more on display than with this book, which involves the strangest research materials yet and is about her least-favorite topic in the world: Space. Thank you, KB.

Garrett M. Graff
Burlington VT
August 1, 2023

Notes

PROLOGUE: WAR OF THE WORLDS

ix   *Just after 8 p.m.*: John Dunning, *On the Air: The Encyclopedia of Old-Time Radio* (New York: Oxford University Press, 1998), 452–54; "Orson Welles—War of the Worlds—Radio Broadcast 1938 Complete Broadcast," audio, 57:02, https://www.youtube.com /watch?v=Xs0K4ApWl4g.

x   *"Good heavens, something's"*: "Orson Welles."

xii   *"On the broad wings"*: John Houseman, *Run-Through: A Memoir* (New York: Touchstone, 1972), 305.

xii   *For the week of Halloween*: A. Brad Schwartz, "The Infamous 'War of the Worlds' Radio Broadcast Was a Magnificent Fluke," *Smithsonian*, May 6, 2015, https://www .smithsonianmag.com/history/infamous-war-worlds-radio-broadcast-was-magnifi cent-fluke-180955180/.

xiii   *By 8:48 p.m.*: "Radio Listeners in Panic, Taking War Drama as Fact," *New York Times*, October 31, 1938, 1.

xiii   *"These reports were almost entirely anecdotal"*: W. Joseph Campbell, "Fright Beyond Measure?: The Myth of The War of the Worlds," in *Getting It Wrong: Debunking the Greatest Myths in American Journalism* (Berkeley: University of California Press, 2010), 26–27.

xiii   *Telephone switchboards had been overwhelmed*: Ibid.

xiv   *The team had just been working*: Ibid.

INTRODUCTION

xv   *As folklorist Thomas Bullard notes*: Thomas E. Bullard, *The Myth and Mystery of UFOs* (Lawrence: University Press of Kansas, 2010), 4.

xv   *Historian David M. Jacobs observes*: David M. Jacobs, *UFOs and Abductions: Challenging the Borders of Knowledge* (Lawrence: University Press of Kansas, 2000), 6.

xvi   *"Ufology" today*: Bullard, *The Myth and Mystery of UFOs*, 15.

xvi   *"In the beginning there was an explosion"*: Steven Weinberg, *The First Three Minutes: A Modern View of the Origin of the Universe* (New York: Bantam, 1983), 2.

xvi   *"Neither possibility"*: Ibid.

xvi   *There were no galaxies*: Ibid., 68.

xvi   *In the first three minutes*: Ibid., 5.

xvii   *It took some seven hundred thousand years*: Ibid., 48.

xvii   *What we see in our skies*: Ibid., 13.

xix   *"There's good and growing reason"*: Seth Shostak, *Confessions of an Alien Hunter* (Washington, DC: National Geographic, 2009), 4.

xx   *Giant squids*: Ibid., 11.

xx   *"There is a tendency"*: J. Allen Hynek, "UFO's Merit Scientific Study," *Science* 154, no. 3747 (October 1966): 329.

xx   *"The common thread"*: Joel Achenbach, *Captured by Aliens: The Search for Life and Truth in a Very Large Universe* (New York: Simon & Schuster, 1999), 37.

xxi *It is a story*: James W. Moseley and Karl T. Pflock, *Shockingly Close to the Truth!: Confessions of a Grave-Robbing Ufologist* (Amherst, NY: Prometheus, 2002), 42.

xxii *"Either we're alone"*: Author interview with Herb Lin.

xxii *"In a very real sense"*: Carl Sagan, ed., *Communication with Extraterrestrial Intelligence (CETI)* (Cambridge, MA: MIT Press, 1979), ix–x.

xxii *"rubber strips"*: "Report of Air Force Research Regarding the 'Roswell Incident,'" NSA, July 1994, 4, https://www.nsa.gov/portals/75/documents/news-features/de classified-documents/ufo/report_af_roswell.pdf.

CHAPTER 1: FLYING SAUCERS

3 *The sheriff, guessing*: "Leave It to a Texan—He 'Found' Flying Disk; World's End Predicted," *Statesman Journal* (Salem, OR), July 1, 1947.

4 *Kenneth Arnold had had*: Eric Lacitis, "'Flying Saucers' Became a Thing 70 Years Ago Saturday with Sighting Near Mount Rainier," *Seattle Times*, June 24, 2017, https://www.seattletimes.com/seattle-news/northwest/flying-saucers-became-a-thing-70-years-ago-saturday-with-sighting-near-mount-rainier/.

4 *"I could not find"*: Ibid.

4 *As the light continued*: Kenneth Arnold, interview by Bill Bequette, KWRC, June 25, 1947, http://www.konsulting.com/K-Arnold%20Layer-3.WAV.

5 *One of the major*: Edward J. Ruppelt, *The Report on Unidentified Flying Objects* (Garden City, NY: Doubleday, 1956), 17.

5 *The first version*: Sarah Scoles, "How UFO Sightings Became an American Obsession," *Wired*, March 3, 2020, https://www.wired.com/story/how-ufo-sightings-became-an-american-obsession/.

5 *The idea of a "flying saucer"*: Bullard, *The Myth and Mystery of UFOs*, 27.

6 *"After having checked"*: Ibid.

6 *"It is the personal opinion"*: Frank M. Brown to the Officer in Charge, July 16, 1947, Project 1947, http://www.project1947.com/fig/kabrown.htm.

6 *On June 28, an F-51 Mustang pilot*: Ruppelt, *The Report*, 19.

6 *Citizens also called in*: "The 1947 UFO Sighting Wave: A Comprehensive Chronological Summary of the Period," National Investigations Committee on Aerial Phenomena, November 12, 2018, http://www.nicap.org/chronos/1947ful lrep.htm.

7 *Under a two-level banner headline*: "RAAF Captures Flying Saucer on Ranch in Roswell Region," *Roswell* (NM) *Daily Record*, July 8, 1947, 1.

7 *"In appearance it looked oval"*: Ibid.

7 *At 5:30 p.m. New Mexico time*: "AP Wires Burn with 'Captured Disk' Story," *Daily Illini* (Champaign, IL), July 9, 1947, 5.

8 *Once again, the general explained*: "Flying Saucers Still Mystery," *Philadelphia Inquirer*, July 9, 1947, 1.

8 *One state over*: "Captured New Mexico 'Disc' Proves Dud," *Arizona Republic* (Phoenix, AZ), July 9, 1947, 1.

9 *"Someone will have to show me"*: Joseph C. McHenry to Thomas A. McMillan, affidavit, July 11, 1947, Project 1947, http://project1947.com/fig/muroc47.htm.

9 *"From my actual observance"*: Ibid.

9 *"The object was yellowish white"*: J. C. Wise to Thomas A. McMillan, affidavit, August 13, 1947, Project 1947, http://project1947.com/fig/muroc47.htm.

9 *"As this object descended"*: John Paul Stapp to Thomas A. McMillan, affidavit, August 12, 1947, Project 1947, http://project1947.com/fig/muroc47.htm.

9   *One of the observers*: Ibid.

10 *The day ended with yet another P-51 pilot*: Ruppelt, *The Report*, 22.

10 *One rumor circulated*: "U. S. Planes Hunting Discs, Russ Tells of 'Atom Saucers,'" *Milwaukee Sentinel*, July 7, 1947.

10 *In the media*: "Saucers? Maybe a Mighty Russian Throwing a Discus, Gromyko Hints," *New York Times*, July 10, 1947, 23.

10 *In 1946, diplomat George Kennan*: Harry S. Truman, "Special Message to the Congress on Greece and Turkey: The Truman Doctrine" (speech, Washington, DC, March 12, 1947), American Presidency Project, https://www.presidency.ucsb.edu/documents/special-message-the-congress-greece-and-turkey-the-truman-doctrine.

11 *In April, statesman Bernard Baruch*: Andrew Glass, "Bernard Baruch Coins the Term 'Cold War,' April 16, 1947," *Politico*, April 16, 2010, https://www.politico.com/story/2010/04/bernard-baruch-coins-term-cold-war-april-16-1947-035862.

11 *A military historian characterized*: Geoffrey Wawro, *Sons of Freedom: The Forgotten American Soldiers Who Defeated Germany in World War I* (New York: Basic Books, 2018), 55.

11 *At the start of World War II*: Herman S. Wolk, "Toward Independence: The Emergence of the U.S. Air Force, 1945–1947," Air Force History and Museums Program, 1996, https://apps.dtic.mil/sti/pdfs/ADA433273.pdf.

11 *In 1944, he had published*: Harry S. Truman, "Our Armed Forces MUST Be Unified," *Collier's Weekly*, August 26, 1944, 16, https://www.unz.com/print/Colliers-1944aug26-00016/.

12 *As president*: Ibid., 16.

12 *"The war had ushered in"*: Ibid., 13.

12 *Harry Truman signed the legislation*: *The National Security Act of 1947*, Public Law 235, *U.S. Statutes at Large* 61 (1947).

12 *At its start, the new entity was called*: "Department of Defense, 9/18/1947," National Archives Catalog, https://catalog.archives.gov/id/10455766.

13 *Major General Curtis LeMay*: "Flying Saucers Baffle Radar, but People Keep on Seeing Em," *Washington Post*, July 7, 1947.

13 *Another military spokesman*: David Michael Jacobs, *The UFO Controversy in America* (Bloomington: Indiana University Press, 1975), 42.

13 *In early July, officials at the US Naval Observatory*: " 'Bring One in, Let's See It,' Say Scientists," *Salt Lake Tribune*, July 6, 1947, 8.

13 *David Lilienthal, the head of the Atomic Energy Commission,*: Tom Rogan, "The Roswell Mystique," *Washington Examiner*, July 9, 2020, https://www.washingtonexaminer.com/opinion/the-roswell-mystique.

13 *That reassurance, though, seemed undermined*: "Mysterious 'Flying Saucers' Reported Seen Over 10 States," *Washington Post*, July 4, 1947, 1.

13 *To know one way or another*: "Planes Chasing Disks Find Only Empty Sky," *Milwaukee Journal Sentinel*, July 7, 1947, 19.

14 *Other military bases placed*: "Army Planes Comb Skies for Flying Saucers," *Portland Press Herald*, July 7, 1947.

14 *Even as the military came up*: "Planes Chasing Disks."

14 *"Flying 'Whatsits'"*: "Flying 'Whatsits' Supplant Weather as No. 1 Topic Anywhere People Meet," *Los Angeles Times*, July 7, 1947.

14 *One Oregon minister preached*: "End of World Held Near," *Lodi* (CA) *News-Sentinel*, July 1, 1947, 4.

14 *"As things stand right now"*: Ted Bloecher, *Report on the UFO Wave of 1947* (National Investigations Committee on Aerial Phenomena, 2005), http://nicap.org/waves/Wave47Rpt/ReportOnWaveOf1947.pdf.

15   *Smith describes*: "Eyewitness Account of Flying Discs," *Columbus* (NE) *Telegram*, July 5, 1947, 3.

15   *When an army counterintelligence officer*: Frank Brown to Officer in Charge, July 16, 1947, FBI, https://vault.fbi.gov/UFO/UFO%20Part%203%20of%2016.

CHAPTER 2: THE FOO FIGHTERS

16   *One Illinois report described*: David Michael Jacobs, *The UFO Controversy in America* (Bloomington: Indiana University Press, 1975), 10.

17   *"The strange aerial craft"*: "The Mysterious Airship," *Detroit Free Press*, April 10, 1897, 2.

17   *That same day the* Chicago Tribune *reported*: "See Airship or a Star," *Chicago Daily Tribune*, April 10, 1897, 1.

17   *One rumor circulated*: Jacobs, *The UFO Controversy*, 12–14.

18   *"We saw two lights"*: Jo Chamberlin, "The Foo Fighter Mystery," *American Legion Magazine*, December 1945, 44.

18   *One pilot had an encounter so unsettling*: Graeme Rendall, "The Foo Fighters: Today's Pilots Encounters with UAP Are Nothing New," Debrief, April 15, 2021, https://thedebrief.org/the-foo-fighters-todays-pilots-encounters-with-uap-are-nothing-new/.

19   *The army eventually wrote off the entire episode*: Jacobs, *The UFO Controversy*, 36.

19   *By that August, the* New York Times: "Swedes Use Radar in Fight on Missiles," *New York Times*, August 13, 1946, 4.

20   *Doolittle was touring*: "Doolittle, Sarnoff Stir Swedish Talk," *New York Times*, August 21, 1946, 3.

20   *Doolittle would decline to comment*: "Doolittle Consulted by Swedes on Bombs," *New York Times*, August 22, 1946, 2.

20   *"The weight of evidence"*: Hoyt Vandenberg to Harry S. Truman, August 22, 1946, Project 47, http://www.project1947.com/gr/gr2.gif.

20   *"Most observations are vague"*: Jerome Clark, *The UFO Book: Encyclopedia of the Extraterrestrial* (Detroit: Visible Ink, 1998), 247.

21   *"There is no actual proof"*: Ibid.

21   *By August, Gallup reported*: Jacobs, *The UFO Controversy*, 41.

22   *"Several homesick Americans"*: "Flying Discs," *Courier-Gazette* (McKinney, TX), July 9, 1947, 1.

22   *"By the end of July"*: Jacobs, *The UFO Controversy*, 38.

22   Life *magazine compared*: Ibid., 41.

22   *"It is with considerable disappointment"*: Kenneth Arnold to Commanding General, Wright Field, July 12, 1947, https://www.saturdaynightuforia.com/html/articles/articlehtml/positivelytruestoryofkennetharnold3.html.

23   *"If I saw a ten-story building"*: Kenneth Arnold to the Officer in Charge, July 16, 1947, https://www.saturdaynightuforia.com/html/articles/articlehtml/positivelytruestoryofkennetharnold3.html.

23   *"It is more propaganda"*: "Wright Raps Saucers As War Propaganda," *Cincinnati Enquirer*, July 9, 1947, 1.

23   *"The Air Corps has taken"*: C. G. Fitch to D. M. Ladd, July 10, 1947, FBI, https://vault.fbi.gov/UFO/UFO%20Part%201%20of%2016.

23   *There was also a possibility*: Ibid.

23   *The military, Schulgen had explained:* Ibid.

24   *Assistant Director Daniel Milton "D.M." Ladd recommended*: Ibid.

24   *One of the reports that landed on Ladd's desk*: Unknown author to D. M. Ladd, July 12, 1947, FBI, https://vault.fbi.gov/UFO/UFO%20Part%202%20of%2016.

24   *"I would do it"*: Fitch to Ladd, July 10, 1947.

24   *The mention of an "La. case"*: FBI New Orleans to FBI Director, July 7, 1947, FBI, https://vault.fbi.gov/UFO/UFO%20Part%202%20of%2016.

25   *In early September, the head of the FBI's San Francisco Field Office*: D. M. Ladd to J. Edgar Hoover, September 25, 1947, FBI, https://vault.fbi.gov/UFO/UFO%20Part%204%20 of%2016.

25   *The FBI was no one's junior partner*: Ibid.

25   *In late September, Hoover sent a terse letter*: J. Edgar Hoover to George C. McDonald, September 27, 1947, https://vault.fbi.gov/UFO/UFO%20Part%204%20of%2016.

25   *"Effective immediately, the Bureau has discontinued"*: "(D) Flying Discs," memorandum, October 6, 1947, FBI,https://vault.fbi.gov/UFO/UFO%20Part%204%20of%2016.

CHAPTER 3: THE ROCKET AGE

26   *"Air Force officials could not confirm"*: Kate Dorsch, "Reliable Witnesses, Crackpot Science: UFO Investigations in Cold War America, 1947–1977" (PhD diss., University of Pennsylvania, 2019), 30, https://repository.upenn.edu/cgi/viewcontent.cgi?article=5017&context=edissertations.

26   *While the air force became its own branch*: Wolk, "Toward Independence," 29.

27   *"[Hersey's story was] the first truly effective"*: Lesley M. M. Blume, *Fallout: The Hiroshima Cover-Up and the Reporter Who Revealed It to the World* (New York: Simon & Schuster, 2020), 6.

27   *One army lieutenant who had journeyed*: Ibid., 63.

28   *In World War II*: "History Milestones," US Air Force, https://web.archive.org /web/20121020162322/http://www.af.mil/information/heritage/milestones.asp?dec=1940&sd=01%2F01%2F1940&ed=12%2F31%2F1949.

28   *On September 23*: N. F. Twining to Commanding General, Army Air Forces, September 23, 1947, https://medium.com/on-the-trail-of-the-saucers/twining-memo-ufo -c719bed1d287.

29   *Within a short period*: Edward J. Ruppelt, *The Report on Unidentified Flying Objects* (Garden City, NY: Doubleday, 1956), 16.

29   *In an era before hard-shell flying helmets*: Chuck Yeager and Leo Janos, *Yeager: An Autobiography* (London: Century, 1985), 110.

29   *"Anyone with brain cells"*: Ibid., 119.

30   *"Do you want to jeopardize"*: Ibid., 122.

30   *In flight, he'd only planned*: Ibid., 129–30.

30   *"There should've been a bump"*: Ibid., 130.

30   *"Light buffet"*: Ibid., 150.

31   *"My husband is a little firm"*: Ibid., 3.

32   *"The V-2 Panel was born"*: David DeVorkin, "Organizing for Space Research: The V-2 Rocket Panel," *Historical Studies in the Physical and Biological Sciences* 18, no. 1 (1987): 2.

32   *The V-2 Panel, organized quickly*: Ibid., 3–4.

32   *Over the course of the program*: Ibid., 21.

33   *"The system, the law"*: Mark O'Connell, *The Close Encounters Man: How One Man Made the World Believe in UFOs* (New York: Dey St., 2017), 14.

33   *He pursued science*: Ibid., 17.

33   *The observatory looked far grander*: Ibid., 18.

33   *"The doctor said [Hynek]"*: Ibid.

33   *A genius born to an aristocratic family*: Kevin Krisciunas, "Otto Struve," in National

Academy of Sciences, *Biographical Memoirs* 61 (Washington, DC: National Academies Press, 1992), 351–52, https://nap.nationalacademies.org/read/2037/chapter/17.

34 *he received the Gold Medal*: Alan H. Batten, *Resolute and Undertaking Characters: The Lives of Wilhelm and Otto Struve* (Dordrecht, Holland: D. Reidel, 1988), 239.

34 *Hynek loved working alongside*: O'Connell, *The Close Encounters Man*, 19.

35 *Hynek had felt uncomfortable*: Ibid., 31.

CHAPTER 4: PROJECT SIGN

36 *The US captured*: H. M. McCoy to Commanding General, Army Air Forces, September 24, 1947, https://www.fold3.com/image/11885481/blank-blank-page-50-project-blue-book-ufo-investigations.

36 *"Are you positive"*: Edward J. Ruppelt, *The Report on Unidentified Flying Objects* (Garden City, NY: Doubleday, 1956), 22.

36 *In late December, an air force intelligence memo*: H. M. McCoy to Chief of Staff, United States Air Force, December 19, 1947, https://www.fold3.com/image/11885484/blank-blank-page-51-project-blue-book-ufo-investigations.

37 *He wrote, "It is Air Force policy"*: L. C. Craigie to Commanding General, Air Material Command, December 30, 1947, Project 47, http://project1947.com/shg/condon/appndx-s.html.

37 *He was able to spot*: "Check-List—Unidentified Flying Objects," January 7, 1948, https://documents2.theblackvault.com/documents/projectbluebook/projectbluebook-thomasmantell-allfiles.pdf.

37 *"The object observed"*: Guy F. Hix, written statement, January 9, 1948, https://documents2.theblackvault.com/documents/projectbluebook/projectbluebook-thomasmantell-allfiles.pdf.

38 *Around 2:45 p.m., the fighters headed south*: Quinton A. Blackwell, written statement, January 9, 1948, https://documents2.theblackvault.com/documents/projectbluebook/projectbluebook-thomasmantell-allfiles.pdf.

38 *A Kentucky native, Mantell was an experienced combat pilot*: Curtis Peebles, *Watch the Skies!: A Chronicle of the Flying Saucer Myth* (Washington, DC: Smithsonian Institution Press, 1994), 18.

38 *"It appears to be a metallic object"*: Ibid., 19.

38 *"It's above me"*: Ruppelt, *The Report*, 32.

38 *"I was seeing double"*: "Did Airman Hit 'Saucer,' Fall to Death?," *Tennessean* (Nashville, TN), January 9, 1948, 1.

39 *"The fact that a person had dramatically died"*: David Michael Jacobs, *The UFO Controversy in America* (Bloomington: Indiana University Press, 1975), 45.

39 *A Vanderbilt astronomer later came forward*: Peebles, *Watch the Skies!*, 20.

40 *Interestingly, though, as historian Kate Dorsch has noted*: Kate Dorsch, "Reliable Witnesses, Crackpot Science: UFO Investigations in Cold War America, 1947–1977" (PhD diss., University of Pennsylvania, 2019), 40, https://repository.upenn.edu/cgi/viewcontent.cgi?article=5017&context=edissertations.

40 *Overall, Sign's investigation procedures*: Ibid., 47.

40 *To better understand the design*: L. H. Truettner and A. B. Deyarmond, *Unidentified Aerial Objects: Project "SIGN,"* February 1949, 3, https://archive.org/details/ProjectSIGN/page/n11/mode/2up.

40 *The plans had come together so rapidly that*: Alex Abella, *Soldiers of Reason: The Rand Corporation and the Rise of the American Empire* (Boston: Mariner Books, 2009), 12.

40 *In March 1946, James E. Lipp*: Mark Wade, "Lipp, James Everett," http://www.astronautix.com/l/lipp.html.

40   *"Before long, someone will start"*: J. E. Lipp, "RAND Report RA-15032," February 1, 1947, quoted in Robert L. Perry, "Origins of the USAF Space Program, 1945–1956," History of DCAS, 1961, https://www.nro.gov/Portals/65/documents/foia/declass /WS117L_Records/288.PDF.

41   *Now, as RAND became a stand-alone nonprofit*: Peebles, *Watch the Skies!*, 33.

42   *Lipp also assumed that*: Ibid.

42   *"A trip from another star system"*: Ibid., 34.

43   *With a decade of astronomy study under his belt*: Mark O'Connell, *The Close Encounters Man: How One Man Made the World Believe in UFOs* (New York: Dey St., 2017), 35.

43   *As Hynek's biographer wrote, "Wherever there was a star"*: Ibid.

43   *"When I first heard of the UFO's"*: J. Allen Hynek, "Are Flying Saucers Real?," *Saturday Evening Post*, December 17, 1966, 18.

43   *After some consideration, he agreed*: J. Allen Hynek, *The UFO Experience: A Scientific Inquiry* (Collector's Library of the Unknown) (Alexandria, Va.: Time-Life Books, 1989), 1.

43   *"The sky and stars"*: O'Connell, *The Close Encounters Man*, 27.

44   *The realization had come in the final months*: A. C. B. Lovell, "Meteor Research in Great Britain," *Physics Today* 1, no. 8 (1948): 26.

44   *"A new daytime stream"*: Ibid., 27.

CHAPTER 5: THE CLASSICS

45   *"Look, here comes a new Army"*: Curtis Peebles, *Watch the Skies!: A Chronicle of the Flying Saucer Myth* (Washington, DC: Smithsonian Institution Press, 1994), 22.

45   *"As if the pilot"*: Ibid., 22–23.

45   *Together, the men were sure*: Edward J. Ruppelt, *The Report on Unidentified Flying Objects* (Garden City, NY: Doubleday, 1956), 40.

45   *Interestingly, "no disturbance was felt"*: Peebles, *Watch the Skies!*, 22.

45   *That same evening, another pilot flying near*: Ruppelt, *The Report*, 40.

46   *Luckily, the media had largely given up*: David Michael Jacobs, *The UFO Controversy in America* (Bloomington: Indiana University Press, 1975), 46.

46   *One afternoon in 1948*: Robert B. Landry, interview by James R. Fuchs, February 28, 1974, Harry S. Truman Library & Museum, https://www.trumanlibrary.gov/library /oral-histories/landryr.

46   *"If there was any evidence"*: Ibid.

46   *Over the rest of Truman's presidency*: Ibid.

47   *In one memo, project scientists speculated*: Ruppelt, *The Report*, 28.

47   *"The situation was the UFO's"*: Ibid., 41.

47   *"The general wouldn't buy"*: Ibid., 45.

48   *"No other corroborating evidence"*: Kate Dorsch, "Reliable Witnesses, Crackpot Science: UFO Investigations in Cold War America, 1947–1977" (PhD diss., University of Pennsylvania, 2019), 88, https://repository.upenn.edu/cgi/viewcontent.cgi?article =5017&context=edissertations; Ruppelt, *The Report*, 41; Jacobs, *The UFO Controversy*, 309n25.

48   *Gorman is usually*: Peebles, *Watch the Skies!*, 24.

48   *"Dairy Line Salesman"*: Paul J. Sherry, "Flying Saucers," agent report, December 23, 1948, http://www.nicap.org/docs/MAXW-PBB4-768-770.pdf.

49   *"I guess I got scared"*: Richard Hall, "Gorman 'Dogfight,'" in Ronald D. Story, ed., *The Encyclopedia of UFOs* (New York: Dolphin Books, 1980), 151.

49   *"It is hard to believe"*: "Those Discs Again," *National Guardsman*, 26, http://www.nicap .org/docs/MAXW-PBB4-774-777.pdf.

49   *"The object was moving very swiftly"*: Hall, "Gorman 'Dogfight,'" 152.

49   *After he was on the ground*: Ruppelt, *The Report*, 42.

49   *"I am convinced"*: Hall, "Gorman 'Dogfight,'" 152.

50   *The investigators also noted*: "Incident w172, a, b, c—Fargo, North Dakota—1 October 1948," Aerospace Studies Institute Archives, http://www.nicap.org/docs/MAXW -PBB4-685-701.pdf.

50   *"I have a normal amount"*: George F. Gorman to Kenneth Arnold, December 10, 1948, National Investigations Committee on Aerial Phenomena, http://www.nicap.org/re ports/gorman.htm.

50   *That pilot watched his radarscope*: Ruppelt, *The Report*, 46.

50   *Then a landmark report from Germany arrived*: Ibid.

51   *"1. Flying disks"*: L. H. Truettner and A. B. Deyarmond, *Unidentified Aerial Objects: Project "SIGN,"* February 1949, iv, https://archive.org/details/ProjectSIGN/page/n11 /mode/2up.

51   *All of the first three categories*: Ibid., 6.

51   *For instance, wind-tunnel tests*: Ibid., 8.

51   *As for the last, fourth, category*: Ibid., 9.

52   *"One would like to assume"*: G. E. Valley, "Some Considerations Affecting the Interpretation of Reports of Unidentified Flying Objects," in Truettner and Deyarmond, *Unidentified Aerial Objects*, 24–25.

52   *All told, about 20 percent of the sightings*: Truettner and Deyarmond, *Unidentified Aerial Objects*, iv.

52   *Some chunk of the sightings*: Ibid., 2.

52   *"The possibility that some of the incidents"*: Ibid., v.

52   *"[The air force] just couldn't"*: J. Allen Hynek, *The Hynek UFO Report* (New York: Barnes & Noble Books, 1997), 3.

52   *"Proof of non-existence"*: Ibid., vi.

53   *"It would be necessary"*: Truettner and Deyarmond, *Unidentified Aerial Objects*, 9.

53   *Future investigations, they advised*: Ibid., vii.

53   *"Such a civilization"*: Valley, "Some Considerations," 25.

54   *Based on the reports gathered*: Ibid., 35.

54   *"It is hard to believe"*: Lipp to Putt, December 13, 1948, 29.

54   *"They must have been satisfied"*: Ibid.

54   *As a final note, Lipp stated*: Ibid.

54   *The notion that the flying objects*: Truettner and Deyarmond, *Unidentified Aerial Objects*, 9–10.

CHAPTER 6: PROJECT GRUDGE

55   *"Whenever a reporter"*: Curtis Peebles, *Watch the Skies!: A Chronicle of the Flying Saucer Myth* (Washington, DC: Smithsonian Institution Press, 1994), 17.

56   *"If the American people"*: Sidney Shalett, "What You Can Believe About Flying Saucers," *Saturday Evening Post*, April 30, 1949, 36, 184, https://www.saturdayeveningpost .com/reprints/what-you-can-believe-about-flying-saucers/.

56   *"Forget it!"*: Ibid.

56   *"I have found that if there is a scrap"*: Ibid., 20.

56   *"If you've really seen"*: Ibid., 186.

56   *As the*: "Flying Saucers Hold 'No Joke' to Air Force," *New York Times*, April 27, 1949, 29.

57   *an air force*: "Air Force Disowns 'Flying Disk' Finds," *New York Times*, August 21, 1949, 39.

57   *"HAVE BEEN INVESTIGATING"*: Donald Keyhoe, *The Flying Saucers Are Real* (Greenwich, CT: Fawcett, 1950), https://www.gutenberg.org/files/5883/5883-h/5883-h.htm.

57 *He'd been injured*: Edwin N. McClellan, ed., *The Marines Corps Gazette* (Philadelphia: Marine Corps Association, March 1922), 227.

58 *"There's something damned queer"*: Keyhoe, *The Flying Saucers Are Real.*

58 *"The evidence was more impressive"*: Ibid.

58 *"We had produced the A-bomb"*: Ibid.

58 *"I've been told it's all bunk"*: Ibid.

59 *"One, the saucers don't"*: Ibid.

59 *the first red flag*: H. W. Smith and G. W. Towles, eds., *Unidentified Flying Objects: Project "GRUDGE,"* August 1949, iii, https://www.academia.edu/43389931/Project _GRUDGE_Report_1949.

59 *Hynek estimated*: Ibid., 5.

60 *"We have found nothing"*: Ibid., iv.

60 *The conclusion felt*: Kate Dorsch, "Reliable Witnesses, Crackpot Science: UFO Investigations in Cold War America, 1947–1977" (PhD diss., University of Pennsylvania, 2019), 46, https://repository.upenn.edu/cgi/viewcontent.cgi?article=5017&con text=edissertations.

60 *Again, it was concluded*: Ibid., vi.

60 *Having apparently satisfied*: Smith and Towles, *Unidentified Flying Objects*, vii.

60 *As more reports*: Edward J. Ruppelt, *The Report on Unidentified Flying Objects* (Garden City, NY: Doubleday, 1956), 63.

61 *"More and more, I became convinced"*: Keyhoe, *The Flying Saucers Are Real.*

61 *"The explorers would first"*: Ibid.

61 *In January 1950*: Donald E. Keyhoe, "The Flying Saucers Are Real," *True*, May 1949, 11–12, https://www.saturdaynightuforia.com/library/fsartm/truemagazinetheflying saucersarereal1950.html.

62 *"The sudden spurt"*: Ibid., 17.

63 *"I am convinced that it was a flying saucer"*: Robert B. McLaughlin, "How Scientists Tracked a Flying Saucer," *True*, March 1950, 96, http://www.nicap.org/articles/True Mar1950.pdf.

63 *"Where the saucers come from"*: Ibid., 99.

64 *"At first I had a queer feeling"*: Keyhoe, *The Flying Saucers Are Real.*

64 *The author of*: Frank Scully, *Behind the Flying Saucers* (New York: Henry Holt, 1950), 2.

64 *The original 1948*: Peebles, *Watch the Skies!*, 47.

64 *"Anything remotely scientific"*: Scully, *Behind the Flying Saucers*, xi.

64 *"Every citizen who thought"*: Ibid., 10.

65 *"Measured for scientific credibility"*: "Science: Saucers Flying Upward," *Time*, September 25, 1950, https://content.time.com/time/subscriber/article/0,33009,813368,00.html.

65 *In the end*: Peebles, *Watch the Skies!*, 67–71.

65 *Scully, meanwhile*: Ibid., 71.

65 *"These searchers and explorers"*: Gerald Heard, *Is Another World Watching?* (New York: Harper & Brothers, 1951), 28.

65 *"When we twice struck Japan"*: Ibid., 166.

CHAPTER 7: CAPTAIN RUPPELT ARRIVES

66 *"General annihilation"*: David McCullough, *Truman* (New York: Simon & Schuster, 1992), 915.

67 *On his second day on the job*: Edward J. Ruppelt, *The Report on Unidentified Flying Objects* (Garden City, NY: Doubleday, 1956), 84.

68 *"I'd only been at"*: Ibid., 85.

68 *"The powers-that-be"*: Ibid., 87.

68   *In May 1951, it was renamed*: *Wright-Patterson Air Force Base: The First Century*, Wright-Patterson Air Force Base History Office, 2015, 11, https://www.wpafb.af.mil /Portals/60/documents/Index/History-of-WPAFB.pdf.

68   *The airfield, named in part*: Ibid.

68   *"Besides the aviation-related advances"*: "National Air and Space Intelligence Center History," https://web.archive.org/web/20121025053015/http://www.afisr.af.mil/shar ed/media/document/AFD-120627-049.pdf.

69   *After the war, the base*: Ibid., 15.

70   *"Who in hell has been giving"*: Ruppelt, *The Report*, 93.

70   *Ruppelt says in his memoir*: Ibid.

71   *"As long as I was chief"*: Ibid., 114.

71   *"Sufficient specific information"*: *Amending the Act Relating to U.S. Participation in the Hemisfair 1968 Exposition: Hearing on H.R. 15098*, 89th Cong. 334 (1966), https:// books.google.com/books?id=grmguksdXhAC&pg=RA4-PA334.

72   *" 'These witnesses were overwhelmingly male' "*: Kate Dorsch, "Reliable Witnesses, Crackpot Science: UFO Investigations in Cold War America, 1947–1977" (PhD diss., University of Pennsylvania, 2019), 57, https://repository.upenn.edu/cgi/viewcontent .cgi?article=5017&context=edissertations.

72   *"If a spaceship flew wing-tip to wing-tip"*: Curtis Peebles, *Watch the Skies!: A Chronicle of the Flying Saucer Myth* (Washington, DC: Smithsonian Institution Press, 1994), 55.

72   *"We don't like the name"*: Brad Steiger, ed., *Project Blue Book: The Top Secret UFO Findings Revealed* (New York: Ballantine, 1976), 394.

CHAPTER 8: THE MYSTERIOUS DEATH OF CAPTAIN MANTELL

74   *"Both the tests"*: Edward J. Ruppelt, *The Report on Unidentified Flying Objects* (Garden City, NY: Doubleday, 1956), 131.

74   *His astronomy class was one of the most popular*: Mark O'Connell, *The Close Encounters Man: How One Man Made the World Believe in UFOs* (New York: Dey St., 2017), 66.

75   *Finding the air force back*: J. Allen Hynek and Jacques Vallée, *The Edge of Reality: A Progress Report on Unidentified Flying Objects* (Chicago: Henry Regnery, 1975), 74.

75   *"The first man to sight"*: Ruppelt, *The Report*, 37.

75   *The Blue Book*: Brad Steiger, ed., *Project Blue Book: The Top Secret UFO Findings Revealed* (New York: Ballantine, 1976), 51–52.

76   *Nearly 100 feet in diameter*: Earl G. Droessler, " 'Skyhook' Plastic Balloons for High-Altitude Soundings," *Bulletin of the American Meteorological Society* 31, no. 6 (June 1950): 191.

76   *A one-hundred-foot-diameter balloon*: Curtis Peebles, *Watch the Skies!: A Chronicle of the Flying Saucer Myth* (Washington, DC: Smithsonian Institution Press, 1994), 19.

77   *To address*: *How to Make FLYOBRPTS*, Air Technical Intelligence Center, Wright-Patterson Air Force Base, July 25, 1953, 2, http://www.cufon.org/cufon/FLY OBRPT.pdf.

77   *"Have we visitors"*: H. B. Darrach Jr. and Robert Ginna, "Have We Visitors from Space?," *Life*, April 7, 1952, 80.

77   *The article walked*: Ibid., 96.

77   *"The least improbable explanation"*: Ibid.

77   *"Isn't it true that if you make"*: Peebles, *Watch the Skies!*, 60.

78   *"With the present world unrest"*: David Michael Jacobs, *The UFO Controversy in America* (Bloomington: Indiana University Press, 1975), 73.

CHAPTER 9: THE WASHINGTON MERRY-GO-ROUND

79   *"Here's a fleet"*: Harry G. Barnes, "Radar Man Tells How He Tracked Flying Saucers over Washington," *Kingsport* (TN) *Times*, July 31, 1952, 18.

79   *Not long after, the pilot of Capital Airlines*: "Flying Objects Near Washington Spotted by Both Pilots and Radar," *New York Times*, July 22, 1952, 27.

80   *"A single flight of planes"*: E. B. White, *Here Is New York* (New York: Little Bookroom, 1999), 54.

80   *Truman had recently approved*: *Report to the National Security Council by the Acting Executive Secretary of the Council*, December 31, 1952, NSC files, lot 63 D 351, NSC 139, Office of the Historian, https://history.state.gov/historicaldocuments/frus1952 -54v06p2/d958.

80   *"Files filled with reports"*: Kate Dorsch, "Reliable Witnesses, Crackpot Science: UFO Investigations in Cold War America, 1947–1977" (PhD diss., University of Pennsylvania, 2019), 54, https://repository.upenn.edu/cgi/viewcontent.cgi?article=5017& context=edissertations.

80   *"It would be extremely difficult"*: Harry G. Barnes to Chief, Facility Operations, "Unidentified Targets," July 20, 1952, http://www.nicap.org/docs/1952_07_19_US_DC _Radar_968_970.pdf.; Mark O'Connell, *The Close Encounters Man: How One Man Made the World Believe in UFOs* (New York: Dey St., 2017), 73.

80   *"The only recognizable behavior"*: Barnes, "Radar Man Tells."

81   *"I tried to make contact"*: Edward J. Ruppelt, *The Report on Unidentified Flying Objects* (Garden City, NY: Doubleday, 1956), 166.

81   *"One thing I would like"*: John G. Norris, "Jets Poised for Pursuit; 'Saucer' Peril Discounted," *Washington Post*, July 29, 1952, 7.

81   *"We have no evidence"*: Paul Sampson, " 'Saucer' Outran Jet, Pilot Reveals," *Washington Post*, July 28, 1952, 1, https://archive.org/details/per_washington-post_1952-07-28 _27801/.

81   *Everyone was looking for answers*: Ruppelt, *The Report*, 168.

82   *"there has been no pattern"*: Donald Keyhoe, *Flying Saucers from Outer Space* (New York: Henry Holt, 1953), 76.

82   *"There have remained a percentage"*: Ruppelt, *The Report*, 18.

82   *"If an enemy should"*: Harry S. Truman, "Statement by the President on the Ground Observer Corps' 'Operation Skywatch,'" July 12, 1952, Harry S. Truman Library & Museum, https://www.trumanlibrary.gov/library/public-papers/202/statement-presi dent-ground-observer-corps-operation-skywatch.

82   *One volunteer in a remote mountain post*: W. Patrick McCray, *Keep Watching the Skies!: The Story of Operation Moonwatch & the Dawn of the Space Age* (Princeton, NJ: Princeton University Press, 2008), 30.

83   *Normal air force intelligence*: " 'Flying Saucer' Queries Hamper Air Force Work," *New York Times*, August 1, 1952, 19.

83   *"The almost simultaneous appearance"*: Ibid., 156.

83   *"Targets were larger"*: Ibid., 157.

83   *"A few minutes later"*: Dr. Edward U. Condon, *Scientific Study of Unidentified Flying Objects* (London: Vision Press, 1970), 155.

84   *Stork, known internally as PPS-100*: *Analysis of Reports of Unidentified Aerial Objects*, May 5, 1955, US Air Force Historical Archives, 1, https://archive.org/details/Project BlueBookSpecialReport14/page/n8/mode/1up.

84   *Ultimately, about four thousand reports were coded*: *Second Status Report on Project Stork, PPS-100*, June 6, 1952, National Archives and Records Administration, 1–15; *Analysis of Reports*, 2, 4, https://www.cufon.org/cufon/stork1-7.htm.

84   *The sightings had no apparent trends*: Ibid., viii.
85   *"Whenever possible, I brought"*: J. Allen Hynek and Jacques Vallée, *The Edge of Reality: A Progress Report on Unidentified Flying Objects* (Chicago: Henry Regnery, 1975), 190.
85   *Whenever possible*: O'Connell, *The Close Encounters Man*, 77.
85   *"Their general lethargy"*: Ibid., 78.
85   *"A scientist will confess"*: Ibid., 77.
85   *There were still steps to be taken*: Ibid., 78.

CHAPTER 10: THE ROBERTSON PANEL

86   *The day of Ruppelt's air force press conference*: Curtis Peebles, *Watch the Skies!: A Chronicle of the Flying Saucer Myth* (Washington, DC: Smithsonian Institution Press, 1994), 73.
86   *While the agency believed*: Ibid., 74.
86   *Out of the reports, CIA analysts created*: Ibid., 75.
86   *Plus, the CIA*: Ibid.
87   *"Air Force is watching this organization"*: Ibid., 77.
87   *"We will run the increasing risk"*: Ibid.
88   *"I consider this problem"*: Ibid., 80.
88   *Beloved by colleagues*: "Howard Percy Robertson—IN—2464," July 5, 1949, FBI, https://documents2.theblackvault.com/documents/fbifiles/scientists/howardrobert son-fbi1.pdf.
88   *In the middle of World War II*: Peebles, *Watch the Skies!*, 81.
88   *his work focused on*: Jesse L. Greenstein, "Howard Percy Robertson, 1903–1961," National Academy of Sciences, 1980, 358, http://www.nasonline.org/publications/bi ographical-memoirs/memoir-pdfs/robertson-howard-p.pdf.
88   *From 1950 to 1952, he had served*: Steven Aftergood, "Documenting the Weapons System Evaluation Group," Federation of American Scientists, March 8, 2018, https://fas .org/blogs/secrecy/2018/03/wseg/.
89   *Page later said he suspected*: Thornton Page to James L. Klotz, October 3, 1992, http:// www.cufon.org/cufon/tp_corres.htm.
89   *"H. P. Robertson told us"*: Ibid.
89   *Supplementing those video*: F. C. Durant, *Report of Meetings of Scientific Advisory Panel on Unidentified Flying Objects*, February 15, 1953, CIA, 3, https://documents.theblack vault.com/documents/ufos/robertsonpanelreport.pdf.
89   *"vigorous effort should"*: Durant, *Report of Meetings*, 5.
90   *"When he was at Mather"*: Jan. L. Aldrich, "Brigadier General William Madison Garland, USAF," Project 1947, http://www.project1947.com/fig/garland.htm.
90   *"In the normal intelligence"*: Dewey J. Fournet, Jr. to Robert E. Barrow, January 6, 1976, Robert Barrow Collection, https://ufothemovie.blogspot.com/2008/06/maj-dewey-j -fournet-man-who-knew-too.html.
91   *"If the whole Robertson panel"*: Robert Emenegger, *UFO's Past, Present, & Future* (New York: Ballantine, 1974), 53.
91   *"Their basic attitude"*: Ibid., 54.
91   *"The absence of any 'hardware'"*: Durant, *Report of Meetings*, 10.
91   *In the end, the Robertson Panel concluded*: Ibid., Tab A.
92   *"It was noted by Dr. Goudsmit"*: Ibid., 11.
92   *To course correct, the military*: Ibid., 9, 19.
92   *"When the CIA Scientific Panel"*: Fournet to Barrow, January 6, 1976.

93   *"They're not going to have a scientific investigation"*: Mark O'Connell, *The Close Encounters Man: How One Man Made the World Believe in UFOs* (New York: Dey St., 2017), 90.

CHAPTER 11: SAUCER-MANIA

95   *"Now I understand why I'm different"*: Michael L. Fleisher, *The Great Superman Book* (New York: Warner Books, 1978), 392.

95   *"I think that Nova Herculis"*: Laura Poppick, "Superman's Origins Possibly Born from Star Explosion," Space.com, July 12, 2013, https://www.space.com/21949-super man-origin-star-explosion.html.

95   *"The Thing was not only"*: Todd McCarthy, *Howard Hawks: The Grey Fox of Hollywood* (New York: Grove Press, 1997), 482.

96   *"Not since Dr. Frankenstein"*: Bosley Crowther, "The Screen: Two Films Have Local Premieres," *New York Times*, May 3, 1951, 34; McCarthy, *Howard Hawks*, 483.

96   *"The World's First Flying Saucer Convention"*: James W. Moseley and Karl T. Pflock, *Shockingly Close to the Truth!: Confessions of a Grave-Robbing Ufologist* (Amherst, NY: Prometheus, 2002), 72–73.

96   *"Why, then, have so many"*: Ibid., 53.

97   *"The meteorologist cannot"*: Ibid.

97   *"This game of 'cosmic hide-and-seek' "*: Ibid., 275.

97   *"We can define a flying saucer"*: J. A. Hynek, "Unusual Aerial Phenomena," *Journal of the Optical Society of America* 43, no. 4 (April 1953): 311–13.

99   *Titled only*: Donald Keyhoe, *Flying Saucers from Outer Space* (New York: Henry Holt, 1953), 8.

99   *The book kicked*: "Jet Liner Crashes in Storm in India with 40 on Board," *New York Times*, May 3, 1953, 1.

99   *"was keeping the answer secret"*: Keyhoe, *Flying Saucers from Outer Space*, 8.

99   *"Don, I swear"*: Ibid., 35–36.

99   *"fictitious characters"*: Moseley and Pflock, *Shockingly*, 45.

99   *"There's no other possible answer"*: Ibid.

100 *"[We're] aware of Major Keyhoe's conclusion"*: Keyhoe, *Flying Saucers from Outer Space*, 248.

100 *Most readers would see*: David Michael Jacobs, *The UFO Controversy in America* (Bloomington: Indiana University Press, 1975), 103.

100 *Going forward, the military would only provide*: N. F. Twining, "Unidentified Flying Objects Reporting," Air Force Regulation 200-2, August 12, 1954, https://www.cufon .org/cufon/afr200-2.htm.

100 *Known as Joint-Army-Navy-Air Force Publication (JANAP) 146*: "General Description and Purpose of Communication Instructions for Reporting Vital Intelligence Sightings," National Security Administration, 1, https://www.nsa.gov/portals/75/docu ments/news-features/declassified-documents/ufo/janap_146.pdf.

101 *In 1954, the air force began exploring options*: James C. Hagerty, statement, July 29, 1955, https://www.eisenhowerlibrary.gov/sites/default/files/research/online-documents/igy /1955-7-29-press-release.pdf.

101 *"When man talks"*: W. Patrick McCray, *Keep Watching the Skies!: The Story of Operation Moonwatch & the Dawn of the Space Age* (Princeton, NJ: Princeton University Press, 2008), 63; "A New Moon in the Sky," *New York Times*, July 30, 1955, 16.

101 *"The United States did not exploit"*: Robert L. Perry, *Origins of the USAF Space Program, 1945–1956*, History Office, Space and Missile Systems Center (1997), https://spp.fas .org/eprint/origins/part05.htm.

CHAPTER 12: FROST'S FLYING SAUCER

102 *And he believed, too*: Joe Pappalardo, "Declassified: America's Secret Flying Saucer," *Popular Mechanics*, February 11, 2013, https://www.popularmechanics.com/military /a8699/declassified-americas-secret-flying-saucer-15075926/.

103 *In March 1955, the air force revised*: 4602d Air Intelligence Service Squadron, *UFOB (Unidentified Flying Objects) Guide*, March 1955, 4, 6, https://documents.theblackvault .com/documents/ufos/4602HistoryUFOs.pdf.

104 *The air force also reorganized*: Jared V. Crabb, "General Orders Number 47," October 17, 1952, https://www.cufon.org/cufon/4602smpl1.htm.

104 *It had no other distinct peacetime mission*: Leo Orlovsky, "Historical Data for 4602d Air Intelligence Service Squadron," May 26, 1953, 2, https://www.cufon.org/cu fon/4602smpl1.htm.

104 *"The new methods of investigating"*: David Michael Jacobs, *The UFO Controversy in America* (Bloomington: Indiana University Press, 1975), 135.

104 *"Nothing has come to me"*: Dwight D. Eisenhower, "The President's News Conference" (Washington, DC, December 15, 1954), American Presidency Project, https://www .presidency.ucsb.edu/documents/the-presidents-news-conference-363.

104 *In 1955, the military also released*: *Analysis of Reports of Unidentified Aerial Objects*, May 5, 1955, US Air Force Historical Archives, 1, https://archive.org/details/Project BlueBookSpecialReport14/page/n8/mode/1up.

105 *In 1954*: "California Committee for Saucer Investigation," memorandum, February 9, 1953, http://www.project1947.com/shg/csi/csicia1.html.

106 *"APRO was shaped"*: Jerome Clark, *The UFO Encyclopedia: The Phenomenon from the Beginning*, 3rd ed. (Detroit, MI: Omnigraphics, 2018), EPUB. "Lorenzen, Coral E. Lightner (1925–1988) and Leslie James (Jim) Lorenzen (1922–1986)."

106 *"Actually the Air Force"*: Curtis Peebles, *Watch the Skies!: A Chronicle of the Flying Saucer Myth* (Washington, DC: Smithsonian Institution Press, 1994), 111.

106 *As their interest continued in parallel*: Jacobs, *The UFO Controversy*, 133.

CHAPTER 13: THE CONTACTEES

107 *In general, Blue Book*: Donald Keyhoe, *Flying Saucers from Outer Space* (New York: Henry Holt, 1953), 120.

107 *"The contactees represented"*: David Michael Jacobs, *The UFO Controversy in America* (Bloomington: Indiana University Press, 1975), 109.

107 *Thomas Bullard, one of*: Thomas E. Bullard, "Abduction Phenomenon," in Jerome Clark, *The UFO Encyclopedia: The Phenomenon from the Beginning*, 3rd ed. (Detroit, MI: Omnigraphics, 2018), EPUB.

108 *"I fully realized I was in the presence"*: Desmond Leslie and George Adamski, *Flying Saucers Have Landed* (New York: British Book Centre, 1953), 194.

108 *"I felt that part of me"*: Ibid., 210.

108 *These extraterrestrials*: George Adamski, *Inside the Space Ships* (London: Neville Spearman, 1966), 79.

108 *Jerome Clark*: Clark, *The UFO Encyclopedia*, "Adamski, George (1891–1965)."

108 *"To put it politely"*: James W. Moseley and Karl T. Pflock, *Shockingly Close to the Truth!: Confessions of a Grave-Robbing Ufologist* (Amherst, NY: Prometheus, 2002), 45.

109 *A photograph he provided*: Clark, *The UFO Encyclopedia*, "Adamski, George (1891–1965)."

109 *The FBI had met*: Ibid.

109 *Months later, Adamski*: Ibid.

109 *Truman Bethurum*: Truman Bethurum, *Aboard a Flying Saucer* (Los Angeles: DeVorss & Co., 1954).

110 *"Non-Fiction—A True Account"*: Ibid., "Bethurum Contact Claims."

111 *He followed it*: Orfeo Angelucci, *The Secret of the Saucers* (Stevens Point, WI: Worzalla, 1955), 5.

111 *When he stopped*: Ibid., 5.

111 *"Orfeo, you are looking"*: Ibid., 24–25.

112 *As the out-of-this-world*: Ibid., 34.

112 *Pulsing with energy*: Ibid., 46.

112 *"War will come again"*: Ibid., 46.

112 *New York overnight*: Long John Nebel, *The Way Out World* (Englewood Cliffs, NJ: Prentice Hall, 1961), 37.

CHAPTER 14: THE MEN IN BLACK

114 *"Everything about these books"*: Isabel L. Davis, "Meet the Extraterrestrial," *Fantastic Universe* 8, no. 5 (1957): https://archive.org/details/Fantastic_Universe_v08n05_1957 -11_Gorgon776The_Elves/page/n57/.

115 *As the air force*: Edward J. Ruppelt, *The Report on Unidentified Flying Objects* (Garden City, NY: Doubleday, 1956), 9.

115 *Moseley had gotten*: James W. Moseley and Karl T. Pflock, *Shockingly Close to the Truth!: Confessions of a Grave-Robbing Ufologist* (Amherst, NY: Prometheus, 2002), 25.

115 *Later, with his family*: Ibid., 26.

115 *"This will solve my problem"*: Ibid., 30.

115 *Through the experience*: Ibid., 54.

116 *"Nationally there was a vacuum"*: Ibid., 108.

116 *Near the site of*: Gray Barker, "The Monster and the Saucer," *Fate*, January 1953, https://www.fatemag.com/post/the-monster-and-the-saucer; Joe Nickell, "The Flatwoods UFO Monster," *Skeptical Inquirer*, November/December 2000, 15, https://cdn.center forinquiry.org/wp-content/uploads/sites/29/2000/11/22164839/p15.pdf.

117 *The work, Barker*: Gray Barker, *They Knew Too Much About Flying Saucers* (New York: University Books, 1956), 81.

117 *"The mystery of the flying saucers"*: Ibid., 138.

118 *Occult journalist*: John A. Keel, "Beyond the Known: Return of the Men in Black," *Fate*, December 1994, 24.

117 *One such note*: Curtis Collins, "George Adamski, R. E. Straith and the Seven Letters of Mischief," February 10, 2014, https://www.jimmoseley.com/2014/02/george-adamski -r-e-straith-and-the-seven-letters-of-mischief/.

119 *APRO's Carol Lorenzen*: Moseley and Pflock, *Shockingly*, 121.; Ibid., 223.

119 *"Those drawn to saucers"*: Ibid., 119.

119 *The Flying Saucer Discussion Group*: Jim G. Lucas, "Group Formed to Seek Answer on 'Saucers,'" *Albuquerque Tribune*, October 24, 1956, 34.

119 *In October 1956*: " 'Toward a Broader Understanding . . .': The Story of How NICAP Began," *UFO Investigator*, October 1971, 2, http://www.cufos.org/UFOI_and_Selected_ Documents/UFOI/067%20OCTOBER%201971.pdf/; Lucas, "Group Formed."

120 *Once at the helm*: Ibid.

120 *"There are objects coming"*: "Guided Missile Expert Says: 'Saucers' Reported Entering Our Atmosphere," *Arizona Daily Star* (Tucson, AZ), January 17, 1957, 1.

121 *"Flying Saucers Now Respectable"*: "Flying Saucers Now Respectable," *Victoria* (TX) *Advocate*, January 22, 1957, 4.

121   *An editorial in Vermont's*: "'Operation Skylight,'" *Bennington* (VT) *Banner*, January 22, 1957, 2.

121   *It's not clear when*: "Adm. Fahrney Quits Saucer Probers," *Washington Daily News*, April 10, 1957, https://web.archive.org/web/20120222013443/http://www.bluebookarchive.org/page.aspx?PageCode=NARA-PBB89-856; Vince Anselmo, "Guided Missile Expert Enjoys Farm in County," *Chester* (PA) *Times*, February 21, 1957, 6.

121   *Under his tenure, NICAP*: Delmer S. Fahrney, "Statement on Unidentified Flying Objects," FBI, https://vault.fbi.gov/National%20Investigations%20Committee%20on%20Aerial%20Phenomena%20%28NICAP%29/National%20Investigations%20Committee%20on%20Aerial%20Phenomena%20%28NICAP%29%20Part%201%20of%203/view.

122   *"Most important of all"*: Donald E. Keyhoe, letter, April 3, 1957, FBI, https://vault.fbi.gov/National%20Investigations%20Committee%20on%20Aerial%20Phenomena%20%28NICAP%29/National%20Investigations%20Committee%20on%20Aerial%20Phenomena%20%28NICAP%29%20Part%201%20of%203/view.

122   *NICAP leadership praised*: Charles A. Maney and Richard Hall, *The Challenge of Unidentified Flying Objects* (Washington, DC: National Investigations Committee on Aerial Phenomena, 1961), 84, http://www.nicap.org/books/coufo/partII/chVIII.htm.

122   *"Our UFO-reporting network"*: Donald E. Keyhoe, *Flying Saucers: Top Secret* (New York: G. P. Putnam's Sons, 1960), 48.

122   *To manage the new influx*: "Report on Unidentified Flying Object(s)," *UFO Investigator*, November 1976, https://archive.org/details/sim_u-f-o-investigator_1976-11/page/n1/.

122   *A syndicated feature*: Douglas Larsen, "Afraid the Neighbors Will Laugh? Tell It to Confidential Service for Saucer-Seers," *Sandusky* (OH) *Register*, August 26, 1957, 17.

123   *In some cases*: Ruppelt, *The Report*, 212–13.

123   *As part of its reviewing*: "8 Point Plan Offered Air Force," *UFO Investigator*, July 1957, 1, http://www.cufos.org/UFOI_and_Selected_Documents/UFOI/001%20JULY%201957.pdf.

123   *Most of the plan consisted*: Ibid., 25.

123   *To say that the air force*: Curtis Peebles, *Watch the Skies!: A Chronicle of the Flying Saucer Myth* (Washington, DC: Smithsonian Institution Press, 1994), 117.

123   *"Certainly the experience"*: Lawrence J. Tacker, *Flying Saucers and the U.S. Air Force* (Princeton, NJ: D. Van Nostrand, 1960), 29.

123   The Report on Unidentified Flying Objects: Clark, *The UFO Encyclopedia*, "Ruppelt, Edward J. (1923–1960)."

CHAPTER 15: SPUTNIK

125   *The IGY*: Mark O'Connell, *The Close Encounters Man: How One Man Made the World Believe in UFOs* (New York: Dey St., 2017), 122.

126   *"The manufacture of the camera"*: Ibid., 123.

126   *Twelve of the so-called Baker-Nunn*: W. Patrick McCray, *Keep Watching the Skies!: The Story of Operation Moonwatch & the Dawn of the Space Age* (Princeton, NJ: Princeton University Press, 2008), 79.

126   *It required large teams*: Ibid., 103.

126   *As W. Patrick McCray*: Ibid., 98.

126   *Many Moonwatch recruits*: O'Connell, *The Close Encounters Man*, 126.

126   *In May 1957*: McCray, *Keep Watching*, 136.

127   *All they could do*: O'Connell, *The Close Encounters Man*, 128.

127   *It was a shocking moment*: Ibid.

127   *In the coming weeks*: Ian Ridpath, "The Man Who Spoke Out on UFOs," *New Scientist*, May 17, 1973, 424.

127   *"We had a world-wide nerve center"*: O'Connell, *The Close Encounters Man*, 128.

128   *Two weeks after the launch*: C. C. Furnas, "Why Did U.S. Lose the Race? Critics Speak Up," *Life*, October 21, 1957, 25.

128   *The article in Life*: Ibid., 22.

128   *"This is really and truly"*: "Common Sense and Sputnik," *Life*, October 21, 1957, 35.

128   *The somewhat extreme*: Furnas, "Why Did U.S. Lose," 23.

128   *As the light approached*: " 'Great Sound, Rush of Wind'—Flaming, Flying Object Leaves Public Puzzled," *Shreveport* (LA) *Journal*, November 4, 1957, 1.

129   *A college student reported*: O'Connell, *The Close Encounters Man*, 135–36.

129   *The local sheriff*: "Texan Thinks Weird Object Came from Another Planet," *Nashville Banner*, November 4, 1957, 2.

129   *All told, more than*: George Dolan, "Whatnik Sidelines Sputnik, Woofnik," *Fort Worth Star-Telegram*, November 4, 1957, 1.

129   *Two weeks later*: Air Force Press Release No. 1108-57, November 15, 1957, quoted in "The Levelland Sightings," J. Allen Hynek Center for UFO Studies, 2, http://www.cufos.org/cases/1957_11_23_US_TX_Levelland_NICAP_MultWit_CEII_PartII.pdf.

129   *The breadth of sightings*: O'Connell, *The Close Encounters Man*, 136.

129   *In the month after*: Curtis Peebles, *Watch the Skies!: A Chronicle of the Flying Saucer Myth* (Washington, DC: Smithsonian Institution Press, 1994), 126.

130   *For a few minutes*: Ibid., 163.

131   *The apparent act*: "Author Digresses on TV, Sound Is Cut," *New York Times*, January 23, 1958, 55.

131   *"What makes me boil"*: Unknown to Donald Keyhoe, January 23, 1958, quoted in Richard H. Hall, "Air Force Censorship of TV Broadcast about UFOs Stirred Controversy in 1958," *Journal of UFO History*, January/February 2005, 4, http://www.nicap.org/jufoh/JournalUFOHistoryVol1No6.pdf.

131   *"This program had been carefully cleared"*: Herbert A. Carlborg to I. E. Epperson, January 31, 1958, http://www.nicap.org/cbs_letter.htm.

131   *Convinced anew*: Donald Keyhoe, interview by Mike Wallace, March 8, 1958, video, 29:53, Harry Ransom Center, University of Texas at Austin, https://hrc.contentdm.oclc.org/digital/collection/p15878coll90/id/51/.

132   *The press*: "Russia Just Repeats U.S. Self-Criticism on Rocket," *Dayton Daily News*, December 8, 1957, 20.

132   *As one Moonwatcher*: McCray, *Keep Watching*, 177.

132   *The cameras they used*: Ridpath, "The Man Who Spoke Out," 424.

133   *Moonwatch itself*: McCray, *Keep Watching*, 230.

133   *"I came here to work"*: O'Connell, *The Close Encounters Man*, 147.

133   *The astronomer*: Ridpath, "The Man Who Spoke Out," 422.

133   *Despite promising*: G. Jacquemin, *Stress Analysis of 1/12 Scale Hovering and Transition Model*, September 1957, Avro Aircraft Limited, https://www.secretsdeclassified.af.mil/Portals/67/documents/AFD-121113-024.pdf.

133   *"The aircraft can be satisfactorily"*: Project 1794: Final Development Summary Report, U.S. Air Force, June 1, 1956, 33, https://www.secretsdeclassified.af.mil/Portals/67/documents/AFD-121113-019.pdf.

133   *Its first tethered*: Bernard Lindenbaum and William Blake, "The VZ-9 'Avrocar,'" 5, https://www.robertcmason.com/textdocs/avro-car-VZ9.pdf.

133   *Design changes*: Ibid.

134 *"The cockpit was cramped"*: Ibid., 7.
134 *While* Popular Mechanics: Air Force Declassification Office, "Project 1794 Documents (Saucer-Type Aircraft)," November 13, 2012, https://www.secretsdeclassified.af.mil /News/Article-Display/Article/459834/project-1794-documents-saucer-type-air craft/.

CHAPTER 16: BRIEFING CAPITOL HILL

135 *The group was surviving*: Curtis Peebles, *Watch the Skies!: A Chronicle of the Flying Saucer Myth* (Washington, DC: Smithsonian Institution Press, 1994), 135.
135 *And in 1957*: *A History of the Committee on Science and Technology*, August 1, 2008, U.S. House of Representatives, https://republicans-science.house.gov/_cache/files/b/1 /b164acf0-738a-490a-8c00-c9b7d827a16d/AB2938CE6D7DBB932F6F601EBB EC10D5.committee-history-50years.pdf.
135 *Arriving by train*: Thomas S. Ryan, *Report No. IR 193-55*, October 14, 1955, 1–2, http:// www.nicap.org/reports/551004russia_report_swords38C.pdf.
136 *As Congress's own history*: Marcia S. Smith, *The UFO Enigma*, March 9, 1976, Congressional Research Service, 60, https://digital.library.unt.edu/ark:/67531/metadc993849 /m2/1/high_res_d/76-52SP_1976march9.pdf.
136 *While the FBI*: J. Edgar Hoover to SAC, New Orleans, July 17, 1961, FBI, https:// vault.fbi.gov/National%20Investigations%20Committee%20on%20Aerial%20 Phenomena%20%28NICAP%29/National%20Investigations%20Committee%20 on%20Aerial%20Phenomena%20%28NICAP%29%20Part%202%20of%203 /view.
137 *In a statement of the times*: "National Investigations Committee on Aerial Phenomena (NICAP)," FBI, https://vault.fbi.gov/National%20Investigations%20Committee%20 on%20Aerial%20Phenomena%20%28NICAP%29.
137 *In 1960*: Milton Viorst, "FBI Invokes New Law to Arrest Woman in Debt-Collection Scheme," attached in Lawrence J. Tacker to J. Edgar Hoover, August 23, 1960, FBI, https://vault.fbi.gov/National%20Investigations%20Committee%20on%20Ae rial%20Phenomena%20%28NICAP%29/National%20Investigations%20Com mittee%20on%20Aerial%20Phenomena%20%28NICAP%29%20Part%201%20 of%203/view.
137 *"As you well know"*: Tacker to Hoover, August 23, 1960.
137 *The program had sorted*: *Study by AFCIN-4E4: Unidentified Flying Objects—Project #5771*, September 28, 1959, https://www.saturdaynightuforia.com/html/articles/arti clehtml/saucsum13.html.
138 *In 1960, he tried to fund*: Peebles, *Watch the Skies!*, 135.
138 *"I feel that the [Air Force]"*: "New Capitol Hill Backing for NICAP," *UFO Investigator*, April–May 1961, 2, http://www.cufos.org/UFOI_and_Selected_Documents /UFOI/012%20APR-MAY%201961.pdf; "Congressman Confirm AF Secrecy: Pressure for Investigation Increasing," *UFO Investigator*, December–January 1960–61, 1, http://www.cufos.org/UFOI_and_Selected_Documents/UFOI/011%20DEC-JAN %201960-61.pdf.
138 *Finally, the House agreed*: "Majority Leader Support Indicates Early Congressional Action," *UFO Investigator*, October 1961, 1, http://www.cufos.org/UFOI_and_Selected _Documents/UFOI/014%20OCT%201961.pdf.
138 *Keyhoe responded*: David Michael Jacobs, *The UFO Controversy in America* (Bloomington: Indiana University Press, 1975), 182.
139 *As historian David Jacobs wrote* Ibid., 184.

CHAPTER 17: FERMI'S PARADOX

144   *"Edward," he asked, "what do you think"*: Eric M. Jones, " 'Where Is Everybody?': An Account of Fermi's Question," Los Alamos National Laboratory, 2, https://www.osti.gov/servlets/purl/5746675.

144   *Many accounts of this*: Ibid., 3.

144   *"In spite of Fermi's question"*: Ibid.

145   *The announcement of*: "New Radio Waves Traced to Centre of the Milky Way," *New York Times*, May 5, 1933, 1.

145   *According to his son, Jansky*: Ronald Smothers, "Commemorating a Discovery in Radio Astronomy," June 9, 1998, https://www.nytimes.com/1998/06/09/nyregion/commem orating-a-discovery-in-radio-astronomy.html.

146   *"A universe of radio sounds"*: John Kraus, "The First 50 Years of Radio Astronomy, Part 1: Karl Jansky and His Discovery of Radio Waves from Our Galaxy," *Cosmic Search* 3, no. 4 (Fall 1981): http://www.bigear.org/CSMO/HTML/CS12/cs12p08.htm.

147   *That September*: Robert Buderi, *The Invention That Changed the World: How a Small Group of Radar Pioneers Won the Second World War and Launched a Technological Revolution* (New York: Touchstone, 1997), 33–35.

147   *Now, in the weeks*: Ibid., 48.

147   *The team's evening drinking sessions*: Ibid., 98.

147   *A plane using the Rad Lab's breakthroughs*: Ibid., 149.

148   *That fall*: Ibid., 168–69.

148   *By then, radar*: Ibid., 225.

148   *On January 25, 1946, the front page of the* New York Times: Jack Gould, "Contact with Moon Achieved by Radar in Test by the Army," *New York Times*, January 25, 1946, 1.

148   *Since the first time*: "Radar Scientists Hoping to Detect Life on Moon," *Fort Myers* (FL) *News-Press*, January 26, 1946, 1.

148   *"[Radio astronomy] led to information"*: Smothers, "Commemorating a Discovery."

148   *Radio astronomy centers*: Buderi, *The Invention*, 279.

148   *The Australians relied*: Ibid., 287.

149   *"No one believed radio noise"*: Ibid., 288.

149   *By the mid-1950s*: Bart J. Bok, "Toward a National Radio Observatory," National Radio Astronomy Observatory, August 7, 1956, 5, https://www.nrao.edu/archives/items /show/21729.

149   *"The number of active radio astronomers"*: *Symposium on Radio Astronomy*, C.S.I.R.O. Radiophysics Laboratory, September 1956, https://books.google.com/books?id=r -jPAAAAMAAJ.

CHAPTER 18: PROJECT OZMA

150   *"Not only was it one of many"*: Frank Drake and Dava Sobel, *Is Anyone Out There?: The Scientific Search for Extraterrestrial Intelligence* (New York: Delta, 1992), 5.

150   *"Everything I had read"*: Ibid., 8.

150   *"He raised the practice"*: Ibid., 11.

151   *"In the space of a few moments"*: Ibid., 12.

151   *The significance of Struve's*: "Messenger Lecture Explains Nebulae, Star Origin Theory," *Cornell Daily Sun*, December 6, 1951, 3.

151   *"I realized that a radio telescope"*: Drake and Sobel, *Is Anyone Out There?*, 18.

152   *As Drake recalled, "Any scientifically savvy civilization"*: Ibid., 19.

152   *"What I felt was not a normal emotion"*: Ibid.

152   *"I sat down, sweating"*: Ibid.

153 *"Radio telescopes needed big collecting dishes"*: Ibid., 15.

153 *After a nationwide survey of thirty suitable locations*: Richard Emberson, "National Radio Astronomy Observatory," *Science* 130 (1959): 1307, https://www.gb.nrao.edu/~fghigo /biwf/biwf2/biwf2016final7opt.pdf; Bart J. Bok, "Toward a National Radio Observatory," National Radio Astronomy Observatory, August 7, 1956, 5, https://www.nrao .edu/archives/items/show/21729, 23.

153 *Construction for the remote site*: Eggers and Higgins, *Feasibility Report for the National Science Foundation*, May 5, 1955, 17, https://www.nrao.edu/archives/files/orig inal/3672bc248757ed6fc145276db88e474b.pdf.

153 *The town of Green Bank*: D. S. Heeschen to L. V. Berkner, November 12, 1957, https:// www.nrao.edu/archives/files/original/e2543ba8b7515aa9acb84cf93d7404a3.pdf.

153 *The groundbreaking took place*: Graham DuShane, "Groundbreaking at Green Bank," *Science* 126 (November 1957), https://www.gb.nrao.edu/~fghigo/biwf/biwf2/biwf 2016final7opt.pdf.

154 *Ultimately, though*: John W. Finney, "Radio Telescope to Expose Space," *New York Times*, June 19, 1959, 6.

154 Popular Mechanics *called*: Martin's Mann, "New Radio Telescope Is Man's Biggest Machine," *Popular Science*, December 1959, 85.

154 *"In reports by"*: James Bamford, "The Agency That Could Be Big Brother," *New York Times*, December 25, 2005, https://www.nytimes.com/2005/12/25/weekinreview/the -agency-that-could-be-big-brother.html.

154 *The two telescopes*: Drake and Sobel, *Is Anyone Out There?*, 24–25.

155 *"It was a remarkable idea"*: Seth Shostak, *Confessions of an Alien Hunter* (Washington, DC: National Geographic, 2009), 9.

155 *"He had a reputation in science"*: Drake and Sobel, *Is Anyone Out There?*, 27.

155 *Drake named the effort:* Drake and Sobel, *Is Anyone Out There?*, 27; Karl S. Guthke, *The Last Frontier: Imagining Other Worlds, from the Copernican Revolution to Modern Science Fiction*, trans. Helen Atkins (Ithaca, NY: Cornell University Press, 1990), 2.

156 *"For centuries Platonists"*: Ibid., 4.

156 *Goethe wrote, "Of all discoveries and convictions"*: Ibid., 45.

156 *As Guthke traces*: Ibid., ix.

156 *As Guthke notes, "Galileo himself, soon widely hailed"*: Ibid., 95.

156 *In many ways, the debate for centuries paralleled*: Ibid., 50.

157 *The Bishop of Chester*: Ibid., 148.

157 *By the 1700s and 1800s*: Ibid., 200.

157 *Discoveries around 1860*: Ibid., 325.

157 *"For the first time"*: Drake and Sobel, *Is Anyone Out There?*, 215.

157 *As Drake recalled, "There's something aesthetically appealing"*: Ibid., 43.

158 *Radio telescopes*: Giuseppe Cocconi and Philip Morrison, "Searching for Interstellar Communications," *Nature* 184 (September 1959): 846.

158 *"SETI has always made me unhappy"*: Philip Morrison, interview by Owen Gingerich, February 22, 2003, Niels Bohr Library & Archives, American Institute of Physics, https://www.aip.org/history-programs/niels-bohr-library/oral-histories/30591-1.

CHAPTER 19: PHANTOM SIGNAL

159 *Others were about to claim*: Kenneth I. Kellermann, Ellen N. Bouton, and Sierra S. Brandt, *Open Skies: The National Radio Astronomy Observatory and Its Impact on US Radio Astronomy* (Cham, Switzerland: Springer, 2021), 234.

159 *"It is probable that a good many"*: H. Paul Shuch, ed., *Searching for Extraterrestrial Intelligence: SETI Past, Present, and Future* (Chichester, UK: Praxis, 2011), 15.

159   *The presence of the two women*: Ibid., 33.
160   *"It had the simplest possible output device"*: Ibid., 36–37.
161   *"The rate at which the phantom signal"*: Ibid., 15.
162   *"We had failed to detect"*: Ibid., 41.
162   *Thus, since 1955*: Annie Jacobsen, *Area 51: An Uncensored History of America's Top Secret Military Base* (New York: Little, Brown, 2011), 5.
163   *Project staff could dine at the nation's first McDonald's*: Michael R. Beschloss, *Mayday: Eisenhower, Khrushchev and the U-2 Affair* (New York: Harper, 1986), 90.
163   *Through World War II*: Ibid., 91.
163   *"The entire project became the most"*: Richard M. Bissell Jr., Jonathan E. Lewis, and Frances T. Pudlo, *Reflections of a Cold Warrior: From Yalta to the Bay of Pigs* (New Haven, CT: Yale University Press, 1996), 105.
163   *Information was so sensitive*: Gregory W. Pedlow and Donald E. Welzenbach, "Developing the U-2," in *The Central Intelligence Agency and Overhead Reconnaissance: The U-2 and Oxcart Programs* (Central Intelligence Agency, 1992), 59–60, https://nsarchive2.gwu.edu/NSAEBB/NSAEBB434/docs/U2%20-%20Chapter%202.pdf.
164   *It could stay in the air*: Beschloss, *Mayday*, 92.
164   *"Manufacturing this special fuel"*: Pedlow and Welzenbach, "Developing the U-2," 62.
164   *"With 12,000 feet of film"*: Beschloss, *Mayday*, 92.
164   *Pilots for the program were plucked*: Ibid., 108–09.
165   *"Once U-2s started flying"*: Pedlow and Welzenbach, "Developing the U-2," 72.
165   *By the CIA's secret estimate*: Ibid., 73.
165   *As one CIA memo noted*: Jacobsen, *Area 51*, 88.

CHAPTER 20: THE DRAKE EQUATION

167   *He hung a sign*: Frank Drake and Dava Sobel, *Is Anyone Out There? The Scientific Search for Extraterrestrial Intelligence* (New York: Delta, 1992), 45.
167   *Born in the working-class*: Carl Sagan, "Growing Up with Science Fiction," *New York Times Magazine*, May 28, 1978, 24.
167   *By age ten*: Ibid.
167   *The final two sentences*: William Poundstone, *Carl Sagan: A Life in the Cosmos* (New York: Henry Holt, 1999), 12.
167   *As a high school student*: Ibid., 15.
168   *"Not a single adult"*: Ibid., 20.
168   *At just sixteen years old*: Keay Davidson, *Carl Sagan: A Life* (New York: John Wiley, 1999), 49.
168   *Urey, the recipient*: Poundstone, *Carl Sagan*, 23.
168   *They wanted to build*: Melvin Calvin, "Chemical Evolution," *American Scientist* 63, no. 2 (March–April 1975): 169.
169   *In fact, later analysis after Miller's death*: *The Cell*, episode 3, "The Spark of Life," aired August 26, 2009, on BBC, https://www.bbc.co.uk/programmes/b00mbvfh.
169   *It would become*: Jeffrey L. Bada and Antonio Lazcano, "Prebiotic Soup—Revisiting the Miller Experiment," *Science* 300, no. 5620 (May 2, 2003): 745–46.
169   *"The scientists who designed NASA experiments"*: Poundstone, *Carl Sagan*, 39.
169   *With a vote of confidence*: Ibid., 40.
169   *"I believe that this nation"*: John F. Kennedy, "The Goal of Sending a Man to the Moon" (Washington, DC, May 25, 1961), Miller Center, University of Virginia, https://millercenter.org/the-presidency/presidential-speeches/may-25-1961-goal-sending-man-moon.
170   *In a strong Oxford accent*: Drake and Sobel, *Is Anyone Out There?*, 46.

171   *"Yup," the man replied*: Ibid., 49.

172   *This, he now explained*: Ibid., 52.

172   *Closer examination, though, raised more questions*: Walter Sullivan, *We Are Not Alone: The Search for Intelligent Life on Other Worlds* (New York: McGraw-Hill, 1966), 254.

173   *At one point, Su-Shu Huang joined in*: Ibid., 249.

173   *Calvin's own recollection*: Drake and Sobel, *Is Anyone Out There?*, 54.

173   *"Let's imagine what"*: Ibid., 60.

174   *Life might take many forms*: Sullivan, *We Are Not Alone*, 252.

174   *Lilly, for his part, raised a final challenge*: Poundstone, *Carl Sagan*, 59.

174   *By the conference's end*: Drake and Sobel, *Is Anyone Out There?*, 62.

174   *"This is work for society"*: Ibid., 63.

175   *"To the value of* L*"*: Poundstone, *Carl Sagan*, 59.

CHAPTER 21: THE SEARCH EXPANDS

176   *"The adjacent possible is a kind of shadow future"*: Steven Johnson, *Where Good Ideas Come From: The Natural History of Innovation* (New York: Riverhead, 2010), 31.

177   *"It makes a compelling argument"*: Frank Drake and Dava Sobel, *Is Anyone Out There?: The Scientific Search for Extraterrestrial Intelligence* (New York: Delta, 1992), 68.

177   *"Under normal circumstances"*: Iosif Shklovsky, *Five Billion Vodka Bottles to the Moon: Tales of a Soviet Scientist*, trans. Mary Flemin Zirin and Harold Zirin (New York: W. W. Norton, 1991), 250.

177   *The book was a huge success*: "Is Communication Possible with Intelligent Beings on Other Planets? by I. S. Shklovskiy," card catalog entry, CIA, https://www.cia.gov/read ingroom/docs/CIA-RDP91-00772R000200960023-6.pdf.

177   *"The early world-leading space exploration program"*: Lev M. Gindilis and Leonid I. Gurvits, "SETI in Russia, USSR and the Post-Soviet Space: A Century of Research," *Acta Astronautica* (2019), 2, https://arxiv.org/pdf/1905.03225.pdf.

178   *A talented artist*: David W. Swift, *SETI Pioneers: Scientists Talk about Their Search for Extraterrestrial Intelligence* (Tucson: University of Arizona Press, 1990), 168–69.

178   *As technology improved, Harvard astronomer*: Drake and Sobel, *Is Anyone Out There?*, 97.

178   *According to Sagan's biographer*: William Poundstone, *Carl Sagan: A Life in the Cosmos* (New York: Henry Holt, 1999), 77.

178   *"It was impossible not to like him"*: Drake and Sobel, *Is Anyone Out There?*, 98.

179   *The book went through fourteen*: Poundstone, *Carl Sagan*, 92.

179   *There, over three days*: Shklovsky, *Five Billion Vodka Bottles*, 254; L. M. Gindilis, "Conference on Extraterrestrial Civilizations," *Soviet Astronomy* 9, no. 2 (March–April 1965): 370.

179   *Together, they called for*: Rebecca A. Charbonneau, "Mixed Signals: Communication with the Alien in Cold War Radio Astronomy" (PhD diss., University of Cambridge, 2021), 79, https://api.repository.cam.ac.uk/server/api/core/bitstreams/7e186d38-914c -4175-bd0c-d9501279dd98/content.

179   *One of the conference's most notable*: Leonid I. Gurvits, Yuri Y. Kovalev, and Philip G. Edwards, "Nikolai Kardashev," *Physics Today*, December 16, 2019, https://pubs.aip .org/physicstoday/Online/5586/Nikolai-Kardashev; "Nicolay S. Kardashev," International Astronomical Union, https://www.iau.org/administration/membership/individ ual/3990/.

180   *It was of the "utmost importance"*: N. S. Kardashev, "Transmission of Information by Extraterrestrial Civilizations," *Soviet Astronomy* 8, no. 2 (September–October 1964): 220.

180   *"Should there even exist"*: Ibid., 219.

181 *As Kaku wrote, "These time scales are insignificant"*: Michio Kaku, "The Physics of Inter-stellar Travel," https://mkaku.org/home/articles/the-physics-of-interstellar-travel/.

181 *"It is speculated that even some sources"*: Kardashev, "Transmission of Information," 217.

181 *Now, with the broader resources*: Kellermann, Bouton, and Brandt, *Open Skies*, 249.

182 *"Many of the details of Sholomitskii's observation"*: Charbonneau, "Mixed Signals," 72.

182 *At an April 1964 colloquium*: Ibid., 81–82.

183 *The elder Shklovsky*: Ibid., 83.

183 *On April 13, 1965*: Walter Sullivan, "Russians Say a Cosmic Emission May Come from Rational Beings," *New York Times*, April 13, 1965, 1.

183 *"I saw Jane Fonda"*: Drake and Sobel, *Is Anyone Out There?*, 104.

183 *"It is rather sad"*: "People in Space? 'No Proof Yet,'" *Evening Standard* (London, UK), April 13, 1965, 11.

CHAPTER 22: THE SOCORRO INCIDENT

184 *"UFOs had been reported"*: Mark O'Connell, *The Close Encounters Man: How One Man Made the World Believe in UFOs* (New York: Dey St., 2017), 146.

184 *"Professional astronomy is a field"*: Jacques Vallée, *Forbidden Science: Journals 1957–1969* (Berkeley, CA: North Atlantic Books, 1992), 71–72.

185 *"The great tradition"*: Ibid., 72.

185 *A Grenoble farmer*: Ibid., 67–68.

185 *Worried about the sightings*: Wilkins, *Flying Saucers Uncensored*, 59.

185 *Vallée shared*: Joshua Malin, "The 1954 French UFO Craze that Led to the World's Weirdest Wine Law," VinePair, July 7, 2015, https://vinepair.com/wine-blog/chateau-neuf-du-pape-ufo-wine-law/.

186 *"[Our first meeting] lasted"*: Vallée, *Forbidden Science*, 72.

186 *"He is a warm and yet a deeply scholarly man"*: Ibid.

186 *Vallée remembered: "Hynek watched us fight"*: Ibid., 76.

186 *In January*: Ibid., 84.

187 *"We only have vague theories"*: Ibid., 87.

187 *Even as the conversations*: Ibid., 88.

187 *On the afternoon*: "Unidentified Flying Object, Socorro, New Mexico, April 24, 1964," statement by Lonnie Zamora, May 8, 1964, FBI, 2, https://documents2.theblackvault .com/documents/fbifiles/paranormal/FBI-UFO-Socorro-fbi1.pdf.

187 *Then, he saw "two figures in what resembled white coveralls"*: Clark, *The UFO Encyclopedia*, "Socorro CE2/CE3."

187 *"10-44 [accident]"*: "Unidentified Flying Object, Socorro," 5.

188 *He heard a couple*: Ibid., 5–8.

188 *A New Mexico State*: Clark, *The UFO Encyclopedia*, "Socorro CE2/CE3."

188 *The local FBI agent*: "Unidentified Flying Object, Socorro, New Mexico, April 24, 1964," statement by Arthur Byrnes, May 8, 1964, FBI, 1, https://documents2.theblackvault .com/documents/fbifiles/paranormal/FBI-UFO-Socorro-fbi1.pdf.

188 *The FBI report*: Ibid., 2.

189 *As he told*: Clark, *The UFO Encyclopedia*, "Socorro CE2/CE3."

189 *At the meeting*: Vallée, *Forbidden Science*, 100.

189 *"The attitude of the Air Force"*: Ibid., 92.

189 *As historian Jerome Clark notes*: Clark, *The UFO Encyclopedia*, "Socorro CE2/CE3."

189 *In a confidential memo*: Ibid.

190 *Interestingly, one of the FBI reports on the incident*: Albuquerque 62-1028 3P to Direc-tor, teletype, April 27, 1964, FBI, https://documents2.theblackvault.com/documents /fbifiles/paranormal/FBI-UFO-Socorro-fbi1.pdf.

190   *Writing in the CIA's*: Hector Quintanilla, Jr., "The Investigation of UFO's," CIA, 18, https://www.cia.gov/static/835f2989f8b975cc31ebbfd2f78e7d34/Investigation-of -UFOs.pdf.

190   *Local legend eventually*: Ibid.

190   *The "unusual case"*: David Michael Jacobs, *The UFO Controversy in America* (Bloomington: Indiana University Press, 1975), 190–91.

CHAPTER 23: EXPLORING MARS

192   *In 1610*: Sarah Stewart Johnson, *The Sirens of Mars: Searching for Life on Another World* (New York: Crown, 2021), 11.

192   *"If we could believe with any probability"*: Ibid.

192   *It would be another*: Rebekah Higgitt, "Mapping Mars: A Long and Highly Imaginative History," *Guardian*, August 6, 2012, https://www.theguardian.com/science/the-h -word/2012/aug/06/mapping-mars-history.

193   *"During those nights up on the rooftop"*: Johnson, *The Sirens of Mars*, 25.

193   *"The evidence of handicraft"*: Percival Lowell, *Mars* (Boston: Houghton, Mifflin, 1895), 208, https://books.google.com/books?id=w9JJAAAAMAAJ.

193   *As one of Lowell's*: W. W. Campbell, "Mars," Publications of the Astronomical Society of the Pacific, August 1, 1896 (Vol. 8, No. 51), p. 209, https://www.jstor.org/sta ble/40667612?seq=3.

194   *Even as pieces*: Johnson, *The Sirens of Mars*, 29.

194   *"My first observations positively terrified"*: Nikola Tesla, "Talking with the Planets," *Collier's Weekly*, February 9, 1901, https://earlyradiohistory.us/1901talk.htm.

194   *One of Tesla's biographers*: Marc J. Seifer, "Nikola Tesla: The Lost Wizard," *Extra-Ordinary Technology* 4, no. 1 (January–March 2006), https://teslatech.info/ttmagazine /v4n1/seifer.htm.

194   *Science fiction was a popular*: Johnson, *The Sirens of Mars*, 13.

195   *As they saw it*: Ibid., 7.

196   *On November 28, 1964*: Ibid., 5.

196   *President Johnson touted*: Lyndon B. Johnson, "Inaugural Address" (Washington, DC, January 20, 1965), Miller Center, University of Virginia, https://millercenter.org /the-presidency/presidential-speeches/january-20-1965-inaugural-address.

196   *"Looking at a planet"*: Johnson, *The Sirens of Mars*, 15.

197   *"My God, it's the moon"*: Ibid., 17.

197   *"As a member of the generation"*: Lyndon B. Johnson, "Remarks Upon Viewing New Mariner 4 Pictures from Mars" (Washington, DC, July 29, 1965), American Presidency Project, https://www.presidency.ucsb.edu/documents/remarks-upon-viewing -new-mariner-4-pictures-from-mars.

197   *The next day's*: Walter Sullivan, "Mariner 4's Final Photos Depict a Moonlike Mars," *New York Times*, July 30, 1965, 1.

197   *"Those who had been on the periphery"*: David Michael Jacobs, *The UFO Controversy in America* (Bloomington: Indiana University Press, 1975), 193.

198   *"The picture was overexposed"*: Frank Edwards, *Flying Saucers—Serious Business* (New York: Bantam, 1966), 165; "The Sherman, Texas, Photo Case," National Investigations Committee on Aerial Phenomena, http://www.nicap.org/650802sherman_dir.htm.

198   *"Something is going on"*: Jacobs, *The UFO Controversy*, 194.

198   *"Maybe it's time"*: Richard H. Hall, *The UFO Evidence: A Thirty-Year Report*, Vol. 2 (Lanham, MD: Scarecrow Press, 2001), 4.; " 'Saucers' Are Flying," *Fort Worth Star-Telegram*, August 4, 1965, 4.

198   *Even some who had*: Jacobs, *The UFO Controversy*, 196.

199 *On September 3*: Clark, *The UFO Encyclopedia*, "Exeter CE1."

199 *"At this time I have been unable"*: Ibid.

199 *The responding officers*: Ibid.

199 *J. Allen Hynek, for his part*: Jacobs, *The UFO Controversy*, 198.

200 *"In 19 years and more than 10,000 sightings"*: Ibid.

200 *UFO researchers have obtained*: "Appendix I," *Special Report of the USAF Scientific Advisory Board: Ad Hoc Committee to Review Project "BLUE BOOK,"* March 1966, http://www.cufon.org/cufon/obrien.htm.

201 *Jacques Vallée was less*: Jacques Vallée, *Forbidden Science: Journals 1957–1969* (Berkeley, CA: North Atlantic Books, 1992), 170.

201 *As the youngest member*: William Poundstone, *Carl Sagan: A Life in the Cosmos* (New York: Henry Holt, 1999), 92; Jacobs, *The UFO Controversy*, 198.201 *One night after giving*: Carl Sagan, "UFO's: The Extraterrestrial and Other Hypotheses," in Carl Sagan and Thornton Page, eds., *UFO's—A Scientific Debate* (Ithaca, NY: Cornell University Press, 1972), 272–73.

202 *That belief was only*: Poundstone, *Carl Sagan*, 64–65.

202 *Two years later*: Ibid., 66.

CHAPTER 24: SWAMP GAS

203 *To him, it didn't seem*: David Michael Jacobs, *The UFO Controversy in America* (Bloomington: Indiana University Press, 1975), 213.

203 *"The unwillingness of government"*: Oscar Handlin, "Reader's Choice," *Atlantic*, August 1966, https://www.theatlantic.com/magazine/archive/1966/08/readers-choice/659614/.

204 *In a six-part series*: "Those 'Flying Saucers'... Air Force Explainings-Away of UFOs Deepens Mystery," *Evening Express* (Portland, ME), January 17, 1966, 2.

204 *"For anyone who didn't live through it"*: James W. Moseley and Karl T. Pflock, *Shockingly Close to the Truth!: Confessions of a Grave-Robbing Ufologist* (Amherst, NY: Prometheus, 2002), 193–94.

205 *"We saw a real brilliant light"*: Jack Butler, "UFO: In 1966, Hillsdale Had Its Own Close Encounter," *Collegian* (Hillsdale, MI), March 19, 2015, https://hillsdalecollegian.com/2015/03/ufo-in-1966-hillsdale-had-its-own-close-encounter/.

205 *"All three networks are talking"*: Jacques Vallée, *Forbidden Science: Journals 1957–1969* (Berkeley, CA: North Atlantic Books, 1992), 173.

205 *The Washington Post*: *Unidentified Flying Objects: Hearing by Committee on Armed Services*, 89th Cong. 6050 (1966), https://archive.org/details/ufo_1966_1/ufo_1966_2/page/n11/mode/2up.

205 *In response*: Mark O'Connell, *The Close Encounters Man: How One Man Made the World Believe in UFOs* (New York: Dey St., 2017), 242.

205 *There was also a clear*: J. Allen Hynek, "Are Flying Saucers Real?," *Saturday Evening Post*, December 17, 1966, 20.

205 *"Men spilled out"*: O'Connell, *The Close Encounters Man*, 184.

206 *"So far," he said at the time*: Ibid., 187.

206 *Matters were only made*: Ibid., 191.

206 *"Half-heartedly, he settled on"*: Hynek, "Are Flying Saucers Real?," 20.

206 *"It would seem to me"*: O'Connell, *The Close Encounters Man*, 191.

206 *"I'm just a simple fellow"*: Paul O'Neil, " 'Invasion'—by Something," *Life*, April 1, 1966, 29; William B. Treml, "Findings on 'Saucers' Draw Sharp Reactions," *Ann Arbor News*, March 26, 1966, https://aadl.org/taxonomy/term/9218.206 *It was perhaps*: O'Connell, *The Close Encounters Man*, 194.

207 *The quick, dismissive*: Vallée, *Forbidden Science*, 175.

207   *Ford acknowledged his "special interest"*: Gerald R. Ford to L. Mendel Rivers, March
       28, 1966, in *Unidentified Flying Objects*, 6046–47; Gerald R. Ford, "Radio Tape for
       Fifth District Stations" (Washington, DC, March 30, 1966), Gerald R. Ford Pres-
       idential Library and Museum, https://www.fordlibrarymuseum.gov/library/docu
       ment/0054/4526519.pdf.

207   *When the White House's*: Gerald R. Ford, statement, March 29, 1966, Gerald R. Ford
       Presidential Library and Museum, https://www.fordlibrarymuseum.gov/library/docu
       ment/0054/12130682.pdf.

208   *"Let me assure you that the Air Force"*: *Unidentified Flying Objects*, 5992.

208   *It was a powerful declaration*: Ibid., 6004–05.

208   *Hynek tried to salvage things*: Ibid., 6007–08.

208   *Later, he added, "Puzzling cases exist"*: Ibid., 6009.

209   *"In seriousness, the people in Vermont"*: Ibid., 6067.

209   *While "the theme of the show"*: Jacobs, *The UFO Controversy*, 203.

209   *Cronkite seemed*: Ibid.

209   *That summer a Gallup poll*: Ibid., 200.

CHAPTER 25: THE UFO GAP

210   *"There were times when I would"*: J. Allen Hynek and Jacques Vallée, *The Edge of Reality:
       A Progress Report on Unidentified Flying Objects* (Chicago: Henry Regnery, 1975), 193.

210   *He was also conscious*: Ibid., 193–94.

211   *When McDonald reported*: Ann Druffel, *Firestorm: Dr. James E. McDonald's Fight for
       UFO Science* (Columbus, NC: Wild Flower Press, 2003), 20.

211   *That spring*: Ibid., 52.

211   *"You've been involved in a foul-up"*: Ibid., 61.

211   *"The explanations [are] pure bullshit"*: Jacques Vallée, *Forbidden Science: Journals 1957–
       1969* (Berkeley, CA: North Atlantic Books, 1992), 186–87.

211   *"This man has many contacts"*: Ibid., 186.

212   *The conversation*: Hynek and Vallée, *The Edge of Reality*, 204.

212   *"I am a Buddhist"*: Vallée, *Forbidden Science*, 190–91.

212   *The Pentagon decreed*: Ibid., 191.

213   *His international ties*: Lewis M. Branscomb, "Edward U. Condon, Ph.D., 1958–1964,"
       Washington University in St. Louis University Libraries, https://libguides.wustl.edu/c
       .php?g=338660&p=2280746.

213   *Condon responded*: Jessica Wang, "Edward Condon and the Cold War Politics of Loy-
       alty," *Physics Today* 54, no. 12 (December 2001): 38.

213   *A few years before*: Grace Marmor Spruch, "Reporter Edward Condon," *Saturday Re-
       view*, February 1, 1969, 55.

214   *Even though he wouldn't*: J. Allen Hynek, "Are Flying Saucers Real?," *Saturday Evening
       Post*, December 17, 1966, 21.

214   *As the committee started*: Ibid., 20–21.

215   *Now Edward Condon had about $500,000*: David Michael Jacobs, *The UFO Controversy
       in America* (Bloomington: Indiana University Press, 1975), 208–11.

215   *Upon arrival*: Vallée, *Forbidden Science*, 229.

215   *As they left*: Ibid., 231.

215   *That fall*: Hynek and Vallée, *The Edge of Reality*, 202.

216   *That December*: Mark O'Connell, *The Close Encounters Man: How One Man Made the
       World Believe in UFOs* (New York: Dey St., 2017), 229.

216   *"What little 'hard' information"*: J. Allen Hynek, "The UFO Gap," *Playboy*, December 1967,

146, https://www.cia.gov/readingroom/docs/CIA-RDP81R00560R000100010006-5 .pdf.

216 *At best, Hynek*: Ibid., 144.

217 *"The expense is trivial"*: Ibid., 271.

217 *Instead, they focused*: Edward U. Condon, *Final Report of the Scientific Study of Unidentified Flying Objects* (New York: E. P. Dutton, 1969), 60.

217 *To help with photographic data, the committee enlisted*: Vallée, *Forbidden Science*, 245.

218 *Shortly after, "he picked up his questionnaire"*: David R. Saunders and R. Roger Harkins, *UFOs? Yes!: Where the Condon Committee Went Wrong* (New York: World Publishing, 1969), 69.

218 *Project coordinator Robert Low*: Ibid., 135.

218 *Perhaps even more troubling*: Jacobs, *The UFO Controversy*, 211.

218 *In January 1967*: Ibid., 212.

218 *As the weeks went by*: Vallée, *Forbidden Science*, 236.

219 *The confidential internal*: Saunders and Harkins, *UFOs*, 129.

CHAPTER 26: THE CONDON REPORT

220 *Perhaps not surprisingly*: Donald H. Menzel to J. Edward Roush, July 24, 1968, in *Symposium on Unidentified Flying Objects: Hearings Before the Committee on Science and Astronautics*, 90th Cong. 205 (1968), https://books.google.com/books?id=Yx4v AAAAMAAJ.

220 *With more humility*: *Symposium on Unidentified Flying Objects*, 1.

220 *To start, Hynek*: Ibid., 4–5.

221 *"We are not dealing with publicity seekers"*: Ibid., 21.

221 *The testimonies and witnesses*: Ibid., 26–27.

222 *"I do not think the evidence is at all persuasive"*: Ibid., 86.

222 *As it turned out*: William Poundstone, *Carl Sagan: A Life in the Cosmos* (New York: Henry Holt, 1999), 171.

222 *"[He] has dashed"*: Ibid., 172.

223 *One of Gold's maxims*: Ibid., 173.

223 *The opportunity*: John Yaukey, "Life on Mars," *Ithaca Journal*, August 19, 1966, 4A.

223 *Sagan noted that*: *Symposium on Unidentified Flying Objects*, 86–87.

224 *"For varying reasons, UFO-related pranks"*: Edward U. Condon, *Final Report of the Scientific Study of Unidentified Flying Objects* (New York: E. P. Dutton, 1969), 62.

224 *In his portion of the document*: Ibid., 1.

225 *A few pages later*: Ibid., 5.

225 *The lack of urgency*: J. Allen Hynek, "The Condon Report and UFOs," *Bulletin of the Atomic Scientists*, April 1969, 39.

225 *Condon took the criticism*: David Michael Jacobs, *The UFO Controversy in America* (Bloomington: Indiana University Press, 1975), 252.

225 *In March 1969*: David J. Shea, "NCAS Presentation," September 8, 2018, 6–7, https://www.politico.com/f/?id=00000168-3213-db11-ab7d-33fb55e70000.

225 *Later that year*: "Air Force to Terminate Project 'BLUE BOOK,' " news release, December 17, 1969, 1, https://www.esd.whs.mil/Portals/54/Documents/FOID/Reading%20 Room/UFOsandUAPs/asdpa1.pdf.

225 *Throughout the summer*: Sarah Stewart Johnson, *The Sirens of Mars: Searching for Life on Another World* (New York: Crown, 2021), 34.

226 *"Just like that, the concept"*: Ibid., 48.

226 *NASA had wrestled*: W. David Compton, *Where No Man Has Gone Before: A History*

of Apollo Lunar Exploration Missions, NASA, 1989, https://www.hq.nasa.gov/pao/History/SP-4214/ch4-3.html.

227 *"Maybe it's sure to 99 percent"*: "Space: Is the Earth Safe from Lunar Contamination?," *Time*, June 13, 1969, https://content.time.com/time/subscriber/article/0,33009,942095,00.html.

CHAPTER 27: THE BYURAKAN CONFERENCE

228 *"Never, before or afterward"*: Iosif Shklovsky, *Five Billion Vodka Bottles to the Moon: Tales of a Soviet Scientist*, trans. Mary Flemin Zirin and Harold Zirin (New York: W. W. Norton, 1991), 257.

228 *The proceedings were almost derailed*: Frank Drake and Dava Sobel, *Is Anyone Out There?: The Scientific Search for Extraterrestrial Intelligence* (New York: Delta, 1992), 111.

228 *As Drake recalled, "Our American contingent"*: Ibid., 109.

228 *Such an occasion*: V. A. Ambartsumian, "Prospect," in Sagan, *Communication*, 3.

229 *He also noted*: Ibid., 5.

229 *The dissident Soviet*: Shklovsky, *Five Billion Vodka Bottles*, 259.

229 *Almost exactly thirty years later*: Ibid., 41.

229 *Ironically, under the Soviet system*: Drake and Sobel, *Is Anyone Out There?*, 96.

229 *It also meant that information*: Ibid., 107.

230 *"They did not make any educated guesses"*: Ibid.

230 *One of the conference's most intriguing*: F. H. C. Crick and L. E. Orgel, "Directed Panspermia," *Icarus* 19 (1973): 341.

230 *At that point*: Ibid.; Thomas Gold, " 'Cosmic Garbage,' " *Space Digest*, May 1960, 65.

231 *In colorful conversations, Gold was known to lightheartedly imagine*: Carl Sagan, "Is There Life Elsewhere, and Did It Come Here?," *New York Times Book Review*, November 29, 1981, 32.

231 *Now, in Armenia*: Crick and Orgel, "Directed Panspermia," 342.

231 *According to a 1973 article*: Ibid., 343, 344.

231 *Normal science held that life*: Ibid.

232 *The scientists were also puzzled by the "anomalous abundance"*: Ibid., 345.

232 *"Perhaps the galaxy is lifeless"*: Ibid.

232 *Even Crick's wife told him, "It is not a real theory"*: Francis Crick, *Life Itself: Its Origin and Nature* (New York: Simon & Schuster, 1981), 148; Crick and Orgel, "Directed Panspermia," 345.

232 *Later, Crick published a book*: Nicholas Wade, "Francis Crick, Co-Discoverer of DNA, Dies at 88," *New York Times*, July 30, 2004, https://www.nytimes.com/2004/07/30/us/francis-crick-co-discoverer-of-dna-dies-at-88.html.

233 *"This joyful event serves"*: Ibid., 261.

CHAPTER 28: THE ARECIBO MESSAGE

234 *"It is . . . overwhelmingly probable"*: Freeman J. Dyson, "Search for Artificial Stellar Sources of Infrared Radiation," *Science* 131, no. 3414 (1960): 1667.

235 *In that heady time*: Robert Dixon, "Project Cyclops: The Greatest Radio Telescope Never Built," in Shuch, *Searching for Extraterrestrial Intelligence*, 20.

235 *"The Exobiology Division"*: Seth Shostak, *Confessions of an Alien Hunter* (Washington, DC: National Geographic, 2009), 166.

236 *This band, Oliver wrote*: Ibid., 64.

236 *In announcing a reprint*: "Announcing the Reprint of the Cyclops Report," SETI League, http://www.setileague.org/articles/cyclops.htm.

236 *"The search for extraterrestrial intelligent life"*: Ibid., 171.

236 *"Each passing year has seen"*: *Astronomy and Astrophysics for the 1970's: Report of the Astronomy Survey Committee*, Vol. 1 (Washington, DC: National Academy of Sciences, 1972), 51.

237 *"You have to see it"*: Frank Drake and Dava Sobel, *Is Anyone Out There?: The Scientific Search for Extraterrestrial Intelligence* (New York: Delta, 1992), 73.

238 *The telescope, Drake learned*: Ibid., 76.

239 *In 1820, German mathematician*: Willy Ley, *Rockets, Missiles, and Space Travel* (New York: Viking, 1957), 32.

239 *Whether Gauss himself*: Michael J. Crowe, *The Extraterrestrial Life Debate, 1750–1900* (Mineola, NY: Dover, 1999), 205.

239 *In France, a scientist thought*: Ibid., 36–37.

239 *Drake compared the conundrum*: Drake and Sobel, *Is Anyone Out There?*, 164.

240 *To test its efficacy*: Ibid., 167.

240 *Shortly after*: Ibid., 169.

240 *"Their minds are uncommonly well prepared"*: Ibid.

241 *As conference-goers moved*: Ibid., 176.

242 *In the end*: Ibid., 180.

243 *Drake believed that it could detect*: Ibid., 183.

243 *At the telescope dedication ceremony*: Dava Sobel, "New Radio Telescope: A Greeting from Arecibo Speeds to the Stars," *Cornell* (Ithaca, NY) *Chronicle*, November 21, 1974, 2.

243 *Then a loud siren*: Dava Sobel, "The Long Hello," http://www.davasobel.com/blog/124.

244 *By the time the ceremony participants*: Drake and Sobel, *Is Anyone Out There?*, 184.

244 *Far beyond the island*: Carl Sagan, *Murmurs of Earth: The Voyager Interstellar Record* (New York: Random House, 1978), 65–66.

CHAPTER 29: CLOSE ENCOUNTERS OF THE THIRD KIND

246 *"For too long"*: Leonard H. Stringfield, *Situation Red: The UFO Siege* (Fawcett Crest Books, 1977), 15.

246 *Altogether, by his count*: Leonard H. Stringfield, "Retrievals of the Third Kind—Part 3: A Case Study of Alleged UFOs and Occupants in Military Custody," *Flying Saucer Review*, https://ilpoliedrico.com/wp-content/uploads/2017/07/Retrievals-of-the-Third-Kind.pdf.

247 *Later, he alleged that plainclothes policemen*: James W. Moseley and Karl T. Pflock, *Shockingly Close to the Truth!: Confessions of a Grave-Robbing Ufologist* (Amherst, NY: Prometheus, 2002), 255.

247 *In the years ahead*: "Retrievals of the Third Kind—Part 1: A Case Study of Alleged UFOs and Occupants in Military Custody," *Flying Saucer Review*, https://ilpoliedrico.com/wp-content/uploads/2017/07/Retrievals-of-the-Third-Kind.pdf.

247 *"More than any other single ufologist"*: Moseley and Pflock, *Shockingly*, 253.

248 *there were seven photos taken*: Curtis Peebles, *Watch the Skies!: A Chronicle of the Flying Saucer Myth* (Washington, DC: Smithsonian Institution Press, 1994), 249.

248 *The book sold widely*: Clark, *The UFO Encyclopedia*, "Crashes and Retrievals of UFOs in the Twentieth Century."

248 *"If one accepted these tales"*: Moseley and Pflock, *Shockingly*, 261.

248 *He called it "Cosmic Watergate"*: Jerome Clark, *UFOs in the 1980s: The UFO Encyclopedia*, Vol. 1 (Detroit, MI: Apogee, 1990), 117.

248 *The same month*: Ibid., 232.

249 *After more than a decade*: David Michael Jacobs, *The UFO Controversy in America* (Bloomington: Indiana University Press, 1975), 257.

249   *The closure of Blue Book*: Ibid., 283.

249   *In 1972, he had published*: J. Allen Hynek, *The UFO Experience: A Scientific Inquiry* (Collector's Library of the Unknown) (Alexandria, Va.: Time-Life Books, 1989), viii.

250   *Written for a popular audience*: Ibid., 229.

251   *The second grouping gathered*: Ibid., 138.

251   *It was a category*: Ibid., 143.

251   *"It is in Close Encounter cases"*: Ibid., 87.

252   *Acknowledging these cases*: Ibid.

252   *These were, he emphasized*: Ibid., 234.

252   *Its five major areas of research*: Ibid.

252   *"The interdisciplinary nature"*: Ibid.

252   *The center launched*: "Center for UFO Studies Explained," *Skylook: The UFO Monthly*, March 1974, 7, https://dailydialectics.com/space/MUFON/MUFON%20UFO%20Journal%20-%201974%203.%20March%20-%20Skylook.pdf/.

254   *Simon put great stock*: Ibid., 61.

254   *While the case, Simon decided*: Ibid., 63; Peebles, *Watch the Skies!*, 226.

255   *Over the years*: Clark, *The UFO Encyclopedia*, "Hill Abduction Case."

255   *In the mid-1970s, Astronomy magazine reported*: Terence Dickinson, "The Zeta Reticuli (or Ridiculi) Incident," *Astronomy*, https://astronomy.com/bonus/zeta.

255   *Betty Hill had actually "recovered"*: William Poundstone, *Carl Sagan: A Life in the Cosmos* (New York: Henry Holt, 1999), 130.

255   *Fish, presented with later evidence*: Colin Johnston, "The Truth about Betty Hill's UFO Star Map," Armagh Observatory and Planetarium, August 19, 2011, https://armagh planet.com/betty-hills-ufo-star-map-the-truth.html.

255   *As UFO expert*: Clark, *The UFO Encyclopedia*, "Hill Abduction Case."

256   *"Efforts to explain"*: Clark, *UFO Encyclopedia*, Vol. 1, 451.

256   *But Hynek was dubious*: J. Allen Hynek and Jacques Vallée, *The Edge of Reality: A Progress Report on Unidentified Flying Objects* (Chicago: Henry Regnery, 1975), 54.

257   *"From the facial expressions"*: Mark O'Connell, *The Close Encounters Man: How One Man Made the World Believe in UFOs* (New York: Dey St., 2017), 262.

257   *New technology was being*: Hynek and Vallée, *The Edge of Reality*, 55.

257   *"Why would they frighten animals"*: Ibid., 51–52.

258   *"It just laid up"*: O'Connell, *The Close Encounters Man*, 273.

258   *Over the course of six*: Ibid., 276.

258   *As he told the press, "There's simply no question in my mind"*: Ibid., 279.

258   *As he wrote late in the decade*: Alan Hendry, *The UFO Handbook* (Garden City, NY: Doubleday and Co., 1979), p. 285.

CHAPTER 30: THE DICK CAVETT DUEL

259   *On October 18, 1973*: David Michael Jacobs, *The UFO Controversy in America* (Bloomington: Indiana University Press, 1975), 293.

259   *The military never seemed*: Clark, *The UFO Encyclopedia*, "Coyne CE2."

259   *"I don't understand it—their exclusive story"*: David J. Skal, *Screams of Reason: Mad Science and Modern Culture* (New York: W. W. Norton, 1998), 200–01.

259   *Sagan, who was becoming*: Ralph Blum and Judy Blum, *Beyond Earth: Man's Contact with UFOs* (New York: Bantam, 1974), 203.

260   *Hynek, meanwhile*: Jacques Vallée, *Forbidden Science, Volume Two: Journals 1970–1979* (San Francisco: Documatica Research, 2017), 213.

260   *Ahead of the event*: O'Connell, *The Close Encounters Man*, 299.

260   *To mitigate further damage*: Ibid., 302–03.

261   *"A standard," Hynek's biographer notes*: Ibid., 303.

CHAPTER 31: THE TEHRAN INCIDENT

262   *Over the years*: Matthew Hayes, *Search for the Unknown: Canada's UFO Files and the Rise of Conspiracy Theory* (Montreal: McGill-Queen's University Press, 2022), introduction, EPUB.

262   *After deciding*: Ronald D. Story, ed., *The Encyclopedia of UFOs* (New York: Dolphin Books, 1980), 276.

263   *"It was impossible to do much more"*: Ibid., chap. 4.

263   *"By erecting a façade of ridicule"*: O. H. Turner, "Scientific and Intelligence Aspects of the UFO Problem," May 27, 1971, Department of Defence Joint Intelligence Organization, i, https://documents.theblackvault.com/documents/ufos/australia/A13693_3092-2-0 00_30030606.pdf.

264   *According to a report*: Frank B. McKenzie, message, undated, Department of Defense, 2, http://www.nicap.org/reports/iran22.htm.

264   *As the second fighter*: Ibid.

265   *This was, analysts could tell*: Lawrence Fawcett and Barry J. Greenwood, *The UFO Cover-Up: What the Government Won't Say* (New York: Fireside, 1984), 84.

266   *It was a scenario that Hynek*: J. Allen Hynek, "The UFO Gap," *Playboy*, December 1967, 270, https://www.cia.gov/readingroom/docs/CIA-RDP81R00560R000100010006-5 .pdf.

266   *After the French translation . . . in earnest*: Gildas Bourdais, "From GEPAN to SEPRA: Official UFO Studies in France," *International UFO Reporter*, Winter 2000–2001, 11, https://web.archive.org/web/20160604010219/http://www.ufoevidence.org/newsite /files/GEPANSEPRA.pdf.

267   *Much of its first year*: "French Government UFO Study," National Security Agency, https://www.nsa.gov/portals/75/documents/news-features/declassified-documents /ufo/french_gov_ufo_study.pdf.

267   *The committee's final report*: Claude Poher, *GEPAN Report to the Scientific Committee*, June 1978, https://ufologie.patrickgross.org/rec/claudepoher.htm.

267   *Two years later*: Jim Wilson, "When UFOs Land," *Popular Mechanics*, May 2001, 66.

268   *"I clearly saw the device"*: Peter A. Sturrock, *The UFO Enigma: A New Review of the Physical Evidence* (New York: Warner, 1999), 264–66.

268   *GEPAN's resulting sixty-six-page report*: Clark, *The UFO Encyclopedia*, "Trans-en-Provence CE2."

CHAPTER 32: THE WOW SIGNAL

269   *"He was like the movie star"*: William Poundstone, *Carl Sagan: A Life in the Cosmos* (New York: Henry Holt, 1999), 188.

269   *In 1973, since the facility lacked*: Ibid., 187.

269   *"It was an actual feeling of depression"*: Ibid., 189.

269   *"It was a big trip"*: Ibid., 188.

270   *"I had never seen any signal"*: Robert Krulwich, "Aliens Found in Ohio? The 'Wow!' Signal," NPR, May 28, 2010, https://www.npr.org/sections/krulwich/2010/05/28/126510251 /aliens-found-in-ohio-the-wow-signal.

270   *The so-called "Wow signal"*: John Kraus, "The Tantalizing 'Wow!' Signal," National

Radio Astronomy Observatory, 1, https://www.nrao.edu/archives/files/original/2ec
6ba346ab16e10a10d09462507beda.pdf.

271   *In a shared cottage at the Kahala Hilton*: Ibid., 232.

271   *When the design phase was completed*: Frank Drake and Dava Sobel, *Is Anyone Out There?:
The Scientific Search for Extraterrestrial Intelligence* (New York: Delta, 1992), 186.

271   *"Now, let's see if I got"*: Poundstone, *Carl Sagan*, 235.

272   *The engaged Druyan*: Ibid., 247.

272   *If they could decode*: Drake and Sobel, *Is Anyone Out There?*, 186.

272   *There were also greetings*: "Greetings to the Universe in 55 Different Languages," NASA
Jet Propulsion Laboratory, https://voyager.jpl.nasa.gov/golden-record/whats-on-the
-record/greetings/.

272   *After thinking it over*: Drake and Sobel, *Is Anyone Out There?*, 189–90.

273   *He imagined another planet*: Ibid., 190.

273   *Aside from music sounds*: Jimmy Carter, "Voyager Spacecraft," statement, July 29, 1977,
American Presidency Project, https://www.presidency.ucsb.edu/documents/voyager
-spacecraft-statement-the-president/.

273   *Carter's opponent in 1976*: Frances Lewine, "Star Trek Fans Win on Space Shuttle,"
Lewiston (ME) *Daily Sun*, September 6, 1976, 20.

274   *At about 7:15 p.m.*: Wil S. Hylton, "The Gospel According to Jimmy," *GQ*, December 5,
2005, https://www.gq.com/story/jimmy-carter-ted-kennedy-ufo-republicans.

274   *The Lions Club*: Bob Reddick, "Lionism Changed Jimmy Carter's Life," Westport
Lions Club, April 9, 2020, https://westportlions.ca/2020/04/09/lionism-changed-jim
my-carters-life/.

274   *There, a bright light appeared*: Howell Raines, "Carter Once Saw a UFO on 'Very Sober
Occasion,'" *Atlanta Constitution*, September 14, 1973, 1D.

274   *Instead, the governor*: Ibid.

275   *Justus knew this because*: C. G. Justus, "What Was That 'UFO' Jimmy Carter Saw?,"
February 2020, 6–7, http://www.debunker.com/texts/What%20Jimmy%20Carter%20
Saw.pdf.

275   *"The rapid growth in apparent cloud size"*: Ibid., 19.

275   *This wasn't entirely rare*: Ibid., 23.

275   *"One thing's for sure"*: Bryce Zabel, "UFOs Hovered over the 1976 Election," *Trail of the
Saucers*, September 8, 2020, https://medium.com/on-the-trail-of-the-saucers/the-ufo
-factor-in-the-1976-election-d1ac7cdc1b31/.

275   *In April 1977*: Curtis Peebles, *Watch the Skies!: A Chronicle of the Flying Saucer Myth*
(Washington, DC: Smithsonian Institution Press, 1994), 204.

276   *For the first time, Hynek's grandly named center*: Mark O'Connell, *The Close Encounters
Man: How One Man Made the World Believe in UFOs* (New York: Dey St., 2017), 324–25.

277   *The movie, film critic*: Charlene Engel, "Language and the Music of the Spheres: Steven
Spielberg's *Close Encounters of the Third Kind*," *Literature/Film Quarterly* 24, no. 4 (1996):
376, https://archive.org/details/literaturefilmqu0023vari/page/380/mode/2up/.

277   *When Spielberg was asked*: Joseph Mcbride, *Steven Spielberg: A Biography* (New York:
Simon & Schuster, 1997), 17.

277   *"There are two kinds of cover-ups"*: Ibid., 348.

CHAPTER 33: SITUATION RED

278   *Then, in the final months*: Stephen Webbe, " 'Stealth' Plane: A Secret That's Been Out
Since 1976," *Christian Science Monitor*, August 25, 1980, https://www.csmonitor
.com/1980/0825/082544.html.

278 *The A-12 had a radar cross-section*: Peter Westwick, *Stealth: The Secret Contest to Invent Invisible Aircraft* (New York: Oxford University Press, 2020), 39.

279 *Once it passed into Northrop's hands*: Ibid., 44.

279 *Flight tests*: Ibid., 78.

280 *The victim was Lady*: Clark, *The UFO Encyclopedia*, "Animal Mutilations and UFOs."

280 *While they found little interesting*: Ibid.

280 *In Kansas, a 1973 wave*: Ibid.

281 *The following year*: Ibid.

281 *"Mutilated Livestock, Helicopters"*: "Are UFO Sightings and Mutilations Related? Mutilated Livestock, Helicopters and UFOs Source of Wonder, Worry," *Daily Tribune* (Hastings, NE), August 29, 1974, 8, https://vault.fbi.gov/Animal%20Mutilation /Animal%20Mutilation%20Part%201%20of%205/view#document/p4.

281 *"The problem became so widespread"*: Michael J. Goleman, "Wave of Mutilation: The Cattle Mutilation Phenomenon of the 1970s," *Agricultural History* 85, no. 3 (2011): 403.

281 *On some level, ranchers*: Lorraine Boissoneault, "How the Death of 6,000 Sheep Spurred the American Debate on Chemical Weapons," *Smithsonian*, April 9, 2018, https:// www.smithsonianmag.com/history/how-death-6000-sheep-spurred-american-de bate-chemical-weapons-cold-war-180968717/.

282 *"The federal government betrayed"*: Goleman, "Wave of Mutilation," 413.

282 *In 1979, a retired FBI agent*: Ibid., 410.

282 *"It is a rule rather than the exception"*: Clark, *The UFO Encyclopedia*, "Animal Mutilations and UFOs."

282 *A South Dakota social behavior professor*: Goleman, "Wave of Mutilation," 409.

282 *Carl Whiteside*: Grace Lichtenstein, "11 States Baffled by Mutilation of Cattle," *New York Times*, October 30, 1975, 77.

282 *Ultimately, the investigations*: Clark, *The UFO Encyclopedia*, "Animal Mutilations and UFOs"; Grace Lichtenstein, "11 States Baffled by Mutilation of Cattle," *New York Times*, October 30, 1975, 77.

283 *Unsatisfied by the first round of findings*: Harrison Schmitt, press release, July 17, 1979, FBI, https://vault.fbi.gov/Animal%20Mutilation/Animal%20Mutilation%20Part%20 5%20of%205/view#document/p16.

283 *"We didn't know what could have happened"*: Curtis Peebles, *Watch the Skies!: A Chronicle of the Flying Saucer Myth* (Washington, DC: Smithsonian Institution Press, 1994), 218.

283 *Unlike the broader UFO phenomenon*: Clark, *The UFO Encyclopedia*, "Animal Mutilations and UFOs."

283 *In the end, the Center for UFO Studies doubted*: Ibid.

284 *"Mutilation phenomenon can tell you"*: Goleman, "Wave of Mutilation," 409.

284 *"The whole point was the believers"*: Peebles, *Watch the Skies!*, 221.

285 *According to a memo written*: Charles I. Halt to RAF, "Unexplained Lights," January 13, 1981, https://upload.wikimedia.org/wikipedia/commons/thumb/b/bd/Halt_Memo randum.jpg/1024px-Halt_Memorandum.jpg.

285 *Decades later, the two lead*: Nick Pope, John Burroughs, and Jim Penniston, *Encounter in Rendlesham Forest: The Inside Story of the World's Best Documented UFO Incident* (New York: Thomas Dunne, 2014), xvi.

286 *In* Encounter in Rendlesham Forest: Ibid., 7.

CHAPTER 34: EXPLORING THE COSMOS

287 *Sagan was now*: William Poundstone, *Carl Sagan: A Life in the Cosmos* (New York: Henry Holt, 1999), 285.

288   *Sagan brushed the affront aside*: Joel Achenbach, *Captured by Aliens: The Search for Life and Truth in a Very Large Universe* (New York: Simon & Schuster, 1999), 108.

288   *Eight years later*: Poundstone, *Carl Sagan*, 264.

288   *Spielberg pledged*: Frank Drake and Dava Sobel, *Is Anyone Out There? The Scientific Search for Extraterrestrial Intelligence* (New York: Delta, 1992), 219.

288   *Sagan and MEGA's Paul Horowitz*: Poundstone, *Carl Sagan*, 350.

288   *"How fitting," Frank Drake later noted, "that some of the box office"*: Drake and Sobel, *Is Anyone Out There?*, 198.

289   *More often than not*: Martin Tolchin, "The Perplexing Mr. Proxmire," *New York Times Magazine*, May 28, 1978, 8, 56.

289   *"The overwhelming odds"*: ". . . But Proxmire Debunks Space Encounters," *Miami News*, February 15, 1978, 14A.

289   *"In my view, this project"*: "Outer Space Signals to Pass Us by," *Sioux City Journal*, August 9, 1978, A15.

289   *Drake was later surprised:* Drake and Sobel, *Is Anyone Out There?*, 193.

290   *As Drake ruefully noted, "He did what a good politician does"*: Drake and Sobel, *Is Anyone Out There?*, 196.

290   *"It is hard to imagine a more exciting"*: Ibid., 199.

291   *"There could no longer be any question"*: Ibid., 201.

291   *After his hit*: Poundstone, *Carl Sagan*, 268.

291   *In high school*: Sarah Scoles, *Making Contact: Jill Tarter and the Search for Extraterrestrial Intelligence* (New York: Pegasus Books), 37.

291   *Proctor & Gamble assumed*: Ibid., 42–43.

292   *In a three-hundred-student*: Ibid., 36–37.

292   *"You three ladies"*: Ibid., 52.

292   *"I just knew I'd found"*: Ibid., 67.

292   *Hat Creek was so remote*: Ibid., 66.

292   *Her marriage to Welch*: Ibid., 159.

293   *The team called it*: Ibid., 145.

293   *In October and November*: Ibid., 146.

294   *Classified histories*: "The Longest Search: The Story of the Twenty-One-Year Pursuit of the Soviet Deep Space Data Link, and How It Was Helped by the Search for Extraterrestrial Intelligence," National Security Administration, 1, https://nsarchive2.gwu.edu/NSAEBB/NSAEBB501/docs/EBB-49.pdf.

294   *the US lost both its Ethiopian and Turkish*: Ibid.

294   *"Before its successful career"*: James D. Burke, "The Missing Link," National Security Administration, 3, https://nsarchive2.gwu.edu/NSAEBB/NSAEBB501/docs/EBB-28.pdf.

295   *"The SETI specialists were given sanitized"*: "The Longest Search," 3.

295   *In a rush*: Scoles, *Making Contact*, 147.

295   *In his office that day*: Ibid., 148.

296   *Lovell might have been intended*: "Sir Bernard Lovell Feared 'Poisoning To Remove Memories,'" BBC, September 21, 2012: https://www.bbc.com/news/uk-england-manchester-19674135; John Hodgson, "Sir Bernard Lovell (1913-2012)," University of Manchester, September 24, 2012: https://rylandscollections.com/2012/09/24/sir-bernard-lovell-1913-2012/.

296   *Tarter, at first*: Ibid., 152.

296   *It's mission*: Ibid.

297   *"In that mirror," she thought, "we are all"*: Ibid., 25.

CHAPTER 35: THE ALONE THEORY

298   *"If intelligent life was abundant"*: Iosif Shklovsky, *Five Billion Vodka Bottles to the Moon: Tales of a Soviet Scientist*, trans. Mary Flemin Zirin and Harold Zirin (New York: W. W. Norton, 1991), 19.

299   *"Shklovsky's point was that intelligence"*: William Poundstone, *Carl Sagan: A Life in the Cosmos* (New York: Henry Holt, 1999), 320.

299   *One of Frank Drake's students*: Frank Drake and Dava Sobel, *Is Anyone Out There?: The Scientific Search for Extraterrestrial Intelligence* (New York: Delta, 1992), 205.

299   *"I feel it in my bones"*: Joel Achenbach, *Captured by Aliens: The Search for Life and Truth in a Very Large Universe* (New York: Simon & Schuster, 1999), 53.

299   *His counterargument*: Sebastian von Hoerner, "The Search for Signals from Other Civilizations," *Science* 134, no. 3493 (December 8, 1961): 1839.

300   *As Sagan argued*: Achenbach, *Captured*, 55.

300   *Stephen Hawking later*: Joseph Packer, *Alien Life and Human Purpose: A Rhetorical Examination Through History* (Lanham, MD: Lexington Books, 2015), 188.

300   *Later, when the new*: Drake and Sobel, *Is Anyone Out There?*, 207.

301   *"I must confess I'm weary"*: David W. Swift, *SETI Pioneers: Scientists Talk about Their Search for Extraterrestrial Intelligence* (Tucson: University of Arizona Press, 1990), 101.

301   *Congress, he continued*: Ibid., 107.

CHAPTER 36: VOODOO WARRIOR

302   *Reagan's pilot that night*: Jerome Clark, *UFO Encounters: Sightings, Visitations, and Investigations* (Lincolnwood, IL: Publications International, 1992), 53.

303   *As Gorbachev later recounted*: Jimmy Orr, "Reagan and Gorbachev Agreed to Fight UFOs," *Christian Science Monitor*, April 24, 2009, https://www.csmonitor.com/USA /Politics/The-Vote/2009/0424/reagan-and-gorbachev-agreed-to-fight-ufos.

304   *Later, Reagan would use*: Ronald Reagan, "Address to the 42d Session of the United Nations General Assembly" (New York, September 21, 1987), Ronal Reagan Presidential Library & Museum, https://www.reaganlibrary.gov/archives/speech/address-42d -session-united-nations-general-assembly-new-york-new-york.

305   *Knowing the ins and outs*: John B. Alexander, *UFOs: Myths, Conspiracies, and Realities* (New York: Thomas Dunne, 2011), 15.

305   *To ensure they*: Ibid., 16.

306   *"Everyone from an organization"*: Ibid., 17.

306   *"What civilian UFO researchers did not know"*: Ibid., 18.

307   *One by one*: Ibid., 27.

307   *In 1968, he'd authored a position paper for NSA leaders*: "UFO Hypothesis and Survival Questions," National Security Administration, https://web.archive.org/web /20160409041818/https://www.nsa.gov/public_info/_files/ufo/ufo_hypothesis.pdf.

308   *"Bureaucrats are just like your scientists"*: Jacques Vallée, *Forbidden Science: Journals 1957– 1969* (Berkeley, CA: North Atlantic Books, 1992), 160.

308   *"The scientific capability at LANL"*: John B. Alexander, *UFOs: Myths, Conspiracies, and Realities* (New York: Thomas Dunne, 2011), 25.

309   *They had given*: Sharon Weinberger, "Col. John Alexander Plants UFO Doubts in New Book: Exclusive Interview," *Popular Mechanics*, February 9, 2011, https://www.pop ularmechanics.com/space/a6488/colonel-john-alexander-plants-ufo-doubts-in-new -book/.

309   *"The key assumption across all agencies"*: Alexander, *UFOs*, 17.

309   *In one briefing*: Ibid., 34.

310   *"Ufology penetrated the Iron Curtain"*: Alvin Powell, "A Fact Is No Match for a Martian," Harvard Radcliffe Institute, May 20, 2021, https://www.radcliffe.harvard.edu/news -and-ideas/a-fact-is-no-match-for-a-martian.

310   *Speaking on Soviet*: Timothy Good, *Above Top Secret: The Worldwide UFO Cover-Up* (New York: William Morrow, 1988), 233.

310   *To his core*: Ibid., 240.

311   *Then, in 1977*: Ibid., 247.

311   *The incident made national headlines*: Ibid., 237.

311   *As it was, the Soviet Union even had its own*: Joseph Kellner, "The End of History: Radical Responses to the Soviet Collapse" (PhD diss., University of California, Berkeley, 2018), 135, https://escholarship.org/content/qt148662nt/qt148662nt_noSplash _c2c303c1364d5af8804cb6a13be4c38a.pdf.

311   *"If a scientist is faced with something"*: Matthew Bodner, "Little Green Men: A Look at the Official Soviet X-Files Investigation," *Moscow Times*, March 31, 2016, https://www .themoscowtimes.com/2016/03/31/little-green-men-a-look-at-the-official-soviet -x-files-investigation-a52335.

312   *As The Moscow Times wrote later*: Ibid.

CHAPTER 37: MJ-12

313   *When Shandera opened the thick package, closed with brown tape*: Howard Blum, *Out There: The Government's Secret Quest for Extraterrestrials* (New York: Simon & Schuster, 1990), 240–41.

313   *Upon closer examination*: "Briefing Document: Operation Majestic 12," November 18, 1952, in Timothy Good, *Above Top Secret: The Worldwide UFO Cover-Up* (New York: William Morrow, 1988), 548–51.

314   *One thing leaning them toward*: "Request for Photo Imagery Interpretation Your Msg 292030Z Oct. 80," November 1980, in Good, *Above Top Secret*, 528.

315   *Dated July 14, 1954*: Howard Blum, *Out There: The Government's Secret Quest for Extraterrestrials* (New York: Simon & Schuster, 1990), 259.

315   *"After more than a year of inquiries"*: Ibid., 263–64.

316   *"We've gone knocking"*: Ibid., 266–67.

316   *The briefing paper*: "Briefing Document: Operation Majestic 12," 547.

316   *Today, the National Archives even*: "Majestic 12 or 'MJ-12' Reference Report," National Archives, https://www.archives.gov/research/military/air-force/ufos#mj12.

316   *In the end, the most damning piece of evidence*: Blum, *Out There*, 252–53.

CHAPTER 38: CROP CIRCLES

318   *Strange patterns*: Rob Irving and Peter Brookesmith, "Crop Circles: The Art of the Hoax," *Smithsonian*, December 15, 2009, https://www.smithsonianmag.com/arts-cul ture/crop-circles-the-art-of-the-hoax-2524283/.

318   *Tourists and enthusiasts*: Ibid.; Matt Ridley, "Crop Circle Confession," *Scientific American* 287, no. 2 (2002): 25.

318   *"I could feel the energy"*: Soo Youn, "Inside the Mystical World of Crop Circle Tourism," *National Geographic*, October 19, 2018, https://www.nationalgeographic.com/travel /article/pictures-crop-circles-tourism-wiltshire-england.

319   *Some started to believe*: Irving and Brookesmith, "Crop Circles."

319   *He proclaimed the circle*: William Touhy, " 'Crop Circles' Their Prank, 2 Britons Say," *Los*

Angeles Times, September 10, 1991, https://www.latimes.com/archives/la-xpm-1991 -09-10-mn-2463-story.html.

319 *As one Whiltshire*: Daniel Stables, "England's Crop Circle Controversy," BBC, August 23, 2021, https://www.bbc.com/travel/article/20210822-englands-crop-circle -controversy.

320 *The site advertised itself as "the world's first international news organization"*: Michael Corbin, "Welcome to ParaNet," email, https://www.abovetopsecret.com/forum /thread992225/pg1.

320 *"The United States government has been in business"*: John Lear, statement, December 29, 1987, https://cdn.preterhuman.net/texts/alien.ufo/UFOBBS/1000/1953.ufo.

322 *Soon after, while riding his motorcycle*: Mark Jacobson, *Pale Horse Rider: William Cooper, the Rise of Conspiracy, and the Fall of Trust in America* (New York: Blue Rider Press, 2018), ch. 5, EPUB.

322 *"There was no doubt as to what we had seen"*: Ibid., ch. 7.

323 *"Without the aliens, you can't"*: Ibid.

323 *The fact that Cooper*: Curtis Peebles, *Watch the Skies!: A Chronicle of the Flying Saucer Myth* (Washington, DC: Smithsonian Institution Press, 1994), 274–75.

323 *There had been some sixteen UFO crashes*: Ibid.

323 *Even though corners*: Ibid., 278.

324 *"Oh stop it"*: Jacobson, *Pale Horse Rider*, ch. 7.

324 *That speech, Cooper*: Ibid., ch. 8.

324 *His whistleblowing partner*: Ibid.

324 *"[Cooper and Lear] were the tip"*: Colin Dickey, "A Pioneer of Paranoia," *New Republic*, August 28, 2018, https://newrepublic.com/article/150922/pioneer-paranoia.

324 *He became a fixture*: Jacobson, *Pale Horse Rider*, ch. 8.

325 *In the years ahead*: Ibid., ch. 19.

CHAPTER 39: THE BELGIAN WAVE

326 *"Suddenly, they told me they were seeing"*: Jeva Lange, "30 Years Later, We Still Don't Know What Really Happened During the Belgian UFO Wave," *Week*, March 30, 2020, https://theweek.com/articles/905215/30-years-later-still-dont-know-what-really -happened-during-belgian-ufo-wave.

326 *"I forwarded the question"*: Leslie Kean, *UFOs: Generals, Pilots, and Government Officials Go on the Record* (New York: Harmony, 2010), 36.

326 *For more than an hour*: Ibid., 37.

327 *Later analysis showed*: Ibid., 38.

327 *"No priority was given"*: Ibid., 37.

327 *"There must have been air activities"*: Ibid., 35.

327 *"The UFO of Petit-Rechain"*: Robert Sheaffer, "'Classic' UFO Photo from Belgian Wave—the Hoaxer Confesses," July 26, 2011, https://badufos.blogspot.com/2011/07 /classic-ufo-photo-from-belgian-wave.html.

CHAPTER 40: INTERRUPTED JOURNEY

328 *As best as anyone could determine*: Robert Sheaffer, "'Classic' UFO Photo from Belgian Wave—the Hoaxer Confesses," July 26, 2011, https://badufos.blogspot.com/2011/07 /classic-ufo-photo-from-belgian-wave.html. "Villas-Boas CE3"; David M. Jacobs, *Secret Life: Firsthand Accounts of UFO Abductions* (New York: Simon & Schuster, 1992), 39.

329   *The* New York Times: Ralph Blumenthal, *The Believer: Alien Encounters, Hard Science, and the Passion of John Mack* (Albuquerque, NM: High Road, 2021), 92.

329   *In fact, his life*: Ibid.

329   *In 1981, he published*: Budd Hopkins, *Missing Time: A Documented Study of UFO Abductions* (New York: Richard Marek, 1981), 217.

330   *Hopkins's book had kicked*: Blumenthal, *The Believer*, 91.

330   *He'd found Fuller's*: Jacobs, *Secret Life*, 20.

330   *"Why, if they were extraterrestrial"*: Ibid., 21.

330   *"Researchers writ large*: Ibid., 43.

330   *"After all, people have always claimed"*: Ibid., 22–23.

331   *"They all told the same stories"*: Ibid., 24.

331   *"From the first few seconds of an abduction"*: Ibid., 29.

331   *"At one point, he said the image"*: Will Bueché, "Ted Seth Jacobs: An Interview with the Artist," Beyond Communion, October 6, 1999, http://www.beyondcommunion.com /communion/9910tsjacobs.html.

332   *The book, which the author*: Whitley Strieber, *Communion* (New York: William Morrow, 1987), 15.

332   *"Evident in Mack's prodigious research"*: Blumenthal, *The Believer*, 37.

333   *As his longtime friend*: Ibid., 76.

333   *"A human black hole"*: Ibid., 68.

333   *Mack was a somewhat*: Ibid., 39.

333   *After Danny and his father*: Ibid., 72.

334   *Mack, now opened up*: Ibid., 87.

334   *He also began to experiment*: Ibid., 100.

334   *On January 10, 1990*: Ibid., 91.

334   *The meeting*: Ibid., 98.

334   *"I like to be able to explain things"*: Ibid., 103.

335   *"Lester," he told Grinspoon*: William Poundstone, *Carl Sagan: A Life in the Cosmos* (New York: Henry Holt, 1999), 360. This story is related similarly, with minor differences, in Blumenthal, *Believer*, pp. 100-102.

335   *"In no case so far have I found"*: Ibid., 116.

335   *Collectively, Mack argued*: Ibid., 107.

336   *As Mack's biographer*: Blumenthal, *The Believer*, 121.

336   *In February, he presented*: Ibid., 119.

336   *"I want to go forward with what I believe"*: Ibid., 121.

336   *"Clearly an abduction!"*: Blumenthal, *The Believer*, 131.

337   *When, toward the end*: Ibid., 139.

CHAPTER 41: SEX WITH ALIENS

338   *David Jacobs*: David M. Jacobs, *Secret Life: Firsthand Accounts of UFO Abductions* (New York: Simon & Schuster, 1992), 28.

338   *Over dozens of pages*: Ibid., 256.

339   *Jacobs understood that some*: Ibid., 285.

339   *Nor did it seem*: Ibid., 287–88.

339   *"The more I learned about the abduction phenomenon"*: Ibid., 317.

339   *As Mack's biographer summarized*: Ralph Blumenthal, *The Believer: Alien Encounters, Hard Science, and the Passion of John Mack* (Albuquerque: High Road, 2021), 147.

340   *"I'll never do anything like that again"*: Ibid., 150.

340   *As the conference ended*: Ibid.

340   *In 1994, a profile*: Stephen Rae, "John Mack," *New York Times Magazine*, March 20, 1994, 30.

340   *An article in* Psychological Inquiry: Leonard S. Newman and Roy F. Baumeister, "Toward an Explanation of the UFO Abduction Phenomenon: Hypnotic Elaboration, Extraterrestrial Sadomasochism, and Spurious Memories," *Psychological Inquiry* 7, no. 2 (1996): 122.

341   *They saw a possible conclusion*: Ibid., 100.

341   *As he said*: Ibid., 182.

341   *When another reporter later*: Blumenthal, *The Believer*, 166.

341   *He remained confused by*: Ibid., 196.

342   *How did one account*: Jacques Vallée, *Dimensions: A Casebook of Alien Contact* (San Antonio, TX: Anomalist, 2008), 163.

342   *And how did one account*: Ibid., 179.

342   *"In antiquity their occupants"*: Ibid.

342   *"The concept current"*: Ibid., 178–79.

342   *Alien abductions*: James Gleick, "The Doctor's Plot," *New Republic*, May 30, 1994, 31–32.

343   *Meanwhile, warning signs*: Rae, "John Mack."; Blumenthal, *The Believer*, 192.

343   *It cautioned him*: Ibid., 224.

344   *In the paperback*: John E. Mack, *Abduction: Human Encounters with Aliens* (New York: Ballantine, 1994), ix.

344   *Asked whether Harvard*: Mary Roach, "Probed in Space," *Salon*, July 30, 1999, https://www.salon.com/1999/07/30/abductions/.

344   *He wrote about how*: John E. Mack, *Passport to the Cosmos: Human Transformation and Alien Encounters* (Largo, FL: Kunati, 2008), xi.

344   *"I do not consider that abduction reports"*: Ibid., 30–31.

344   *"Rather, I am more concerned"*: Ibid., xi–xii.

344   *"One cannot begin to consider"*: Ibid., xii.

345   *"What I have been finding has been"*: Ibid., 8.

345   *At his memorial service*: Blumenthal, *The Believer*, 274.

CHAPTER 42: ROSWELL REVISITED

346   *As what you might*: Karl T. Pflock, *Roswell: Inconvenient Facts and the Will to Believe* (Amherst, NY: Prometheus, 2001), 14.

346   *As "pro-UFO" "ufologist"*: Ibid., 19.

346   *"Like all good stories, Roswell"*: Frank Kuznik, "Aliens in the Basement," *Air & Space*, August/September 1992, 34–39.

347   *The change and attention*: William Claiborne, "GAO Turns to Alien Turf in Probe," *Washington Post*, January 14, 1994, A21.

347   *As he referred*: Steve Brewer, "Letters Lead to UFO Inquiry," *Albuquerque Journal*, January 14, 1994, 3D.

347   *As one example of the report's*: Richard L. Weaver and James McAndrew, *The Roswell Report: Fact Versus Fiction in the New Mexico Desert*, United States Air Force, 1995, 14, https://books.google.com/books?id=2Kp4oWwUKwwC.

347   *A multipage summary*: Ibid., 16.

348   *Instead, the air force swiftly*: Ibid., 15–16.

348   *It also produced*: Ibid., 21.

348   *"Determining whether the Soviets were testing"*: Ibid.

349   *It was considered such a critical program*: Pflock, *Roswell*, 146.

349   *While it was hard*: Ibid., 147.

350 *When it took off:* Ibid., 158.

350 *It was probably:* Weaver and McAndrew, *The Roswell Report*, 3.

350 *The air force report:* Ibid., 8.

350 *"It was kind of a standing joke":* Albert C. Trakowski, statement, June 29, 1994, in Weaver and McAndrew, *The Roswell Report*.

351 *"It seems that there was overreaction":* Weaver and McAndrew, *The Roswell Report*, 30.

351 *"Pro-UFO groups will strongly object":* Ibid., 5.

351 *"It's a bunch of pap":* William J. Broad, "Wreckage in the Desert Was Odd but Not Alien," *New York Times*, September 18, 1994, 40.

351 *Almost exactly a year later:* "Combined History 509th Bomb Group and Roswell Army Air Field: 1 July 1947 through 31 July 1947," 39, in Weaver and McAndrew, *The Roswell Report: Results of a Search for Records Concerning the 1947 Crash Near Roswell, New Mexico*, United States General Accounting Office, July 28, 1995, 5, 7, https://media.defense.gov/2021/Jul/13/2002761373/-1/-1/0/GENERAL_ACCOUNTING_OFFICE_S_SCHIFF.PDF.

352 *As he told one interviewer:* Philip J. Klass, "The GAO Roswell Report and Congressman Schiff," *Skeptical Inquirer*, November/December 1995, 21, https://cdn.centerforinquiry.org/wp-content/uploads/sites/29/1995/11/22165051/p22.pdf.

353 *In the end:* Ibid., 22.

353 *It was a clip:* Richard Corliss, "Autopsy or Fraud-Topsy?," *Time*, November 27, 1995, https://content.time.com/time/subscriber/article/0,33009,983764,00.html.

353 *All told, only about:* C. Eugene Emery, Jr., " 'Alien Autopsy' Show-and-Tell: Long on Tell, Short on Show," *Skeptical Inquirer*, November/December 1995, 15, https://cdn.centerforinquiry.org/wp-content/uploads/sites/29/1995/11/22165051/p17.pdf.

353 *"The details are still intriguing":* Ibid.

354 *"The fact is, an autopsy":* Ibid., 16.

354 *In an episode that aired late:* Jake Rossen, "E.T. or B.S.? When Fox Aired Its Infamous 'Alien Autopsy' in 1995," *Mental Floss*, October 6, 2022, https://www.mentalfloss.com/posts/fox-1995-alien-autopsy-hoax.

355 *As the* Tucson Weekly: Jim Nintzel, "Crash Fest," Tucson Weekly, July 10, 1997, https://www.tucsonweekly.com/tw/07-10-97/curr1.htm.

355 *"I know we're no longer the only ones":* Joel Achenbach, *Captured by Aliens: The Search for Life and Truth in a Very Large Universe* (New York: Simon & Schuster, 1999), 229.

356 *Our ancient forebears:* Ibid., 224.

356 *This time, the Pentagon:* James McAndrew, *The Roswell Report: Case Closed*, United States Air Force, 1997, 1, https://www.esd.whs.mil/Portals/54/Documents/FOID/Reading%20Room/UFOsandUAPs/RoswellReportCaseClosed.pdf.

356 *There had also been a series:* Ibid., 23.

357 *At the time, dummy-recovery:* Ibid., 30.

357 *It was entirely possible:* Ibid., 33.

357 *Altogether, the historical record:* Pflock, *Roswell*, 185.

358 *As Karl Pflock:* Ibid., 17, 185.

358 *They include such testimonies:* Ibid., 187.

358 *Six months later:* Ibid.

358 *Later, secret CIA:* Ibid., 190.

358 *As the UFO prankster James Moseley:* James W. Moseley and Karl T. Pflock, *Shockingly Close to the Truth!: Confessions of a Grave-Robbing Ufologist* (Amherst, NY: Prometheus, 2002), 318.

CHAPTER 43: "WHO KILLED JFK?"

359   *When Webb*: Web Hubbell, *Friends in High Places: Our Journey from Little Rock to Washington, D.C.* (New York: William Morrow, 1997), 282.

359   *Responding to a question: Public Papers of the Presidents of the United States: William J. Clinton*, Book II, Government Publishing Office, November 30, 1995, 1815, https://www.govinfo.gov/content/pkg/PPP-1995-book2/html/PPP-1995-book2-doc-pg1813-2.htm.

360   *A briefing memo from Jack Gibbons*: John Gibbons to William J. Clinton, "Inquiry from Laurance Rockefeller," August 4, 1995, http://www.paradigmresearchgroup.org/Rockefeller%20Documents/RID-8-4-95.htm.

360   *Rockefeller had been funding*: Laurance S. Rockefeller to William J. Clinton, "Lifting Secrecy on Information about Extraterrestrial Intelligence as Part of the Current Classification Review," attached in Henry L. Diamond to John Gibbons, November 1, 1995, http://www.paradigmresearchgroup.org/Rockefeller%20Documents/RID-11-1-95.htm#1.

360   *In 1995, Hillary was photographed walking*: Robin Seemangal, "Extraterrestrial Lobbyist Explains Hillary Clinton's Controversial UFO Statements," January 16, 2016, https://observer.com/2016/01/extraterrestrial-lobbyist-explains-hillary-clintons-controversial-ufo-statements/.

360   *Despite Hillary Clinton's*: "Hillary Clinton Adopts Alien Baby," *Weekly World News*, June 15, 1993, 1.

360   *For much of the previous decade*: Sarah Scoles, *Making Contact: Jill Tarter and the Search for Extraterrestrial Intelligence* (New York: Pegasus Books), 164.

361   *Her efforts had helped*: Ibid., 166.

361   *A decade of bruising*: William J. Broad, "Hunt for Aliens in Space: The Next Generation," *New York Times*, February 6, 1990, C12.

361   *In the end, the institute*: Jacob V. Lamar, Jr., "Jake Skywalker: A Senator Boards the Shuttle," *Time*, April 22, 1985, https://content.time.com/time/subscriber/article/0,33009,966871,00.html.

361   *While the shuttle trip*: John Hollenhorst, "Former Senator Garn Memorialized with 'Garn Scale,'" KSL, December 19, 2005, https://www.ksl.com/article/141307/former-senator-garn-memorialized-with-garn-scale.

361   *"The law of large numbers ought to indicate"*: Lee Davidson, " 'E.T.' Garn Trying to Save Program That Seeks Aliens," *Deseret News* (Salt Lake City, UT), June 8, 1990, https://www.deseret.com/1990/6/8/18865595/e-t-garn-trying-to-save-program-that-seeks-aliens.

361   *Garn's patronage helped*: Broad, "Hunt for Aliens," C12.

362   *"This is the big step"*: Ibid., C1.

362   *"You can theorize forever"*: Ibid., C12.

362   *"We sail into the future, just as Columbus did"*: John Noble Wilford, "Astronomers Start Search for Life Beyond Earth," *New York Times*, October 13, 1992, C1.

362   *The SETI program*: Scoles, *Making Contact*, 174.

362   *Moreover, as one NASA*: Stephen J. Garber, "Searching for Good Science: The Cancellation of NASA's SETI Program," *Journal of the British Interplanetary Society* 52 (1999): 9, https://history.nasa.gov/garber.pdf.

362   *There was also what NASA*: Ibid., 5.

363   *"Not a single Martian"*: Scoles, *Making Contact*, 180–81.

363   *Bryan spent two terms*: "Richard Bryan," Wikipedia, accessed May 16, 2023, https://en.wikipedia.org/wiki/Richard_Bryan.

363   *The team, including CEO*: Seth Shostak, *Confessions of an Alien Hunter* (Washington, DC: National Geographic, 2009), 155–57.

363   *"This number has been disconnected"*: "This Number Has Been Disconnected," *New York Times Magazine*, November 14, 1993, 25.

363   *Once again, SETI*: Scoles, *Making Contact*, 188.

363   *Barney Oliver was livid*: Bernard M. Oliver, "Congress Spurns Unique Silicon Valley Jewel," *Signals* 9, no. 10 (November 1993), http://www.naapo.org/NAAPO-News /Vol09/v09n10.htm.

364   *In December 1993, astronauts aboard*: William Harwood, "How NASA Fixed Hubble's Flawed Vision—and Reputation," *CBS News*, April 22, 2015, https://www.cbsnews .com/news/an-ingenius-fix-for-hubbles-famously-flawed-vision/.

364   *"The human life is more than survival"*: Joel Achenbach, *Captured by Aliens: The Search for Life and Truth in a Very Large Universe* (New York: Simon & Schuster, 1999), 25.

364   *"There was not a hint of life"*: William Poundstone, *Carl Sagan: A Life in the Cosmos* (New York: Henry Holt, 1999), 205.

364   *What has once been hailed*: Gilbert V. Levin, "The Curiousness of Curiosity," *Astrobiology* 15, no. 2 (2015): 101.

365   *"That's the ball game"*: Poundstone, *Carl Sagan*, 219.

365   *As SETI scientist*: Shostak, *Confessions*, 39.

365   *Resilient Martian life*: Ibid., 41.

365   *The planet, he understood*: Sarah Stewart Johnson, *The Sirens of Mars: Searching for Life on Another World* (New York: Crown, 2021), 168.

365   *Perhaps if scientists looked*: Achenbach, *Captured*, 27.

CHAPTER 44: THE MARS ROCK

366   *The bacteria of Yellowstone*: Seth Shostak, *Confessions of an Alien Hunter* (Washington, DC: National Geographic, 2009), 79.

366   *Scientists were finding*: Keith Cooper, *The Contact Paradox: Challenging Our Assumptions in the Search for Extraterrestrial Intelligence* (Dublin: Bloomsbury, 2021), 133.

366   *In the 1990s, the field originally known as "exobiology"*: Ibid., 28.

367   *As Tufts University*: Joel Achenbach, *Captured by Aliens: The Search for Life and Truth in a Very Large Universe* (New York: Simon & Schuster, 1999), 304.

367   *The duo kept the potential*: Ibid., 133.

368   *He'd written hundreds*: Mimi Swartz, "It Came from Outer Space," *Texas Monthly*, November 1996, https://www.texasmonthly.com/news-politics/it-came-from-outer -space/.

368   *"We do not want you to tell anybody"*: Achenbach, *Captured*, 133.

368   *Thomas-Keprta went*: Swartz, "It Came from Outer Space."

368   *"This could be the coolest day"*: Ibid.

368   *Their final sentence*: David S. McKay et al., "Search for Past Life on Mars: Possible Relic Biogenic Activity in Martian Meteorite ALH84001," *Science* 273, no. 5277 (August 16, 1998): 929.

368   *"There were an infinite number of ways"*: Achenbach, *Captured*, 134.

368   *The thirty-minute meeting*: Swartz, "It Came from Outer Space."

369   *"We have it nailed"*: Achenbach, *Captured*, 134.

369   *Goldin paused to take that in*: Swartz, "It Came from Outer Space."

369   *President Clinton grilled*: Achenbach, *Captured*, 135.

369   *Vice President Al Gore*: Swartz, "It Came from Outer Space."

369   *"Today, rock 84001 speaks to us"*: William J. Clinton, "Statement Regarding Mars Meteorite Discovery" (Washington, DC, August 7, 1996), NASA, https://www2.jpl.nasa .gov/snc/clinton.html/.

370   *Goldin proclaimed it*: David L. Chandler, "Online Document: Clinton Calls for

Intensified Search for Life on Mars," *Deseret News* (Salt Lake City, UT), August 8, 1996, https://www.deseret.com/1996/8/8/19259540/online-document-clinton-calls -for-intensified-search-for-life-on-mars.

370 *"This was undoubtedly the most exciting thing"*: Ibid.

370 *"I'm certain we will find life elsewhere"*: Achenbach, *Captured*, 137.

370 *One science peer*: William Poundstone, *Carl Sagan: A Life in the Cosmos* (New York: Henry Holt, 1999), 379.

370 *Clinton called for an*: Blaine Friedlander, "CU Scientists Laud Research on Mars Rock," *Cornell Chronicle* (Ithaca, NY), August 15, 1996, https://news.cornell.edu/sto ries/1996/08/cu-scientists-laud-research-mars-rock; Cynthia Hanson, Yvonne Zipp, and Sally Steindorf, "News in Brief," *Christian Science Monitor*, August 9, 1996, https:// www.csmonitor.com/1996/0809/080996.news.news.1.html.

371 *A years-long battle*: Poundstone, *Carl Sagan*, 381.

371 *By the time Clinton's*: Sarah Stewart Johnson, *The Sirens of Mars: Searching for Life on Another World* (New York: Crown, 2021), 85.

371 *In his final days*: *Cosmos*, episode 12, "Encyclopaedia Galactica," directed by Adrian Malone, Geoffrey Haines-Stiles, and Rob McCain, written by Carl Sagan, Ann Druyan, and Steven Soter, aired December 14, 1980, on PBS.; Poundstone, *Carl Sagan*, 379.

371 *As part of the service*: "Voyager 1's Pale Blue Dot," NASA, February 13, 2020, https:// solarsystem.nasa.gov/resources/536/voyager-1s-pale-blue-dot/.

371 *"That's here. That's home"*: Achenbach, *Captured*, 369.

CHAPTER 45: THE PHOENIX LIGHTS

373 *"Damn politicians"*: Sarah Scoles, *Making Contact: Jill Tarter and the Search for Extra-terrestrial* Intelligence (New York: Pegasus Books), 185.

373 *"In retrospect, this early, easy success"*: Seth Shostak, *Confessions of an Alien Hunter* (Washington, DC: National Geographic, 2009), 178.

374 *To outfit their quarters*: Scoles, *Making Contact*, 192, 193.

374 *To Tarter's annoyance*: Ibid., 193.

374 *"We could pick from only two"*: Ibid., 13.

375 *Finally, the team tried*: Ibid., 14.

375 *The issue resolved itself*: Ibid., 17–18.

376 *As Shostak recounted*: Ibid., 18.

376 Heck, *Shostak thought*: Ibid., 16.

377 *As Joel Achenback wrote*: Joel Achenbach, *Captured by Aliens: The Search for Life and Truth in a Very Large Universe* (New York: Simon & Schuster, 1999), 285.

377 *Witness reports varied*: Leslie Kean, *UFOs: Generals, Pilots, and Government Officials Go on the Record* (New York: Harmony, 2010), 248.

377 *"We're going to get to the bottom"*: Ibid., 249.

377 *"This just goes to show that you guys"*: Ibid.

378 *It wouldn't be until*: Ibid., 254.

378 *"I witnessed something that defied logic"*: Ibid., 262.

379 *"If I had to do it all over again"*: Ibid., 256.

379 *As the comet Hale-Bopp*: Diedtra Henderson, "Internet Rife with Chatter of Comet's 'Companion'—Debate Raged on Whether Saturn-Like Object Is a Star or UFO," *Seattle Times*, May 27, 1997, https://archive.seattletimes.com/archive/?date=199703 27&slug=2530904.

379 *"Hale-Bopp brings closure"*: "Hale-Bopp Brings Closure to Heaven's Gate," captured February 19, 1999, Internet Archive, https://web.archive.org/web/19990219190134 /http://www.sunspot.net/news/special/heavensgatesite/2index.shtml.

CHAPTER 46: COMETA

383   *"Without a doubt, the phenomenon remains"*: UFOs and Defense: What Should We Pre-pare For?, COMETA, 1999, 7, https://ia800403.us.archive.org/17/items/pdfy-NRI Qie2ooVehep7K/The%20Cometa%20Report%20%5BUFO%27s%20And%20De fense%20-%20What%20Should%20We%20Prepare%20For%5D.pdf.

383   *Over the course of its research*: Ibid., 34.

383   *In fact*: Ibid., 56–57.

384   *Similarly, they added*: Ibid., 7.

384   *A native of New York*: Gideon Lewis-Kraus, "How the Pentagon Started Taking U.F.O.s Seriously," *New Yorker*, May 10, 2021, https://www.newyorker.com/maga zine/2021/05/10/how-the-pentagon-started-taking-ufos-seriously.

385   *"The UFO story was journalistically elusive"*: Ibid., 4.

386   *"There's stuff out there that is strange"*: Mary Manning, "At Last, a Glimpse of Area 51," *Las Vegas Sun*, April 18, 2000, https://lasvegassun.com/news/2000/apr/18/at-last-a -glimpse-of-area-51/.

386   *Robert Bigelow had spent nearly his entire life*: Adam Higginbotham, "Robert Bigelow Plans a Real Estate Empire in Space, *Bloomberg Businessweek*, May 2, 2013, https:// www.bloomberg.com/news/articles/2013-05-02/robert-bigelow-plans-a-real-estate -empire-in-space.

386   *"It's as suite as it gets!"*: Ibid.

387   *A 2000 PowerPoint*: Colm A. Kelleher, "What Is NIDS?," July 15, 2000, 4, https://web .archive.org/web/20071012102520/http://www.nidsci.org/pdf/mufon2000.pdf.

387   *Headquartered in a two-story building*: Ibid., 8, 11.

387   *"The Holy Grail in the UFO field"*: Brandon M. Mercer, "The UFO Hunters—Scientists at National Institute for Discovery Science Study Anomalous Phenomena," *TechTV*, January 16, 2003, https://web.archive.org/web/20030124024516/http://www.techtv .com/news/culture/story/0%2C24195%2C3414589%2C00.html.

387   *"We wouldn't be there just for the weather"*: Zack Van Eyck, "Private UFO Study Takes a Public Turn," *Deseret News* (Salt Lake City, UT), August 10, 1998, https://www .deseret.com/1998/8/10/19395824/private-ufo-study-takes-a-public-turn.

387   *The property, which came*: James T. Lacatski, Colm A. Kelleher, and George Knapp, *Skinwalkers at the Pentagon: An Insiders'* [sic] *Account of the Secret Government UFO Program* (self-published, 2021), xxvi.

388   *"We call this the jacks experiment"*: Higginbotham, "Robert Bigelow Plans."

388   *Outside of Utah, Bigelow continued to invest millions*: Ibid.

388   *One of the phenomena*: Leonard David, " 'Flying Triangle' Sightings on the Rise," *NBC News*, September 2, 2004, https://www.nbcnews.com/id/wbna5897539.

388   *As Kelleher told*: Ibid.

388   *As he said later*: Geoffrey Little, "Mr. B's Big Plan," *Air & Space*, January 2008, https:// www.smithsonianmag.com/air-space-magazine/mr-bs-big-plan-23798796/.

CHAPTER 47: SKINWALKER RANCH

390   *He was hoping*: James T. Lacatski, Colm A. Kelleher, and George Knapp, *Skinwalkers at the Pentagon: An Insiders'* [sic] *Account of the Secret Government UFO Program* (self-published, 2021), 17.

390   *According to him*: Ibid., 39.

390   *The US senator*: Ibid., 14.

391   *In an age before*: Ibid., 13.

391   *In August 1996*: Brandon M. Mercer, "The UFO Hunters—Scientists at National

Institute for Discovery Science Study Anomalous Phenomena," *TechTV*, January 16, 2003, https://web.archive.org/web/20030124024516/http://www.techtv.com/news /culture/story/0%2C24195%2C3414589%2C00.html.

391   *"I'm terribly interested in this"*: Lacatski, Kelleher, and Knapp, *Skinwalkers*, xv.

391   *As they sat down:* Ibid.

392   *"I've been waiting to do this"*: Helene Cooper, Ralph Blumenthal, and Leslie Kean, "Glowing Auras and 'Black Money': The Pentagon's Mysterious U.F.O. Program," *New York Times*, December 16, 2017, https://www.nytimes.com/2017/12/16/us/politics /pentagon-program-ufo-harry-reid.html.

392   *A mock-up of the supposed car-sized acorn UFO*: David Templeton, "The Kecksburg Files," *Pittsburgh Post-Gazette*, September 9, 1998, https://old.post-gazette.com/mag azine/19980908ufo1.asp.

392   *To assist in her efforts*: Lloyd Grove, "John Podesta: Clinton's Mr. Fix-It," *Washington Post*, September 30, 1998, https://www.washingtonpost.com/wp-srv/politics/special /clinton/stories/podesta093098.htm.

392   *When he was promoted*: Doris O. Matsui to John Podesta, email, October 20, 1998, https://pbs.twimg.com/media/Fs8JLelXwAA9uhh?format=jpg&name=medium.

393   *"I think it's time to open the books"*: John Podesta, "Remarks at a Press Conference Sponsored by the SciFi Channel" (Washington, DC, October 22, 2002), https://www.para digmresearchgroup.org/Podesta_2002_Statement.htm.

393   *The support was meaningful*: Leonard David, "Is Case Finally Closed on 1965 Pennsylvania 'UFO Mystery'?," *Space.com*, November 249, 2009, https://www.space.com/7589 -case-finally-closed-1965-pennsylvania-ufo-mystery.html.

393   *"There was nothing that provided any clarity"*: Gideon Lewis-Kraus, "How the Pentagon Started Taking U.F.O.s Seriously," *New Yorker*, May 10, 2021, https://www.newyorker .com/magazine/2021/05/10/how-the-pentagon-started-taking-ufos-seriously.

394   *The sighting leaked*: "O'Hare Workers Say They Saw a UFO," *Chicago Tribune*, January 2, 2007, https://www.chicagotribune.com/news/ct-xpm-2007-01-02-0701020212-story .html.

394   *"Do you see anything above United concourse?"*: Richard F. Haines et al., *Report of an Unidentified Aerial Phenomenon and Its Safety Implications at O'Hare International Airport on November 7, 2006*, National Aviation Reporting Center on Anomalous Phenomena, May 14, 2007, 12, https://static1.squarespace.com/static/5cf80ff422b5a90001351e31/t /5d02ec731230e20001528e2c/1560472703346/NARCAP_TR-10.pdf.

394   *"I haven't seen anything"*: Ibid., 29.

394   *The incident was ultimately*: David Bates, "The O'Hare Field UFO Remains a Great Case," *Trail of the Saucers*, September 17, 2021, https://medium.com/on-the-trail-of -the-saucers/why-skeptical-inquirers-debunking-of-the-o-hare-field-ufo-is-ridicu lous-428d4ee077ad.

394   *"The FAA treats the smallest safety issue"*: Leslie Kean, *UFOs: Generals, Pilots, and Government Officials Go on the Record* (New York: Harmony, 2010), 69.

394   *As she'd later write*: Ibid., 72.

394   *In March 2007*: "GEIPAN UAP Investigation Unit Opens Its Files," Centre National D'Études Spatiales, March 26, 2007, https://cnes.fr/en/web/CNES-en/5866-geipan -uap-investigation-unit-opens-its-files.php.

395   *"I believe that our government should take"*: "Pilots to Tell Their UFO Stories for the First Time," press release, November 7, 2007, https://www.prweb.com/releases/un identified_flying/object_ufo_event/prweb567548.htm.

395   *The experiences, which ranged*: Lewis-Kraus, "How the Pentagon."

395   *Some of Kean's*: Ibid., 22.

396   *In the main text*: Kean, *UFOs*, 13.

396   *In the book's forward*: Ibid., xii.
396   *As a* New Yorker *profile*: Lewis-Kraus, "How the Pentagon."

CHAPTER 48: STARCHIPS

397   *Philip Morrison*: Ronald D. Ekers et al., eds., *SETI 2020: A Roadmap for the Search for Extraterrestrial Intelligence* (Mountain View, CA: SETI Press, 2002), xxix.
397   *Jill Tarter, too, marveled*: Ibid., xxxv.
397   *In 1980, it had required about a million dollars*: Ibid., xlii–xliii.
398   *"At the conference, the attendees' main conclusion"*: Benjamin Svetkey, "Making *Contact*: The Story Behind the Controversial Space Odyssey," *Entertainment Weekly*, July 18, 1997, https://ew.com/article/1997/07/18/making-contact/, 71.
398   *It was, as Tarter*: Tarter, "Join the SETI Search," TED Talks, 2009, https://www.ted.com/talks/jill_tarter_join_the_seti_search
398   *"A concerted attempt should be made"*: Ekers, *SETI 2020*, xlvii.
399   *"At least we're not wasting your money"*: Scoles, *Making Contact*, 74.
399   *SETI agreed, but struggled*: Ibid., 76.
400   *The closure idled*: Michael D. Lemonick, "ET, Call Us—Just Not Collect," *Time*, April 28, 2011, https://content.time.com/time/health/article/0,8599,2067855,00.html.
400   *Eventually, the SETI Institute*: Scoles, *Making Contact*, 80–81.
400   *"All of the concerted SETI efforts"*: Tarter, "Join the SETI Search."
400   *"Each of these short observations"*: Seth Shostak, *Confessions of an Alien Hunter* (Washington, DC: National Geographic, 2009), 13.
401   *As Tarter's biographer*: Scoles, *Making Contact*, 90.
402   *"In many ways, a public announcement"*: "The Rio Scale," International Academy of Astronautics, 1, https://iaaspace.org/wp-content/uploads/iaa/Scientific%20Activity/setirio.pdf.
402   *"It's absolutely crucial"*: Meghan Bartels, "To Fight Fake News, SETI Researchers Update Alien-Detection Scale," *Scientific American*, August 1, 2018, https://www.scientificamerican.com/article/to-fight-fake-news-seti-researchers-update-alien-detection-scale/.
402   *"Throughout the life"*: "The Rio Scale," 2.
402   *"A confirmed detection of extraterrestrial"*: "Declaration of Principles Concerning Activities Following the Detection of Extraterrestrial Intelligence," International Academy of Astronautics, 1989, https://iaaseti.org/en/declaration-principles-concerning-activities-following-detection/.
403   *For fun and science*: Seth Shostak and Ivan Almar, "The Rio Scale Applied to Fictional SETI Detections," International Academy of Astronautics, 2002, 4, 7, http://resources.iaaseti.org/abst2002/rio2002.pdf.
403   *Additionally—and notably*: Ibid.
403   *As critic John Billingham*: "Who Speaks for Earth?," *Seed*, July 11, 2009, https://web.archive.org/web/20090711205859/http://seedmagazine.com/content/article/who_speaks_for_earth.

CHAPTER 49: THE TIC TAC INCIDENT

404   *"One aspect of the future"*: "B—Advanced Aerospace Weapon System Applications Program—Solicitation HHM402-08-R-0211," August 18, 2008, http://www.fbodaily.com/archive/2008/08-August/20-Aug-2008/FBO-01643684.htm.
404   *"This was a UFO program"*: James T. Lacatski, Colm A. Kelleher, and George Knapp, *Skinwalkers at the Pentagon: An Insiders'* [sic] *Account of the Secret Government UFO Program* (self-published, 2021), 25.

405 *In its contract, the Bigelow:* Ibid., 22–26.

405 *The new Star Team Impact Project:* "Air Traffic Control," Federal Aviation Administration, February 11, 2010, https://web.archive.org/web/20100412064244/http://www.faa.gov:80/air_traffic/publications/atpubs/ATC/atc0908.html.

406 *Worried about a malfunction:* Tim McMillan, "The Witnesses," *Popular Mechanics*, November 12, 2019, https://www.popularmechanics.com/military/research/a29771548/navy-ufo-witnesses-tell-truth/.

406 *When the* Princeton *announced:* Greg Taylor, "Tic-Tac Tactics: Pilot Discusses the U.S. Military's Engagement with a UFO in 2004," *Daily Grail*, June 18, 2021, https://www.dailygrail.com/2021/06/tic-tac-tactics-pilot-discusses-the-u-s-militarys-engagement-with-a-ufo-in-2004/.

406 *"We describe [it] as a 'tic-tac'":* Pavithra George, " 'Normalizing' UFOs—Retired U.S. Navy Pilot Recalls Tic Tac Encounter," video, *Reuters*, June 25, 2021, https://www.reuters.com/lifestyle/science/normalizing-ufos-retired-us-navy-pilot-recalls-tic-tac-encounter-2021-06-25/.

406 *"We don't know what it was":* Ibid., article text.

407 *A recorded video:* "FLIR1: Official UAP Footage from the USG for Public Release," To the Stars Academy of Arts & Sciences, December 16, 2017, 2:45, https://www.youtube.com/watch?v=6rWOtrke0HY.

407 *It was never found again:* Paco Chierici, "There I Was: The X-Files Edition," March 14, 2015, Fighter Sweep, https://fightersweep.com/1460/x-files-edition/.

407 *When the first set:* Jonathan Axelrod, "Executive Summary," Advanced Aerospace Weapon System Applications Program, 9, https://www.theblackvault.com/casefiles/wp-content/uploads/2018/01/tictac.pdf.

407 *That night, one of:* Helen Cooper, Leslie Kean, and Ralph Blumenthal, "2 Navy Airmen and an Object That 'Accelerated Like Nothing I've Ever Seen," *New York Times*, December 16, 2017, https://www.nytimes.com/2017/12/16/us/politics/unidentified-flying-object-navy.html.

407 *"These two guys show up":* McMillan, "The Witnesses."

407 *The USS* Nimitz *incident:* Chierici, "There I Was."

408 *"It was completely ignored":* George Knapp, "Robert Bigelow Opens Up About AAWSAP, the Tic Tac Incident, Weird Events on the Skinwalker Ranch, the Connection to Consciousness," video, *Mystery Wire*, January 25, 2021, https://www.mysterywire.com/ufo/robert-bigelow-aawsap/.

408 *One of its investigators interviewed:* Lacatski, Kelleher, and Knapp, *Skinwalkers*.

408 *As the Bigelow team's:* Axelrod, "Executive Summary," 1.

408 *"In order to support":* Lacatski, Kelleher, and Knapp, *Skinwalkers*, 91.

408 *"After a while the consensus":* Bryan Bender, "The Pentagon's Secret Search for UFOs," *Politico*, December 16, 2017, https://www.politico.com/magazine/story/2017/12/16/pentagon-ufo-search-harry-reid-216111/.

409 *Meanwhile, a special team:* Lacatski, Kelleher, and Knapp, *Skinwalkers*, 81.

410 *His program, known as:* Gideon Lewis-Kraus, "How the Pentagon Started Taking U.F.O.s Seriously," *New Yorker*, May 10, 2021, https://www.newyorker.com/magazine/2021/05/10/how-the-pentagon-started-taking-ufos-seriously.

410 *In a showing of:* "Aliens Exist," Genius, https://genius.com/Blink-182-aliens-exist-lyrics.

410 *Over the years, he'd taken:* Patrick Doyle, "Tom DeLonge on 'Scary' UFO Footage, Angels and Airwaves and Blink-182's Future," *Rolling Stone*, June 4, 2019, https://www.rollingstone.com/music/music-features/tom-delonge-interview-ufo-footage-angels-airwaves-blink-182-843812/.

410 *"I have 10 people that":* Ibid.

410 *It seemed like an unlikely claim*: Bryan Bender, "How Harry Reid, a Terrorist Interrogator and the Singer from Blink-182 Took UFOs Mainstream," Politico, May 28, 2021, https://www.politico.com/news/magazine/2021/05/28/ufos-secret-history-government-washington-dc-487900.

411 *Podesta, for his part*: Al Kamen, "Obama Aide John Podesta Says 'Biggest Failure' Was Not Securing the Disclosure of UFO Files," *Washington Post*, February 13, 2015, https://www.washingtonpost.com/blogs/in-the-loop/wp/2015/02/13/obama-aide-john-podesta-says-biggest-failure-was-not-securing-the-disclosure-of-ufo-files/.

411 *"There is sufficient credible evidence"*: Bender, "The Pentagon's Secret Search."

411 *Right away, Blumenthal emailed*: Ralph Blumenthal, "On the Trail of a Secret Pentagon U.F.O. Program," *New York Times*, December 18, 2017, https://www.nytimes.com/2017/12/18/insider/secret-pentagon-ufo-program.html.

412 *"Internationally, we are the most backward"*: Helene Cooper, Ralph Blumenthal, and Leslie Kean, "Glowing Auras and 'Black Money': The Pentagon's Mysterious U.F.O. Program," *New York Times*, December 16, 2017, https://www.nytimes.com/2017/12/16/us/politics/pentagon-program-ufo-harry-reid.html.

412 *Midway through the article*: Ibid.

412 *The* Times *article also contained*: Ibid.

413 *On the video, the flight crews*: Christopher Mellon, "The Military Keeps Encountering UFOS. Why Doesn't the Pentagon Care?," *Washington Post*, video, March 9, 2018, https://www.washingtonpost.com/outlook/the-military-keeps-encountering-ufos-why-doesnt-the-pentagon-care/2018/03/09/242c125c-22ee-11e8-94da-ebf9d112159c_story.html.

413 *"As with Sputnik, the national"*: Ibid., article text.

CHAPTER 50: LIFE SCIENCE

414 *But as science writer Daniel Stone*: Daniel Stone, *Sinkable: Obsession, the Deep Sea, and the Shipwreck of the Titanic* (New York: Dutton, 2022), p. 46.

414 *Plus, there's evidence that water*: Alvin Powell, "How Earth Was Watered," *Harvard Gazette*, February 27, 2014, https://news.harvard.edu/gazette/story/2014/02/how-earth-was-watered/.

415 *She proposed that the tiny*: Linda T. Elkins-Tanton, "Formation of Early Water Oceans on Rocky Planets," *Astrophysics and Space Science* 332 (2011): 359–64.

415 *"All of our planetary water"*: Stone, *Sinkable*, 47.

415 *"If water oceans were present"*: Bruce Dorminey, "Earth Oceans Were Homegrown," *Science*, November 29, 2010, https://www.science.org/content/article/earth-oceans-were-homegrown.

416 *"It is very possible"*: Powell, "How Earth Was Watered."

416 *Recent experiments conducted*: Eric Hand, "Old Rocks Drown Dry Moon Theory," *Nature* 464, no. 7286 (March 11, 2010): 150.

416 *Elkins-Tanton called*: Ibid.

416 *"They are finding a lot more water"*: Andrew Fazekas, "Moon Has a Hundred Times More Water Than Thought," *National Geographic*, June 15, 2010, https://www.nationalgeographic.com/science/article/100614-moon-water-hundred-lunar-proceedings-science.

416 *"That shallowness, though"*: Stone, *Sinkable*, 48.

417 *"If life arose so shortly"*: Seth Shostak, *Confessions of an Alien Hunter* (Washington, DC: National Geographic, 2009), 96.

417 *Mega volcanoes and meteors*: Steve Brusatte, *The Rise and Reign of the Mammals: A New History, from the Shadow of the Dinosaurs to Us* (New York: Mariner, 2022), 42–43.

417   *For several hundred thousand years*: Ibid., 45.

417   *That extinction gave space*: Ibid., 68.

418   *"The dinosaurs had 150 million years"*: Shostak, *Confessions*, 100.

418   *"Mammals almost died out"*: Brusatte, *The Rise and Reign*, 169.

418   *Just 7 percent*: Ibid., 175.

418   *We are all their descendants*: Ibid., 6.

418   *"All modern-day mammals"*: Ibid., xviii.

418   *Humans, in turn*: Ibid., 259.

419   *"Initially humans were an endemic group"*: Ibid., 382.

419   *As Brusatte says, "Our single"*: Ibid., 383.

419   *Even this history*: Ibid., 390.

420   *"In my view, once you"*: Keith Cooper, *The Contact Paradox: Challenging Our Assumptions in the Search for Extraterrestrial Intelligence* (Dublin: Bloomsbury, 2021), 58.

420   *ALH84001 was hardly anomalous*: Ibid., 170.

420   *Calculations showed that billions*: Avi Loeb, *Extraterrestrial: The First Sign of Intelligent Life Beyond Earth* (New York: Houghton Mifflin Harcourt, 2021), 169–72.

420   *As one astronomer would write*: Ibid., 171.

420   *Scientists reported, too*: Meilan Solly, "Ancient Roundworms Allegedly Resurrected from Russian Permafrost," *Smithsonian*, July 30, 2018, https://www.smithsonian mag.com/smart-news/ancient-roundworms-allegedly-resurrected-russian-perma frost-180969782/.

CHAPTER 51: BREAKTHROUGH LISTEN

421   *In one fell swoop*: Seth Shostak, *Confessions of an Alien Hunter* (Washington, DC: National Geographic, 2009), 6.

421   *Astronomers now were able*: Ibid., 75.

421   *"Today we may be"*: Ibid., 77.

421   *He'd been fascinated by extraterrestrial*: Avi Loeb, *Extraterrestrial: The First Sign of Intelligent Life Beyond Earth* (New York: Houghton Mifflin Harcourt, 2021), 54.

421   *"I am fully committed"*: Lee Billings, "Search for Extraterrestrial Intelligence Nets Historic Cash Infusion," *Scientific American*, July 20, 2015, https://www.scientificamerican .com/article/search-for-extraterrestrial-intelligence-nets-historic-cash-infusion/.

422   *"We are the beginners"*: Ibid.

422   *There was always the question*: Shostak, *Confessions*, 284–85.

422   *Beyond simply listening*: "Gravity Assist: If They Call, Will We Listen? The Search for Technosignatures," NASA, June 26, 2020, https://www.nasa.gov/mediacast/gravity -assist-if-they-call-will-we-listen-the-search-for-technosignatures.

422   *The researchers found precisely zero*: Paul Gilster, "G-HAT: Searching for Kadashev Type III," *Centauri Dreams*, April 16, 2015, https://www.centauri-dreams .org/2015/04/16/g-hat-searching-for-kardashev-type-iii/.

423   *"Looking for alien cities"*: "City Lights Could Reveal E.T. Civilization," Harvard & Smithsonian Center for Astrophysics, November 3, 2011, https://www.cfa.harvard .edu/news/city-lights-could-reveal-et-civilization.

423   *As Starshot unfolded*: "Proxima Centauri b," NASA, https://exoplanets.nasa.gov/exo planet-catalog/7167/proxima-centauri-b/.

423   *Loeb and others came up*: Loeb, *Extraterrestrial*, 57.

424   *Milner calculated it would take*: Dennis Overbye, "Reaching for the Stars, Across 4.37 Light Years," *New York Times*, April 12, 2016, https://www.nytimes.com/2016/04/13 /science/alpha-centauri-breakthrough-starshot-yuri-milner-stephen-hawking.html.

425   *As Loeb wrote, "This scout"*: Loeb, *Extraterrestrial*, 4.

425 *Finally, on November 14*: "The IAU Approves New Type of Designation for Interstellar Objects," International Astronomical Union, November 14, 2017, https://www.iau.org/news/announcements/detail/ann17045/.

425 *"We determined that Oumuamua needed to be"*: Loeb, *Extraterrestrial*, 65.

425 *"Could Solar Radiation Pressure Explain"*: Shmuel Bialy and Abraham Loeb, "Could Solar Radiation Pressure Explain 'Oumuamua's Peculiar Acceleration?," *Astrophysical Journal Letters* 868, no. 1 (2018): 1–5.

425 *"Do you believe there are alien civilizations"*: Loeb, *Extraterrestrial*, 67.

426 *"It's possible that the civilization is not alive"*: Isaac Chotiner, "Have Aliens Found Us? A Harvard Astronomer on the Mysterious Interstellar Object 'Oumuamua," *New Yorker*, January 16, 2019, https://www.newyorker.com/news/q-and-a/have-aliens-found-us-a-harvard-astronomer-on-the-mysterious-interstellar-object-oumuamua.

426 *The object, he suspected*: Loeb, *Extraterrestrial*, 177.

426 *That same year, two Arizona State*: Dennis Overbye, "Why Oumuamua, the Interstellar Visitor, Looks Eerily Familiar," *New York Times*, March 23, 2021, https://www.nytimes.com/2021/03/23/science/astronomy-oumuamua-comet.html.

427 *The object, whatever it was*: Mike Sullivan, "Harvard professor Avi Loeb believes he's found fragments of alien technology," CBS News Boston, July 7, 2023, https://www.cbsnews.com/boston/news/avi-loeb-harvard-professor-alien-technology-fragments/.

EPILOGUE: THE TRUTH IS OUT THERE

428 *"That was always out there"*: Dennis Overbye, Kenneth Chang, and Joshua Sokol, "Webb Telescope Reveals a New Vision of an Ancient Universe," *New York Times*, July 12, 2022, https://www.nytimes.com/2022/07/12/science/james-webb-telescope-images-nasa.html.

429 *As Seth Shostak, one of the leading*: Ibid., 139.

429 *As Shostak calculated*: Ibid., 66.

430 *"Humans are woefully ill prepared"*: Avi Loeb, *Extraterrestrial: The First Sign of Intelligent Life Beyond Earth* (New York: Houghton Mifflin Harcourt, 2021), xii.

430 *"Human science still needs to mature"*: Ibid., 94.

430 *"Bet that Oumuamua was an exotic rock"*: Ibid., 162.

430 *"Mainstream theoretical physicists now widely accept"*: Ibid., 50.

431 *"Today, a young theoretical astrophysicist"*: Ibid., 97.

431 *The general state of support*: Daniel Alarcón, "The Collapse of Puerto Rico's Iconic Telescope," *New Yorker*, April 5, 2021: https://www.newyorker.com/magazine/2021/04/05/the-collapse-of-puerto-ricos-iconic-telescope.

431 *As the* New Yorker *wrote*: Gideon Lewis-Kraus, "How the Pentagon Started Taking U.F.O.s Seriously," *New Yorker*, May 10, 2021, https://www.newyorker.com/magazine/2021/05/10/how-the-pentagon-started-taking-ufos-seriously.

432 *The Senate Intelligence Committee*: Ryan Browne, "Pentagon to Launch Task Force to Investigate UFO Sightings," *CNN*, August 13, 2020, https://www.cnn.com/2020/08/13/politics/pentagon-ufo-task-force/index.html.

433 *"I've seen some of those videos"*: John O. Brennan, interview by Tyler Cowen, *Conversations with Tyler*, December 16, 2020, https://conversationswithtyler.com/episodes/john-o-brennan/.

433 *The next year, former president Obama*: Duncan Phenix, "Barack Obama Talks About UFOs Again on Late Night Television," WGN 9, May 18, 2021, https://wgntv.com/news/barack-obama-talks-about-ufos-again-on-late-night-television/.

433   *Many have admitted suspecting*: Tim McMillan, " 'Fast Movers' and Transmedium Vehicles—The Pentagon's Unidentified Aerial Phenomena Task Force," *The Debrief,* December 2, 2020, https://thedebrief.org/fast-movers-and-transmedium-vehicles -the-pentagons-uap-task-force/.

434   *"I was told for decades that Lockheed"*: Ibid.

434   *After prodding by Congress*: *Preliminary Assessment: Unidentified Aerial Phenomena,* Office of the Director of National Intelligence, June 25, 2021, 5, https://www.dni.gov /files/ODNI/documents/assessments/Prelimary-Assessment-UAP-20210625.pdf.

434   *As Christopher Mellon wrote*: Christopher Mellon, "Key Takeaways from 2023 ODNI UAP Report," January 12, 2023, https://www.christophermellon.net/post/key-take aways-from-2023-odni-uap-report.

434   *That same year, the House Intelligence Committee*: Alex Rogers, "House Panel Will Hold First Public Hearing on UFOs in Decades," *CNN,* May 10, 2022, https://www.cnn .com/2022/05/10/politics/ufo-hearing-house-intelligence-committee/index.html.

435   *"When it comes to material that we have"*: *Unidentified Aerial Phenomena,* transcript of a meeting of the U.S. House Permanent Select Committee on Intelligence, Subcommittee on Counterterrorism, Counterintelligence, and Counterproliferation, May 17, 2022, 34, https://www.congress.gov/117/meeting/house/114761/documents/HHRG -117-IG05-Transcript-20220517.pdf.

435   *As it was, swarms of mysterious*: Adam Kehoe and Marc Cecotti, "Multiple Destroyers Were Swarmed by Mysterious 'Drones' Off California Over Numerous Nights," *War Zone,* May 23, 2021, https://www.thedrive.com/the-war-zone/39913/multi ple-destroyers-were-swarmed-by-mysterious-drones-off-california-over-numerous -nights.

435   *"We do not want potential adversaries"*: Julian E. Barnes, "Many Military U.F.O. Reports Are Just Foreign Spying or Airborne Trash," *New York Times,* October 28, 2022, https://www.nytimes.com/2022/10/28/us/politics/ufo-military-reports.html.

436   *Days of strange official silence*: Libby Cathey, "White House Says 'No Indication of Aliens' as Questions Swirl about Objects Shot Down," *ABC News,* February 13, 2023, https://abcnews.go.com/Politics/white-house-indication-aliens-questions-swirl-ob jects-shot/story?id=97090516.

436   *At least one of the US shootdowns appeared*: Matt Berg and Lee Hudson, "A Hobby Group May Have the Answer to What the U.S. Shot Down Over Canada Last Week," *Politico,* February 16, 2023, https://www.politico.com/news/2023/02/16/mystery-ob ject-balloon-illinois-biden-00083355.

436   *The military's new engagement*: "NASA Announces Unidentified Anomalous Phenomena Study Team Members," NASA, October 21, 2022, https://www.nasa.gov/feature /nasa-announces-unidentified-aerial-phenomena-study-team-members/.

436   *As NASA Administrator Bill Nelson*: Whitelaw Reid, "Space Jam: Former Senator Talks Aliens, Asteroids and 'Star Trek' with Larry Sabato," *UVAToday,* October 20, 2021, https://news.virginia.edu/content/space-jam-former-senator-talks-aliens-asteroids -and-star-trek-larry-sabato.

436   *As Kean told an interviewer*: Soo Youn, "The Woman Who Forced the US Government to Take UFOs Seriously," *Guardian,* June 14, 2021, https://www.theguardian.com /world/2021/jun/14/leslie-kean-ufo-reporter-us-government-report.

437   *In 2022, Jacques Vallée*: Chantel Tattoli, "Jacques Vallée Still Doesn't Know What UFOs Are," *WIRED,* April 2022: https://www.wired.com/story/jacques-Vallée-still -doesnt-know-what-ufos-are/.

437   *The truly "unexplained" cases*: Paul Scott Anderson, "Has the Ball Lightning Mystery Been Solved?" EarthSky, June 14, 2019, https://earthsky.org/earth/ball-light ning-lightning-atmosphere-earth-optik/.

437   *(3) weird terrestrial stuff: London's Roll of Fame* (London: Cassell & Company, 1884), 305, https://books.google.com/books?id=ne6yXTyC61wC.

437   *The life span of the average species*: Ronald D. Ekers et al., eds., *SETI 2020: A Roadmap for the Search for Extraterrestrial Intelligence* (Mountain View: SETI Press, 2002), xxx.

437   *As British biologist J. B. S. Haldane*: J. B. S. Haldane, *Possible Worlds and Other Essays* (London: Chatto and Windus, 1937), 286.

438   *"I think they enjoy the anticipation"*: George, " 'Normalizing' UFOs."

Index

conspiracy theories, xxii, 245–46, 322, 324, 359, 379n
UFO, *see* UFO conspiracy theories
Contact (film), 376n, 403n
Contact (Sagan), 291, 376n
contactees, 106, 107–13, 114–15, 203, 330, 331
Cooper, Bill, 321–25
Cooper, Helene, 412
Copernicus, Nicolaus, 33, 156, 192
Corden, James, 433
Cordes, James, 269n
Cornell Chronicle, 244
Cornell Daily Sun, 151n
Cornell University, 222, 237, 269n, 272, 291
Corson, Dale, 291
cosmic evolution, 367n
cosmic pluralism, 155–56
Cosmos: A Personal Voyage, 287, 290, 291
Costa Rica, 264
Cowen, Tyler, 433
Coyne, Larry, 259, 260
Craigie, L. C., 37
Creutz, Albert, 326
Crichton, Michael, 227
Crick, Francis, 230–32
Cronkite, Walter, 209
crop circles, 318–19
Crowe, Michael J., 239n
Crowther, Bosley, 96
CSI (Civilian Saucer Intelligence), 105, 114, 116, 119
CTA-102, 181–83, 255n
Cuban Missile Crisis, 166n, 195
Cummings, Jerry, 69–71
Cutler, Robert, 315, 316

Daily Mail, 9
Dalai Lama, 337
DARPA (Defense Advanced Research Projects Agency), 278
Darrach, H. B., Jr., 77
Davidson, Leon, 116n
Davies, Paul, 360, 422
Davis, Isabel, 114
Davis, John, 243
Davis, Patti, 303n
Day After, The, 303
Day the Earth Stood Still, The, 303
De Brouwer, Wilfried, 326, 327

Defense Department (DoD), 12n, 60, 347, 354, 388, 404, 408, 410
Defense Intelligence Agency, *see* DIA
de Gaulle, Charles, 266
DeLonge, Tom, 410–11
Democratic National Convention, 79, 81
Desch, Steven, 426–27
Detroit Free Press, 17
de Vaucouleurs, Gérard Henri, xviiin
DeVorkin, David, 32
Dewey, John, 220
Dexter, Mich., 205
DIA (Defense Intelligence Agency), 265, 306, 307, 315, 389, 390, 391, 404, 405, 408–9
  AAWSAP program of, 392, 404–5, 408–9, 430n
Dick Cavett Show, The, 259–60
Dickey, Colin, 324
Dietrich, Alex, 406–7, 438
dinosaurs, xx, 417–18
Dir, Gary, 281
dirigibles, 17, 59
Discovery space shuttle, 363
Disney, Walt, 94n
Disneyland, 94
DNA, 169, 230, 232, 243, 418
Dolan, RIchard, 306
dolphins, 171–75, 430
Doolittle, James, 20
Doomsday Clock, 27
Doppler, Christian Johann, 34n
Doppler shift, 34, 152, 270n
Dorsch, Kate, 26, 40, 48n, 60, 70n, 72, 80, 276n
Doty, Richard, 314
Douglas Aircraft, 40–41
Dragons of Eden, The (Sagan), 332n
Drake, Frank, 150–55, 157–58, 165–66, 167, 170–74, 176, 178, 236–42, 269–70, 277, 288, 290–91, 361, 362, 371, 377n, 421, 422, 427
  Arecibo message of, 242–44
  at Byurakan Conference, 228, 230
  equation of, 171–72, 174, 176–77, 229, 232, 300, 367, 397
  hydrogen line and, 151–52, 157, 158, 236, 270
  Ozma project of, 155, 157, 159–62, 166, 167, 170, 171, 230, 234, 235, 269, 300
  Proxmire and, 289, 290n

Image Credits

INSERT 1:

1. Courtesy, *Fort Worth Star-Telegram* Photograph Collection, Special Collections, The University of Texas at Arlington Library, Arlington, Texas.
2. Roswell Daily Record, Wikimedia Commons
3. Chronicle / Alamy Stock Photo
4. Chronicle / Alamy Stock Photo
5. Photo Courtesy of Bettman Archive, Getty Images
6. Daily Grail Publishing, WikiMedia Commons
7. Photo Courtesy of Bettman Archive, Getty Images
8. US Air Force Photo, History Office, Air Force Life Cycle Management Center, Air Force Materiel Command, Wright-Patterson Air Force Base
9. US Navy Photo
10. US Navy Photo, Naval History and Heritage Command
11. US Air Force Document, US Air Force
12. Chronicle / Alamy Stock Photo
13. Photograph by Cloyd Teter, *Denver Post* Collection, Getty Images
14. National Archives 6981836
15. US Air Force Photo, National Museum of the US Air Force
16. US Army Illustration
17. AP Photo/Alvin Quinn
18. Drawing released by Washtenaw County Sheriff's Office, Ann Arbor, Mich.
19. Smithsonian Institution Archives, Record Unit 371, Box 4, Folder: December 1983
20. *International UFO Reporter*, published by Center for UFO Studies
21. US Government Photo
22. Smithsonian Institution Archives, Record Unit 9520, Box 1, Fred L. Whipple Oral History Interviews
23. National Radio Astronomy Observatory
24. Photo by Carl Iwasaki, *The Chronicle Collection*, Getty Images
25. NRAO/AUI/NSF
26. Arne Nordmann, Creative Commons Attribution-Share Alike 3.0 Unported, Wiki-Media Commons
27. NASA
28. NASA

INSERT 2:

1. Irene P. Ertman Science Fiction Book Collection, Digital Commons at Pittsburg State University
2. Instituto Geográfico Nacional de Costa Rica, WikiMedia Commons
3. FBI Records: The Vault, https://vault.fbi.gov/Majestic%2012
4. NASA, WikiMedia Commons
5. National Radio Astronomy Observatory
6. World History Archive / Alamy Stock Photo

About the Author

GARRETT M. GRAFF has spent nearly two decades covering politics, technology, and national security. The former editor of *POLITICO Magazine* and a contributor to *WIRED* and CNN, he's written for publications from Esquire to Rolling Stone to the New York Times, and today serves as the director for cyber initiatives at the Aspen Institute. Graff is the author of multiple books, including the FBI history *The Threat Matrix*; *Raven Rock*, about the government's Cold War Doomsday plans; and the *New York Times* bestsellers *The Only Plane in the Sky* and *Watergate*, which was a finalist for the Pulitzer Prize in history.